CIVIL PROCEDURE

Examples and Explanations

CIVIL PROCEDURE

Examples and Explanations
Second Edition

Joseph W. Glannon

Professor of Law
Suffolk University Law School

LITTLE, BROWN AND COMPANY
Boston   Toronto   London

Library of Congress Catalog Card No. 91-77970

ISBN 0-316-31596-6

EB
Second Edition

Fifth Printing

Published simultaneously in Canada by Little, Brown & Company (Canada) Limited

Printed in the United States of America

I wish to dedicate this book to my parents, Edward and Helen Glannon.

Contents

Preface to Students

Everyone comes to law school with some idea of what a contract is or of the meaning of assault and battery, but who ever heard of supplemental jurisdiction, impleader, or res judicata? Abstract concepts such as these make civil procedure the most unfamiliar and intimidating of the basic law school courses.

However, civil procedure can also be fascinating if you can get by the initial strangeness. Many of the topics covered in the course appear baffling upon first acquaintance but begin to make sense when you see how they apply in particular cases and how they relate to other topics in the course. The goal of this book is to demystify civil procedure by providing concrete examples of procedural doctrines and rules in operation, together with full explanations of how these abstract concepts apply to each example.

Most case books contain major or representative cases but provide little discussion of what the cases mean or "what the law is" on a particular topic. I hope that you will find, as my students have, that the discussion in this book helps to tie the cases together into a coherent picture of the law. In addition, the opportunity to try your hand at the examples and then to compare your answers with mine will provide an incentive to analyze the examples and make that process more rewarding — perhaps even enjoyable.

Each chapter (except for the pleading chapters in Part Six) includes an introduction that gives a basic explanation of the relevant procedural concept followed by a series of examples. The "Explanations" section of each chapter presents my analysis of the examples in that chapter. The most effective way to use the book is to read each chapter when that topic is covered in your civil procedure course and to try to answer the questions yourself, based on my introductions and your reading for class. To keep yourself honest, write out your own analysis of each example, if only in a few sentences, before comparing it to mine. You may also want to review the chapter again after class coverage or discuss with your civil procedure professor any issues that you don't fully understand.

One of my principal frustrations as a first year law student was that the questions posed in the casebooks were too hard. (Many are still beyond me, even after teaching procedure for a number of years.) I think you will find that the examples in this book are geared to cover the basics as well as more sophisticated variations; you really will be able to answer many of them, and the explanations will help to deepen your understanding of the issues.

You certainly will want to use Civil Procedure: Examples and Explanations for reviewing your civil procedure course at the end of the year. My students have found that these chapters are an excellent way to test their understanding of each topic and to fill in any gaps in class discussion or case reading. The examples provide an efficient means of learning the material because they help you to actively apply the concepts. You will learn a lot more by doing that than by passively rereading cases. In addition, the process will give you a sense of mastery of the material. As the year progresses, you will find that your ability to analyze the examples improves markedly, and that this positive feedback will help you feel more confident of your analytical skills. Surely every first year law student will be thankful for that.

Acknowledgments

In addition to those who assisted in the original creation of this book, I would like to express my appreciation to Dean Paul Sugarman and Suffolk University Law School for their support in the preparation of the Second Edition. I also appreciate the assistance of Professors Karen Blum, Victoria Dodd, Steven Eisenstat, and Thomas Finn of the Suffolk faculty in reviewing various chapters. Thanks, also, to my student research assistants, Lisa Sherman ('92), Salina Millora ('93), and Rob Schwandt ('93), for their help in updating the law.

As always, I appreciate the excellent support provided by the Law Division at Little, Brown, especially Richard Heuser, Carol McGeehan, Betsy Kenny, Dana Wilson, and Julie Nahil. And special thanks to my wife, Annie, for her advice as well as her good nature in tolerating my preoccupation with these revisions.

Special Notice

For several frequently cited treatises I have used shortened forms after the initial citation to the work. These are as follows: Casad, Jurisdiction in Civil Actions (2d ed. 1991), cited as Casad; Friedenthal, Kane, and Miller, Civil Procedure (1985), cited as Friedenthal, Kane, and Miller; James and Hazard, Civil Procedure (3d ed. 1985), cited as James and Hazard; Moore's Federal Practice, cited as Moore's; Wright, Federal Courts (4th ed. 1983), cited as Wright; and Wright and Miller, Federal Practice and Procedure, cited as Wright and Miller. (My apologies to supplementary co-authors of the Moore's and Wright and Miller treatises.) For multivolume treatises (Moore's and Wright and Miller) the volume number has been retained before the authors' names.

CIVIL PROCEDURE

Examples and Explanations

PART ONE

Choosing a Proper Court

1

Personal Jurisdiction: The Enigma of Minimum Contacts

Introduction

There is no place to start like the beginning, and the usual beginning for the defendant is the receipt of a summons from the court with an order to appear and defend a lawsuit. It is never a prospect that evokes much enthusiasm, but the reception is likely to be even chillier if the suit has been filed in a distant state. The defendant will want to know why on earth the plaintiff has chosen to sue in a court a thousand miles away and, perhaps more to the point, whether she *can* sue there. The answer to the second question lies shrouded in one of the foggiest realms of civil procedure, the doctrine of personal jurisdiction.

Ever since the landmark case of *Pennoyer v. Neff*, 95 U.S. 714 (1877), the Supreme Court has consistently held that plaintiffs are not free to bring suit wherever they choose. The fourteenth amendment to the United States Constitution forbids the states from "depriv[ing] any person of life, liberty or property, without due process of law." A state would violate this guarantee if its courts entered judgments against defendants without following a fair judicial procedure, and fair procedure includes not only such traditional elements as the right to counsel or to cross-examine witnesses, but also appropriate limits on the places where a defendant can be required to defend a lawsuit.

The Supreme Court has repeatedly attempted to define the appropriate limits on the power of state courts to "exercise personal jurisdiction over" defendants, that is, to require them to come into the state to defend lawsuits there. A number of bases for personal jurisdiction have evolved, including domicile, consent, physical presence, and the enigmatic "minimum contacts" standard. In many cases in which the defendant is not from the forum state (the state where suit is brought), the only basis for exercising personal jurisdiction over her will be the minimum contacts test developed in *International Shoe v. Washington*, 326 U.S. 310 (1945). This chapter focuses on the meaning of that test.

The Minimum Contacts Test

In *International Shoe*, the Supreme Court held that the courts of a state may exercise personal jurisdiction over a defendant if she has such minimum contacts with the state that it would be fair to require her to return and defend a lawsuit in that state. The Court did not elucidate this somewhat circular proposition by providing a list of what minimum contacts are sufficient, nor did it base the test on the number of contacts with the state. Instead, the Court suggested that whether jurisdiction is permissible depends on the "quality and nature" of the contacts with the state. 326 U.S. at 319. In some cases, the Court indicated, even a single contact will do, but not contacts that are "casual" or "isolated."

This language is too vague to provide much guidance in applying the minimum contacts test, but the rationale of *International Shoe* is more helpful. The *Shoe* Court suggested that a corporation that chooses to conduct activities within a state accepts (implicitly, of course) a reciprocal duty to answer for its in-state activities in the local courts. A defendant should understand that her activities within the state will have an impact there, that those activities may lead to controversies and lawsuits there, and that the state has a right to enforce the orderly conduct of affairs within its borders by adjudicating disputes that arise from such in-state activities. The defendant who deliberately chooses to take advantage of the "benefits and protections of the laws" (326 U.S. at 319) of a state will not be heard to cry "foul" when that state holds her to account in its courts for her in-state acts.

This rationale suggests an important limitation on minimum contacts jurisdiction. Because the court's power to exercise jurisdiction derives from the defendant's voluntary relation to the state, the power should be limited to cases arising out of that relation. *International Shoe* implies such a limitation, and subsequent cases have confirmed that minimum contacts jurisdiction is limited to claims arising from (or, perhaps, related to) the defendant's contacts with the forum state. In *Shoe*, for example, the corporation was held subject to personal jurisdiction in Washington for claims arising out of its shoe sales in that state, but the corporation could not have been required to defend a claim in Washington arising from shoe sales in Texas under a minimum contacts analysis. Sales in Texas are unrelated to Washington; the corporation would certainly not expect to be sued in Washington by a Texas shoe buyer; nor does the corporation take advantage of the benefits and protections of the laws of Washington by its activities in Texas. The analysis must always consider the relationship between the contacts that gave rise to the suit and the state where the suit is brought. Miscellaneous contacts are not minimum contacts. It is the contacts that spawned the lawsuit that are crucial to the minimum contacts analysis.

Specific and General Jurisdiction: The "Shoe Spectrum"

Although *International Shoe* is primarily viewed as a minimum contacts case, the opinion analyzes a broad spectrum of possible contacts with a state and their jurisdictional consequences. Figure 1-1 illustrates this spectrum of increasing contacts.

At one end of the "*Shoe* spectrum" are cases in which a defendant has no contact with the forum state. In such cases, *Shoe* indicates that the state has no authority to exercise personal jurisdiction over the defendant, unless she consents to it. "Casual" or "isolated" contacts (whatever they may be) are also insufficient to support jurisdiction. But other single acts, because of their "quality and nature," will support "specific in personam jurisdiction," that is, jurisdiction over claims arising out of that single act. See, e.g., *McGee v. International Ins. Co.*, 355 U.S. 220 (1957) (upholding jurisdiction over claim arising out of a single contract solicited in the state). Continuous activity in the forum state, such as the ongoing business relationship in *Burger King Corp. v. Rudzewicz*, 471 U.S. 462 (1985), will also support "specific" jurisdiction, that is, jurisdiction over claims arising out of that continuous activity. In each of these categories of cases, the in-state activity is limited. In each, the defendant is only subject to jurisdiction for claims arising out of those "minimum contacts."

The *Shoe* opinion also suggests that if the defendant's forum contacts fall at the far right end of the spectrum, that is, the in-state contacts are very substantial, the defendant is subject to "general in personam jurisdiction." This means that the defendant may be sued in the state for any claim, even one completely unrelated to its in-state activities. Several cases since *International Shoe* affirm that general in personam jurisdiction is sometimes permissible (see *Helicopteros Nacionales de Colombia, S.A. v. Hall*, 466 U.S. 408 (1984); *Perkins v. Benguet Consolidated Mining Co.*, 342 U.S. 437 (1952)), but the Supreme Court has not clearly indicated where the line (marked "G" on Figure 1-1) lies between contacts that support general in personam jurisdiction and those that support only specific, minimum contacts jurisdiction.

Extent of Contacts	Decreasing ◀——— contacts			Increasing ———▶ contacts	
	no contacts	casual or isolated	single act	continuous and systematic	G ──────── substantial or pervasive
Jurisdictional Consequences	no jurisdiction	no jurisdiction	specific jurisdiction	specific jurisdiction	general jurisdiction

Figure 1–1: The *Shoe* Spectrum

General jurisdiction is apparently appropriate when the defendant's activities in the state are so substantial and continuous that she would expect to be subject to suit there on any claim and would suffer no inconvenience from defending there. See generally Friedenthal, Kane, and Miller, Civil Procedure §310 (1985) (hereinafter cited as Friedenthal, Kane, and Miller).

Under general in personam jurisdiction analysis, for example, a major American oil company would be subject to personal jurisdiction in many, if not all states, regardless of whether the claim arose in the state where suit was brought. Companies that have such extensive activities and facilities in a state may fairly be considered "at home" there and, therefore, subject to the burden of submitting generally to jurisdiction there.[1] This approach is analogous to general jurisdiction over individual defendants based on domicile in the state, which was approved in *Milliken v. Meyer*, 311 U.S. 457 (1940).[2]

Some Guidelines in Applying Minimum Contacts

Several important aspects of the minimum contacts test have been settled by cases since *International Shoe*. *First,* the minimum contacts test applies to individual as well as corporate defendants. See, e.g., *Kulko v. Superior Court,* 436 U.S. 84 (1978). This makes good sense, since individuals benefit from their voluntary in-state contacts just as corporations do and should likewise understand that those benefits may carry with them the burden of related litigation. *Second,* the limitations on personal jurisdiction found in long-arm statutes are distinct from the constitutional limit imposed by the minimum contacts test. See Chapter 2, which compares these two related concepts.

Third, it is clear that a defendant may have sufficient contacts *with* a state to support minimum contacts jurisdiction there even though she did not act *within* the state. If a defendant commits an act outside the state that she knows will cause harmful effects within the state, she will be subject to minimum contacts jurisdiction there for claims arising out of that act. In

---

1. Be careful not to confuse general in personam jurisdiction over a corporation with the corporation's domicile for diversity purposes under 28 U.S.C. §1332(c). A corporation will almost certainly be subject to general in personam jurisdiction in the states where it is incorporated and has its principal place of business, but it may also be subject to general in personam jurisdiction in many additional states, as in the oil company example described above. General in personam jurisdiction is explored more fully in Chapter 8.

2. A recent Supreme Court opinion suggests in dicta that general in personam jurisdiction based on extensive in-state contact may only apply to corporations. *Burnham v. Superior Court of California,* 495 U.S. 604 (1990). Whether or not this is true, the overwhelming majority of general in personam cases involve corporate defendants. Individuals' contacts with states other than their domicile are seldom so extensive as to support an argument for general in personam jurisdiction.

Calder v. Jones, 465 U.S. 783 (1984), for example, the defendant was held subject to personal jurisdiction in California for an allegedly defamatory article written in Florida, since the article was circulated in California, the plaintiff lived there, and the plaintiff's career was centered there. Similarly, if Healy, a Minnesota lawyer, calls a Missouri client on a regular basis to give her legal advice and bills the client for that advice, Healy derives benefits from conducting activities in Missouri. Even if she has never visited Missouri, she will have to answer there for a legal malpractice claim that arises from her deliberate business activity there.

Fourth, minimum contacts analysis focuses on the time when the defendant acted, not the time of the lawsuit. Even if Healy stopped representing her Missouri client a year before being sued and now has no contacts with Missouri, Healy is subject to jurisdiction in Missouri for claims arising from these prior contacts. Minimum contacts jurisdiction is based on the premise that parties who conduct activities in a state accept the risk that those activities will give rise to suits and understand that they may have to return to the state where the activity was conducted to defend such suits. This rationale applies whether or not the defendant is still acting in the state at the time the suit is actually filed. Compare jurisdiction based on service of process on the defendant within the state, recently reaffirmed in *Burnham v. Superior Court of California,* 495 U.S. 604 (1990). Jurisdiction based on in-state service only requires that the defendant be present in the state at the time that the summons and complaint is served upon her. The defendant need not have had *any* contact with the state at the time of the events giving rise to the suit.

Purposeful Availment

The toughest problem in applying the minimum contacts test has been defining the "quality and nature" that makes a contact sufficient to support jurisdiction. Many cases have relied on the statement in *Hanson v. Denckla* that the defendant must have "purposely avail[ed] itself of the privilege of conducting activities within the forum State, thus invoking the benefits and protections of its laws." 357 U.S. 235, 253 (1958). This language emphasizes that the defendant must have made a deliberate choice to relate to the state in some meaningful way before she can be made to bear the burden of defending there. Unilateral contacts of the plaintiff or others will not do.

Although scholars have criticized this emphasis on the defendant's purposeful in-state contacts,[3] the Court has consistently required it. In *World-Wide Volkswagen v. Woodson,* 444 U.S. 286 (1980), for example, the Court concluded that the Audi dealer, Seaway, had not purposely availed itself of the opportunity to conduct activities in Oklahoma, although it could foresee

---

3. See, e.g., M. Weber, Purposeful Availment, 39 S.C.L. Rev. 815, 865-871 (1988).

that others would take its cars there. The dealer had not sold cars there, advertised there, cultivated Oklahoma customers, or deliberately focused on Oklahoma as a market. Thus, it had not sought any direct benefit from Oklahoma activities sufficient to require it to submit to jurisdiction there. In *Keeton v. Hustler Magazine, Inc.*, 465 U.S. 770, 780 (1984), by contrast, the defendant had purposely availed itself of the opportunity to engage in in-state activities, by distributing its magazines within the state. Those contacts supported jurisdiction even though the defendant's acts had greater impact in other states, and the plaintiff had few contacts with the forum state.

Much debate has swirled around application of this purposeful availment requirement in cases where the defendant's goods reach the forum state through the so-called stream of commerce. This often happens in two ways. *First,* an out-of-state component manufacturer sells components to a manufacturer of a finished product outside the state. That manufacturer then incorporates the component into a finished product and sells the finished product in the forum state. *Asahi Metal Industry Co. v. Superior Court,* 480 U.S. 102 (1987), is an example of this situation. *Second,* a manufacturer sells finished products to a wholesaler outside the state, the wholesaler then resells to a retailer in the forum state, and the retailer resells to the consumer.[4] In each of these situations, the defendant did not itself import the product into the forum. Instead, it resold to others who did. The original maker may know that such resales take place in the state, may think it highly likely, or may not know or care about the ultimate destination of its product.

In *Asahi,* the Court split on the question of whether the mere act of selling goods outside the forum state, which will likely be imported into the forum state for resale, suffices to support jurisdiction. Justice O'Connor's opinion, joined by three other Justices, rejected the premise that "mere awareness" that the stream of commerce may sweep goods into the state after they leave the defendant's hands suffices to satisfy "purposeful availment." O'Connor would require clearer evidence that the defendant seeks to serve the market in the particular state, such as designing the product for the market in that state or advertising there. 480 U.S. at 112-113. However, the concurring Justices in *Asahi* would find that sending goods into the stream of commerce, at least in substantial quantities, constitutes "purposeful availment," whether or not the original maker knows that the goods will be sold in a particular state or cultivates customers there. The rationale for this view is that the maker both foresees and benefits from such sales in other states, whether it distributes them there directly or simply takes advantage of the fact that another entity conveniently does so in its place.

Since the *Asahi* Court split sharply on this issue, and since two of the

---

4. A case may also involve both situations, that is, a component is sold to an out-of-state manufacturer, which then incorporates it into a product that is resold to a wholesaler and imported into the forum state, thus reaching the ultimate consumer.

Asahi Justices have left the Court, it is difficult to say what "the law" is on stream of commerce cases. "The only certainty is that the present court is deeply divided over the scope and validity of the stream of commerce theory." K. Dayton, Personal Jurisdiction and the Stream of Commerce, 7 Rev. of Litig. 239, 246 (1988). That's not very satisfying to an attorney who has to advise a client, or to a first year law student, but it is, as of this writing, the state of the law.[5] It is clear, however, that if the defendant's contacts satisfy Justice O'Connor's test they will support jurisdiction, since the other *Asahi* opinions would require a lesser showing.

Other Factors in the Jurisdictional Calculus

There is also a great deal of talk in the cases about factors other than the defendant's in-state contacts, such as the interest of the forum state in providing redress to its citizens, the interest of the plaintiff in obtaining relief in a convenient forum, the interest of the states in enforcing their substantive law or policy, and the extent of the inconvenience to the defendant if she is forced to defend away from home. The cases have repeatedly cited such factors in determining whether it would be fair to assert personal jurisdiction over the defendant. See *Keeton*, 465 U.S. at 775-780; *Burger King*, 471 U.S. at 476-477. Indeed, the *Asahi* Court concluded that these factors made it unreasonable to take jurisdiction in the case before it, even if minimum contacts were established.

However, while the plaintiff's interest, the forum state's interest, and other fairness issues enter the balance once minimum contacts are found, they are not sufficient to support jurisdiction if those contacts are not present. The defendant must first have purposely availed herself of the opportunity to conduct activities in the state. It is only when such deliberate contacts exist between the defendant and the forum state (and when those contacts give rise to the claim) that other factors will be weighed in determining whether the exercise of jurisdiction would comport with "fair play and substantial justice."

Thus, although some principles are established in the minimum contacts area, the test still remains difficult to state and even more difficult to apply in close cases. Over the course of your lawyering life it will take on clearer meaning as you handle personal jurisdiction issues and begin to see how courts give flesh to the bare-bones test. The following examples will provide a start in that direction. In answering them, focus on the constitutional issue of minimum contacts only; do not worry about statutory problems under long-arm statutes. Also, assume that the contacts mentioned are the only contacts the defendant has with the forum state.

---

5. For the author's prediction on this point, see infra example 11 and n.8.

EXAMPLES

Opening Rounds

1.   Austin is a traveling salesman who lives in North Dakota and sells Fuller brushes in parts of North Dakota, South Dakota, and Minnesota. While en route to deliver brushes to a Minnesota customer, he is involved in an auto accident in Minnesota with Healy, a Minnesota citizen. He brings suit against Healy in North Dakota for his injuries in the accident. Does the court have personal jurisdiction over Healy?

2.   As a result of the same accident, Healy brings suit against Austin for her injuries. She sues in South Dakota. Does the court have jurisdiction over Austin based on minimum contacts?

3.   To be on the safe side, Healy also files suit against Austin in Minnesota. Does that court have personal jurisdiction over Austin based on minimum contacts?

A Parade of Perplexities

4.   *The Volkswagen.* Many of the most difficult personal jurisdiction cases involve commercial contacts, that is, contacts that arise out of business done in the state, either directly or indirectly, by a corporation acting outside the state. *World-Wide Volkswagen v. Woodson,* 444 U.S. 286 (1980), sets out the basic framework for analyzing these cases. The motorcade of hypotheticals that follows may help you assess the importance of various contacts with the forum state.

Hudson, an Ohio citizen, buys a Volkswagen from Smoky Mountain VW, located on the east side of the Smoky Mountains in North Carolina, while she is on vacation in North Carolina. Shortly after she returns home, all four wheels fall off while she is driving, and Hudson is injured. Understandably upset, Hudson sues Smoky Mountain in an Ohio court for negligence. Does the court have personal jurisdiction over the dealer?

5.   *The Chevy.* After Hudson leaves, Ford pulls into Smoky Mountain's lot with his engine belching smoke. His car is clearly a total loss, and he tells De Soto, the salesman, that he must have a car to get back home to Florida. De Soto sells him a (very) used Chevy. After crossing into Florida, Ford pushes the windshield wiper button, and the engine automatically ejects into the Everglades. Ford sues De Soto and Smoky Mountain in Florida. Is personal jurisdiction proper there?

6.   *The Maserati.* De Soto has an eye for fast cars. At the moment, he has a nice Maserati on the lot, with all the extras (engine, wheels, brakes). A customer tells him that a trucker buddy of his, Packard, from Pennsylvania, might be interested in buying the Maserati. De Soto calls Packard in Pennsylvania, extolls the Maserati's virtues and encourages her to come in and test drive the car on her next delivery in North Carolina. Packard does stop to see

the car, likes it, and buys it. She makes the mistake of towing it home, only to discover upon arrival that the engine, lights, carburetor, and exhaust system are missing. She sues De Soto in Pennsylvania. De Soto has no other contacts with Pennsylvania. Will the Pennsylvania court have personal jurisdiction over De Soto?

7. *The Audi*. After lunch, Rambler comes in. Rambler lives across the border in Tennessee, where he read in a Tennessee paper Smoky Mountain's ad for a one-year-old Audi for $1,100. Because the Smoky Mountain dealership is located ten miles from the Tennessee border, it advertises frequently in Tennessee, as well as in North Carolina. Rambler visits the dealership, talks De Soto down to $1,025 and buys the car. He barely gets across the Tennessee line when the steering wheel comes off in his hand, and the body comes entirely loose from the frame of the car. Rambler sues Smoky Mountain in Tennessee. Does the court have personal jurisdiction over Smoky Mountain?

8.   Assume, on the facts of example 7, that Smoky Mountain only advertises occasionally in Tennessee and derives only 5 percent of its business ($20,000 of its annual gross sales of $400,000) from sales to Tennessee customers. The rest of its sales are in North Carolina. Rambler sees the ad and buys the Audi at Smoky Mountain's dealership; it breaks down in Tennessee on the way home. Can Rambler sue Smoky Mountain in Tennessee?

Sports Cars

9.   *The Ferrari*. You can't work all the time. When De Soto relaxes, he likes to go to the Georgia coast for some deep sea fishing. While drinking at a bar in the fishing lodge there, he gets to talking with Lenoir, another guest at the lodge. Lenoir asks De Soto about his work. The two get into a car lovers' debate over the relative merits of various sports cars. Before leaving the bar, Lenoir asks De Soto for his card.

Two months later, Lenoir visits Smoky Mountain and buys a jazzy looking Ferrari from De Soto. Imagine for yourself what happens to the Ferrari when Lenoir gets it back to Georgia. Lenoir sues De Soto in Georgia. Will the court have personal jurisdiction over De Soto?

Changing Cars in Midstream

10. *The Off-Road Vehicle*. Nippon Auto Unlimited is a Japanese corporation that manufactures off-road vehicles in Japan for sale worldwide. It sells substantial numbers of these vehicles in Japan to A-1 Wholesalers, Inc., a California dealer in off-road vehicles. A-1 imports them into the United States and resells them to dealers throughout the western United States. Nippon sells an off-road vehicle to A-1, which then sells it to A-1's Recreational Emporium in Reno, Nevada. A-1's sells the off-road vehicle to Lincoln, who is injured

when the vehicle collapses while driving over a crack in the sidewalk. Lincoln sues Nippon in a state court in Nevada.

    a. Does the court have jurisdiction over Nippon? *— Split*

    b. Would it have jurisdiction over A-1 if Lincoln sued it in Nevada? *Yes, purposeful*

11. Assume that A-1 bought the off-road vehicle from Atlanta Importers, Inc., a large importer of off-road vehicles in Atlanta, Georgia. A-1 has the off-road vehicles shipped to California and resells some to A-1's, where Lincoln bought hers. Could Lincoln sue Atlanta Importers in Nevada? *split*

12. *The Edsel.* Andretti is an Indiana race car driver whose hobby is collecting antique cars. He notices an ad in *Antique Auto,* a national magazine, for a mint condition Edsel for sale by a Michigan collector, Studebaker. He calls Studebaker, gets further information on the car, and decides to go up to look at it. While he is in Michigan, he and Studebaker discuss price but do not settle the deal. After Andretti returns to Indiana, he calls Studebaker back, agrees to his price, and arranges to pick up the car the following month. After buying the car and returning with it to Indiana, he discovers that it is a cleverly disguised Dodge Dart. He sues Studebaker in Indiana. Will the court dismiss for lack of personal jurisdiction?

Fundamental (Un)truths

13. Every year, the following statements sprout like dandelions in civil procedure bluebooks. What is wrong with them?

    a. "Even if the defendant lacks minimum contacts with the state, the plaintiff may be able to get jurisdiction over him if he has taken advantage of the benefits and protections of the laws of the state."

    b. "The defendant may be sued in the state because she has engaged in deliberate acts there and thus has minimum contacts sufficient to support personal jurisdiction."

EXPLANATIONS

Opening Rounds

1. In this case Austin has sued Healy in a state with which Austin has contacts, but Healy has none. As far as the example tells us, Healy has never been there, has not formed any deliberate relationship to or performed acts within the state, and has done nothing to derive benefits from North Dakota. Consequently, she has no reason to expect to be sued there and has not impliedly swallowed that bitter pill in exchange for the benefits of in-state activity. She lacks minimum contacts with North Dakota and may not be sued there on this claim.

    As this conclusion suggests, the personal jurisdiction rules are defendant-oriented. The plaintiff's contacts with the forum state will not do; the court must find some basis for forcing the defendant, the unwilling litigant, to appear before it.[6] One might well ask why Austin should have to go to Healy instead of Healy coming to Austin. If someone will have to be inconvenienced by the suit, shouldn't it be the defendant rather than the injured plaintiff? On the other hand, the defendant may be completely blameless: Plaintiffs lose law suits as well as win them. If so, it seems unfair to add the insult of distant litigation to the injury of being sued in the first place. Perhaps more importantly, the defendant (unlike the plaintiff, who started the suit) has not chosen the forum and ought to have some veto power over unreasonable choices by the plaintiff.

2.   The South Dakota court will not have personal jurisdiction over Austin under the minimum contacts test. It is true that Austin has some contacts with South Dakota because he travels there to sell brushes. However, *International Shoe* does not hold that a defendant may be sued in a state simply because she has some contacts with that state. *Shoe* holds that a defendant may, by committing limited acts within a state, submit herself to jurisdiction for claims arising out of the in-state acts themselves. Here, Healy's claim is unrelated to Austin's brush sales in South Dakota. Austin had no reason to believe that he was submitting himself to the jurisdiction of the South Dakota courts for auto accidents in Minnesota by selling brushes in South Dakota. The situation would be different if the claim were for faulty brushes sold to a South Dakota customer. In that case, the claim would arise directly from Austin's voluntary contacts with the state, and jurisdiction would be proper.

However, Healy may still be able to sue Austin in South Dakota for the auto claim. Ever since *Pennoyer v. Neff,* 95 U.S. 714 (1877), it has been permissible to obtain personal jurisdiction over an individual defendant (that is, a person) by serving her with the summons in the state where suit is brought. Although some scholars had suggested that the Supreme Court would ultimately reject jurisdiction based solely on in-state service,[7] the Court recently reaffirmed that such "transient jurisdiction" is permissible, even if the defendant is only in the state briefly or for reasons unrelated to the litigation. *Burnham v. Superior Court of California,* 495 U.S. 604 (1990). Thus, if Healy is determined for one reason or another to sue in South Dakota, she may bring suit there and have the process server await Austin's next sales trip into the state.

---

6. Conversely, if the defendant has minimum contacts with the forum state, it is irrelevant (at least, for personal jurisdiction purposes) that the plaintiff has none.

7. A number of scholars argued that such jurisdiction based on "transient presence" of the defendant in the forum state was inconsistent with *Shaffer v. Heitner,* 433 U.S. 186 (1977), which held that all exercises of personal jurisdiction must be measured against the minimum contacts standard. See, e.g., Friedenthal, Kane, and Miller at §3.17.

3.   Healy has gotten it right by suing Austin in Minnesota. Austin's act of driving in Minnesota provides a minimum contacts basis for a suit against him there for injuries suffered in the accident. Motorists who use the roads of a state should realize that this purposeful activity in the forum subjects other drivers to serious risks, that people may be injured and may sue. It would be unfair to allow drivers to take advantage of Minnesota's highways but not to call them to account there for accidents they are involved in on those highways.

Even if causing the accident in Minnesota were Austin's only contact with the state, it would support specific in personam jurisdiction in this case. The "quality and nature" of this single, purposeful act, and the consequences that may predictably ensue from it, are so serious as to make it reasonable to force the driver to return to defend a suit that arises from the accident. This is true whether Austin causes an accident while in Minnesota on business or in Florida on vacation.

A Parade of Perplexities

4.   As the heading suggests, this case bears some resemblance to *World-Wide Volkswagen v. Woodson*. Here, as in *World-Wide,* the plaintiff purchased the car in one state and took it to another where she suffered injury from alleged defects in the car. As in *World-Wide,* the plaintiff sues where the injury is suffered, although the defendant acted in a distant state and is still in that state. And, as in *World-Wide,* the court will dismiss this case for lack of personal jurisdiction. Smoky Mountain (like Seaway in the *World-Wide* case) has committed no deliberate act that affiliates it with Ohio. It does not sell cars there, has not availed itself of the protection of Ohio's laws, and has no reason to expect that it will be sued there. Although it is foreseeable that the car will be driven through or end up in Ohio, it is equally foreseeable that it will go to many other states. A rule that such foreseeability establishes jurisdiction would essentially subject the seller of any portable product to nationwide jurisdiction, making "the chattel [product] his agent for service of process" (*World-Wide Volkswagen* at 296) wherever the buyer takes it.

5.   This case is somewhat stronger than Hudson's, since De Soto at least knew that he was dealing with a Florida citizen who would use the Chevy in Florida. However, it is very doubtful that this knowledge is enough to support jurisdiction over De Soto or Smoky Mountain in Florida. Personal jurisdiction is the price defendants pay for deliberate efforts to derive benefits from or conduct activities in a state. These defendants did not solicit any business in Florida; they did not even solicit business from a Floridian. Ford rolled into the dealership under his own steam (and smoke) and initiated the transaction in North Carolina. It was only by chance that Ford told De Soto why he needed the car; it is reasonable to infer that it was irrelevant to De Soto that Ford planned to drive it to Florida. (A sale is a sale, right?) De Soto

and his employer derived benefits from dealing with a Floridian in North Carolina, not from conducting business activities in Florida. Ford's Florida domicile is a unilateral contact of the *plaintiff*, not the defendant, with the forum state. See *Hanson v. Denckla,* 357 U.S. 235, 253 (1958); compare *Burger King,* 471 U.S. at 478-482, in which jurisdiction was upheld because the defendants had an on-going contractual relationship with a large Florida franchise, agreed that Florida law would govern the relationship, and regularly related to the Florida headquarters of the franchise regarding important aspects of their business.

It is true that the Supreme Court cases, especially the recent ones, emphasize that the plaintiff's interest in a remedy and the forum state's interest in providing one are part of the personal jurisdiction calculus. See, e.g., *Asahi,* 480 U.S. at 113-115; *Keeton v. Hustler Magazine,* 465 U.S. at 775. However, before those factors can be weighed in favor of jurisdiction, the defendant must be shown to have appropriate purposeful contacts with the state asserting jurisdiction. *Burger King Corp. v. Rudzewicz,* 471 U.S. at 474-478. De Soto's relation to Florida on these facts appears too attenuated to support such a finding.

Nor is it sufficient that the defendants could anticipate that the car would be used in Florida. If that were sufficient to support jurisdiction, then the local store that sells a defective mountain climbing rope could be sued in any mountainous state, or a farmer who sells rancid tomatoes to railroad dining cars could be sued in any state the railroad serves. The Court has chosen a narrower view of personal jurisdiction, focusing on the scope of the activity of the seller, rather than the predictable area of use of the product by the buyer.

6.   Here, as in example 5, De Soto has consciously dealt with an out-of-stater, but here, unlike the earlier situation, he has voluntarily affiliated himself with the plaintiff's state. He cannot only anticipate that his acts will have consequences in the other state, but he has also deliberately set those events in motion by his own in-state act. De Soto voluntarily reached into Pennsylvania to conduct business with a Pennsylvanian. He made representations to Packard in Pennsylvania that encouraged her to come to North Carolina to buy the car. He can reasonably anticipate that Packard will use the car extensively in Pennsylvania and likely suffer harm there from any defects in the car. De Soto should realize that his deliberate relationship with a Pennsylvanian, which he initiated by calling into that state, may lead to a lawsuit and that if a claim arises out of the sale, Packard will likely bring the suit in Pennsylvania. Thus, De Soto will be subject to personal jurisdiction in this action. His single contact with Pennsylvania is sufficient to support specific in personam jurisdiction (that is, jurisdiction for claims arising out of the contact itself), although it would not support jurisdiction for claims that did not arise out of the sale.

7.   In this case the dealership has reached into Tennessee to solicit business. It has attempted to draw customers from there into North Carolina, and in Rambler's case it succeeded. Although the actual sale took place in North Carolina, the claim arises directly out of deliberate efforts to serve the Tennessee market. Smoky Mountain can hardly plead unfairness or surprise when suits that arise from those efforts are brought in Tennessee. Even Justice O'Connor should have no problem upholding jurisdiction in this case, since the defendant has intentionally attempted to derive profits from dealing with Tennessee customers.

It is important that the dealership is the defendant here, instead of De Soto, because it is the dealership that solicited the business in Tennessee, not the salesman. It is unlikely that the dealership's contacts with Tennessee will be imputed to its employees. (Compare example 6, in which De Soto personally initiated contacts with the forum state.) Thus, if Rambler wanted to sue De Soto and Smoky Mountain together, he would probably have to bring suit in North Carolina.

8.   This hypo makes an important point. Personal jurisdiction is not based on the most contacts or the best contacts but on minimum contacts. Here, Smoky Mountain has a great deal more contact with North Carolina than it has with Tennessee, but the dealership has solicited business in Tennessee, and the claim arises out of its efforts to obtain that business. That is enough to support jurisdiction in Tennessee. Smoky Mountain will not be able to defeat jurisdiction there by arguing that it has more contacts with North Carolina.

A corollary of this point is that a defendant may be subject to minimum contacts jurisdiction in more than one state for a claim that arises from a transaction involving contacts with a number of states.

Sports Cars

9.   In my estimation, this is the kind of "casual" or "isolated" contact (*International Shoe*, 326 U.S. at 317) that is insufficient to subject the defendant to personal jurisdiction. Although De Soto did act in the state, he was not soliciting business and did not initiate the conversation for business purposes. He gave Lenoir his card at Lenoir's request. He did not encourage Lenoir to go to North Carolina to buy a car. In the "but-for" sense, this contact did give rise to the claim Lenoir asserts, but it was not a purposeful act intended to take advantage of the benefits and protections of conducting activity in Georgia. De Soto would be justifiably upset if this off-hand inter-action led to a suit in Georgia. He would hardly expect that to be the consequence of responding to a request for a business card, and jurisdictional doctrine is largely based on a common sense appraisal of what people should expect.

There is room for debate on this case, but it is doubtful that this constitutes deliberate in-state activity intended to exploit the local market or affect local citizens. In this regard, it is clearly distinguishable from the Maserati case, in which De Soto deliberately initiated a business contact with the in-state plaintiff, or *McGee v. International Ins. Co.,* 355 U.S. 220 (1957) (in which the insurer reached into California by sending an offer there to reinsure a Californian).

Changing Cars in Midstream

10a. This is a relatively typical stream of commerce example, in which an out-of-state (in this case, out-of-country) manufacturer sells its product to a wholesaler outside the forum state, which then independently imports the product into the state for final sale to consumers. As in most cases, the original seller, Nippon, does not control the subsequent flow of the "stream." Nippon may or may not know that A-1 resells in Nevada, though it certainly could predict that it will. Doubtless, it hopes that A-1 will sell as widely as possible and profits from those sales regardless of what it knows about A-1's market area.

In the first edition of this book, I offered the following analysis of a similar example:

> *World-Wide Volkswagen* clearly supports jurisdiction over such out-of-state (or out-of-country) suppliers who deliver "products into the stream of commerce with the expectation that they will be purchased by consumers in the forum State." 444 U.S. at 298.
>
> Here, Nippon has purposely taken advantage of the benefits and protections of the laws of Nevada by importing cars to that state and deriving a profit from those sales. It cannot insulate itself from the jurisdictional consequences of that activity by using wholesalers to channel the goods into the state.

Since *Asahi,* however, it is not so clear that putting goods into the stream of commerce constitutes sufficient "purposeful availment" to support jurisdiction over Nippon in Nevada. Nippon has not done any of the things Justice O'Connor would require to cultivate the Nevada market. It neither markets directly there, nor advertises there, nor designs its goods for Nevada buyers. It just sells its product in Japan to a foreign wholesaler.

Arguably, this example is distinguishable from *Asahi*: The defendant there was a component maker, not a manufacturer of a final product. Also, it was a third-party defendant, not a direct defendant as here. More importantly, Nippon sold to an American buyer, while Asahi sold to a Taiwanese corporation. But it does not appear that these distinctions would make a difference to Justice O'Connor. O'Connor's position requires an active effort to serve the forum state market to support stream-of-commerce jurisdiction; Nippon merely sells its off-road vehicles to wholesalers in Japan. If O'Connor's view were "the law," or becomes the law, Nippon would apparently not be subject to jurisdiction in Nevada.

The concurring opinions in *Asahi* suggest that jurisdiction would be proper in cases like this, assuming a reasonable quantity of goods coming into the country, since Nippon predictably derives benefits from the ultimate sale of its goods in Nevada. Those benefits are the same, whether Nippon directs A-1 to sell in Nevada, knows that it does, suspects that it does, or deliberately avoids finding out. Arguably, that economic reality should support jurisdiction over Nippon, even though it does not control the means by which its product enters the forum state.

b. There is no question about jurisdiction over A-1 in Nevada on this claim. It imported the vehicle into the state, a purposeful contact, which directly gives rise to the claim.

11. The main difference here is that the defendant is an out-of-state corporation, not a corporation from another country. This might influence the second prong of the jurisdictional inquiry: the reasonableness of taking jurisdiction. Almost all the Justices considered it relevant to the fairness analysis that *Asahi* would be dragged into a foreign court halfway around the world. Here, unlike *Asahi,* the defendant, Atlanta Importers, has imported the product into the United States. Clearly, it is trying to serve the United States market.

It is not clear, however, that these distinctions would lead Justice O'Connor to a different conclusion on the issue of purposeful availment. Atlanta Importers has still sold a product to a buyer in Georgia, with no special knowledge or effort to serve the Nevada market where its buyer resold the product. If the O'Connor view would reject jurisdiction in cases like this, and if it becomes the position of the Court, this would be a very substantial change in the limits of jurisdiction in stream of commerce cases. (Compare *World-Wide,* 444 U.S. at 297-298 (reasonable to subject manufacturer to suit if it "serves, directly or indirectly, the market for its product" in the state)). Indeed, this reasoning could lead to a rejection of jurisdiction, even if Atlanta *manufactured* the off-road vehicles in Georgia but sold to wholesalers there for marketing in other states.[8]

---

8. If you want this author's view on how this will be resolved, it is that it won't be. The Court is likely to proceed on a case by case basis, and each will turn, as personal jurisdiction cases inevitably do, on its facts. If the Court ultimately requires more than placing goods into the stream, it is likely to require *very little more*. On the facts of this example the Court would likely recognize the economic reality that the very purpose of the importer is to serve the United States market, not just the Georgia market. Thus, the resale of its off-road vehicles in Nevada is consistent with Atlanta Importer's goals and expectations, and the company should be subject to jurisdiction there, even if it does not have the various in-state contacts referred to in the O'Connor plurality.

12. This is a close case indeed, perhaps too close to call. Studebaker does have a contact with Indiana: He advertised in a magazine circulated there with the express purpose of selling his Edsel. On the other hand, the magazine is a specialty publication circulated nationally. Studebaker was not specifically soliciting an Indiana buyer but was willing to sell to anyone, in or out of the state. Once Andretti learned of the car's availability, he took the initiative: He went to Michigan to see the car; he called back to make an offer; and he picked up the car in Michigan. Studebaker remained in Michigan and passively responded. It was irrelevant to him that Andretti was from Indiana. He may not even have known where Andretti was from.

I think this is a case in which the defendant does have a deliberate contact with the forum state, but the totality of the circumstances weighs against jurisdiction in Indiana. At least eight of the *Asahi* Justices agreed that, once a jurisdictionally significant contact with the forum state is found, the Court must consider whether it would be fair and reasonable under all the circumstances to take jurisdiction. 480 U.S. at 113-116. Given the lack of deliberate acts by Studebaker in Indiana, that all the negotiations took place at Andretti's initiative, and that Studebaker never left Michigan, it appears unreasonable to expect Studebaker to defend this claim in Indiana. Once again, compare example 6, in which the seller solicited the sale in the forum state.

Fundamental (Un)truths

13a. This statement implies that taking advantage of the benefits and protections of the laws of the state is an alternative basis for personal jurisdiction, independent of the minimum contacts test. On the contrary, the purpose for asking whether the defendant has taken advantage of the benefits and protections of the state's laws is to *evaluate* the defendant's contacts with the state, to ascertain whether they are of the "quality and nature" to support jurisdiction. If the defendant's in-state acts demonstrate a deliberate effort to take advantage of the benefits and protections of the forum state's laws, it is a fair inference that these acts satisfy the minimum contacts test, since minimum contacts jurisdiction is based on the defendant's deliberate decision to act in the forum state for her own purposes.

b. The problem with this statement is that it suggests that a defendant is subject to jurisdiction in a state for any claim if she has *some* contacts with the state. Not so. Conducting some activity in a state does not support such wide jurisdiction. Unless the contacts are so substantial as to pass that ambiguous "G" line in Figure 1-1, the defendant is only subject to jurisdiction for claims *related to the in-state contacts*.

Precision and clarity are the stock-in-trade of the law student as well as the lawyer. A few students who make statements like this on the exam have not really grasped the distinction between specific and general in personam jurisdiction. Most really mean to say, "The defendant may be sued in the state on this claim under the minimum contacts test because it has purposely conducted activities there, and the claim arises out of this purposeful contact." This second statement is not only a great deal more precise than the first, but it is accurate, while the other, as it stands, is not. It is differences like this that separate the daffodils from the dandelions in the Merry Month of May.

2

Statutory Limits on Personal Jurisdiction: The Reach and Grasp of the Long-Arm

Introduction

As Chapter 1 explains, the due process clause of the fourteenth amendment to the Constitution imposes fundamental limitations on the power of state courts to exercise personal jurisdiction over defendants in civil suits. Under that clause states may only assert jurisdiction over defendants who have established a significant relationship to the forum state, such as domicile, in-state presence, continuous and substantial business within the state, consent to suit in that state, or minimum contacts with the state that gave rise to the claim in suit. If the defendant is not subject to personal jurisdiction within the forum state on one of these limited bases, the court will be unable to adjudicate the plaintiff's claim.

However, even if it is constitutionally permissible for a court to exercise personal jurisdiction in a case, that court may still lack the power to call the defendant before it. The due process clause does not actually confer any jurisdiction on state courts; it only defines the outer bounds of permissible jurisdictional power. It is up to the legislature of each state to actually grant the power to its courts to exercise personal jurisdiction through jurisdictional

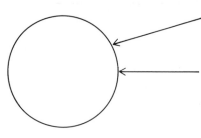

Constitutional scope of jurisdiction
under the due process clause

Statutory power to exercise jurisdiction
under California Civil Procedure Code
§410.10 (same as constitutional scope)

Figure 2-1

statutes. Thus, every personal jurisdiction issue involves a two-step analysis. *First,* the court must ask whether there is a state statute that authorizes it to exercise personal jurisdiction under the circumstances of the case. *Second,* if there is, the court must ask whether it would be constitutional under the due process clause to do so.

State legislatures are free to grant their courts the power to exercise personal jurisdiction to the limits of the due process clause or to confer only part of the constitutionally permissible jurisdiction. In some states the legislature has granted the courts the full scope of personal jurisdiction permissible under the due process clause. California's statute, for example, authorizes its courts to exercise jurisdiction "on any basis not inconsistent with the Constitution of this state or of the United States." Cal. Civ. Proc. Code §410.10 (West 1973 & Supp. 1986). In states with statutes like California's, the two inquiries are collapsed into one: If the court has the constitutional power to assert jurisdiction, it automatically has the statutory power to do so as well. Visually the relationship may be (somewhat simplistically) portrayed in Figure 2-1. One advantage of such expansive provisions is that they are "self-adjusting"; that is, if the courts reinterpret the due process clause to allow the exercise of personal jurisdiction in additional circumstances, these statutes automatically authorize the courts of the state to exercise jurisdiction in such cases. See Beyler, The Illinois Long-Arm Statute: Background, Meaning and Needed Repairs, 12 S. Ill. L.J. 293, 319, 320 (1988).

"Enumerated Act" Long-Arm Statutes

Other states, however, have not given their courts blanket authority to exercise personal jurisdiction to the limits of due process. Instead, these states have passed "long-arm" statutes, which authorize their courts to exercise jurisdiction over defendants based on specific types of contact with the forum state. Historically, these "enumerated act" long-arm statutes were passed in reaction to *International Shoe* and its progeny. See generally R. Casad, Jurisdiction in Civil Actions ¶4.01 (2d ed. 1991) (hereinafter cited as Casad). Once *International Shoe* and succeeding cases established that certain types of contacts were constitutionally sufficient bases for exercising personal jurisdiction over nonresidents, the states adopted long-arm statutes to authorize

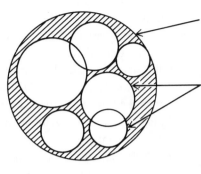

Figure 2-2

their courts to hear cases arising out of such contacts. Thus, enumerated act long-arm statutes generally authorize state courts to exercise jurisdiction over cases arising out of contacts such as committing a tortious act within the state, transacting business in the state, or owning property in the state.[1]

Visually the relation of such statutes to the due process clause is represented by Figure 2-2. Such provisions convey a good deal of the jurisdiction authorized by the due process clause, but not necessarily all of it. Some areas remain (represented by the shaded area in the diagram) in which jurisdiction could be exercised, but the statute does not authorize it.

Students often ask why a state would enact an enumerated act long-arm when the California model is simpler and broader. One reason is historical: The first modern long-arm statute, the Illinois statute, used the enumerated act approach, and many states later used it as a model. Even if California's mellow approach is preferable in the abstract, many states are reluctant to tinker with statutes that have worked satisfactorily for years and have been construed repeatedly by their courts. In addition, the list of jurisdictionally sufficient acts in enumerated act long-arm statutes provides some guidance to nonresidents about the jurisdictional consequences of their choice to conduct particular activities in the state. Finally, some legislatures may not want to authorize jurisdiction in every case that barely passes constitutional muster. The enumerated act statutes give courts some leeway to reject jurisdiction in cases having little connection to the state, without making constitutional pronouncements.[2]

---

1. A fairly typical provision is the Uniform Interstate and International Procedure Act, 13 U.L.A. 355 (West 1986), which has served as the model for the long-arm statutes of some 20 states. It is reproduced on p.28 for use in the examples in this chapter.

2. A few states have taken the curious approach of *adding* a California-type, anything-constitutional-goes provision to their enumerated act statute. This seems calculated to confuse: Why specify enumerated acts which support jurisdiction, if everything else within due process limits does too? For a defense of this strategy, see K. Beyler, The Illinois Long-Arm Statute: Background, Meaning, and Needed Repairs, 12 S. Ill. L.J. 293, 412-414 (1988).

Long-arm statutes take their colorful name from their primary purpose, which is to reach out of the state to call nonresident defendants back into the state to defend lawsuits.[3] Even though a defendant has left the forum state before he is sued (or in some cases has never been in the state at all), he may be required to defend a suit there under the *International Shoe* analysis if the suit arises out of his prior contacts with the forum. Legislatures tend to grant such long-arm jurisdiction liberally since it is usually invoked by plaintiffs who live in the state and prefer to sue at home.

Be careful, however, not to conclude that every assertion of jurisdiction under a long-arm statute is automatically constitutional simply because the statute apparently covers it. In the area of personal jurisdiction, it is not always easy to tell what is and is not constitutional. Consequently, the reach of a state's long-arm statute may sometimes exceed its constitutional grasp. Suppose, for example, that an Iowa long-arm statute authorized its courts to take jurisdiction in all cases brought by resident plaintiffs. It would certainly be unconstitutional to apply such a statute to a case arising out of the plaintiff's purchase of goods from a Colorado defendant in Colorado. Assuming that the defendant has no other contacts with Iowa, there would be no constitutional authority to assert personal jurisdiction over the defendant, since the claim does not arise out of any minimum contacts with Iowa. This case falls within the "bulge" area in Figure 2-3, in which the statute authorizes jurisdiction (because the plaintiff is a resident), but it would exceed the limits of due process to exercise that jurisdiction.

However, the statute could be applied in other cases without violating due process. For example, if the case arose from a sale by the defendant to the plaintiff that took place in Iowa, the exercise of jurisdiction would be constitutionally permissible because the defendant's voluntary contacts with Iowa gave rise to the claim. This case would fall in the shaded area on the diagram. In such cases, where the statute may be constitutional as applied to some cases but not all, the courts do not invalidate the statute entirely; they simply refuse to apply it to cases that fall outside the bounds of due process. Consequently, the statute remains in force and may be applied in other cases that are within due process limits.

All long-arm statutes that base personal jurisdiction on specific minimum contacts require that the claim sued upon arise out of the contact itself. See, e.g., Uniform Interstate and International Procedure Act §1.03(b), infra

---

3. Such statutes are usually unnecessary to obtain jurisdiction over in-state defendants. Individuals who are domiciled in the state are subject to personal jurisdiction on that basis. *Milliken v. Meyer,* 311 U.S. 457 (1940). Individuals present within the state may be personally served and are subject to jurisdiction under the ancient (but still viable) theory of *Pennoyer v. Neff.* In-state corporations are subject to jurisdiction on the basis of substantial and continuous activities in the forum state. See *International Shoe* at 318. In each of these cases, however, there must also be a statutory basis for the exercise of jurisdiction. See, e.g., Uniform Interstate and International Procedure Act §1.02 (jurisdiction based on domicile or incorporation in the forum state).

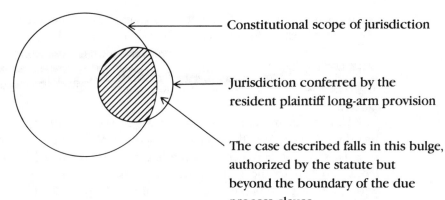

Figure 2–3

p.29. This limitation is rooted in the *International Shoe* analysis, which holds that limited in-state contacts only support jurisdiction over claims that arise from those contacts. See the "*Shoe* spectrum" at p.6. By echoing that limitation in the long-arm statute itself, the legislature insures that the statute will not be used to reach cases beyond the constitutional bounds of due process.

Going to the Limits of Due Process

You will frequently read in the cases that an enumerated act long-arm statute is "intended to reach to the limits of due process." This is one of the most frequently misunderstood phrases in the civil procedure lexicon. Although innumerable cases broadly hold that the long-arm statute in question is intended to extend jurisdiction to the constitutional limits, this is *not* generally intended to mean that a statute like the Uniform Act occupies the entire constitutional field, as the California statute does. It would make little sense for the legislature to pass a statute enumerating specific contacts that support jurisdiction if it actually intended all minimum contacts to do so. Instead, this phrase is better interpreted to mean that the *specific categories* of jurisdiction conveyed by the long-arm statute are to be interpreted as liberally as the due process clause will allow.

For example, the phrase "transacting business" in a long-arm statute might be interpreted quite narrowly, to apply only in cases where the defendant has ongoing commercial activities and permanent employees within the state. Alternatively it might be interpreted more broadly, to apply whenever the defendant enters into a single business transaction with an in-state party. If the statute is intended to go to the limits of due process, the court will interpret this language to reach all cases that are arguably within the statutory language and can be reached under the due process clause. See Casad at ¶4.01[1][b]. Since a single business transaction (depending on the facts) may be sufficient under due process analysis to give rise to personal jurisdiction over claims arising out of it, the statute should be broadly interpreted to reach such a case. In other words, the going-to-the-limits-of-due-process language commands liberal interpretation of the specific provisions of the long-arm statute; it does not fill in any interstices those provisions fail to cover.

Unfortunately, courts have not always grasped this distinction between broad interpretation of the enumerated acts and absorbing the whole constitutional sphere. Many decisions holding that the relevant long-arm is intended to "go to the limits of due process" really do mean, rightly or wrongly, that it fills all the shaded interstices in Figure 2-2.[4] Thus, if you are researching a case and find such language, it should set off a little alarm in the personal jurisdiction corner of your brain, stimulating some very careful reading of the cases under your long-arm statute to determine what the court really means to say.

In analyzing the following examples, consider first whether the applicable long-arm statute authorizes the court to exercise jurisdiction. Then consider whether it would be constitutional under the minimum contacts test for the court to exercise jurisdiction on the facts given. The Uniform Act, which is used in most of the examples, is set forth below.

UNIFORM INTERSTATE AND INTERNATIONAL PROCEDURE ACT

§1.03. [Personal Jurisdiction Based upon Conduct]

(a) A court may exercise personal jurisdiction over a person, who acts directly or by an agent, as to a [cause of action] [claim for relief] arising from the person's

(1) transacting any business in this state;

(2) contracting to supply services or things in this state;

(3) causing tortious injury by an act or omission in this state;

(4) causing tortious injury in this state by an act or omission outside this state if he regularly does or solicits business, or engages in any other persistent course of conduct, or derives substantial revenue from goods used or consumed or services rendered, in this state; [or]

(5) having an interest in, using, or possessing real property in this state [; or

(6) contracting to insure any person, property, or risk located within this state at the time of contracting].

---

4. For an example of the confusion such loose language has generated under one long-arm provision, see Comment, Georgia's Not-So-Long Arm Statute: Exposing the Myth, 6 Ga. St. L. Rev. 487 (1990).

(b) When jurisdiction over a person is based solely upon this section, only a [cause of action] [claim for relief] arising from acts enumerated in this section may be asserted against him.

EXAMPLES

Torts and the Long-Arm: Basic Cases

1.   Hardy throws a pie at Fields while the two are making a movie in New York. Fields fails to see the joke and sues Hardy for assault in Pennsylvania, where Fields lives. Hardy has no other contacts with Pennsylvania.
    a. Could the Pennsylvania court assert jurisdiction over Hardy if the Uniform Act applied in Pennsylvania? N
    b. Would it be constitutional for the court to do so? N

2.   Assume that Hardy, a comedian, performs two or three times a year at clubs in Pennsylvania. Fields sues him in Pennsylvania for the New York assault.
    a. Is jurisdiction proper under the Uniform Act?
    b. Would it be constitutional for the court to take jurisdiction?

3.   While traveling to Pittsburgh for a performance, Hardy collides with Fields on Interstate 83 near Harrisburg. After the performance, Hardy returns to New York. Fields, fast losing his sense of humor, sues Hardy in Pennsylvania.
    a. May Fields do so under the Uniform Act?
    b. Would it be constitutional for the Pennsylvania court to take personal jurisdiction over Hardy?

4.   West, in California, learns that Paramount Pictures plans to offer Fields a lucrative contract to make a movie in New York. She calls the producer in New York and tries to talk him out of it. During the conversation, she offers several vivid and distinctly uncomplimentary opinions concerning Fields's sense of humor. Fields is not amused; he sues West in New York for defamation.
    a. Does the Uniform Act authorize jurisdiction on these facts?
    b. Would it be constitutional for the New York court to exercise jurisdiction over West on this claim?

Torts and the Long-Arm: *Gray* Areas of Products Liability

5.   Chaplin manufactures stunt cars in Michigan for use in movie and television chase scenes. Paramount Pictures of Hollywood, California, a regular customer of Chaplin's, orders ten cars from Chaplin, which are shipped to California. One of the cars is used to film a cliff-hanging scene in Rocky Mountain Park, Colorado. Brice, the star of the show, is injured when the brakes fail at 14,000 feet. Brice sues Chaplin in Colorado.

   a. Would jurisdiction be authorized by a long-arm statute that allowed jurisdiction for claims "arising out of a tortious act committed in this state"?

   b. Would long-arm jurisdiction be proper under the Uniform Act if it applied in Colorado?

   c. Would it be constitutional for the Colorado court to exercise jurisdiction over Chaplin in this action?

6.   Assume the same facts as example 5, except that the accident took place on location in Hollywood.

   a. Would jurisdiction be proper under the Uniform Act if it applied in California (instead of California's anything-constitutional-goes version quoted at p.24)?

   b. Would it be constitutional for the California court to exercise personal jurisdiction on these facts?

7.   In this same case against Chaplin in California, Brice also sues Gleason Brake Corporation, the Michigan manufacturer of the brakes in the stunt car.

   a. Would the Uniform Act authorize jurisdiction if it were applicable in California?

   b. Would it be constitutional to require Gleason to defend this action in California?

Famous Foibles

8.   The following dandelion sprouts all too frequently in student answers to personal jurisdiction questions involving out-of-state acts and in-state torts:

> If the defendant does not have minimum contacts with the state, he may still be required to defend a suit there if the court concludes that the tort takes place where the injury occurs rather than where the defendant's negligent act took place.

What is wrong with this analysis?

Transacting and Contracting

9.   Chaplin sells ten stunt cars to Paramount in California. Paramount sues Chaplin for breach of contract and breach of warranty after one of the cars repeatedly breaks down during filming in Hollywood. Assume that suit is brought in California and that the Uniform Act applies. (Assume for purposes of examples 9, 10, and 11 that breach of warranty is not a tort action.)

   a. Does the Uniform Act authorize jurisdiction over the suit?

   b. Does the court have power to hear the suit under the due process clause?

10. Chaplin manufactures stunt cars and sells them to a distributer, Indestructible Auto, Inc., of Denver, Colorado; Indestructible in turn sells the cars to movie studios. Indestructible sells ten of Chaplin's specials to Paramount in California. Paramount sues Chaplin in California for breach of warranty after three of the cars break down repeatedly during filming.

    a. Is jurisdiction proper under the Uniform Act?

    b. Is jurisdiction permissible under due process analysis?

11. Tucker, understandably anxious about the chase scene in her new movie, shops around for the best stunt car she can find. She visits Chaplin's plant in Detroit, is impressed with Chaplin's work, and agrees to buy a Chaplin stunt car. When the car is ready, Chaplin calls to find out where to deliver it, and Tucker asks him to ship it to a town in Colorado where the movie is to be filmed. The car breaks down repeatedly, and Tucker sues Chaplin in Colorado for breach of warranty.

    a. Would the suit be proper under the Uniform Act?

    b. Would it be constitutional to sue Chaplin in Colorado on this claim?

12. Lloyd, a Californian, calls Rae, a New York lawyer he has not previously dealt with, to ask her about the advisability of signing a contract to make a movie about an opera. The call is placed from California. Rae advises him not to sign the contract because several key provisions are unenforceable. The contract goes to Marx. Lloyd sues Rae in California for legal malpractice.

    a. Could the California court exercise jurisdiction over Rae under the Uniform Act?

    b. Would it be constitutional for the court to do so?

EXPLANATIONS

Torts and the Long-Arm: Basic Cases

1.   Long-arm jurisdiction: No   Constitutional power: No

    a. The Uniform Act does not provide statutory authority for Fields to sue Hardy in Pennsylvania. Although §1.03(a)(3) and 1.03(a)(4) of the Uniform Act authorize jurisdiction in tort cases, neither applies in the circumstances of this case. Subsection 1.03(a)(3) authorizes jurisdiction over claims arising out of tortious injuries caused by an act or omission in the state (meaning the state where suit is brought). This subsection does not apply because Hardy's act took place in New York. Subsection 1.03(a)(4) allows the plaintiff to sue in Pennsylvania if he suffered tortious injury in Pennsylvania from an out-of-state act and if the defendant does business in the state or derives revenues from goods used or consumed in the state. This doesn't help Fields either. *First,* any injury he suffered took place in New York, where the assault occurred. *Second,* the example states that Hardy does not do business in Pennsylvania or have any other contacts with the state. No matter how liberally interpreted, the long-arm is too short to reach this case.

b. Had the statute purported to confer jurisdiction over this case, its reach would have exceeded its constitutional grasp. Although Fields has minimum contacts with Pennsylvania, Hardy does not. Nor do the facts suggest any other basis for personal jurisdiction, such as consent or domicile. Fields's domicile in Pennsylvania is irrelevant; it is the defendant who is being forced into the state to defend. The plaintiff's unilateral contacts with the forum do not create a constitutional basis for requiring the defendant to defend there. *Hanson v. Denckla,* 357 U.S. 235 (1958).

2.   Long-arm jurisdiction: No   Constitutional power: No

a. Hardy's occasional forays into Pennsylvania do not lead to a different result from example 1. Subsection (a)(3) of the Uniform Act still doesn't apply because the tortious act took place in New York. Nor does subsection (a)(4) reach this case because the injury also occurred in New York. Even if the injury could be construed to take place in Pennsylvania, it is doubtful that the proviso in (a)(4) could be met. Such sporadic performances in Pennsylvania probably do not amount to "regularly do[ing] business" in the state or "deriving substantial revenue from . . . services rendered" in the state.

Fields might argue that Hardy has "transacted business" (Uniform Act §1.03(a)(1)) in Pennsylvania by his performances there. Indeed he has, but this is insufficient to subject him to personal jurisdiction for Fields's New York tort claim. The Uniform Act and all long-arm provisions limit jurisdiction based on specific contacts to claims *arising out of* the contacts. Indeed, this point is so fundamental that the Act says it twice, in the first sentence of §1.03(a) and in §1.03(b) as well. Hardy could be sued in Pennsylvania under §1.03(a)(1) for a breach of contract claim resulting from his performances there, but not for an unrelated claim arising in New York.

b. In this case, Hardy has contacts with Pennsylvania, but the claim doesn't arise from them. As the "*Shoe* Spectrum" on p.6 illustrates, when the defendant's contacts with the state are limited, he is only subject to "specific in personam jurisdiction," that is, jurisdiction for claims that arise out of those in-state contacts. It is because of this constitutional limitation that long-arm statutes also restrict jurisdiction to claims arising from the listed contacts. Otherwise, their reach would frequently exceed their constitutional grasp in cases like this one.

3.   Long-arm jurisdiction: Yes   Constitutional power: Yes

a. In this case, Fields gets the last laugh. The case is clearly covered by subsection (a)(3) of the Uniform Act because Hardy's tortious act (the negligent driving) took place in Pennsylvania. An argument might also be made, since Hardy was driving to a performance, that the claim arose out of Hardy's doing business in Pennsylvania (subsection (a)(1)). It is certainly possible for a defendant's acts to satisfy more than one provision of a long-arm statute, as illustrated by the intersecting circles in Figure 2-2. The argument is dubious here, however, since the claim is for a tort to a person not involved in Hardy's in-state business. In any event, it is unnecessary, since subsection (a)(3) squarely applies.

b. Courts have consistently held that committing a tortious act within the state is a minimum contact of the "quality and nature" that gives rise to personal jurisdiction. Because the claim arises out of this in-state act, jurisdiction is proper under the minimum contacts test. The fact that Hardy left the state before suit was brought does not preclude jurisdiction. *International Shoe* premises jurisdiction on the in-state contacts that gave rise to the claim, not presence at the time of suit.

4.   Long-arm jurisdiction: Maybe   Constitutional power: Yes

a. Assuming that West has no other contacts with New York, the only likely basis for jurisdiction is subsection (a)(3) of the Uniform Act. The problem, of course, is that that section requires that the tortious injury result from an "act or omission in this state," yet West has not entered New York. In *Gray v. American Radiator and Standard Sanitary Corp.,* 176 N.E.2d 761 (Ill. 1961), the Illinois Supreme Court stretched to conclude that a "tortious act" took place where a negligently constructed product caused an injury. The Uniform Act precludes this extravagant interpretation by specifying that the act or omission that causes the injury, not the injury itself, must take place in the state. See §1.03(a)(3). Indeed, provisions like §1.03(a)(3) and (a)(4), which distinguish between in-state tortious acts and out-of-state tortious acts causing in-state injuries, were drafted to clarify the statutory ambiguity discussed in *Gray*.

However, a strong argument can be made that West did commit the tortious act in New York. West has deliberately projected her voice into the state via the telephone wires for the purpose of making the defamatory statement to a person in that state. (Compare *Gray,* in which the tortious act was done entirely in Ohio, but the harm was suffered after the water heater was shipped into Illinois.) Some courts have concluded in such cases that the act takes place where the statements are heard, rather than where they are uttered. Other courts have concluded that the act takes place where the actor acts, not where the statement is heard. These latter courts view such cases as out-of-state act/in-state injury cases and refuse to take jurisdiction unless the defendant has engaged in business or other persistent activity in the state under subsection (a)(4). See generally Casad at ¶7.07[1][b].

This is a good example of a case in which interpreting the long-arm statute to "go to the limits of due process" makes a difference. If this is the governing rule of interpretation, the court should interpret the "act or omission within this state" language as broadly as due process allows and conclude that the act took place in New York.

b. West's act is deliberately aimed at causing harm to Fields in New York. Such an act, undertaken with the intent to injure the plaintiff in New York and involving direct contact with the producer there, constitutes a voluntary affiliation with the forum of the "quality and nature" to support jurisdiction under the due process clause. West can hardly claim surprise when the harm she intended eventuates where she intended it, and Fields sues her there. See *Calder v. Jones,* 465 U.S. 783, 788 (1984).

Torts and the Long-Arm: *Gray* Areas of Products Liability

5.   Long-arm jurisdiction: (a) Possibly   (b) No
     Constitutional power: No

   a. The long-arm statute quoted here is similar to the Illinois statute interpreted in *Gray v. American Radiator and Standard Sanitary Corp.,* 176 N.E.2d 761 (Ill. 1961). In *Gray* the court interpreted this language to apply if the injury occurred in the state, even though the defendant's negligence occurred elsewhere. 176 N.E.2d at 763. However, other courts have refused to accept this strained interpretation. See *Feathers v. McLucas,* 209 N.E.2d 68, 79 (N.Y. 1965), in which the court concluded that the *Gray* interpretation "disregards [the statute's] plain language and exceeds the bounds of sound statutory interpretation" and that the phrase only applies to cases in which the defendant's tortious conduct took place in the state. Thus, whether Chaplin is subject to jurisdiction under this long-arm provision depends on the court's willingness to stretch the language as the court did in *Gray.*

   b. The Uniform Act does not reach this case. Subsection (3) does not apply; it focuses specifically on the place where the negligent act (negligent manufacture) took place, which was Michigan in this case. Subsection (4) does not apply either. Although Chaplin may have caused tortious injury within the state by his out-of-state act, there is no indication that the additional requirement of regular in-state conduct or profits is met.

   c. The only contact Chaplin has with Colorado in this case is that the motion picture company took one of his stunt cars from California to Colorado to make a movie, and the brakes failed there. Like the Volkswagen in *World-Wide Volkswagen v. Woodson,* the car reached Colorado by the unilateral act of a third party, not as the result of any deliberate contact by Chaplin with Colorado. Although it may be foreseeable that Paramount will use the car to make chase scenes in the Rockies, this foreseeability is not a sufficient basis for exercising jurisdiction over Chaplin there. *World-Wide Volkswagen v. Woodson,* 444 U.S. 286, 295-296 (1980). It would exceed the limits of due process for the Colorado court to exercise jurisdiction over Chaplin wherever Paramount chooses to film movies. Thus, this is another example in the "bulge" area of Figure 2-3, in which the long-arm statute might be interpreted to authorize jurisdiction (under the *Gray* approach), but it would exceed the bounds of due process to exercise that jurisdiction.

6.   Long-arm jurisdiction: Yes   Constitutional power: Yes

   a. If Brice's accident takes place in California, subsection (4) will authorize jurisdiction. Chaplin has caused Brice's injuries in California by an out-of-state act. In addition, he apparently does business with Paramount in California on a regular basis. Note that subsection (4) includes two requirements: an in-state injury from an out-of-state act and an ongoing relationship to the state. The second requirement may be satisfied by one of several alternative showings: regular solicitation of business, regularly doing business, any other persistent course of conduct in the state, or deriving substantial revenue from goods or services used or consumed in the state.

It may also be possible to argue that Brice's claim in this case arises from Chaplin's "transacting business" in California, under §1.03(a)(1) of the Uniform Act. Although Brice's claim does not arise directly out of the transaction itself (as a claim by Paramount for defects in the cars would, for example), it does "arise out of" the sale of the cars in California in a more general sense. Some courts would uphold jurisdiction in these circumstances under §1.03(a)(1). See Casad at ¶4.02[1][b]. However, others have held that "transacting business" provisions like §1.03(a)(1) are intended to apply to business-related claims such as contract claims, so that a plaintiff such as Brice must satisfy subsection (a)(3) or (a)(4) in order to sue Chaplin on this tort claim in California. See, e.g., *Whitaker v. Krestmark of Alabama, Inc.*, 278 S.E.2d 116, 118 (Ga. App. 1981).

b. There is a constitutionally significant difference between this case and the last. Here, the brake failure and resulting injury is not the sole contact Chaplin has with the forum state. The presence of the car in California arose through deliberate efforts by Chaplin to serve the market for his product in California. This is a voluntary affiliation with the state that changes the "quality and nature" of Chaplin's in-state act of causing injury in California. The Supreme Court's stream-of-commerce analysis in *World-Wide Volkswagen* supports jurisdiction over out-of-state defendants in these circumstances on the theory that a defendant who persistently takes advantage of the opportunity to market its product in the state may fairly be called to account in the state if his product causes tortious injury there.

Even under Justice O'Connor's view in *Asahi*, jurisdiction would be proper in this case. Unlike the valve maker in *Asahi*, Chaplin in this example has deliberately shipped his cars — including the one that caused the injury — to California. Thus, there is no question of being subjected to jurisdiction due to the unilateral acts of a subsequent distributor. Chaplin has chosen to sell cars directly to California, and this purposeful conduct gives rise to the claim in suit.

7.   Long-arm jurisdiction: Yes   Constitutional power: Maybe

a. The issue here is whether the component part manufacturer, who has dealt with the final manufacturer but has not directly done business or sold goods in California, can be required to defend there in a products liability case arising out of injury in California allegedly resulting from a defect in its product. Gleason is analogous to Titan Valve Company in *Gray*. Gleason caused tortious injury in California by an out-of-state act and derives substantial revenue from goods used or consumed in California, since Chaplin, and perhaps others as well, sell cars in California made with Gleason brakes. Jurisdiction has generally been upheld over component part manufacturers in these circumstances, under §1.03(a)(4) of the Uniform Act, and perhaps §1.03(a)(1) as well.

It will not always follow that the component part manufacturer will fit subsection (4) just because the final manufacturer does. For example, if Chaplin sold only 50 cars in California, this may be enough to constitute doing or soliciting business there or deriving substantial revenue from goods sold there. The company that makes the windshield wipers, however, at $2 a pair does not derive substantial revenue from goods used or consumed in California if the only wipers that go there are on Chaplin's 50 stunt cars. If the wipers failed and caused the accident, Chaplin would be subject to jurisdiction under this language but the wiper manufacturer probably would not.

b. Prior to *Asahi,* a number of courts held it within the bounds of due process to exercise jurisdiction over an out-of-state component manufacturer in this type of case. These courts reasoned that a component maker who derives revenue from substantial sales of its product in a state should not be able to accept that benefit without submitting to jurisdiction when the product causes injury there. Some courts reached this conclusion even if the component maker was unaware that the finished product for which it provided parts was being sold in the forum state. See, e.g., *Bean Dredging Corp. v. Dredge Technology Corp.,* 744 F.2d 1081 (5th Cir. 1984).

However, as Chapter 1 indicates, *Asahi* has thrown some doubt on the question of whether component makers who do not direct their goods into a state or cultivate the market there are subject to personal jurisdiction if their product reaches the forum state through resale of the finished product and causes injury there. The O'Connor approach would require more to establish "purposeful availment." The other five Justices (two of whom have since retired) apparently would not. A distinction might be premised on the fact that the component maker is in Michigan rather than Japan, but this seems to go more to the second prong of the analysis (reasonableness once minimum contacts are shown) rather than to the issue of minimum contacts themselves.

Famous Foibles

8.   Obviously, this reasoning is based on *Gray v. American Radiator,* in which the Illinois court concluded that the "tortious act" provision of its long-arm statute applies in cases where the injury to the plaintiff takes place in the state, even though the negligent act that led to the injury (in *Gray,* the negligent manufacture of the valve) took place elsewhere. The fallacy in this foible is the conclusion that satisfying the terms of a long-arm statute is enough to obtain personal jurisdiction. This is never the case: The statutory

analysis only determines whether the legislature has granted jurisdiction, not whether it would be constitutional to exercise it.

Suppose, for example, on the facts of *World-Wide* that Oklahoma had had a statute authorizing jurisdiction over a defendant who "commits a tortious act in the state"; and assume further that the Oklahoma courts interpreted it as the *Gray* court did, to be satisfied if the plaintiff suffers injury in Oklahoma. On these assumptions, the long-arm statute would have authorized jurisdiction over Seaway, the New York dealer, since its negligent act in New York caused injury in Oklahoma when the Audi blew up there. But the *World-Wide* court held that it was not constitutionally permissible for the Oklahoma court to take jurisdiction over Seaway on these facts, since Seaway had not purposely availed itself of the benefits of conducting activities in Oklahoma. No matter how Oklahoma interpreted the "tortious act" provision in its statute, it could not make such an exercise of jurisdiction constitutional.

Transacting and Contracting

9.   Long-arm jurisdiction: Yes   Constitutional power: Yes

a. This claim squarely fits subsection (2) of the Uniform Act because it arises directly out of Chaplin's agreement to sell the allegedly defective car to Paramount in California. It would likely satisfy subsection (1) as well. Even if Chaplin does not have a business office in California, most courts would hold that he transacts business there by selling his product to a California buyer, at least where the sale is as substantial as this one.

b. The decision to sell goods to buyers in another state is a deliberate, profit-oriented contact with that state. When the sale is substantial (as here) or part of a series of such sales, the seller enjoys the benefits and protections of doing business in the state and may have a significant effect on the commerce of the state. In such cases, the seller should expect to defend suits there arising out of those business transactions with forum-state customers. See *Burger King*, 471 U.S. at 475-476.

10.   Long-arm jurisdiction: Probably   Constitutional Power: Probably

a. Paramount might argue that several provisions of the Uniform Act apply but will probably have to fall back on §1.03(a)(1), the "transacting business" provision. Subsection 1.03(a)(2) was probably meant to apply to cases in which the defendant directly contracted to supply goods in the state, not stream of commerce cases where a distributor resells the defendant's goods in the state. Section 1.03(a)(4), the tortious-act-outside/injury-inside-the-state provision probably can't be stretched to reach the case either: The claim is for failure of the goods to perform properly, not for personal injury or property damage.

However, many courts would conclude that Chaplin did "transact business" in California, albeit indirectly. Chaplin has delivered his goods into the stream of commerce. He may well know that they are destined for California or hope that they are. Where he profits from these resales in the state, it appears likely that the legislature would intend to reach his conduct even though he used a distributor rather than sending the goods directly to California. See, e.g., *Stabilisierungsfonds Fur Wein v. Kaiser Stuhl Wine Distributors Pty. Ltd.*, 647 F.2d 200, 204-206 (D.C. Cir. 1981).

b. This is another stream of commerce case. It differs from *Asahi* and example 7 in that Chaplin is a final manufacturer rather than a component maker. But it is still indirect, as Chaplin sold his cars to Colorado, and they were then reimported into California. The reasoning of Justice O'Connor's opinion would seem to bar taking jurisdiction in both types of cases. Because of the split in the court and the change in its composition, it is hard to say whether jurisdiction is proper in such cases, in which a predictable stream of commerce sweeps the defendant's goods into the state.

Note that, should the O'Connor view prevail, interpreting "transacting business" provisions to apply to defendants who indirectly sell their goods in the state would often exceed the bounds of due process. This example, then, would fall in the bulge area of Figure 2-3, in which the statute authorizes jurisdiction but exceeds due process limits to assert that jurisdiction.

11. Long-arm jurisdiction: Unlikely   Constitutional power: Doubtful

a. It is unlikely that Chaplin's shipment of a single car into Colorado at Tucker's order is sufficient to support jurisdiction under the Uniform Act. First, it is doubtful that a court would conclude that Chaplin has transacted business (subsection (1)) in Colorado by shipping a single car there at Tucker's request. Although many courts (but not all) have concluded that a single shipment of goods into the state is sufficient to establish "transaction of business" (see Casad ¶¶4.02[1][a][iv], 8.01[2][a][i]), such cases have usually involved a deliberate effort by the defendant to serve the in-state market or to direct a flow of goods into the state. In this case, Chaplin did not deliberately seek a business affiliation with Colorado or even agree in advance to ship the goods to Colorado. He simply followed the shipping directions of his buyer in delivering goods previously ordered elsewhere.

It also seems unlikely that jurisdiction could be found under §1.03(a)(2), which authorizes jurisdiction based on contracting to supply goods in the state. This transaction was initiated by Tucker in Michigan. The facts suggest that Chaplin did not know where the car was to be shipped or used at the time that the sale was made. He contracted to supply a car to Tucker, but not to supply it in any particular place; Tucker could have ordered him to send it anywhere. Although the car was ultimately shipped to Colorado, there is a substantial difference between passively agreeing to ship a car to the destination chosen by a buyer and deliberately agreeing from the beginning to supply goods in a particular state. It is clear that the drafters of this section intended to reach the latter conduct, but they probably did not mean to include the former.

b. It is doubtful that this isolated shipment of a single car to Colorado, at the buyer's request, is a sufficient contact with Colorado to support jurisdiction under the minimum contacts test. Chaplin has not deliberately taken advantage of the benefits and protections of Colorado law. The sale was made to a Californian in Michigan, apparently without specific knowledge that the car would be used in Colorado. Tucker's order to ship the car to Colorado is more a unilateral contact of Tucker with Colorado than of Chaplin. See *Hanson v. Denckla,* 357 U.S. 235, 253 (1958). Merely following the buyer's shipping orders is not the type of deliberate affiliation with a state that *International Shoe* contemplates as a basis for personal jurisdiction.

12. Long-arm jurisdiction: Unlikely   Constitutional power: Also
                                                                 unlikely

a. This case could be analyzed as a "transacting any business" case under subsection (1) of the Uniform Act. While there is an argument to be made that Rae has transacted business in California by offering legal advice to Lloyd there, most courts would conclude otherwise. Rae did not initiate the contact, never entered the state, and perhaps did not even know what state Lloyd was calling from. This one-shot, passive, forum-related activity is probably too fortuitous to rise to the level of "transacting business," which implies a calculated intent to benefit from business activities in the state.

Alternatively, Lloyd might argue, since his claim is for legal malpractice, that Rae committed a tortious act in the state, analogous to West's call in example 4. This is a close issue, but there is a significant difference between the two situations. West deliberately called the New York producer with the intent to affect his actions there. Rae simply picked up the phone and responded to inquiries from Lloyd. It is a fine distinction, but the interpretation of long-arm statutes frequently turns on such delicate judgments about what the legislature must have intended in enacting a statute that uses rather general language.

b. It is unlikely that it would be constitutional to sue Rae in California on the basis of this single, passive contact with the state. She has not deliberately formed an affiliation to the state but simply responded to a call initiated by Lloyd, which could have come from anywhere. While Rae may receive some protection from the laws of California (for example, the right to sue Lloyd there to collect her fee), this relation to the state seems too casual to make it fair to sue her there. Even if the court concludes that she committed a tortious act in California within the meaning of the long-arm statute, it does not seem fair on these facts to subject Rae to jurisdiction there. See *McBreen v. Beech Aircraft Corp.,* 543 F.2d 26 (7th Cir. 1976) (no jurisdiction over defendant who made allegedly defamatory statements outside the state to a reporter calling from the forum state).

It would be different if Rae were Lloyd's regular counsel, and she frequently provided him legal advice in California over the phone. On those facts the call would not be a chance occurrence, but part of an ongoing course of business in the state. In that case, Rae would be advising Lloyd in much the same way as if she had an office in Hollywood, and it would not be unreasonable for her to expect that a suit arising from this advice to a Californian in California would be brought there.

3

Seeking the Home Field Advantage: Challenges to Personal Jurisdiction

Introduction

Surely one of the most fundamental principles of civil procedure is that the courts of a state may not exercise judicial power over a defendant unless that defendant has, in one way or another, submitted to the jurisdiction of the courts of that state. A century of case law has given some specificity to this requirement. As Chapter 1 indicates, defendants may be subject to jurisdiction under due process analysis on the basis of domicile in a state, in-state service of process, consent to jurisdiction, continuous or substantial in-state contacts, or as a result of "minimum contacts" with the forum state that give rise to a particular cause of action.

It is not always clear when a plaintiff sues a defendant in a particular state whether one of these bases for personal jurisdiction is met. Suppose, for example, that Wolfe, a North Carolina novelist, gives a newspaper interview in North Carolina in which he disparages Hemingway's writing abilities. Hemingway sues Wolfe in Oregon for libel. When Wolfe is served with the complaint, he may be unsure whether the Oregon court has the right to exercise jurisdiction over him. For example, he may not know whether the newspaper that interviewed him is circulated in Oregon or whether Hemingway has suffered any injury in Oregon as a result of the alleged libel. If Wolfe has no other connections with Oregon, he may well conclude that the courts of Oregon have no right to order him to appear and defend the suit.

This chapter explores the options available to a defendant like Wolfe to present his objection to the exercise of personal jurisdiction over him by the courts of another state. Generally, these options involve a challenge either in the court in which the original action is brought (the rendering state) or in another state where enforcement of the original judgment is sought (the enforcing state).

Challenging Jurisdiction in the Rendering State

The defendant's first option is to appear in the original action at the beginning of the suit and object to the court's exercise of jurisdiction over her. For example, Wolfe may decide to appear in the Oregon court and ask the court to dismiss the action for lack of personal jurisdiction. The procedure for doing this varies from state to state. In some states, the defendant who objects to jurisdiction files a "special appearance." Under a special appearance, the defendant is allowed to appear before the court at the beginning of the action for the sole purpose of challenging its power to exercise personal jurisdiction over her. If the defendant is careful to appear "specially," she may litigate the jurisdictional question without submitting to jurisdiction by the very act of appearing before the court.

However, the defendant who files a special appearance must exercise extreme care not to raise any other issue: If she raises any objection or argument that the court can construe as a defense on the merits, the court may conclude that she has waived her jurisdictional objection. For example, in *Koplin v. Saul Lerner Co.*, 201 N.E.2d 763 (Ill. App. 1964), the defendant entered a special appearance to object to the court's jurisdiction and also moved to strike the complaint for vagueness. The court held that this hapless defendant, by raising the vagueness issue, had submitted to the court's jurisdiction. The pitfalls of making a successful special appearance are discussed in Casad ¶3.01[5][a].

A growing number of states have abandoned the common law special appearance device in favor of the more liberal approach to challenging personal jurisdiction used in federal courts. Under the Federal Rules, as under the special appearance, a defendant may appear before answering to the merits of the complaint and object to personal jurisdiction. Fed. R. Civ. P. 12(b)(2). However, under the Federal Rules approach, the defendant may also raise other objections at the same time, without waiving the objection to personal jurisdiction. For example, under Fed. R. Civ. P. 12(b), a defendant may move to dismiss for lack of personal jurisdiction and, at the same time, for failure to state a claim upon which relief can be granted (see Rule

12(b)(6)). This second objection clearly goes to the merits of the suit; if a defendant did this in a state that adheres to the older special appearance rule, the court would hold that she had waived her objection to personal jurisdiction by bringing up matters going to the merits of the case.[1]

Thus, in the federal courts under Rule 12(b), and in the numerous state courts that have adopted the same approach, the defendant has a little more flexibility in raising the objection and is less likely to be tripped up by the procedural technicalities of doing so. But under either approach, the objection to jurisdiction must be raised immediately or be lost: A defendant who answers on the merits and later concludes that personal jurisdiction is lacking will have waived the objection by failing to raise it at the outset. See generally Chapter 17.

If Wolfe properly raises his objection in the rendering court, under either the special appearance approach or the Federal Rules approach (whichever applies in that state), the court will hold a hearing on the issue. If the court concludes that there is no basis to exercise jurisdiction over Wolfe, it will dismiss the suit. However, if the court concludes that it does have the power to exercise jurisdiction over him (at least for the cause of action asserted by Hemingway), it will proceed with the case.

In most states a defendant who challenges jurisdiction at the beginning of the suit and loses may proceed to defend the merits of the suit without waiving her objection to the court's jurisdictional ruling. If she loses the suit on the merits, she may appeal to an appellate court in the rendering state, claiming that the trial court's conclusion that it had personal jurisdiction was wrong. This scenario is hardly palatable to Wolfe, of course, since it requires him to do exactly what he believes he should not have to do, defend the action in a state that (allegedly) lacks personal jurisdiction over him. However, it at least leaves him an avenue to correct the trial judge's mistake and to avoid being bound by a decision rendered by a court that lacks jurisdiction to render it.

Challenging Jurisdiction in the Enforcing Court

The second option for the defendant who objects to personal jurisdiction is to ignore the original suit entirely. If Wolfe is truly convinced that Oregon lacks personal jurisdiction over him, he may view the suit as mere harassment, an ineffective proceeding that can give rise to no binding judgment and that

---

1. Under Fed. R. Civ. P. 12(b), the defendant could also raise the jurisdictional objection in the answer, if she did not file a pre-answer motion. The crucial thing is to raise it immediately, either in the answer or a pre-answer motion. See Chapter 17, p.279. For an example where the objection was raised in the answer, see the defendant's answer in the Schulansky case, infra p.462.

can therefore be ignored with impunity. If the Oregon court lacks personal jurisdiction over Wolfe, any judgment it enters in Hemingway's suit will be unenforceable anyway. If that's true, why bother to respond at all?

Procedurally, it is true that Wolfe has a right *not* to appear in Oregon if the Oregon court lacks jurisdiction over him for the claim asserted in the suit. However, this course poses a serious risk: If Wolfe fails to appear at all in Oregon, either to object to personal jurisdiction or to defend on the merits of the libel claim, the court will enter a default judgment for Hemingway — that is, a judgment that Wolfe is liable to Hemingway on the claims asserted in the complaint. If that judgment is enforceable, Wolfe will have lost his suit without ever having had a chance to defend it.

The usual method of enforcing money judgments against out-of-state defendants is for the plaintiff to take her judgment against the defendant to a state where the defendant has property and seek a court order from the courts of that state authorizing the sheriff to sell the defendant's assets to satisfy the judgment. Hemingway, for example, may take his Oregon judgment to North Carolina, where Wolfe lives, and ask the court to authorize a judicial sale of Wolfe's house to pay off the judgment.

However, the North Carolina court will not automatically enforce the Oregon judgment. Hemingway must first obtain recognition of the Oregon judgment (called "domesticating the judgment," like finding a home for a wild animal) in one of two ways. The traditional procedure is to file a new action on the judgment in the enforcing state — North Carolina in this case — seeking a "judgment on the judgment." In about half the states, the legislature has provided an alternative procedure for domesticating foreign[2] judgments. The judgment creditor (Hemingway in our example) simply registers a certified copy of the Oregon judgment in the North Carolina court, eliminating the need to file a new suit there.[3] In states that have such a procedure, the judgment creditor may either file a traditional action on the judgment or use the registration procedure.

The Full Faith and Credit Clause of the United States Constitution (article IV, §1) requires the courts of each state to honor the judgments of other states by entering judgments upon them and allowing out-of-state creditors like Hemingway to use court process to collect them. Once Hemingway obtains a judgment on the judgment (or under a registration statute, registers the judgment in the enforcing state), he may invoke North

---

2. The word "foreign" in this context refers to a judgment of another state, not that of another country.

3. Most registration statutes are based on a model act, the Uniform Enforcement of Foreign Judgments Act (1964 Revised Act), 13 U.L.A. 152 (1986). There is also a federal statute authorizing registration of federal judgments in other federal districts. 28 U.S.C. §1963.

Carolina procedures for collecting it, including placing liens on Wolfe's assets in the state, forcing sale of those assets, or initiating court hearings to determine Wolfe's ability to pay.

There is, however, one important exception to a state's duty to give full faith and credit to a judgment of another state: The enforcing court may always inquire as to whether the rendering state had jurisdiction in the original action and refuse enforcement if it did not. See *Pennoyer v. Neff,* 95 U.S. 714, 732 (1877). For example, if the North Carolina court concludes after a hearing on the jurisdiction issue that the Oregon court had jurisdiction over Wolfe, the North Carolina court must enforce the Oregon default judgment by entering a North Carolina judgment on the original judgment and making its procedures for execution of judgments available to Hemingway. However, if the North Carolina court concludes that the Oregon court did *not* have jurisdiction over Wolfe, it will refuse to honor the Oregon judgment, and Hemingway will not be able to levy on Wolfe's property in North Carolina.

Thus, if Wolfe ignores the Oregon proceeding, he will still have an opportunity to protect his property from being sold on execution in North Carolina. Even though a default judgment will be rendered in the original Oregon law suit, Wolfe may oppose enforcement of that judgment by asserting in the North Carolina enforcement action that the Oregon court lacked personal jurisdiction over him.[4] This is referred to as a "collateral attack" on the judgment because the defendant challenges the original court's jurisdiction in the enforcement action rather than in the original suit. Collateral attack is clearly more convenient for Wolfe because he does not have to go to Oregon, something that from his point of view he shouldn't have to do. It also allows him to litigate the jurisdictional issue in his home state. While the issue of whether the Oregon court had jurisdiction over Wolfe will theoretically be the same in either state, it is at least possible that a North Carolina court will be more sympathetic to Wolfe's objection than the Oregon court would be.

However, this strategy poses a great risk for Wolfe. The Full Faith and Credit Clause allows Wolfe to question the rendering court's jurisdiction but not to reopen the merits of the underlying libel action. If the North Carolina court concludes that the Oregon court had jurisdiction over Wolfe, it will automatically enforce the Oregon default judgment. If Wolfe's original conclusion that the Oregon court lacks jurisdiction is wrong (and most conclusions in this area are only educated guesses), the default judgment will be

---

4. If Hemingway brings a suit to obtain a judgment on the original judgment, Wolfe can raise this objection as a defense to the enforcement suit. If Hemingway registers the judgment directly, Wolfe can raise the objection by a motion to vacate the registration. See Uniform Enforcement of Foreign Judgments Act §2, 13 U.L.A. at 154.

valid and enforceable, in Oregon or any other state. The idea is that a defendant has the right to stay away if a court lacks jurisdiction but not if it has jurisdiction. In the latter situation, the defendant is deemed to have waived her defense on the merits by failing to appear. That is a very considerable price to pay to avoid contesting the jurisdictional issue in the plaintiff's chosen forum.

All this is complex enough, but one further wrinkle is also important. It is true that the Full Faith and Credit Clause allows defendants such as Wolfe to challenge the validity of another state's judgment on the ground that the rendering state never obtained personal jurisdiction over them. But there is an exception to this rule as well: A defendant may not challenge personal jurisdiction in the enforcement action if she has already done so in the original action. Suppose, for example, that Wolfe had appeared in the Oregon action and moved to dismiss for lack of personal jurisdiction. If he lost and then defaulted on the merits, he could not renew his challenge to jurisdiction in an enforcement action in North Carolina because he had already litigated and lost on that issue. Once is enough; the rules of collateral estoppel provide that a party who has fully litigated an issue in one action may not relitigate it in another. See Chapter 23. Thus, Wolfe gets his choice to raise the objection in one court or the other but not to resurrect it after it has been fully litigated and decided.

While the explanation of these principles is lengthy, their application is fairly straightforward. The following examples should help. Please assume that all cases are brought in state court unless the example specifies otherwise. Also assume that the special appearance rule applies in Mississippi.[5]

EXAMPLES

Novel Developments

1.   Lewis publishes books in Ohio. He agrees to sell a thousand copies of *Brandywine, Ohio,* a popular novel, to Faulkner, a book wholesaler with offices in Mississippi. At Faulkner's request Lewis ships the books to Faulkner's Louisiana warehouse. Faulkner subsequently discovers that the books are damaged and sues Lewis in Mississippi to recover the price of the books. Lewis claims that the books were damaged later, while stored in Faulkner's warehouse. He also doubts that the Mississippi court has jurisdiction over him because all the negotiations took place in Ohio and the parties

---

5. Until 1982 Mississippi practice required defendants to raise objections to personal jurisdiction by special appearance. Mississippi now follows the Federal Rules model, which allows defendants to raise the objection by a pre-answer motion to dismiss. Miss. R. Civ. P. 12(b)(2). Assume in analyzing the examples that the special appearance rule still applies.

contemplated from the beginning that the books would be shipped to Louisiana.

Lewis makes a special appearance in Mississippi to contest the Mississippi court's jurisdiction over him. The court concludes after holding a hearing that it lacks jurisdiction. What will the court do?

2.   When first served with the complaint in *Faulkner v. Lewis,* Lewis is confident that he can win on the merits and therefore answers the complaint and defends the case on the merits. Just before trial, however, he gets nervous about the outcome and decides to move to dismiss for lack of personal jurisdiction. How will the court respond to the motion?

3.   Assume that Lewis decides to appear in the Mississippi action, despite his doubts that the court has jurisdiction over him. He defends the action on the merits and loses. Judgment is entered for Faulkner. Faulkner brings a suit on the judgment in Ohio, and Lewis opposes enforcement of the judgment on the ground that the Mississippi court lacked personal jurisdiction over him. What will the court do?

The Silent Treatment

4.   Lewis is convinced from the outset that the Mississippi court lacks jurisdiction over him. Consequently, he does not respond to the complaint, and a default judgment is entered for Faulkner, who then brings an action on the judgment in Ohio.

   a. Lewis defends the Ohio enforcement action on the ground that he is not liable for the damage because the books were damaged after delivery. Assuming that Lewis can prove this, what will the court do?

   b. Lewis defends the enforcement action on the ground that the Mississippi court never obtained personal jurisdiction over him. Assuming this is true, what will the court do?

   c. Lewis defends the enforcement action on the ground that the Mississippi court lacked jurisdiction over him. The Ohio court, however, concludes that the Mississippi court *did* have jurisdiction. What will the court do?

5.   Lewis appears specially in the original suit in Mississippi to challenge personal jurisdiction. The court holds that it has personal jurisdiction. Lewis, convinced that the court is wrong, defaults. Faulkner gets a default judgment and seeks enforcement in Ohio. Lewis defends on the ground that the Mississippi court lacked jurisdiction over him. What result?

6.   Assume that Faulkner's suit is brought in a state that follows the Federal Rules model. Lewis appears and moves to dismiss for failure to join an indispensable party. The motion is denied. He then moves to dismiss for lack of personal jurisdiction. How will the court rule?

The Plot Thickens

7.   Assume that Faulkner brings suit in Louisiana, the state where Lewis has agreed to deliver the books, and the Louisiana long-arm statute authorizes personal jurisdiction over a nonresident defendant as to all claims arising out of "contracting to supply goods in the state." The Ohio long-arm statute, however, has no such provision, nor any other that would apply on the facts of the case. Lewis defaults in the Louisiana action. When Faulkner seeks to enforce his default judgment in Ohio, Lewis defends on the ground that the court lacked personal jurisdiction under the Ohio long-arm statute. Will his defense be upheld?

8.   Assume that Lewis is sued in Mississippi and makes a special appearance to object to the court's exercise of personal jurisdiction over him. The court concludes that it has jurisdiction and therefore refuses to dismiss the case. Lewis, fearful lest he lose his right to defend on the merits, decides to defend the case on the merits in Mississippi and loses. May he appeal the court's initial decision that it had personal jurisdiction over him?

9.   Lewis makes a special appearance in Mississippi to challenge personal jurisdiction and loses. He is frustrated; he knows that decision is wrong. He foresees the following scenario: litigating the merits, losing, appealing on jurisdiction, winning the appeal, the case being dismissed for lack of jurisdiction, and Faulkner starting over in Ohio (where he ought to have started anyway). Is there any way that Lewis can short-circuit this procedural nightmare?

Double Trouble

10. Lewis defaults in Mississippi and challenges enforcement of the resulting default judgment in Ohio. The Ohio court refuses to enforce the Mississippi judgment, on the ground that the Mississippi court lacked personal jurisdiction over Lewis. Faulkner, convinced that the Ohio decision is wrong, brings another action on the judgment in Illinois, where Lewis owns property subject to execution. What do you think the Illinois court will do?

EXPLANATIONS

Novel Developments

1.   In most cases, the court will dismiss the case because it lacks the power to render a binding decision if it lacks personal jurisdiction over the defendant. Thus, by entering a special appearance (or a motion to dismiss in a state that follows the Federal Rules model), Lewis will avoid litigating the merits in Mississippi without risking a default judgment that might be enforced in Ohio or some other state where Lewis has property.

In a few cases the court may agree with Lewis that it has not acquired jurisdiction over Lewis and yet still refuse to dismiss. For example, if the defendant is subject to jurisdiction in the forum state but has not been properly served with process, the court may simply order process to be served in an appropriate manner and then proceed. See Chapter 16 on the proper methods for service of process. In most cases, however, the defendant's objection will not be to the method of service but to the power of the court to exercise jurisdiction. This objection, if valid, will usually require dismissal.

2. In this case Lewis has waived his objection to personal jurisdiction by appearing and defending on the merits without raising his jurisdictional challenge. In states that follow the special appearance rule, the defendant waives her jurisdictional objection unless she raises it immediately, before pleading to the merits. The states that follow the federal approach similarly provide that objections to personal jurisdiction are waived unless raised by motion before answering or in the initial answer to the complaint. See Fed. R. Civ. P. 12(g), (h). Thus, under either approach, objections to personal jurisdiction must be raised immediately, or they are waived. Lewis may not hold back on this defense and spring it on the plaintiff later if things go badly on the merits. The motion will be denied.

3. The answer to this example follows from the last. Lewis has waived his jurisdictional objection and is barred from raising it either by direct attack in the Mississippi court or by collateral attack in the Ohio enforcement action. It is true that it is ordinarily open to the defendant to defend the enforcement suit on the ground that the original, rendering court lacked personal jurisdiction over her. Here, however, Lewis waived the objection by appearing on the merits in the initial action. He may not sandbag the plaintiff by trying to win on the merits in one court and saving the jurisdictional objection to raise in the other.

The Silent Treatment

4a. Lewis defaulted on the merits in Mississippi. That precludes him from litigating any of the underlying substantive issues that Faulkner had to prove to recover, such as whether the books were damaged and whether the damage resulted from Lewis's negligence. Even if Lewis can conclusively prove that the damage was not his fault, the Ohio court will not listen. The Full Faith and Credit Clause prevents it from reexamining issues that have been settled (even by default) in another state's courts.

If this seems like a victory of form (or procedure) over substance, consider what would happen if the opposite were true. If defendants could litigate the merits in the enforcement action, they could simply ignore the plaintiff's original suit and have the substantive issues heard in the forum of the defendant's choice instead. The plaintiff's traditional right to choose the forum (subject, of course, to venue and jurisdictional restrictions) would be replaced by the defendant's right always to litigate at home.

b. In this hypo, Lewis exercised his prerogative to ignore the Mississippi action because he is convinced that the rendering court had no power to order him to appear there. He may raise the defense of lack of personal jurisdiction in the Ohio enforcement action since jurisdiction is the one issue that the enforcing court may consider before giving full faith and credit to the Mississippi judgment. If it is true that the Mississippi court lacked jurisdiction, the Ohio court will refuse to enter a judgment on the Mississippi judgment, Faulkner will be unable to collect on his default judgment, and Lewis will suffer no harm from it — except, of course, the anxiety over whether the Ohio court will agree with him on the jurisdictional question. If I were Lewis, I would prefer to litigate the jurisdictional issue in the Mississippi court, by filing a special appearance there, rather than risk losing the chance to litigate the merits entirely by staking all on the chance that the Ohio court will agree that the Mississippi court lacked jurisdiction over him.

c. As in example 4b, it is open to Lewis to challenge the personal jurisdiction of the original court in this enforcement action. However, if Faulkner proves that the Mississippi court had jurisdiction, the Ohio court is bound under the Full Faith and Credit Clause to enter judgment on the original judgment and order execution of it on Lewis's assets. Thus, by postponing his jurisdictional challenge, Lewis has abdicated his chance to defend the substance of the claim in either Mississippi or Ohio. This is an extreme price to pay for the convenience of litigating the jurisdictional issue in your home state. This price was paid, for example, in *McGee v. International Life Ins. Co.*, 355 U.S. 220 (1957), in which the insurer ignored the original California suit, and the California judgment was subsequently held enforceable in Texas.

5.   Once again, Lewis has run afoul of the rules. He has already raised his challenge to jurisdiction in the initial action. One bite at the apple is all that he gets; he may not challenge jurisdiction in Mississippi, lose, and try again in the enforcing court in hopes of getting a more favorable reading from an Ohio judge. See *Baldwin v. Iowa State Traveling Men's Association*, 283 U.S. 522 (1931). The plaintiff should not have to prove twice that the first court had jurisdiction, nor should the defendant be allowed to keep raising the issue until she finds some court that agrees with her. If Lewis insists on challenging jurisdiction in Ohio, he must default in Mississippi to preserve his right to do so.

6.   Alas, poor Lewis. All these arbitrary rules and traps for the unwary. Here, he has fallen into another by misconstruing Rule 12. That rule, as well as state rules modeled on it, allows the defendant to raise the jurisdictional objection along with other objections but not to raise other objections first and then challenge the court's personal jurisdiction in a subsequent motion.

Responding with other objections and defenses (such as failure to join an indispensable party, failure to state a claim, or denials on the merits) without raising the personal jurisdiction objection operates as a waiver of that objection. See Fed. R. Civ. P. 12(g), (h). The jurisdictional challenge must always be raised in the defendant's first response to the complaint. The motion will be denied.

The Plot Thickens

7.   This example raises two important points. First, the rendering court must have jurisdiction not only under the minimum contacts standard of *International Shoe* but also under the applicable long-arm statute. Thus, even if Lewis's contacts with Louisiana are sufficient to support jurisdiction under the constitutional standard, Lewis could still argue (in the original suit or the enforcement action) that the rendering court lacked jurisdiction under the applicable long-arm statute.

The second point is, what *is* the applicable long-arm statute? Ohio's, where enforcement is sought? or Louisiana's, where the initial suit was brought? The relevant issue is whether the Louisiana court had the right to exercise jurisdiction over Lewis. Therefore, the Ohio court must ask whether the Louisiana long-arm statute authorized jurisdiction in Louisiana, not whether the Ohio statute would have allowed it if Faulkner had sued there. Lewis's defense fails again.

8.   As the introduction indicates, most states allow the defendant, after raising the jurisdictional objection and losing, to take the safer course of defending on the merits and appealing the decision on jurisdiction.[6] This way, Lewis may still obtain appellate review of the decision on personal jurisdiction without abandoning his opportunity to defend the case on its merits. If he wins on the merits, he will be content and obviously will not appeal the decision on jurisdiction. If he loses on the merits, he may appeal the trial court's decision that he was subject to personal jurisdiction in Mississippi. If the appellate court concludes that he was subject to jurisdiction, it will affirm the judgment. If, however, it concludes that he was not subject to jurisdiction in Mississippi, it will order the case dismissed, even though there has been a full trial on the merits.

A few states still follow the older, more formalistic rule that the defendant waives the jurisdictional objection by defending the case on the merits. The theory behind this approach is that it is inconsistent for the defendant to appear and litigate in that court and at the same time claim that the court lacks jurisdiction over her. If you object to jurisdiction, these courts hold, you

---

6. Mississippi follows the majority rule. See *E. B. Kaiser Co. v. Ludlow,* 243 So. 2d 62, 66 (Miss. 1971).

should stick to your guns by refusing to litigate the merits and appeal solely on the jurisdictional issue. See, e.g., *Jewett v. Jewett,* 296 A.2d 11 (N.H. 1972).

9.   Clearly the most efficient course for Lewis would be to file an immediate appeal in the Mississippi appellate court, challenging the trial court's decision that it had jurisdiction. That way he could avoid going through a trial on the merits in Mississippi, assuming that the trial judge was wrong.

This strategy would not be open to Lewis in the federal courts. Ordinarily, parties in federal cases can only take appeals from final judgments of the district courts. 28 U.S.C. §1291. The Supreme Court has held that decisions upholding personal jurisdiction are "interlocutory" orders because they do not finally resolve the suit and are therefore not appealable until the end of the suit. See *Catlin v. United States,* 324 U.S. 229, 236 (1945).

However, state practice varies considerably on this issue. Some states allow interlocutory appeals of orders upholding personal jurisdiction or appellate relief through some extraordinary method of review. A good example is *World-Wide Volkswagen v. Woodson,* 444 U.S. 286 (1980), in which the Oklahoma Supreme Court entertained a "writ of prohibition" to prohibit the trial judge from acting in excess of his jurisdiction. Some states even *require* the defendant to seek interlocutory review of these decisions, presumably on the rationale that early dismissal of cases in which jurisdiction is improper will save everyone the useless exercise of a trial destined to be vacated later. See Casad at ¶601[5][c]. The lesson is to check carefully the applicable state practice to see whether you may or must take an immediate appeal.

Double Trouble

10. This is an interesting strategy on Faulkner's part. Because Court Number Two has held that Court Number One lacked jurisdiction, Faulkner tries Court Number Three, in hopes that it will disagree with Two and enforce One's judgment. It is reminiscent of Lewis's attempt in example 5 to have the enforcing court reexamine the jurisdictional issue already litigated and decided in the rendering court.

For the same reasons, it won't work. The issue of whether the original court had personal jurisdiction over Lewis was litigated and decided in Ohio. Under the principle of collateral estoppel Faulkner will be barred from relitigating the jurisdiction issue in Illinois or any other state. Note that the Illinois court, by refusing to reopen the jurisdiction issue, is not choosing between the two courts and deciding to honor the judgment of one over the other. Only the Ohio court decided the issue of jurisdiction over Lewis in the original action; the Mississippi court never did because Lewis defaulted. Thus, the Illinois court is honoring the holding of the one court that reached the jurisdictional issue.

Figure 3–1: Challenges to Personal Jurisdiction: Some Common Scenarios

Defendant's Response to the Original Suit	Action in the Rendering Court	Action in the Enforcing Court
D appears, defends on merits, and loses	Enters judgment for *P*	Must enforce the rendering court's judgment, even if *D* challenges the rendering court's jurisdiction; *D* has waived his objection
D makes special appearance or 12(b)(2) motion; court agrees that it lacks jurisdiction	In most cases, dismisses action for lack of jurisdiction; in some, may order proper service to cure jurisdictional defect	If original suit dismissed, there will be no judgment to enforce
D makes special appearance or 12(b)(2) motion; court upholds jurisdiction; *D* defaults	Enters judgment for *P*	Must enforce judgment because *D* already litigated the rendering court's jurisdiction and lost
D loses on objection to jurisdiction; defends action on the merits; loses; appeals	In most states, appellate court may review decision that jurisdiction was proper; a few treat defense on merits as a waiver of the jurisdictional objection	If jurisdiction upheld on appeal, or objection waived by defense on merits, must enforce
D defaults, contests jurisdiction in enforcing court	Enters default judgment for *P*, unless lack of jurisdiction is clear from the complaint	Enforcing court may decide whether rendering court had jurisdiction; if it holds it did not, it refuses enforcement. If it holds that it did, it must enforce the judgment
D defaults, denies liability on the merits in the enforcing court	Enters default judgment for *P*, unless lack of jurisdiction is clear from the complaint	Enforces the judgment; full faith and credit clause precludes reexamination of merits, which are settled by default

4

Diversity Jurisdiction: When Does Multiplicity Constitute Diversity?

Introduction

A major premise underlying our Constitution is that the states function quite well in most respects and that federal interference should be confined to those areas where there is a special need for national policy. For example, in 1787, when the Constitution was drafted, every state already had its own system of courts. The framers of the Constitution saw no need to abolish those courts in favor of federal courts administered by the national government. Instead, they authorized the creation of a separate federal court system (see U.S. Const. art. III, §1), but they only authorized those courts to hear limited categories of cases that, for one reason or another, involved a particular national interest. U.S. Const. art. III, §2. Jurisdiction of all other cases was left to the courts of the states.

One of the major categories of cases that the framers authorized federal courts to hear is the so-called diversity jurisdiction, described in Article III, §2 as cases "between citizens of different states." In diversity cases, as in some others enumerated in Article III, §2, the subject matter jurisdiction of the federal courts is defined by who the parties to the suit are, rather than the subject matter of the underlying dispute.[1] The plaintiff in a diversity case may

---

1. Other examples in Article III that authorize jurisdiction based on the nature of the

55

$ 75,000

seek recovery on a battery theory, a fraud claim, a right created by state statute, or any other state law cause of action. So long as he sues a diverse defendant and the claim is for more than $50,000, the federal court will have subject matter jurisdiction on the basis of diversity.

The framers' apparent reason for singling out diversity cases for federal jurisdiction was a fear that out-of-state citizens would suffer prejudice if they were forced to litigate against local citizens in the local state courts. That rationale has been long disputed by the scholars,[2] and repeated efforts have been made to abolish diversity jurisdiction. The latest example is the 1990 report of the Federal Courts Study Committee, which recommended abolishing diversity jurisdiction in all but a few unusual types of cases. Report of the Federal Courts Study Committee (April 2, 1990) pp.38-42. However, reports of its death, in the words of Sam Clemens, have been greatly exaggerated.[3]

Although Article III authorizes jurisdiction over diversity cases, it does not directly confer the diversity jurisdiction, or any other category of jurisdiction, on the lower federal courts. Rather, it authorizes Congress to create lower federal courts and to confer jurisdiction upon them to hear the types of cases enumerated in Article III, §2. This important additional requirement is succinctly explained by Judge Sirica in one of his Watergate opinions:

> [F]ederal courts may assume only that portion of the Article III judicial power which Congress, by statute, entrusts to them. Simply stated, Congress may impart as much or as little of the judicial power as it deems appropriate and the Judiciary may not thereafter on its own motion recur to the Article III storehouse for additional jurisdiction. When it comes to jurisdiction of the federal courts, truly, to paraphrase the scripture, the Congress giveth, and the Congress taketh away.[4]

Thus, a plaintiff invoking federal jurisdiction must always be prepared to show that his case is not only within the constitutional bounds of Article III but also within some congressional grant of jurisdiction as well.

In the case of diversity jurisdiction, Congress has granted to the federal courts some, but not all, of the Article III diversity jurisdiction. The statutory

2 part test:
- Constitution
- Congress

---

parties include cases to which the United States is a party; cases involving ambassadors, ministers, and foreign citizens; and cases between states.

2. For a review of the debate, see Wright, Federal Courts §23 (4th ed. 1983) (hereinafter cited as Wright).

3. The Study Committee impliedly acknowledged the resistance to eliminating diversity by including a "back-up proposal" for more limited changes in §1332. As this book went to print, neither set of changes had been adopted.

4. *Senate Select Committee v. Nixon*, 366 F. Supp. 51, 55 (D.D.C. 1973).

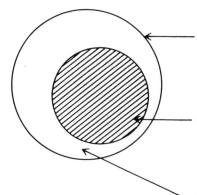

Scope of possible diversity jurisdiction under Article III, §2 ("the Article III storehouse")

Scope of the diversity jurisdiction conferred by Congress in 28 U.S.C. §1332

In this area lie cases in which some parties are diverse, but there is not complete diversity. Also cases in which diversity is complete but the amount-in-controversy requirement is not met.

Figure 4-1

grant, in 28 U.S.C. §1332, is narrower than Article III, for example, in that it includes an amount-in-controversy requirement, while Article III authorizes jurisdiction over all diversity cases, regardless of the sum in dispute. Chief Justice Marshall further narrowed the reach of the statute in *Strawbridge v. Curtiss*, 7 U.S. 267 (1806). *Strawbridge* holds that a case is not within the statutory grant of diversity jurisdiction unless there is "complete diversity" between the parties, that is, all plaintiffs in a suit are from different states than all defendants at the time suit is brought.

As a result of these restrictions, many cases within "the Article III storehouse" may not be brought in federal court as diversity cases. This relationship between the constitutional and statutory requirements is reminiscent of the separate limits on personal jurisdiction in the fourteenth amendment and long-arm statutes. See Chapter 2, pp.23-27. Here, as there, the legislature may grant less than all of the constitutionally available jurisdiction but not more. See Figure 4-1.

The Meaning of State Citizenship

Constitutions establish grand principles but seldom explain exactly how to apply them. In the area of diversity jurisdiction, for example, it has been left to the courts to determine what it means to be "citizens of different states." For natural persons (that is, human beings), the courts have equated state citizenship for diversity purposes with the common law concept of domicile.

"domicile"

A person's domicile is generally defined as the state where he has taken up residence with the intent to reside indefinitely. Under this definition, residence is not equivalent to domicile; having a residence in the state is necessary but not sufficient to establish a domicile for diversity purposes. If Hawes owns houses in Missouri and Wyoming and spends a good deal of time in both states, he will still have only one domicile. Which state it is depends on his subjective intent — sometimes almost impossible to ascertain — to make one particular state his "home." See Wright at 147.

The major problem in applying the domicile concept is determining what it means to "intend to stay indefinitely" in a state. It is not necessary to make an irrevocable commitment to stay in a place "permanently" to establish intent under the domicile test. That would be an unduly stringent requirement; few of us make such a firm decision about what we will do in the long term. Rather, "indefinitely" means that a person's presence in the state is open-ended: That is, he has no definite intent to leave to make a home elsewhere. This test can be met, even though a person expects that he probably *will* move on at some point, so long as he has no definite plans to do so at a particular time or upon the occurrence of a particular event. A person who is not committed to leaving is thought to be "at home" even though, like all of us, he may choose to leave at some time in the future.

For example, if Hawes quits his job and goes to Florida in hopes of finding a good job, he establishes a new domicile, even though he may leave if the job market proves unpromising. However, if Hawes goes to Florida for a few months as an undercover agent for the FBI, with the intent to return to his home in Missouri when the case is closed, he remains domiciled in Missouri, even if the exact length of time it will take to crack the case is unknown. Although the exact date of his departure from Florida is unknown, Hawes does not intend to stay "indefinitely" but rather to leave upon the occurrence of a particular event.

In addition, subjective intent to stay indefinitely is necessary but not sufficient: It must coincide with physical presence within the new domicile. Even if Hawes firmly intends to move to Florida after he retires next month, he does not acquire a domicile there until he physically arrives there to stay. Until then, he keeps his last domicile.

Although it is hardly a foregone conclusion from the language of Article III and §1332, corporations have long been held to be "citizens" authorized to invoke the diversity jurisdiction. Until 1958 they were held to be citizens of the state in which they were incorporated, regardless of where they actually conducted their daily business activity. In 1958 Congress enacted 28 U.S.C. §1332(c), which provides a statutory definition of the state citizenship of corporations for diversity purposes. Under §1332(c) corporations are citizens for diversity purposes of both the state where their principal place of business is located and the state in which they are incorporated. Consequently, if an opposing party is a citizen of either of those states, diversity does not exist.

The "principal place of business" provision in §1332(c) has also created some interpretive problems. Most corporations carry on their business totally or predominately in one state, so it is clear that they are citizens of that state for diversity purposes. In other cases, however, particularly cases involving very large corporations or corporations whose business involves commerce or transportation among numerous states, it is difficult to point definitively to one state as the corporation's principal place of business. If there is a definable center of the productive activities of the corporation, that is, the manufacturing or other profit-making activity that the corporation is engaged in, most courts tend to choose that state. The term "place of business," after all, connotes the place where you do what you exist to do, and the term "principal" place of business suggests the place where you do the most of it. This is sometimes referred to as the "place of operations" test. The asserted rationale for diversity jurisdiction, to avoid prejudice against "outsiders," supports the use of this test: the corporation will most likely be perceived as "local" where it employs the most people, conducts the most activities, and has the most interaction with the public. See generally Wright and Miller §3625.[5]

However, the day-to-day activities of some corporations may be so dispersed as to make it artificial to characterize one state as the center of their productive activities. For example, it may be difficult to say that the productive activity of an insurance company that insures risks in many states or an airline that flies to destinations in many states is centered in any one of those states. In cases involving such widely dispersed corporate activities, courts have sometimes looked to the so-called "nerve center" of the corporation, the corporate headquarters or home office from which its activities are coordinated, to determine the principal place of business. See, e.g., *Egan v. American Airlines, Inc.*, 211 F. Supp. 292 (E.D.N.Y. 1962).[6]

Assume in analyzing the following examples that all actions are brought in federal court, that the amount-in-controversy requirement is met in each case, and (unless otherwise specified) that each case is based on state law.

EXAMPLES

The Basic Diversity Requirements

1. Is there diversity between the parties in the following cases?
   a. Marlowe, from California, sues Archer, from California, in a federal district court in Illinois.

---

5. On the other hand, this logic suggests that corporations should *not* be deemed citizens of their state of incorporation, if, as is often true, they conduct no activities in that state. But, of course, under §1332(c), they are.

6. Like so many procedural issues, however, this one is not entirely settled. The Seventh Circuit uses the nerve center test alone to establish a corporation's principal place of business. *Wisconsin Knife Works v. National Metal Crafters*, 781 F.2d 1280, 1282-1283 (7th Cir. 1986).

    b. Carella, from New York, sues Marlowe (California) and Archer (California).

    c. Carella (New York) sues Marlowe (California) and McGee, a Floridian, in a federal district court in California.

    d. Carella (New York), McGee (Florida), and Spenser (Massachusetts) sue Marlowe (California), Archer (California), and Meyer (New York).

    e. Marlowe (California) sues Carella (New York) and Marple, an Englishwoman.

    f. Same facts as (e), except that Marple, still an Englishwoman, lives in California.

2. Marlowe (California) sues Archer (California) in federal court in California for damages under a federal firearms control statute. May the court hear the case?

3. Marlowe (California) sues Carella (New York) for breach of contract in state court. Can he do this?

4. Marlowe (California) sues McGee (Florida) and Archer (California). Marlowe's claim against McGee is for defamation, a state law claim. His claim against Archer arises from the same incident but is based on federal law. Will the federal court have jurisdiction?

5. Marlowe (California) sues McGee (Florida) for libel. He subsequently learns that Archer (California) co-authored the offending article and amends his complaint to assert a libel claim against Archer as well. Will the federal court have jurisdiction over the action?

Homes Away from Home

6. Carella (New York) collides with McGee (Florida) during a car chase in New York City. Carella is disabled in the accident, retires to Florida, and sues McGee in a federal district court in Florida. Is the suit proper?

7. Meyer, a New Yorker, decides to move to Arizona. He buys an Audi from Isola Volkswagen, a New York dealership incorporated in New York, and sets off with his family for Arizona. While driving through Oklahoma, he is involved in an accident and hospitalized.

    a. Four months later, while still in the hospital, Meyer files suit against Isola in an Oklahoma federal court. May the court entertain the action?

    b. While in the hospital, Meyer receives an offer to stay in Oklahoma and work as a detective for an oil company. He accepts and several months after beginning work sues Isola in federal court. Is the suit proper?

    c. Meyer is released from the hospital after six months. The company he had planned to join in Arizona has rescinded its job offer since he was unable to start work when it needed him. He still has six months of rehabilitation ahead of him in Oklahoma. After that he plans to begin looking for a job as a detective in the oil drilling industry, wherever one turns up. Is he diverse from Isola?

Corporate Diversity

8.   Carella (New York) sues Underworld, Inc., incorporated in Delaware, doing business in every state, with its principal place of business in Florida. Suit is brought in the federal district court for the Northern District of Florida. Does the court have jurisdiction?

9.   McGee (Florida) sues Underworld in a New York federal court. Is the suit proper?

10. Marlowe (California) sues Gamblers International, Inc., a corporation incorporated in Nevada. Gamblers has two casinos: one very large casino in Reno, Nevada, which grosses $40 million per year, and another casino in California, which does $35 million in business each year. The corporate offices are in Reno. Is there diversity jurisdiction in Marlowe's suit?

11. Prior to the 1958 amendment that provided for dual citizenship of corporations for diversity purposes, corporations were considered citizens of their state of incorporation only. Did the amendment expand or contract corporate access to federal court?

The Amount-in-Controversy Requirement

As stated above, Article III, §2 broadly grants federal court jurisdiction over cases "between citizens of different states" without any requirement that a particular amount be in dispute between the parties. But Congress has always chosen to keep minor diversity cases out of the federal courts by providing that such cases can only be brought there if the amount in controversy exceeds a given figure. The figure started out at $500 in 1789, and has been periodically increased in pursuit of inflation. For thirty years, from 1958 to 1988, the amount was required to exceed $10,000; now, it must exceed $50,000. The Federal Courts Study Committee has already recommended another increase, to $75,000.

It is important to realize that §1332(a) requires that more than $50,000 be "in controversy," not that the plaintiff will definitely receive that much. A plaintiff might legitimately seek considerably more than $50,000, yet recover less if the jury values his injuries at less than he thinks they should. This is particularly true in the case of intangible injuries, such as pain and suffering, emotional distress, loss of consortium, or loss of goodwill in a business. Lawyers often vary widely in predicting what damages a jury will assess in such cases, since there is no objective yardstick for lawyers to use in making such predictions or for juries to use in awarding such damages.

Indeed, a plaintiff may legitimately seek more than $50,000 and recover nothing: The jury may conclude that the defendant was not negligent or that some defense to the claim is established. The paradox that arises in applying the amount-in-controversy requirement is that it is impossible to know what value the jury will put on plaintiff's claim, or whether they will find for him at all, until the case is tried. How is the court to determine its power to hear the case without hearing the case?

This paradox has been resolved by the very sensible rule in *St. Paul Mercury Indemnity Co. v. Red Cab Co.,* 303 U.S. 283 (1938), which holds that a plaintiff's good faith claim for more than the amount required controls, unless it "appear[s] to a legal certainty that the claim is really for less. . . ." 303 U.S. at 288-289. What this means is that the court must find the amount-in-controversy requirement met unless it is quite clear that there is no way the recovery will reach $50,000.01. The *St. Paul Mercury* rule is heavily weighted toward the plaintiff. Where the plaintiff might get more or might get less, the amount-in-controversy requirement is deemed satisfied. Where he will probably get less, but just might get more, it is deemed satisfied. It is only where the judge, looking at the pleaded facts, concludes "to a legal certainty" that he could only be awarded less that the amount-in-controversy requirement is not met.

This rule makes sense because Congress has not provided that jurisdiction only exists where the plaintiff *recovers* more than $50,000. The requirement is that more than $50,000 be *in dispute*. Where there is legitimate debate as to whether the jury might return a verdict above that amount, the Congressional mandate is satisfied. However, while the *St. Paul Mercury* rule makes sense, it is ineffective in keeping many types of diversity cases out of federal court. Where intangible damages are at issue, it will seldom be possible to conclude that there is no way the plaintiff will recover more than the amount required.

A second interpretive problem raised by the amount-in-controversy requirement is how to measure the amount in cases involving multiple claims or multiple parties. The basic rules on "aggregation of damages" are that a single plaintiff may aggregate any claims he has against a single defendant to reach the required sum. However, he cannot add claims he has against different defendants to reach the magic number. Nor may he add his own claim to that of another plaintiff. Except in rare cases involving "common undivided interests" (such as joint owners of property), each plaintiff must have a colorable claim for more than $50,000 against each defendant. A useful way to look at such multiple party cases is to ask, "if each plaintiff alone were suing each defendant alone, would he satisfy the amount-in-controversy requirement?" For a full (but skeptical) discussion of the confusing aggregation rules, see Wright at 196-201.

The following examples will help you apply the aggregation rules, if not appreciate them.

EXAMPLES

Aggravation of Damages

12. Is the amount-in-controversy requirement met in each of the following cases? (Assume that diversity is otherwise proper and that there is no common undivided interest involved in the suit.)

    a. Hammer sues Holmes for $40,000 for his personal injuries suffered in an auto accident and for $15,000 for damage to his car in the same accident.

    b. Hammer sues Holmes to recover $30,000 on a loan he made to Holmes and for $30,000 for an unrelated libel.

    c. Hammer sues Holmes for $80,000 for injuries suffered in an auto accident. He also claims that Dr. Watson negligently treated his injuries, causing $20,000 in additional damages.

    d. Hammer sues Holmes for $40,000 for damages suffered in an accident. In the same action, Marlowe, who was a passenger in Hammer's car, sues Holmes for $25,000 for his injuries.

Adding Insult to Injury

    e. McGee sues Spenser for causing $30,000 worth of damage to McGee's houseboat. His complaint contains two counts. Count One seeks $30,000 from Spenser for negligently ramming the boat while docking in Fort Lauderdale. Count Two seeks $30,000 from Spenser on the theory that he intentionally damaged the boat.

    f. McGee's $75,000 houseboat is completely destroyed in a collision with boats piloted by Spenser and Carella. He claims that either Spenser, Carella, or both, were negligent and sues them both to recover for the damage to the boat.

    g. McGee sues Spenser for $40,000 for intentionally injuring his boat and for $50,000 in punitive damages.

Another Famous Foible

13. Here is another dandelion from the bluebook garden. What is wrong with it?

> The plaintiff's claim must be dismissed for failure to meet the amount-in-controversy requirement unless it appears to be a legal certainty that he will recover more than fifty thousand dollars.

EXPLANATIONS

The Basic Diversity Requirements

1a. Marlowe and Archer are both from California. You can't get any less diverse than this, under any definition of diversity. The fact that Marlowe has sued in an Illinois federal court is irrelevant. No matter which district he chooses, the parties are from the same state. Don't be thrown off the track by the fact that suit is brought in a third state. For diversity purposes (unlike personal jurisdiction purposes), the crucial question is where the opposing parties live, not where they sue.

b. This is a proper diversity case even though both defendants are from California. The *Strawbridge* rule requires that all defendants be from different states than all plaintiffs; parties on the same side of the "v" may be co-citizens. While this might not satisfy one's intuitive notion of "complete diversity," it is diverse enough to satisfy Chief Justice Marshall and §1332.

c. This is the completest of all possible diversities because all parties are from different states. It is therefore a proper diversity case. Once again, the place of suit is irrelevant to the diversity analysis. Carella's choice of the defendant's home state does not destroy diversity, just as the choice of forum could not create it in example 1a.

d. There is no diversity jurisdiction here. While there are diverse citizens on both sides of the "v," there are also New Yorkers on both sides, which violates the *Strawbridge* rule. This is an ironic result: Why should a New York state court jury be any less prejudiced against Marlowe and Archer, simply because Meyer has been sued as well? Indeed, might not the jury shift the blame from the in-state defendant to the out-of-state defendants? It is easy to poke holes in the *Strawbridge* rule in cases like this; indeed, Chief Justice Marshall is said to have regretted the decision himself. Wright at 141.[7] But any effort to amend the diversity statute to revise the *Strawbridge* rule would probably lead to an expansion of diversity jurisdiction. In an age when diversity is in disrepute such an amendment is unlikely.

Note the various ways in which the plaintiffs could restructure this suit to use the federal courts. All three plaintiffs could sue Marlowe and Archer, or McGee and Spenser could sue all three defendants. In either case, diversity would exist, but some part of the controversy would have to be heard separately in state court.

e. This is a suit between diverse citizens with an additional party who is an alien (a harsh-sounding term for a person who is a citizen or subject of another country). Article III, §2 does not specifically provide for this kind of case, but it does separately authorize jurisdiction over cases between citizens of different states and cases between citizens and aliens ("between a State, or the Citizens thereof, and foreign States, Citizens or Subjects"). It is a fair inference that a combination of the two is also proper. Congress has expressly authorized jurisdiction in such cases in 28 U.S.C. §1332(a)(3).

f. Marple is an alien whether she is currently living in California or England. She cannot become a state citizen without first becoming a United States citizen. Thus, even if she is domiciled in California, this is a proper

---

7. On the other hand, this application of the rule is not entirely irrational. Carella could not sue Meyer in federal court alone, since they are both from New York. Why should he be able to do so simply by joining other defendants who are diverse?

diversity case.[8] See, e.g., *Mas v. Perry*, 489 F.2d 1396 (5th Cir. 1974). For an interesting variation on this case, see *Twentieth Century-Fox Film Corp. v. Taylor*, 239 F. Supp. 913 (S.D.N.Y. 1965), in which Elizabeth Taylor was sued for various claims arising out of the filming of the movie "Cleopatra." Although Taylor was an American citizen at the time suit was filed, she was domiciled abroad. Consequently, she was not subject to suit in federal court under the diversity statute since she was not a citizen of any state, nor was she an alien since she had not relinquished her American citizenship. Id. at 914 n.2.

2.   This example is meant to dispel one potential source of confusion. It is only necessary to have one basis of federal jurisdiction to sue in federal court. Here, Marlowe's suit is brought under a federal statute. It is a case "arising under federal law," a separate basis for federal subject matter jurisdiction authorized by Article III and 28 U.S.C. §1331. It is therefore irrelevant that the parties are from the same state, since diversity is not needed.

3.   This is a fundamental question, and one that breeds much confusion. Clearly, this is a proper diversity case. However, that does not mean that Marlowe *must* go to federal court, only that he *may*. The fact that a federal court is empowered to hear a case does not automatically mean that state courts cannot. State courts have very broad subject matter jurisdiction, including jurisdiction over most cases that are within federal court jurisdiction. The usual rule is that state courts have "concurrent jurisdiction" over cases that federal courts can hear unless Congress provides that federal jurisdiction is exclusive. For an example where Congress has done so, see 28 U.S.C. §1338(a) (making federal court jurisdiction exclusive in patent, plant variety and copyright cases). In diversity cases, however, plaintiffs may choose to bring suit in state court even though they also could choose a federal court.

4.   This suit is proper even though Archer and Marlowe are both from California. Marlowe has a federal claim against Archer, a separate basis for suing him in federal court. Thus, he is not relying on diversity between himself and Archer as a basis for jurisdiction. In determining diversity, you can disregard parties who are properly before the federal court on another basis and focus on the part of the case for which diversity is the claimed source of jurisdiction. *Kauth v. Hartford Ins. Co. of Illinois*, 852 F.2d 951 (7th Cir.1988). Because Marlowe is diverse from Carella, his claim against him is proper, so there is a proper basis for jurisdiction over all claims in the case.

Put another way, it is clear that on these facts Marlowe could sue McGee and Archer in separate actions in federal court, one based on federal question jurisdiction and the other on diversity. It would hardly make sense to allow him to do that, but not to allow him to sue them in a combined action.

---

8. However, a recent amendment to §1332 treats an alien "admitted to the United States for permanent residence" as a citizen of the state where he is domiciled. See the last paragraph of 28 U.S.C. §1332(a).

5.   The federal court would be forced to dismiss this action for lack of diversity jurisdiction. Marlowe's amendment has "destroyed diversity" by adding a party from his home state. Even though the court had jurisdiction over the action as originally filed, it must dismiss once the nondiverse party is added. Otherwise, the plaintiff would be able to gain access to federal court by suing diverse parties in the initial action and adding home-state defendants later on. See *Owen Equipment & Erection Co. v. Kroger,* 437 U.S. 365 (1978).

As a practical matter, Marlowe will not offer this amendment if he wishes to remain in federal court and knows that his amendment will destroy diversity. He will sue Archer separately in state court. If unified litigation is more important than access to federal court for part of his claim, he will bring a separate action against both defendants in state court and dismiss his federal suit against McGee.

Homes Away from Home

6.   Although the parties were diverse at the time of the incident that gave rise to Carella's claim, they are not diverse at the time of the suit: Carella has apparently changed his domicile by retiring to Florida. Although it is unclear from the statute, courts have held that the magic date for determining diversity is the date of filing suit. *Hawes v. Club Equestre El Comandante,* 598 F.2d 698, 701 (1st Cir. 1979). If the parties are not diverse on that date, there is no jurisdiction. If they are, it does not matter that they were from the same state when the claim arose. Nor is the fact that the accident took place in New York of any help; the place of the underlying events in suit, like the place where the plaintiff brings the action, is irrelevant to the determination of diversity.

7a.   You may recognize this hypo as a slightly modified version of the facts in *World-Wide Volkswagen v. Woodson,* 444 U.S. 286 (1980). The case could not properly be brought as a diversity case, since Meyer is still a New Yorker. Even though he intends to settle in Arizona and has left New York, perhaps never to return, he has not yet established a domicile in Arizona. To do so, he must physically arrive in the state with the intent to remain indefinitely.

Nor may Meyer argue that he is domiciled in Oklahoma, based on his four-month stay there. He has arrived there and established a "residence" of sorts,[9] but as far as we know, he has not changed his intent to go on to live in

---

9. Establishing a residence for domicile purposes need not entail purchasing a house or leasing an apartment. Even an overnight stay in a hotel or a night spent in the family camper may suffice. See Restatement (Second) of Conflicts of Laws §12, illustration 2; cf. *T. P. Laboratories v. Huge,* 197 F. Supp. 860, 863 (D. Md. 1961). Some authorities state the requirement as one of "physical presence" rather than residence. See, e.g., *Holmes v. Sopuch,* 639 F.2d 431, 433 (8th Cir. 1981).

Arizona. Residence in Oklahoma without the necessary intent is just as inef-fective to create a new domicile as intent to live in Arizona without residence there. Until the two coincide in a new state, Robinson remains a New York domiciliary.

b. A frequent mistake in applying the domicile rule is to conclude that intent and residence must coincide when a person originally arrives in the state. That is not so; as long as the two coincide at some time while he is there, a new domicile is established. In this case, Meyer does not intend to stay in Oklahoma when he arrives but forms that intent later, while residing there. When he does form that intent, Oklahoma becomes his domicile. Restatement (Second) of Conflicts of Laws §15, illustration 2 (1971). Con-sequently, this is a proper diversity case.

c. This is a difficult case. Meyer has not made any commitment to stay in Oklahoma after he finishes rehabilitation; nor does he have a reason any longer to go on to Arizona; nor is he likely to return to New York (they don't drill an awful lot of oil there, last I heard); nor can you argue that he is in Oklahoma for a definite period of time, the six-month rehabilitation period. He will definitely be there for *at least* six months, but he is not definitely there for *only* six months. He may stay until Armageddon, for all we know.

Of course, the rule is that you don't lose your old domicile until you acquire a new one. But I would conclude that Meyer has acquired domicile in Oklahoma. He might stay in Oklahoma — where they clearly do have oil wells — or he might go elsewhere. While he's not irrevocably committed to staying, he's not committed to leaving either. Meyer's plans are "indefinite."

Nearly a generation of civil procedure students have done battle with me over examples like this, resisting the idea that a person can be domiciled in a state where they have so little commitment or expectation of remaining. Many argue that Meyer remains domiciled in New York, since he is not committed to staying in Oklahoma; but I say he is domiciled in the state where he currently resides unless he is committed to going somewhere else. Meyer was committed to leaving in example 7a, but that isn't true here.

Corporate Diversity

8.   Diversity jurisdiction is proper here, since Carella is not from either Underworld's state of incorporation or the state where it has its principal place of business. The fact that Underworld does business in New York, the plaintiff's home state, does not affect diversity as long as New York is not Underworld's principal place of business. Distinguish personal jurisdiction over the corporation, which may be established (in appropriate cases) in a state where the corporation does business, even though it does a great deal more business in other states. See Chapter 1, example 8.

9.   There is no diversity jurisdiction here because the plaintiff is a citizen of the state in which Underworld has its principal place of business. McGee may

not claim diversity on the ground that he is from Florida and Underworld from Delaware: Underworld is *also* from Florida under §1332(c). Neither the corporation nor the opposing party may pick and choose between these two states in order to establish diversity. The corporation is from both states, and therefore, complete diversity is lacking.

10. In this case, the defendant has very large facilities in two states, both of which might ordinarily be deemed "principal" places of business. While it may seem artificial to designate either as more "principal" than the other, §1332(c) has been consistently interpreted to mean that a corporation can have only one principal place of business for diversity purposes. See 28 U.S.C. §1332(c) ("*the* state where it has its principal place of business") (emphasis supplied). Thus, the court will have to choose California or Nevada; because the corporate headquarters and the larger casino are both in Nevada, the court will likely conclude that Gamblers' principal place of business is Nevada. Thus, it will be a citizen of Nevada on this basis as well as on the basis of its incorporation there and will be diverse from Marlowe. (In many cases, as in this one, corporations will be citizens of only one state under §1332(c) because they are incorporated in the state where their principal place of business is located.)

11. The amendment restricted corporate access to the federal courts by increasing the number of cases in which corporations share the same state citizenship with opposing parties. For example, a mining corporation might incorporate in Delaware, for tax or legal reasons, but do all its mining business in Colorado. Under the earlier interpretation, it was diverse from a Colorado citizen and could invoke federal jurisdiction even though, in day-to-day reality, it functioned as a local Colorado corporation. Under §1332(c), however, that corporation is deemed a citizen of Colorado as well as a citizen of Delaware and confined to the state courts in suits against Colorado citizens.

Aggravation of Damages

12a. Hammer may aggregate any claims he has against Holmes, a single defendant, to reach the required jurisdictional amount. Because the two claims combined exceed $50,000, the amount-in-controversy requirement is met.

b. Aggregation is proper because the plaintiff may aggregate his claims against a single defendant even if, as here, the two parties are totally unrelated.

c. Hammer satisfies the amount requirement against Holmes, but not against Watson. He may not bootstrap his $20,000 claim against Watson onto his claim against Holmes; aggregation only allows a plaintiff to aggregate claims against a single defendant. Hammer's claim against Watson will be dismissed for lack of jurisdiction.

d. Both of these claims will be dismissed. Just as Hammer was barred from aggregating claims against separate defendants, he may not aggregate his claims with those of another plaintiff to reach the $50,000-plus threshold. When you look separately at each plaintiff's claim against each defendant, neither satisfies the amount-in-controversy requirement.

For an interesting decision applying this rule to class actions, see *Zahn v. International Paper Co.*, 414 U.S. 291 (1973). In *Zahn*, the named plaintiffs claimed more than $10,000 in damages, but many members of the class they sought to represent did not. The Court stuck to its guns on the traditional aggregation rules and held that the class members' claims had to be dismissed for failure to meet the amount-in-controversy requirement.

Adding Insult to Injury

e. If you thought carefully about this case, you should have concluded as a matter of common sense that the amount-in-controversy requirement is not met. The rule that the plaintiff may aggregate his claims against a single defendant applies to claims for *separate losses,* such as those asserted in example 12b, not to demands for the same damages based on different theories. McGee has only suffered $30,000 in damages; that is what he is suing to recover. Granted, he has two possible theories of relief, but he will clearly not recover $30,000 on each theory. Spenser could not have been negligent *and* intentionally caused the damage. If McGee wins at all, he will win on only one theory and will only recover the amount of his loss.

Indeed, even in cases where a plaintiff might recover on both theories, he will not be awarded more than his actual damages, absent a claim for punitive damages. For example, McGee might sue a truck dealer for breach of contract and breach of implied warranty to recover for a truck worth $30,000 less than he paid for it. Even if the court finds for McGee on both counts, he will still recover only the $30,000 he has lost; no court will give him double damages simply because he advances two theories for relief.

f. In this case McGee is claiming that one or both defendants' negligence contributed to cause the loss of his boat. If only Spenser was at fault, McGee would recover the entire $75,000 from him. If Carella caused the collision, McGee will recover the $75,000 loss from him. If they are both found negligent, the law in most states would allow McGee to collect the full $75,000 from either, assuming that McGee was not negligent himself. Thus, since either defendant might be liable for the entire $75,000, the amount-in-controversy requirement is satisfied against both. Of course, either might be absolved completely, but as long as each *might* be liable for more than the jurisdictional amount, the requirement is met.

g. Here, McGee's actual damages are $40,000, but he may recover more than his actual damages if the law of the state allows recovery of punitive damages. If the state allows punitive damages in the kind of action McGee brings, the amount requirement is likely met. Under *St. Paul Mercury*, the plaintiff's demand controls, unless it appears to be a legal certainty that he could not recover the jurisdictional amount. It is extremely difficult to say for sure that McGee will not recover $10,000.01 in punitive damages, since punitive damages turn on a jury's subjective assessment of the extremity of the defendant's conduct and, at the time the defendant challenges the sufficiency of the amount sought, the court will have little familiarity with the underlying facts of the case.

However, if the relevant state law bars punitive damages, the amount-in-controversy requirement will not be met, and the case will be dismissed, since the only allowable damages do not exceed $50,000.

Another Famous Foible

13. This too-frequent misstatement of the *St. Paul Mercury* rule exactly reverses its meaning: It requires the plaintiff to prove that he *will* recover more than $50,000 to satisfy the amount-in-controversy requirement and stay in federal court. On the contrary, the rule gives the plaintiff every benefit of the doubt: If looking at the pleaded facts it appears that the plaintiff *might* recover more than $50,000, the requirement is met. It is only where it is clear to a legal certainty that the plaintiff *definitely will not* recover that much on the claim he has asserted that the court dismisses for failure to meet the monetary threshold.

5

Personal and Subject Matter Jurisdiction Compared: The First Two Rings

Introduction

Much of the civil procedure course is devoted to the fundamental issue of choosing the proper court in which to bring a lawsuit. As you probably already know, there is quite a choice: Each of the 50 states has its own court system, not to mention the District of Columbia and other territories. In addition, there is a separate system of federal courts, established and administered by the federal government but geographically located throughout the United States. Thus, in any particular state there will be both the local state courts and one or more "branches" or districts of the federal court system.

The plaintiff is not free to choose indiscriminately among the various federal and state courts in the 50 states. There are three basic requirements that limit the proper courts for any lawsuit. *First* is the need to find a court that can exercise personal jurisdiction over the defendant. *Second*, not all courts can hear all types of cases: The plaintiff must choose a court that has "subject matter jurisdiction" over the kind of case she wishes to litigate. *Third*, the chosen forum must be a proper "venue" under the applicable venue statutes. I call these the three rings of civil procedure and visualize them as in Figure 5-1.[1] As a rule, courts can only hear those cases that satisfy

---

1. I am indebted to Professor Abram Chayes of Harvard Law School, my own civil procedure teacher, for this helpful diagram.

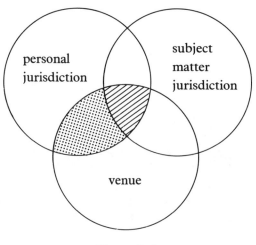

Figure 5-1

all three rings (the shaded area on the diagram). Frequently, a case will satisfy one or two of these prerequisites but fail the third. For example, the plaintiff may have chosen a court that has personal jurisdiction over the defendant and is a proper venue under the relevant venue statute (see the dotted area in the diagram), but the court will still have to dismiss the action if the third ring, subject matter jurisdiction, is not met.

This chapter compares the first two rings, personal and subject matter jurisdiction. The reasons for these two limitations on the right to bring an action are quite different, yet the concepts used to define them are sometimes confusingly similar. It is worth getting the distinctions clear in your mind before wading too deeply into the procedural morass.

Basic Distinctions

Personal jurisdiction, as Chapter 1 explains, is a geographical limitation on the places where a plaintiff may choose to sue a defendant for a particular claim. It is intended, as a matter of basic fairness, to prevent a plaintiff from suing a nonresident defendant in a state unless that defendant has established a relationship to that state which would reasonably lead her to anticipate being sued there.

Personal jurisdiction turns in each case on the relationship between the defendant and the state where suit is brought. Consequently, it may be proper to bring a particular action in one state but not in another. For example, if Gable sues Leigh, a Texan, for assault arising out of threats Leigh made at a Hollywood movie opening, it would be unreasonable to force

Leigh to defend the action in Minnesota. She has (presumably) no minimum contacts with Minnnesota, did not make the threats in Minnesota, and has no reason to expect this suit to be brought there. However, she could be sued in California for this claim, since she has relevant contacts with California: She made the threats there and can expect them to injure Gable there.

Similarly, the courts of a single state may have jurisdiction over one suit between particular litigants but not over another between the same parties, if the second suit is unrelated to that state. Although Gable's first assault action could not be brought in Minnesota, he might well be able to sue Leigh there for another assault if Leigh repeats her threatening statements at a Minneapolis opening. Thus, the answer depends in every case on the defendant's contacts with the state where suit has been brought.

Subject matter jurisdiction, by contrast, concerns the court's authority to hear generic types of cases. All state court systems have a set of trial courts with very broad subject matter jurisdiction. These courts (sometimes confusingly referred to as courts of "general jurisdiction") have subject matter jurisdiction over a wide range of suits, such as torts, contracts, property, and other common types of disputes. These state courts of broad subject matter jurisdiction have different names in different states. In California they are called the Superior Courts; in Pennsylvania, the Courts of Common Pleas; in New York, perversely, they are called the Supreme Courts. In addition, a state may create specialized courts to hear certain types of claims, such as landlord/tenant cases (housing courts) or family and inheritance matters (probate courts).

The subject matter jurisdiction of the federal district courts is much more limited than that of the state courts. The federal courts were not created to displace the preexisting state systems, but only to provide a federal forum for specific categories of cases of federal concern. The federal courts have jurisdiction over cases arising under federal law, cases between citizens of different states (the so-called diversity jurisdiction), and other more limited categories of cases. United States Constitution, Article III, §2. By contrast, they have no jurisdiction over most common types of suits, such as tort suits, contract actions, or actions seeking recovery under state statutes (unless the parties are diverse or some other category of federal jurisdiction applies).

Unlike personal jurisdiction, the subject matter jurisdiction of a court does not usually depend on the location of the particular court the plaintiff chooses. For example, if a case arises under federal law, any federal district court will have subject matter jurisdiction over it. Since Article III and 28 U.S.C. §1331 authorize "the [federal] district courts" to hear cases arising under the laws of the United States, they all have jurisdiction over such cases. If subject matter jurisdiction were the only limit on a plaintiff's right to sue, she could bring a case arising under federal law in any federal district court in the country.

Sources of Confusion

A number of factors conspire to make these differing concepts difficult to sort out. First, although Article III, §2 of the Constitution confers jurisdiction over various categories of cases on federal courts, it does not withdraw jurisdiction over those cases from the state courts. The state courts have "concurrent jurisdiction" over cases within the federal judicial power unless Congress has made federal court jurisdiction exclusive for a particular type of claim. Thus, a state court may hear many claims arising under federal law, such as federal civil rights cases, even though the plaintiff would have the option to bring the action in federal court as well. By contrast, the federal courts do not have concurrent jurisdiction over state law actions (unless the parties are diverse); they may only hear those cases specifically provided for in Article III of the United States Constitution and jurisdictional statutes passed by Congress.

The framers of the Constitution made the situation particularly confusing by creating the diversity jurisdiction (see U.S. Const. article III, §2), which authorizes the federal courts to hear cases between citizens of different states. In most situations, subject matter jurisdiction is defined by the nature of the controversy (such as housing cases, probate cases, or tax cases), but here the framers chose to confer upon federal courts the power to hear cases on the basis of who the parties are. Despite this focus on the domicile of the parties, this is *not* personal jurisdiction; it does not focus on the geographical relationship of the events giving rise to the suit to the state where suit is brought but broadly grants subject matter jurisdiction to any federal court, no matter where located, so long as the case is between citizens of different states. For example, if Flynn, from Oregon, sues Peck, from Maryland, for a breach of contract arising in Montana, the case is a proper diversity case (assuming the amount in controversy exceeds $50,000). Any federal district court will have subject matter jurisdiction over it, though many will not have personal jurisdiction over Peck.

Another potential source of confusion arises from the fact that the concept of domicile is relevant to both personal and subject matter jurisdiction. A natural person (that is, a human being–type defendant) is subject to personal jurisdiction in the state where she is domiciled, that is, the last state where she has established a residence with the intent to reside indefinitely. See Restatement (Second) of Conflicts of Law §27 (1971). An individual's state citizenship for purposes of determining diversity jurisdiction is also determined by this same domicile concept. But in applying the concept to determine personal jurisdiction, the court will ask whether the defendant's domicile is in the state where suit is brought. When invoking this concept to determine subject matter jurisdiction based on diversity, the court will simply compare the plaintiff's domicile to the defendant's to make sure they differ.

Yet another piece of terminology that breeds confusion is the concept of "general jurisdiction," which is used in connection with both personal and subject matter jurisdiction. The basic trial courts of each state, for example, are said to exercise "general jurisdiction." This means that they have very broad subject matter jurisdiction over many types of suits, unless the type of dispute has been delegated to a specialized state court or is within those few categories of cases in which Congress has made federal subject matter jurisdiction exclusive. By contrast, when used in the personal jurisdiction context, "general jurisdiction" refers to the authority of a state's courts to hear any claim against a particular defendant, related or unrelated to the defendant's in-state contacts. Such general in personam jurisdiction may be based on domicile in the state, substantial and continuous in-state business activities, or in-state service of process. See Chapter 1, pp.5-7.

Personal Jurisdiction in the Federal Courts

For the purposes of this chapter, it is necessary to touch briefly on a problem that puzzles lawyers as well as law students — the reach of personal jurisdiction in the federal courts. As a matter of *constitutional power*, the federal courts' power to exercise personal jurisdiction is limited not by the fourteenth amendment due process analysis of the *International Shoe* line of cases, but instead by the due process clause of the fifth amendment. Under fourteenth amendment analysis, state courts may only exercise personal jurisdiction over parties who have formed a relationship to that state. By contrast, under the fifth amendment a defendant need only have an appropriate relationship to the United States — such as being found or domiciled in the United States or having minimum contacts here that give rise to the claim — in order to be subject to personal jurisdiction in a federal court. Thus, it is generally held that Congress has the power to authorize federal courts to exercise nationwide jurisdiction, that is, to require parties with contacts anywhere in the United States to respond to suits brought in any federal district court. See generally Casad at ¶5.01.[2]

In some types of actions Congress has authorized nationwide jurisdic-

---

2. A frequent argument in support of this conclusion is that Congress did not have to create separate federal courts in each state. It might have created regional courts or a single court located at the seat of the federal government. Had Congress taken this course, it would obviously have been necessary to authorize such a court to exercise broad jurisdiction over defendants from all over the country. Since such nationwide jurisdiction might well have been necessary, it would be incongruous to hold that it is constitutionally impermissible. See, e.g., *Briggs v. Goodwin*, 569 F.2d 1, 8-10 (1st Cir. 1977), rev'd on other grounds sub nom. *Stafford v. Briggs*, 444 U.S. 527 (1980).

tion in the federal courts through special jurisdictional provisions governing particular types of actions. An example is 28 U.S.C. §2361, which authorizes nationwide service in interpleader actions. Unless such a special provision applies, however, the authority for federal courts to serve process outside the state where they sit is restricted by the Federal Rules of Civil Procedure. Under Fed. R. Civ. P. 4(e), a federal court is authorized to serve process out of state "under the circumstances" prescribed by state law, that is, to exercise personal jurisdiction only to the extent it could be exercised by the courts of the state in which the federal court sits. *Omni Capital Intl. v. Rudolf Wolff & Co., Ltd.*, 484 U.S. 97, 105 (1988). Thus, if Gable sues Leigh in federal court in California, and Congress has not authorized broader jurisdiction for the type of suit involved, the court will only exercise personal jurisdiction over Leigh if the California courts could do so under the California long-arm statute and the due process clause of the fourteenth amendment.

This is really a very sensible rule. By generally confining the reach of personal jurisdiction in the federal court to that of the state courts of the same state, the Rules eliminate a potential ground for "forum-shopping" based on purely procedural considerations. As indicated above, in many cases plaintiffs will have a choice of state or federal court because both systems have concurrent subject matter jurisdiction over many types of suits. If the reach of personal jurisdiction were generally broader in federal court, plaintiffs would frequently choose to bring suit there for this reason alone, even though state court would otherwise be a more appropriate forum.

The following examples should help you sort out these related concepts. Assume in all cases that the relevant long-arm statute authorizes exercise of all constitutionally permissible jurisdiction. See the California statute supra p.24.

EXAMPLES

Distinctions and Differences

1.   Stewart, a California citizen, wishes to sue Cagney, also a Californian, for battery, to recover for injuries he suffered in a fight between them on a Los Angeles street. Stewart prefers to sue Cagney in California.
   a. Would a California state court have personal jurisdiction over Cagney?
   b. Would a California federal court have personal jurisdiction over Cagney?
   c. Would a California state court have subject matter jurisdiction over the action?
   d. Would a California federal court have subject matter jurisdiction over the action?

2.   Assume that Cagney is from New York and that he attacked Stewart while visiting California to make a movie. Stewart, a California citizen, prefers to sue Cagney in California.

  a. Would the California state court have personal jurisdiction over Cagney?
  b. Would the California federal court have personal jurisdiction over Cagney?
  c. Would a California state court have subject matter jurisdiction over the action?
  d. Would a California federal court have subject matter jurisdiction over the action?

3. On the facts of example 2, could Stewart have sued Cagney in either a state or federal court in New York?

4. On the facts of example 2, could Stewart have sued Cagney in either a state or federal court in Nevada?

Variations

5. One more variation on the facts of example 2: Assume that after the Los Angeles battery but before bringing suit, Cagney moves to California.
  a. May Stewart sue him in federal court in California?
  b. May Stewart sue him in a New York state court?

6. Colbert sues Hepburn in the federal district court for the Southern District of California for breach of a contract to star in a movie. Both parties are domiciled in New York, the contract was made there, and the movie was to be made there. However, Colbert prefers to sue in California, where she is currently working, and also prefers to sue in federal court. Hepburn, who is currently working in Arizona, does not object to the California court hearing the case. May it do so?

7. Colbert, a New Yorker, sues Kojak for a violation of her federal civil rights. Suit is brought under 42 U.S.C. §1983, the statute that authorizes suits for such violations. The claim arises out of an unlawful arrest, which took place in New York, and Kojak is domiciled there.
  a. May Colbert bring the suit in a New York state court?
  b. May she bring the suit in a California federal court?
  c. Assume, on the same facts, that Colbert is from California. Could she bring the action in a California federal court?

8. May Colbert sue Hepburn in a New York state court for violation of a copyright she holds on a book about the golden age of the movies? See 28 U.S.C. §1338(a).

EXPLANATIONS

Distinctions and Differences

1a. The California state court will have personal jurisdiction over Cagney on several bases. First, the California court may exercise personal jurisdiction over Cagney on the basis of his California domicile. Domicile in the forum state has been held an adequate basis for asserting personal jurisdiction, even if the claim sued upon did not arise in the state. *Milliken v. Meyer,* 311 U.S. 457 (1940). A person who has chosen the state as his domicile may fairly be said to have submitted himself generally to the judicial power of that state's courts, as a quid pro quo for enjoying the benefits and protections of living within the state.

In addition, Cagney has (allegedly) committed an in-state tortious act by assaulting Stewart in California. Virtually every state's long-arm statute authorizes personal jurisdiction over defendants for claims arising out of torts committed within the state, and this assertion of jurisdiction is clearly constitutional under *International Shoe.* Where Cagney has entered the state and consciously committed an act intended to harm Stewart in California, it is both fair and foreseeable to require him to respond to a California suit arising out of those in-state acts. See Chapter 2, example 4.

b. As stated in the introduction, the federal district courts' reach of personal jurisdiction is restricted in most cases to that of the courts of the state, since Rule 4(e) requires the federal court to look to the statutes or court rules governing personal jurisdiction in the state where the federal court sits. For example, the Idaho federal court will look to the Idaho long-arm statute. If the statute authorizes the assertion of jurisdiction and such an exercise of jurisdiction would not exceed the due process limits on *state* court jurisdiction, then the federal court will have personal jurisdiction. Similarly, the California federal court will look to the California jurisdiction statutes as well as the constitutional limits on state jurisdiction. Since the California state court will have personal jurisdiction over Cagney, the federal court will too.

One interesting consequence of this rule is that the reach of personal jurisdiction may vary from one federal court to another because each exercises jurisdiction to the extent permitted in the state in which it sits, and the reach of long-arm statutes varies from state to state.

c. Every state court system has a set of courts that has broad subject matter jurisdiction over state law claims, including battery claims. These courts of "general jurisdiction" are the workhorses of the state court systems because they are the basic trial courts for most types of claims. In California they are called the superior courts, and their jurisdiction includes tort claims such as the battery alleged in *Stewart v. Cagney.* Note that the analysis here for subject matter jurisdiction focuses on the nature of the case Stewart is asserting, rather than the relationship of the underlying events to the state of California, as in the personal jurisdiction analysis.

d. The California federal district court will not have subject matter jurisdiction over this case. The federal courts are not courts of general jurisdiction, but are limited to the types of cases listed in Article III, §2 and the federal statutes, such as 28 U.S.C. §§1331 and 1332, which confer this subject matter jurisdiction on the federal courts. Because nothing in Article III grants federal courts jurisdiction over battery cases, Stewart's suit may not properly be brought in federal court.

It is true that cases involving state claims, such as battery, negligence, or breach of contract may be brought in federal court if there is diversity between the parties. The framers, in their wisdom, saw fit to allow even cases based on state theories of recovery to be brought in federal court, if the parties are from different states. But here they are not, so there is no basis for federal subject matter jurisdiction. Only the California state court has both personal and subject matter jurisdiction over Stewart's suit; if venue is also proper, it may proceed to hear the case.

2a. On these facts Cagney is not subject to personal jurisdiction in California on the basis of his domicile, but the minimum contacts analysis in example 1a remains unchanged. Cagney has still committed a tortious act in California, which is likely to injure Stewart there. He will be subject to specific in personam jurisdiction there for suits arising out of this in-state tortious act. Even though it may be extremely inconvenient for Cagney to return to California to defend the action, under due process analysis the California court may require him to do so.

   b. As suggested above, the federal court under Fed. R. Civ. P. 4(e) will exercise personal jurisdiction to the same extent as the state court. Since the California state court may require Cagney to return and defend, the federal court may as well.

   c. The answer here is the same as example 1c: The California superior court is a court of general subject matter jurisdiction that may hear tort claims. Thus, as in example 1, the California state court satisfies both rings; if venue is proper, it may hear this case.

   d. It is still true, as in example 1d, that the federal courts have no subject matter jurisdiction over battery cases because nothing in Article III bestows jurisdiction of common law tort claims on the federal courts. However, Article III does authorize federal courts to hear cases between citizens of different states, regardless of the nature of the underlying dispute between them, and Congress has conferred that jurisdiction on the federal district courts in 28 U.S.C. §1332, subject to the amount-in-controversy requirement. Because Cagney and Stewart are diverse in this example, the federal court has subject matter jurisdiction over the suit between them if Stewart seeks more than $50,000 in damages. So here, too, the two rings intersect: Stewart may choose a California state or federal court for this suit, assuming that he can satisfy the third ring, venue, in both courts.

3. Stewart may sue Cagney in state or federal court in New York. Here, there is no minimum contacts basis for personal jurisdiction, but Cagney is subject to personal jurisdiction there because New York is his domicile. When jurisdiction is based on domicile it is irrelevant that the cause of action did not arise there. See Chapter 1, p.7. Thus, the state courts in New York may exercise personal jurisdiction over him, and a New York federal court may do so as well, under Fed. R. Civ. P. 4(e).

   Subject matter jurisdiction is also proper in the state or federal court in

New York. The state trial courts of New York, the inaptly named supreme courts, have broad subject matter jurisdiction, including battery cases. That does not mean "battery cases arising in New York," but battery cases *as a class*. Thus, it does not matter, for subject matter jurisdiction purposes, that this battery took place in California.

The federal district court in New York also has subject matter jurisdiction based on diversity since Stewart and Cagney are still diverse. Note that Cagney's New York domicile is essential to establish a basis for personal jurisdiction over him in this case. For subject matter jurisdiction, however, he need only be domiciled in some state other than California. The fact that he happens to be domiciled in the state where suit is brought is not essential for establishing diversity. Forty-eight other states would do as well.

4. If Stewart sues in Nevada, the subject matter analysis is the same as example 3. Nevada's trial level courts (called district courts) have broad subject matter jurisdiction, including tort claims. Further, the federal district court in Nevada will have diversity jurisdiction over this case; Stewart and Cagney are just as diverse there as they are anywhere else.

The personal jurisdiction analysis differs, however, because Cagney has no minimum contacts with Nevada that gave rise to this claim, and he is not domiciled there. Absent consent or service of process on Cagney in Nevada, neither the Nevada state court nor the federal court sitting in that state will have the power to require Cagney to come to Nevada to defend this particular suit. Here, Stewart will come up at least one ring short.

Note, in particular, that the existence of diversity here does not substitute for personal jurisdiction; diversity is a separate requirement for a separate purpose. To rephrase the old song, you *can* have one without the other.

Variations

5a. Personal jurisdiction would be proper in this case based on minimum contacts analysis, but subject matter jurisdiction is not. Cagney and Stewart were diverse at the time of the events giving rise to the suit. However, as a result of Cagney's move, they no longer are diverse when suit is brought. Because the relevant date for determining diversity is the date suit is filed (*Smith v. Sperling*, 354 U.S. 91, 93 n.1 (1957)), there is no diversity. Nor is there a federal claim or other basis for federal subject matter jurisdiction.

b. There would be subject matter jurisdiction in the state court, since it has broad jurisdiction over common law claims, but personal jurisdiction is not proper. This claim arises out of events that took place in California. Because the claim is unrelated to New York, the only possible basis for personal jurisdiction is Cagney's domicile. Cagney was domiciled in New York at the time of the assault but is not at the time of suit.

The rationale for allowing a state to exercise personal jurisdiction on the basis of domicile is that a party living in the state is so integrally related to the state that it is fair to require him to appear in its courts. *Milliken v. Meyer,* 311 U.S. at 463. In addition, it is unlikely to be inconvenient to defend in the state of one's domicile. This rationale suggests that domicile jurisdiction should apply (as it does) to domicile at the time of suit, not at the time of the events that led to the suit. *Nicholas v. Inglimo,* 421 N.E.2d 1014, 1016-1017 (Ill. App. 1981). The New York court therefore lacks personal jurisdiction over Cagney.

Minimum contacts (specific in personam) jurisdiction provides an interesting contrast. Cagney can be required to return to defend a California suit arising out of the assault there, even if he has had no contact with California since then. The rationale underlying minimum contacts jurisdiction is that performing certain acts in a state carries with it predictable consequences, including a duty to return to defend those acts in court. The defendant cannot avoid those consequences by subsequently avoiding the state. If he could, minimum contacts jurisdiction would be meaningless.

6.   This example highlights an important distinction between personal and subject matter jurisdiction. The California court lacks any basis for personal jurisdiction over Hepburn on this claim, which arose in New York. However, personal jurisdiction is deemed a privilege of the defendant, which will be waived if she fails to assert it. *Rauch v. Day & Night Manufacturing Corp.,* 576 F.2d 697, 701 (6th Cir. 1978). Consequently, a court that lacks personal jurisdiction over a case may still hear it if the defendant does not object. Because Hepburn is willing to litigate the claim in California, she will presumably waive her objection by failing to raise it. See Fed. R. Civ. P. 12(b)(2), (g), (h).

However, the California federal court also lacks subject matter jurisdiction over this action. Nothing in Article III, §2, or the federal jurisdictional statutes gives the federal courts jurisdiction over state contract claims between nondiverse citizens. Hepburn's willingness to have the federal court hear the case is irrelevant: The parties cannot confer subject matter jurisdiction on the court. Subject matter jurisdiction allocates governmental power among different tribunals. That allocation is made by the Constitution and Congress, not the parties. Consequently, even if neither party objects to the federal court hearing the case, it will refuse to do so. See Fed. R. Civ. P. 12(h)(3).

7a.   This suit is proper in state court in New York. Personal jurisdiction is satisfied because the claim arises out of alleged deprivation of rights taking place in New York. Under the minimum contacts test, Kojak could fairly be required to defend a suit arising out of these in-state acts in a New York court. In addition, he is subject to personal jurisdiction in New York on the basis of his domicile in the state.

Subject matter jurisdiction is also proper in the New York state court, even though this is a case arising under federal law. As a rule, the general trial courts of each state have subject matter jurisdiction of almost any kind of case, unless it has been exclusively delegated to a specialized state court or (for some cases within the federal subject matter jurisdiction) to the federal courts. Even though federal civil rights cases arise under federal law and are therefore properly brought in federal court under 28 U.S.C. §1331, Congress has not made federal jurisdiction over such cases exclusive. Consequently, the state courts retain concurrent jurisdiction to hear such claims.

b. Because the case arises under federal law, the California federal court will have subject matter jurisdiction. 28 U.S.C. §1331. However, the federal court will not exercise personal jurisdiction if the California state court could not do so. Fed. R. Civ. P. 4(e). Here, the claim does not arise out of any contacts with the state of California. The California courts therefore lack personal jurisdiction over Kojak (absent some other basis such as in-state service), since there are no "minimum contacts" among the claim, Kojak, and the forum state.

c. Moving Colbert's domicile to California creates some distinctions from the prior case, but distinctions without any relevant difference. Colbert's California domicile would be an adequate basis for personal jurisdiction over *her*, were she the defendant, but it does not alter the due process requirement that the defendant, the party being unwillingly haled before the court, must have minimum contacts with the state that is doing so. Kojak lacks any such contacts, at least for this claim. Personal jurisdiction is therefore lacking.

The other difference here is that the parties in this case are diverse. This gives the court an alternate source of subject matter jurisdiction (which is unnecessary, since it is a federal-question case anyway), but it is irrelevant to personal jurisdiction. Innumerable first-year exam answers notwithstanding, diversity is *not* a substitute for personal jurisdiction.

8. Although the general rule is that jurisdiction over cases arising under federal law is concurrent, Congress may create exclusive federal jurisdiction over cases within the Article III power. It has done so for copyright cases, presumably because of the specialized nature of these suits and the national scope of the protection conferred by the copyright laws. See 28 U.S.C. §1338(a). Consequently, the state court lacks subject matter jurisdiction over this case.

6

Second-Guessing the Plaintiff's Choice of Forum: Removal

Introduction

The traditional rule in American courts has been (and largely, still is) that the plaintiff chooses the forum in which to bring a suit, subject to the limitations of personal jurisdiction, subject matter jurisdiction, and venue. He may choose the geographical place of suit by suing in the courts of the state he prefers. And, assuming proper subject matter jurisdiction, he may also choose the court system in which to litigate by starting the action in either a federal or state court. In this respect, and in others, it is said that "the plaintiff is master of his claim."

Removal is an exception to this rule, however. The federal removal statutes allow the defendant, after the plaintiff has chosen a state court, to "second-guess" that choice by "removing" some types of cases from the state court to a federal court. Once properly removed the case becomes a federal case, and the state court loses jurisdiction over it. Both pretrial litigation and trial will take place in the federal court.

The rationale for removal is that defendants as well as plaintiffs should have the option to choose federal court for cases within the federal jurisdiction — that jurisdiction is intended to protect both parties, and therefore, both parties should have access to it. If a federal court is particularly qualified to decide cases arising under federal law, then a defendant should be able to ask it to do so, just as a plaintiff may. Similarly, if an out-of-state defendant may suffer prejudice from litigating in a state court, he should have the same right as an out-of-state plaintiff to avoid that prejudice by invoking federal diversity jurisdiction.

A natural corollary of this rationale is that removal jurisdiction should be available to the defendant only in cases that the plaintiff could have commenced in federal court. Removal is not meant to expand federal jurisdiction but merely to make it available to defendants. Therefore, 28 U.S.C. §1441(a) only authorizes removal of state court actions "of which the district courts of the United States have original jurisdiction." If the plaintiff could not have chosen to bring the action in federal court initially, the defendant cannot remove it. For example, if Oakley sues Cody, a fellow Kansan, on a state law contract claim, she could not sue in federal court, since there is neither diversity nor a federal question. Consequently, her action against Cody in state court will not be removable. By contrast, if she sued Cody under a federal age discrimination statute, or if they were citizens of different states, Cody could remove because Oakley could have chosen to sue him on that claim in federal court.

A caution is in order here, however. While it is generally true that a defendant cannot remove a case if the federal court would not have had original jurisdiction over it, some cases are not removable *even though* the plaintiff could have brought them in federal court originally. In particular, 28 U.S.C. §1441(b) provides that a diversity case is only removable if "none of the parties in interest properly joined and served as defendants is a citizen of the State in which such action is brought." In other words, if a defendant is sued in his home state, he may not remove on the basis of diversity. If Oakley, from Nevada, sues Cody, from Kansas, on a state law claim in Kansas state court, Cody cannot remove. The rationale for this exception is that Cody has no need to be protected from local prejudice, since he is from the forum state. And Oakley is protected from such prejudice by the option to bring the action in federal court initially.

Interestingly, there is no explicit authority in the Constitution for snatching cases out of the hands of state courts by removal to federal court. Yet the First Congress provided for removal in the Judiciary Act of 1789, and it has been with us in one form or another ever since. The courts have consistently upheld the constitutionality of the removal procedure. See Wright at 209. Because removal only applies to cases that could have been brought *originally* in federal court, there seems little constitutional distinction between allowing the plaintiff to choose the federal court in a case within the federal court's jurisdiction and allowing the defendant to do so by removing a state court action.[1]

---

1. However, §1441(c), the enigmatic provision for removal of "separate and independent" claims, may be an exception to this principle.

Traditionally, removal jurisdiction depended not only on the scope of original federal jurisdiction, but also on the jurisdiction of the state court from which it was removed. The federal court's removal jurisdiction was said to be "derivative" (Wright at 212) of the state court's. Thus, removal jurisdiction was only proper if the removed case was properly before the state court to begin with. For example, if Butterfield brought a patent infringement action in state court, it could not be removed because the federal courts have exclusive jurisdiction over patent cases. 28 U.S.C. §1338(a). Thus, because only the federal court had jurisdiction, it had to dismiss the case! However, if Butterfield was not too bewildered to press on (and if the statute of limitations had not passed), he could bring an *original* action on the patent claim in federal court.

This long-standing but impractical rule was changed by statute in 1986. Congress added §1441(e) to the removal statute, providing that the federal court is not precluded from hearing the case simply because the state court lacked jurisdiction over it. Thus, a case like Butterfield's would now be removable, despite the fact that the state court had no power to hear his patent claim. Clearly, however, §1441(e) does not change the requirement that the case be within *federal* jurisdiction to be removable. Section 1441(a) still requires that.

Even if a state court case satisfies the jurisdictional requirements for removal, there are drastic limits as to which court it may be removed *to*. You can't remove to another state court or to a state court in a different state. You can't remove to a federal court in another state or even in another district in the same state. There is only one lonely court that can host a removed action: the federal district court "for the district and division embracing the place where such action is pending [in the state court]." 28 U.S.C. §1441(a). Thus, removal only partially displaces the plaintiff's choice of forum: He still gets to choose the state where the action will be litigated, even if he ends up in federal court in that state due to removal by the defendant.

The usual federal venue rules do not apply in removed actions. A case that is removable must be removed to the "district and division embracing the place where such action is pending" (§1441(a)), even if that federal district would not have been a proper venue under 28 U.S.C. §1391 if the case had been brought there initially. In the *Schulansky* case (see Part Six), for example, Ronan may only remove to the District of Massachusetts because the Plymouth County Superior Court, where the suit was initiated, falls within that district. Even if the District of Massachusetts would not have been a proper venue if Schulansky started her suit in federal court, it is the proper district when Ronan removes it on these facts.

It may be helpful to compare removal under §1441 with transfer of venue under 28 U.S.C. §1404(a). Section 1404(a) provides for geographical transfer from one district court within the federal system to another in a different state or district. See Jones's motion to transfer venue in the Schulansky case, infra Chapter 30. Removal, by contrast, authorizes transfer from the state court system to the federal court system within the same state. Transfer displaces the plaintiff's geographical choice for litigation, while removal displaces the plaintiff's choice of the state court system in favor of a federal court within the same geographical area. As the Schulansky papers suggest, it may be possible to use both devices in a single suit. For a case that was removed and then transferred (and then dismissed for forum non conveniens!), see *Piper Aircraft Co. v. Reyno,* 454 U.S. 235 (1981).

The right to remove applies to cases, not claims: When the defendant properly removes a suit to federal court, the defendant's entire suit is removed, including not only the specific claim that gives rise to removal jurisdiction, but also any related claims that the federal court has the power to hear under supplemental jurisdiction. Suppose, for example, that Colter sues Bridger (a citizen of the same state) for violation of Colter's federal civil rights (a claim based on federal law, which state courts as well as federal courts may hear) and asserts a claim for relief on a state law battery theory as well. If Bridger removes, the federal court acquires jurisdiction of the entire action, including the civil rights claim that provides the basis for federal court jurisdiction and the supplemental state law claim. Neither the plaintiff nor the defendant can dissect a single case and send only parts of it to the federal forum.[2] In addition, remember that removal is a one-way street: A defendant who is properly sued in federal court cannot remove to state court.

After removal, a case proceeds in federal court under the Federal Rules. See Fed. R. Civ. P. 81(c). Essentially, that court picks up the ball in mid-air and continues to juggle it. The state court complaint and answer (if one has been filed before removal) will be filed with the notice of removal. 28 U.S.C. §1446(a). See the notice of removal in *Schulansky v. Roman,* infra p.449. The court may order the parties to file discovery material and other filings from the state court in the federal court for use in the action. 28 U.S.C. §1447(b). If the state court has entered any orders prior to removal, such as a preliminary injunction or a protective order concerning discovery, those orders remain in effect in the federal court, unless modified by the federal judge. 28 U.S.C. §1450. It's a little like the Red Sox being whisked out of Fenway Park to Dodger Stadium in the fourth inning and being told to just finish the game under the National League rules.

The following examples illustrate the substantive limits on removal jurisdiction. The second set of examples deals with removal procedure. For purposes of this chapter, I have stubbornly ignored the murky mysteries of §1441(c), dealing with removal of "separate and independent" claims. You should do the same in analyzing the examples. Also, where it is relevant, assume that the amount-in-controversy requirement is met.

---

2. However, the federal court may, in its discretion, remand or dismiss supplemental state law claims in appropriate cases. See 28 U.S.C. §§1367(c), 1441(c); *United Mine Workers v. Gibbs,* 383 U.S. 715, 726-727 (1966).

EXAMPLES

The Power to Remove

1.   Earp, from Kansas, sues Dillon, also a Kansan, in a state court in Kansas. His claim is based on violation of the federal civil rights laws. May Dillon remove?

2.   Suppose Earp (still from Kansas) sues Carson, from Colorado, in the *diverse* Colorado state court on a state law assault claim. May Carson remove?

3.   Assume the same facts as example 2, but Earp sues a second defendant, Hickok, as well. Hickok is from Missouri. Can the defendants remove?

4.   Consider the same facts again, with another twist: Earp, from Kansas, sues Carson (Colorado) and Hickok (Missouri) on the assault claims in a Kansas state court. Can the defendants remove?

5.   Chester, from Iowa, sues Carson, a Coloradan, and James, a Kansan, in Kansas state court on a federal civil rights claim.
    a. May the defendants remove? y
    b. If so, to which court or courts?

6.   Recall that old chestnut case, *Louisville and Nashville R.R. v. Mottley,* 219 U.S. 467 (1911), in which the Supreme Court dismissed for lack of subject matter jurisdiction because the federal question in the case arose as a defense. Suppose that the plaintiffs in that case sued the (nondiverse) railroad in state court for breach of contract. Ten days later the railroad answered, raising the defense that the federal statute precludes it from renewing the Mottleys' passes. Ten days after answering, the railroad removes the case to federal court. Is removal proper?

Some Refinements

7.   Suppose, on the facts of example 4, that Carson wants to remove, but Hickok likes the state court. Can Carson remove the case? See 28 U.S.C. §1441(a).

8.   Earp sues James, a fellow Kansan, on a state law assault claim. Six months later Earp's lawyer decides, on the basis of his further knowledge of the case gleaned from discovery, that Earp also has a claim against James for a federal civil rights violation arising out of the same facts. Earp amends to assert the federal claim. May James now remove?

9.   Earp, a Kansan, sues Bean, a Texan, on a state law abuse-of-process claim in an Iowa state court. Bean removes to federal court. Subsequently, Earp amends to add James, a fellow Kansan, as a second defendant. Should the federal court remand the case to state court?

10. On the facts of example 9, suppose that Earp (Kansas) has claims against Bean (Texas) and James (Kansas) for abuse of process. Earp deliberately decides to sue them jointly in a single action in state court in order to avoid removal to federal court. Is this permissible? Will it work?

11. Suppose, on the facts of example 9, that Earp sues Bean in state court. Anticipating removal, Earp seeks only $45,000 in damages, leaving out a demand for consequential damages worth $8,000. May Bean remove?

12. James sues Earp, his fellow Kansan, on an assault claim. Earp counter-claims for damages for violation of his federal civil rights, arising out of the same encounter. (See Fed. R. Civ. P. 13(a).) Does §1441 allow James to remove?

Unlucky Number 13

13. Dillon (a Kansan) sues Greeley (a New Yorker) for $75,000 for breach of contract. Dillon claims that he had contracted with Greeley to allow Greeley to manufacture electrical circuits upon which Dillon held a patent. In return, Greeley agreed to pay Dillon royalties but has failed to do so. Dillon also claims that Greeley, by making the circuits covered by his patent, has committed patent infringement. Suit is brought in state court in Kansas. Greeley removes.

    a. If suit had been brought prior to 1986, how would this case have been resolved?

    b. How would it be resolved under current removal law?

The Procedure for Removal

The procedure for removal, set forth in §1446, is relatively straightforward. The defendant (or defendants) must file a notice of removal in the appropriate federal district court, together with all pleadings, process, and other papers on file in the state action. 28 U.S.C. §1446(a). The notice must be filed within 30 days of receiving the plaintiff's pleading in the state suit. 28 U.S.C. §1446(b). Once the notice is filed and the state court is notified, the state court loses control of the case automatically. It may not proceed with discovery, try the case, or issue orders to the parties. 28 U.S.C. §1446(d). The Schulansky case in Part Six provides a full example of the removal process.

Although the state court loses power over the case once it has been removed, the removal decision is not irrevocable. If the plaintiff contends that the case is not removable, or that the defendant has not properly followed the requirements of removal procedure, his recourse is to move in the federal court to remand the case back to state court. If the basis for the motion is failure to comply with the procedural requirements (such as failure of all defendants to join in the notice or failure to notify the state court), the motion must be made within 30 days of removal, or the objection is waived. 28 U.S.C. §1447(c). A motion to remand on the basis of lack of subject matter jurisdiction, however, may be made at any time prior to final judgment in the case. Id.

This procedure, under which removal takes place automatically, prevents any confusion as to which court has jurisdiction to proceed: Even if the federal court has no jurisdiction, the state court loses power to proceed. That way, the decision as to whether the federal court has jurisdiction over the case will be made, quite properly, by the federal court when the plaintiff challenges its jurisdiction by moving to remand. If that court lacks jurisdiction, it will remand the case to the state court, which will once more pick up the ball and run with it.

In many cases, the right to remove will not be clear from the face of the complaint. For example, most states do not require the plaintiff to allege the citizenship of the parties because state court jurisdiction does not depend upon it. Compare Fed. R. Civ. P. 8(a)(1); see p.439. Thus, a defendant who claims the right to remove on the ground of diversity may have to ascertain the citizenship of the plaintiff and allege in his notice of removal that diversity exists. Section 1446(a) explicitly allows the removing defendant to allege in the notice of removal any facts that are necessary to demonstrate the right to remove.

EXAMPLES

Some Technicalities

14. Chester, an Iowa citizen, sues Holiday, of Kansas, for malpractice in a leg operation. Suit is brought in an Iowa state court. His complaint does not state a dollar demand for relief (some states don't require it; others don't even allow it). Holiday wants to remove. Can he?

15. Suppose the Long Branch Saloon, a corporation, sues Holiday (a Kansan) in Nebraska to collect $60,000 rent due on Holiday's offices above its Dodge City, Kansas, saloon. Several months later Holiday discovers, much to his surprise, that the Long Branch Saloon in Dodge City is the smallest of three such establishments run by Long Branch. Its principal place of business and state of incorporation is Colorado. Holiday removes on the basis of diversity. Can he do so?

16. Assume that Earp removes James's suit against him within 30 days. However, James disputes the right to remove since he claims that his action is based on state law rather than federal law.

    a. James moves in the state court to have the case remanded for lack of removal jurisdiction. The court agrees that removal was improper. What should it do?

    b. James moves for remand in the federal court. That court agrees that removal was improper. What should it do?

17. Masterson (Nebraska) sues Hickok (Missouri), Earp (Kansas), and Bean (Texas) for assault, arising out of a fight at a corral. He serves Hickok on June 1 and Earp on June 15. As of June 25 Bean has not yet been served. If Earp wants to remove, what should he do?

Two Bemusing Variations on Example 17

18. Assume on the facts of example 17 that Earp and Hickok remove the case on June 27. On July 12 Bean is served. If he prefers state court, does he have any recourse? Should he?

19. Assume that Earp and Hickok do not remove. On July 12 Bean is served. If he wants to remove, what should he do?

A Final, Fundamental Point

20. Chester (Iowa) sues Holiday (Kansas) in an Iowa state court. Holiday removes. Three days later Holiday moves to dismiss the complaint, on the ground that the court lacks personal jurisdiction over him. Is this motion permissible?

EXPLANATIONS

The Power to Remove

1. Earp has asserted a right to relief arising under federal law. Had he chosen to do so, he could have commenced this case in federal court under 28 U.S.C. §1331. Thus, the case satisfies the requirement of §1441(a) — that the federal courts have original jurisdiction over the action (or, more accurately, *would* have had original jurisdiction over it had it been brought in federal court).

However, §1441(b) must also be considered since it places some further restrictions on removal jurisdiction. That section does not restrict removal of Earp's suit. It provides that cases "founded on a claim or right arising under the Constitution, treaties or laws of the United States shall be removable without regard to the citizenship or residence of the parties." Since Earp's claim is based on a federal question, it is irrelevant that the parties are not diverse and that there is an in-state defendant in the action. Removal is proper.

2. This is a straightforward diversity case. A federal district court would have original jurisdiction over the case, but this illustrates the situation in which the federal courts' removal jurisdiction is narrower than their original jurisdiction. Section 1441(b) provides that actions based on diversity ("[a]ny other such action") cannot be removed if any defendant is from the forum state. Under this provision Carson is barred from removing this case.

The logic behind this limitation is that diversity jurisdiction was intended to protect out-of-state parties from local prejudice, so there is no need to extend it to cases where suit is brought in the defendant's home state. Of course, that rationale would support a similar restriction on *original* diversity jurisdiction in the plaintiff's home state, but there is no such restriction: Logic has its limits.

3.   This example makes one narrow point: §1441(b) precludes removal of a diversity case if *any* defendant is from the state where the state court action is brought ("only if none of the parties . . ."). Carson is still in the case; ergo, no removal. Here again, Earp could have initiated the action in federal court as a diversity action in Colorado or elsewhere, but removal is narrower.

4.   Moving the case back to Kansas changes the result. The case is still within the federal court's diversity jurisdiction, but now no defendant is from the forum state, so they may remove under §1441(b). Note that this configuration, with the Kansas plaintiff using the Kansas state courts to recover from two non-Kansas defendants, presents the strongest risk of prejudice to the defendants and therefore is the best candidate for removal jurisdiction.

5a. This case, like that in example 1, is a federal question case and is still removable as such. Here, however, there is also diversity of citizenship, a separate basis for federal jurisdiction. The interpretive problem raised is whether it is removable "without regard to the citizenship or residence of the parties" (§1441(b)) when there is *both* a claim under federal law and diversity. If not, removal would be barred due to the presence of an in-state defendant, James. The answer is "yes"; the case may be removed because it is just as squarely founded on a claim under federal law when there *is* diversity as when there is *not*.

   b. Carson would clearly prefer to remove to the Colorado district court, to get the benefit of the home forum. However, removal is not meant to give the defendant a geographical choice of forum, only a choice to use the federal court system. The action can only be removed to the federal district court for the District of Kansas. If there were more than one federal district in Kansas (as there is in New York, for example), the defendants could only remove the case to the district in which the state court where Chester brought suit is located.

6.   On the facts given here, there is no original federal jurisdiction because it is a state law claim between nondiverse parties. Of course, when the railroad answers the complaint in the state court, raising the federal statute as a defense, it becomes clear that a federal issue exists in the case. However, that does not make it a case that "arises under" the laws of the United States. Jurisdiction is determined by looking at the plaintiff's complaint, to determine if he seeks recovery under federal law. The Mottleys did not. The only difference between this hypo and *Mottley* is that in the hypo we *know* the railroad relies on a federal defense at the time when removal is sought. But it is a defense nonetheless, and it does not convert the Mottleys' contract action into a federal question case. Because the federal issue does not arise on the face of the well-pleaded complaint, there is no original federal jurisdiction. No original jurisdiction, no removal jurisdiction.

   A number of commentators have suggested that this rule, like *Mottley* itself, makes little sense because the assertion of the federal defense clearly indicates that the case involves federal issues. See, e.g., American Law Institute, Study of the Division of Jurisdiction Between State and Federal Courts §1312(a)(2) and accompanying commentary (1969).

Some Refinements

7.   The answer to this example depends on the meaning of §1441(a), which provides that the "defendant or defendants" may remove. Although it is not a foregone conclusion from the language of the statute, the courts have held that the alternative reference to the "defendants" means that, in a multi-defendant case, all defendants must join in the notice of removal. See *Chicago, Rock Island & Pacific Railway Co. v. Martin*, 178 U.S. 245 (1900); *Tri-Cities Newspapers, Inc. v. Tri-Cities Printing Pressman and Assistants' Local 349*, 427 F.2d 325, 326-327 (5th Cir. 1970).[3] Carson will be stuck in state court, even though he may be subject to prejudice as an out-of-stater. While this is a reasonable interpretation of the statute, it prevents removal in cases in which the policy underlying diversity jurisdiction would support it.

8.   Again, removal jurisdiction turns on original jurisdiction. In this example there was no original federal jurisdiction over the case when it was filed; the claim was based on state law and was between nondiverse parties. However, once Earp amends to assert a federal claim, the case looks different. Earp is now relying on federal law as a basis for relief. If the case had been brought in this amended form in federal court, the court would have had jurisdiction under 28 U.S.C. §1331.

The removal statute specifically provides for removal in cases like this, when the case becomes removable after the filing of the original complaint. See 28 U.S.C. §1446(b), second paragraph, which gives the defendant 30 days from the amendment to file a notice of removal. This approach is clearly necessary; otherwise plaintiffs could avoid removal by suing in state court on a state law theory alone, later amending to assert their federal claims.

Once the case is removed, both the federal claim and the related state assault claim will be heard in the federal court. If the combined action had been brought originally in federal court, the court could have heard the state law claim under principles of supplemental jurisdiction. See Chapter 14, example 1. Consequently, the court may also do so in a removed action.

9.   Whatever answer you come up with for this example is troubling. By adding a Kansas defendant after removal, Earp has "destroyed diversity." If he had started this case in federal court and later added James, the court would have dismissed for lack of subject matter jurisdiction. *Owen Equipment & Erection Co. v. Kroger*, 437 U.S. 365, 373-374 (1978). On the other hand,

---

3. It is not entirely clear that the unanimity requirement applies in federal question cases. Cf. *Charles D. Bonanno Linen Service, Inc. v. McCarthy*, 708 F.2d 1, 11 (1st Cir. 1983) (defendant on federal question claim permitted to remove though related claims not removable).

if Earp can win a remand by this device after Bean removes, it allows Earp to defeat the right to removal by his subsequent choice of defendants, a choice he was not inclined to make until the defendant invoked the removal jurisdiction.

Because the addition of the nondiverse party destroys the basis for subject matter jurisdiction, the court will have to remand the case if the amendment is allowed. In some cases, when the amendment was apparently offered for the sole purpose of defeating removal, courts simply refused to allow the amendment, thus preserving diversity jurisdiction. *Boyd v. Diebold Inc.,* 97 F.R.D. 720, 722-723 (E.D. Mich. 1983). In other cases, however, in which the nondiverse party was added in good faith for independent reasons (such as efficiency or belated discovery of a claim against the added party), courts have allowed the amendment and then remanded the case to state court under 28 U.S.C. §1447(c). See, e.g., *McIntyre v. Codman & Shurtleff, Inc.,* 103 F.R.D. 619, 621-623 (S.D.N.Y. 1984). In 1988 Congress codified this practice by adopting 28 U.S.C. §1447(e), which authorizes the court to refuse the amendment or allow it and remand the case.

10. There is nothing improper in Earp's choice here. It will work, so long as he really has colorable claims against both defendants. The joinder rules in most states allow Earp to choose to sue the defendants together. The fact that he has exercised that option in part to secure the forum of his choice is a permissible form of "forum shopping." However, were he to assert a frivolous claim against James for the sole purpose of avoiding removal, he would violate the procedural rules governing pleadings, as well as his professional responsibility as an officer of the court. In such a case, Bean could remove on the basis of diversity and argue to the federal court that James should be disregarded, since no meaningful claim is asserted against him.

11. Here again Earp has structured his lawsuit to prevent removal by seeking damages that do not satisfy the amount-in-controversy requirement of §1332. This is permissible even if Earp could have sought higher damages. If Earp is willing to pay the price — foregoing his other $8,000 claim — to buy a state forum, he may do so. *St. Paul Mercury Indemnity Co. v. Red Cab Co.,* 303 U.S. 283, 294-295 (1938).

12. The issue here is whether a plaintiff can remove. James could not have started in federal court because he had no basis upon which to invoke federal jurisdiction. However, if Earp had started the litigation by suing on the civil rights claim first, James could have removed. Shouldn't James have the same right to remove, whether as the original defendant or as the "defendant" on the counterclaim? The Supreme Court says no, as a matter of statutory interpretation. Section 1441(a) authorizes removal by "the defendant or defendants." In *Shamrock Oil and Gas Corp. v. Sheets,* 313 U.S. 100 (1941), the Court concluded that only the original defendant satisfied this language, so that a plaintiff may not remove under the statute. See generally 1A Moore's at ¶0.157[7].

Unlucky Number 13

13a. Even before 1986, this case would have been removable in part. Dillon's first claim is for breach of contract. True, it is a claim for breach of a contract involving a patent, but the source of the claim is still state contract law. See *Schwarzkopf Development Corp. v. Ti-Coating, Inc.,* 800 F.2d 240, 244 (Fed. Cir. 1986) (contracts for patent royalties have consistently been held to arise under state contract law). Since the parties are diverse and the amount in controversy is over $50,000, this part of the case is removable.

However, the related claim for patent infringement was barred by the "derivative" jurisdiction doctrine. Since Congress has made federal jurisdiction exclusive in patent cases (28 U.S.C. §1338(a)), the state court in which the claim was brought lacked jurisdiction, and the federal court could not acquire jurisdiction of the infringement claim on removal. The federal court would have had to dismiss it. Then, presumably, Dillon would have moved to amend the contract action (now in federal court) to add a claim for patent infringement.

b. As the Introduction states, Congress has jettisoned the derivative jurisdiction rule by adding §1441(e), which provides that the federal court acquires jurisdiction on removal even if the state court where the case was brought lacked the power to hear it. Under §1441(e) the patent claim would be proper in the federal court so both could proceed. Even if there were no diversity between the parties, there would be supplemental jurisdiction over the contract claim (see Chapter 14), so the federal court would have jurisdiction over the entire action.

Some Technicalities

14. The problem for Holiday here is that removal turns on original federal jurisdiction, in this case, diversity jurisdiction. The federal court only has diversity jurisdiction if more than $50,000 is in dispute, but the court can't tell from the complaint whether this prerequisite is met, and Holiday must remove within 30 days or waive his right to do so. Section 1446(a) allows the defendant in situations like this to include in his notice of removal any further allegations that are necessary to demonstrate his right to remove. Thus, Holiday could allege in the notice that Chester's claim might support damages in excess of $50,000. Such allegations are subject to the same ethical standards as the allegations in pleadings. See §1446(a) (incorporating by reference the pleading standard in Fed. R. Civ. P. 11).

15. The smart aleck answer to this example is "yes": You can always remove, even if you have no valid ground, by filing a notice of removal, which automatically removes the action whether it is within federal jurisdiction or not. But of course it will be remanded on the plaintiff's motion if that jurisdiction is lacking.

The more meaningful answer is that Holiday's motion comes too late. If a case is removable as originally filed, the notice of removal must be filed within 30 days after the complaint is served on the defendant. 28 U.S.C. §1446(b). Although there was no way to know it from the original pleadings, this case was removable from the beginning. The system puts the burden on the defendant to *find out* if the case is within the removal jurisdiction within the 30-day period. Holiday's plea — "But I didn't realize we were diverse!" — will likely fall on deaf ears.

16a. Although the state court is convinced that it alone has jurisdiction over the case, it can do nothing to help Earp. Once the case is removed, the state court loses all power over it, even if it was improperly removed. 28 U.S.C. §1446(d). The court should advise Earp to lodge his objection in the proper forum, the federal court.

   b. Here, Earp has followed the proper procedure for objecting to removal: a motion in the federal court to remand the action to the state court. The federal court will hear the motion and resolve any factual issues necessary to determine its jurisdiction. If it concludes that jurisdiction is lacking, it will remand the case to the state court. Note that it does not *dismiss* the case, but *remands* it. The plaintiff need not refile, pay a new fee, or worry about the statute of limitations, since the original suit continues its wobbly way in the state court.

17. The problem here is that §1441(a) has been interpreted to require all defendants to join in the notice of removal. See example 7. Bean has not even been informed of the suit yet. Do the other defendants have to find Bean, tell him the bad news, and convince him to join in removing the case?

   Although it is not entirely clear from the statute, the cases hold that only the defendants actually served need join in the removal. See 28 U.S.C. §1441(b) (referring to "parties in interest properly joined and served as defendants"); *DiCesare-Engler Productions, Inc. v. Mainman Ltd.*, 421 F. Supp. 116, 120 (W.D. Pa. 1976). But see the next two examples as to what happens when the last defendant is served.

Two Bemusing Variations on Example 17

18. If all defendants are served at the same time, each will have the power to prevent removal by refusing to join in the removal. In this case, however, Bean finds himself in federal court without having had the chance to forestall removal by refusing to agree to removal. It appears that Bean may still prevent the case from being heard in federal court by moving to remand on the ground that he does not consent to removal. Cf. *Hutchins v. Priddy*, 103 F. Supp. 601, 607 (W.D. Mo. 1952) (subsequently served defendant may move to remand to state court).

19. This is an interesting twist. Here, Hickok and Earp did not choose to remove, but Bean would like to. Even if Bean can convince them to join in removing the case, it is too late: Hickok and Earp waived their right to removal by failing to file within 30 days. This result is unfair to Bean. Hickok and Earp may be entirely indifferent on the removal issue. Had Bean been

timely served, he might have convinced them to join and obtained the federal forum. By serving him late, the plaintiff has essentially defeated Bean's right to remove. The cases hold that Bean is out of luck in this situation, at least where there is no evidence of a deliberate attempt on the part of the plaintiff to defeat removal by staggered service on successive defendants. See *Brown v. Demco, Inc.*, 792 F.2d 478, 481-482 (5th Cir. 1986).

A Final, Fundamental Point

20. The motion is proper. Holiday does not waive his objection to personal jurisdiction just because he prefers to litigate in federal court. Indeed, he may have removed precisely because he believes that a federal judge will take a more objective view of the jurisdiction question. Removal does not affect Holiday's right to raise any objections or defenses he may have; it only changes the court in which they will be presented. On the other hand, had Holiday waived his personal jurisdiction objection by answering in state court before removal without raising the jurisdiction objection (compare Fed. R. Civ. P. 12(b), (g), (h)), removal would not revive it.

7

Proper Venue in Federal Courts: A Rough Measure of Convenience

Introduction

Earlier chapters have considered personal and subject matter jurisdiction, two crucial restrictions on the forums in which a lawsuit may be brought. Frequently, these "first two rings" will dramatically limit the plaintiff's choice of forum. For example, if Jones comes to Alabama, Smith's home state, and is injured there in a collision with Smith, Jones will likely be able to obtain personal jurisdiction over Smith only in Alabama.

However, personal and subject matter jurisdiction will not always limit the plaintiff's choice of forum so significantly. Suppose, for example, that Smith travels a great deal in her work, so that she could be personally served with process in other states. Under *Burnham v. Superior Court of California*, 495 U.S. 604 (1990), such personal service in any state — say Illinois or Oregon — would suffice to support jurisdiction in that state. And, because Smith and Jones are diverse, the federal district courts in every state would have subject matter jurisdiction. Even if they were not diverse, the broad subject matter jurisdiction of the state courts in every state would support jurisdiction over this ordinary tort case. Thus, if only the first two "rings" limited Jones's choice of courts, she might well be able to sue Smith in any state in the United States, quite possibly in either federal or state court in each one.

Venue rules are meant to further restrict the places the plaintiff may choose to bring suit, to assure that suits are tried in a place that bears some sensible relationship to the claims asserted or to the parties to the action. Such venue rules form a third "ring," apart from and in addition to personal and subject matter jurisdiction, which must be satisfied (or waived) if a court is to hear a particular case. Every court system, state or federal, has venue rules, generally established by statute. State court venue provisions often provide that cases must be brought where one of the parties resides or does business, where the claim arose, or where property in dispute is located. See generally Friedenthal, Kane, and Miller at §2.15.

The Basic Federal Venue Provisions

To provide an example of how venue provisions work, this chapter will focus on the federal venue statute, 28 U.S.C. §1391. That statute has been substantially revised in recent years. Sections 1391(a) and (b), which provide the basic options for laying venue in most federal cases, were amended in 1990. Section 1391(c), which determines the "residence" of corporate defendants under the venue statute, was amended in 1988.

Currently, venue in diversity cases is governed by 28 U.S.C. §1391(a), which provides that a diversity case may be brought in

(1) a judicial district where any defendant resides, if all defendants reside in the same state,
(2) a judicial district in which a substantial part of the events or omissions giving rise to the claim occurred, or a substantial part of property that is the subject of the action is situated, or
(3) a judicial district in which the defendants are subject to personal jurisdiction at the time the action is commenced.

All other cases ("a civil action wherein jurisdiction is not founded solely on diversity of citizenship") are governed by §1391(b), which provides that such cases may be brought in

(1) a judicial district where any defendant resides, if all defendants reside in the same State,
(2) a judicial district in which a substantial part of the events or omissions giving rise to the claim occurred, or a substantial part of property that is the subject of the action is situated, or
(3) a judicial district in which any defendant may be found, if there is no district in which the action may otherwise be brought.

Thus, the options are much the same in diversity cases and others, since subsections (1) and (2) are the same in both statutes. However, diversity cases allow an extra option (§1391(a)(3)) based on districts where the defendants are subject to personal jurisdiction. For other cases, §1391(b)(3) provides a narrow "fallback" provision, authorizing venue where any defendant "may be found." This subsection of §1391(b) only applies when there is no district that is a proper venue under §1391(b)(1) or (2).

Venue Based on Individual "Residence"

Let's address the various bases for venue in turn. Both §1391(a)(1) and (b)(1) authorize venue in a judicial district where any defendant resides, *if they all reside in one state*. First, note that these provisions focus on judicial districts, not on states. Suppose, for example, that Sherman sues Stuart, from the Western District of Virginia, and Lee, from the Eastern District of Virginia, in a diversity case. Venue would be proper in either district, because both are from the state and §1391(a)(1) authorizes jurisdiction in such cases in any district in which a defendant resides. The same would be true if the case arose under federal law, since §1391(b)(1) parallels §1391(a)(1).

However, if Stuart was from the Southern District of California and Lee from the Central District of California, suit would not be proper in the Northern District of California under either §1391(a)(1) or (b)(1), since no defendant is from that district. This focus on districts contrasts with personal jurisdiction doctrine: A person who is subject to personal jurisdiction in a state is subject to jurisdiction *anywhere* in that state.

As in other areas of civil procedure, the venue provisions in §1391 include ambiguous terms, which have required judicial interpretation. For example, the term "reside" in these sections had spawned contradictory holdings prior to the 1990 revisions. Some courts equated it with the state citizenship/domicile analysis used in the diversity context. Others concluded that a person may "reside" in several districts if she maintains residences in more than one, even though she would have only one domicile for diversity purposes. The trend of authority, prior to the 1990 amendment, was to equate "residence" under these provisions with domicile. See, e.g., *Lee v. Hunt,* 410 F. Supp. 329, 332 (M.D. La. 1976).[1]

Since Congress carried over the term "reside" from the old venue statute, the courts will likely conclude that "residence" is to be equated with the district of domicile under the amended statute as well. If so, a defendant will be deemed to reside only in the district where she actually lives. If Greeley lives in Manhattan, he will "reside" only in the Southern District of New York for venue purposes, even though the State of New York has three other districts.

---

1. Professor Wright suggests that the drafters used the term "reside" instead of "domicile" because the venue statute restricts suit to the *district* in which the party is domiciled; Congress used "reside" to avoid awkward references to parties as "citizens" or "domiciliaries" of a district. Wright at 243-244.

Venue Based on Events or Omissions Giving Rise to the Claim

Prior to the 1990 amendments, §1391(a) and (b) authorized venue in the judicial district "where the claim arose." This created interpretive problems in cases involving activities in a number of states. For example, an action for violation of the federal trademark laws might involve: 1) a decision made in one state to market the goods in violation of the trademark; 2) sales of the goods by the defendant in several states; and 3) harm to the plaintiff's business in other states where it manufactured goods or had its headquarters. The Supreme Court never established a single test for where a claim "arose" under §1391.

The 1990 amendments clarify this issue considerably. Section 1391(a)(2) and (b)(2) authorize venue in a judicial district in which "a substantial part of the events or omissions giving rise to the claim occurred, or a substantial part of property that is the subject of the action is situated." Although there will certainly be close questions as to what constitutes a "substantial part" of the relevant events, these provisions will often authorize venue in several different districts.[2] In the trademark example above, for example, this language would presumably authorize venue in the district where the infringing decision was made and where the goods were actually sold. In a products liability case, this language would likely authorize venue in both the district where the product was manufactured and the district where it caused injury. This is a perfectly sensible result. The purpose of this venue provision is to assure a relation between the underlying events that are litigated and the place where the case is tried. Such a relation will exist in each of the districts where significant events involved in the case took place.

Venue Where the Defendant Is Subject to Jurisdiction

Section 1391(a)(3) authorizes venue in a diversity case in a judicial district in which the defendants are subject to personal jurisdiction. At this writing, there is considerable confusion about what this means, and little judicial interpretation to help. In part, the confusion arises from disbelief at the breadth of the provision; §1391(a)(3) appears to authorize venue wherever

---

2. Under the earlier version of §1391, a number of courts held that a claim "arose" in any state that had "significant contacts" with the claim (see, e.g., *Data Disc, Inc. v. Systems Technology Associates, Inc.,* 557 F.2d 1280 (9th Cir. 1977). Under this approach, venue was proper in more than one district if a case involved contacts with several states. Section 1391(a)(2) and (b)(2) basically codify this approach.

personal jurisdiction is proper, which may be very broad and may substantially overlap sections (a)(1) and (a)(2).

The legislative history implies, somewhat equivocally, that subsection (3) was meant to apply only if no other proper venue could be found. See House Report No. 101-734, p.23. But that is not what the statute says. Congress was quite explicit in imposing such a restriction in §1391(b)(3), but no similar language appears in (a)(3). In fact, §1391(c) (discussed at p.104) authorizes venue where corporations are subject to personal jurisdiction, so the idea is not really that radical.

It has also been suggested, based on the reference in subsection (3) to "the defendants," that it may only apply in multi-defendant cases. 15 Wright and Miller §3802.1 (1991 Supp.). But a more plausible reason for the plural is to require that, if there is more than one defendant, all be subject to personal jurisdiction in the district. Before the 1990 revision §1391(a) required that "all defendants" reside in a district to support venue, but that was always held to apply in single defendant cases. It appears likely that §1391(a)(3) will likewise be held applicable where there is only one defendant. So the provision may very well mean what it says: If all defendants are subject to personal jurisdiction in the district, it is a proper venue. Until the courts determine otherwise, we have to work under the above assumption, and I will do so for purposes of this chapter.

Even read on its face, however, §1391(a)(3) will raise some interpretive problems. Suppose, for example, that Smith is a saleswoman and sells some products in the Northern District of Georgia. Surely, she would be "subject to personal jurisdiction" there for a claim arising from those sales. Does that make the Northern District a proper venue in Jones's action against Smith for an auto accident in Alabama? It is very doubtful that Congress meant to authorize venue in the Northern District solely on the ground that someone else might get personal jurisdiction over Smith in that district for a completely unrelated claim. That interpretation would not assure any relationship between the case being tried (Jones's) and the place of trial. This provision will almost certainly be interpreted to require that Smith is subject to personal jurisdiction in the district for *the particular claim* Jones is bringing against her.

Assume that the latter interpretation of §1391(a)(3) is proper, requiring that the defendant be subject to personal jurisdiction in the district on the plaintiff's claim. Suppose that Smith was served with process in the Northern District of Georgia in a suit for the Alabama auto accident. That would make her "subject to personal jurisdiction" in the Northern District, since service of process within a state supports personal jurisdiction over a defendant even for a claim that arose elsewhere. *Burnham v. Superior Court of California*, 495 U.S. 604 (1990). Does such service make the Northern District a proper venue?

It hardly seems that §1391(a)(3) was meant to authorize venue wherever the defendant could be served. The goal of venue restrictions is to authorize suit in a district that has a meaningful relationship to the case or the parties. Such a relationship is assured where the defendants reside (§1391(a)(1)) or where substantial events relating to the claim took place (§1391(a)(2)) or where a defendant has minimum contacts that gave rise to the claim (§1391(a)(3)). But simply being served with process in a district does not establish such a relationship between the suit or the parties and the district. The courts will doubtless have to decide this question. For what it is worth, this author would argue that §1391(a)(3) should be construed to require that the defendants be subject to personal jurisdiction based on their contacts in the district, not based on the mere fact that the defendant is served with process there.[3]

Two Other Important Points

Venue, like personal jurisdiction, is considered a personal privilege of the defendant, which may be waived. See *Neirbo Co. v. Bethlehem Shipbuilding Corp.*, 308 U.S. 165, 168 (1939). Under the Federal Rules of Civil Procedure, the defendant waives her objection to venue by failing to raise it when she responds to the plaintiff's complaint. See Fed. R. Civ. P. 12(b), (g), (h); Chapter 17, p.279. Parties may even agree in advance to a particular venue for suits that may arise between them. Many contracts contain such "forum selection clauses," and these have generally been held enforceable in the federal courts, even if they lay venue in a district that would not be proper under §1391. See *Carnival Cruise Lines, Inc. v. Shute*, 111 S. Ct. 1522 (1991) (upholding forum selection clause in absence of showing of unfairness).

Section 1391(a) and (b) broadly cover all diversity and federal question claims "except as otherwise provided by law." An important caveat is in order based on this exception: Specialized venue provisions govern many types of claims that appear to be covered by §1391(a) and (b). For example, one would reasonably conclude from §1391(b) that patent infringement claims, which arise under federal law, may be brought wherever the defendant resides or the claim arose. Not so; lurking elsewhere in the Code is 28 U.S.C. §1400(b), which restricts venue in patent infringement actions to the district where the defendant resides or where she committed acts of infringement *and* has a regular and established place of business. Special venue provisions also govern copyright suits, interpleader actions, actions against federal officials, and others. See generally 15 Wright and Miller §§3810-3825. There is no

---

3. What little commentary there is concludes to the contrary, however. See D. Siegel, Changes in Federal Jurisdiction and Practice Under the New (Dec. 1, 1990) Judicial Improvements Act, 133 F.R.D. 61, 72-73 (1991).

way to guard against such pitfalls other than a careful search of the statutes prior to bringing suit.[4]

Although these venue provisions appear daunting at first, they basically provide that the defendants must be sued where they reside or where important events relevant to the suit took place or where the personal jurisdiction ring is satisfied. In at least a rough way, these provisions assure some reasonable connection between the court where suit may be brought and the suit itself. The first set of examples below considers venue in cases involving individual defendants. The second set deals with the further complexities of cases in which suit is brought against corporations. In considering the examples, assume that all actions are brought in federal court, that the amount-in-controversy requirement is met where it is relevant, and that no special venue statute applies.

EXAMPLES

The Basic Venue Provisions

1. Grant, who lives in the Northern District of Ohio, sues Lee, who lives in the Eastern District of Virginia and has his architectural office there, for breach of a contract to design a building. Grant claims that Lee agreed, after extensive negotiations in the Northern District of Ohio, to design a building to be built in Nashville, in the Middle District of Tennessee. Subsequently, however, Lee refused to follow through on the contract. In which of the following districts would venue be proper?
    a. The Eastern District of Virginia?
    b. The Western District of Virginia?
    c. The Middle District of Tennessee?
    d. The Northern District of Ohio?

2. Grant sues Lee and Stuart, Lee's partner who lives in the Western District of Virginia. What venues in Virginia are proper?

3. Assume that Grant sues Lee and Longstreet (from the District of South Carolina) for breach of contract. Longstreet, an engineer, had represented to Lee (in a conversation that took place at Longstreet's Charleston, South Carolina, office) that he would do the mechanical engineering on the building for a certain price but then backed out. Lee then recalculated the cost of doing the job with the higher engineering costs and decided to renege on his contract with Grant. In which of the following districts would venue be proper?

---

4. Similar traps for the unwary may await the state court plaintiff. In Massachusetts, for example, there is a general venue statute, Mass. Gen. L. ch.223, §1, analogous to 28 U.S.C. §1391, but an ancient venue statute provides that an action in replevin "shall be brought in the county where the goods or beasts are detained." Mass. Gen. L. ch.223, §4.

    a. The Eastern District of Virginia?
    b. The Western District of Virginia?
    c. The Middle District of Tennessee?
    d. The Northern District of Ohio?

4.   On the facts of example 3, assume that Grant also asserts a federal question claim against Lee. How would this affect the available venues?

5.   Assume, on the facts of example 3, that Longstreet also does design projects for Davis, an architect with offices in the Western District of Virginia, and has on several occasions conducted meetings at Davis's offices on design projects for Davis's clients. Is the Western District of Virginia a proper venue in Grant's diversity case?

6.   Assume that Longstreet had two meetings with Lee at Lee's office in the Eastern District of Virginia. During the first, Longstreet made the representations about the cost of his services which led Lee to enter into the contract with Grant. During the second, Longstreet reneged on his offer to do the mechanical engineering for the original price, causing Lee to change his mind about doing the job. Longstreet has no other contacts with Virginia. Would venue be proper in the Western District of Virginia?

7.   Assume that venue is improper in Grant's case against Lee, but Lee does not raise an objection. May the judge dismiss the case sua sponte (on her own initiative, without a request to do so by the parties)?

Venue in Cases Involving Corporations

These venue rules can be seriously confusing; worse, I think, than the ones they replaced. But the real topper is 28 U.S.C. §1391(c), concerning venue in cases involving corporate defendants. That provision was amended in 1988 and substantially changed the rules. As amended, it reads as follows:

> For purposes of venue under this chapter, a defendant that is a corporation shall be deemed to reside in any judicial district in which it is subject to personal jurisdiction at the time the action is commenced. In a State which has more than one judicial district and in which a defendant that is a corporation is subject to personal jurisdiction at the time an action is commenced, such corporation shall be deemed to reside in any district in that State with which its contacts would be sufficient to subject it to personal jurisdiction if that district were a separate State, and if there is no such district the corporation shall be deemed to reside in the district within which it has the most significant contacts.

This is formidable language, but on closer examination it is not really as bad as it seems.

    First, to clear away a little underbrush, note that §1391(c) applies only to corporate defendants. It says nothing about cases in which corporations bring suit as plaintiffs. Because §1391(c) does not apply, venue in such cases is governed by the basic venue provisions in §1391(a) and (b).

Second, it is crucial to understand that §1391(c) is not a separate, exclusive provision governing venue in cases against corporations. All it does is define corporate "residence" for purposes of applying §1391(a)(1) and (b)(1). Thus, it is proper to lay venue in a case against a corporation, for example, in a district where a substantial part of the events giving rise to the claim took place, under §1391(a)(2) or (b)(2). Section 1391(c) is irrelevant in applying these sections because venue under them does not depend on where the corporation "resides."

If, however, the plaintiff wants to lay venue in the district where a corporate defendant "resides," under either §1391(a)(1) or (b)(1), she must look to §1391(c) to determine where the corporation resides. Section 1391(c) defines corporate "residence" as any district in which the corporation is subject to personal jurisdiction. Suppose, for example, that Mead sues Jackson Corporation for breach of a contract that the parties made and performed in South Carolina (which only has one district, the District of South Carolina). If Mead bases venue on Jackson's residence under §1391(a)(1), he must refer to §1391(c) to determine where Jackson "resides." Under that section, it "resides" in the District of South Carolina because it would be subject to personal jurisdiction there based on the contacts of negotiating and performing the contract in South Carolina.

Jackson may also "reside" in other districts under §1391(c). For example, if it is incorporated in Delaware, the District of Delaware would be a proper venue, since corporations are subject to general in personam jurisdiction in the state where they are incorporated. Or, if Jackson has extensive production facilities in the District of Maryland, it will be subject to general in personam jurisdiction there (see Chapter 1, pp.5-7), and thus "resides" there as well under §1391(c). Consequently, it may be sued in those districts in a diversity case under §1391(a)(1).

The more confusing part of the new §1391(c) is the second sentence, which applies this concept of corporate "residence" to states with more than one judicial district.

> In a state which has more than one judicial district and in which a defendant that is a corporation is subject to personal jurisdiction at the time an action is commenced, such corporation shall be deemed to reside in any district in that State with which its contacts would be sufficient to subject it to personal jurisdiction if that district were a separate state. . . .

Suppose, for example, that Jackson corporation negotiated and breached the contract with Mead in Richmond, Virginia, but has no other contacts with Virginia. As Figure 7-1 shows, Virginia is divided into an Eastern District and a Western District, and Richmond is in the Eastern District of Virginia. Under §1391(c) venue would be proper in the Eastern District of Virginia: If the Eastern District were a separate state, Jackson's contacts in that district — negotiating and breaching the contract with Mead — would support personal jurisdiction there for this lawsuit under the minimum contacts test.

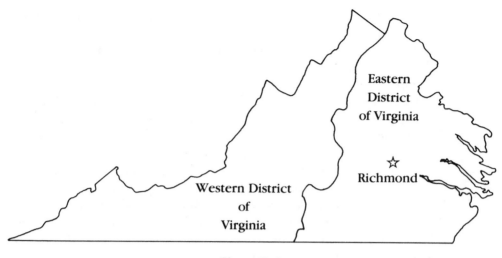

Figure 7–1

However, there would not be jurisdiction over Jackson in the Western District, if it were a separate state, since the corporation has no contacts in the Western District. Therefore, the Western District would not be a proper venue under §1391(c).

Now, suppose that Jackson has a permanent production facility in Atlanta, Georgia, but no other contacts with Georgia. As Figure 7-2 shows, Georgia has three districts. Mead could sue Jackson in the Northern District of Georgia since, if that district were treated as a separate state, Jackson's permanent facility there would support general in personam jurisdiction over it there. Thus, the Northern District is a proper venue. However, because Jackson has no contacts in the Middle or the Southern District of Georgia, venue would not be proper in either of those districts under §1391(a)(1) and (c).[5]

EXAMPLES

Applying §1391(c)

8.   Mead, who lives and works in the Northern District of Ohio, sues Dixie Corporation for a libelous statement made about him by an officer of the corporation. Dixie is incorporated in Maryland and has large factories in Atlanta, Georgia (in the Northern District of Georgia), and Nashville, Tennessee (in the Middle District of Tennessee). The statement about Mead was made in Philadelphia, in the Eastern District of Pennsylvania. As a result of the statement, Mead was fired from his job.

---

5. Though venue in those districts may be proper under §1391(a)(3).

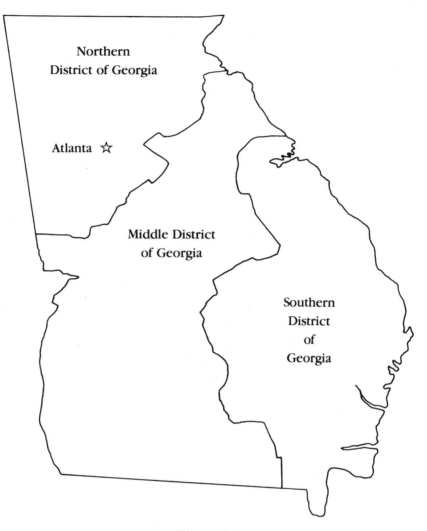

Figure 7–2

If Mead sues Dixie, which of the following districts would be proper venues?

    a. The District of Maryland?

    b. The Middle District of Tennessee?

    c. The Southern District of Georgia?

    d. The Eastern District of Pennsylvania?

    e. The Northern District of Ohio?

9.   On the same facts, suppose Mead sues both Dixie and Calhoun, the officer who made the statement. Calhoun lives in Atlanta. Which of the following districts is a proper venue?

    a. The Northern District of Georgia?

    b. The Southern District of Georgia?

    c. The Eastern District of Pennsylvania?

    d. The Middle District of Tennessee?

10. Suppose that Dixie Corp. sues Mead for a violation of the federal trade-mark laws, arising from Mead's distribution throughout Ohio of products bearing the Dixie logo. What venues are proper? (Ohio has two districts, the Northern and Southern.)

A Subtle Variation

11. Dixie Corporation makes and sells shotguns for hunting. It regularly ships guns to Outdoor Product Sales, a sporting goods store in Asheville, in the Western District of North Carolina. Boone moves to Durham, in the Middle District of North Carolina, from Georgia, and brings a Dixie shotgun with him, which he bought in Georgia. Boone is injured when he stumbles in his yard and the gun fires even though the safety catch was on. He sues Dixie for negligence. Is venue proper in the Western District of North Carolina?

12. Consider the facts of *World-Wide Volkswagen Corp. v. Woodson,* 444 U.S. 286 (1980), in which the Robinsons were injured when an Audi they bought from Seaway in New York exploded while driving across Oklahoma. Assuming that the Robinsons are diverse from Seaway (a New York corporation doing business only in the Northern District of New York), can you think of a district in which venue would be proper but personal jurisdiction would not?

EXPLANATIONS

The Basic Venue Provisions

1a. Because this is a diversity case, §1391(a) prescribes the proper venues. Under §1391(a)(1) the Eastern District of Virginia is proper, since "a defendant" resides there and all defendants (Lee only) are from the same state. In addition, if §1391(a)(3) means what it says, the Eastern District would be proper under that provision as well, since Lee, who is domiciled in Virginia, would be subject to personal jurisdiction there.

    b. The Western District of Virginia is not a proper venue under §1391(a)(1), since Lee doesn't "reside" there. It is true that the concept of "residence" in the venue statute is generally equated with domicile and that Lee is domiciled in the *state* of Virginia. But for venue purposes, the term "reside" has been interpreted to mean the district within the state in which Lee actually has his domicile, that is, where he actually lives.

    However, the Western District may be a proper venue under a broad reading of §1391(a)(3). Because Lee is domiciled in Virginia, he is subject to general in personam jurisdiction anywhere in the state. *Milliken v. Meyer,* 311 U.S. 457 (1940). Thus, Lee is arguably "subject to personal jurisdiction at the time the action is commenced" in the Western District of Virginia, making it a proper venue under §1391(a)(3). Under this interpretation a defendant would be "subject to personal jurisdiction" in every district in the state in which she resides, since an individual is subject to general in personam jurisdiction throughout the state in which she is domiciled.

Section 1391(a)(3) might be interpreted to limit venue to the particular district within a state where the contacts supporting jurisdiction are located. However, the statute does not say this, and it must have been clear to the drafters that they were authorizing venue in other districts within the state. Section 1391(c), revised two years before this provision was written, explicitly confines corporate venue to the districts where the contacts exist, but §1391(a)(3) contains no similar restriction.

c. The Middle District of Tennessee is a proper venue under §1391(a)(2), since "a substantial part of the events or omissions giving rise to the claim" occurred there: Lee "omitted" to build the building there.

d. The Northern District of Ohio may be a proper venue under §1391(a)(2) on the ground that "a substantial part of the events or omissions giving rise to the claim occurred" there. The courts will have to decide whether the negotiations that took place in the Northern District "gave rise to the claim." Arguably, the claim arose from the failure to follow through on the agreement rather than the contract formation. However, given the purpose of venue provisions — to site the litigation in a place with a substantial connection to the case — the court may well take the more flexible view of this phrase and conclude that venue is proper where the parties negotiated the contract.

Under §1391(a)(3) venue is apparently proper in any district in which Lee is subject to personal jurisdiction. The Northern District of Ohio would be proper under this provision, since the extensive negotiations there would likely support minimum contacts jurisdiction over Lee in Ohio on this claim.

2. On these facts either district in Virginia is a proper venue under §1391(a)(1), since all defendants reside in the same state and one of the defendants ("any defendant") resides in each district. It is also proper under §1391(a)(3), since both defendants, as Virginia domiciliaries, are subject to general in personam jurisdiction in the state.

3a. This is also a diversity case, so §1391(a) applies. Subsection (1) authorizes venue in a judicial district where any defendant resides, if they all reside in the same state. Here, they don't, so §1391(a)(1) is no help. Section 1391(a)(3) is also unlikely to support jurisdiction in the Eastern District of Virginia. Lee is subject to personal jurisdiction there, based on his domicile. However, Longstreet is not domiciled there, nor is there any evidence that he committed any acts there to support minimum contacts jurisdiction in this case. The mere fact of making an agreement in South Carolina with a Virginia architect to work on a Tennessee building would not support jurisdiction over Longstreet in Virginia.

But how about §1391(a)(2), which makes a district a proper venue if "a substantial part of the events or omissions giving rise to the claim" occurred there? If Lee did his recalculations at his office in the Eastern District, this language in §1391(a)(2) is apparently satisfied, even though Longstreet was not involved in that "event." Of course, there would still have to be personal jurisdiction over Longstreet in Virginia, under the three ring analysis, before suit could be brought against him there.

b. Venue is not proper in the Western District of Virginia. All defendants are not from the same state, so §1391(a)(1) does not apply. Nor does §1391(a)(2) apply, since none of the relevant events took place there. Finally, the facts do not suggest any basis for personal jurisdiction over Longstreet in Virginia, so §1391(a)(3) does not apply, even though Lee would be subject to personal jurisdiction there. One defendant is not enough; the subsection requires that "the defendants" be subject to personal jurisdiction in the district.

c. Venue is proper in the Middle District of Tennessee, since a substantial part of the omissions giving rise to the claim took place there. 28 U.S.C. §1391(a)(2). Again, it appears that it would not matter that it was *Lee's* omission, not Longstreet's, that took place there: The standard in §1391(a)(2) focuses on the events or omissions giving rise to the claim, not the acts or omissions of each individual defendant. Here again, however, Grant would have problems with personal jurisdiction over Longstreet.

d. The Northern District of Ohio would be a proper venue under §1391(a)(2), based on the extensive negotiations between Grant and Lee there. It would not be proper under §1391(a)(3): Lee would be subject to personal jurisdiction there, but it seems doubtful that Longstreet would be, since he dealt only with Lee and did nothing in Ohio. Note again that, though venue is proper here, Grant will probably not be able to satisfy the personal jurisdiction "ring" as to Longstreet in Ohio.

4. Because Grant has asserted a federal claim against one of the defendants, the case is "not founded solely on diversity of citizenship." Consequently, §1391(b) applies rather than §1391(a). However, this doesn't provide any additional venue options in this case. Subsections (1) and (2) are the same in sections (a) and (b), and §1391(b)(3), which authorizes venue in a district where any defendant may be "found," does not apply because there are other districts that are proper venues under the first two subdivisions of §1391(b). This "catch-all" provision is apparently included to assure that there will be some proper venue in federal question cases, even if the events giving rise to the claim took place outside the United States. It does not apply unless no district is a proper venue under subsections (1) and (2). Section 1391(a) is broader than §1391(b), since it allows venue where the defendants are subject to personal jurisdiction, regardless of whether there is an alternative venue under (a)(1) or (a)(2).

Ironically, one goal of the 1990 amendments to the venue statute was to eliminate broader venue in diversity cases by eliminating the option of laying venue in the district of the plaintiff's residence in diversity cases. However, the statute has introduced a new distinction, which still makes venue broader in diversity cases. Grant would have a broader choice of venue if he based jurisdiction on diversity rather than on a federal claim, since §1391(a)(3) would then apply.[6]

5.   As example 3b indicates, venue is not proper in the Western District of Virginia based on the residence of the defendants (§1391(a)(1)) or the occurrence of events giving rise to the claim (§1391(a)(2)). The only arguable basis is §1391(a)(3), which authorizes venue in a district where the defendants are subject to personal jurisdiction. Lee is subject to personal jurisdiction in the Western District of Virginia on any claim, since he is domiciled in Virginia. Longstreet would also be subject to personal jurisdiction there on claims arising out of his meetings and work there for Davis. But this claim does not arise out of those contacts, and there appears to be no basis for exercising personal jurisdiction over Longstreet in Virginia *on this claim.*

The drafters presumably intended to restrict venue under §1391(a)(3) to districts in which the defendants would be subject to personal jurisdiction on the particular claim in suit. Otherwise, venue could be laid in a district that had absolutely nothing to do with the dispute, on the fortuitous basis that the defendant would be subject to personal jurisdiction there on some completely unrelated matter. Thus, venue is not proper in the Western District.

6.   In this case, Longstreet has minimum contacts with the Eastern District of Virginia. Because these minimum contacts gave rise to the claim, they would clearly suffice to support personal jurisdiction over him in any court in Virginia. Does this mean that venue is proper in the Western District of Virginia under §1391(a)(3), since Lee is subject to jurisdiction there on the basis of his domicile and Longstreet on the basis of his contacts in the Eastern District?

Section 1391(a)(3) apparently applies on these facts, since both defendants are subject to personal jurisdiction in the Western District, even though neither has contacts with the Western District. While it might make sense to restrict venue on this basis to districts in which the defendant actually has contacts, it does not appear that Congress has done so. See example 1b.

7.   Several cases have held that it is improper for the court to dismiss an action sua sponte for improper venue, since venue is a privilege of the defendant, which she may waive. See, e.g., *Concession Consultants, Inc. v. Mirisch,*

---

6. It is unclear why Congress authorized venue where the defendants are subject to personal jurisdiction in diversity cases but not federal question cases. One possibility is that some statutes authorize federal courts to exert nationwide personal jurisdiction in some federal question cases. Authorizing venue wherever jurisdiction is proper would have allowed venue in such cases in any district in the country.

355 F.2d 369, 371 (2d Cir. 1966); see also 15 Wright and Miller at §3826 (p.257). However, the court ought to have some control over inappropriate venue choices even if the parties are satisfied. The purpose of venue statutes is not only to prevent inconvenience to defendants, but also to allocate judicial business to courts with some connection to the case. See *Gulf Oil Corp. v. Gilbert,* 330 U.S. 501, 508-509 (1947) (listing various private interests and public interests, which may make a court an inappropriate venue). The public interest may suggest that a particular venue is inappropriate even if the parties are willing to litigate there. However, this public interest may be protected by 28 U.S.C. §1404(a), which authorizes a court to transfer cases to other districts when justice so requires.

Applying §1391(c)

8a. This is a diversity case, so venue is governed by §1391(a). Under that section, venue is proper where the defendant resides. A corporation's "residence" is defined by §1391(c) to include any district in which it would be subject to personal jurisdiction. Because corporations are subject to general in personam jurisdiction in the state where they are incorporated, Dixie would be subject to jurisdiction in the District of Maryland (which encompasses the entire state of Maryland). Thus, it is a proper venue.

Note that this analysis makes the District of Maryland a proper venue even though the case does not arise out of events that took place there. But venue provisions often lay venue where the defendant has important connections such as a residence or a place of business, even if the claim arose somewhere else. Thus, it is not anomalous that the place of incorporation is a proper venue under §1391(c). Note also that venue would apparently be proper in the District of Maryland under §1391(a)(3) as well.

b. Once again, venue will be proper under §1391(a)(1) if Dixie "resides" in the Middle District of Tennessee. And again, §1391(c) provides that Dixie resides in any district in which its contacts would subject it to personal jurisdiction. Here, Dixie is subject to general in personam jurisdiction in the district based on its large factory there. Thus, the Middle District is a proper venue. It would also be proper under §1391(a)(3), assuming that that section applies to single defendant cases.

c. Dixie does not "reside" in the Southern District of Georgia under §1391(c). True, Dixie is subject to personal jurisdiction throughout Georgia because of its large factory in Atlanta. But, under §1391(c), Dixie is only deemed to "reside" in those districts within a state in which its contacts would support jurisdiction if the district were a state. Thus, since Georgia is a multi-district state, we must look at the contacts Dixie has with each district, not at its contacts with the state as a whole. Here, Dixie has no contacts with the Southern District of Georgia. If that district were a state, Dixie would not be subject to personal jurisdiction in it for this claim. Thus, it does not "reside" there under §1391(c), even though it has substantial and continuous contacts with another district within the state.

However, venue is apparently proper there anyway, under §1391(a)(3), because Dixie's substantial and continuous contacts anywhere in the state subject it to general in personam jurisdiction throughout the state. This result, which authorizes venue under §1391(a)(3) even though it is not proper under §1391(c), is one reason why some commentators have doubted that §1391(a)(3) really means what it says.

d. The Eastern District of Pennsylvania is a proper venue on several grounds. First, venue is proper there under §1391(a)(2), since a substantial part of the events giving rise to the claim took place there. Second, venue is apparently proper under §1391(a)(3), since the corporation would be subject to personal jurisdiction where the allegedly defamatory statement was made. Third, venue is proper under §1391(a)(1), since the corporation "resides" (so says §1391(c)) in districts where its contacts would support personal jurisdiction. Note here that §1391(c) is only relevant to the analysis of venue under §1391(a).

e. It is not clear whether the Northern District of Ohio is a proper venue. Although the venue statute used to allow venue in a diversity case in the district where the plaintiff resides, it no longer does, so Mead's residence in the Northern District won't support venue. The other possible basis is that "a substantial part of the events or omissions giving rise to the claim" took place in the district, since Mead lost his job there because of the statements. This will be an important interpretive question under the new statute: whether a district in which the plaintiff sustains damages as a result of the defendant's acts qualifies as "a judicial district in which a substantial part of the events or omissions giving rise to the claim occurred." 28 U.S.C. §1391(a)(2). It seems likely that the courts will hold that a district where the plaintiff suffers substantial injury from the defendant's acts satisfies this language.

9a. Section 1391(a)(1) authorizes venue where any defendant resides, if they both reside in the same state. Calhoun resides in Georgia, as does Dixie, as "residence" is defined for corporations in §1391(c). Thus, any district in Georgia in which either defendant resides is a proper venue. Because they both "reside" in the Northern District of Georgia, that is a proper venue.

b. Although both defendants "reside" in Georgia, neither resides in the Southern District of Georgia. Consequently, it is not a proper venue under §1391(a)(1). However, Calhoun is subject to general in personam jurisdiction in Georgia based on his domicile, and Dixie is as well, based on its extensive in-state business (even though it is in the Northern District, not the Southern). Consequently, each is subject to personal jurisdiction in the Southern District, and (if §1391(a)(3) is taken at face value) it is a proper venue. Tricky, isn't it?

c. The Eastern District of Pennsylvania is a proper venue under

§1391(a)(2), since a substantial part of the events giving rise to the claim took place there. Again, note that §1391(c) is irrelevant to this analysis.

    d. Dixie "resides" in the Middle District of Tennessee (see example 8b), but Calhoun does not. Hence, it is not a proper venue under §1391(a)(1); nor does it meet the requirements of the other subsections.

10. In this case Dixie is the plaintiff, so section 1391(c) does not apply. In addition, the claim is not based "solely on diversity," so §1391(b) applies. Venue is proper where Mead resides, in the Northern District, or in the districts where a substantial part of the events giving rise to the claim took place. Because the goods were distributed throughout Ohio, this would include both the Northern and the Southern districts. However, these are not proper venues based on the fact that Mead may be "found" in them or subject to personal jurisdiction in them: §1391(b)(3) only applies if there is no district that is a proper venue under §1391(b)(1) or (2). Here there is, so subsection (3) does not apply.

A Subtle Variation

11. Bear with me through the analysis of this complex example. To begin with, §1391(a)(2) does not apply, since the events giving rise to the claim did not take place in the Western District of North Carolina: This claim arises out of a gun sold in Georgia, which caused injury in the Middle District of North Carolina.

    Now let's consider whether venue is proper under §1391(a)(1) and (c). If the Western District were viewed as a separate state, Dixie would not be subject to personal jurisdiction there based on its limited shipment of goods to a store there. Such limited shipments are not enough for general in personam jurisdiction, and the claim does not arise from those sales, so there is no specific in personam jurisdiction based on those sales. Thus, Dixie does not "reside" there under §1391(c). Nor would there be personal jurisdiction in the Middle District if it were viewed as a state. All that happened there was the explosion of the gun, which the plaintiff brought from another state. Basing jurisdiction on this contact alone would "appoint the chattel [the defendant's] agent for service of process," which the Supreme Court clearly disapproved in *World-Wide Volkswagen Corp. v. Woodson,* 444 U.S. 286, 296 (1980).

    However, this may be a case within the last part of §1391(c), in which the contacts with a state as a whole suffice to support personal jurisdiction over the defendant, but the contacts in any single district within the state do not. Here, the sales in the Western District and the injury caused by one of Dixie's products in the Middle District may, together, support "hybrid" jurisdiction over Dixie in North Carolina based on the total contacts with the state. See, e.g. Uniform Interstate and International Procedure Act §1.03(a)(4) (supra p.28) (jurisdiction may be based on regular business in state, together with injury in state caused by out-of-state tortious act). If so, §1391(c) tells us that venue may be laid in the district "within which it has the most significant contacts." Even if this line of reasoning applies, it is doubtful whether the sales contact in the Western District is as "significant" as the injury that directly gives rise to the claim. So the bottom line in this example is probably still that the Western District is not a proper venue under this arcane provision, though the Middle District might be.

But wait! Section 1391(a)(3) authorizes venue in a district where the defendant would be subject to personal jurisdiction. Based on the combined contacts with the state, Dixie may be subject to personal jurisdiction throughout North Carolina for this claim, so the Western District may be a proper venue anyway.

Is all of this really what Congress meant to subject us to when it amended the statute?

12.   This one is easy. Venue would be proper in the district within Oklahoma in which the accident occurred, under §1391(a)(2), since a "substantial part of the events giving rise to the claim" took place there. But the Supreme Court held in *World-Wide* that the Oklahoma court did not have personal jurisdiction over Seaway. Of course, without jurisdiction over Seaway, the plaintiffs will take little advantage from the fact that another ring, venue, is satisfied.

8

Choosing a Proper Court: The Three Rings Reconsidered

Introduction

A major purpose of this book is to introduce procedural concepts, such as personal jurisdiction, subject matter jurisdiction, and venue, and to illustrate their operation through a variety of examples. However, an equally important goal is to help you to see the interrelatedness of things, to explore how these procedural doctrines interact to form a rather elegant system for adjudication of law suits. This chapter reconsiders the three rings analyzed in earlier chapters in order to emphasize how these separate constraints operate together to circumscribe the plaintiff's choice of a proper forum.

As a preliminary matter it is important to reemphasize that all three of these prerequisites must be satisfied in order to bring suit in a particular forum. It is no answer to an objection to personal jurisdiction that diversity (or some other basis for subject matter jurisdiction) is present or that the venue provisions of 28 U.S.C. §1391 are satisfied. Each of the three doctrines has a different legal source, serves a distinct purpose, and employs a different standard. The limits on federal subject matter jurisdiction are found in Article III, §2 of the Constitution, which authorizes federal jurisdiction over certain limited types of cases. Personal jurisdiction, on the other hand, arises from due process limitations in the fourteenth amendment and limits the power of states to require out-of-state defendants to defend suits in their courts. The third ring, venue, does not have a constitutional source: It is a statutory limit that imposes separate constraints on the place of trial to protect parties from inconvenient litigation.

While the three rings are distinct in theory, the potential for confusing them is great because the standards that govern personal jurisdiction, subject matter jurisdiction, and venue are closely related. For example, the concept of domicile may be relevant to analysis of all three rings. Courts use the domicile test to determine the state citizenship of individuals (that is, natural persons) under 28 U.S.C. §1332(a)(1), the basic diversity provision. Domicile in the forum state is also a proper basis for exercising personal jurisdiction over an individual defendant. *Milliken v. Meyer,* 311 U.S. 457 (1940). Finally, domicile is relevant (with a twist) to venue because most courts have held that an individual "resides" under the venue statute in the judicial district where he is domiciled. Wright at 243-244. (The "twist" is that venue is only proper in the particular district within the state in which the individual has his domicile, not in the entire state.)

The concept of domicile, in the traditional common law sense of a place of residence where one intends to remain indefinitely, does not apply to corporations because they cannot have intent in the same sense that individuals do. However, the analogous doctrines of corporate citizenship or presence within the state are also relevant to all three rings. For the purpose of establishing subject matter jurisdiction on the basis of diversity, a corporation is deemed to be a "citizen" of the state of its principal place of business, as well as the state where it is incorporated. 28 U.S.C. §1332(c). To establish personal jurisdiction over corporations, however, the courts invoke the separate but confusingly similar concept of general in personam jurisdiction. Under general in personam jurisdiction analysis, a corporation is subject to personal jurisdiction in states in which it conducts substantial and continuous business activities. See Chapter 1, pp.5-7. The state in which a corporation is incorporated and the state of its principal place of business would almost certainly satisfy this standard, but other states may satisfy it as well.

For example, a major airline would be subject to general in personam jurisdiction in many states, due to the volume of flights it operates from those states and the facilities and employees it maintains there. Yet only one state will be its "principal place of business" for diversity purposes under 28 U.S.C. §1332(c). Thus, both of these related inquiries consider the amount of business activity in the state, but the two standards do differ, and the states that meet the standards will overlap but may not be exactly the same.

Venue in suits against corporations requires yet another related analysis. Under 28 U.S.C. §1391(a)(1), venue in a diversity case will lie in any judicial district in which a defendant "resides," if they all reside in the same state. For individuals, residence for venue purposes is generally equated with domicile, but, as explained above, corporations do not have a domicile in the common law sense of the term. Instead, corporate "residence" for venue purposes is defined in the venue statute. 28 U.S.C. §1391(c). Under §1391(c), a corporate defendant resides for venue purposes in any judicial district in which its contacts would suffice to support personal jurisdiction.

Thus, corporate activity or presence in the district is relevant to determining venue in cases against corporate defendants, just as it is relevant to determining their state citizenship for diversity purposes and their amenability to personal jurisdiction. However, a much smaller quantum of corporate activity will satisfy the venue requirement than is needed to establish a corporation's "principal place of business" for diversity purposes, or "substantial and continuous activities" for general in personam jurisdiction. Under §1391(a) and (c), for example, a district would be a proper venue based on a single act by a corporate employee in the district, if that act gave rise to the claim. Such a single act would support personal jurisdiction over the corporation for that claim, and therefore, under §1391(c), venue would be proper there as well.

Relation of the Claim to the Forum

Another understandable source of confusion in applying the three-ring analysis is the fact that one of the rings may require a relationship between the state in which the suit is brought and the claim the plaintiff asserts, while that relationship is irrelevant to applying the other rings. Suppose, for example, that Santini, a California high-wire artist, sues Robinson Shows, Inc., a Virginia corporation with its principal place of business in Virginia. If Santini brings suit in an Alabama federal court for a negligence claim that arose in Missouri, it is irrelevant to diversity analysis that the claim did not arise in Alabama. Diversity jurisdiction turns on a comparison of the citizenship of the parties, not on the relationship between the parties or the claim and the forum state. So long as the parties are from different states (and the amount-in-controversy requirement is met) diversity is satisfied.

Similarly, the fact that Santini's claim did not arise in Alabama may be irrelevant to the venue and personal jurisdiction analysis. If the circus does sufficient business in Alabama, it will be subject to general in personam jurisdiction there. And, if that is true, venue will be proper in the Alabama district where the business activity takes place, under 28 U.S.C. §1391(a)(1) and (c), even though the claim does not arise out of the business done in that district.[1] For example, if Robinson does extensive business in the Southern District of Alabama, that activity would support general in personam jurisdiction over Robinson, if the Southern District were a state, even though Santini's claim did not arise there. This suffices to make that district a proper venue under §1391(a) and (c).

Because venue in cases against corporations is proper where the corporation is subject to personal jurisdiction, under §1391(c), it should follow that

---

1. Robinson's corporate business activity in the Southern District would also support venue under §1391(a)(3), for the same reason, that it suffices for general in personam jurisdiction.

wherever a corporation is subject to personal jurisdiction will also be a proper venue. Not quite true, unfortunately. *First*, of course, it would not suffice that it was subject to personal jurisdiction on some other claim unrelated to the case before the court. *Second*, the combination of §1391(a)(1) [or (b)(1)] and (c) authorizes venue only in the particular districts within a state where the defendant has contacts. So a corporate defendant may be subject to personal jurisdiction in a state, but some districts in that state may still be improper venues. It is true that §1391(a)(3) appears to authorize venue wherever the corporation is subject to personal jurisdiction. But that subsection only applies if "the defendants" are subject to jurisdiction in the district, so it will not apply where the corporation is but other defendants are not. Further, this provision only applies to diversity cases; §1391(b)(3), governing venue in federal question cases, authorizes venue wherever a defendant may be "found," but only if no district is a proper venue under the other subsections.

The subtlety of these interrelations suggests that they were deliberately designed to intimidate first year law students. However, the situation is not really so bad once you have worked with the related doctrines in the context of specific facts. The following examples will help you sort out the various rings. Assume, unless the example specifies otherwise, that the relevant long-arm statute is like California's (see supra p.24), which authorizes the exercise of all constitutionally permissible jurisdiction and that all suits are brought in federal court. You may wish to refer to 28 U.S.C. §133 (found in most of the civil procedure supplements), which lists the federal judicial districts in each state.

EXAMPLES

Into the Rings

1.   Barnum, a citizen of Maine, sues Ringling Brothers, Inc. for injuries suffered when Leo, a trained lion, escaped from the circus train near Bangor, Maine. Ringling Brothers is incorporated in Wisconsin with its principal place of business in New York. The circus winters in Florida, has permanent facilities for training performers in Ohio, and performs for three weeks to a month in every state on the eastern seaboard.[2]

   a.   Could the suit be brought in federal district court in Maine? (Maine has only one judicial district.)

   b.   Could the suit be brought in the Northern District of New York? (New York has Southern, Northern, Eastern, and Western Districts.)

---

2. For those whose geography is rusty, the eastern seaboard states include Maine, New Hampshire, Massachusetts, Connecticut, Rhode Island, New York, New Jersey, Delaware, Maryland, Virginia, North Carolina, South Carolina, Georgia, and Florida.

    c. Could the suit be brought in any federal district court in Ohio?

    d. Could the suit be brought in any federal district court in New Jersey?

2.   Barnum sues Ringling Brothers and Kelly, the clown who let the lion escape from the train. Barnum claims that Kelly left Leo's cage unlocked while the train was refueling in Bangor. Kelly is domiciled in Florida.

    a. May Barnum sue in federal district court in Maine?

    b. May he sue in a Florida federal district court?

    c. May he sue in a New York federal district court?

3.   Barnum sues Ringling Brothers and Kelly in the Eastern District of Pennsylvania for the injuries Barnum suffered in Maine. Barnum serves the summons and complaint on Kelly and on T. Thumb, General Manager of Ringling Brothers, while the circus train is stopped just west of Philadelphia to feed the animals. Is the suit proper under the three rings?

Juggling Acts

4.   Suppose the circus sues Kelly, from Florida, and Rice, a Vermont citizen, for allowing Leo to escape. The circus alleges that Rice was negligent in failing to lock the cage when the train left Rutland, Vermont, and that Kelly was negligent in failing to check the lock when the train stopped to refuel in Bangor. The suit is brought in Maine.

    a. Will the Maine federal district court have subject matter jurisdiction over the action?

    b. Will the court have personal jurisdiction over the parties?

    c. Is Maine a proper venue?

5.   Beatty, an Arizona citizen, sues the Bailey Circus Corporation for an injury suffered when Elmer, a willing but occasionally clumsy elephant, fell on him while Beatty was watching a circus performance in Phoenix, Arizona. When the accident occurred, in 1988, Bailey was incorporated in Delaware with its principal (and only) place of business in Phoenix. Since 1988, however, the circus has prospered. As of 1992, when suit was brought, its principal place of business was California, although it still performed extensively in Arizona as well. May Beatty bring suit in federal court in California?

Procedural Acrobatics

6.   In 1992, Beatty sues the Bailey Circus and Stenk, Elmer's trainer, for the circus accident. Suit is brought in the New Mexico district court, the *state* court of general jurisdiction in New Mexico. Stenk is from New Mexico. Assume that the relevant New Mexico venue statute authorizes venue in the county where any defendant resides and that the suit is brought in the county where Stenk resides.

    a. Is the suit properly before the court?

    b. May the defendants remove to federal court?

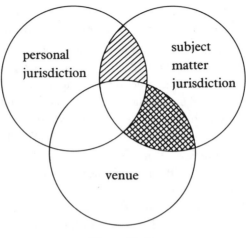

Figure 8–1

A Two-Ring Circus

7.   A representative of Ringling Brothers visits Adler, a retired clown who lives in Cedar Rapids, Iowa, in the Northern District of Iowa. The agent explains that the circus wishes to get Adler's permission to use a famous poster of Adler in promoting the circus, for a small royalty. Adler agrees. Ringling Brothers uses the picture in advertising in New York but does not pay Adler. Adler decides to sue Ringling Brothers for breach of contract and federal copyright infringement. (Assume, contrary to fact, that the general venue statute applies to copyright claims.)

    a. Can you think of a court or courts that would fall in the shaded area of Figure 8-1, that is, in which personal jurisdiction and subject matter jurisdiction are satisfied but venue is not? (The relevant facts concerning Ringling Brothers' business activities are found in example 1.)

    b. Assume that the contract involved was made in New York while Adler was visiting there, rather than in Iowa. Can you think of a court or courts that would fall in the hatched area of Figure 8-1, in which venue and subject matter jurisdiction are proper, but the court would not have personal jurisdiction over Ringling Brothers?

EXPLANATIONS

Into the Rings

1a. As pointed out in the Introduction, the suit may only be brought in those federal courts that satisfy all three rings of the analysis for choosing a proper court. There is clearly no problem with subject matter jurisdiction.

Barnum is a Maine citizen, and Ringling Brothers is a citizen of Wisconsin and New York under 28 U.S.C. §1332(c). As long as Barnum's claim is for more than $50,000 the requirements for federal subject matter jurisdiction based on diversity are met. The fact that Barnum is a citizen of the state where suit was brought is unnecessary to the diversity analysis; that analysis is satisfied as long as he and Ringling Brothers are citizens of different states, regardless of which states those are.

The Maine court will also have personal jurisdiction over Ringling Brothers in this action. The claim arises out of a negligent act by its employee, which evidently took place in the state and caused injury in the state. The defendant's negligent in-state conduct is sufficient to support specific in personam jurisdiction under the minimum contacts test, that is, jurisdiction over a claim such as Barnum's, which arises out of the in-state act itself.

Venue is also proper in Maine. Venue in diversity cases is governed by 28 U.S.C. §1391(a), which authorizes laying venue in the district where the defendants reside, where a substantial part of the events giving rise to the claim took place, or where the defendants are subject to personal jurisdiction. Venue is proper in the District of Maine under all three subsections of §1391(a). *First,* venue would be proper on the ground that Ringling Brothers "resides" in Maine for venue purposes. Under 28 U.S.C. §1391(c) a corporate defendant "resides" in every district in which it is subject to personal jurisdiction. Because the circus is subject to minimum contacts jurisdiction in the District of Maine for this claim, it "resides" there under 28 U.S.C. §1391(c). *Second,* venue is proper under §1391(a)(2), since a substantial part of the events giving rise to the claim took place in the district. *Third,* the district is apparently a proper venue under 28 U.S.C. §1391(a)(3), which authorizes venue in a district where the defendants (here only Ringling Brothers) are subject to personal jurisdiction.[3]

b. This suit could apparently be brought in any district in New York, including the Northern District. The analysis of the court's subject matter jurisdiction is exactly the same as in example 1a. A diversity case is a diversity case is a diversity case: If the parties are from different states and the amount-in-controversy requirement is satisfied, any federal court will have subject matter jurisdiction on the basis of diversity.

Personal jurisdiction over Ringling Brothers is proper in New York because it has its principal place of business there, which in virtually every case will establish the type of substantial and continuous contacts necessary to support general in personam jurisdiction over a corporation. Be careful, however, to distinguish this personal jurisdiction analysis from the diversity

---

3. As Chapter 7 explains, there is a great deal of uncertainty as to the proper interpretation of §1391(a)(3). This chapter assumes that it means what it says on its face: Venue is proper in any district in which all defendants are subject to personal jurisdiction, and §1391(a)(3) applies even if there is only one defendant.

analysis. For personal jurisdiction, the question is whether Ringling Brothers' activities in the state are so substantial and continuous as to make it fair to subject it to personal jurisdiction for any claim. By contrast, whether the corporation is a citizen of the state for diversity purposes turns on whether that state is the one state in which the corporation's business activities are centered under the various tests for determining a corporation's principal place of business. See Chapter 4, pp.58-59.

If venue in Barnum's suit is analyzed under §1391(a), we look to §1391(c) to determine whether Ringling Brothers "resides" in any New York district. Section 1391(c) provides (for states that have more than one judicial district) that a corporation resides in any district in which its contacts would subject it to personal jurisdiction. Once again, the analysis of the rings is similar but a little bit different. If New York is Ringling Brothers' principal place of business because its corporate offices are located in Manhattan, in the Southern District of New York, and it has no activities in the other judicial districts in New York State, venue would only be proper in the Southern District under §1391(a)(1) and (c). Thus, Barnum's suit could not be brought in the Northern District under those provisions.

However, §1391(a)(3) authorizes venue in any district in which "all defendants" are subject to personal jurisdiction. If §1391(a)(3) applies to single defendant cases (see the discussion in Chapter 7, p.101), the Northern District is a proper venue, since Ringling Brothers is subject to personal jurisdiction in any court in New York, based on general in personam jurisdiction.

Even if Barnum has filed suit in a forum where all three rings intersect, it is still not certain that the suit will be heard there. The court has the power under 28 U.S.C. §1404(a) to transfer cases "for the convenience of parties and witnesses, in the interest of justice," including cases in which the plaintiff has properly chosen that court under the three-ring analysis. This example, where suit is filed in a district with no connection to the claim, would be a good candidate for transfer.

c. Suit would also be proper in Ohio for this claim, on much the same reasoning as example 1b. Subject matter jurisdiction is no problem since, as indicated above, the parties are just as diverse if suit is brought in Ohio as they are if suit is brought anywhere else. Note that Ringling Brothers is not a "citizen" of Ohio for diversity purposes even though it has substantial business activities there that would subject it to general in personam jurisdiction in that state.

General in personam jurisdiction would probably be proper over Ringling Brothers in Ohio because they have a substantial, continuous presence in the state, due to their permanent training facility there. Presumably, they own or rent property there and have regular employees in the state, contacts that frequently support general in personam jurisdiction. Venue would also be proper in the judicial district within Ohio in which Ringling Brothers' training facility is located, under §1391(a)(1) and (c), since the corporation's contacts would subject it to personal jurisdiction there. And, apparently, venue would be proper in any Ohio district under §1391(a)(3).

If Barnum brings suit in Ohio, the circus will have a good case for transfer of venue under 28 U.S.C. §1404(a) because the claim did not arise in Ohio and the defendant's activities in the forum, though substantial, are completely unrelated to the cause of action before the court.

d. At last we have happened upon a forum where this law suit cannot be brought. Although diversity still exists, there is no basis for personal jurisdiction over Ringling Brothers in New Jersey for this claim. The claim does not arise out of any contacts of the defendant with New Jersey, so minimum contacts jurisdiction is not appropriate under *International Shoe*. Further, the three-week tour that the circus makes in the state is unlikely to satisfy the substantial and continuous contact requirement for general in personam jurisdiction. In addition, because the corporation is not subject to personal jurisdiction in New Jersey, neither §1391(a)(1) and (c) combined, nor §1391(a)(3) supports venue there.

2a. This suit may properly be brought in Maine. Complete diversity is present: Barnum is a citizen of Maine; Kelly is a citizen of Florida; and Ringling Brothers is a citizen of New York and Wisconsin. Personal jurisdiction is proper over both defendants under minimum contacts analysis, based on Kelly's negligent act of allowing Leo to get loose. This is a minimum contact of Kelly personally, since she actually performed the negligent act in the state. It is also a minimum contact of the corporation because Kelly's negligence occurred in the course of her work for the circus, and the contacts of the corporation's agents while acting on its behalf will be attributed to the corporation.

Venue is also proper under subsections (a)(2) and (a)(3) of §1391. A substantial part of the events giving rise to the claim took place in Maine, and, as already indicated, both defendants are subject to personal jurisdiction there. Note that §1391(a)(1) does not apply because Kelly does not "reside" in Maine, even though Ringling Brothers does under §1391(a)(1) and (3) combined.

b. Barnum will also have the option to sue in Florida under the three-ring analysis. Diversity is still present; here again it is irrelevant to diversity analysis that one of the parties (Kelly) is from the forum state. Personal jurisdiction is also likely to be proper over both defendants in Florida. Kelly is subject to jurisdiction there because she is domiciled there, and the circus is subject to general in personam jurisdiction there if it has its permanent winter quarters in Florida.

Venue is also proper on multiple bases. Under 28 U.S.C. §1391(a)(1) venue is proper in the district where any defendant resides if they all reside in the same state. For venue purposes, Kelly "resides" in the district within the state where she actually lives. See Chapter 7, example 1. If Kelly's home is in the Northern District of Florida, she "resides" there but not in the Southern District. Ringling Brothers resides, under §1391(a)(1) and (c), in whichever district its winter quarters is in, since this extensive and permanent contact would support general in personam jurisdiction. On these facts, venue would be proper in either the district where Kelly lives or the district in which Ringling Brothers' winter quarters are located. See §1391(a)(1) (the district "where any defendant resides, if all defendants reside in the same State"). In addition, venue is evidently proper in *any* Florida district under §1391(a)(3), since both defendants are subject to personal jurisdiction in Florida.

c. Suit will not be proper in New York because personal jurisdiction could not be asserted over Kelly in New York, under either minimum contacts analysis or general in personam analysis. Venue would also be a problem, since Kelly does not reside there and is not subject to personal jurisdiction there, and none of the events giving rise to the claim took place there.

3. The diversity analysis is unchanged here, but personal jurisdiction and venue are improper. Barnum may obtain "transient" personal jurisdiction over Kelly by serving her with process while she is passing through the state. *Burnham v. Superior Court of California,* 495 U.S. 604 (1990). But this "gotcha" theory, based on physical presence within the state, applies to individual, warm-body defendants, not to corporations: They are not necessarily "in" the state just because someone who works for them is. Because the claim arose in Maine, and the facts do not suggest any basis for general in personam jurisdiction over Ringling Brothers in Pennsylvania, the personal jurisdiction ring is not satisfied.

Nor is venue proper under §1391(a). Neither defendant resides there, and none of the events giving rise to the suit took place there. It is unclear whether obtaining personal jurisdiction by in-state service makes venue proper under §1391(a)(3). See Chapter 7, pp.101-102 (arguing that it should not be). Even if it does, that section does not apply here because personal jurisdiction was only obtained over Kelly by the in-state service; thus, "the defendants" are not subject to personal jurisdiction in the district.

Juggling Acts

4a. The Maine federal court, like any federal court, will have subject matter jurisdiction in this case, since there is complete diversity. Of course, the amount-in-controversy requirement will have to be met, but my guess is that more than $50,000 goes into your basic trained lion. If Leo falls in love with a moose and never returns, the circus might recover more than that amount; that's all that's needed to meet the amount requirement.

b. Personal jurisdiction presents a more difficult issue. Since neither defendant is domiciled in Maine, the circus will have to rely on specific jurisdiction, based on minimum contacts analysis. Kelly is clearly subject to jurisdiction in Maine under the *International Shoe* analysis because the claim arose from her negligent act (actually, her omission) in Maine. However, Rice's alleged negligence took place in Vermont, and it is doubtful that the mere foreseeability that the door would swing open in another state is sufficient to support jurisdiction over Rice there. Compare Chapter 1, example 1. Absent personal service in Maine or consent by Rice, the court will not have personal jurisdiction over her.

c. The District of Maine would be a proper venue in this action under §1391(a)(2), since a substantial part of the events or omissions giving rise to the claim took place in Maine. It would not be proper under §1391(a)(1), since neither defendant resides in Maine; and §1391(a)(3) does not apply, since Rice is not subject to personal jurisdiction there.

5. The interesting aspect of this example is that none of the three rings would have been satisfied if Beatty had brought suit immediately after the injury. The parties were not diverse at the time of the accident, but have become diverse in 1992, due to the change in Bailey's principal place of business. It is settled that diversity jurisdiction turns on the state citizenship of the parties when the suit is filed. See Chapter 4, example 6. Diversity jurisdiction is therefore proper in this case if the amount in controversy exceeds $50,000. In a case as weighty as this, that sounds likely.

Similarly, Bailey would not have been subject to personal jurisdiction in California in 1988. Because the claim arose in Arizona, Bailey was not (and still is not) subject to specific jurisdiction in California for this claim. Nor was Bailey subject to general in personam jurisdiction in California in 1988. Bailey had no contacts with California then; its continuous and substantial business in California has all developed since 1988. May it be sued there in 1992 based on general in personam jurisdiction, even if it was not subject to such jurisdiction at the time the claim arose?

Logically, it should not matter that the corporation was not subject to general in personam jurisdiction in California when the claim arose. No one was trying to assert jurisdiction over it then. The rationale underlying general in personam jurisdiction is that extensive corporate presence within the state reduces the inconvenience of litigation and affiliates the corporation with the state in such a substantial way as to make it fair to sue it there for any claim. If that presence exists at the time the suit is brought, the rationale for subjecting the corporation to jurisdiction is satisfied. In addition, any inconvenience to the corporation from litigating in the state occurs when the litigation takes place, and at that time Bailey had a substantial presence in the forum state.

If this personal jurisdiction analysis is right, then venue will also be proper in the federal districts in California where Bailey does substantial business. Looking at those districts as though they were states, the contacts there would support general in personam jurisdiction over Bailey, even though the claim arose elsewhere; consequently §1391(c) applies. Apparently, §1391(a)(3) applies as well, authorizing jurisdiction in any California district.

Procedural Acrobatics

6a. This chapter deals primarily with the choice of a proper federal forum. The same three rings must also be satisfied if suit is brought in state court, but the standards for meeting those tests differ in a state suit. All states have a trial court that exercises broad subject matter jurisdiction over most types of claims, including negligence claims. In New Mexico, these courts of general jurisdiction are called district courts. They have subject matter jurisdiction over garden variety tort claims such as Beatty's, as well as a broad range of other common law and statutory causes of action. There is no need to consider the state citizenship of the parties, since the diversity requirements of 28 U.S.C. §1332 apply to subject matter jurisdiction of the federal courts, not that of the state courts.

Venue analysis also differs in state court actions. Each state has its own statutes defining proper venue for claims brought in its courts, which may vary considerably from the federal venue provisions. Here, the New Mexico statute is satisfied if Stenk "resides" (whatever that may mean under the New Mexico statute) in the county where the suit is filed. By contrast, venue would not be proper in this example under 28 U.S.C. §1391, since the circus has no contacts there and the events giving rise to the claim took place elsewhere.

Personal jurisdiction analysis, however, is likely to be the same whether the suit is brought in state or federal court. As indicated in Chapter 5, the federal courts generally exercise personal jurisdiction only to the extent that it would be exercised by the state courts in that state, under Fed. R. Civ. P. 4(e). See pp.75-76. In this case, jurisdiction would be proper over Stenk, on the basis of her New Mexico domicile, but not over Bailey, since the claim did not arise in New Mexico and the facts do not indicate that Bailey would be subject to general in personam jurisdiction there.

b. By now you may wish you had run away and joined the circus instead of going to law school. Taming lions or swallowing swords might not be a bad alternative.

The personal jurisdiction analysis will not be affected by the defendant's decision to remove, since both courts apply the same statutory and constitutional standards for exercising personal jurisdiction, unless a federal statute authorizes the federal courts to exercise broader jurisdiction. Fed. R. Civ. P. 4(e). The defendants do not waive their right to object to personal jurisdiction by removing to federal court. See Chapter 6, example 20. Thus, Bailey could seek dismissal on this ground in the federal court after removal.

Venue and subject matter jurisdiction, however, require further analysis. Venue would not be proper under §1391 because all defendants do not reside in Arizona, the events giving rise to the claim did not take place there, and there is not personal jurisdiction over both defendants there. However, the usual federal venue provisions do not apply in removed actions. For removed cases, the applicable provision is 28 U.S.C. §1441(a), which requires that the case must be removed to the district and division embracing the place where the state action was brought. See *Polizzi v. Cowles Magazines,* 345 U.S. 663, 665 (1953). Thus, as long as the defendants remove to the federal district that includes the county where the state action was filed, venue will not be a problem.

The subject matter jurisdiction analysis requires a two-level inquiry. First, the removal statute requires that the case have been within the original subject matter jurisdiction of the federal court. 28 U.S.C. §1441(a). Assuming that suit was brought after Bailey moved its principal place of business to California, that requirement would be met, based on diversity. However, even if a case satisfies the basic diversity requirements, §1441(b) bars removal if any defendant is a citizen of the forum state. So, the short version of this long-winded answer is that the case cannot be removed, since Stenk is a citizen of New Mexico.

A Two-Ring Circus

7a. It appears that the Southern District of Iowa falls in this area. Federal subject matter jurisdiction would be proper if the suit were brought in that district, as in any other. Adler asserts a claim under the federal copyright laws, and supplemental jurisdiction will apply to his related breach of contract claim. (The court would also have independent jurisdiction over the contract claim on diversity grounds.) Personal jurisdiction is likely to be upheld in any Iowa court since the claim results, at least indirectly, from Ringling Brothers' deliberate contact in going to Iowa to make the royalty agreement with Adler. This would likely suffice for specific in personam jurisdiction under the *International Shoe* minimum contacts test.

However, venue would not be proper in the Southern District of Iowa. This case is not founded solely on diversity, so the analysis must be under §1391(b). Ringling Brothers does not "reside" there under §1391(b)(1) and (c) because it has no contacts there if the district is viewed as a state; nor did a substantial part of the events giving rise to the claim take place there; nor does §1391(b)(3) apply. That section authorizes venue where any defendant may be "found." Even if this language is equated with "subject to personal jurisdiction" (which Ringling Brothers would be, under minimum contacts analysis), venue is not proper under §1391(b)(3) unless there is no district in which venue would otherwise be proper. Here, there are other districts in which venue is proper under §1391(b)(1) and (2), so the third subsection does not apply.

There could be numerous other districts that fall in this area as well. In any state where the circus does enough business to support general in personam jurisdiction, the diversity and personal jurisdiction rings will be satisfied. If the circus does business in some districts of those states but not others, venue will only be proper in the districts where it does business. (Got that?)

b. The Northern District of Iowa might fall into this area on the diagram, depending on the interpretation of §1391(b)(2). Subject matter jurisdiction is proper based on the federal question and supplemental jurisdiction. Venue may be proper under §1391(b)(2) since the claim arises in part from an "omission" — Ringling Brothers' failure to pay Adler the agreed royalties — which arguably took place in the Northern District of Iowa. However, it is doubtful that the circus would be subject to personal jurisdiction in Iowa if its only contact was the failure to send the royalty checks to Adler there.

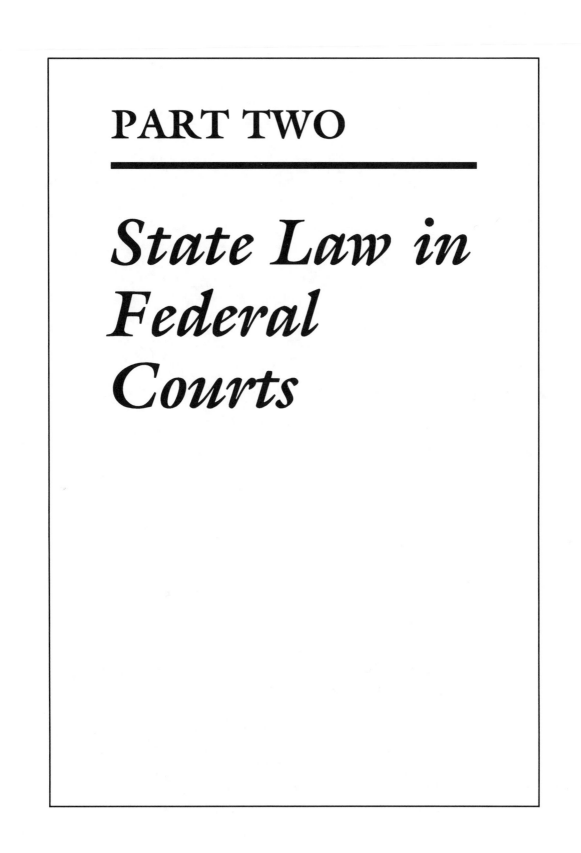

PART TWO

State Law in Federal Courts

9

Easy Erie: *The Law of Rome and Athens*

A Personal Fantasy

It is December, and the pace of the first year of law school is picking up. Glannon sits numbly in Civil Procedure class. The professor is droning on, quite learnedly. Subject: the *Erie* doctrine. Glannon cowers as unobtrusively as possible in the middle of the class. All around him, students listen intently, with apparent comprehension. Glannon understands nothing.

Suddenly, the Archangel Gabriel appears, hovering resplendent above the class. No one else takes notice; the discussion moves on obliviously. Pointing a star-studded scepter at the object of his visit, Gabriel speaks. "Glannon," he declaims, "listen well, for you, *you* shall be called upon to explain the *Erie* doctrine to a future generation of students."

Astonished by the apparition and appalled at his message, Glannon streaks from the room. After a long convalescence and many setbacks, he takes a job watering flowers in a nursery.

Introduction

If old Gabe had really put in an appearance back then, I would surely have given the nursery job some serious thought. But even if I had stoically accepted the archangel's charge, I would never have contemplated calling anything about the *Erie* doctrine "easy." I certainly found it impenetrable then, and there is much about it that remains a mystery to me today. However, some aspects of *Erie* really are fairly straightforward, and, luckily, those

133

are the aspects that it is particularly important for you to understand. This chapter deals with these comprehensible aspects of *Erie*.

The whole problem is really the framers' fault. They decided to craft a federal form of government, in which most power would remain with the states, but certain limited powers would be delegated to the new national government. They spent a summer thinking about what legislative powers the national government really had to have and set them forth in Article I, §8 of the Constitution. All other powers, anything they hadn't mentioned (or by fair implication "necessary and proper" to the exercise of these "delegated" powers), "are reserved to the States respectively, or to the people." U.S. Const., amend. X.

At the same time, the framers adopted Article III of the Constitution, which authorizes the creation of federal courts and defines their jurisdiction. In defining the federal judicial power, they authorized federal courts to hear claims that arise under federal law ("cases arising under this Constitution, the Laws of the United States, or Treaties made, or which shall be made, under their Authority"). Thus, when Congress makes law under its delegated powers in Article I, §8 and cases arise in which plaintiffs seek recovery under those laws, the federal courts have jurisdiction.

However, the framers went further in Article III. They also created the diversity jurisdiction, which authorizes federal courts to hear cases that do not involve federal law at all. In fact, by definition a diversity case does not arise under federal law. If Plato, from Montana, sues Lucan, from South Dakota, for violation of the federal patent laws, the parties are diverse; but it is not a diversity case, since the claim arises under federal law. Plato's right to recover is created by federal law, a law Congress had the power to pass because the power to regulate patents is delegated to the federal government under Article I, §8. This is a federal question case; it is irrelevant that the parties are from different states.

On the other hand, if Plato's claim is for breach of contract, the federal court will have jurisdiction (if the amount in controversy is sufficient) based on diversity of citizenship. However, the substantive law that governs the claim cannot be created by Congress, since it has no delegated power to create a general law of contracts. The federal court has *judicial* power to hear the case, even though there is no federal *legislative* power to create the governing law. The question addressed in *Erie* — and in its infamous predecessor, *Swift v. Tyson*, 41 U.S. 1 (1842) — was what law should be applied in this anomalous situation.

The Rule of Swift v. Tyson

There was no real reason why this had to be such a problem. The First Congress had considered the issue in 1789 and passed a statute to deal with it. The Rules of Decision Act, 1 Stat. 92 (1789), provides:

> The laws of the several states, except where the constitution, treaties or statutes of the United States shall otherwise require or provide, shall be regarded as rules of decision in trials at common law in the courts of the United States in cases where they apply.

The Rules of Decision Act (referred to herein as "the RDA") is still in force today, virtually unchanged from the original of 200 years ago. See 28 U.S.C. §1652.

Much controversy could have been avoided if the Supreme Court had simply interpreted the RDA differently in 1842, when Justice Story decided *Swift v. Tyson*. In *Swift,* the plaintiff, Swift, brought a federal diversity suit to collect on a bill of exchange. The bill had been given by Tyson to a third party, Norton, who endorsed it over to Swift in New York. As consideration for the bill, Swift had cancelled an antecedent debt owed him by Norton. Swift, a "holder in due course," was entitled to collect on the bill if he had given "a valuable consideration" for it. The less than earth-shaking issue in the case was whether Swift's cancellation of Norton's pre-existing debt constituted such consideration. 41 U.S. at 14-16.

Tyson, the defendant, argued that the RDA required the court to apply New York law to determine the validity of consideration, since the case involved a bill executed in New York and no federal statute applied. Under New York law, Tyson contended, such consideration was insufficient. Justice Story doubted that New York law was so clear, but concluded that it didn't matter anyway. The RDA, he concluded, did not require the federal court to follow New York's view of this question of general commercial law. In Story's view, the phrase "the laws of the several states" in the RDA referred only to the statutes and certain established local usages of the state, not to judicial decisions interpreting general principles of common law.

If the federal court did not have to apply the common law decisions of the state in a diversity case, what law should it apply? In Story's view, the federal court should examine all the common law authorities — including cases from the state in which it sat, from other states, from federal courts, English courts, and respected commentators — to ascertain the proper rule. The federal judge's job, like that of any judge, was to choose the right rule of consideration, rather than to follow a rule that some other judge deemed to be the right one.

The Philosophical Underpinnings of Swift

It is not hard to see behind this conclusion a fundamental premise about the nature of law. The law, declared Justice Story, cannot be one thing in Rome and another in Athens. 41 U.S. at 19. The law is the Law, a body of absolute "right" rules, existing apart from a particular place, time, or judge. Under this "natural law" view (said to derive from Blackstone,[1] but doubtless more fundamentally from the Greek philosophers), the task of every judge was to look to all the available evidence to ascertain the ideal "right" rule on any common law question, such as the proper consideration for a contract or true duty owed to a trespasser on a railroad right of way.[2] In the lofty search for this "transcendental body of law,"[3] it is hardly surprising that one judge seeking the true rule of adequate consideration should not feel bound by a prior judge's perceptions. All looked to the same sources in their efforts to approximate the ideal outcome.

This natural law view ran into some problems along the way. *First,* it was clear that the law *could* be one thing in Rome and another in Athens, if the legislature so declared it. If the New York legislature passed a statute declaring that railroads owed a duty of due care to frequent trespassers, that became the law of New York. There was no question that the RDA required the federal diversity court to apply that law to New York cases. If Pennsylvania passed a statute declaring that the railroad need only avoid wilful or wanton negligence, the federal court sitting in diversity would have to apply that rule in a Pennsylvania case. The federal courts under *Swift* also followed many so-called local usages, such as established state common law rules concerning interests in land, for reasons of stability and predictability of titles.

Second, the *Swift* rule created potential for manipulation of the sort upheld in *Black & White Taxicab Co. v. Brown & Yellow Taxicab Co.,* 276 U.S. 518 (1928). In that case, the Brown and Yellow Taxicab Company sought to enforce a contract with the railroad, providing it the exclusive right to pick up and discharge passengers at a train station in Kentucky. Aware that the Kentucky courts did not enforce such contracts, Brown & Yellow reincorporated in Tennessee, thus creating diversity between it and the defendant, Black & White. It then brought suit in federal court — in Kentucky, no

---

1. W. Castro, The *Erie* Doctrine and the Structure of Constitutional Revolutions, 62 Tul. L. Rev. 907, 913 (1988).

2. The language of the pre-*Erie* opinions nicely reflects this premise. In *Swift,* for example, Story speaks of "the true result of the commercial law upon the question now before us." 41 U.S. at 19. In *Black & White Taxicab Co. v. Brown & Yellow Taxicab Co.,* 276 U.S. 518 (1928), the high-water mark of the *Swift* doctrine (or, perhaps, its low-water mark), the majority speaks of "the discovery" of common law principles and of looking to past cases as "evidence of the existing applicable rule." 276 U.S. at 529-530.

For a very provocative dissent on the meaning of *Swift,* see L. Teply, Civil Procedure (1991) 280ff. Professor Teply argues that the Court in *Swift* actually did follow New York's view, which was to apply the "general common law." However, Teply concedes that cases following *Swift* usurped much state authority by deciding purely state law issues as matters of "general common law." Id. at 301-302.

3. *Black & White Taxicab Co. v. Brown & Yellow Taxicab Co.,* 276 U.S. 518, 533 (1928) (Holmes, J., dissenting).

less — to enjoin Black & White from interfering with its contract. The Kentucky federal court held, as other federal cases had, that the true rule was that the monopoly contract was enforceable and enjoined the defendant from interfering with it. The Supreme Court upheld the decision on the ground that the federal court had the authority under *Swift* to reach its own conclusion on the common law issue of whether such exclusive contracts should be enforced. Thus, by invoking diversity jurisdiction, the plaintiff was able to choose a substantive rule of law which upheld rather than barred the contract.

The Legal Realist Attack on Swift

Justice Oliver Wendell Holmes wrote a marvelous dissent in *Black & White Taxicab,* in which he attacked *Swift*'s basic philosophical premise about the nature of law. *Swift,* he wrote, was based on

> the impression that there is one august corpus, to understand which clearly is the only task of any Court concerned. If there were such a transcendental body of law outside of any particular State but obligatory within it unless and until changed by statute, the Courts of the United States might be right in using their independent judgment as to what it was. But there is no such body of law. The fallacy and illusion that I think exist consist in supposing that there is this outside thing to be found.

276 U.S. at 533.

If there is no "august corpus" of true rules of law, just what is the law anyway? The law, declares Holmes, is a set of rules laid down by those with the power to do so, to govern behavior in a given place and at a given time:

> Law is a word used with many meanings, but law in the sense in which courts speak of it today does not exist without some definite authority behind it. The common law so far as it is enforced in a State, whether called common law or not, is not the common law generally but the law of that State existing by the authority of that State.

Id. For Holmes, the rule that a railroad owes a duty of due care to a trespasser — or doesn't — derives its force not from its inherent "rightness," but from the fact that the authorities empowered to make such a rule have made it. The law *can* be one thing in Rome and another in Athens because the people who make Roman laws are different from those who make the Athenian laws. Since Athens is a different place, with different conditions and problems, its lawmakers may well choose different rules than the Romans do. And later Athenian lawmakers may choose different rules than their predecessors. Each rule may be "right" in the sense that it is appropriate to its time and place, but it is not "right" because it is the one true rule for all time on a particular issue.[4]

If this "legal realist" view of the judge's role is correct, what should a federal judge do in a case like *Black & White*? According to Holmes, he should ask what body has the authority to make rules governing the enforcement of contracts. The answer to that question is usually the states, since the Constitution delegates no general law-making authority over contracts to the legislative or judicial branches of the federal government. Whether the state speaks through its legislature or through its "other voice" (its courts), it must be heeded because it is the body with the authority to create the applicable law under our constitutional distribution of powers.[5]

The Erie Decision

Justice Holmes died in 1935, so it fell to Justice Brandeis to sound the death knell for *Swift*. It was doubtless a task Holmes would have relished, since the Court in *Erie* dramatically repudiated the 100-year tradition represented by *Swift*.

The facts of the case were simple: Tompkins lost an arm when hit by a projection from an Erie Railroad train while walking on a pathway along the tracks. His injury was quite likely the result of negligence; however, there was no evidence that the railroad's employees had acted wilfully or wantonly in creating the danger, which was the standard for recovery under Pennsylvania law.[6] The federal district court, relying on *Swift*, concluded that it was not bound by the Pennsylvania decisions and instead followed federal decisions, which held that railroads owed a duty of due care to users of lateral pathways along the track. Tompkins recovered in federal district court, though he would have lost if the case had been brought in state court.

Interestingly, no party argued that *Swift* should be overruled: The defendant in *Erie* argued instead that the federal court should have followed the Pennsylvania rule because it was a matter of "local usage" rather than general common law. I. Younger, What Happened in *Erie*, 56 Tex. L. Rev. 1011, 1025-1026 (1978). The *Erie* Court, however, dramatically rephrased the issue: "The question for decision is whether the oft-challenged doctrine of

---

4. Holmes' language in *Black & White*, like that of the natural law judges, reflects his premise. He speaks of state courts "establishing," "declaring," or "adopting" rules of law, of "say[ing] . . . that thus the law is and shall be." 276 U.S. at 534-535. His is not the language of discovery, but of creation.

5. Ironically, while the obvious implication of Holmes' argument was the overruling of *Swift*, he did not argue for that in *Black & White*. Instead, he would "leave *Swift v. Tyson* undisturbed, . . . but . . . would not allow it to spread the assumed dominion into new fields." 276 U.S. at 535. His position shows that he was a political realist as well as a legal realist.

6. All involved assumed that, if state law applied at all, Pennsylvania law would apply.

Swift v. Tyson shall now be disapproved." 304 U.S. at 69 (footnote omitted). To its own question, the Court answered "yes" for a number of reasons.

First, Swift had failed to achieve one of the main goals of its supporters. It was hoped that the gradual accumulation of "general common law" decisions by eminent federal judges would induce state judges to recognize the "rightness" of those decisions and fall into line, leading to broad uniformity in the common law throughout the nation. But state judges had the temerity to believe that they too could examine the "evidence" and "discover" true principles for themselves. Rather than docilely following federal cases, the state judges persisted in taking their own views. The result was a multiplicity of rules on recurrent issues, not only from different state courts, but also from federal and state courts within a single state.

Second, Justice Brandeis concluded, the federal practice of making common law had led to grave discrimination in the administration of justice. As *Black & White Taxicab* illustrates, it allowed an out-of-state plaintiff to choose a different rule of substantive law because he could choose federal court. While a local company would have to sue in a Kentucky state court, which would refuse to enforce exclusive contracts, a diverse plaintiff could go to federal court and get a more favorable outcome.[7] Ironically, while diversity was created to prevent prejudice against out-of-staters — to assure a "level playing field" as they said in the 1980s — *Swift* had introduced discrimination in favor of the out-of-stater.

Third, and most fundamentally, Justice Brandeis declared the *Swift* doctrine unconstitutional, since it authorized federal judges to "make" law in areas in which the federal government has no delegated powers. *Erie* emphatically adopts Holmes's view that, in choosing its rules of decision, the federal court must look to the body with the authority to make those rules. When it comes to common law matters not within the delegated powers, that body is the state, whether it speaks by statute or judicial decision. Thus, ignoring

---

7. Arguably, there is no discrimination here between the parties to the case. After all, defendants get a choice of forum too: they can remove cases from state to federal court. But this is not true of in-state defendants. 28 U.S.C. §1441(b). Thus, in *Black & White,* if the Kentucky rule had been more favorable to the plaintiff than the "federal common law" rule, Brown & Yellow could have sued in state court, and the defendant would have been stuck in state court. In addition, when the diverse plaintiff chooses federal court initially, the defendant is stuck with it, since there is no such thing as removal to state court. In *Black & White,* for example, the out-of-state plaintiff sued in federal court because the federal rule was more favorable. Once again, the defendant was stuck with that court and that rule.

Finally, there is another type of discrimination here, between out-of-state plaintiffs and in-state plaintiffs with similar claims against local citizens. A Kentucky taxi driver who sued Black & White on a similar claim would not have had the same opportunity that Brown & Yellow had to choose the applicable law by choosing the "right" court.

state common law rules invades rights reserved to the states under our federal system of divided powers:

> Notwithstanding the great names which may be cited in favor of the [*Swift*] doctrine . . . there stands, as a perpetual protest against its repetition, the constitution of the United States, which recognizes and preserves the autonomy and independence of the states, — independence in their legislative and independence in their judicial departments. Supervision over either the legislative or the judicial action of the states is in no case permissible except as to matters by the constitution specifically authorized or delegated to the United States.

Erie, 304 U.S at 78-79, quoting from *Baltimore & Ohio R. Co. v. Baugh,* 149 U.S. 368, 401 (1893) (Field, J., dissenting).

I suggested earlier that Justice Story could have avoided the entire problem by interpreting the RDA a little differently. That act requires the federal courts to apply "the laws of the several States," unless the federal Constitution, treaties, or statutes require otherwise. If Story had concluded that the phrase "the laws of the several States" includes state common law decisions, the federal courts would have been required *by the RDA itself* to apply those decisions, and lofty questions of constitutional power to do otherwise would have been avoided. He didn't interpret it that way. In *Erie,* however, Justice Brandeis concluded that it would be unconstitutional to interpret it any other way. It was Justice Story's interpretation of the act, not the act itself, that the court rejected in *Erie.*

What's Easy about Erie

Whatever its fascination may be as a triumph of legal realism or a constitutional landmark, the central command of *Erie* is basic. In diversity cases, federal courts must apply the law that would be applied by the courts of the state in which they sit. They are not free to decide for themselves the "right" rule of consideration, the duty that a railroad owes to a trespasser, or the enforceability of exclusive contracts. Rather than create "general common law," their job is to *apply* state common law. In those broad areas where the law is largely judge-made, such as contracts, torts, probate, and property issues, state law reigns supreme because "there can be no other law." *Hanna v. Plumer,* 380 U.S. 460, 472 (1965).

In 97 percent of the cases, this *is* easy. Lawyers and federal courts apply *Erie* every day without the slightest difficulty because all parties recognize that state law provides the governing rules of decision and there is little question as to what the state law is. There's been a lot of fuss about some fringe cases — we'll fuss over them ourselves in the next chapter — but in the overwhelming number of diversity cases *Erie* functions simply and effectively to determine the applicable principles of substantive law.

The following examples consider the basic mechanics of applying the

Erie doctrine. In considering them, assume, unless otherwise specified, that all actions are brought in federal court on the basis of diversity. After the initial examples, we will consider a related question: How does a judge determine what the law of the state actually is?

EXAMPLES

When in Rome . . .

1.   Plato was injured in an accident in Minnesota when his car collided with those of Solon and Ovid. He sued Solon and recovered $200,000 in damages, which Solon paid. Solon then sued Ovid for contribution, that is, to get a judgment that Ovid, as a joint tortfeasor, must reimburse Solon for half of the damages he paid to Plato. The contribution action was brought in federal court in Minnesota.

   At the time of Solon's contribution suit, the law on contribution was in a state of flux throughout the United States. Most courts refused to order contribution between joint tortfeasors. A few courts, however, had adopted the opposite view, that a tortfeasor who had paid the plaintiff could require other negligent parties to pay their share of the loss. Several states had adopted statutes authorizing contribution. Minnesota had no statute on point, but its courts had followed the minority rule, allowing contribution.
      a.   How should the federal district court decide the issue of Solon's right to contribution, if the case arose prior to *Erie*?
      b.   How should the court decide the issue after *Erie*?

2.   Assume that Solon's contribution action arose in 1925, and most *federal* courts that had considered the issue had concluded that contribution should be allowed between joint tortfeasors. However, Judge Quintus, the federal trial judge in *Solon v. Ovid,* agreed with the reasoning of the courts that deny contribution. What should he do?

3.   Assume that, prior to *Solon v. Ovid,* Minnesota had passed a statute that authorized contribution among joint tortfeasors.
      a.   How should the federal district court decide the contribution question, if the case arose before *Erie*?
      b.   How should the court decide the issue after *Erie*?

4.   Assume that Minnesota had a statute authorizing contribution among joint tortfeasors. Most states with contribution statutes had held that they are not intended to allow a party who acted wilfully or wantonly to seek contribution. However, assume that the Minnesota Supreme Court had construed its statute to authorize a tortfeasor to seek contribution even if her conduct was wilful or wanton. If Solon seeks contribution, and Ovid argues that the statute does not authorize it because Solon's conduct was wilful or wanton, how should Judge Quintus rule if
      a.   the case arose prior to *Erie*?
      b.   the case arose after *Erie*?

History Repeats Itself

5.   Assume that Harry Tompkins III is walking on a lateral pathway along the tracks of the Erie Railroad in Pennsylvania in 1991. He is injured when hit by something projecting from a passing train. He sues the Erie Railroad under the Federal Interstate Railway Act, which (we will assume) authorizes suits for damages arising from railroad accidents. He also claims damages for common law negligence. On the negligence claim, the railroad raises the defense that Pennsylvania law does not allow trespassers on the right of way to recover damages, absent wilful or wanton negligence, but Tompkins argues that the court should apply a due care standard to the negligence claim. What should Judge Quintus do, and why?

Ascertaining State Law

Because *Erie* requires federal courts to apply state law in diversity cases, federal judges obviously must decide what the state law is. In many cases that is easy because the issue has been clearly decided by the state's highest court. If there is a recent case from the Pennsylvania Supreme Court holding that railroads are only liable to trespassers if the railroads act wilfully, the federal court knows its course and will dismiss a future Tompkins' case if there is no evidence of such aggravated fault. For example, if the Kentucky decisions consistently refuse to enforce exclusive contracts like that in *Black & White,* the federal court in Kentucky will also refuse to enforce them.

Many cases, however, are not so squarely resolved by the case law. For example, there may be older cases from the Pennsylvania Supreme Court requiring wilful conduct but recent tort cases in related areas that suggest a trend to expand duties in tort cases generally. Or perhaps the Kentucky courts have refused to enforce exclusive contracts, but those cases are distinguishable because they involved matters of particular public interest. Or there may be no state supreme court case on the point, but there may be one from an intermediate appellate court. Or perhaps no appellate court from the state has decided the question in dispute, but a trial judge has. Or going one step further, perhaps another *federal* judge has decided the point, but no state judge has. Or one step further, perhaps there is absolutely no decision on point, though there are decisions on analogous tort issues.

The early post-*Erie* cases suggested that the federal court, in deciding what state law is, should follow any existing state precedent, without making creative projections about how that precedent might be treated in a future case. In *West v. American Tel. & Tel. Co.,* 311 U.S. 223 (1940), for example, the Court held that, where there was no decision on point from the state supreme court, a decision of the state's intermediate appellate court was binding, "even though it [the federal district court] may think that the state Supreme Court may establish a different rule in some future litigation." 311

U.S. at 238. The furthest extension of this approach came in *Fidelity Trust Co. v. Field,* 311 U.S. 169 (1940), in which the Supreme Court required the federal court to follow two trial court decisions on a question of New Jersey law, in the absence of any appellate cases on point, even though no other New Jersey judge would have been bound by those decisions. This led Judge Frank of the Second Circuit to complain that the federal judge was to woodenly follow existing state cases like a "ventriloquist's dummy." *Richardson v. Commissioner,* 126 F.2d 562, 567 (2d Cir. 1942).

The Supreme Court has since suggested, however, that federal judges have more flexibility in determining state law under *Erie.* In *Commissioner v. Bosch,* 387 U.S. 456, 465 (1967), the Court held that a federal court construing state law should give "proper regard" to decisions of trial and intermediate appellate courts, but that its job is to apply the law as announced, or as it *would be announced,* by the state's highest court. Thus, the federal judge must predict how the issue before it would be decided by the state supreme court if that court decided the issue today. In making that prediction, the judge may look to all available data, including lower court decisions, developing trends in the area of law that cast doubt on the earlier decisions, and dicta or legislative developments that weaken (or reaffirm) the existing precedents. The judge is not free to make up state law, but he is entitled to make an educated judgment on what rule the state supreme court would apply to the case *today,* rather than merely parroting what the rule was when the last case on point was decided.

The federal court may have an additional option in determining state law. Some states have "certification" procedures, which allow a federal court faced with a thorny state law issue to certify the issue to the state supreme court. See, e.g., Kan. Stat. Ann. §§60-3201 to 60-3212; W. Va. Code §§51-1A-1 to 51-1-12. When the federal judge certifies the issue, a statement of the issue and the relevant facts is sent to the state court. The case then goes into the regular appellate pipeline: The parties brief and argue the issue before the state court as though it were a regular appeal from a lower state court. Ultimately, the state supreme court issues an opinion, much like that on any other appeal, resolving the issue. Then, armed with the answer to their question, the parties return to the *federal* court and pick up the litigation there.

While certification assures an accurate reading of state law (assuming the state court accepts the certification), a mere description illustrates why it can only solve the problem of ascertaining state law in a small percentage of cases. It is a lengthy and expensive diversion from the federal litigation. In addition, it creates the anomalous situation of federal courts determining the state supreme court's workload. For this latter reason, certification statutes are usually optional, giving the state supreme court the power to accept or refuse the certification. Only those cases that the federal court chooses to certify and the state court accepts will lead to authoritative pronouncements of state law.

. . . Do As the Romans Do

6.   Assume that the Minnesota Supreme Court, in *Aristotle v. Caesar*, a 1952 decision, refused to allow contribution between joint tortfeasors, reasoning that each tortfeasor who caused the plaintiff's injury may justly be made to pay the entire damages and that the legislature is the proper body to change this basic tort principle if it is dissatisfied with the common law no-contribution approach. In 1984, the issue comes before the Minnesota Court of Appeals, the state intermediate appellate court, in *Justinian v. Lycurgus*. It reviews the broad changes in many areas of tort law since 1952, including the very wide adoption by other states of the right of contribution. On balance, it concludes that if the state supreme court reconsidered the issue it would likely overrule *Aristotle* and allow contribution.

  a.   What should the Minnesota Court of Appeals do in *Justinian v. Lycurgus*?

  b.   Assume that, shortly before the decision in *Justinian,* Solon brings an action against Ovid for contribution in federal court. Judge Quintus, the federal judge, reviews the *Aristotle* opinion, as well as the broad trend of tort law decisions in Minnesota, and concludes (as did the court of appeals in *Justinian*) that the Minnesota Supreme Court would overrule *Aristotle.* How should Judge Quintus rule?

  c.   Suppose that Solon sues Ovid for contribution in federal court after the Minnesota Court of Appeals (the intermediate state court) had predicted in *Justinian* that the Minnesota Supreme Court would overrule *Aristotle.* However, Judge Quintus, who is handling the *Solon* case, does not agree with the Court of Appeals' prediction. What should he do?

  d.   If you represented Solon in the contribution action against Ovid, would you file suit in federal court or state court?

Role Reversal

7.   Justinian is held liable to Draco in a negligence action and sues Charondas in a Minnesota state court for contribution as a joint tortfeasor. Judge Ulpian, the state trial judge, prior to ruling on the right to contribution, researches the law on contribution and finds that there is no Minnesota case addressing the right to contribution between joint tortfeasors. However, in *Solon v. Ovid* (a diversity case applying Minnesota law), the Federal Court of Appeals for the Eighth Circuit had concluded that the Minnesota Supreme Court, if it considered the question, would allow contribution. How should Judge Ulpian rule?

8.   Assume that Justinian's contribution action is brought in federal district court. Judge Quintus's research uncovers *Solon v. Ovid* from the Eighth Circuit. How should Judge Quintus decide the contribution question?

Figure 9–1: Judicial Districts of Illinois Appellate Court

High Fidelity

9.   The State of Illinois has not one, but five intermediate appellate courts. Each handles appeals from a separate geographical area of the state. See Figure 9-1. A case tried in Washington County, for example, in the Fifth District, would be appealed to the Fifth Judicial District of the Illinois Appellate Court. A case tried in Cook County goes on appeal to the First Judicial District. (In fact, Cook County is the only county in the First District because Chicago is located there and creates as much judicial business as many other counties put together.)

Assume that Gaius sues Draco in Cook County Circuit Court (the Illinois trial court of general jurisdiction) for contribution as a joint tortfeasor. Assume further that the Illinois Supreme Court has never decided whether contribution is available between tortfeasors. The Fourth and Second Districts of the Illinois Appellate Court have held that it is, but the First District has held that it is not.

   a.   What rule should the state trial judge in *Gaius v. Draco* follow?
   b.   Now, assume that the *Gaius* case is brought in Cook County but is removed to the federal district court for the Northern District of Illinois, which includes Cook County. What rule should the federal district judge apply?

EXPLANATIONS

When in Rome . . .

1a.   If this case arose under the *Swift* regime, the federal judge would not be bound by the Minnesota decisions on the right to contribution. *Swift* authorized federal judges to make independent judgments as to what the proper rule should be on issues of "general common law." Contribution was a question of tort law, which had long been governed by the common law decisions of courts rather than by statute. Thus, the judge was not bound to follow the Minnesota decisions, even though, had the suit been brought in a Minnesota state court, contribution would have been allowed.

Nor would he have been bound by the majority position of the other states: The rule was not necessarily "right" because it was more widely followed. The judge would look to all the cases and authorities, assess their reasoning, and reach the decision that, in his judgment, represented the proper rule on the issue.

   b.   After *Erie,* the judge would clearly be bound to follow the Minnesota rule, even though it is a judge-made common law rule rather than a statute. *Erie* held that the RDA requires federal courts to apply state law in diversity cases, whether judge-made or statutory, rather than following their own perception of the best rule. The rationale of *Erie* is that the grant of jurisdiction over diversity cases in Article III is not a grant of authority to displace state substantive rules of decision, but only to apply those rules in a federal, presumably neutral forum. Since only the state has the power to make law on general tort issues like the right of contribution among joint tortfeasors, the federal court must apply the state's law rather than creating its own law.

Note that the court must apply the Minnesota rule, not the rule that the majority of states would choose. Where the case is governed by Minnesota law, the issue is not how most state courts would rule, but how the Minnesota courts would.

2. This is an interesting dilemma for the judge under *Swift*. He was not bound by the state decisions — either those of Minnesota or of other states — but was he bound by the trend in the federal cases? One of the arguments for the *Swift* doctrine was that eventually uniform common law rules would evolve as a body of "general common law" decisions on similar issues accumulated. But the basic rationale of *Swift* is that each judge looks to the common law sources to reach an independent judgment as to the proper rule. Presumably, if a judge did that and concluded that the majority of his federal colleagues had reached the wrong result, he should not follow them any more than state judges who had missed the mark. Thus, he would not be bound by decisions from other federal district courts either. Although such decisions might be persuasive (just as the Minnesota decisions might be) he would make an independent judgment as to the proper contribution rule.

3a. In this case the state rule is the same as in the previous examples, but it has been established by statute rather than by judicial decision. Even under *Swift* it was consistently held that the RDA required federal courts to apply state statutes in diversity cases. 1A Moore's (Part 2) ¶0.302[2]. Thus, the federal court had to apply the state rule if the legislature made it but was free to ignore it if the state supreme court did.

b. *Erie* held that the RDA must be interpreted to require federal courts to apply state common law decisions in diversity cases. It did not in any way impair the long-established view that the act required federal courts to apply state statutes in diversity cases. Indeed, under *Erie* this is not only the proper interpretation of the RDA, but the only permissible one. Since Congress has no delegated power to enact laws governing contribution among joint tortfeasors, state law must govern because "there can be no other law." *Hanna v. Plumer*, 380 U.S. 460, 472 (1965). Thus, after *Erie*, as before, the court would apply the Minnesota statute.

4a. Here, there is a state statute on point, and the issue is the proper interpretation of it. Minnesota courts construe their statute one way, though other states construe similar provisions differently. Under *Swift*, the federal court had to follow state statutes in diversity cases, but did the federal court have to follow state court cases construing the meaning of those statutes?

Even under *Swift* it was recognized that the issue in such cases was not what the "right" rule should be, but what the Minnesota law was. The RDA required application of the Minnesota statutes, whatever they meant, and the Minnesota courts were the proper body to determine their meaning. It is one thing for the federal courts to take an independent view of what the common law rule of contribution *should be*. It would be quite another for them to ignore the local courts' conclusions as to what their own state statutes *actually say*. On this question, the Minnesota courts were the acknowledged experts.

b. The same result is clearly appropriate under *Erie*. The source of the applicable law is the state, since the question is not within the federal legislative authority. The federal diversity court must therefore follow the law of the state, as laid down in the statute and construed by the state court. This follows as a matter of *Erie* policy as well as constitutional division of powers: If the federal court were free to construe the statute differently, parties would invoke the diversity jurisdiction to get a more favorable substantive result, just as they did under *Swift*.

History Repeats Itself

5.   Strictly speaking, this case does not raise an *Erie* problem at all. The case is a federal question case, since Tompkins III has sued under the Federal Interstate Railway Act. However, as plaintiffs are wont to do, Tompkins has asserted a state law negligence claim as well.

The state negligence claim would be properly before the federal court under supplemental jurisdiction, which authorizes a federal court to entertain related state claims that arise from the same facts as a federal claim. See 28 U.S.C. §1367; Chapter 14. However, supplemental jurisdiction is another example of a situation — like diversity — in which federal courts have jurisdiction to hear state claims but no power to create the governing law. Here, as in diversity cases under *Erie,* the court's job is to apply state law to the supplemental claim, not to make up its own rule. Thus, Judge Quintus should have his law clerk research Pennsylvania law to determine whether it requires a showing of wilful or wanton negligence. If it does, he must apply that rule to the supplemental claim.

Obviously, the court would apply federal law to the interpretation of the Federal Interstate Railway Act claim. It may "make" law on that claim if necessary to decide the case, but it would have to follow state law, or predict it, on the state negligence claim. Thus, in many federal cases that are *not* diversity cases the court must indulge in the same exercise of guessing at the content of state law that is required in diversity cases under *Erie*. Even if the foes of diversity jurisdiction ultimately achieve its repeal, ascertaining and applying state law will still be necessary in every case involving supplemental state law claims.

. . . Do As the Romans Do

6a. The Minnesota Court of Appeals is a mid-level appellate court, bound by the decisions of the highest court of the state. *Aristotle v. Caesar* is such a case, and it is directly on point. An intermediate appellate court would almost certainly consider itself bound by *Aristotle*. The role of the lower courts is to follow the law established by the highest court of the state, not to speculate about how that court might change it in the future. Unless *Aristotle* had been utterly eviscerated and effectively overruled by more recent Minnesota Supreme Court decisions, the Minnesota Court of Appeals would feel bound to follow *Aristotle* and deny contribution. The court of appeals might well write an opinion encouraging the state supreme court to review the case and change the law, but it cannot do so itself.

b. In this case, the only Minnesota Supreme Court case on point denies contribution, but Judge Quintus (like the court of appeals in the previous example) has strong grounds to believe, in light of other tort law developments, that the state supreme court would adopt a more liberal approach on this issue if it came before that court today.

The federal judge's role in a diversity case is to predict how the case would ultimately be decided if it wended its wobbly way through the state system and reached the highest court of the state. Judge Quintus may be very circumspect about making such a prediction — and consequently ignoring *Aristotle* — but if he is convinced that the Minnesota Supreme Court would approve contribution today, he should apply that rule.

c. The only difference on this scenario is that Judge Quintus, when he rules, has the benefit of the intermediate appellate court's prediction of what the state supreme court will do. That is certainly useful data in determining what the highest court would say; indeed it is highly persuasive. But it is not absolutely dispositive. The federal judge's role is to predict what the Minnesota Supreme Court would do, not to follow what the court of appeals thinks the supreme court would do. See, e.g., *Dimidowich v. Bell & Howell,* 803 F.2d 1473, 1482 (9th Cir. 1986) (intermediate court decisions are data to be followed unless the court is convinced by other persuasive data that the state's highest court would decide otherwise). If Judge Quintus is convinced from his general review of the law in the area that the Minnesota Supreme Court would follow *Aristotle,* he must do so.

d. If I had strong arguments that the Minnesota Supreme Court would change the rule, I might well go to federal court. In state court there is a good chance of losing on a motion to dismiss, since *Aristotle* is mandatory precedent, which the state trial judge must follow. Even if the case goes to the court of appeals, I would still lose under *Aristotle,* since the intermediate appellate court is likely to consider itself bound by that decision. Only if the Minnesota Supreme Court takes the case (a matter vested in its discretion, which is sparingly exercised)[8] will I have a chance of winning.

In federal court, on the other hand, if the trial judge is convinced that the supreme court would adopt contribution, he will allow the case to go forward. This will keep the case alive. Maybe it will settle. If it goes up on appeal, the federal Court of Appeals will not be bound by *Aristotle,* if convinced it is a derelict waiting to be interred by its creator. Federal judges are not anxious to disregard state supreme court decisions, but they can do it upon strong evidence, and sometimes it is pretty clear that the law will change.

The irony here is that the federal judge's freedom to predict what the law *will be,* rather than woodenly applying what it has been, opens up a narrow opportunity for diversity plaintiffs to choose more favorable substantive law despite *Erie.* Theoretically the ultimate result would be the same because the Minnesota Supreme Court, if the case got up there, would do what the federal court predicts it would. But, as a practical matter, the case probably won't get there. The result in state court is likely to be dictated by the (perhaps outdated) *Aristotle* case but might not be in federal court.[9]

Role Reversal

7.   Judge Ulpian should rule any way he wants to: He is not bound by the Eighth Circuit's conclusion that Minnesota law allows contribution. The Eighth Circuit under *Erie* cannot make the law of Minnesota, it can only predict what the Minnesota courts will do or follow what they have done.

---

8. See *Abbott Laboratories v. Granite State Ins. Co.* 573 F. Supp. 193, 198 & 198 n.5 (N.D. Ill. 1983), in which Judge Shadur argues that the chance of getting the Illinois Supreme Court's view on an issue of Illinois law is miniscule. For 1982, he notes, 706,893 cases were disposed of in the Illinois trial courts, but the Illinois Supreme Court only wrote 199 opinions.

9. Perhaps because of this disparity, some federal courts have expressed considerable reluctance to recognize new state law rights in diversity cases. See, e.g., *Tritle v. Crown Airways, Inc.,* 928 F.2d 81, 84-85 (4th Cir. 1991). These courts reason that the plaintiff who seeks recognition of new rights under state law should sue in state court:

> We have warned, time and again, that litigants who reject a state forum in order to bring suit in federal court under diversity jurisdiction cannot expect that new [state-law] trails will be blazed.

Carlton v. Worcester Ins. Co., 923 F.2d 1, 3 (1st Cir. 1991) (quoting from *Ryan v. Royal Ins. Co.,* 916 F.2d 731, 744 (1st Cir. 1990); cf. *Spector Motor Service, Inc. v. Walsh,* 139 F.2d 809, 823 (2d Cir.) (Hand, J., dissenting), vacated 323 U.S. 101 (1944) (warning lower courts against "embrac[ing] the exhilarating opportunity of anticipating a doctrine which may be in the womb of time, but whose birth is distant").

Minnesota judges are not bound by federal judges' predictions about Minnesota law, even federal appellate judges.

Although not bound by the Eighth Circuit's decision, Judge Ulpian is likely to give the opinion in *Solon v. Ovid* serious consideration in deciding Justinian's case. A panel of three august federal judges has looked at Minnesota tort law and concluded that the Minnesota Supreme Court would allow contribution. Judge Ulpian may not be bound to follow that conclusion, but he may well be persuaded by a well-reasoned opinion by judges who, though they do not make Minnesota law, are fully conversant with it. Put another way, *Solon v. Ovid* is persuasive authority, though not mandatory.

8.   Federal district courts are normally bound to follow the precedents of their supervisory court of appeals. Certainly, if the Eighth Circuit Court of Appeals decided an issue of federal law, Judge Quintus would be bound to follow it. That's what the whole system of mandatory precedent means. However, in diversity cases, federal courts do not make the law, they just guess at it. Should the federal district judge be bound by the court of appeals' guess as to what the Minnesota Supreme Court would do?

As a practical matter, if Judge Quintus makes a different guess, the losing party will appeal, and the Eighth Circuit will overrule him based on its view announced in the *Solon* case. So it makes sense for the district court judge to follow the Eighth Circuit's conclusion even though the Eighth Circuit does not "make" Minnesota law.

Suppose, however, that after *Solon* the Minnesota Supreme Court decided several cases in related areas, which indicated their intent to change the rule on contribution. At this point, Judge Quintus may be convinced that the Eighth Circuit would no longer make the same prediction on Minnesota law that it did in *Solon* because the evidence as to what Minnesota law "is" has changed. In such cases, where the court is convinced that later developments render the federal appeals court's prediction obsolete, it may disregard it. See, e.g., *Scadron v. City of Des Plaines*, 734 F. Supp. 1437, 1451-1452 (N.D. Ill. 1990).

High Fidelity

9a.   The Illinois Supreme Court has held that the trial courts within each judicial district must follow the rule established by the appellate court for that district, even though other appellate courts of equal stature have ruled otherwise. Consequently, the judge in *Gaius v. Draco* must follow the holding of the First District that contribution is not allowed between joint tortfeasors.

Under this approach, if there is a split among the districts of the Illinois Appellate Court, the "law" of Illinois will differ from one part of the state to another until the Illinois Supreme Court takes a case on further review and resolves the split in the appellate decisions.

b. The *Erie* doctrine requires the federal judge to follow the law of the state, but in this case, the "law" of the state differs, depending on which judicial district the case is filed in. What should the federal judge do?

There are several possible answers in this situation. One, perhaps the most obvious in light of the earlier examples, is to predict how the Illinois Supreme Court would rule on the issue. The federal court's job, after all, is to predict what "the law" of Illinois is, not the law of the First Appellate District or the Third.

. . . Or is it? Judge Shadur of the Northern District of Illinois has consistently ruled otherwise. He argues that the federal judge's job is to assure that the suit comes out the same way in federal court as it would in state court. See, e.g., *Abbott Laboratories v. Granite State Ins. Co.*, 573 F. Supp. 193, 196-200 (N.D. Ill. 1983). Allowing Gaius to avoid the First District's no-contribution rule by going to federal court, Judge Shadur argues, will undermine the *Erie* goal of uniformity and encourage choice of the federal court to obtain a "better rule of law." Consequently, he concludes that the federal district court must follow the rulings of the Illinois Appellate District in which the case arose.

Most courts, however, have followed the "Supreme Court predictive approach," which asks how the state supreme court would decide the issue if the case got up that far. Judge Shadur finds this an illusory rule because few cases *do* get that far: For most parties "the law" is the rule of the appellate court for their judicial district. Thus, he argues, the "Supreme Court predictive approach" will often yield a result quite different from the one the parties would obtain in state court. See *Abbott Laboratories* at 198 & 198 n.5.

Like example 6, the case demonstrates that, despite the command of *Erie,* it is very difficult to assure absolute uniformity in treatment within the two court systems.

10

Eerie Erie: The Substance/ Substance Distinction

Introduction

As "Easy *Erie*" suggests, the *Erie* doctrine is applied without substantial difficulty in most diversity cases. *Erie* and the Rules of Decision Act (RDA) require the federal court to apply state law, and the court does. It uses the state rules governing the standard of care to a trespasser, enforceability of contracts, the validity of wills and property transfers, and myriad other state rules of law, whether pronounced by statute or by common law.

It sounds easy, and often it is easy. But not always. Lurking behind the majestic and simple truths of the *Erie* case were some complex implications, which, if not foreseen by the *Erie* justices, have certainly bedeviled their successors. These implications are so subtle and important to our ideas of federalism that they have fascinated law professors as well. Consequently, while they play a relatively minor part in the daily administration of diversity jurisdiction, they figure prominently — too prominently, perhaps — in the first-year Civil Procedure course.

The most puzzling problem, of course, has been determining which issues are governed by the command of *Erie*. Clearly, *Erie* requires federal courts to apply state law to issues upon which there is no federal law-making power. For example, neither Congress nor the federal courts have any authority to establish the standard of care owed to trespassers. Thus, the RDA, as interpreted in *Erie,* requires the federal court to apply state law on this "substantive" issue. But it is doubtful that the Court ever thought that *Erie*'s command would require federal courts to follow state law on clearly *procedural* issues in diversity cases.

The Emergence of the Problem

It didn't take long for the implications of *Erie* to begin to emerge. The very next term the Court was confronted with an *Erie* problem that challenged the limits of the doctrine. In *Cities Service Oil Co. v. Dunlap,* 308 U.S. 208 (1939), the issue was which party had the burden of proof on a question of title to land. Texas law put the burden of proof on the party challenging the legal title, but federal procedure placed it on the party who brought suit, in this case the holder of legal title. The court of appeals concluded that *Erie* was inapplicable, since the issue was "a matter of practice or procedure and not a matter of substantive law." 101 F.2d 314, 316 (1939). But the Supreme Court reversed, holding that the burden of proof issue "relates to a substantial right" so that *Erie* mandated application of state law. 308 U.S. at 212.

The *Dunlap* decision must have sent shock waves through the legal community. The decision suggested that *Erie* required diversity courts to defer to state law not only on "substantive" rules but also on matters of procedure that related to the enforcement of state rights. If the federal court had to apply state law on burden of proof in a diversity case, why not on the time for filing a complaint, the right to amend, or the admissibility of evidence? At its most extreme, this would mean that federal courts would have to abandon the Federal Rules of Civil Procedure in diversity cases and apply instead the entire *procedural* law of the state in which they sat. Federal courts would then operate under a dual system of procedure: the Federal Rules in federal question, admiralty, and other types of cases within federal subject matter jurisdiction, but state procedural law when jurisdiction was based on diversity.[1]

The next major post-*Erie* case did little to allay these concerns. In *Guaranty Trust Co. v. York,* 326 U.S. 99 (1945), the issue was whether a federal diversity court must apply the state statute of limitations to a claim, or whether it was free to apply its own more flexible "laches" doctrine to the case. The Court, speaking through Justice Frankfurter, refused to distinguish

---

1. This prospect was enormously ironic because up until 1938 federal courts *had* followed state procedural rules in all cases. The Federal Rules of Civil Procedure took effect in 1938, the same year that *Erie* was decided. Prior to 1938 the Conformity Act of 1872 provided that federal courts should follow the procedural rules of the state in which they sat. Thus, under the Conformity Act the procedural rules differed from one federal court to another because each applied the procedure of the state in which it sat. The Federal Rules introduced uniformity in federal procedure for the first time . . . and the progeny of *Erie* promptly threatened to destroy it.

Erie on the basis that it involved state "substantive" law while *York* involved "procedure." Instead, the Court held that the state limitations statute must be applied, in order to implement the "policy" of *Erie* that

> in all cases where a federal court is exercising jurisdiction solely because of the diversity of citizenship of the parties, the outcome of the litigation in the federal court should be substantially the same, so far as legal rules determine the outcome of a litigation, as it would be if tried in a State court.

york

326 U.S. at 109. If following a federal practice not available in state court might "significantly affect the result of a litigation," (id.) the court must apply the state rule instead, to prevent diverse parties from gaining unfair advantages simply because they can choose federal court. In *York*, this "outcome-determinative" test dictated use of the state limitations statute, since the claim was barred under that statute but might have been allowed to proceed under the federal laches doctrine.

In retrospect, it is clear that *York* broadened the *Erie* doctrine considerably. *Erie* required the lower federal court to apply the state duty of care because neither the federal courts nor Congress has constitutional authority to create rules of tort law.[2] However, *York* extended the doctrine well beyond the area in which it is constitutionally compelled by the limits on federal power. There is constitutional authority to make federal *procedural* rules, even in diversity cases: The Constitution grants Congress the power to establish lower federal courts (Article I, §8; Article III) and to make laws "necessary and proper" for exercising that power. U.S. Const. Article I, §8. However, because many clearly procedural rules may affect outcome, *York*'s outcome-determinative test required federal courts to apply state law in many cases in which there would be federal power under Articles I and III to apply a separate rule.

Suppose, for example, that state law allows 30 days to answer and federal law only allows 20. If Clinton files suit in federal court, and Fisk answers on the twenty-fifth day, that difference could be outcome determinative. If Clinton serves Fisk by leaving the summons and complaint at his last and usual place of abode (see Fed. R. Civ. P. 4(d)(1)), but state law requires personal delivery to Fisk, that difference may be outcome determinative. If federal law allows Clinton to amend his pleadings to add new claims after the limitations period passes, but state law does not, that also may be outcome determinative. At its broadest, *York* would mandate use of the state rule in each of these

---

2. This is often, but not always, true. In many situations various constitutional provisions would support federal power to enact tort legislation. For example, the interstate commerce power in Article I, §8 would doubtless support federal legislation dealing with products liability claims. And scholars have argued that Congress could have enacted a standard of care governing the *Erie* facts under the Interstate Commerce power. See, e.g., 19 Wright and Miller §4505 at 55-56.

cases, although there is federal constitutional authority to establish a different rule. If so, it should be clear that there would not be much left of the Federal Rules of Civil Procedure in diversity cases.

The Pendulum Swings Back . . . a Little

Next in this intimidating line of post-*Erie* decisions is *Byrd v. Blue Ridge Rural Electrical Cooperative, Inc.*, 356 U.S. 525 (1958). The *Erie* issue in *Byrd* was whether the judge or the jury should determine the plaintiff's status as an "employee" of the defendant. State law left the question to the judge, but the practice in federal court was to send such issues to the jury.

Although *Byrd* is often viewed as a departure from *York*, the Court actually reaffirmed the holdings of both *Erie* and *York*. First, the Court noted, federal courts must honor the "definition of state-created rights and obligations by the state courts." 356 U.S. at 535. I take this to mean that the federal court must follow state law in those areas where it has no power to create law. This is the constitutional prong of the *Erie* doctrine, exemplified by *Erie* itself, in which the rule at issue involved clearly "substantive" law — duty of care to a trespasser — which the Constitution reserved to the states. In *Byrd*, however, Justice Brennan concluded that the South Carolina rule authorizing the judge to decide "employee" status was *not* "bound up with the definition of the rights and obligations of the parties" but "merely a form and mode of enforcing" the compensation scheme. 356 U.S. at 536. Thus, the issue was a matter of procedure as to which the federal court was not *constitutionally* compelled to apply the state practice.

Justice Brennan also acknowledged that *York* evinced a "broader policy" that federal courts should follow state practices even of "form and mode," if ignoring them would substantially affect the outcome of the litigation. 356 U.S. at 536. Thus, *Byrd* reaffirmed the broader approach of *York,* under which the federal court applies outcome-determinative state law even on procedural issues as to which there is federal constitutional authority to apply a separate rule. Brennan even conceded in *Byrd* that, absent other considerations, the outcome-determinative test would very likely require the court to apply state law to the issue before it. 356 U.S. at 537.

However, he went on to hold that, in deciding whether to follow state law in matters of "form and mode" (that is, the area in which the court follows state law as a matter of policy rather than constitutional command), the federal court must consider not only the *York* policy of uniform outcomes in diversity cases, but also any countervailing federal policies that arise from the federal court's status as an independent judicial system. In *Byrd,* the constitutional right to jury trial under the seventh amendment to the Constitution was at least tangentially implicated in making the choice between judge and jury. Given the importance of that right in the administration of federal courts, Justice Brennan concluded that the *Erie* policy of maximizing uniformity of outcome should yield to the federal policy of broad availability of jury trial. 356 U.S. at 538-539.

Because *Byrd* reaffirmed that state rules of form and mode should usually be applied if they might prove outcome determinative, it still appeared after *Byrd* that state procedural rules would often supersede the Federal Rules of Civil Procedure in diversity cases. It remained for the Warren Court to rescue the Rules in *Hanna v. Plumer,* 380 U.S. 460 (1965).

The Rules Rescued: Hanna v. Plumer

The issue in *Hanna,* like many of these post-*Erie* cases, was less than titillating. The plaintiff served process on the defendant, the executor of a Massachusetts estate, by leaving the summons and complaint at his home with "a person of suitable age and discretion," as required by Fed. R. Civ. P. 4(d)(1). However, a Massachusetts statute required in-hand service upon the executor. Mass. Gen. L. ch.197, §9. While the issue was dull, the stakes were high: If service was valid, the case would go forward. If it was not, it would have to be dismissed, since the executor had not been served within the limitations period. Validity of service turned, of course, on whether the federal court was required to apply the state service rule instead of Rule 4(d)(1).

The defendant made a seemingly airtight argument for application of the state rule: *York* says "use state law if doing so will affect the outcome." I win immediately if the state statute is applied, since service was not made within the limitations period. But the case goes forward if service was valid under the Federal Rule. Certainly, that difference is outcome determinative, so the state rule must be applied.

The argument was a good one, but Chief Justice Warren found several reasons for rejecting it. In the first part of the opinion (which I will call *Hanna* Part 1) he analyzed the conflict between the two service rules under a modified outcome-determinative test. Whether a federal procedure is outcome determinative, Warren concluded, must be viewed in light of the policies underlying *Erie,* to prevent forum shopping and inequitable administration of the laws. Not every difference between state and federal rules leads to those problems. It is very doubtful, for example, that a plaintiff would choose federal court over state court simply to avoid serving the defendant in person, since the effort required to do so is only marginally greater than that required to serve under the federal rule. Nor is the difference in litigation effort between "last and usual" service and in-hand service sufficient to be viewed as "inequitable administration of the laws." Thus, the Court concluded, the outcome-determinative test, viewed in light of the aims of the *Erie* doctrine, did not require the federal court to substitute the state rule for its own.

Hanna *Part 2: A Distinct Analysis for Federal Rules Conflicts*

The major *Erie* cases, before *Hanna,* involved conflicts between federal judicial practices (that is, informal practices of federal judges not required by federal statute or Federal Rule) and state law. For example, *Erie* involved the practice of federal judges of "making" common law on tort issues, despite differing state common law. *York* involved the federal judicial practice of applying the laches doctrine, rather than state statutory limitations periods. *Byrd* involved the choice by federal judges, not commanded by statute or Rule, to send certain issues to the jury, which were determined by the judge under corresponding state practice. Thus, the Court in these cases had no occasion to decide whether the standard for deferring to state law in a diversity case would be the same if the state law conflicted with a formal Federal Rule of Civil Procedure.

In *Hanna* Part 1, the Court analyzed the service issue before it *as though* it involved the typical "relatively unguided *Erie* choice" between an uncodified federal judicial practice and state law. It concluded that such conflicts should be addressed under a "modified outcome determinative test" based on avoidance of forum shopping and inequitable administration of the laws. However, in the second part of *Hanna,* the Court noted that the service provision at issue (Rule 4(d)(1)) was a Federal Rule of Civil Procedure, recommended by the Advisory Committee on the Civil Rules, officially promulgated by the Supreme Court under the Rules Enabling Act (see 28 U.S.C. §2072, hereinafter referred to as the REA), and implicitly endorsed by Congress.[3] In *Hanna* Part 2, the Court established an entirely different analysis for cases in which an official Federal Rule of Civil Procedure conflicts with state law.

The REA was enacted in 1934 and is still in effect. The first section of the REA authorizes the Supreme Court to "prescribe general rules of practice and procedure" for the federal courts. Pursuant to this authority, an advisory committee appointed by the Supreme Court drafted the Federal Rules. They were then promulgated by the Supreme Court and, as required by the REA (28 U.S.C. §2074), submitted to Congress for review before taking effect.

Thus, there is both constitutional and statutory authority for the adoption of the Federal Rules. In *Hanna,* the Court held that Article III and the Necessary and Proper Clause provide broad *constitutional* authority to

---

3. The relevant provisions of the REA, as it presently reads, are as follows:

> §2072. (a) The Supreme Court shall have the power to prescribe general rules of practice and procedure and rules of evidence for cases in the United States district courts (including proceedings before magistrates thereof) and courts of appeals.
>
> (b) Such rules shall not abridge, enlarge, or modify any substantive right. . . .

> make rules governing the practice and pleading in [federal] courts, which in turn includes a power to regulate matters which, though falling within the uncertain area between substance and procedure, are rationally capable of classification as either.

380 U.S. at 472. This language suggests, as some have concluded, that Congress and the Court have broad constitutional authority to promulgate any rule that is "arguably procedural."[4]

The first section of the REA also provides broad *statutory* authority to promulgate procedural rules. In *Hanna* the court endorsed an equally broad construction of this statutory grant:

> The test must be whether a rule really regulates procedure — the judicial process for enforcing rights and duties recognized by substantive law and for justly administering remedy and redress for disregard or infraction of them.

Hanna, 380 U.S. at 464 (quoting from *Sibbach v. Wilson,* 312 U.S. 1, 14 (1941)). Like *Hanna*'s broad definition of the constitutional grant, this somewhat tautological definition suggests that Congress and the Court have the authority under the REA to enact any Federal Rule that is "arguably procedural." And, for what it is worth, Congress's acquiescence in the rules (by failing to intercept them after they are promulgated and submitted for review) provides a little extra dose of credibility. To invalidate one of the Rules, the Court would have to conclude that the Advisory Committee, the Supreme Court, and Congress had all erred in their judgment that the rule could validly be applied in federal court.

Due to *Hanna's* very broad construction of the constitutional and statutory authority to promulgate the Federal Rules, a party who argues that a Federal Rule is beyond the bounds of federal authority because it is not "procedural" faces a very steep uphill battle. However, the second subsection of the REA (28 U.S.C. §2072(b)) opens another avenue of attack: It provides that "[s]uch rules shall not abridge, enlarge, or modify any substantive right." Thus, alas, the elusive substance/procedure distinction also emerges in assessing the validity of Federal Rules under the REA. A Rule, though "procedural" under the first subsection of the REA, is invalid under the second if it impinges on "substantive rights."

Well, this is a little eerie: A federal judicial practice may not be applied, under *Hanna* Part 1, if it is "substantive" in the sense that it fails the modified outcome-determinative test. And a formal Federal Rule may not be applied if it impinges on "substantive" rights under the second subsection of the REA. However, "substance" must mean something different in the Federal Rules context than it does under the outcome-determinative test (hence the enig-

---

4. See *Hanna,* 380 U.S. at 476 (Harlan, J., concurring) (describing the majority's test for validity as "arguably procedural, *ergo* constitutional").

matic title of the chapter) or there would be no need for separate analyses under *Hanna* Part 1 and *Hanna* Part 2.

A Framework for Analysis

Although cases since *Hanna* have fine-tuned the analysis somewhat, *Erie, York, Byrd,* and *Hanna* provide the basic framework for determining when the federal court must defer to state law. What follows are some basic ground rules that should help you identify the proper arguments to make in such cases.

There are four basic types of federal provisions that may conflict with state law. *First,* a federal constitutional provision might mandate a federal court procedure that differs from state law (as, for example, requiring a unanimous jury verdict, even though state law would allow a majority verdict). *Second,* a federal statute may govern federal practice but conflict with state law. An example might be a statute that requires federal courts to enforce arbitration agreements, even though the courts of a state would not. *Third,* a formal Federal Rule of Civil Procedure may apply in federal court and conflict with state law, such as the conflicting service provisions in *Hanna. Last,* federal judges may develop judicial practices, that is, procedures applied as a matter of common practice not embodied in a Federal Rule or statute, which differ from state law (the situation discussed in *Hanna* Part 1). For example, federal judges may, as a matter of accepted judicial practice, comment to the jury on the evidence or allow alternate jurors to deliberate on cases or allow juries to decide certain issues, even though state practice is different. Each of these conflicts requires a slightly different analysis.[5]

A. Conflicts between a Federal Constitutional (wins) Provision and State Law

The United States Constitution is the "supreme Law of the Land." U.S. Const., Article VI, ¶2. Its provisions apply even if they conflict with state law, substantive or procedural, because we all agreed to that, by proxy, back in 1789, without any "ifs," "ands," "buts," or "outcome-determinative" modifiers. If the constitution mandates a practice different from state law, the constitutional requirement prevails. For example, if the seventh amendment requires unanimous jury verdicts (an issue still unclear at this writing), the federal court would apply that requirement in a diversity case even though state practice allowed majority verdicts, as some do.

---

5. This discussion, and my understanding of the entire *Erie* doctrine, owes much to the fine article by Westen and Lehman, Is There Life for *Erie* After the Death of Diversity, 78 Mich. L. Rev. 311 (1980). I highly recommend it to those who want to explore these issues further.

"procedural"

if valid, wins

B. Conflicts between a Federal Statute and State Law

If the conflict is between a federal statute and state law, the issue is whether the federal statute is valid. *Hanna* holds that Congress has the constitutional authority to enact statutes governing procedure in the federal courts if, "while falling in the uncertain area between substance and procedure, [they] are rationally capable of classification as either." *Hanna*, 380 U.S. at 472. The duty-to-trespassers rule in *Erie* would fail this test, but most statutes related to the litigation process will not. If this "arguably procedural" test is met, the statute must be applied if it conflicts with state practice because Congress has the authority to enact the statute, and valid federal statutes are the "supreme Law of the Land" even if they conflict with state law. U.S. Const., Article VI, ¶2.

In *Stewart Organization, Inc. v. Ricoh Corp.*, 487 U.S. 22 (1988), the Supreme Court upheld application of 28 U.S.C. §1404(a), governing transfer of cases between federal district courts, on this reasoning. In *Stewart* the Court found a state practice refusing to enforce forum selection clauses in conflict with §1404(a), which calls for case-by-case discretion in deciding whether to transfer a case. Since the question of which federal court should hear a particular case is "arguably procedural," the Court concluded that Congress has the power to enact §1404(a). Thus, the statute is valid and applies in federal court even if the state court would decide differently.

C. Conflicts between a Federal Rule and State Law

If a Federal Rule of Civil Procedure conflicts with state law, the Federal Rule applies if it is valid. *Hanna* Part 2. Congress has the constitutional power to authorize the Supreme Court to adopt a Federal Rule, *Hanna* concludes, if it is "rationally capable of being classified" as a procedural regulation. And the first section of the REA authorizes the Court to adopt the rule if it is procedural under the broad definition in *Sibbach,* that is, it "really regulates procedure — the judicial process for enforcing rights and duties recognized by substantive law and for justly administering remedy and redress for disregard or infraction of them." Virtually all Federal Rules will satisfy these broad tests. So the Federal Rules are valid, unless they "abridge, enlarge, or modify" a substantive right under the second subsection of the REA. (This exception is discussed further at p.163.)

D. Conflicts between a Federal Judicial Practice and State Law

Federal judges have to run their courtrooms. That means they often make rulings resolving recurring issues, which arise in the day-to-day administration of justice but are not addressed by the Constitution, federal statutes, or Federal Rules. Under *Erie* itself, such federal judicial practices are invalid if they purport to establish rules of primary behavior (like the duty to trespassers rule in *Erie*), which there is no federal constitutional power to make. In other cases, where the practice relates to the conduct of litigation (so that there is federal authority to make a separate rule), *Hanna* Part 1 indicates that a diversity court should still choose the state rule if the difference between it and the federal practice could prove "outcome determinative." The difference is outcome determinative if following a separate federal practice could lead to forum shopping or inequitable administration of the laws. Whether the difference leads to those evils may be problematic in a particular case, but at least it is fairly clear that the argument should be framed under *Hanna* Part 1.

Problems in Applying the Hanna *Analyses*

The principles above provide a framework for analyzing these eerie *Erie* problems. However, they do not answer the really hard questions which arise in working through the analysis. Here are some sticky parts:

- When is there a direct conflict between a federal statute or Rule and state law?

There is no need to choose between a Federal Rule or federal statute and state law unless there is a "direct conflict" between them, but it is not clear when such a conflict exists. Some cases have avoided displacing state law by concluding that there was no conflict between the Federal Rule and the state provision. In *Walker v. Armco Steel Corp.,* 446 U.S. 740 (1980), for example, the issue was whether the plaintiff had to file suit or serve process on the defendant within the limitations period. The plaintiff filed suit within the limitations period but did not serve the defendant with the summons and complaint until well after. The Supreme Court avoided a difficult *Hanna* Part 2 clash by holding that Federal Rule 3, which provides that a suit is commenced by filing, is not intended to govern when the limitations period is tolled; it only prescribes the point for calculating various time requirements under the Federal Rules (such as the time for filing an answer (Rule 12(a)), taking depositions (Rule 30(a)), or sending interrogatories (Rule 33(a))).

Since the *Walker* Court concluded that Rule 3 did not apply, it turned to *Hanna* Part 1 to determine whether tolling the limitations period upon filing rather than upon service was permissible as a *federal judicial practice.* The Court concluded that ignoring the state rule would lead to inequitable administration of the laws because the suit would go forward in federal court even though it would have been barred in state court under the state's tolling-upon-service rule.

A similar analysis must be done to determine whether a federal statute or constitutional provision will apply in the face of contrary state law. A federal statute will not "trump" state law unless the two conflict. There would be such a conflict, for example, if a federal statute required unanimous verdicts and state law provided for majority verdicts: The two would require contradictory procedures and could not coexist. But in other cases, in which there is no obvious contradiction in the terms of the state and federal provisions, it will be less clear whether both can apply without interfering with the operation of the federal provision.[6]

• When does a Federal Rule, which is constitutionally valid and "procedural" under the first subsection of the REA, violate the second subsection because it "abridges, enlarges, or modifies substantive rights"?

This is a real toughie. A short answer is "seldom"; very few cases have rejected use of a Federal Rule under this subsection of the REA.[7] The Federal Rule will have to have a substantial impact on a state policy unrelated to litigation to be declared invalid under the second paragraph of the REA, given the heavy presumption of validity for formal rules promulgated by the Court.

Various tests have been proposed to determine when a federal rule impermissibly trenches on state "substantive" rights to this extent. See, e.g., Ely, The Irrepressible Myth of *Erie,* 87 Harv. L. Rev. 693, 725 (1974) (a right is "substantive" in the REA sense if it is "granted for one or more nonprocedural reasons, for some purpose or purposes not having to do with the fairness or efficiency of the litigation process").

The Supreme Court has yet to meaningfully clarify the reach of this limiting language. However, the Court's recent treatment of the issue in *Burlington Northern R.R. Co. v. Woods,* 480 U.S. 1, 8 (1987), suggests that it is a very limited limit. The Court in *Burlington Northern* held that procedural rules that "incidentally" affect substantive rights are permissible under the second sentence of the REA and rather casually concluded that Federal Rule of Appellate Procedure 38 passes muster because it "affects only the process of enforcing litigants' rights and not the rights themselves." 480 U.S. at 8.

• What differences are sufficient to lead to "inequitable administration of the laws" under *Hanna* Part 1?

---

6. See, e.g., *Burlington Northern R.R. Co. v. Woods,* 480 U.S. 1 (1987), in which the Court found a conflict although there was a good argument that the two provisions could both be applied. See 480 U.S. at 6-8.

7. For some examples of cases that might fall afoul of this limitation, see Braman and Neumann, The Still Unrepressed Myth of *Erie,* 18 Balt. L. Rev. 403, 448, 456 (1989).

Here again, the cases provide a framework for analysis but little clarity as to how the court will apply the relevant concepts. *Hanna* Part 1's modified outcome-determinative test is certainly narrower than *York*'s, which required use of state law any time the difference could be outcome determinative.[8] But it evidently requires more deference to state law than the second section of the REA, which bars Federal Rules that abridge, enlarge, or modify substantive rights. Some practices will pass muster if the Court and Congress formally require them, but not if federal judges simply adopt them as a matter of practice.

For example, *Walker* held that the state practice of tolling the limitations period upon service must prevail over a contrary federal judicial practice but suggested that this difference would pass muster if the tolling-on-commencement rule were embodied in a formal Federal Rule, despite the effect on outcome. 446 U.S. at 753. Thus, there is a tough "substance/substance distinction" between the analysis under *Hanna* Part 1 and *Hanna* Part 2.

• What is the current status of *Byrd*?

It is not clear whether *Hanna* effectively displaces *Byrd*'s balancing of federal and state interests or whether *Byrd* somehow factors into at least the *Hanna* Part 1 analysis. If the cases are any indication, *Byrd* is very much alive: Many lower federal courts rely on *Byrd*'s emphasis on the importance of the federal interests as a factor in resolving conflicts under *Hanna* Part 1.[9] But it is not clear that this is the intent of *Hanna,* or, if it is, how the federal and state interests are to be weighed.

This introduction may not help you all that much in "answering" hard *Erie* problems. However, the discussion and the following examples should provide a framework for analyzing these problems, so that you will be able to properly search for applicable precedents and formulate your arguments in appropriate terms.

EXAMPLES

Collisions and Close Calls

1.   Assume that Colorado's comparative negligence statute provides that the plaintiff's recovery in a negligence case is to be reduced in proportion to his own negligence but that the plaintiff may not recover at all if his negli-

---

8. But see *Walker v. Armco Steel,* 446 U.S. at 743, in which the Court concluded that applying the federal rule would be inequitable because the case would go forward instead of being barred. This appears to simply resurrect the *York* outcome-determinative test.

9. See Braman and Neumann, 18 Balt. L. Rev. at 416-440 (reviewing many post-*Hanna* cases applying *Byrd* analysis).

gence was "as great as" the defendant's. The statute also specifies that the jury shall be instructed that the plaintiff will not recover if his negligence is as great as (or greater than) the defendant's.[10] The evident purpose of this provision is to let the jury know that, if they find the plaintiff 50 percent or more at fault, he will take nothing.

Assume that Morgan brings a diversity suit against Harriman in federal court for negligently causing a motor vehicle accident. The Colorado statute applies, but no one thinks to request the instruction on the effect of plaintiff's negligence. The jury is not so instructed and returns a finding that Morgan was 60 percent at fault. The judge enters judgment against Morgan, and he appeals, claiming a right to a new trial because the jury was not instructed in accordance with the statute.

The Colorado courts hold that a plaintiff in these circumstances is entitled to a new trial (at which the required instruction is given), even if he did not request the instruction. However, Fed. R. Civ. P. 51 provides that "[n]o party shall assign as error the giving or the failure to give an instruction unless that party objects thereto before the jury retires to consider its verdict. . . ." Harriman argues that Rule 51 applies, while Morgan argues that *Erie* principles require the court to follow Colorado law and order a new trial.

a. How would this issue be resolved under Justice Frankfurter's analysis in *York*?
b. How do you think it would come out after *Byrd*, but before *Hanna*?
c. If the case arose after *Hanna*, should the issue be analyzed under *Hanna* Part 1 or Part 2?
d. How would the issue be resolved under *Hanna* Part 2?
e. How would it come out if there were no Federal Rule on point, but federal judges followed a judicial practice of refusing to review errors that were not objected to below?

2. Morgan sues Harriman for negligence in federal court. The relevant state negligence law recognizes contributory negligence of the plaintiff as a complete defense and provides that the plaintiff bears the burden of proving that he was not negligent. Morgan argues, however, that the defendant should bear the burden of proving that he (Morgan) *was* negligent because Fed. R. Civ. P. 8(c) requires defendants to plead contributory negligence as an "affirmative defense." How should the court rule?

3. Assume that the *York* case arose immediately after *Hanna v. Plumer* was decided. How would the issue in *York* be decided under the principles of *Hanna*?

10. The Colorado comparative negligence statute contained such a provision for some years, but it has now been repealed. See Colo. Rev. Stat. §13-21-111(4), as amended by 1975 Colo. Sess. Laws 570, §1; repealed by 1986 Colo. Sess. Laws 679, §5.

4.   Assume that the judges in the courts of the state of Aroostook, as a matter of judicial practice, give the jury instructions in writing, but that the federal judicial practice is to read the instructions to the jury without giving them a copy. Underwood sues Drew for negligence in federal court. Because jurisdiction is based on diversity, Aroostook law governs the underlying negligence claim. Must the federal judge instruct the jury in writing?

The Ultimate Test

5.   Assume that the Aroostook legislature has enacted a statute authorizing its supreme court to promulgate rules of procedure for the Aroostook courts, and it has adopted Aroos. R. Civ. P. 49(c), which requires the judge to give the jury a written copy of the instructions. Assume further that federal judges, as a matter of judicial practice, instruct the jury orally. Underwood sues Drew for negligence in the federal court. Aroostook law again governs the underlying negligence claim. Must the federal judge instruct the jury in writing?

Switching Tracks

6.   Clinton brings a diversity suit in federal court against Fisk for negligence. To prove Fisk's negligence, Clinton offers two days of testimony by an eminent (and expensive) expert on accident reconstruction. Clinton wins at trial, and moves to collect as "costs" a $10,000 fee he paid to the expert to review the facts, perform experiments, and prepare for trial. The relevant federal statute, 28 U.S.C. §1920, provides that the prevailing party may recover certain limited types of costs of suit from the losing party. These costs include a $40-per-day attendance fee for witnesses who testify at trial, but include no provision for recovering an expert's fee for preparing for trial. By contrast, a state statute provides that the prevailing party in a negligence case may recover the full costs of retaining expert witnesses.

    a. Is there a conflict between the federal and state statutes? *y*

    b. How should the judge rule on the motion?

7.   The State of Aroostook, concerned by skyrocketing medical malpractice insurance premiums, passes a statute limiting recovery for intangible damages (such as pain, suffering, and emotional distress) in malpractice cases. The statute provides that recovery for intangible injuries from any incident shall not exceed $250,000 and that such damages shall be determined by the judge. Morgan sues Dr. Drew in federal court for medical malpractice. The judge concludes that, under the seventh amendment, the jury must determine the intangible damages in federal court and that it need not apply the cap in the Aroostook statute. The jury returns a verdict for Morgan, which includes $400,000 for pain and suffering.

    Dr. Drew appeals, arguing that the federal court should have followed the Aroostook statute, since its jurisdiction is based on diversity. Thus, the

$250,000 cap on damages should apply, and the judge rather than the jury should assess the damages for intangible injuries. Morgan argues that the verdict should be upheld, since the seventh amendment mandates jury trial of factual issues such as the amount of the damages — which it does. How should the court rule?

The Late Train

8.   Morgan sues Harriman but discovers after the passage of the limitations period that it was actually Gould who was driving the car that hit him, not Harriman. He seeks to amend his complaint to name Gould as a defendant. The relevant state law does not allow amendments to add a defendant who was not sued and served within the limitations period. Assume that Federal Rule 15(c), however, allows a plaintiff to amend the complaint to add a party if the party: 1) received notice of the action within the limitations period; and 2) knew that, "but for a mistake concerning the identity of the proper party," the action would have been against him. Assume that Harriman was aware of the suit within the limitations period and that he was actually the intended defendant. Morgan argues that, since the requirements of Rule 15(c) are satisfied, the amendment should be allowed. Should the court allow the amendment?

9.   Assume that the same version of Federal Rule 15(c) applies, but the state in which Morgan brings his action has a statute that provides:

> In any civil action, the court may, at any time, allow an amendment adding or changing a party, and allow any other amendment in matter of form or substance which may enable the plaintiff to sustain the action for the cause or recovery for which the action was intended to be brought. Such an amendment shall relate back to the time of the original pleading.[11]

After the passage of the limitations period, Morgan makes a motion in the federal action to name Gould as a defendant. Assume that Gould had no prior notice that Morgan intended to sue him. What rule should the court apply?

EXPLANATIONS

Collisions and Close Calls

1a.   In *York,* Justice Frankfurter concluded that federal courts should follow state rules if the difference between the state and the federal rules could be "outcome determinative." If *York*'s outcome-determinative test were applied to this example, there appears little doubt that the court would have to defer

---

11. This statute is an edited version of a statute recently enacted in Massachusetts. See Mass. Gen. L. ch.231, §51.

to state law. If the federal court sticks with its rule, Morgan loses because the appellate court will not consider the error. But if the federal court applies the Colorado approach, Morgan will get a new trial. At the new trial, the jury will be told the effect of finding Morgan more at fault and may well find him less faulty (say, perhaps, 49 percent?). Of course, we can't say Morgan will definitely win if he gets the new trial, just as the *York* Court could not say for sure that the plaintiffs there would win if they were allowed to proceed to trial. However, applying the federal rule could make a difference, so the *York* test would require use of the state rule.

b. The Court in *Byrd* reaffirmed that the federal courts *must* follow state rules that define the "rights and obligations" of the parties. 356 U.S. at 535. This presumably refers to those clearly "substantive" rights, which (as *Erie* declared) the federal government has no authority to create. This matter of instructing the jury, however, seems more like a "matter of form and mode" for the conduct of the litigation itself, as to which there is federal authority to apply a separate rule. *Byrd* reaffirmed that the federal court should generally defer to state rules even in matters of "form and mode," if they are likely to be outcome determinative, in order to implement the policy of uniformity pronounced in *Erie* and reaffirmed in *York*. 356 U.S. at 536-537. Thus, unless affirmative countervailing considerations require application of the federal rule, *Byrd* would also support application of the state practice in this case.

A problem with the *Byrd* analysis is that it does not specify what federal policies will outweigh the *Erie/York* policy of assuring that diversity cases come out the same in state and federal court. Here, the federal objection rule is meant to assure that objections are presented to the trial court so they can be considered and resolved there, thus reducing errors and appeals. That is certainly a meaningful policy, aimed at increasing accuracy and efficiency of federal trials, but it is probably not such an overriding "countervailing consideration" as to outweigh *Erie*'s policy of uniformity. It certainly isn't as lofty a concern as the constitutional right to jury trial implicated in *Byrd*.

c. As the introduction states, where there is a direct conflict between a state rule or statute and a Federal Rule of Civil Procedure, the court must analyze the problem under *Hanna* Part 2. Here the Colorado practice (ordering a new trial if the instruction is left out) and Fed. R. Civ. P. 51 (barring reversal if no objection is made) are clearly incompatible. The court will affirm the verdict for the defendant if it follows the Federal Rule but will reverse if it follows state law. Thus, there is a direct conflict, and the REA analysis of *Hanna* Part 2 applies.

d. There can be little doubt about the Court's authority to promulgate Rule 51. On the constitutional level, it is certainly "arguably procedural," since it governs the process of instructing the jury at trial and reviewing those instructions on appeal. It also passes muster under the similar test of "procedurality" under the first subsection of the REA, since it relates to "the judicial process for enforcing rights and duties recognized by substantive law. . . ." Thus, it is valid unless it "abridge[s], enlarge[s], or modif[ies]" substantive rights: The second subsection of the REA prohibits enacting rules — even procedural rules — that alter substantive rights.

As discussed in the introduction, it is at this stage that the analysis becomes murky. Professor Ely would ask whether the statute was enacted for any "nonprocedural" reason. Interestingly, the Colorado provision involved here was not found in Colorado's procedural code, but was part of the comparative negligence statute itself, suggesting a "nonprocedural" purpose. While it governs behavior in the courtroom, it is evidently aimed at affecting the substantive outcome of suits: More plaintiffs will win if juries know that they must be less than 50 percent at fault to recover.

Despite this argument, the case on which this example is based concluded (relying on Ely's article!) that following Rule 51 would not transgress the restriction in the second paragraph of the REA:

> This effect [denying review of the failure to give the instruction] however, is not an enlargement, abridgment or modification of the comparative negligence doctrine, which is the substantive rule of law at issue. It is rather a procedural directive, aimed at augmenting the fairness and efficiency of the litigation process in federal court.

Platis v. Stockwell, 630 F.2d 1202, 1206 (7th Cir. 1980). This reasoning, of course, is circular: The Rule does not abridge substantive rights because it is procedural. But, despite the Ely test, my sense is that most courts would reach the same conclusion, based on the heavy presumption of validity that *Hanna* accords to the Federal Rules and the fact that the plaintiff can avoid any abridgement of the "right" involved by the simple expedient of asking for the instruction.

e. If the refusal to grant a new trial in the absence of an objection were a matter of federal judicial practice, rather than a Federal Rule, the analysis would proceed under *Hanna* Part 1. This may be an example of a rule that would be "substantive" under *Hanna* Part 1, although it does not affect "substantive" rights under *Hanna* Part 2. Under *Hanna* Part 1, the question would be whether the twin aims of *Erie* would be compromised by allowing the federal courts to ignore the state statute in favor of their usual practice. It is very clear that using the federal practice instead of the state statute would *not* lead to forum shopping. Any plaintiff who knows about the jury instruction rule would have no need to base his forum choice on the difference: He would simply be sure to ask for the instruction in either court, so the difference would make no difference!

However, it would arguably be "inequitable administration of the laws" for the federal court to refuse a new trial where a state court would be bound to grant one. Compare *Walker v. Armco,* in which the Court concluded that it would foster inequitable administration of the laws to allow a suit to go forward in federal court that would be barred in state court.[12]

2.   The first issue here is whether there is a direct conflict between the state practice requiring the plaintiff to prove that he is free of negligence and Fed. R. Civ. P. 8(c). If there is such a conflict, the court must consider whether Rule 8(c) is valid under the REA. It certainly is "procedural" under the first sentence of the REA, since it regulates the process of proof at trial. However, it is a tough question whether the Rule would "abridge, enlarge, or modify" a substantive right under the second paragraph of the REA. The burden of proof can have a profound impact on the case, particularly where one or both of the parties is unable to produce evidence (as, for example, when one of the parties is killed in the accident).

In *Palmer v. Hoffman,* 318 U.S. 109 (1943), the Supreme Court nicely avoided tackling this REA issue by concluding that there is no direct conflict between Rule 8(c) and state burden of proof rules. The *Palmer* Court concluded that Rule 8(c) only addresses who must *plead* contributory negligence, not who bears the burden of proof on it. Based on this cramped reading of the Rule, the Court concluded that there was no conflict with state law, since federal law said nothing about who bore the burden of proof. Consequently, the state rule applied. As in *Walker v. Armco,* the Court construed the Rule narrowly to avoid a hard problem under the second section of the REA.

3.   *York* involved a conflict between a state statute and a federal judicial practice, not a formal rule or statute. Thus, it presents the "relatively unguided" *Erie* choice analyzed in *Hanna* Part 1. The Court would have to consider whether allowing federal courts to use their own limitations principles would lead to forum shopping or inequitable administration of the laws.

Very likely, ignoring the state limitations period in federal court would encourage both of these "twin evils." Clearly, a plaintiff whose claim was barred under the state statute would shop for the federal forum if the claim might not be barred under federal limitations principles. And, as the Court

---

12. Many differences look "inequitable" if viewed retrospectively, but not if viewed prospectively. The difference here, for example, hardly seems inequitable when viewed at the outset of the litigation: Any inequity can be avoided by careful trial planning. But looking back, after the plaintiff has failed to seek the instruction, the difference is crucial to his case.

The Court in *Hanna* Part 1 appeared to call for a prospective analysis. It emphasized that the prospective burden to comply with the two rules was not very different, though the plaintiff could no longer comply with the state rule at all at the time of the appeal. However, in *Walker* the Court appeared to revert to a retrospective approach, relying on the fact that the plaintiff would lose if the state rule applied but might win if allowed to proceed in federal court. 446 U.S. at 753.

concluded in analogous circumstances in *Walker,* allowing such dramatic disparity in results would be inequitable:

> There is simply no reason why, in the absence of a controlling federal rule, an action based on state law which concededly would be barred in the state courts by the state statute of limitations should proceed through litigation to judgment in federal court solely because of the fortuity that there is diversity of citizenship between the litigants.

446 U.S. at 753.

4.   This case should be analyzed under *Hanna* Part 1, since the conflict is between a judge-made federal practice and state practice. The issue is whether the difference between written instructions and oral instructions will trigger the "twin evils" of forum shopping and inequitable administration of the laws. Neither seems at all likely from such a relatively minor discrepancy between state and federal practice. *First,* it is unlikely that a litigant would choose federal court based on this procedural difference; if he is concerned that the jury clearly understands a particular instruction, he can make sure the judge instructs on it clearly and emphasize it in closing argument, rather than make the choice of forum turn on it.

Nor is there a substantial inequity in allowing this discrepancy between the administration of diversity cases in federal court and similar cases in state court. For one thing, it is not at all clear that it favors one litigant over the other, or (if it does) which one it will be in any particular case. Further, as suggested, any anticipated problem can probably be alleviated by careful argument to the jury. Thus, the federal court should apply this simple "housekeeping rule" despite contrary state practice, since doing so will not foster the "twin evils" discussed in *Hanna* Part 1.

The Ultimate Test

5.   If this example did not throw you off the track, you are well on your way to understanding the *Erie* doctrine. The analysis here is so straightforward that it's almost impossible to get it right.

In all of these cases, *it is the nature of the federal provision, not the competing state provision,* that determines the analysis. The issue is when *federal law,* whether made by the framers, Congress, the Supreme Court, or federal judicial practice, is valid and therefore applies in federal court. If the federal provision is valid it prevails over a contrary state provision, whether found in the state constitution, a state statute or rule, or a state judicial practice.

A federal judicial practice is valid federal law if it governs the litigation process and passes the *Hanna* Part 1 test. The oral instruction rule here is valid, since the difference between the federal practice of giving oral instructions to the jury and the state written-instruction rule is unlikely to lead to forum shopping or inequitable administration of the laws. Consequently, the federal court may follow its own practice despite contrary state law. See example 4. It does not matter that the state provision is found in a formal Rule. The question is not whether a "higher" form of law (such as a constitutional provision, statute, or Rule) prevails over a "lower" one (such as a judicial practice). The question is whether the federal provision, from whatever source derived, is valid and applicable.

On the same analysis, a Federal Rule that passes muster under the constitutional and statutory analysis of *Hanna* Part 2 is valid federal law, which will apply despite a conflicting state provision, even if the state provision is found in a state constitution or statute. This is because federal law, made with the authority to make it, is the "supreme Law of the Land." See *Hanna* Part 2, in which the Court held that the Federal Rule prevailed over a state statute. See also *Hanna* Part 1, where the Court stated that the federal last-and-usual service provision would prevail over the state statute, even if it was a matter of judicial practice rather than a formal rule. 380 U.S. at 466-469.

Switching Tracks

6a.   Clinton will probably argue that the two statutes are not in conflict. The federal statute only addresses the costs for a witness's testimony at trial; since it says nothing about fees for experts' preparation time, the matter is not covered by the federal statute, there is no direct conflict, and the issue should be analyzed under *Hanna* Part 1. This argument makes some sense, but it has been rejected by the Supreme Court. In *Crawford Fitting Co. v. J.T. Gibbons, Inc.*, 482 U.S. 437 (1987), the Court held that the statute, by specifying those items that may be recovered as costs, implicitly rejects taxing others, such as the expert's preparation fee. See 482 U.S. at 441-443 (§§1920 and 1821 "comprehensively addressed" the taxation of fees for litigant's witnesses, barring further fees for expert witnesses). Since the state statute allows full reimbursement for expert witness expenses, while the federal statute only authorizes minimal attendance fees, the two are in direct conflict.

b.   Assuming that there is a direct conflict between the state and federal statutes, the federal statute governs, if it is constitutional, because the Constitution provides that federal statutes are the "supreme Law of the Land." U.S. Const., Article VI.

The Court's discussion in *Hanna* certainly supports the conclusion that these cost statutes are constitutional under Article III and the Necessary and Proper Clause. *Hanna* concludes that Congress has power under those provisions to "regulate matters which, though falling within the uncertain area between substance and procedure, are rationally capable of classification as either." 380 U.S. at 472. A statute specifying which expenses in the conduct of a lawsuit may be collected by the winning party can rationally be classified as procedural. Thus, Congress had the power to enact this statute, and the statute applies despite the contrary state law.

Note that the second paragraph of the REA is irrelevant to this analysis.

That provision limits *the Supreme Court's rule-making authority*, not Congress's own power to enact procedural statutes. Only the Constitution does that, and the constitutional authority (so says *Hanna*) is broad enough to encompass a statute of this sort, since it can rationally be classified as addressing a procedural issue.

7.   Interestingly, the analysis of this example doesn't have much to do with *Byrd*. In *Byrd* the "influence" of the seventh amendment lurked in the background, but it appears that it did not directly *require* that the jury decide the question. Here, by contrast, the seventh amendment directly conflicts with the state statute. That statute requires the judge to make the factual finding as to the amount of the intangible damages, while the seventh amendment requires factual questions such as the amount of damages to be decided by the jury.

Because there is a direct conflict between the constitutional provision and the state statute, the analysis derives from Part 2 of *Hanna*. That analysis makes clear that if a federal statute or rule is valid and covers the issue, the federal court must apply it. A fortiori, if a constitutional provision applies, it will control despite a contrary state statute or practice. U.S. Const., Article VI. Thus, since the assessment of Morgan's damages is an issue of fact, it must be decided by the jury if suit is brought in federal court.[13]

However, the type and measure of damages recoverable in a tort case is a classically "substantive" issue, in the basic *Erie* sense. States are free to expand, define, or eliminate tort causes of action. See *Martinez v. California*, 444 U.S. 277, 282 (1980). The Aroostook legislature could eliminate recovery for intangible damages entirely; it may also establish a cap on such damages instead. By doing so, the statute creates a state law "right" (or, better phrased, partial *immunity* for doctors), which must be honored under the command of *Erie* to follow state law on issues where only the states have the authority to create it. Thus, the $250,000 limit on damages for intangible injuries will apply in Morgan's federal action. The judge should enter judgment on the jury's verdict but reduce the amount for intangible damages to $250,000.

The Late Train

8.   This is a direct conflict case: State law would bar the amendment, but Gould could be brought in if the version of Fed. R. Civ. P. 15(c) given in the example applies. Because the conflict is between a formal federal rule and a

---

13. The seventh amendment does not apply to the courts of the states. However, all state constitutions include a similar guarantee of jury trial. The statute hypothesized here might be unconstitutional under the Aroostook constitution but is still useful for illustration purposes.

state practice, the analysis comes under *Hanna* Part 2. There appears to be little doubt that Rule 15(c) is within the "arguably procedural" arena, so that Congress may authorize federal courts to apply their own rules. There is also little doubt that it passes muster under the first subsection of the REA, since it regulates the "judicial process for enforcing rights and duties recognized by substantive law. . . ."

The battleground in this case will be under the limiting language of the second subsection of the REA. Does the rule, which extends the right to sue a party beyond the limitations period, "abridge, enlarge, or modify" a substantive right? There is a nice analysis of this conflict in Westen and Lehman's article, 78 Mich. L. Rev. at 363-364. They argue that the "substantive" purpose of a limitation period is to provide notice to the defendant within the limitations period. Because the federal rule in the example only allows the amendment if the defendant has such notice and is aware that he is the intended target of the suit, this substantive purpose is not "abridged" and Rule 15(c) is valid. There is some difference in the state and federal approaches, but it is not sufficiently substantial to violate the REA limitation concerning substantive rights. In effect, there is a difference, but it does not significantly trench upon the policy underlying the state's approach, so (the authors conclude) it is a tolerable difference. See 19 Wright and Miller §4509, at 149-150 for a similar analysis.

9.   There is also a direct conflict between the statute and the Rule in this case: The amendment may be allowed under the state rule but would not be permissible under the version of Fed. R. Civ. P. 15(c) in this example, since Gould had no notice within the limitations period that anyone intended to sue him. Thus, a *Hanna* Part 2 analysis is again in order.

In this case there is a dramatic difference between the state statute and the Federal Rule. In example 8 the state rule required notice within the limitations period, and the Federal Rule, while slightly more liberal, did too. Here, however, the state rule is much more indulgent than the Federal Rule. It allows Morgan to amend to sue a person who had no notice of the action within the limitations period, so long as he sued *somebody* before that period expired. Thus, Morgan's possibilities are a great deal broader under the state statute than under the federal version.

On the constitutional level, the analysis is the same as in example 8. The federal government has authority to regulate procedure in the federal courts, including matters like this, which, while within the "uncertain area between substance and procedure," can rationally be classified as procedural. Further, the first section of the REA authorizes the rule, since it regulates court procedure.

The problem, again, is that nasty second subsection of the REA, and this time it is a much more substantial problem. There is a dramatic difference between the reach of Rule 15(c) (as set forth in the example) and the state statute. The policy behind the state statute is to maximize litigants' ability to assert causes of action, at the expense of the policy of repose behind limitations periods. Rule 15(c) draws a very different balance between these policies. This is an example, I think, where the difference so affects the right to recover that it would abridge state substantive rights to apply the federal rule. Cf. *Marshall v. Mulrenin,* 508 F.2d 39 (1st Cir. 1974) (reaching the same conclusion under an earlier version of this statute); see also 19 Wright and Miller at 152-158.

For many years Rule 15(c) contained the provisions stated in example 8. However, in 1991 the Court amended Rule 15 to provide that an amendment will relate back if it would relate back under state law. Fed. R. Civ. P. 15(c)(1). Evidently the rulemakers were concerned about the validity of Rule 15(c) under the second subsection of the REA and therefore amended it to conform to state law in cases such as this. Under new Rule 15(c), Morgan's amendment would be proper, and the potential problem under the second subsection is avoided.[14]

---

14. However, the amended version of Rule 15 says nothing about the situation illustrated by example 8, in which the state practice is more restrictive than the federal relation back rule.

11

Erie *and State Choice of Law: Vertical Uniformity and Horizontal Chaos*

Introduction

Chapter 9 suggests that the whole *Erie* problem was the framers' fault, for creating a federal form of government. See p.134. But that isn't really true. *Another* part of the problem is the colonists' fault because they settled in separate colonies. Those colonies developed more or less independently for 150 years before they became states and retain a great deal of autonomy under our constitution. This autonomy — from each other as well as from federal control — has some very interesting consequences for our judicial system.

A fundamental consequence, not generally appreciated, is that "the law" governing many types of claims can differ from state to state. The law of torts can be, and often is, one thing in Rome, Wisconsin, and another in Athens, Ohio. As "Easy *Erie*" explains, there is no general federal authority to "make" common law in areas such as tort law, so each state has to make its own. Also, there is nothing in the Constitution or in nature that says Wisconsin has to make the same tort law that Ohio does. Very frequently they don't, so that a tort case might come out differently if it were decided under Ohio law than it would if it were decided under Wisconsin law. The same is true in many other areas, such as commercial law, probate, contracts, and property. In this respect, the states are a little like independent countries, each of which has the authority to choose the proper rules of law to apply to its own cases.

This phenomenon, that the 50 states may have 50 different rules on the duty of care to a trespasser, or the enforcement of exclusive contracts, is in itself surprising but tolerable. It is part of the price we pay for having a system of divided sovereignty, in which the states retain the power to make law in the many areas not delegated to the federal government. But this doctrine of state autonomy has a very unruly stepchild, the problem of "choice of law," which bedevils state courts as well as federal ones. This chapter explores the interaction of *Erie*'s state law mandate with the curious quagmire* known as choice of law.

The Dismal Swamp: The Problem of Choosing the Proper State Law

The problem of choice of law is exactly what the phrase suggests, the need to choose a body of substantive law to apply to the dispute before the court. The *Erie* case itself involved a choice of law problem, since the Supreme Court had to determine whether federal courts in diversity cases were free to choose "federal common law" or were required to follow state law. But choice of law problems also arise when the plaintiff sues in *state* court, and the state court must choose whether to apply its own law to the claim or the law of another state.

The answer may appear obvious: The court should apply its *own* law, that is, the law of the state where the suit is brought. If Pogo sues Albert in Ohio for injuries suffered in a boat collision, the Ohio court should apply Ohio law. If he sues in Wisconsin, that court should apply Wisconsin law. Adopting this as the universal choice of law rule would have one great advantage: Everyone would know what law would be applied in each court, and there would be no litigation over choice of law.

Despite the simplicity of this choice of law rule, courts have not opted to apply their own substantive law in all cases, for several reasons. *First,* this approach would obviously encourage plaintiffs like Pogo to "forum shop" by suing in the state with the "best" (i.e., the most Pogo-oriented) tort law. Suppose, for example, that Wisconsin applies contributory negligence, which would bar recovery if Pogo was negligent in any degree, but Ohio applies comparative negligence, which would allow him to recover but would reduce that recovery to account for his negligence. If Ohio always applied its own law, and Pogo was 10 percent at fault, he could sue in Ohio and recover 90

---

* The "quagmire" and "dismal swamp" metaphors are from Prosser's famous quotation, see p.179.

percent of his damages. However, if he brought the suit in Wisconsin, he would get nothing.[1] That's a big difference. If Ohio's courts always chose to apply its own law, Ohio could become a magnet for tort cases that had no relation to that state or had more significant connections with other states.

In addition, as a matter of policy, it seems unwise to decide a controversy under a substantive rule completely foreign to the events in dispute. If Pogo lived in Wisconsin when the accident took place, the accident took place in Wisconsin, and Albert is a Wisconsin citizen, it would make little sense to apply Ohio law to the case, even if, for one reason or another, Pogo could sue in Ohio. The events and the parties had substantial connections to Wisconsin, but none at all to Ohio. At the time of acting, the parties had no expectation that Ohio law would determine the legal consequences of their conduct. In addition, Ohio has little interest in regulating or compensating this occurrence, but Wisconsin does. Pogo's choice of an Ohio court looks like a blatant attempt to avoid application of Wisconsin's contributory negligence rule to a Wisconsin accident between Wisconsin citizens. In such cases, where the case has little connection to the forum state but strong connections to another, many states would choose to apply the substantive law of the other state.

Similarly, suppose that Schulansky, from Massachusetts, goes to New Hampshire to meet with Ronan, a New Hampshire contractor. They negotiate there for the construction of an addition to her vacation home in Alton, New Hampshire, and enter into an agreement there for the work. If Schulansky has a problem with the quality of the work and sues Ronan in Massachusetts, the court would likely decide that the dispute has such significant ties to New Hampshire, and so few to Massachusetts, that it ought to be decided under New Hampshire contract law. Again, the result may be that a court in one state hears the suit but chooses to apply the substantive law of another.

Intellectual Quicksand: Approaches to Choice of Law

If courts do not always apply the law of the state in which they sit, they need to develop "choice of law" rules for deciding when they will choose the law of another state instead. They have done so, and they are indeed a quagmire:

> The realm of the conflict of laws is a dismal swamp, filled with quaking quagmires, and inhabited by learned but eccentric professors who theorize about mysterious matters in a strange and incomprehensible jargon. The ordinary court, or a lawyer, is quite lost when engulfed and entangled in it.

---

1. Whether Pogo *can* sue in Ohio (or Wisconsin, or Idaho, or any other state) depends on the three ring analysis explored in Part One. Often, Pogo will be able to satisfy the rings in a number of states, potentially giving him a choice of substantive tort rules as well as forums.

W. Prosser, Interstate Publication, 51 Mich. L. Rev. 959, 971 (1953).

Stated less poetically, the various approaches that courts use for choosing the proper law in cases with connections to several states are complicated and in flux. The rules used to be fairly mechanical, based on "objective" connections between the claim and the state. See W. Richman and W. Reynolds, Understanding Conflict of Laws, pp.131-152 (1984) (describing the "vested rights" principles of the First Restatement of Conflicts of Laws). Under the First Restatement approach, tort cases were usually determined under the law of the place of injury, contracts cases under the law of the place of making, and property cases under the law of the place where the property was located. It wasn't quite that neat, but that was the general idea. Under this approach Pogo's case would be decided under Wisconsin law (where the injury occurred), and Schulansky's under New Hampshire law (where the contract was made).

Many courts have concluded that the First Restatement principles are too mechanical to yield satisfying solutions to choice of law problems. Led primarily by conflicts scholars, they have attempted to formulate choice of law rules that are more responsive to underlying policy considerations. One "modern" approach to conflicts of law weighs the interests of each affected state in applying its law to the case. See Richman & Reynolds at 174-191 (describing the "interest analysis" approach to conflicts). Suppose that Churchy and Howland, two Florida neighbors, decide to take a canoe trip in the Okefenokee Swamp, just over the Georgia border. A half mile into Georgia, the canoe swamps due to poor maintenance, causing serious injuries to Howland, who is hospitalized in Florida and permanently disabled. The First Restatement would require the court to apply the "lex loci delicti," the law of the place where the injury occurred, which is Georgia. However, a court that applies an "interest analysis" approach to conflicts might conclude that Florida has a greater interest in the case than Georgia, since the parties are domiciled there, the injured plaintiff was treated there, and the negligent maintenance, which caused the accident, took place there. Thus, "interest analysis" might lead the court to apply Florida law.

Another current approach to conflicts problems is to apply the law of the state with the "most significant relationship" to the case, in light of various policy considerations, including the expectations of the parties, the policy interests of the states with connections to the case, uniformity in enforcement, and others. See Richman and Reynolds at 157-174 (describing the approach of the Second Restatement of Conflict of Laws to torts, contracts and property issues). There are also other approaches and variations on all of them.[2] It is not crucial for our purposes to understand these theories, but

---

2. See *Ferens v. John Deere Co.*, 494 U.S. 516, 538 (1990) (Scalia, J., dissenting) (variety in state approaches to choice of law "has become kaleidoscopic"). Take the course in conflicts of laws if you want to delve into these mysteries. It is a fascinating area and useful background for law practice.

rather to realize that *different approaches exist*, that they may lead the court in one state to choose different substantive law than another would apply to the same case, and that the selection of the applicable law will depend on the choice of law approach of the court in which the suit is filed.

Quirks in the Quagmire: Federal Courts Choosing State Law

The situation is made even more complicated by the fact that the plaintiff often has the choice not only of state courts in different states, but also federal courts in each of those states. Suppose, for example, that Pogo, now an Ohio citizen, sues Albert, from Wisconsin, for his injuries in the Wisconsin accident. Because the parties are diverse, Pogo may choose federal court and chooses the federal district court in Ohio. What law should that court apply? Clearly, the answer under *Erie* is "state law," since it is a diversity case. That is not the whole answer, however, because there are several states whose law might apply. Should the federal court choose Ohio law or Wisconsin law?

Three years after *Erie,* the Supreme Court answered this question in *Klaxon v. Stentor Manufacturing Co.,* 313 U.S. 487 (1941). In *Klaxon,* the Court held that the policy underlying *Erie* mandates the application of the forum state's choice of law rules as well as its substantive law:

> We are of opinion that the prohibition declared in *Erie R. Co. v. Tompkins,* 304 U.S. 64, against such independent determinations by the federal courts, extends to the field of conflicts of laws. The conflict of laws rules to be applied by the federal court in Delaware must conform to those prevailing in Delaware's state courts. Otherwise, the accident of diversity of citizenship would constantly disturb equal administration of justice in coordinate state and federal courts sitting side by side.

313 U.S. at 496 (footnote omitted). Under *Klaxon,* the federal court must do whatever the state court within that state would do. If an Ohio state judge would choose Ohio law, so must the federal judge if the case is brought in an Ohio federal district court. If the Ohio state judge would choose Wisconsin law, the federal judge in Ohio must do so as well.

The *Klaxon* rule makes a certain amount of sense, as a matter of policy. *Erie* teaches that plaintiffs should not obtain an advantage due to the "accident of diversity," which they would not have in state court. If the state court would apply Ohio tort law to Pogo's case, but the federal court were free to choose Wisconsin's, the case could still come out differently simply because Pogo was able to invoke diversity jurisdiction. In the words of Judge Magruder, if federal diversity courts could follow their own choice of law rules, "the ghost of *Swift v. Tyson* . . . still walks abroad, somewhat shrunken in size, but capable of much mischief." *Sampson v. Channell,* 110 F.2d 754, 761 (1st Cir. 1940). The *Klaxon* rule puts the ghost to rest, since the federal court must again do whatever the state court would.

Klaxon has been met with some skepticism by the scholars. Although *Erie* clearly requires diversity courts to apply state law, it is certainly arguable that it is both constitutional and appropriate for a federal court to choose *which state's law* to apply in diversity cases. Choice of law involves the relations among the states, and the framers might well have considered that a federal diversity court should be available to litigants as a neutral decisionmaker in choosing the proper body of state law. See, e.g., H. Hart, The Relations Between State and Federal Law, 54 Colum. L. Rev. 489, 514-515 (1954) (arguing that *Klaxon* impedes development of conflicts law and promotes forum shopping).

Whatever the merits of these arguments may be, the Supreme Court continues to adhere to the *Klaxon* rule. The issue was raised again in *Day & Zimmerman v. Challoner,* 423 U.S. 3 (1975), a case involving strict liability claims for serious injuries to military personnel in Cambodia during the Vietnam War. The *Klaxon* approach required application of the Texas conflicts of law rule to the case, which in turn would lead to application of Cambodian law, which did not recognize strict liability. Despite these implications, the Supreme Court unanimously reaffirmed *Klaxon* in a brief per curiam opinion.[3]

Because *Klaxon* requires the federal court in a diversity case to apply the conflicts law that would be applied by the courts of the state in which it sits, the combination of *Klaxon* and *Erie* produces substantial "vertical uniformity" between the state and federal courts within each state. However, a side effect of the two decisions is to destroy "horizontal uniformity" among the federal courts in different states. If Ohio would apply Ohio's comparative negligence principle to Pogo's accident, and Michigan would apply Michigan's contributory negligence law, the federal court in Ohio will apply a different rule than the federal court in Michigan would. Thus, *Erie* has not ended the game of forum shopping for a more favorable substantive law, it has just changed the rules of that game. Instead of choosing between federal and state court to obtain more favorable substantive law, plaintiffs may get the same result by choosing between federal courts in different states or between state courts in different states.

The following examples illustrate the effect of *Erie* and *Klaxon* on the law applied to the facts of the *Erie* case. Assume that all example cases arise after *Erie* and *Klaxon* were decided. After these examples, we will wade a little

---

3. *Challoner* is a nice example of a situation in which interest analysis would yield a different result than the place-of-the-injury rule. The plaintiffs in *Challoner* were American servicemen; the defendant was an American corporation; and the shell that caused the injury was manufactured in Texas. As the Fifth Circuit pointed out in its opinion (reversed on other grounds by the Supreme Court), Cambodia had no interest in enforcing its fault requirement under the circumstances, while Texas had a substantial interest in applying its strict liability policy to the claim. See 512 F.2d at 80.

further into the mire by considering the implications of transfer of venue under 28 U.S.C. §1404(a).

EXAMPLES
Wading In

1.   The unfortunate Harry Tompkins, Jr., a Pennsylvania citizen, is injured while walking on a track along the Erie Railroad near Hughestown, Pennsylvania. Evidently he was hit by an object, perhaps a door, projecting from the side of the train. He brings suit in federal court, based on diversity, against the Erie Railroad, a New York corporation with its principal place of business in New York.

Assume that, under Pennsylvania law, a trespasser like Tompkins is only entitled to recover if the railroad's conduct was wilful and wanton. New York law, on the other hand, holds railroads to a duty of due care to trespassers on a frequently used pathway along the tracks. Assume further that the Pennsylvania choice of law rule requires the court to apply the law of the place of the injury (lex loci delicti) in tort cases, and that the New York choice of law rule is the same.

   a. If Tompkins sues in a state court in Pennsylvania, what standard of care rule should the court apply?
   b. If Tompkins sues in a federal court in Pennsylvania, what standard of care rule should the court apply?
   c. If Tompkins sues in a state court in New York, what standard of care rule should the court apply?
   d. If Tompkins sues in a federal court in New York, what standard of care rule should the court apply?

2.   On the same basic facts, assume that Pennsylvania tort law requires a showing of wilful and wanton conduct under the circumstances, and that it applies the place-of-the-injury choice of law rule. However, New York applies a due care standard to trespassers in Tompkins, Jr.'s position, and New York's choice of law rule involves a balancing of interests, which would lead to the application of New York law on the facts of Tompkins's case.

   a. If Tompkins sues in a state court in Pennsylvania, what standard of care rule should the court apply?
   b. If Tompkins sues in a federal court in Pennsylvania, what standard of care rule should the court apply?
   c. If Tompkins sues in a state court in New York, what standard of care rule should the court apply?
   d. If Tompkins sues in a federal court in New York, what standard of care rule should the court apply?

3.   Tompkins, Jr., is injured near Hughestown and two months after the accident is transferred to a hospital in West Virginia. His wife moves to West

Virginia to be near him. He is released three months later, is bedridden for nine more months, and does not recover fully for over two years. The Tompkins decide to stay in West Virginia, and they bring a diversity suit against the Erie Railroad in federal court there. Mr. Tompkins seeks recovery for his injuries, and Mrs. Tompkins seeks recovery for loss of consortium, that is, for the interference with her relationship to her husband during the time he was incapacitated due to the injury. See *Hopson v. St. Mary's Hospital*, 408 A.2d 260 (1979) (loss of consortium includes the " 'constellation of companionship, dependence, reliance, affection, sharing and aid' " which flows from marriage) (quoting from W. Prosser, Handbook of The Law of Torts, 881-882 (4th ed. 1971). Assume that West Virginia applies the place-of-the-injury choice of law rule in tort cases.

> a. What state's tort law should the federal court apply to Mrs. Tompkins's claim?
> b. If the judge is unsure which law to apply, to which state court should she certify the issue?

A Quagmire Quandary

4.   Tompkins is injured near Hughestown, Pennsylvania, and decides to sue the Erie Railroad. He consults Webster, a local lawyer. Webster would like to sue "at home," of course, as most lawyers would. However, she is aware that Pennsylvania law requires wilful and wanton conduct in cases like this, and that a Pennsylvania court would apply its own law to the case, under the lex loci rule.

In preparation for filing suit, Webster researches New York law on the duty of care to trespassers. She finds no case directly on point. Some older cases applied the wilful/wanton standard in analogous circumstances, but more recent New York cases have "modernized" some related doctrines of premises liability.

Webster also researches New York conflicts of law doctrine, and finds (we will assume) that New York used to follow the mechanical conflicts rules of the First Restatement. A recent case rejected the First Restatement's approach to contract cases in favor of interest analysis, but no case has arisen asking the court to abandon the First Restatement's place-of-the-injury rule for tort cases. In short, it looks like change may be coming both in the conflicts law and the tort law, but it hasn't arrived yet, and may not arrive at all.

> a. Should Webster sue in New York or Pennsylvania?
> b. Should she choose state or federal court?

The Procedure/Procedure Distinction

5.   Assume that New York would choose Pennsylvania tort law in the Tompkins case under the place-of-the-injury approach. Webster decides to

sue in state court in New York. She sues the Erie Railroad Company and also Hepzibah, the conductor in charge of the train that hit Tompkins. Webster learns that Hepzibah lives with her mother in Queens and serves process on Hepzibah by delivering the summons and complaint to her mother at the house. Hepzibah moves to dismiss for improper service, on the ground that New York law requires service in hand upon her. Assume that New York law does indeed require in-hand service but that leaving it at the house with the mother would suffice under Pennsylvania law.

    a. How should the court decide the motion?

    b. If Webster had sued in federal court in New York, how would it have ruled? See Fed. R. Civ. P. 4(d)(1).

6.   Two-and-a-half years after his accident, Tompkins goes to see Webster. Assume that the statute of limitations on tort claims in New York is four years, but that it is two in Pennsylvania. Assume further that New York choice of law rules would lead to the application of Pennsylvania tort law to the case. Webster files a diversity suit in federal district court in New York against the Erie Railroad. The Erie brings a motion for summary judgment on the ground that the claim is barred due to passage of the limitations period. What should the federal court do?

Totally Swamped: The Impact of Transfer

All of this is exquisitely complex. So let's make matters worse by considering another procedural wrinkle, transfer of venue under 28 U.S.C. §1404(a). Because the basic federal venue rules provide a wide choice of venues (see Chapter 7), the plaintiff will often have the right to bring suit in courts that have little connection to the events in suit. Section 1404(a) provides federal courts with the discretionary authority to transfer a case to another federal district "for the convenience of parties and witnesses, and in the interest of justice," where the plaintiff has chosen one district but it makes more sense to litigate the case in a different district.[4] If a case is based on diversity, and if the judge transfers it to another district, even more elaborate complications arise in determining the applicable law.

An example may help. In *Van Dusen v. Barrack,* 376 U.S. 612 (1964), the plaintiffs were the personal representatives of passengers who died when an airplane crashed upon takeoff from a Boston airport, en route to Philadel-

---

4. The factors to be considered in deciding whether a transfer is appropriate include the private interests of the parties, such as their residences, access to sources of proof, ability to subpoena witnesses, the need for a view of premises involved in the litigation, whether a judgment can be enforced in the forum, and others. There are also systemic interests involved, including appropriate distribution of cases among the federal districts, local decision of local cases, distribution of the burden of jury service, and the trial court's familiarity with the applicable law. See *Gulf Oil Corp. v. Gilbert,* 330 U.S. 501, 508-509 (1947).

phia. They brought a diversity action in federal district court in Pennsylvania against the airline, the manufacturer of the plane, and other defendants. The defendants moved for transfer to the District of Massachusetts under §1404(a).

There were some good practical reasons for the court to grant the motion. The site of the accident and many witnesses and documents were in Massachusetts. In addition, other actions arising from the crash had been filed there; if the Pennsylvania suits were transferred, they could be consolidated with those and litigated more efficiently, which is presumably "in the interest of justice."

However, the defendants' motion may have been motivated less by these practical factors than by several significant differences between the wrongful death statutes of Massachusetts and Pennsylvania. The Massachusetts statute limited damages to $20,000 per decedent, while the Pennsylvania court did not. Liability under the Massachusetts statute turned on the culpability of the defendant (so that even the $20,000 figure was limited to egregious conduct), while Pennsylvania law viewed wrongful death damages as compensatory. Because of these differences, recovery under Pennsylvania law might be substantial in each case, while recovery under Massachusetts law might not even equal the expenses of litigation.

In *Van Dusen* much turned, then, on what law the Massachusetts federal court (called the "transferee court") would apply if the case were bounced up there. If the defendants could convince the Pennsylvania federal court to transfer, and the transferee court applied Massachusetts law, *they could forum shop too*. After the plaintiffs chose a federal court in Pennsylvania, to have the case decided under Pennsylvania's more favorable wrongful death statute,[5] the defendants could trump that choice with a strategic coup of their own, by seeking transfer to a court that would apply the somewhat stingy Massachusetts wrongful death remedy.

The Supreme Court refused to take the gambit. In *Van Dusen* the Court held that a transfer of venue under §1404(a) should effect a change of court but not a change of law. That is, the transferee court should apply the law that the transferor court would have applied if the case had not been transferred. On the *Van Dusen* facts, if the case were transferred to the Massachusetts court, that court should choose whatever law the Pennsylvania federal court would have applied because the plaintiffs had the right to file suit there and had done so. Put a bit more cynically, the court should honor the plain-

---

5. This assumes, of course, that the Pennsylvania courts would have applied Pennsylvania law, while the Massachusetts courts (and therefore the Massachusetts federal court, if bound to do the same) would have applied Massachusetts law to the case. It is entirely possible, under current choice of law principles, that this would have happened on the *Van Dusen* facts.

tiffs' forum-shopping choice, rather than allowing the defendants to displace it through transfer.

The combination of *Erie, Klaxon,* and *Van Dusen* places the federal judge in a transferred case in a position wondrous to contemplate. Under *Van Dusen* and *Klaxon,* she must determine what the choice of law rules of the transferor state are, and what state's law the courts of the transferor state would have chosen under that choice of law rule. Then, under *Erie,* she must determine what the substantive law of *that* state is and apply it. As Judge Friendly wryly observed in a related context:

> Our principal task, in this diversity of citizenship case, is to determine what the New York courts would think the California courts would think on an issue about which neither has thought.

Nolan v. Transocean Airlines, Inc., 276 F.2d 280, 281 (2nd Cir. 1960).

EXAMPLES

Games People Play

7. Assume for the purposes of this example the same facts concerning Tompkins, Jr.'s accident. Tompkins goes to see Webster two-and-a-half years after the accident, inquiring about suing the railroad and wishing to sue at home. Webster researches the law and learns that Pennsylvania tort law would allow Tompkins to recover on a showing of simple negligence, but New York law would require him to prove wilful or wanton conduct. She also learns that New York applies the place-of-the-injury choice of law rule to tort cases. Last, she finds that Pennsylvania has a two-year limitations period for tort claims, but that New York's limitations period for tort claims is four years.

   a. Tompkins brings suit in state court in New York. The Erie Railroad moves to transfer the case to Pennsylvania, arguing that the accident took place, the plaintiff, and all the witnesses are there, and that Pennsylvania law will apply, so it makes more sense to litigate the case in Pennsylvania. What will the court do?

   b. Tompkins sues in federal court in the Southern District of New York, based on diversity. The Erie Railroad then moves to transfer the case to the Middle District of Pennsylvania, in which Hughestown is located. If the court grants the motion, what law will be applied to the limitations question and to the merits?

   c. Suppose that Tompkins sues in the Southern District of New York, and then *he* moves to transfer to the Middle District of Pennsylvania. If the court grants the motion, what law will apply to the limitations question and to the merits?

EXPLANATIONS

Wading In

1a. This case has some connections to both New York and Pennsylvania, since it involves a New York corporation and a Pennsylvania citizen, and the accident occurred in Pennsylvania. In such cases a court must choose which state's law to apply. Pennsylvania's choice of law principles (the example assumes) require its courts to apply the law of the place of the injury in tort cases, so the Pennsylvania state court will apply Pennsylvania law to this case. Tompkins will lose unless he can prove wilful and wanton conduct.

b. If this case is brought in federal court in Pennsylvania, the federal district judge must, under *Klaxon,* apply Pennsylvania choice of law rules to determine the applicable tort standard. She must first decide which state's tort law Pennsylvania courts would apply, and then she must decide what the law of the chosen state is on the tort issue. Here, because Pennsylvania applies the place-of-the-injury choice of law rule to tort cases, the federal judge must apply Pennsylvania tort law, since the accident took place there. Under Pennsylvania law (the example assumes) the railroad is only liable for wilful or wanton conduct toward a trespasser, and the federal court must apply this standard. *Klaxon* assures "vertical uniformity" within Pennsylvania, because Tompkins, Jr., will be stuck with the same rule in Pennsylvania federal court that would apply in the state court.

c. If Tompkins sues in a state court in New York, that court must use its choice of law rules to determine what state's substantive law to apply. Since New York applies the place-of-the-injury choice of law rule (the example assumes), New York will apply the tort law of Pennsylvania to this case. Since Pennsylvania law requires a showing of wilful and wanton conduct to recover, the New York state court will do so as well. Even though a plaintiff injured in a similar accident in New York would be entitled to recover on a showing of simple negligence, the "lex loci" choice of law rule means that the New York court will apply another state's law to the case.

An interesting consequence of this scenario is that the New York state court will end up doing the same kind of exercise that federal courts do in diversity cases, making their best guess at the content of another state's substantive law. New York courts cannot "make" Pennsylvania tort law, so when they choose to apply Pennsylvania tort law to a case, they have to engage in an *Erie*-type analysis of what the Pennsylvania law is on the point.[6]

d. The federal judge in New York must apply the same choice of law rule that a state court in New York would apply. Since the state court would look to Pennsylvania law, the New York federal judge must do so as well.

---

6. It would be interesting to know whether state courts use the same kind of predictive approach in this context that the federal courts use under *Erie* or whether they try to act like a trial court of the other state in following any binding precedent on point.

Thus, the combination of New York choice of law doctrine and Pennsylvania tort law again leads to application of the wilful/wanton rule.

In this example the case comes out the same way in all four courts because the choice of law principles in all four courts point to application of the same state's law. If all states used the same choice of law rules, all cases would theoretically be decided under the same substantive law no matter where suit was brought, since the choice of law rules would always direct the court — whatever court it was — to the same law.[7] That would eliminate forum shopping for more favorable substantive law.

The First Restatement rules aspired to this legal nirvana, but exceptions and idiosyncratic application made uniformity elusive. The more recent approaches, because they are based on judgmental balancing of interests and policies unique to each case, are less likely to lead courts in different states to apply the same state's law. Consequently, they create greater opportunities for forum shopping. However, because modern choice of law "rules" involve an ambiguous (one might even say, slushy) balancing of policy considerations, it is also harder to predict what state's law the forum court will choose. Thus, plaintiffs can only *try* to forum shop; they may end up mired in a different state's law because the court drew the balance differently than they predicted.

2a. The Pennsylvania state court judge will apply Pennsylvania choice of law doctrine, which points to Pennsylvania tort law. As in example 1a, the result is application of the wilful/wanton rule.

b. The Pennsylvania federal judge, under *Klaxon*, will also choose Pennsylvania's wilful/wanton rule, as in example 1b.

c. The New York state judge will apply New York's balancing of interests approach to conflicts law, which leads (the example assumes) to the conclusion that New York tort law should apply to the case. This is a realistic possibility under modern choice of law principles. A number of factors, such as the residence of the parties at the time of the accident, the interests promoted by application of a particular tort principle, the place of the negligence that led to the accident, and the place in which the effect of the injuries is felt, might lead a court to apply its own law even though the accident took place in another state.[8]

If New York does choose its own law in this case, Tompkins will be able to recover by showing that the railroad was negligent, even though he would have to show wilful or wanton conduct in a Pennsylvania court. He will have exactly the choice of two different substantive rules, which the Court decried in *Erie*. However, the result arises because *different states* apply different tort law, not because the results differ between the state and federal courts within the same state, as was true under *Swift*.

---

7. Unless, of course, the choice of law rule was to always apply forum law.

8. See, e.g., *Challoner*, discussed in note 3.

d. Once again, *Klaxon* requires the New York federal judge to achieve "vertical uniformity" by applying the same law that the New York state judge would. Therefore, the federal judge will apply the New York simple negligence rule. "Horizontal" uniformity is lost because the New York federal court applies different law than the Pennsylvania federal court would. Compare example 2b. The Court in *Klaxon* acknowledged that its decision would destroy horizontal uniformity among the federal courts:

> Whatever lack of uniformity this may produce between federal courts in different states is attributable to our federal system, which leaves to a state, within the limits permitted by the Constitution, the right to pursue local policies diverging from those of its neighbors.

313 U.S. at 496. The different results in these examples are illustrated in Figure 11-1. Note that in each scenario, there is vertical uniformity in the law applied between the federal court and the state court in which the federal court sits. However, in example 2 this vertical uniformity leads to horizontal disuniformity: The federal courts in Pennsylvania and New York apply different standards of care to the case because the state courts of those states would too.

3a. *Klaxon* requires the West Virginia federal court to apply the choice of law approach of West Virginia courts, which is the lex loci delicti (place-of-the-injury) rule. The problem, however, is in determining whether Mrs. Tompkins's consortium injury took place in Pennsylvania, where her hus-

Figure 11–1: Choice of Courts and Choice of Law

	Pennsylvania	New York
Example 1		
State Court:	Chooses Pa. law, wilful/wanton rule applies	Chooses Pa. law, wilful/wanton rule applies
	↕	↕
Federal Court:	Chooses Pa. law, wilful/wanton rule applies	Chooses Pa. Law, wilful/wanton rule applies
Example 2		
State Court:	Chooses Pa. law, wilful/wanton rule applies	Chooses N.Y. law, negligence rule applies
	↕	↕
Federal Court:	Chooses Pa. law, wilful/wanton rule applies	Chooses N.Y. law, negligence rule applies

band was injured, or in West Virginia, where they lived during most of the time that her relationship with him was impaired by his injury. Or did part of her "injury" take place in Pennsylvania (where she suffered two months of consortium losses) and part in West Virginia?

The First Restatement had a mechanical solution for this problem. Under Section 377 the court looked to "the state where the last event necessary to make the actor liable for the alleged tort takes place." Presumably, this would be Pennsylvania, since the Erie Railroad became liable to Mrs. Tompkins as soon as she started to suffer consortium losses. If West Virginia followed the First Restatement approach, the federal court would do so as well, and apply Pennsylvania tort law to her loss of consortium claim. But it is hardly self-evident that the law of Pennsylvania *should* govern this injury, which primarily affects Mrs. Tompkins in another state. Such rigidities led to a revolt against the First Restatement, which is still going on.

b. The ambiguity here is not as to the content of the tort law of either state, but rather as to how a West Virginia court would identify the "place of the injury" in applying its choice of law rule. Because the federal judge must apply the place-of-the-injury rule as the West Virginia court would, it should certify the issue to the West Virginia Supreme Court, if it has a certification procedure.

Suppose that the judge were unsure whether West Virginia's choice of law rule would point to Pennsylvania law and whether Pennsylvania tort law allowed recovery for loss of consortium. Presumably, the judge would have to certify the choice of law issue to West Virginia and (if it determined that Pennsylvania law should apply) then the substantive law issue to the Pennsylvania court.

A Quagmire Quandary

4a. This is a quandary indeed. Several important strategic considerations point to suing at home: The witnesses will likely be available in Pennsylvania; it is convenient for Tompkins; and it is convenient for Webster. It is *not* so convenient for the Erie Railroad, which will have to hire local counsel and monitor litigation in another state. However, the wilful/wanton rule looms as a serious stumbling block to recovery, and one certainty in the case is that the wilful/wanton rule will apply if Webster sues in Pennsylvania. On the other hand, suing in New York is inconvenient for Tompkins, who wants to sue at home and wants Webster to do it. In addition, important witnesses may be beyond the subpoena power of the New York court.

Yet suing in New York has some important potential advantages. If the court decides to apply New York law, and if New York tort law would allow recovery based on simple negligence, Tompkins's case looks a good deal stronger on the merits. Naturally, Tompkins has a strong interest in the merits.

This is a difficult tactical decision because the advantage New York offers turns on several contingencies. *First,* Webster must convince the New York court that the lex loci delicti rule has effectively been overruled by recent New York choice of law decisions adopting interest analysis for contract cases, so that it should apply interest analysis to tort cases as well. *Second,* if the court applies interest analysis to the case, Webster must also demonstrate that that approach supports application of New York law to this accident. Just because the court applies a different choice of law *rule* does not necessarily mean it will choose the law of New York. The court might assess the interests of the parties and the states involved and conclude that they weigh in favor of Pennsylvania law anyway. *Last,* if she convinces the New York court to look to New York law, she must still convince that court that New York tort law now allows recovery based on simple negligence.

All of this is a little chaotic, isn't it? It is hard to give up the home forum on the speculative chance that all those decisions will go your way in a distant court. These contingencies will certainly act as a check on forum shopping in many cases. Webster's decision will turn on how strong her arguments are on these legal issues and, conversely, how weak her case would be if she sued in Pennsylvania and had to meet the wilful/wanton standard.

b. If Webster does choose to sue in New York, she might be well advised to choose a federal court in New York. If New York law — both tort law and conflicts law — is in the process of change, the federal court may have more flexibility to anticipate those changes than the state trial court would. Presumably, the federal diversity court must apply New York conflicts law in the same way it would apply New York substantive law; that is, it must ask what the state's highest court would do if the issue were before it today. If the case law strongly suggests that the highest court would no longer apply the place-of-the-injury rule, the federal court may be more willing to reject it than a state trial court, which will feel bound by the highest court's past precedents unless they are clearly eviscerated by later holdings. See Chapter 9, example 6d.

The Procedure/Procedure Distinction

5a. This example raises the issue of whether the New York court, when it chooses the law of another state, must apply the whole law of the other state, including matters of procedure. Sound familiar? It is akin to the dilemma explored in "Eerie *Erie,*" as to when the federal court must select state law and when it may apply its own procedures. In the "horizontal" choice of law context, as in the *Erie* context, things get dicey because, generally speaking, state courts apply their own procedural law even if they have chosen the substantive law of another state under their choice of law rules.

It isn't hard to see why this dichotomy has long been accepted in the horizontal choice of law context. Just as federal diversity courts would have to abandon the Federal Rules entirely if *Erie* required them to exactly imitate the state court, the New York court would have a very difficult task if, once it chose to apply Pennsylvania tort law, it *also* had to apply Pennsylvania procedural law. The problem would be even worse than the federal judge's under *Erie*. Since New York courts might choose the law of many different states in different cases, the New York judge would have to learn the procedural quirks of many states. Effectively, she would be forced to run her courtroom under 50 different procedural systems instead of one. See G. Gelfand and H. Abrams, Putting *Erie* On The Right Track, 49 U. Pitt. L. Rev. 937, 963 (1988). That is insupportable; to avoid it, the substance/procedure distinction has emerged in conflicts of law doctrine as it has under *Erie*. Thus, the New York court would require compliance with its in-hand service of process rule, even though Pennsylvania would not.

b. If Webster sued in federal court in New York, the court would deny the motion to dismiss. While *Erie* mandates application of state law in diversity cases, it does not require wholesale abandonment of federal procedure. Where a valid Federal Rule covers an issue, it may be applied in a federal diversity case despite contrary procedure in the state court. *Hanna v. Plumer*, 360 U.S. 460 (1965). Here, Fed. R. Civ. P. 4(d)(1) clearly provides that leaving the papers at Hepzibah's home with a person residing therein is sufficient. The federal court need not ask (under *Erie*) what New York law would require, nor must it ask (under *Klaxon*) whether New York would look to Pennsylvania law. It may apply the Federal Rule.

6.   You don't know enough to "answer" this example, but you do know enough to see the quizzical problem it poses. The case is in federal court. Under *Erie*, the judge must look to state law on "substantive" issues — "substantive," that is, in the *Erie* sense of the term. In *Guaranty Trust Co. v. York*, the Supreme Court concluded that the state limitations period for a claim was "substantive" for *Erie* purposes, so that state law applied. So, the judge has to apply the state limitations period.

That much is easy, but only gets us part of the way. There remains the question as to *which* limitations period should be applied, New York's or Pennsylvania's? Well, that's easy too: *Klaxon* requires the federal court to do what the New York court would do. That turns on whether New York would apply the Pennsylvania limitations period or its own longer one.

If the issue is "substantive" (see *Guaranty Trust Co. v. York*), presumably the New York court would apply the Pennsylvania limitations period. Unfortunately, they very well might not. The line between substance and procedure has been drawn differently in the horizontal choice of law cases than it has in the vertical choice of law under *Erie*. Limitations periods are an example. While the statute of limitations issue is "substantive" for *Erie* purposes, many courts apply their own limitations law to a case even if their conflicts of law rules mandate application of the substantive law of another state. See *Sun Oil Co. v. Wortman*, 486 U.S. 717 (1988) (approving application of Kansas limitations period to claim even though Kansas lacked sufficient connections to the case to apply its own substantive law); Restatement (Second) of Conflict of Laws §142; Richman and Reynolds at 229-230 (stating and criticizing this approach). Thus, New York might apply its limitations period to the claim, because it is "procedural" for choice of law purposes, while the federal court would be required to make the same choice because it is "substantive" for *Erie* purposes![9]

Games People Play

7a.   The one thing that the New York state court will *not* do is transfer the case. A New York court has no authority to send a case to a Pennsylvania court; these are different, autonomous court systems, which decide for themselves which cases they will hear. The situation is different in federal court, because all federal courts are "branches" of the same federal court system and are required under §1404(a) to entertain cases transferred from other branches of the same system.

   That leaves the state court with several options. It could dismiss under "forum non conveniens." The forum non conveniens doctrine is based on a premise similar to §1404(a), that sometimes cases that are properly filed under the three ring analysis still logically belong somewhere else. Under forum non conveniens, which is recognized in many states, the court may dismiss a case where the interests of justice indicate that it should be litigated elsewhere.[10]

   If the court dismisses Tompkins's case he will lose: If he refiled in Pennsylvania, the Erie Railroad would plead the two-year statute of limitations as a complete defense. That prospect is likely to convince the New York court not to dismiss for forum non conveniens. So the court is likely to take the alternative course of entertaining the action. If, as many courts do, New York applied its own limitations statute (see example 6), Tompkins would get the benefit of the four-year limitations period and — since New York looks to Pennsylvania tort law under the place-of-the-injury rule — the simple negligence standard of care.

   b.   Tompkins gets a pretty good result under the first scenario, but he would still have to go to New York to litigate. Maybe he can do better by

---

9. Another area that has been subject to this schizophrenic classification is burden of proof. See *Sampson v. Channell,* 110 F.2d 754 (1st Cir. 1940), in which the court looked to the Massachusetts choice of law rule under *Erie* (anticipating *Klaxon*) and chose to apply the Massachusetts rule on burden of proof, even though the accident took place in Maine.

10. The doctrine is also applied in the federal courts, where the appropriate forum is in another country. Just as a New York court cannot order a Pennsylvania court to hear a case, a United States court cannot order a court in another country to do so. If, therefore, the case clearly should be litigated in another country, the federal court's only option is to dismiss under forum non conveniens.

suing in federal court in New York. Since the federal court under *Klaxon* must act like the New York state court, it will apply New York's longer limitations period and Pennsylvania's simple negligence rule. In addition, if the federal court transfers the case to the Middle District of Pennsylvania under §1404(a), he will get the best of both worlds. The suit will be litigated in Pennsylvania, and, under *Van Dusen*, the court will apply New York limitations law and Pennsylvania tort law.

In the forum-shopping business, this is the highest form of art: The plaintiff shops for New York law on some issues and Pennsylvania law on others . . . maybe it should be called "issue shopping." In this case there will be a good argument for transfer, since the accident took place in Pennsylvania, most of the witnesses are likely to be there, Tompkins is there, and Pennsylvania law will apply to the case.

Even this scenario is chancy, however. The railroad may not move to transfer, since it is from New York and will have the advantage of litigating at home. Even if it does, the court may deny the motion.

c. This is the ultimate in chutzpah: Tompkins sues in New York and then asks the court to send the case to his home forum, taking the New York statute of limitations — but not New York tort law — with it. *Van Dusen* was not quite this egregious, since the defendants sought the transfer.

The scholars had predicted that the Supreme Court would discourage this game by holding that the law of the *transferee* forum would apply if the plaintiff sought transfer. In Tompkins's case, that would mean that the Pennsylvania court would apply its own two-year limitations period (which would mean, in turn, that Tompkins wouldn't seek the transfer). However, in *Ferens v. John Deere Co.,* 494 U.S. 516 (1990), the Supreme Court perplexed the prognosticators by holding (by a 5-4 majority) that the *Van Dusen* rule applies even where the plaintiff seeks transfer. The reasons are complicated, and the arguments on both sides of the issue are close. Read the case if you can. The bottom line, however, is that Tompkins could sue in the inconvenient forum, get back into Pennsylvania, obtain the benefit of Pennsylvania tort law, and invoke the longer New York limitations period.[11]

If this isn't chaos, it certainly is a peculiar form of order.

---

11. Actually, this is not the ultimate in chutzpah; there is a more extreme possibility. A plaintiff who has missed the local limitations period might file in a district that does not even have personal jurisdiction (but does have a long statute of limitations) and ask the court to transfer under 28 U.S.C. §1406(a). See *Goldlawr v. Heiman,* 369 U.S. 463 (1962), which held that the court has the power to transfer such a case to another jurisdiction, which has jurisdiction over the defendant. In this scenario, most courts have held that the law of the *transferee* forum should apply, but the Supreme Court has not yet decided the issue. See Friedenthal, Kane and Miller at 216.

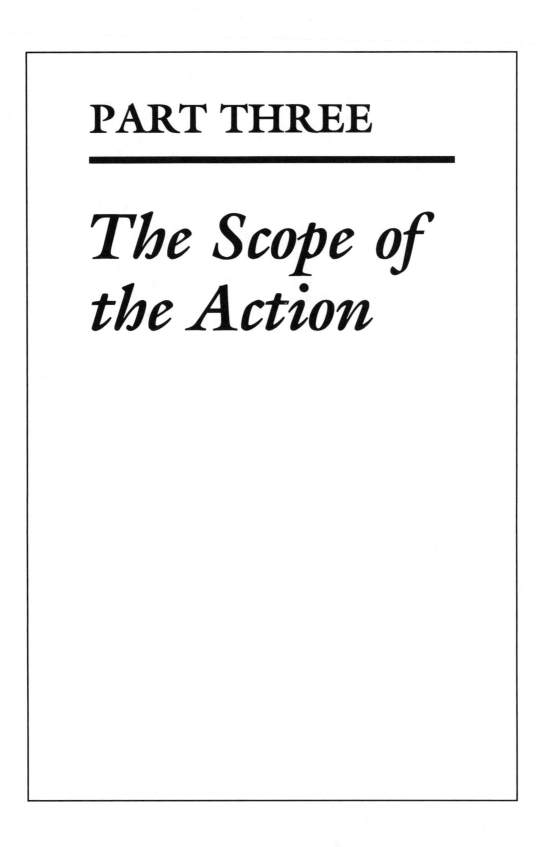

PART THREE

The Scope of the Action

12

Sculpting the Lawsuit: The Basic Rules of Joinder

Introduction

A great deal of time is spent during the first year of law school analyzing decided cases, doing postmortems on past lawsuits. But every lawsuit also has a beginning, and at the beginning someone must make important tactical decisions about the scope of the lawsuit, that is, whom to sue and which claims to assert. The traditional rule in American courts has been, and largely still is, that "the plaintiff is master of his claim," that it is up to the plaintiff (or his lawyer) to decide who the parties to the suit will be and which claims will be asserted in the action.

An example may help to frame the problem. Assume that Wright is the main contractor on a construction job in Erie, Pennsylvania. The electrical subcontractor is Edison Electric. While driving an Edison truck to the construction site, Edison's site manager, Volt, collides with Wright's cement truck, as well as with a private vehicle driven by Ellsworth. All three drivers are injured, and the two trucks are heavily damaged.

If Volt decides to bring suit against Wright to recover for his injuries, he will have to decide whether to sue alone or to bring a combined action along with Edison Electric, which will seek to recover for the damage to its truck. Ellsworth may also wish to join as a plaintiff to recover for her personal injuries and property damage. Alternatively, Volt may wish to sue both Wright and Ellsworth on the theory that each was negligent or, for whatever reason, to sue one tortfeasor but not the other.

Volt's options as to which defendants he may sue and which potential plaintiffs he decides to sue with are defined by the rules of "joinder of parties." In the federal courts, initial joinder of parties is governed by Fed. R. Civ. P. 20(a), which authorizes plaintiffs to sue together if: (1) they assert claims arising out of the same transaction or occurrence; and (2) their claims against the defendant or defendants will involve a common question of law or fact. In Volt's suit, for example, Volt and Edison may join as plaintiffs because their claims arise out of the same accident, and the factual issue of whose negligence caused the accident is common to both their claims.

Similarly, Rule 20 allows the plaintiff to sue multiple defendants in a single action if the same criteria are met. Volt could sue Ellsworth and Wright as codefendants in the same action, since he claims relief from each arising from the same accident and there will be a common question as to whose negligence caused the accident. Here are some configurations that would be permissible under the rule:

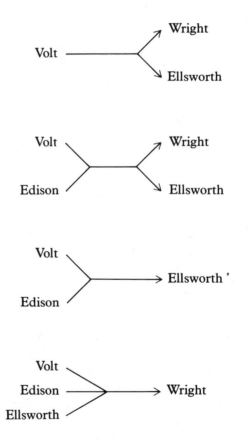

It makes good sense to allow parties to join as plaintiffs or to sue defendants jointly in a single action if the criteria in Rule 20(a) are met. When a number of claims involve a single transaction or occurrence, and the same issue or issues will have to be litigated to resolve each claim, it is more efficient to litigate those issues once in a combined action, rather than repeatedly in separate suits. In addition, resolving those issues in a single action avoids the possibility of inconsistent judgments on the same issue. For example, if Volt sues Ellsworth and recovers, but Edison sues Ellsworth and loses, the two juries must have disagreed on whether Ellsworth was negligent (barring any contributory negligence defense). Such inconsistent results reflect unfavorably on the judicial system and are best avoided where possible. If Volt's and Edison's claims are tried together there will be no inconsistent verdicts, since there will be only one finding on Ellsworth's negligence.

Interestingly, however, Rule 20(a) does not require parties to be joined whenever the criteria in the rule are met. At least initially, the joinder decision is left to the plaintiffs. If they choose to sue some but not all defendants in one action, they may sue the others in a separate action or never sue them at all. If they choose not to join in a suit by other plaintiffs against the defendant, they remain free to pursue their own claims in separate suits.

joinder of parties (20)
not required
joinder of claims in (13)

An Early but Sensible Question

1.   Since it promotes efficiency and consistency to litigate related claims such as Volt's and Edison's together, why doesn't Rule 20(a) *require* joinder of parties where the two criteria in the rule are met?

You should be careful to distinguish Rule 20, which governs joinder of *parties,* from Rules 18 and 13, which authorize parties, once they are properly joined in a law suit, to assert additional *claims* against opposing parties. Rule 13 authorizes a defending party in a suit to assert claims back against a party who has claimed against him. Such counterclaims come in two shapes, compulsory (Rule 13(a)) and permissive (Rule 13(b)). If the defending party's counterclaim arises from the same transaction or occurrence as the claim against him, it is compulsory, which essentially means that he must assert it in the original action or lose it. For example, if Volt sues Ellsworth for his injuries arising out of the accident and Ellsworth suffered injuries in the same accident, which she attributes to Volt's negligence, Ellsworth must assert her claim for these injuries in Volt's action. This rule makes sense; it forces parties who are already adversaries to litigate all claims arising from the same set of facts in a single action.

Another Impromptu Question

2.   Under Rule 20(a), the parties are never forced to bring parties into a particular suit. Rule 13(a), by contrast, compels a party to assert some claims at a time and place not of his choosing. Why did the rulemakers choose to force parties to assert compulsory counterclaims?

Defending parties may also assert counterclaims that are completely unrelated to the original claim under Rule 13(b). This cannot be justified on efficiency grounds, since (by definition) a permissive counterclaim will involve different events from the main claim, and the court will almost certainly order separate trial of the permissive counterclaim. See Rule 42(b). But the rule at least allows a defendant, once brought before the court, to settle all his claims against his opponent, without having to file a separate lawsuit.

Yet another type of claim is addressed in Rule 13(g), which provides for assertion of *cross-claims* arising out of the same transaction or occurrence as the main claim. A cross-claim is a claim asserted by one party against a coparty; that is, someone on the same side of the "v" as the claimant. Again, suppose that Volt sues Wright and Ellsworth for injuries suffered in the accident. If Wright suffered injuries as well and believes that the accident was Ellsworth's fault, she may cross-claim against Ellsworth for her injuries. This is called a cross-claim rather than a counterclaim because it is asserted by one defendant against a codefendant, not against an opposing party. The configuration would look like this:

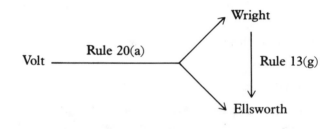

(Volt joins Wright and Ellsworth as defendants under Rule 20(a); Wright cross-claims against Ellsworth under Rule 13(g))

Here again, allowing assertion of these claims in the main action promotes efficiency and consistency because the same underlying facts will be litigated on the main claim and on the cross-claim. Yet here again, the rule makes joinder optional, leaving Wright free to sue separately on her claim against Ellsworth if she prefers to do so.

The various joinder rules may also work in tandem. For example, the counterclaim rules, Rules 13(a) and (b), both authorize "a pleading" to assert a claim against an "opposing party." Once again the rulemakers have chosen the language of the rule with care. This language authorizes any defending party — not just an original defendant — to assert counterclaims against a party who has claimed against him. In the last diagram, Ellsworth is an "opposing party" on Wright's cross-claim. Rule 13 applies to any claim she may have against Wright. If she has a claim against Wright for her injuries in the collision, she must assert it as a compulsory counterclaim once Wright has asserted a claim against her. If she has any unrelated claims against Wright, she may assert, but is not required to, under Rule 13(b).

Rule 18(a) is the last and broadest of the basic joinder rules. Unequivocally, it provides that a party seeking relief from an opposing party may join with his original claim any additional claims he has against that opposing party. Suppose, for example, that Volt exchanges words with Wright after the accident and a fight ensues. Rule 18(a) allows Volt to assert his claim for assault in the same action with the negligence claim. It would also allow Volt to add a completely unrelated claim against Wright for libel, trespass, or anything else. Unlike Rule 20(a), there is no common transaction or occurrence requirement in Rule 18(a).

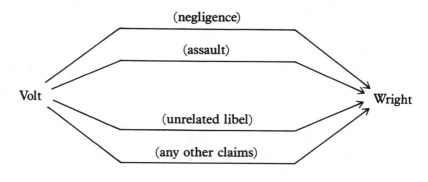

(Rule 18(a) authorizes joinder of all
these claims, related and unrelated)

Rule 18(a), like Rule 13, authorizes "a pleader" to assert as many claims as he has against an opponent. This applies not only to the original plaintiff, but also to any party seeking relief against another party, whether on a counterclaim, a cross-claim, or a third-party claim. Suppose, for example, that Volt sues Ellsworth and Wright for negligence, based on the collision at the construction site, and Ellsworth cross-claims against Wright for her damages arising out of the accident. Rule 18 authorizes Ellsworth, as a party seeking relief, to add on any claim, related or unrelated, that she may have against Wright:

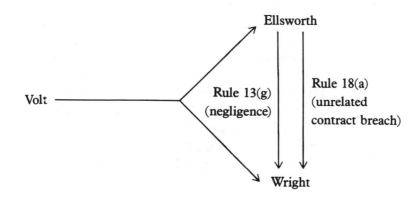

Note that Ellsworth could not have asserted this unrelated contract claim as a cross-claim if it were the only claim she had against Wright: Rule 13(g) only allows cross-claims that arise out of the same transaction or occurrence as the main claim. However, once Ellsworth asserts a proper cross-claim against Wright, Rule 18(a) kicks in, allowing her to add on totally unrelated claims as well.

In puzzling out the following examples, start by identifying the party asserting the claim as a plaintiff or defendant and then consider, given the particular posture of the claim, which of the rules applies. Assume that all suits are brought in federal court.

An Artistic Disaster

3.   Morisot and Cassatt hire Van Gogh and Renoir to paint their studio. Van Gogh and Renoir hire Pissarro as an assistant. Pissarro goes for coffee, leaving the electric paint remover on, and burns the studio to the ground. Morisot breaks her leg jumping from the third-story window, three of Cassatt's priceless masterpieces are burned, and Renoir suffers second-degree burns. Everyone is mad.

    a. Suppose that Morisot and Cassatt are co-owners of the studio. May they join as plaintiffs to sue Pissarro for the damages to the studio from the fire?

    b. Suppose that Cassatt owns the studio on her own. May she and Morisot join as plaintiffs to sue Pissarro for his negligence, if Cassatt seeks recovery for damage to the building and Morisot seeks damages for her broken leg?

    c. Assume that Van Gogh and Renoir are liable for the negligence of Pissarro under the law of respondeat superior, if he acted in the scope of his employment in leaving the heat gun on. May Morisot sue Van Gogh, Renoir, and Pissarro in a single action to recover for her broken leg?

    d. Could Cassatt sue Van Gogh and Renoir for breach of contract for burning down her studio in the process of painting it, and Morisot join as a coplaintiff, asserting a negligence claim against the same defendants for the injury to her leg?

    e. Change the facts a little: Assume that either Pissarro or Gauguin, another employee, left the paint remover on, and Cassatt is unsure which it was. Can she sue them both under Rule 20(a)?

    f. If Cassatt sues Renoir for breach of contract, may Renoir assert claims against Pissarro and Van Gogh in the same suit for negligently causing his injuries? (In considering this example, compare Rule 20(a) with Rule 14(a).)

4.   If Cassatt chooses to sue Renoir alone, may she assert both negligence and breach of contract claims against Renoir for her losses in the fire?

5. If Cassatt sues Renoir and Van Gogh for breach of contract, do the rules authorize her to add a claim against Renoir for breach of a separate contract to paint her home in another village?

6. Cassatt sues Renoir for breach of the studio painting contract. Later, after losing on that claim, she sues Renoir for a previous breach of the unrelated contract to paint her house. Can she do that?

The Tables Turned

7. Assume that Morisot owned the studio and contracted with Renoir and Van Gogh to paint it. Morisot sues Renoir and Pissarro for negligence and breach of contract as a result of the studio fire. Renoir asserts a claim against Morisot in the same action for payments due for part of the painting that had been completed before the building burned. Is Renoir's claim properly joined?

8. Following up on the last example, assume that Renoir also has a claim against Morisot for injuries suffered in an auto accident two months after the fire but before the suit was commenced. Can he assert this claim as well?

9. Suppose on the same facts that the only claim Renoir had against Morisot was for the unrelated auto accident. Could he assert it in this action?

10. If Morisot sues Renoir for her fire losses, may Renoir assert his claim against Morisot for breach of the studio painting contract and also bring in Cassatt (a co-signer of the contract) as a codefendant on that claim?

Acting at Cross-Purposes

11. Suppose that Cassatt sues Renoir, Van Gogh, and Pissarro jointly. She seeks recovery from Pissarro for his negligence and from Renoir and Van Gogh as Pissarro's employers, under the doctrine of respondeat superior. Renoir wishes to assert a claim against Pissarro for indemnification (that is, reimbursement for any damages he — Renoir — must pay if he is found liable to Cassatt) since it was Pissarro's negligence that actually caused the damage to the studio.

    a. May Renoir assert this claim against Pissarro in the same suit?

    b. Why is this claim *not* a counterclaim?

12. On the facts of example 11, could Renoir assert a claim against Pissarro for his own injuries suffered in the fire?

13. If Cassatt sues Renoir and Van Gogh for their negligence in burning the studio, may Renoir assert a claim against Van Gogh for his failure to pay him half of the money they earned on another paint job?

14. Another variation: Suppose that Cassatt sues Renoir and Van Gogh,

and Renoir wishes to assert claims against Van Gogh for his own injuries due to the fire *and* for the money owed him for the other paint job. May he do so?

15. Assume that Van Gogh and Renoir do not agree as to who was negligent in causing the fire. Van Gogh claims that it was Renoir's negligent instructions to Pissarro that caused the blaze. Renoir claims that Van Gogh failed to cut the power to the paint remover when Pissarro left for his break. When Cassatt sues Van Gogh and Renoir, Renoir cross-claims against Van Gogh for indemnification for any damages he must pay Cassatt on the main claim. May Van Gogh assert a claim against Renoir on a similar theory?

Last Impressionists

16. One final example to make a particular point. Suppose Morisot (from Massachusetts) sues Renoir (from Maine) and Van Gogh (from Massachusetts) for their negligence in burning down the studio. Is the suit proper?

EXPLANATIONS
An Early but Sensible Question

1.   While it would serve several goals of our procedural system to force all parties to join in a single action if their claims arise out of the same events, it would raise other serious procedural difficulties. Suppose that Volt and Ellsworth want to sue in federal court, but Edison prefers the state court? Suppose that Volt prefers to sue in Maine, but the others prefer New Hampshire? What if Edison wants to bring suit immediately, but Volt prefers to attempt a settlement first? Will Volt's lawyer represent all parties, or will each have his or her own lawyer? Who will plan litigation strategy? What if they can't agree? Suppose that some of the potential plaintiffs are also potential defendants: Who will decide which side of the "v" to put them on?

In addition to these possible differences of opinion as to tactical choices, the jurisdictional problems would be even more serious. The right to join parties under the Federal Rules does not confer subject matter jurisdiction on the court. Fed. R. Civ. P. 82. For example, suppose that Volt is from Maine, Ellsworth from New Hampshire, and Wright, the intended defendant, from Maine. If Volt and Ellsworth were forced to sue together, the suit could not be brought in federal court because there would not be complete diversity. Under permissive joinder, if Ellsworth prefers federal court she may preserve the option to sue there by *not* joining as a coplaintiff with Volt. Alternatively, assume that Volt wishes to sue Wright, from Maine, and Ellsworth, from New Hampshire, for damages that took place in the Pennsylvania accident. Under Rule 20(a), which allows Volt to sue each defendant separately, he will at least be able to sue Wright at home in Maine because the Maine court will have personal jurisdiction over Wright on the basis of her domicile. If

Volt were forced to join both defendants, he would have to sue in Pennsylvania, the one state where he could obtain personal jurisdiction over both defendants.

Obviously, a compulsory joinder rule would raise a host of procedural problems, which could undermine rather than further the goal of efficiency. The rulemakers wisely chose to stick with the old adage that "the plaintiff is master of his claim," rather than to create a whole new set of procedural complexities.

Another Impromptu Question

2.   Although forcing joinder of parties raises many problems, most of these do not apply to the joinder of an additional *claim* between parties who are already properly before the court. The subject matter jurisdiction problems referred to in the analysis of example 1 will not arise in the compulsory counterclaim situation because there is usually supplemental jurisdiction over compulsory counterclaims. See Chapter 14, example 4. Nor will personal jurisdiction bar assertion of the claim: The plaintiff, by initiating suit, submits to jurisdiction for counterclaims arising out of the transaction or occurrence that is the subject of his claim. 6 Wright and Miller at §1416. Nor does compulsory joinder of the counterclaim pose uncertainties as to who must be joined since no new parties are brought into the suit by the assertion of the counterclaim.

The only substantial argument against making counterclaims compulsory is that it violates the longstanding common law principle that the plaintiff (or, in this case, the defendant) is master of his claim, free to choose where and when to assert any claim he may have. The rulemakers evidently concluded that this was insufficient to outweigh the obvious advantage of litigating the same facts and issues between the same parties in a single action. Some state rulemakers have weighed these policies differently, however, and refused to make any counterclaims compulsory. See Friedenthal, Kane, and Miller at 350 n.15 (1985).

An Artistic Disaster

3a.   This is the simplest example of parties who wish to join as coplaintiffs in a single lawsuit. Rule 20(a) allows it, so long as they are asserting claims arising out of the same transaction or occurrence and their claims will involve at least one common question of law or fact. These criteria are met here because Morisot and Cassatt both seek relief arising out of the fire and both claims involve a common question of fact, whether Pissarro was negligent.[1]

---

1. Indeed, they may even be required to join as plaintiffs, under Fed. R. Civ. P. 19.

b. The only difference between this example and the first is that the two plaintiffs seek compensation for different injuries. However, that does not affect their right to sue together. Rule 20(a) does not require that the plaintiffs seek recovery for exactly the same injuries or on a joint interest. In fact, the rule specifically provides that any one plaintiff "need not be interested in obtaining . . . all the relief demanded." It only requires that the underlying transaction or occurrence be the same and that the two plaintiffs' claims share a common question of law or fact. Those criteria are met here, and joinder is proper under the rule.

This result is appropriate, given the efficiency and consistency goals of Rule 20(a). As long as the claims will require resolution of common issues, joint litigation in a single suit will save time for the parties, the witnesses, and the court.

c. Rule 20(a) applies not only to plaintiffs bringing suit together, but also to one or more plaintiffs bringing suit against multiple defendants. Here, Morisot seeks relief from all three defendants on claims arising out of the same fire, and her right to recover on each claim will require litigation of the negligence issue. Joinder is proper.

d. This example involves multiple plaintiffs and defendants. While Rule 20(a) does not explicitly authorize suit by multiple plaintiffs against multiple defendants, it does authorize suits by multiple plaintiffs and (in the subsequent sentence) against multiple defendants. It is a fair inference that both types of joinder may be used in the same suit. It is proper, therefore, for some or all of the potential plaintiffs to join to sue all of the potential defendants or to sue selected defendants.

The other difference in this example is that the two plaintiffs are proceeding on different theories: Cassatt for breach of contract and Morisot for negligence. Compare example 3b, in which the plaintiffs proceeded on the same theory but for different damages. Nothing in Rule 20(a) requires the plaintiffs to proceed on the same theories in order for joinder to be proper. The idea behind the joinder rule is that there is efficiency and consistency to be gained from litigating the same facts in a single action. These goals are served by joinder criteria that allow a single action even though the plaintiffs are proceeding on different theories.

However, the criteria of Rule 20(a) must still be met. In this case the "same transaction or occurrence" test clearly is met since all claims arise out of the fire. The "common question of law or fact" requirement will likely be met as well: Both Morisot and Cassatt will have to prove that Pissarro's acts caused the fire in order to recover from Van Gogh and Renoir on their respective theories. So long as some such common question exists, joinder is proper, even though many issues (for example, the damages suffered by each plaintiff) will be totally different.

e. In this example either of the defendants may be liable to Cassatt, but not both. However, the requirements of Rule 20(a) are still satisfied, since

Cassatt still claims damages from each defendant, arising from the same occurrence, and the claims against both share the common question of who caused the fire. See Rule 20(a), which allows joinder if relief is sought against the defendants "jointly, severally or in the alternative," as long as the two basic joinder criteria are met.

f. In this case, it is the defendant who has joined multiple parties in the action, not the plaintiff:

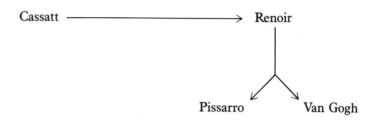

The general language of the second sentence of Rule 20(a), if read in isolation, might be interpreted to allow a defendant to join new parties as "defendants" in the original action. However, a look at Rule 14(a) indicates that this type of situation, a defendant bringing new parties into the suit (whom the plaintiff did not choose to sue), is separately dealt with in that rule, which allows joinder only in much more limited circumstances than Rule 20(a). See Chapter 13.

By contrast, Rule 20(a) only applies to joinder of parties by the original plaintiffs. The rulemakers' meticulous language confirms this: Rule 20(a) speaks specifically of "plaintiffs" and "defendants" rather than "parties claiming a right to relief" or similarly general language. Compare Rules 18 and 13, which are deliberately phrased more generally in order to apply more broadly.

4. This example is typical of the myriad cases in which plaintiffs assert a number of claims against a single defendant for the same injuries but base those claims on different theories of relief. The question here is joinder of claims, not parties, since Cassatt is seeking relief from a single party on two separate claims. Rule 18(a) establishes a refreshingly broad rule for joinder of claims: Once Cassatt decides to sue Renoir, she may join whatever claims she has against Renoir in the suit. Thus, joinder of the negligence and contract claims is proper. It would also be proper if they were totally unrelated.

5. The answer to this question involves application of both Rules 20 and 18. Rule 20 allows Cassatt to sue Renoir and Van Gogh together for breach of the studio-painting contract. Compare example 3c. Rule 18 allows Cassatt, once she has properly asserted a claim against Renoir, to assert her unrelated contract claim against Renoir as well, even though it arises out of a completely separate incident. Visually, the case looks like this:

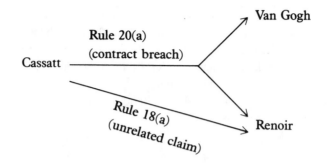

This compound effect of the rules is confusing. It seems to contradict the limitations on joinder established in Rule 20(a), since it allows Cassatt to inject into the case a claim that is completely unrelated to the transaction or occurrence that gave rise to the joint claim she has against the two defendants. After all, if she sued Van Gogh on the studio claim and joined Renoir on the unrelated claim only, joinder would not be proper under Rule 20(a) . . . *n'est-ce pas*? That is true, but the Rules take the position that once you *have* properly gotten the two of them into court, you may add any claims you have against either defendant, related or unrelated. Presumably, the theory is that once the parties become proper adversaries in a lawsuit they ought at least to have the opportunity to resolve all their differences in one suit.

6.   This example is meant to emphasize one point about Rule 18(a): It is permissive. Cassatt may assert unrelated claims against Renoir under Rule 18(a) but is not obligated to do so. Thus, she could bring separate actions against Renoir on these two unrelated contract claims in whatever order she chooses.

One note of caution should be added. While Rule 18 may not force a plaintiff to join all his claims against a defendant in a single action, the rules of res judicata will (at least under federal res judicata principles) if the claims arise out of a single transaction or occurrence. If Morisot has claims for breach of contract and negligence against Renoir and both arise from the studio fire, these would constitute a single "claim" for res judicata purposes that must be litigated in one action, despite the permissive language of Rule 18(a). See Chapter 22, which compares the joinder rules with the principles of res judicata; especially example 2, which specifically addresses the Rule 18 issue. However, because the two claims asserted here are completely unrelated, separate suits will be permissible under res judicata analysis, as well as under Rule 18(a).

The Tables Turned

7.   Morisot's joinder of Renoir and Pissarro as codefendants is proper here under Rule 20(a). Renoir's claim against Morisot is a counterclaim under Rule 13(a), that is, a claim by a defending party against the party suing him.

Not only do the rules authorize Renoir to assert this claim, they require him to do so. Rule 13(a) provides that a defending party's pleading "shall" state as a counterclaim any claim he has that arises out of the same transaction or occurrence as the main claim. Here, Renoir's claim arises out of the performance of the same contract that gave rise to one of Morisot's claims. It is therefore a compulsory counterclaim under Rule 13(a).

8.   Rule 13 provides for the assertion of both compulsory (13(a)) and permissive (13(b)) counterclaims. In this example, Renoir has properly asserted one of each: the compulsory claim against Morisot based on the painting contract and the permissive counterclaim arising out of his auto accident with Morisot. The difference between the two is the source of the claim: The contract claim, which arises out of the same transaction as the original claim, is compulsory, while the claim arising from unrelated events is permissive.

9.   Yes, Renoir is free to assert his unrelated counterclaim, even though it is the only claim he has against Morisot. Rule 13(b) authorizes the assertion of unrelated counterclaims without restriction.

   This may seem illogical. Why drag claims into the lawsuit that will have no factual relation to the main claim? It hardly seems likely to promote efficiency to join the painting contract claim with the auto accident claim, which will present completely different factual and legal issues. The rules allow joinder of such claims, however, on the theory that a defendant, once forced into court by the plaintiff, at least ought to have the option to settle all disputes with that plaintiff in a single action. That way, the defendant can save the cost of filing a new action and serving process again, and perhaps lower the cost of discovery as well. Also, in terms of fairness, the rule gives defendants the same broad authority to join unrelated claims that plaintiffs have under Rule 18(a). If a single trial does not make sense, the court may order separate trials. Fed. R. Civ. P. 42(b).

10.   Here Renoir asserts a counterclaim against Morisot and wants to add Cassatt as an additional party to the counterclaim. Although the plaintiff is ordinarily "master of his claim," to include or exclude possible parties, this is a situation where the defendant also gets some control over the parties. Under Rule 13(h), Renoir is authorized to bring in an additional party on the counterclaim, so long as the requirements of Rule 20(a) (same transaction or occurrence and common question of law or fact) are met. They are met here, so the joinder of Cassatt as an additional party to the counterclaim against Morisot is proper.

Acting at Cross-Purposes

11a. This is the first example in which one defendant seeks to recover against a codefendant. Rule 13(g) authorizes assertion of such "cross-claims" if they arise out of the same transaction or occurrence as the original claim. Renoir's claim qualifies because it arises out of the fire.

   b.   Be careful to distinguish cross-claims from counterclaims. Counterclaims are asserted against a party who has asserted a claim against you. Cross-claims are asserted against a coparty, that is, a party to the action who is on the same side of the "v" as the cross-claimant. Renoir's claim is not a counterclaim since Renoir is not claiming against Cassatt, who sued him, but against Pissarro, his codefendant.

12. This is also a valid cross-claim under Rule 13(g). It differs from the last example because the cross-claimant here seeks recovery for his own injuries, not indemnification for damages he may have to pay the plaintiff. Either type of claim is permissible so long as it arises out of the transaction or occurrence that gave rise to the main claim. The second sentence of Rule 13(g) specifically allows cross-claims for indemnification, such as Renoir asserted in example 11. But the broad language of the first sentence clearly authorizes any cross-claim that arises from the same underlying events as the main claim in the action.

13. This attempt at joinder is improper. As already stated, Rule 13(g) requires that the cross-claim arise out of the same transaction or occurrence as the main claim; this completely unrelated claim is therefore improper. Under the efficiency rationale of the joinder rules, this result is appropriate. There will be little efficiency gained from litigating the unrelated claim in this suit because it involves a completely separate transaction. In addition, litigating these claims separately poses no risk of inconsistent judgments because the judgments rendered on them will not involve the same issues.

14. After the last example, you may be somewhat frustrated by the answer to this one: Joinder of both claims is proper here. Renoir's claim for his own injuries is a proper cross-claim (as in example 12). And, once a proper cross-claim has been asserted against Van Gogh, Renoir may add on any other claims he has against Van Gogh, under Rule 18(a).

It is crucial to understand the differing role of Rule 18(a) in these two cases. Although Rule 18(a) appears on its face to authorize any party to assert any claim he has against an opposing party, the rule actually requires a party to assert one claim that is proper under the other joinder rules before he can add others to it under Rule 18(a). Thus, once Renoir has properly asserted a cross-claim against Van Gogh under Rule 13(g), he may add others under Rule 18(a). Similarly, if Renoir asserted a third-party claim against Pissarro under Rule 14(a), he could add others under Rule 18(a). But Rule 18(a) is not a general hunting license to assert any claim against any party; if it were, all the other rules discussed in this chapter would be unnecessary.

Admittedly, it does not seem logical to allow Renoir to assert the unrelated claim if he asserts a related one (as here), but not if he asserts it alone (as in example 13). Yet, that is just what the Rules do. The apparent rationale is that once Renoir and Van Gogh become adversaries by the assertion of a proper cross-claim, they might just as well resolve all their differences in a single suit. Once again, the court has the discretion to order a separate trial of the unrelated claim if there is no efficiency to be gained from joint litigation.

15. Not only may Van Gogh assert this claim, he *must* do so under Rule 13(a). When Renoir claims against him, Van Gogh becomes a defending party subject to the counterclaim rules of 13(a) and (b). Visually the case looks like this:

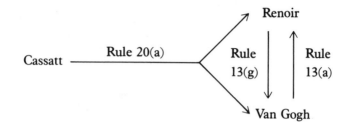

Remember that the counterclaim rules are written in general language to apply to all defending parties, not just original defendants. Since Van Gogh's claim for indemnification from Renoir arises out of the same transaction or occurrence as the cross-claim, it is a compulsory counterclaim and must be asserted in this action or lost.

Last Impressionists

16. The point of this example is so important that I have devoted an entire chapter to it. See Chapter 15. The problem here is that Morisot has properly joined Van Gogh and Renoir as codefendants under Rule 20(a), but the court lacks subject matter jurisdiction because there is neither complete diversity nor a federal claim. The joinder rules do not provide a basis for subject matter jurisdiction, they only govern who may properly be made parties if the court has jurisdiction. Thus, this case is not properly before the court, even though the joinder rules are satisfied.

13

Into the Labyrinth: Joinder of Parties under Rule 14

Introduction

A persistent civil procedure theme explored in the earlier chapters is the right of the plaintiff or plaintiffs to sculpt the lawsuit by their choice of the forum and their initial decisions to join parties as plaintiffs or defendants. An equally persistent theme, however, is the various ways in which the plaintiff's well-laid plans may go awry. For example, she may end up in a different court if the defendant removes or seeks a change of venue; or she may end up *defending* a claim if another party asserts a cross-claim or counterclaim against her.

Rule 14 provides another example of the complexities that await the unwary plaintiff who disregards Dickens's famous advice.[1] Rule 14 gives a defendant a limited right to *implead* (that is, bring into the suit) new parties against whom she has claims related to the main action. Under the rule the defendant may bring in a person not yet a party to the suit who may be liable to her, the defendant, for all or part of any recovery the plaintiff obtains on the main claim.

In many tort cases third parties are impleaded for *contribution,* that is, to obtain a judgment that the third party is liable to pay the main defendant part of the damages she is ordered to pay the plaintiff. For example, suppose that

---

1. "Suffer any indignity that can be done you rather than come [to the courts of chancery]." Charles Dickens, Bleak House 7 (Norton ed. 1977).

Napoleon sues Wellington for negligently injuring him during a polo match. Wellington claims that Robespierre, riding a third horse, was also negligent. Under the usual rules of contribution among joint tortfeasors, Wellington would be entitled to recover from Robespierre half of any damages Wellington pays Napoleon, if he can prove that Robespierre was also negligent. On these facts Wellington may implead Robespierre under Rule 14 since he may be liable to Wellington for part of any damages that Wellington is ordered to pay Napoleon. The case looks like this:

Napoleon ————————————→ Wellington (defendant/third-party
plaintiff)

Rule 14(a)

↓

Robespierre (third-party defendant)

In other cases the defendant may claim that the third party is liable to her for all damages that she may have to pay the plaintiff. In the Schulansky case, for example, in the last claim for relief in the third-party complaint Ronan alleges that Jones is liable to *indemnify* him for any damages that Schulansky recovers from Ronan, since Jones's negligence allegedly caused the damage that led to the action against Ronan. (See infra p.478.) Another common example of a proper impleader claim is a claim for indemnity against an insurer. If Wellington has liability insurance with Lloyds of London, he may implead Lloyds for indemnity. In this example, Wellington claims that if he is held liable to Napoleon, Lloyds should reimburse him as it has contractually agreed to do in the insurance agreement. In both examples in this paragraph, the defendant seeks to pass on all of his liability, not just a part as in the contribution example. This also satisfies the requirement in Rule 14 that the impleaded party may be liable to the defendant for "all or part" of the plaintiff's claim against the defendant.

It is crucial to distinguish these cases from situations in which the defendant contends that another person is liable directly to the plaintiff but not to her. Suppose that Wellington's polo match took place in a jurisdiction that did not allow contribution between joint tortfeasors. In that case Robespierre might still be liable to Napoleon directly, but Wellington could not implead him because Robespierre would not be liable to Wellington at all. He can't offer up Robespierre as an alternate defendant to Napoleon, saying, "Here, Napoleon, you sued me, but you really should have sued us both, so here's Robespierre; go at him." That would allow the defendant to dictate to the plaintiff whom to sue where, in defiance of the conventional doctrine that the plaintiff is master of her claim.

To further illustrate this point, assume that a police officer assaults Dillinger in the course of arresting him for robbery. Dillinger sues Officer Hayes, a six-foot-two, red-headed policeman, for the assault. Hayes claims mistaken identity: It was actually Officer Kelly, another six-foot redhead, who arrested Dillinger. Hayes cannot implead Kelly. He has no claim that Kelly is liable to him. Either one or the other assaulted Dillinger; one or the other will be solely liable to him. Hayes contends of course that Dillinger should have sued Kelly instead of him, but this gives him no right to substitute another defendant or to add one under Rule 14. That rule does not allow defendants to suggest new targets for the plaintiff. Rather, it allows defendants to bring in targets of their own if they may be able to pass on liability to the impleaded party.[2]

It follows from this central requirement of Rule 14 that the third-party defendant's liability depends on the outcome of the main claim. If Napoleon does not recover from Wellington, Wellington will have no right of contribution against Robespierre. Robespierre can hardly be asked to contribute if Wellington doesn't have to pay; nor would Lloyds be liable to indemnify Wellington unless Wellington has to pay a judgment; nor Jones to pay Ronan if Schulansky loses on the main claim. The impleaded party may escape liability by defeating either the plaintiff's original claim or the defendant's derivative claim against her. Consequently, the rule allows her to assert defenses to both. See Rule 14(a), fourth sentence (defenses to third-party claim) and fifth sentence (defenses to the plaintiff's claim against the original defendant).

The impleader claim is treated like an original suit for pleading, service, and other purposes. The defendant, as "third-party plaintiff," must file a third-party complaint against the impleaded "third-party defendant." The complaint must comply with the pleading requirements of Rules 8 through 11 and must be served under Rule 4. The third-party defendant must respond under Rule 12 and has the same options to answer or move to dismiss. The third-party defendant may also file counterclaims against the third-party plaintiff and may implead further parties under Rule 14. That rule also allows

---

2. At one time Rule 14 did allow defendants to add new parties who might be liable directly to the plaintiff. That provision created serious problems that led to the elimination of this option:

> [I]n some cases plaintiff declined to press his claim against the third-party defendant and could not be compelled to amend his complaint in order to do so. When that occurred, the third-party action would have to be dropped since no one had alleged a claim against the third-party defendant. In other cases, an amendment to assert a direct claim against the third-party defendant, if allowed, would have destroyed diversity of citizenship as the basis of federal jurisdiction. For these reasons the rule was amended in 1948 to eliminate defendant's right to implead persons directly liable to plaintiff.

6 Wright and Miller at 287-288.

the plaintiff and the third-party defendant to assert claims against each other if they arise out of the same transaction or occurrence as the main claim. See Rule 14, sixth and seventh sentences.

Under Rule 14 the defendant may implead a third party within ten days of answering the complaint, without obtaining leave of court. This automatic impleader provision suggests that the court must hear the third-party claim if it is filed within the ten-day period. However, the cases establish that it is always within the court's discretion to refuse to entertain the impleader claim. See generally 3 Moore's at ¶14.05[2]. Factors favoring impleader include the efficiency of hearing the related claims together and avoidance of repeated suits or inconsistent judgments. Factors suggesting denial of impleader include undue delay in seeking it, complication of the issues in the main action, and potential prejudice to the plaintiff from impleading a sympathetic third party. In some cases the court may be able to address these concerns by allowing the impleader but separating the main suit and the third-party suit for trial. See Rule 14, eighth sentence; 6 Wright and Miller at §1443.

Two further points should be mentioned concerning the relation of impleader claims to the three-ring analysis in the earlier chapters. First, in determining whether diversity jurisdiction is proper, the citizenship of the third-party defendant is irrelevant; only the citizenship of the original parties is considered. Suppose, for example, that Napoleon is from Maine, Wellington from Connecticut, and Robespierre from Maine:

The original case between Napoleon and Wellington is a proper diversity case. Wellington's impleader of Robespierre does not affect the court's jurisdiction over that case, even though Robespierre is from Maine. Nor would it defeat jurisdiction over the original case if Robespierre was from Connecticut. However, there still must be a basis for subject matter jurisdiction over the impleader claim itself. If Robespierre were from Connecticut, there would be no diversity between the parties to that claim. In most cases subject matter jurisdiction over such added claims will be proper under 28 U.S.C. §1367(a), which authorizes "supplemental jurisdiction" over many claims added under the joinder rules. See Chapter 14, p.227.

The third party is also disregarded in determining whether venue is proper. For example, the case in the illustration could properly be brought in the District of Connecticut, where Wellington resides, under 28 U.S.C. §1391(a)(1), despite the fact that the third-party defendant resides in Maine, not Connecticut. 6 Wright and Miller at §1445, p.348. If the third party's citizenship were counted, defendants would be able to defeat federal jurisdiction in many cases in which the plaintiff had properly invoked it, simply by impleading defendants from the right (that is, the wrong) states.

The examples below may help to dispel some of the darkness that engulfs this murky rule. In considering them, assume that all cases are brought in federal court and that subject matter jurisdiction is proper in each case. In addition, focus on whether the claim would satisfy the requirements of Rule 14, not whether the court (assuming the rule is satisfied) would exercise its discretion to hear the impleader claim.

EXAMPLES

Pleaders and Impleaders

1.   Ali sues Bellefonds, the engineer on a canal construction project, for negligence arising out of faulty engineering calculations in planning the canal. May Bellefonds implead Le Pere, another engineer whom he claims was also negligent in making the calculations?

2.   Ali sues Bellefonds for his faulty engineering calculations. Bellefonds impleads Le Pere, alleging that it was actually Le Pere who did the calculations. Is the impleader proper?

3.   France sues DeLesseps, a general contractor, for faulty canal construction. DeLesseps claims that if there was a breach it was actually the fault of Said, the subcontractor he hired to do the dredging work on the canal, and that Said should therefore bear the loss. Can he implead Said?

4.   Suppose that DeLesseps is unclear as to whether the defective construction work resulted from Said's dredging work or faulty concrete work done by another subcontractor, Ismail. May he implead both?

5.   Assume that France sues DeLesseps on the canal contract, and DeLesseps wishes to recover from Said, his subcontractor, for certain camels Said took away when he left the job. May he implead Said?

6.   In the same contract action, could DeLesseps implead Said and assert both the indemnification claim described in example 3 and the camel-trover claim in example 5?

Heads of the Hydra

7.   Suppose that DeLesseps is sued by France for breach of the canal contract. He impleads Said for faulty subcontract work, and Said wants to assert

a claim against France for intentional interference with his contract with DeLesseps. May he do so?

8.   Notice that the language of the Rule (always *so* carefully chosen by the Solomons of civil procedure) does not call Said's claim against France in the last example a counterclaim. Why isn't it a counterclaim?

9.   Think of three ways in which a counterclaim could insinuate itself into this suit.

10. Assume that DeLesseps impleads Said for indemnification on the theory that his faulty dredging work caused the contract breach. Said claims that his insurer, Cairo Casualty and Indemnity Co., has a duty to pay any damages resulting from his breach. May Said assert a claim against Cairo in the same action?

11. If Said is impleaded, may France assert a claim against Said for shoddy construction on an unrelated job Said did for France?

12. Suppose that DeLesseps counterclaims against France, to collect the contract price for the canal work. May France implead Disraeli, who co-signed the contract along with France and is, therefore, also contractually bound to pay DeLesseps for the contract work?

Another Unlucky Number 13

13. Assume that France is from California, DeLesseps from Texas, and Said from Arizona. The canal work was done in Colorado. France sues DeLesseps in Texas, and DeLesseps impleads Said. Is the impleader proper?

A Last Brainteaser for the Rules Enthusiast

14. Along the same general lines as the earlier examples, assume that France sues DeLesseps, who then impleads Said. Said wishes to assert a claim against France for interference with his contract with DeLesseps. He also claims that Porte (an agent of France not yet a party to the suit) took part in the intentional interference. Can Said add Porte as an additional party to his interference-with-contract claim against France? Visually the hypo looks like this:

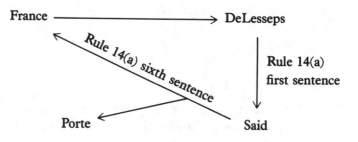

EXPLANATIONS

Pleaders and Impleaders

1.   Here, Bellefonds seeks to implead Le Pere, not yet a party to the suit, to recover part of any judgment Ali recovers from Bellefonds. Assuming that the relevant state law authorizes contribution among joint tortfeasors, this is a proper impleader claim. Le Pere is a new party who "is or may be liable to the third-party plaintiff [Bellefonds] for all or part of the plaintiff's claim against [Bellefonds]." If Bellefonds is found liable to Ali and Le Pere is also found negligent, Bellefonds will be entitled to recover from Le Pere half of the damages Bellefonds pays Ali. Note that at the time he impleads Le Pere, it is not clear that Le Pere will be liable to contribute. That depends on whether Bellefonds is found negligent, whether Le Pere is found negligent, and whether Bellefonds pays more than half of the judgment. But the rule only requires that Le Pere "may" be liable to Bellefonds; Le Pere's liability need not follow automatically from Bellefonds's, nor must Bellefonds have already been adjudged liable before he can implead Le Pere.

2.   As stated in the introduction, impleader under Rule 14 cannot be used to foist alternate defendants on the plaintiff. Ali chose to sue Bellefonds, not Le Pere. If Bellefonds didn't do the faulty calculations, Ali will lose his suit against him. Maybe Ali will then sue Le Pere or maybe he won't. That is his choice. But Bellefonds may not bring Le Pere in on the mere allegation that LePere is liable to Ali. Bellefonds may only implead Le Pere to recover from him part of the damages Bellefonds must pay Ali. If liability is an either/or proposition, Bellefonds has no such claim against Le Pere, and impleader should be denied.

   Ali could have chosen to join Bellefonds and Le Pere as codefendants under Rule 20(a). See Chapter 12, p.201. Alternatively, Bellefonds may defend against Ali's claim on the ground that Le Pere was the offending party instead of him. But he can't use Rule 14 as a backdoor means of forcing Ali to sue Le Pere, which Rule 20(a) allows, but does not require, Ali to do.

3.   This is a proper impleader claim. DeLesseps, as the general contractor, will be liable to France if the work does not meet the contract specifications even though it was a subcontractor's negligence that caused the breach. However, DeLesseps will surely have a contractual right under his separate contract with Said to indemnity for damages caused by Said's faulty subcontract work. Thus, Said "may be liable to the third-party plaintiff [DeLesseps] for all . . . of the plaintiff's claim against [DeLesseps]," and DeLesseps may properly implead Said under the first sentence of Rule 14(a).

4.   In this case Said is unclear as to whether he should be indemnified by one subcontractor or the other or both. Although the rule is not explicit on the point, there is no reason why a defendant should have to limit his impleader claims to one third party when several may be liable to him. As long

as the provisions of Rule 14 are satisfied, a defendant may implead multiple third-party defendants, claiming either joint or alternate liability.

5.   This is not a proper impleader claim. Here, DeLesseps has a claim against Said, arising out of the same transaction (the construction of the canal) as the main claim, but Said's liability to DeLesseps is not derivative of the main suit. DeLesseps has a totally independent claim against Said, which he could assert whether France wins or loses on the main claim or never sues at all.

It might make sense to design the rules of procedure to allow the defendant to expand the lawsuit in this way, but it would certainly introduce many tangential claims sharing few witnesses or factual or legal issues with the main claim. That would be the case here, since the claim for the missing camels is clearly distinct from the faulty construction claim. The rule-makers decided to confine the defendant's options more narrowly, by use of the "may be liable to the third-party plaintiff for all or part of the plaintiff's claim" language. But see, with some perplexity, the following example.

6.   Curiously, despite the previous answer, Rule 18(a) expressly allows DeLesseps, once he has forced Said into the suit on a proper impleader claim, to add on this independent claim. Presumably the rationale for this is that once the third-party defendant is in the case the Rules might as well allow the defendant to settle all her differences with the third-party defendant in a single action. Visually the suit looks like this:

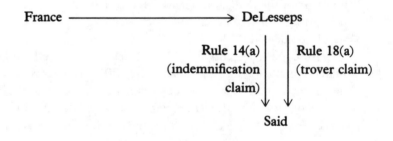

However, Rule 18(a) alone does not allow DeLesseps to bring Said into the suit. To do that, DeLesseps must first assert a claim complying with Rule 14. Rule 18 only allows him to add related (or unrelated) claims once he has properly impleaded Said under Rule 14.

Heads of the Hydra

7.   In this example, Said has been properly impleaded and seeks to assert a related claim against the original plaintiff. The sixth sentence of Rule 14(a) explicitly authorizes Said to do so. The suit now looks like this:

But Said cannot assert any claim he has against France. Under Rule 14(a), his claims against the plaintiff are limited to those that satisfy the same transaction or occurrence test encountered in Rule 20. Assuming the court takes a reasonably broad view of that test, this claim will satisfy it.

8. A counterclaim is defined in both Rules 13(a) and (b) as a claim against an "opposing party." Before Said asserts a claim against France they are not opposing parties. France has a claim against DeLesseps, not Said. Although France and Said are locked in the same litigious dance, they are not yet partners.

9. Counterclaims may be asserted by any defending party against her opponent. Rule 13(a). Obviously, DeLesseps may have some counterclaims against France. Said, once impleaded, may assert counterclaims against DeLesseps. See Rule 14(a), fourth sentence. Indeed, Said *must* assert them if they satisfy the Rule 13(a) test for compulsory counterclaims. For example, he may have a claim against DeLesseps for the subcontract price for his services. This claim arises out of the same transaction as DeLesseps's claim against him and must be asserted in the impleader action under Rule 13(a).

Finally, once Said has asserted a claim against France, they become opposing parties as well. If France has any claim against Said arising from the canal construction, he must assert it. If he has any other claim against Said, he may assert it as well under Rule 13(b). Thus, hydra-like,[3] the suit may grow:

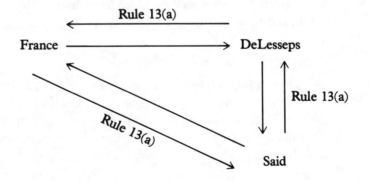

---

3. The hydra, a Greek beast, was reputed to sprout two heads for each lopped off by its unfortunate adversary.

10. Said may indeed implead Cairo under Rule 14(a). The ninth sentence of that rule allows the third-party defendant to assert such telescoping third-party claims against further parties. The suit now looks like this:

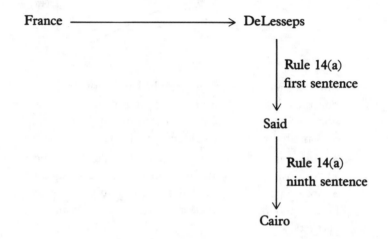

Imagine the title of Cairo's answer to this claim: "Fourth-Party Defendant's Answer to the Third-Party Defendant/Fourth-Party Plaintiff's Third-Party Complaint"!?[4]

11. France's claim here does not arise out of the same transaction or occurrence as the main claim. The seventh sentence of Rule 14 authorizes joinder of claims the plaintiff has against the third-party defendant if those claims satisfy the same transaction or occurrence test. By implication, the rule excludes unrelated claims, so this one fails. As well it should; there has to be some limit to the introduction of unrelated matters into the action, lest it become completely unmanageable.

12. This is an example of a plaintiff, now a defendant on a counterclaim, impleading a party who may be liable to her (the plaintiff) for all or part of a judgment the counterclaiming defendant obtains from her. It is explicitly authorized by Rule 14(b).

Another Unlucky Number 13

13. The fact that you were given the states for each party should have tipped you off that there is some jurisdictional problem here. It can't be diversity: As the Introduction points out, the third party's citizenship is irrelevant to determining diversity, and besides, there is complete diversity anyway. It can't be venue either: The third party's state is disregarded in determining

---

4. For a case taking these antics to the sixth power, see *Bevemet Metais, Ltda. v. Gallie Corp.*, 3 F.R.D. 352 (S.D.N.Y. 1942).

proper venue. Here, at least one district in Texas is a proper venue, since DeLesseps resides there, although Said, the third-party defendant, does not.

It must be personal jurisdiction. Indeed it is, or may be. *Whenever* a party is brought into a suit, whether as an original defendant, a third-party defendant, an additional party to a counterclaim, or whatever, the court must have the power to require that party to appear and defend in that state. Said's due process rights would be as clearly abridged if he were forced to defend a third-party action in a forum with which he lacks contacts as if he were forced into such a court as the original defendant. If Said objects to personal jurisdiction, the court will have to consider whether Said has minimum contacts with Texas or is subject to personal jurisdiction there for this claim on some other basis. Compare Jones's motion to dismiss in *Schulansky v. Ronan,* Chapter 30.

A Last Brain Teaser for the Rules Enthusiast

14. At some point the hydra must be stopped, and it appears that the Rules draw a limit here. Rule 14(a), sixth sentence, allows the third-party defendant to assert claims against the plaintiff if they arise out of the underlying dispute. That sentence makes no mention of adding additional parties. (Compare Rule 13(h), which expressly allows adding parties to counterclaims and cross-claims.) Nor does Rule 20(a) apply here; that rule only applies to the joinder of original defendants. For these more abstruse variants you have to find explicit authority in one of the other joinder rules, and it appears that by providing no such authority the rules stop short of allowing this claim.

14

Jurisdictional Fellow Travelers: Supplemental Jurisdiction

Introduction

The preceding chapters on the federal joinder rules describe a highly flexible system, which liberally allows parties to expand the litigation by joining claims in a single action. However, permission under the joinder rules to assert a claim, while necessary, is not sufficient to allow the court to hear it: From early on, we have seen that the court must always have subject matter jurisdiction over a claim if it is to proceed. As you have already read — and you will hear it repeated ad nauseum for the rest of your professional life — the subject matter jurisdiction of the federal courts is limited to the categories of cases enumerated in Article III, §2 of the Constitution.

These two principles, broad joinder under the Rules of Civil Procedure and the need for subject matter jurisdiction over every claim, are on something of a collision course. Frequently, the rules will authorize joinder of claims over which there is no independent basis of subject matter jurisdiction. Such cases pose a dilemma for the courts: The efficiency goals of the Rules favor inclusion of related claims, but the ineluctable need for subject matter jurisdiction appears to bar the court from hearing them.

Examples of the Problem

The problem can arise in a number of contexts. The simplest is the case in which the plaintiff asserts two claims against a nondiverse defendant, one arising under federal law and one under state law. Assume, for example, that Byron brings suit in federal court against Rossetti (a fellow resident of Wisconsin) for violation of a federal age discrimination statute and also claims that the dismissal constitutes a breach of contract. Visually, the case is illustrated as follows:

Federal Age Discrimination in Employment Act

(jurisdictionally proper under 28 U.S.C. §1331)

Byron
(**Wisconsin**)

Rossetti
(**Wisconsin**)

contract breach

(**no independent basis for federal
subject matter jurisdiction**)

Clearly, these claims are properly joined under the Rules. Rule 18(a). Also, the court clearly has jurisdiction over the federal law claim. But nothing in Article III authorizes jurisdiction over the breach of contract claim: The parties are not diverse, and the claim does not arise under federal law. If Byron sued solely on the contract claim, the federal court would have to dismiss it. Yet the efficiency and consistency goals of the Rules favor hearing Byron's two claims together, since they involve the same occurrence — the dismissal. Doubtless, the witnesses will be the same in both claims, and much of the same evidence will be relevant to both claims. If the federal court is to litigate this case, it would surely be desirable for it to hear the *whole* case, including the federal claim and the related state law claim.

Here is another example: Byron brings his dismissal action against Rossetti under the federal statute, and Rossetti counterclaims against Byron for assault, claiming that at the time of the firing Byron threatened to kill her for firing him. The case now looks like this:

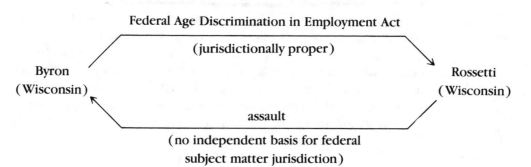

Federal Age Discrimination in Employment Act

(jurisdictionally proper)

Byron
(**Wisconsin**)

Rossetti
(**Wisconsin**)

assault

(**no independent basis for federal
subject matter jurisdiction**)

This is a compulsory counterclaim under Rule 13(a), since it arises from the same occurrence as Byron's claim. However, it is again a state law claim between parties from the same state. If Rossetti sued Byron on this claim alone, the federal court would not have the power to hear it, since nothing in Article III, §2 or the United States Code gives the federal district courts subject matter jurisdiction over state law claims between parties from the same state.

One more frequent example: Burns, from Wyoming, sues Cowper, from Utah, for injuries suffered in an auto accident. Cowper impleads a third driver, Hunt (also from Utah) under Rule 14(a), claiming that Hunt was also negligent and is therefore liable to him for contribution. The case is illustrated here:

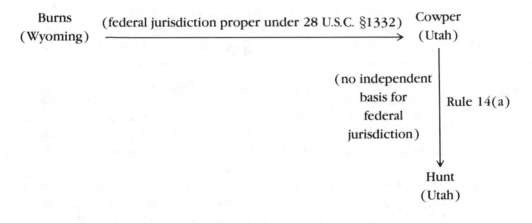

Again, this is proper under the Rules; and again, the existence of common issues argues for allowing the claim to be heard with the main claim. But, once again, there is no independent basis for subject matter jurisdiction: Cowper's claim is a state law claim between two citizens of the same state.

Essential History, Part I: Pendent Jurisdiction

Historically, two doctrines evolved to support jurisdiction over such related claims in federal court. The first, *pendent jurisdiction,* involved the configuration in the first diagram above, in which the plaintiff asserted a jurisdictionally proper claim against a nondiverse party and added on a related state law claim. In *United Mine Workers v. Gibbs,* 383 U.S. 715 (1966), the Supreme Court established guidelines for the exercise of jurisdiction over such "pendent" claims.

In *Gibbs* the plaintiff asserted a federal claim against the defendant under the Labor Management Relations Act and a second claim under state law for interference with contractual relations. Both claims were based on the same dispute, concerning the opening of a particular mine. Because there was no diversity between the parties in *Gibbs* and the interference claim arose under state law, there was no independent basis for subject matter jurisdiction over the interference claim. Yet the *Gibbs* Court held that the federal court had pendent jurisdiction over the state law claim because it was joined with the federal labor law claim.

The Court rationalized this conclusion on the ground that Article III grants jurisdiction over entire "cases," not just over particular claims or issues in a case. If a case includes a claim that is jurisdictionally proper under Article III, the argument goes, the court has constitutional power to hear the *entire dispute* between the parties, not just the claim that is expressly provided for in Article III, §2. Thus, so long as the plaintiff asserts a proper claim based on federal law, diversity, or some other federal ground, the federal court has the power — at least the *constitutional* power — to hear other claims arising out of the same "common nucleus of operative facts."[1] In *Gibbs,* for example, the case was properly before the federal court because the plaintiff asserted a claim under the federal labor laws. The constitutional "case," however, was broader than the federal claim, encompassing all of Gibbs's claims arising out of the same nucleus of operative facts, the opening of the new mine.

This holding in *Gibbs,* that a "case" includes not simply the plaintiff's jurisdictionally sufficient claims, but all claims that arise from the same set of historical facts, is one of the Court's most sensible and enduring procedural decisions. Further, it is consistent with the intent of the framers, who would hardly have contemplated that the federal courts would be required to dissect a single dispute and limit their jurisdiction to certain strands of a logically interrelated set of claims. The language of Article III, §2, after all, speaks in terms of "cases" and "controversies," not of individual causes of action.

While the *Gibbs* Court concluded that the federal courts had the *power* to hear claims that arose from the same nucleus of facts as the jurisdictionally proper claim, it did not *require* the federal court to entertain the related claims. Wisely, the Court provided a second step in the analysis: Once the judge ascertains that he has power to hear the related claim, because it is part of the same "case," he must then determine whether it makes sense to exercise that jurisdiction. See *Gibbs* at 726-727. This discretionary decision depended on a variety of factors in each case, such as whether the state law claim predominated, whether it would require the court to decide sensitive or novel issues of state law, whether hearing the claims together might confuse the jury, and whether the federal issues were resolved early in the case, leaving only a state law claim for decision. These factors might lead the court to

---

1. Chief Justice Marshall is a little more explicit on the point in *Osborn v. Bank of the United States,* 9 Wheat. 738 (1824):

> [W]hen a question to which the judicial power of the Union is extended by the constitution, forms an ingredient of the original cause, it is in the power of congress to give the [federal courts] . . . jurisdiction of that cause, although other questions of fact or of law may be involved in it.

conclude that, while it had power under the first part of *Gibbs* to entertain the pendent claim, it should refuse, in its discretion, to do so.

Essential History, Part II: Ancillary Jurisdiction — *must be logical relationship to the main claim (13(b) not good)*

The courts evolved a similar approach, under the rubric of *ancillary jurisdiction,* to deal with cases like those in the last two diagrams above, in which related claims were asserted by defendants or other additional parties after the initial complaint. In *Moore v. New York Cotton Exchange,* 270 U.S. 593 (1926), the plaintiff sued the defendant under the federal antitrust laws, and the defendant asserted a compulsory counterclaim against the plaintiff under state law. The Court upheld jurisdiction over the state law counterclaim, even though the parties were not diverse and there was no other basis for independent federal jurisdiction over the counterclaim. The Court's discussion in *Moore* is terse, but it did emphasize that the counterclaim (like all compulsory counterclaims) arose out of the same transaction as the main claim. Thus, the decision appears to turn, as did *Gibbs,* on the conclusion that the close connection between the original, jurisdictionally proper claim and the added claim made them part of a single "constitutional case."

From the seed of the *Moore* case, courts extended ancillary jurisdiction to many claims asserted by defending parties that bore a "logical relationship" to the main claim. Third-party claims like that in the last figure above were consistently held ancillary, since they are by definition "logically related" to the main claim: The third-party plaintiff can only recover from the third-party defendant if the plaintiff recovers from the third-party plaintiff. Fed. R. Civ. P. 14. On a similar rationale, ancillary jurisdiction was extended to cross-claims under Rule 13(g) and to intervention as of right under Rule 24(a). But the same logic dictated denial of ancillary jurisdiction for permissive counterclaims (see Rule 13(b)). By definition, such claims arose from different events, and therefore lacked a close logical relation to the main claim. See generally Friedenthal, Kane, and Miller at §2.14.

Essential History, Part III: A Statutory Basis

All of this was complex enough, but the Court multiplied these woes in three major cases by introducing a more sophisticated analysis of the limits of such supplemental jurisdiction. In *Aldinger v. Howard,* 427 U.S. 1 (1976), *Owen Equipment & Erection Co. v. Kroger,* 437 U.S. 365 (1978), and *Finley v. United States,* 490 U.S. 545 (1989), the court reiterated the basic principle that federal jurisdiction is not only limited by the Constitution but also must be conveyed to the federal district courts by Congress in a jurisdictional statute. (Recall Judge Sirica's well-phrased comments on the "Article III storehouse," supra p.56.)

In *Aldinger* the plaintiff was dismissed from her county job and brought suit against Howard and other individual defendants under a federal statute, 28 U.S.C. §1983. She also asserted a second state law claim, based on the same incident, against Spokane County. The case looked like this:

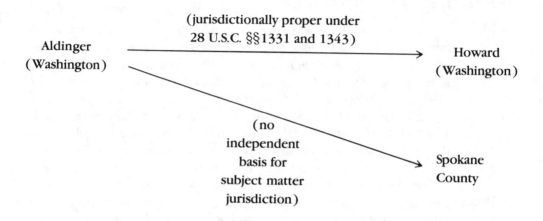

This was an attempt to exercise "pendent party" jurisdiction, that is, to add a jurisdictionally insufficient claim against one defendant to a jurisdictionally proper claim against the other. The claim against Howard was proper, since Aldinger asserted a right to relief under §1983, a federal statute. Jurisdiction was proper under 28 U.S.C. §1331 and under 28 U.S.C. §1343, a separate statute providing for jurisdiction in civil rights cases. However, the claim against the county was based on state law and, thus, not jurisdictionally proper in itself. *Aldinger* at 5. The Court concluded that even though the claim could be viewed as part of a single constitutional case under the first part of *Gibbs,* allowing a state law claim against the county would be inconsistent with the apparent intent of Congress to limit federal civil rights claims against counties.[2] Thus, there was no *statutory* grant of jurisdiction over the pendent party claim.

The second case, *Kroger,* involved an interesting twist on the established types of supplemental jurisdiction. In *Kroger,* the plaintiff sued the Oklahoma Public Power District (OPPD), a diverse defendant who impleaded Owen, a corporation, which (it turned out) was not diverse from either original party. The plaintiff, Kroger, then asserted a direct claim against Owen, as Rule 14(a) allows. The configuration of the parties was as follows:

---

2. At the time *Aldinger* was decided, counties were not considered "persons" subject to suit under §1983. *Monroe v. Pape,* 365 U.S. 167, 187-191 (1961). After *Aldinger* was decided, however, the Supreme Court overruled this aspect of *Monroe.* See *Monell v. Department of Social Services,* 436 U.S. 658, 690-691 (1978).

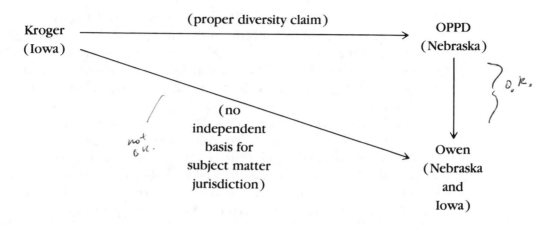

The issue posed was whether the court had jurisdiction over Kroger's claim against Owen.

The *Kroger* Court appeared to assume, under the constitutional analysis in *Gibbs,* that Kroger's claim against Owen was part of the same "constitutional case" as the main claim against OPPD. However, the Court went on to consider whether the relevant jurisdictional statute, 28 U.S.C. §1332, indicated congressional intent to grant federal courts ancillary jurisdiction over a related claim asserted by the plaintiff against a nondiverse third-party defendant. The Court held that extending ancillary jurisdiction to this claim would be inconsistent with the long-standing interpretation of §1332, requiring complete diversity between the parties. Since Mrs. Kroger could not have sued OPPD and Owen together originally, it would ignore the statutory limits on jurisdiction to allow her to do the same thing indirectly.

However, the *Kroger* Court's discussion suggested that ancillary jurisdiction could be exercised over compulsory counterclaims, cross-claims, and third-party claims. The opinion implied, for example, that OPPD's claim against Owen would be ancillary, even though it also abridges the complete diversity requirement. The court emphasized the difference between the claim of a defending party, brought in against its will, and a plaintiff, who presumably had the choice to sue all parties jointly in state court. 437 U.S. at 375-377.

The third important background case, *Finley v. United States,* involved pendent party jurisdiction. The plaintiff, Finley, sued the United States under the Federal Tort Claims Act (FTCA). Jurisdiction over this claim was proper under Article III, §2 because the United States was a party. It was also authorized by 28 U.S.C. §1346(b), which gives the federal district courts exclusive jurisdiction[3] over claims against the United States under the FTCA.

---

3. "Exclusive" jurisdiction means that *only* the federal court can hear such claims. Thus, Mrs. Finley had no chance to bring her claim against the United States in state court, which clearly could have heard her state law claims against the other defendants.

However, Finley also asserted state law claims against other defendants in the action. There was no diversity between the plaintiff and these defendants; instead she asked the court to take jurisdiction over them on the basis of "pendent party" jurisdiction. The configuration of the parties looked much like that in *Aldinger,* in which the court had previously refused to allow pendent party jurisdiction.

Although the pendent party claims in *Finley* arose from the same nucleus of facts as the jurisdictionally proper claim against the United States, the *Finley* Court reiterated that jurisdiction must be granted not only by Article III, but also by statute. The Court found no indication in §1346(b) that Congress meant to convey jurisdiction over any claims other than those against the United States. Consequently, it held that the district court had no jurisdiction over the pendent party claims. As the Court acknowledged, this meant that Mrs. Finley would have to bring two lawsuits, one in federal court against the United States and a second state court action against the other defendants. But that, the court opined, was not a reason to ignore the statutory limits on the federal court's subject matter jurisdiction. 490 U.S. at 555-556.

After *Finley* it appeared that pendent and ancillary jurisdiction had converged into a single doctrine, which required a three-part analysis.

First, the court had to consider whether there was a constitutional basis for the exercise of jurisdiction over the related but jurisdictionally insufficient claim. This analysis, set forth in the first part of *Gibbs,* turned on whether the plaintiff had asserted a substantial claim within the federal court's jurisdiction and whether the state law claim was part of the same "constitutional case" because it arose from the same "nucleus of operative facts."

Second, if the court could constitutionally assert jurisdiction over the entire case, including the state law claims, it would analyze the congressional intent behind the statute that granted jurisdiction over the proper federal claim. If the statute or its legislative history suggested that Congress had "expressly or by implication negated" (*Aldinger* at 18) jurisdiction over the related, jurisdictionally insufficient claim, it could not hear it. If, on the other hand, there was evidence of congressional intent to confer broad jurisdiction over the entire "case," including the added claims, then the court at least had power to entertain all the claims in the case.

Third, if the added claims passed the first two parts of the test so that the court had jurisdictional power to hear them, the court then decided whether it should exercise that jurisdiction, based on the various discretionary factors discussed in *Gibbs*.

A Stroke of the Pen

All of this case law is now history, albeit very important history. In 1990 Congress enacted 28 U.S.C. §1367, which for the first time provides a statutory basis for "supplemental jurisdiction" in the federal courts. With a stroke of the pen, Congress has substantially clarified the authority of the federal courts to entertain claims that are related to proper federal claims, but are not jurisdictionally proper in themselves.

Let's take §1367 one section at a time. Section 1367(a) provides:

> Except as otherwise provided in subsections (b) and (c) or as expressly provided otherwise by Federal statute, in any civil action of which the district courts have original jurisdiction, the district courts shall have supplemental jurisdiction over all other claims that are so related to claims in the action within such original jurisdiction that they form part of the same case or controversy under Article III of the United States Constitution. Such supplemental jurisdiction shall include claims that involve the joinder or intervention of additional parties.

Under this section, if the plaintiff brings a proper federal claim or diversity claim, so that the federal court has "original jurisdiction," the court may hear all the claims that are part of the same "case or controversy under Article III. . . ." While the section does not explicitly define what claims come within a single case or controversy, this phrase will almost certainly be given the same meaning in §1367 that it was given in *United Mine Workers v. Gibbs*. Congress was aware of the widespread use of the *Gibbs* test for a single "constitutional case" in pendent and ancillary jurisdiction cases. Since it chose the same concept in defining the limits of supplemental jurisdiction, the natural inference is that it meant to adopt the same standard. See 13B Wright and Miller §3567.3 [1991 Supp.] (§1367 "ratifies and incorporates" the constitutional analysis in *Gibbs*). Thus, it appears that the section (with certain exceptions discussed below) authorizes the courts to hear all claims that arise out of the same nucleus of operative facts as the proper federal claim. This includes additional claims asserted by the plaintiff, but also those asserted by other parties as well, such as cross-claims and counterclaims.

If *Gibbs* already defined a single constitutional case in those terms, why did Congress pass the statute? Well, in *Aldinger, Kroger,* and *Finley,* the Supreme Court emphasized that it was not enough that the court has constitutional power to hear the related claim. These cases required statutory authority to exercise that jurisdiction as well. This opened up a complex second level of analysis: The court had to look at many different jurisdictional statutes, most of which showed little evidence one way or the other about the intent to allow related state law claims, and divine Congress's intent. Where there was no evidence of intent to allow the related claims, *Finley* strongly suggested that pendent or ancillary jurisdiction could not be exercised, thus severely undermining the efficiency goals of the broad joinder rules.

By enacting §1367, Congress responded to *Finley* (decided the previous year) by *providing the necessary statutory authority to hear the related claims*. The Court in its recent cases had said, "Congress, we can't exercise jurisdiction, even if it would be proper under Article III, unless you give it to us as well." And Congress responded by saying, "Okay federal courts, you say we have to give you jurisdiction over the related claims, so here it is." The authority Congress gave is very broad indeed, reaching in most situations to the outer bounds of the "constitutional case" before the court. For future cases, the statute, not the "essential history" cases reviewed above, provide the governing law. For example, the exercises of pendent party jurisdiction held improper in *Finley* and *Aldinger* would be upheld on similar facts under §1367.

Limits on Supplemental Jurisdiction

There are some exceptions to this broad grant of supplemental jurisdiction. Section 1367(b) provides that supplemental jurisdiction does *not* extend to certain claims by plaintiffs in diversity cases which would be inconsistent with the limits of §1332. Once again, this provision must be read against the "essential history" reviewed above. This section obviously responds to *Kroger,* in which the Court rejected jurisdiction over Mrs. Kroger's claim because it contradicted the complete diversity requirement in §1332. Just as Congress appears to have adopted the broad test of *Gibbs* as the general test for the reach of related claims, it has also endorsed the limitation placed on such claims in *Kroger,* by excepting in §1367(b) claims joined by the original plaintiff, which would be inconsistent with the diversity statute.[4]

Finally, in §1367(c) Congress codified the second holding in *Gibbs.* That section requires the court to exercise discretion in determining whether to take supplemental jurisdiction, based on the factors established 25 years earlier in *Gibbs.*

An Attempted Synthesis

The *Aldinger/Kroger/Finley* trilogy suggested that pendent and ancillary jurisdiction were coalescing into a single doctrine. Congress has confirmed this by adopting a single term, "supplemental jurisdiction," to describe the authority that it provides courts to hear claims that would previously have been classified as either pendent or ancillary. Such supplemental jurisdiction under §1367 still requires a three-part analysis:

First, the court must determine whether there is constitutional power under Article III, §2 to hear the supplemental claim. This analysis has nothing to do with §1367: Congress cannot determine by statute what claims the Constitution authorizes a court to hear. The analysis must still stem from *Gibbs,* which held that the constitutional power to hear the related claim exists if there is a proper claim within the jurisdiction of the federal court and

---

4. In one respect, §1367(b) restricts jurisdiction previously considered proper. Prior to the new statute, claims by intervenors as of right under Fed. R. Civ. P. 24(a) were considered ancillary, even if the intervenor destroyed complete diversity. This anomaly has been eliminated by §1367(b), which bars such claims in diversity cases.

the related claim arises from the same nucleus of operative facts. This level of the analysis is no different now than it was before §1367 was enacted.

Second, the court must determine whether there is a statutory grant of jurisdiction over the related claim. Now, such a grant is provided in most cases by §1367 itself. Because §1367(a) grants jurisdiction over all related claims that are part of the same "case," the answer to the statutory question will be much simpler than it was under *Kroger* and *Finley.* The court need not analyze a variety of jurisdictional statutes (like §§1343 and 1346(b)), which contain little evidence of an intent one way or the other concerning related claims. Statutory authority is broadly granted for all types of cases under §1367(a) if the *Gibbs* constitutional test is met. However, under §1367(b), certain claims in diversity cases, which would contradict the limits on jurisdiction in §1332, are excepted.

Third, Congress has codified the second half of the *Gibbs* analysis in §1367(c). Once the court determines that it has constitutional and statutory authority to hear the related claims, it must decide, based on the various discretionary factors in that section, whether to do so.

To properly analyze the following examples, it would help to read *Gibbs, Kroger,* and *Finley,* as well as §1367 and this Introduction. It will also help to draw quick diagrams of the configuration of the parties and claims in the examples. Then consider whether the constitutional test of *Gibbs* and the similar test in §1367(a) are met. (Disregard for the moment the third, discretionary prong of the analysis.) Assume that all cases are brought in federal court.

EXAMPLES

Simple Addition

1.   Keats, from Minnesota, is arrested by Shelley, a Minnesota police officer, for disturbing the peace. During the arrest, Shelley forcibly restrains Keats, and Keats resists. Keats claims that Shelley used excessive force in making the arrest and sues Shelley under the federal civil rights statute, 42 U.S.C. §1983. Keats also seeks to recover from Shelley on a state law claim for battery based on the scuffle that took place during the arrest.

   a.   Does the court have constitutional power to hear the battery claim?
   b.   Does the court have statutory authority to hear the battery claim?
   c.   Assume that the court concludes that it lacks power to hear the battery claim. What should it do with the §1983 claim?
   d.   Assume that the court declines in its discretion to hear Keats's battery claim. What will happen to the §1983 claim?
   e.   Assume for this example only that there is no statutory authority to exercise supplemental jurisdiction. What would Keats have to do in order to recover on both of his claims?

2.   Apparently there was some prior history to the Keats/Shelley altercation. Shelley owed Keats $500 at the time of arrest as payment for work that Keats had done on his house. Keats was upset because he had not been paid and tempers flared, leading to the arrest. Keats therefore asserts a third claim for the debt in his action against Shelley. Does the court have the power to hear it?

3.   Browning, Blake, and Wordsworth are involved in a three-car collision on Route 192, near Dayton, Ohio. Browning, a New Yorker, sues Blake and Wordsworth, both from Ohio, for $80,000 for her personal injuries. Blake asserts a cross-claim against Wordsworth for his own injuries arising from the same collision. Does the court have jurisdiction over the cross-claim?

4.   Suppose, on the facts of example 3, that Blake (Ohio) asserts a counter-claim against Browning (New York) for $35,000 for his injuries. Does the court have jurisdiction to hear the counterclaim?

5.   May Blake assert a $25,000 counterclaim in the accident case against Browning for Browning's trespass on Blake's property four months prior to the accident?

Important Example, Requiring Thought

6.   Please reconsider example 3, in which Browning sued Blake and Wordsworth for her injuries in an auto accident. In that case could Blake (Ohio) assert a counterclaim against Browning (New York) for an unrelated infringement of a patent Blake holds? Assume that the counterclaim is for $30,000 in damages.

7.   Suppose that Browning (New York) sues Blake (Ohio) for her injuries from the collision, and Blake impleads Wordsworth (Ohio) for contribution if he is found liable to Browning.
   a. Is there independent subject matter jurisdiction over the impleader claim?
   b. Is there supplemental jurisdiction over it?

Complex Equations

8.   If Blake (Ohio) impleads Wordsworth (Ohio), and Browning, the New York plaintiff, then asserts a claim directly against Wordsworth, will the court have the power to hear it?

9.   Blake (Ohio) impleads Wordsworth (Ohio) as a third-party defendant, and Wordsworth asserts a claim against Browning, the New York plaintiff, for $25,000 for his own injuries in the accident.
   a. Will the court have supplemental jurisdiction over the claim?
   b. Assume that, after Wordsworth asserts his claim against Browning, Browning then asserts a claim against Wordsworth for $15,000 for property damage to her car in the same accident. Will the court have supplemental jurisdiction over the claim?

10. Browning, from New York, sues Blake, from Ohio, for $75,000 as a result of her injuries in the auto accident. Coleridge, a New York passenger in Browning's car, joins as a plaintiff, seeking $25,000 for his injuries.

    a. Does the court have the constitutional power to hear Coleridge's claim?

    b. Is there supplemental jurisdiction over it under §1367?

11. Byron (Wisconsin) sues Rossetti (Wisconsin) for patent infringement, arising out of Rossetti's manufacture of inverse roto-turnbuckles on which Byron claims he holds a patent. Byron also asserts a claim against Hunt, a former employee and Wisconsin citizen, for breach of contract, for assisting Rossetti in making the devices.

    a. Is there supplemental jurisdiction over Byron's claim against Hunt under §1367?

    b. Does the court have the constitutional power to hear Byron's claim against Hunt?

EXPLANATIONS

Simple Addition

1a. This is a straightforward example in which the plaintiff asserts a federal question claim and a related state law claim against the same defendant. It is exactly analogous to *Gibbs,* and clearly satisfies *Gibbs*'s criteria for a single constitutional case: The plaintiff has asserted a proper claim under federal law (the §1983 claim), and the state law battery claim arises out of the same "nucleus of operative facts," the scuffle during the arrest. Thus, there is constitutional power to hear the battery claim.

    b. Before Congress enacted §1367, the court would have had to analyze the statute granting jurisdiction over §1983 claims to determine whether Congress intended to allow pendent claims in §1983 cases. Now, however, Congress has answered that question in §1367: If the federal claim and the related claim are part of the "same case or controversy under Article III," the court has supplemental jurisdiction to hear the related claim. Because Congress apparently intended the "same case or controversy" requirement in §1367(a) to mean the same thing as a single "constitutional case" under *Gibbs,* the court should have supplemental jurisdiction, since the battery claim arises from the same nucleus of operative facts as the §1983 claim.

    c. If the court lacked jurisdiction over the related state law claim, it would have to dismiss it. But it could not dismiss the federal claim: The court has jurisdiction over that claim, and (absent some extraordinary situations not discussed here, such as federal abstention) it has a duty to exercise that jurisdiction by hearing and deciding the §1983 claim.

    d. The same result follows if the court concludes that it has jurisdiction over the battery claim but declines to hear the claim as a matter of discretion, which it clearly may under §1367(c). Keats is still entitled to a federal forum on his federal claim even though the related state claim will be heard in state court. If the court dismisses the state law claim, Keats may end up litigating the same facts in state and federal court at the same time.

e. If there is no statutory authority to hear related state claims, Keats would not be able to join his battery claim in the federal suit. He would then have two choices. He could bring two lawsuits, one in federal court on the §1983 claim and the other in state court on the battery claim. Alternatively, he could bring a single action in state court seeking relief on both claims, since state courts have concurrent jurisdiction over federal claims unless Congress makes federal jurisdiction exclusive. If he chose the latter course, the state court would decide Keats's §1983 claim, and, of course, it would decide his state law claim as well.

These alternatives for Keats illustrate the importance of supplemental jurisdiction. Without it, a plaintiff like Keats would have a strong incentive to sue in state court in order to have his entire case resolved in one proceeding. Many federal law cases would be heard in state rather than federal courts, even though a primary purpose of federal courts is to expound and develop federal law. Thus, supplemental jurisdiction assures that plaintiffs who prefer the federal forum will have full access to it.

2.   This example fails at the first level of the analysis, the same-constitutional-case requirement established in *Gibbs*. Under *Gibbs*, jurisdictionally insufficient claims are part of the same case (and therefore within the Article III grant of federal jurisdiction) if they arise out of the same nucleus of operative facts as the federal claim. Here, the assault claim does arise out of the same set of facts, but the debt claim does not. Although there may be a causal relationship between the debt and the eventual arrest and assault, it is too attenuated to make them part of the same nucleus of facts.

3.   This case, illustrated below, is a cross-claim by a defending party against another defendant arising out of the events that gave rise to the original claim. There is no independent basis of federal jurisdiction, since both parties to the cross-claim are from Ohio.

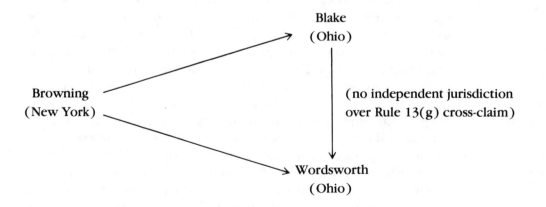

Prior to §1367 the courts routinely took ancillary jurisdiction over cross-claims. Because a cross-claim must arise out of the same transaction or occurrence as the main claim (see Rule 13(g)), it was considered part of the same constitutional case.[5] And, because cross-claims are asserted by a defendant, "haled into court against his will," *Kroger* suggested that they would not be barred even if they abridged the complete diversity requirement of §1332. 437 U.S. at 376.[6]

Now, a statutory basis for supplemental jurisdiction over Blake's cross-claim is provided by §1367(a), which authorizes the court to hear all related claims that arise from the same set of facts. Since Blake's claim arises from the same accident as the proper diversity claim, this requirement is met.

Although §1367(b) limits the broad reach of supplemental jurisdiction in diversity cases, that subsection only bars certain claims by plaintiffs in diversity cases. Here a defendant asserts the related claim, so §1367(b) does not apply.

4. This is the classic ancillary jurisdiction situation, addressed in *Moore v. New York Cotton Exchange,* 270 U.S. 593 (1926). Blake's counterclaim is compulsory because it arises from the same accident as the main claim. Yet the court lacks independent jurisdiction over it because it does not satisfy the amount-in-controversy requirement.

Under the *Gibbs* analysis, the court has constitutional power to hear the added claim since it arises out of the same incident as the main claim. Further, the court has statutory authority to hear the claim because §1367(a) authorizes supplemental jurisdiction over all claims that meet the *Gibbs* standard.

---

5. It is not clear whether the reach of a "common nucleus of operative facts" is exactly the same as the "same transaction or occurrence test" used in the federal joinder rules. One scholar suggests that since the transaction or occurrence test was well established when *Gibbs* was decided, the court must have meant something different — and probably broader — when it formulated the common nucleus test in *Gibbs.* See Matasar, A Pendent and Ancillary Jurisdiction Primer: The Scope and Limits of Supplemental Jurisdiction, 17 U.C. Davis L. Rev. 103, 130 (1983). It is probably safe to assume that the *Gibbs* test is satisfied if the related state claim arises out of the same transaction or occurrence as the federal claim but that it might also be satisfied in some more loosely related situations. Compare the formulation used in the earlier ancillary jurisdiction cases, which required only a "logical relationship" between the two claims.

6. This author takes issue with the Court's analysis here. The Court denied jurisdiction over Kroger's claim on the ground that it abridged the complete diversity requirement. At the same time, for practical reasons, it glossed over the fact that third-party claims like OPPD's claim against Owen or cross-claims or counterclaims may be equally inconsistent with the statute. It seems that the Court should have either taken the logic of the statutory restriction to its limits, by denying jurisdiction over any such claim, or fully recognized the pragmatic argument for jurisdiction over Kroger's claim as well. The decision is a compromise between efficiency and logic. So, in fact, is the statute, which effectively draws the line in much the same place.

The exceptions in §1367(b) do not apply, since the claim is not asserted by the plaintiff.

5.   There is no independent basis for subject matter jurisdiction in this case, since the claim does not meet the amount-in-controversy requirement of 28 U.S.C. §1332(a). Further, because this permissive counterclaim does not arise out of the same events as the main claim, there is no basis for supplemental jurisdiction over it. It founders on the *Gibbs* constitutional analysis, which only allows the court to hear related claims that arise from the same nucleus of operative facts as the main claim. Consequently, there is no basis under Article III to append it to the other claim.

Since this claim fails at the constitutional level of analysis, there is no need to consider whether §1367 provides a statutory basis for jurisdiction over the claim. However, it clearly does not: Section 1367 defines the statutory reach of supplemental jurisdiction by the same test as the outer reach of constitutional authority under *Gibbs*. Because the constitutional test is not met, the statutory test isn't either.

Important Example, Requiring Thought

6.   This example isn't that hard, but it is very important. This case is like example 5, except for one crucial difference. In this case there *is* an independent ground for jurisdiction over the counterclaim. While the court could not take supplemental jurisdiction over the claim under §1367 (because it is not part of the same set of facts, case, or controversy) it has original jurisdiction over the patent claim since it is a claim arising under the federal patent laws. 28 U.S.C. §1338. Blake could have sued Browning directly on this claim in federal court, and the court would have had jurisdiction. Thus, there is no need to invoke supplemental jurisdiction here based on a relationship to Blake's diversity claim.

7a.   The point here is fundamental, but by no means obvious. The impleaded third party, Wordsworth, is diverse from the plaintiff but not from the defendant who impleaded him. Whom do you count in measuring diversity over the third-party claim?

The third-party action by Blake against Wordsworth must be viewed separately for purposes of determining subject matter jurisdiction over it. If the court would not have jurisdiction over this claim as a separate suit, it lacks independent jurisdiction when it is brought as a third-party claim as well. Since Blake and Wordsworth are from the same state, there is no independent ground for jurisdiction over the impleader claim. The fact that Wordsworth is diverse from Browning avails him not. Conversely, if Wordsworth were from New York there would be independent subject matter jurisdiction over the impleader claim even though he was *not* diverse from the plaintiff.

b.   This claim is analogous to the Power District's third-party claim against Owen in *Kroger*. Impleader claims must arise from the same set of facts as the main claim to satisfy the requirements of Fed. R. Civ. P. 14. Thus, they will meet the common nucleus test of *Gibbs* and the statutory test of §1367(a) for supplemental jurisdiction.

Section 1367(b) does not prevent the court from exercising supplemental jurisdiction here. That section bars some "claims against persons made parties under Rule 14(a)," but only such claims *brought by plaintiffs*. This claim is not asserted by the plaintiff, so the general supplemental jurisdiction authority under §1367(a) applies.

Complex Equations

8.   If you diagrammed this case, you will have noticed that it is the same configuration as *Kroger,* with the plaintiff asserting a claim against the third-party defendant. Although it arises from the same set of facts (and therefore satisfies the *Gibbs* constitutional test), *Kroger* clearly held that there was no ancillary jurisdiction over such a claim in a diversity case. And Congress took the same position in §1367(b), which bars supplemental jurisdiction over claims brought by plaintiffs against parties brought in under Rule 14.

However, in this case there may be independent subject matter jurisdiction over the claim. The plaintiff and the third-party defendant here are diverse; if Browning's claim is for more than $50,000 the court will have jurisdiction over it without regard to supplemental jurisdiction.

9a.   This configuration, the reverse of *Kroger,* is a claim by the third-party defendant against the plaintiff. There is no independent jurisdiction over the claim because the amount-in-controversy requirement is not satisfied. But it is part of the same "constitutional case," since the claim arises from the same accident as the main diversity claim. Consequently, the court has both constitutional power to hear the claim under *Gibbs* and supplemental jurisdiction over it under §1367(a), unless it is excepted by §1367(b). Since Wordsworth is a defendant, §1367(b) does not apply. Ironically, supplemental jurisdiction is proper here, even though it was not in example 8 when the plaintiff asserted the claim.

b.   Of course this had to be the next example. Here, the third party has claimed against the plaintiff, and that makes the plaintiff a defending party who must assert any counterclaim he has arising out of the same incident. Fed. R. Civ. P. 13(a). Since Browning's claim arises from the original accident, it satisfies the single "constitutional case" test of *Gibbs* and the basic §1367(a) test for supplemental jurisdiction. Thus, the result turns on whether it is barred by the exception in §1367(b).

This is an interesting one: Section 1367(b) bars "claims by plaintiffs against persons made parties under Rule 14" (and other rules). Browning's claim is against Wordsworth, who was made a party under Rule 14 when Blake impleaded him. So the claim appears to fall within the §1367(b) exception. This makes little sense: Rule 13(a) requires Browning to assert the claim, and much efficiency will be gained by hearing it in the federal action. Yet the plain language of §1367(b) precludes the court from hearing it. Perhaps the courts will blink at the language to achieve a more sensible result.

10a. In this case, there is complete diversity, but Coleridge's claim does not meet the amount-in-controversy requirement. That of course is irrelevant to satisfying the constitutional requirements for diversity jurisdiction: There is no amount-in-controversy requirement in Article III, §2. Since both plaintiffs are diverse from the defendants, there is proper diversity jurisdiction under Article III.

   b. Coleridge's claim arises from the same accident as Browning's, so they are part of the same constitutional case. And the second sentence of §1367(a) specifically authorizes supplemental claims that add additional parties. Consequently, there is supplemental jurisdiction under §1367(a), unless the case falls within the exceptions in §1367(b).

   In fact, it does fall within the §1367(b) exceptions. This is a claim by a plaintiff against a defendant joined under Rule 20, and it is "inconsistent with the jurisdictional requirements of §1332," which has been interpreted to require each plaintiff to separately satisfy the amount-in-controversy requirement. See *Zahn v. International Paper Co.*, 414 U.S. 291, 292-296 (1973); Chapter 4, p.62. One consequence of the exception in §1367(b) (and doubtless one reason why Congress made the exception) is that supplemental jurisdiction will not displace the pesky aggregation rules that are applicable to diversity cases. Coleridge cannot avoid the requirement that each plaintiff separately satisfy the amount-in-controversy requirement by adding his claim as a "pendent party" claim to Browning's. Thus, supplemental jurisdiction does not apply.

11a. This "pendent party" case is closely analogous to *Finley*. The plaintiff asserts a proper federal claim against Rossetti. (In fact, Byron must take this claim to federal court since federal courts have exclusive jurisdiction over patent claims. 28 U.S.C. §1338(a).) Byron then seeks to add a state law claim against Hunt, a nondiverse party. There is no independent jurisdictional basis for this claim.

   It appears clear that Congress intended to authorize supplemental jurisdiction over this type of claim. "Such supplemental jurisdiction shall include claims that involve the joinder or intervention of additional parties." 28 U.S.C. §1367(a). This language suggests that, if the court has jurisdiction based on a proper federal claim, the court's supplemental jurisdiction extends to claims by or against other parties, *even if the plaintiff has not asserted any jurisdictionally sufficient claim against the added party*. For example, this language seems to authorize jurisdiction on the facts of *Finley*.

   This result does not "overrule" *Finley*. On the contrary, it responds to *Finley*'s pronouncement that Congress must provide statutory authority for courts to exert jurisdiction to the reach of their constitutional power. Nor is it inconsistent with example 10: The exception in §1367(b) barred the added claim because it was a diversity case. But that exception does not apply to cases in which the jurisdictionally proper claim is a federal question claim.

The same result would apparently follow if Arnold, another plaintiff, joined with Byron to recover damages for the same acts but not based on federal law. Even if there were no independent basis for federal jurisdiction, the quoted language would allow the added party to sue with Byron. Once again, §1367(b) would not apply since it is not a diversity case.

b. There is at least some question as to whether this expanded authority to hear related claims by different parties comes within the constitutional grant in Article III. *Gibbs* held that a related claim *by the same party* was part of the same constitutional case, but §1367 goes a step further by allowing a new party to be added to the claim because the plaintiff has asserted a jurisdictionally sufficient claim against someone else. In *Finley,* the Court "assumed without deciding that the constitutional criterion for pendent-party jurisdiction is analogous to the constitutional criterion for pendent claim jurisdiction." 490 U.S. at 549. But it clearly is more attenuated to conclude that a "constitutional case" includes jurisdictionally insufficient claims against a different party, against whom Byron has no jurisdictionally proper claim at all.

Certainly, the fact that Congress has purported to grant supplemental jurisdiction over added claims by different parties does not make it constitutional for the court to exercise that jurisdiction. On the other hand, numerous cases prior to the enactment of §1367 exercised "pendent party" jurisdiction,[7] and the Supreme Court, though it had opportunities to do so, never held it unconstitutional. So it is entirely possible that the Court will find pendent parties within the limits of a "constitutional case."

---

7. See 13B Wright and Miller §3567.2.

15

Jurisdiction vs. Joinder: The Difference between Power and Permission

Introduction

Concepts such as supplemental jurisdiction and joinder of parties are difficult enough to grapple with individually. Yet these doctrines do not exist in isolation; they interact to create a system[1] that lawyers must understand as a whole in order to litigate effectively. The real challenge (and fascination) of civil procedure is to try to see how the various pieces of the puzzle fit together into an interrelated, consistent framework for adjudication.

The preceding three chapters have separately analyzed the rules governing joinder of claims and parties, on the one hand, and the doctrine of supplemental jurisdiction on the other. However, a particular suit is proper only if both the joinder rules and the jurisdictional requirements are met. This chapter will explore the interrelations of these affiliated doctrines.

As the earlier chapters on joinder demonstrate, no party may assert a claim against another party in the federal courts unless one of the joinder

---

1. Some lawyers, those unfortunates who have never been captivated by the symmetry and logic of it, might call it a maze, a net, or a trap.

rules — Rules 13, 14, 18, 20, or 24 — authorizes assertion of that claim. However, the fact that the Rules authorize joinder of a particular claim is not sufficient to assure that the federal court may hear it. The court must also have a basis for exercising subject matter jurisdiction over the claim. The federal courts have only limited jurisdictional power; if there is no basis in Article III, §2 to hear a claim, "permission" to join a claim under the Rules cannot substitute for it.

An example may help. If Nimitz is injured in an auto accident involving two other drivers, Spruance and Halsey, Rule 20(a) allows him to sue them both in a single suit. Nimitz's claims against both arise out of a single occurrence and will both involve the common factual issue of whose negligence caused the accident. However, if Halsey and Nimitz are both from Texas, the suit will be dismissed for lack of subject matter jurisdiction since there is no complete diversity and the suit (a basic tort claim) does not arise under federal law.

This need for both power and permission follows from basic constitutional doctrine. All federal jurisdiction must be found in the "Article III storehouse," and it is up to Congress to confer all or part of that jurisdiction on the lower federal courts. See Judge Sirica's comments, p.56. The Federal Rules, on the other hand, are promulgated by the Supreme Court. While the Court has the power to make rules to assure the orderly conduct of business in the federal courts (see 28 U.S.C. §2072), it may not use its rule-making power to expand their jurisdiction. Thus, though the Court has broadly authorized joinder of claims and parties under the Federal Rules, the need for subject matter jurisdiction provides an implicit limitation on joinder in every case. The Court itself reaffirmed this limitation in Fed. R. Civ. P. 82, which provides in part that "[t]hese rules shall not be construed to extend or limit the jurisdiction of the United States district courts or the venue of actions therein."

Although joinder cannot substitute for jurisdiction, it would often make life easier if it could. As we saw in the last chapter, there is a tension between the Rules, which encourage broad joinder of related claims to promote efficiency, and the strict Article III limits on federal court jurisdiction. In cases such as the Halsey example, it would make eminent good sense to hear the related claims together, since the witnesses and much of the evidence will be the same, the legal issues will overlap, and the plaintiff is the same in both claims. The joinder rules encourage and sometimes even require such sensible litigation practice, but good sense may be thwarted at times by the limitations on federal subject matter jurisdiction.

Similarly, in *Owen Equipment & Erection Co. v. Kroger*, 437 U.S. 365 (1978), joinder of Kroger's claim against Owen, the third-party defendant, was permissible under Rule 14. It certainly would have made sense to hear that claim in the same action with the main claim and the third-party claim: The parties were all before the court already, much of the evidence would have been the same, and the judge was already familiar with the case. But the Court balked at extending ancillary jurisdiction to provide a basis for subject matter jurisdiction over the claim. Absolutes are absolutes, and subject matter jurisdiction is as absolute as you get in the civil procedure business.

In many cases supplemental jurisdiction, recently codified by Congress in 28 U.S.C. §1367, *will* provide a jurisdictional base for additional claims. By granting broad authority to hear related claims, Congress acknowledged the good sense of allowing those related claims to be settled in a single action. In other cases, where supplemental jurisdiction does not authorize the additional claims, there may be an independent basis for subject matter jurisdiction. For example, in the *Kroger* case, if Kroger had been from Colorado, there would have been independent diversity jurisdiction over her claim against Owen. Since joinder was proper under Fed. R. Civ. P. 14(a), both power and permission would have been proper. Yet other cases may fall between the cracks, either for lack of jurisdiction or, conversely, because the joinder rules do not authorize assertion of the claim.

The examples below will help you grasp the distinction and the interrelations between these two problems. In analyzing these cases, assume that all are brought in federal court and that personal jurisdiction is proper.

EXAMPLES

Some Basics

1. Nimitz, a citizen of Texas, sues Bradley, from Missouri, and Patton, from California. Nimitz claims that each defendant libeled him, though on different occasions. He claims $100,000 in damages from each. Is the case properly before the court?

2. Nimitz (Texas) sues Bradley (Missouri) for the libel claim and an unrelated breach of contract. He seeks $25,000 in damages on the contract claim and $40,000 on the libel claim. Can the court entertain the claims?

3. Nimitz (Texas) brings suit against Bradley (Missouri) and Clark, a Texas citizen. Nimitz asserts that the two defendants violated his federal civil rights by arresting him under an invalid warrant. Does the federal court have power and permission to hear the claims?

4. Suppose that Nimitz (Texas) sued only Clark (Texas) on the federal civil rights claim and on a state law battery claim arising from the same arrest. Are power and permission both present?

Mixing Apples and Oranges

5. Assume that Nimitz (Texas) sues Clark (Texas) and Bradley (Missouri). He asserts a civil rights claim against Clark for using excessive force in the course of arresting him and a state law battery claim against Bradley, arising from the same arrest. Is the case properly before the court?

6.   Suppose, on the facts of the last example, that Clark counterclaims against Nimitz for $90,000 due on a loan he made to Nimitz six months prior to the arrest? Does the court have both power and permission to hear the claim?

7.   Instead of counterclaiming against Nimitz, Clark (Texas) cross-claims against Bradley (Missouri) to recover on a $90,000 loan to him. Is the claim properly before the court?

8.   Nimitz (Texas) sues both Bradley (Missouri) and Gavin, also from Missouri, for violation of his federal civil rights. Could the federal court entertain a cross-claim by Bradley against Gavin, alleging that Gavin assaulted him (Bradley) in the course of the arrest?

A Few Mazes, Nets, or Traps

9.   Halsey, a New Jersey citizen, brings a negligence action against MacArthur, from Arkansas, seeking $75,000 for injuries arising out of a boating accident. MacArthur impleads Spruance, from Arkansas, who was piloting a third boat involved in the collision. In his impleader complaint, MacArthur seeks contribution from Spruance on any damages he must pay Halsey for the boating injuries, as well as recovery for libel arising out of a newspaper article in which Spruance deprecated his leadership skills. Can a federal district court in Arkansas entertain the entire suit?

10. Suppose on the facts of example 9, that MacArthur (Arkansas) impleaded Spruance (Arkansas) for contribution, and Halsey (New Jersey) then asserted a libel claim against Spruance. Is Halsey's claim against Spruance properly before the court?

11. Assume that Halsey (New Jersey) sues MacArthur (Arkansas) alone on his claim arising out of the boating accident, and MacArthur counterclaims against Halsey and Spruance (Arkansas) for his own injuries in the collision. Can the federal court hear the counterclaims?

12. Halsey (New Jersey) sues MacArthur (Arkansas) for his injuries in the accident, and Spruance (Arkansas) intervenes in the suit to assert a claim against MacArthur for his injuries. May the court hear Spruance's claim?

EXPLANATIONS

Some Basics

1.   Power: Yes   Permission: No

This case in its present form would have to be dismissed. Jurisdiction is proper in the action since there is complete diversity and the amount in controversy exceeds $50,000 against each defendant. However, Nimitz's joinder of Patton and Bradley is improper under the joinder provisions of the Federal Rules. Rule 20(a), which governs joinder of multiple defendants, only authorizes joinder if the plaintiff's claims against both defendants arise out of the same transaction or occurrence. Nimitz alleges libel stemming from two separate incidents; although his theory of liability is the same against each, his claims are based on separate historical occurrences. Thus, joinder under the Rules is not satisfied, though jurisdiction is proper.

Although Nimitz's case can't be heard in its present form, it need not be dismissed in its entirety either. Under Fed. R. Civ. P. 21, the court may drop either Patton or Bradley from the action, eliminating the joinder problem. Nimitz will presumably then file a separate suit against the dropped defendant, perhaps in the same court, which will proceed independent of the original case.

2.   Power: Yes   Permission: Yes

The court in this case has an adequate basis for joinder and jurisdiction. Rule 18(a) authorizes a single plaintiff to join any claims she has against an opposing party, regardless of whether they arise from a single transaction or occurrence. Rule 18(a) is the ultimate in permissiveness: Whatever claims you have, based on the same or separate historical events, may be joined, so long as the various claims are asserted against a single defendant.

Jurisdiction is also satisfied here because the parties are diverse, and the amount-in-controversy requirement is satisfied by aggregation of Nimitz's two claims against Bradley. A single plaintiff like Nimitz may aggregate claims — including totally unrelated claims — against a single defendant but not against multiple defendants. See Chapter 4, p.62.

3.   Power: Yes   Permission: Yes

This case may properly be brought in federal court. Joinder is proper here, unlike in example 1, because the same transaction or occurrence requirement of Rule 20(a) is met; Nimitz seeks damages against both defendants based on the same underlying real-world event. The second requirement of Rule 20(a), that Nimitz's claims against the two defendants share a common question of law or fact, is also met since Nimitz must presumably prove many of the same facts (for example, the invalidity of the warrant) to prevail on both claims.

Jurisdiction is also satisfied in this suit since Nimitz asserts a federal claim against each defendant. 28 U.S.C. §1331. The lack of complete diversity is therefore irrelevant.

4.   Power: Yes   Permission: Yes

This is an easy case. Rule 18(a) authorizes joinder of the two claims, even though they are based on different sources of law. It would similarly authorize joinder of any other claims that Nimitz's creative genius (tempered, of course, by the ethical constraints of Rule 11) might come up with, regardless of whether they arose from the arrest or any other incident.

Jurisdiction over the federal civil rights claim is proper under 28 U.S.C. §1331. Jurisdiction over the state law claim is also proper. This is a classic "pendent claim," a jurisdictionally insufficient claim that arises from the same nucleus of operative facts as the proper federal claim. Prior to the enactment of the supplemental jurisdiction statute it would have been proper (though discretionary) under *United Mine Workers v. Gibbs*. See Chapter 14, pp.229-231. It is now authorized by §1367(a), since that statute authorizes the court to hear claims that are part of the same case or controversy as the jurisdictionally sufficient claim. See Chapter 14, example 1.

Mixing Apples and Oranges

5.   Power: Yes   Permission: Yes

The problem here is clearly not on the joinder issue; Rule 20(a) authorizes joinder of these claims since they both arise out of the same arrest and will likely involve common questions of fact, such as which injuries were caused by Clark and which by Bradley.

Jurisdiction is more difficult. Jurisdiction is proper over Nimitz's claim against Clark because it arises under federal law. However, his claim against Bradley is based on state law; it must have a separate basis for federal jurisdiction. Nimitz and Bradley are diverse . . . but Nimitz and Clark are not. However, since there is a separate basis for jurisdiction over Clark, his citizenship need not be considered in measuring diversity, even though he is a party to the action. See Chapter 4, example 4. Consequently, Clark does not destroy diversity. If Nimitz seeks more than $50,000 from Bradley the suit is proper.

Even if there were no diversity between Nimitz and Bradley, the supplemental jurisdiction statute would provide a basis for jurisdiction over Nimitz's claim against Bradley. Section 1367(a) authorizes jurisdiction over claims that are part of the same case or controversy as the main claim, including such claims against additional parties. This provision would presumably apply here, authorizing supplemental jurisdiction over Nimitz's claim against Bradley, since it is part of the same "case" as his claim against Clark, which is properly before the federal court as a claim arising under federal law.[2] Prior to the enactment of §1367, this would have been referred to as "pendent party" jurisdiction and would have required a complex analysis. See the discussion of "essential history" in Chapter 14, pp.232-234.

6.   Power: No   Permission: Yes

Here, the federal court lacks power to hear the counterclaim, although the Rules grant permission to join it. Clark's counterclaim is permissive

---

2. The limit on such supplemental claims in §1367(b) does not apply, since the case is not "founded solely on §1332," the diversity statute.

because it arises from a transaction unrelated to the main claim. Rule 13(b) authorizes (but does not require) Clark to assert it in this action.

However, there is no independent basis of subject matter jurisdiction over this claim because it is a state law claim between nondiverse parties. Clark would have to rely on supplemental jurisdiction to support this claim. As discussed in Chapter 14, however, the courts will likely apply the "common nucleus of operative fact" test in determining whether the related claims are part of the same case or controversy as the jurisdictionally sufficient claim. Since the loan counterclaim does not arise out of the same nucleus of operative facts as the arrest claim, it is not part of the same case, so it fails both the *Gibbs* test and the similar test of supplemental jurisdiction under §1367. Presumably, this will always be true of Rule 13(b) permissive counterclaims, since, by definition, they are unrelated to the main claim.

7.   Power: Yes   Permission: No

Clark will have to save this claim for another day as well. Jurisdictionally, the claim passes muster since there is diversity between Clark and Bradley (the opposing parties on the cross-claim) and the amount in controversy is sufficient. But the Rules don't authorize assertion of this claim in the Nimitz lawsuit: Rule 13(g) limits cross-claims to those arising out of the same transaction or occurrence as the main claim.

This result makes good sense. There is no relationship between the factual or legal issues relevant to the arrest claim and those relevant to the loan cross-claim and, therefore, no efficiency to be gained from allowing them to be heard in the same suit.

8.   Power: Yes   Permission: Yes

This is a nice contrast to example 7. Here, unlike example 7, joinder is proper under Rule 13(g), since the cross-claim arises out of the same incident as the main claim. There is no independent basis for subject matter jurisdiction, but jurisdiction is supplied by §1367(a), the supplemental jurisdiction statute, because the cross-claim arises out of the same nucleus of facts as the main claim.

Because cross-claims can only be asserted under Rule 13(g) if they arise from the same set of events as the main claim, they should always satisfy the test for supplemental jurisdiction. But see 28 U.S.C. §1367(b), which may sometimes deny supplemental jurisdiction to cross-claims brought by plaintiffs.

A Few Mazes, Nets, or Traps

9.   Power: In part   Permission: Yes

The Rules authorize joinder in this case, but jurisdiction is only proper over part of the case. First of all, I asked whether an *Arkansas* federal district court could hear the action. Really, this was just to blow a little smoke. Personal jurisdiction and venue are satisfied because both defendants are domiciled in Arkansas. *Milliken v. Meyer,* 311 U.S. 457 (1940); 28 U.S.C. §1391(a)(1), (3). And the particular federal district in which the suit is brought is irrelevant to determination of subject matter jurisdiction. See Chapter 4, example 1a.

Joinder is also proper in this action, under Rules 14 and 18. MacArthur properly brought in Spruance under Rule 14(a), since he is seeking to recover from Spruance part of any damages that Halsey recovers from him, MacArthur. MacArthur's claim for contribution satisfies this requirement because he is asking Spruance to pay him half of any judgment Halsey wins, by way of "contribution" to the judgment. MacArthur's libel claim is also proper: Under Rule 18(a) MacArthur may assert any additional claims he has against Spruance, once he has asserted one claim against him that is proper under Rule 14(a). MacArthur could not have impleaded Spruance on the basis of the libel claim since it is an independent claim that does not satisfy the "may be liable to the third-party plaintiff for all or part of the plaintiff's claim" requirement of Rule 14(a). But once he impleads Spruance on a proper Rule 14(a) claim, he can pile on any claims he has against Spruance.

So much for permission. The claims must also be analyzed individually as to jurisdictional power. There is supplemental jurisdiction over MacArthur's contribution claim against Spruance since it arises from the same nucleus of operative facts as Halsey's jurisdictionally sufficient claim against MacArthur. But supplemental jurisdiction does not extend to the libel claim since it is unrelated to the main claim and therefore not part of the same case or controversy under §1367(a). Nor is there an independent basis for subject matter jurisdiction since it is a state law claim between nondiverse parties.

10. Power: Yes   Permission: No

This example involves a state law claim between diverse parties; if the claim is for more than $50,000, it is within the court's diversity jurisdiction. However, the Rules do not authorize joinder of this claim. Claims by plaintiffs against third-party defendants are authorized by Rule 14(a), which limits such claims to those arising from the same transaction or occurrence as the main claim. Halsey's claim is independent of the boating accident and therefore must be sued upon separately.

Curiously, if Halsey asserted a claim against Spruance for injuries arising from the boating accident, he could then pile on the unrelated libel claim under Rule 18(a). Jurisdiction and joinder would both be satisfied, and the court would be able to entertain the claim. However, it would likely be severed for trial under Rule 21(b) and proceed effectively as a separate action anyway.

11. Power: Yes   Permission: Yes

Both joinder and jurisdiction are satisfied in this case. Joinder is proper under Rule 13(a) and (h); MacArthur has asserted a compulsory counterclaim against Halsey, and added Spruance (who destroys diversity) as an additional party to it. Visually the case looks like this:

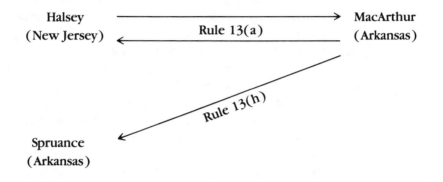

As to the power question, supplemental jurisdiction should provide a basis for jurisdiction. Section 1367(a) is apparently intended to reach these claims, since they arise from the same dispute over the boating accident. Even though MacArthur has added a new party to the compulsory counterclaim, §1367(a) expressly states that supplemental jurisdiction includes "claims that involve the joinder or intervention of additional parties." Further, the exceptions in §1367(b) do not apply, since the party asserting the added claims is not a plaintiff. Thus, even though complete diversity is lacking, or if MacArthur claims less than $50,000 from Spruance and Halsey, the court may hear the counterclaims.

The irony here is that MacArthur may assert a counterclaim that he could not have asserted as an original claim: If he had sued Halsey and Spruance together, the case would have been dismissed for lack of diversity. While this result is ironic, it is not completely illogical. Prior to the enactment of §1367 the courts had given defendants hauled into court against their will broad opportunities to settle all claims arising out of the events that gave rise to the litigation. See *Kroger,* 437 U.S. at 375-377 (distinguishing jurisdictionally insufficient claims by defendants from Kroger's on this basis). In §1367, Congress has preserved this defendant bias by barring claims by plaintiffs that are inconsistent with complete diversity, but allowing similar claims by defending parties.

12. Power: No   Permission: Yes

Permission to join Spruance's claim is provided here by Rule 24(b), which allows a party to seek intervention if her claim shares a question of fact or law with the main claim. Here, Spruance and Halsey will both seek to prove that MacArthur was negligent, thus satisfying the Rule 24(b) standard. Of course, Spruance would need to seek leave to intervene, since permissive intervention under Rule 24(b) is always at the discretion of the court.

However, Congress has barred supplemental jurisdiction over this claim in 28 U.S.C. §1367(b). That section bars supplemental jurisdiction over claims by persons "seeking to intervene as plaintiffs under Rule 24 of such rules, when exercising supplemental jurisdicton over such claims would be inconsistent with the jurisdictional requirements of section 1332." Allowing Spruance to intervene here would be inconsistent with the requirements of §1332, since it would allow a claim by one Arkansas citizen against another, based on state law. If Spruance were allowed to intervene in this case, it would allow him to evade the complete diversity requirement: Instead of suing with Halsey, which would be improper under *Strawbridge v. Curtiss*, 7 U.S. 267 (1806), he could simply allow Halsey to start the suit and then achieve the same result by intervening. Obviously, Congress adopted the view of the Supreme Court, expressed in *Kroger*, that, in an age where diversity is viewed with disfavor by many, supplemental jurisdiction should not provide a means of evading the complete diversity requirement.

This case presents a situation in which it would make good litigation sense to take jurisdiction. The claims arise out of the same nucleus of operative facts, thus satisfying the constitutional test for a single case. In terms of efficiency there is as much justification for hearing this claim as there is for hearing a third-party impleader claim, or MacArthur's counterclaim against Spruance in example 11. But without a statutory basis, the court can't exercise jurisdiction over the claim, and here Congress has quite deliberately withheld the authority to do so.

PART FOUR

Steps in the Litigation Process

16

The Bearer of Bad Tidings: Service of Process in the Federal Courts

Introduction

Some of the most profound protections of our constitutional system are astoundingly simple. "Due process of law" under the fourteenth amendment, for example, guarantees parties the basic right to notice of a court's intention to adjudicate their rights and an opportunity for those parties to be heard before the court proceeds to do so. "An elementary and fundamental requirement of due process in any proceeding which is to be accorded finality is notice reasonably calculated, under all the circumstances, to apprise interested parties of the pendency of the action and afford them an opportunity to present their objections." *Mullane v. Central Hanover Bank*, 339 U.S. 306, 311 (1950). In civil suits, this requirement is fulfilled through service of process.

The term *service of process* is often used to refer to the delivery to a party or witness of various court orders required by the relevant rules of law to be served upon him, including subpoenas, writs, and other orders that are entered in the course of litigation. However, in a stricter sense the term is used — as we will use it here — to refer to service of the initial notice to the defendant of the filing of a lawsuit against him. Service of this initial summons both notifies the defendant that he has been sued and informs him that the court intends to proceed to adjudicate his rights. The summons in the

Schulansky case, for example (infra p.438), specifically warns the defendants that they must respond to the plaintiff's complaint, or judgment by default will be entered against them.

All courts, state and federal, have elaborate provisions governing service of this initial notice to defendants. State service provisions may be found in statutes (see, e.g., N.Y. Civ. Prac. Law §§305-318) or in court rules (see, e.g., Mass. R. Civ. P. 4, set forth on pp.265-266 for use in the chapter). Service of process in the federal courts is governed by Rule 4 of the Federal Rules of Civil Procedure. This chapter explores the intricacies of Federal Rule 4, which has served as a model for service provisions in many states, including the Massachusetts rule used in this chapter.

Rule 4 specifies in detail what documents must be served on the defendant (Rule 4(a) and (b)), how they must be served (Rule 4(c), (d), (e)), when they must be served (Rule 4(j)) and who must do it (Rule 4(c)). For example, look at Form 1 of the Federal Rules Forms, which accompanies the Federal Rules of Civil Procedure. The summons there complies with each of the formal requirements in Rule 4(b). Compare the summons in the Schulansky case (infra p.438), drawn to comply with Mass. R. Civ. P. 4(b), which is very similar to its federal counterpart.

The most complex provisions of Rule 4 are those governing the permissible methods of service, in Fed. R. Civ. P. 4(c), (d), and (e). Under these provisions, the proper method of service depends first on the type of defendant being served. For example, the methods for service on individual defendants differ from those for service on a corporation or on the United States. In addition, the Rule provides different methods of service for in-state defendants (Rule 4(c), (d)) and out-of-state defendants (Rule 4(e)).

These provisions governing the methods of service are particularly confusing, in part because they are scattered throughout subsections (c) through (e) of Rule 4. These subsections have been amended a number of times over the years, as Congress and the Supreme Court have expanded the reach and methods of service. It would be a boon to law students (and to practicing lawyers, who also have trouble with these provisions) if the rule-makers would rewrite the rule in a more understandable fashion.[1] Hopefully the following discussion and the examples in this chapter will help you sort out these service provisions, despite admitted obscurities in the text.

Service on In-State Defendants

Essentially, Fed. R. Civ. P. 4(c) and (d) provide three different methods for serving process on *individual* defendants (that is, natural persons) within the

---

1. A major revision of the rule has recently been proposed by the Advisory Committee on the Civil Rules. If it is ultimately promulgated, it will make the rule considerably easier to understand.

state where the court sits. The most traditional method of service is that found in Rule 4(d)(1), which authorizes service by personal delivery to the defendant, or by leaving copies of the summons and the complaint at his dwelling house or usual place of abode with a person of suitable age and discretion residing there, or by delivering the papers to an agent appointed by the defendant to receive service of process on his behalf.

Until 1983 service by personal delivery under Rule 4(d)(1) had to be made by a United States marshal or a person specially designated by the court to serve process. This provision frequently led to delays in service or motions to the court for appointment of special process servers because the marshals were too busy with other duties to serve process promptly. Consequently, the 1983 amendments to Rule 4 inserted subsection 4(c)(2)(A), which provides that personal service may be made by any person who is over 18 years of age and not a party to the action, except in unusual circumstances set forth in subsection 4(c)(2)(B).

The plaintiff's second option is to serve individual defendants under the provisions for service of process that apply in the courts of the state where the federal court sits. Fed. R. Civ. P. 4(c)(2)(C)(i). The plaintiff in an action in the federal district court in Massachusetts, for example, may use any methods for service of process on individuals that apply in the Massachusetts Superior Courts; that is, any of the methods provided in Mass. R. Civ. P. 4(d) (see infra pp.265-266). If the suit were brought in federal court in Maine, however, the plaintiff would look to the service rules of the Maine courts. Note that the state rules are an alternative to service under the other methods provided in Rule 4(c) and (d); the plaintiff may choose whichever he prefers.

The 1983 amendments to Rule 4 introduced yet a third method for serving individual in-state defendants. Under Rule 4(c)(2)(C)(ii), the summons and a copy of the complaint may be mailed to the defendant with two notice-and-acknowledgment forms and a stamped return envelope. Fed. R. Civ. P. 4(c)(2)(C)(ii); see Federal Rules Form 18-A for a sample of the form. The defendant is supposed to sign one of the forms and return it to the plaintiff or his lawyer. If the defendant fails to return the acknowledgment, the rule requires the plaintiff to re-serve the defendant by one of the methods specified in Rule 4(d)(1) or (3), to insure that the defendant receives proper notice of the action. Practice under the rule indicates that defendants frequently do not cooperate by returning the acknowledgment form. The only penalty prescribed for failing to return the acknowledgment is the costs of serving the defendant another way. Fed. R. Civ. P. 4(c)(2)(D). Thus, while the mail/acknowledgment provision provides a simple method for insuring notice to the defendant without the expense and delay of personal service, it is often ineffective to properly effect service.[2]

---

2. In some cases, using the mail/acknowledgment procedure can even make service more difficult. See, e.g., example 6.

Service on Out-of-State Defendants

One of the reasons that Rule 4 is so confusing is that it does not state explicitly that the three procedures described above apply only to service on defendants who are served within the state. If you look at Rule 4(e), however, you will see that it provides methods for service on "a party not an inhabitant or found within the state." This implies that the separate provisions of Rule 4(c) and (d) apply to *in-state service,* and that is the general reading of the rule. 2 Moore's Federal Practice (2d ed. 1991) ¶4.32[1] (hereinafter cited as Moore's). Most, but not all, courts (see n.8) conclude that service on *out-of-state defendants* must be made under the separate provisions of Rule 4(e).

Rule 4(e) addresses three different situations: 1) instances in which a federal statute authorizes service of process outside the forum state in a particular type of case and specifies how service is to be delivered to the defendant; 2) instances in which a federal statute authorizes service of process outside the state but doesn't specify how it is to be done; and 3) use of the out-of-state service provisions available in the state in which the district court sits. Although the rule is hard to parse, here is what it says:

- In the first situation, in which a federal statute authorizes service of process on an out-of-state defendant and specifies the manner in which it is to be served, the defendant may be served as provided in the statute. Rule 4(e), first sentence. For example, if a special federal statute authorized out-of-state service in securities fraud cases and required that service be made in-hand or as otherwise ordered by the court, that method could be used. In other words, if a federal statute says you can do it, and do it in a particular way, you may. It is hard to quarrel with the good sense of that provision.

- In the second situation, in which out-of-state service is authorized, but the statute doesn't specify how it is to be delivered, the defendant may be served by any appropriate method in Rule 4(c) or (d). Fed. R. Civ. P. 4(e), first sentence. If a federal statute authorized out-of-state service in securities fraud cases but did not specify how it should be delivered, the plaintiff would look to the methods provided in Rule 4(c) and (d). That is also pretty commonsensical, once you realize that that is all the rule says.

- The third option, provided by the second sentence of Rule 4(e), is to serve an out-of-state defendant by any method for service on out-of-state defendants available in the courts of the state where the federal court sits. This provision allows a federal district court to use whatever methods for service of process on an out-of-state defendant that the courts of the state are authorized to use. For example, in a suit in the federal district court for the District of Massachusetts, the defendant may be served in the manner provided under Massachusetts law for service of out-of-state defendants in Massachusetts state court actions.   See Mass. R. Civ. P. 4(e).[3]

It is important to understand that the second sentence of Rule 4(e), authorizing service of process under the provisions of the state in which the federal court sits, is an alternative to service under the first sentence. Even though a federal statute authorizes extraterritorial service, the plaintiff does not have to make service under its provisions; he is always free to serve under state law provisions. Advisory Committee Note to 1963 Amendment to Rule 4(e). Even if there is a federal statute that authorizes extraterritorial service *and* specifies a method for service, the plaintiff still has the option to serve by the method provided in an applicable state rule or statute. On the other hand, if there is no relevant federal statute governing out-of-state service, the *only* proper methods for such service will be those in the state statutes or rules because the first sentence of Rule 4(e) does not apply.

The Relation of Service of Process to Personal Jurisdiction

It is crucial to distinguish the concept of service of process from the related concept of personal jurisdiction. In many cases, particularly older cases, challenges to personal jurisdiction have been framed in terms of "insufficient service of process," although the actual basis of the defendant's objection was insufficient contact between the defendant and the state to support personal jurisdiction. In modern phraseology, a challenge to service of process (a motion to dismiss for insufficiency of service of process under Fed. R. Civ. P. 12(b)(5)) attacks the adequacy of the method used by the plaintiff to give the defendant notice of the action, not the power of the court to exercise personal jurisdiction over him (a motion to dismiss for lack of personal jurisdiction under Fed. R. Civ. P. 12(b)(2)).

It is not surprising that the *Pennoyer*-era cases blended the two concepts. When *Pennoyer* was decided, service of process on the defendant within the forum state was the predominant means of obtaining jurisdiction, as well as giving notice to the defendant of the suit. Thus, under *Pennoyer,* if service was not made properly (that is, delivered personally to the defendant within the state), personal jurisdiction was not obtained. The two requirements were frequently interchangeable; but today the two are quite distinct, and either may be satisfied though the other is not.

---

3. Compare Rule 4(c)(2)(C)(i), which authorizes the state methods for serving in-state defendants to be used to serve in-state defendants in federal suits. Analogously, the second sentence of Rule 4(e) allows state methods for serving out-of-state defendants to be used for serving out-of-state defendants in federal suits.

For example, suppose that Drayton is injured in Utah when Lovelace, a vacationing Marylander, hits him on the street in Salt Lake City. He sues Lovelace in Utah and serves process on Lovelace by publishing notice of the suit in a Salt Lake City newspaper. On these facts, the Utah court would have the constitutional power to exercise personal jurisdiction over Lovelace, based on the in-state contact of causing tortious injury in the state, but service would be improper, since in most cases publication is not an adequate means of informing a defendant that he has been sued. A Rule 12(b)(2) motion would not be granted, but a Rule 12(b)(5) motion would. By contrast, if Drayton sued Lovelace in Alaska for the Salt Lake City accident, personal jurisdiction would be improper, assuming Lovelace has no contacts with Alaska. If Drayton served the summons and complaint on Lovelace by personal delivery (the best possible means of informing him of the suit), service would be proper but the court would not have personal jurisdiction over Lovelace.[4]

Several other mechanical aspects of service should be mentioned. *First,* the person making service must make proof of service (often called "return of service") by promptly filing with the court an affidavit setting forth the manner in which service was made. Fed. R. Civ. P. 4(g). If service is made by a marshal or sheriff, proof of service is usually inserted on the summons itself. See the Schulansky summons (infra p.438), which contains a printed form for proof of service.

Second, the 1983 amendments to Rule 4 added, for the first time, a time limit within which service must be made. Fed. R. Civ. P. 4(j).[5] Prior to the addition of Rule 4(j), service might have been made well after the complaint was filed, so long as there was no unreasonable delay on the plaintiff's part in attempting it. See 2 Moore's at ¶4.46. Under the new rule, the plaintiff will have to demonstrate "good cause" for failure to make service within the 120-day period or face dismissal of the suit.

---

4. Actually, Rule 4(e) governs not only the methods for service of process on out-of-state defendants, but also the amenability of such defendants to personal jurisdiction in the federal court. See Fed. R. Civ. P. 4(e), second sentence, which authorizes service on out-of-state defendants "under the circumstances and in the manner prescribed in the [state] statute or rule." The "under the circumstances" language authorizes each federal district court to assert personal jurisdiction over defendants to the same extent as the courts of the state in which the federal court sits. See Chapter 5, pp.75-76. For the purposes of this chapter, however, we focus on the other aspect of Rule 4(e), authorizing service of process "in the manner" authorized by any relevant federal statute, state statute, or rule.

5. This time limit for service of the summons and complaint is separate from and in addition to the requirements of any applicable statute of limitations. The fact that an action is *filed* within the limitations period (which, in many cases, will satisfy the statute of limitations) does not affect this additional requirement to serve the complaint within the 120-day period prescribed in Rule 4(j).

Third, as noted earlier, many other papers get "served" on parties and witnesses in law suits in addition to the original complaint. All motions, pleadings (other than the complaint), discovery requests, and other papers filed with the court must be served on each party to the action; all parties have a right to notice of these, as well as notice of the commencement of suit. Virtually all such papers may be served under the more flexible provisions of Fed. R. Civ. P. 5, which authorizes service of papers subsequent to the complaint by mailing them to the party's attorney, without requiring an acknowledgment. See the certificate of service for the answer in the Schulansky case, infra p.464 and the accompanying note (p.469). The complaint is singled out for special treatment because it is the first notice the defendant receives of the filing of the suit. If he does not receive this notice, he may never learn of the action at all. Once he has been properly informed of the suit, however, the law presumes that he will keep an eye on the docket and eventually learn of any paper that was served by mail under Rule 5 but, for one reason or another, never reached him.

In analyzing the following examples, assume that all actions are brought in the federal district court for the District of Massachusetts. Because Federal Rule 4 incorporates state provisions for service of process in some circumstances, you will have to also consider the methods of service provided in Mass. R. Civ. P. 4, as well as those in Federal Rule 4. The relevant portions of Massachusetts Rule of Civil Procedure 4 are as follows:

> (c) **By Whom Served.** Except as otherwise permitted by paragraph (h) of this rule service of all process shall be made by a sheriff, by his deputy, or by a special sheriff; by any other person duly authorized by law; by some person specially appointed by the court for that purpose; or in the case of service of process outside the Commonwealth, by an individual permitted to make service of process under the law of this Commonwealth or under the law of the place in which the service is to be made, or who is designated by a court of this Commonwealth. A subpoena may be served as provided in Rule 45. Notwithstanding the provisions of this paragraph (c), wherever in these rules service is permitted to be made by certified or registered mail, the mailing may be accomplished by the party or his attorney.
>
> (d) **Summons: Personal Service within the Commonwealth.** The summons and a copy of the complaint shall be served together. The plaintiff shall furnish the person making service with such copies as are necessary. Service shall be made as follows:
>
> (1) Upon an individual by delivering a copy of the summons and of the complaint to him personally; or by leaving copies thereof at his last and usual place of abode; or by delivering a copy of the summons and of the complaint to an agent authorized by appointment or by statute to receive service of process, provided that any further notice required by such statute be given. . . .
>
> (2) Upon a domestic corporation (public or private), a foreign corporation subject to suit within the Commonwealth, or an unin-

corporated association subject to suit within the Commonwealth under a common name: by delivering a copy of the summons and of the complaint to an officer, to a managing or general agent, or to the person in charge of the business at the principal place of business thereof within the Commonwealth, if any; or by delivering such copies to any other agent authorized by appointment or by law to receive service of process, provided that any further notice required by law be given. . . .

(e) **Same: Personal Service outside the Commonwealth.** When any statute or law of the Commonwealth authorizes service of process outside the Commonwealth, the service shall be made by delivering a copy of the summons and of the complaint: (1) in any appropriate manner prescribed in subdivision (d) of this Rule; or (2) in the manner prescribed by the law of the place in which the service is made for service in that place in an action in any of its courts of general jurisdiction; or (3) by any form of mail addressed to the person to be served and requiring a signed receipt; or (4) as directed by the appropriate foreign authority in response to a letter rogatory; or (5) as directed by order of the court.

EXAMPLES

A Comedy of Errors

1.   Marvell brings a pro se[6] diversity action against Donne for breach of contract. He serves Donne by having a copy of the complaint delivered to Donne personally at his summer home on Cape Cod, in Hyannis, Massachusetts. Is service proper?

2.   The court upholds Donne's objection to the original service and orders Marvell to re-serve Donne properly. Marvell takes a new copy of the complaint and summons, drives to Hyannis, and serves them personally on Donne. Donne moves again to dismiss for improper service of process. Why will the motion be granted?

3.   Disgusted with the whole process (no pun intended), Marvell retains Herbert to represent him. Herbert promptly serves process on Donne by having Marple, an investigator from his office, deliver copies of the summons and complaint to Donne in Hyannis. Donne is not there when the investigator arrives, so she pushes the papers under the front door. Donne renews his objection to the method of service. Is the objection valid?

4.   Herbert changes tactics and orders Marple to serve the summons on Donne at his year-round residence in Boston. Since the elusive Donne is not at home, Marple serves copies of the summons and complaint by leaving them with Donne's sister, who lives in Texas but is visiting Donne to run in the Boston Marathon. Though not to be found at home, Donne reappears

---

6. A pro se action is one brought by a party who is not represented by a lawyer.

faithfully in court to object once again to the manner of service. Has Herbert cured the defect?

5.   If Donne is elusive, Herbert is tenacious. He sends the sheriff to Donne's house in Boston to serve the papers. As the sheriff knocks on the front door, Donne leaves by the back for a pressing appointment. The sheriff slips the papers under the front door and leaves. Is service finally proper?

6.   Assume that Herbert is up on the latest changes in the rules and decides to serve Donne under the new mail/acknowledgment procedure instead of any of the methods in the prior examples. He sends copies of the summons and complaint to Donne at his Boston home, along with the required acknowledgment forms and a stamped return envelope. See Fed. R. Civ. P. Sample Forms, Form 18A. Nothing happens. Consequently, he re-serves Donne by having the sheriff take the papers to Donne's Boston home and (Donne being predictably unavailable) leave them there under the door. Is service proper?

At Your Service

7.   Herrick sues Marlowe for personal injuries arising out of an accident while visiting Marlowe's truck repair garage in Revere, Massachusetts. Marlowe is from Massachusetts, and the action is again brought in the federal district court for the District of Massachusetts. Herrick serves copies of the summons and complaint by having them delivered in hand to Daniel, Marlowe's service manager, at the garage. Is service proper?

8.   Herrick sues both Marlowe and Daniel (also a Massachusetts citizen) for his injuries arising out of the accident at the shop. He serves the complaint by having his investigator, Poirot, deliver a copy of the complaint and summons to Marlowe at the shop. Is service proper?

9.   Herrick sues Marlowe in Massachusetts federal district court for the injuries suffered in the accident at the shop, and Marlowe decides to implead Daniel under Fed. R. Civ. P. 14, on the theory that Daniel, as a joint tortfeasor, is liable to pay half of any judgment Herrick obtains against Marlowe. Marlowe serves the complaint on Daniel, under Fed. R. Civ. P. 5, by mailing a copy to him at his home in Boston. Is service proper?

10. Assume that Marlowe has incorporated his business in Massachusetts, as Poetic Truck Repair, Inc., with himself as president. Herrick decides to sue the corporation for injuries he suffered on its premises.

    a. He serves the complaint by having Poirot deliver copies of the summons and complaint to Daniel at the shop. Is service proper on the corporation?

    b. He serves the complaint by having Poirot take the papers to Marlowe's house and leave them there with Marlowe's wife. Is service proper?

Crossing State Lines

11. Philips sues Datarama Corp., a Texas corporation doing business in Texas, for violation of the federal antitrust laws. Unlike most federal statutes, the antitrust laws specifically authorize nationwide service of process but do not specify how such service is to be made. See 15 U.S.C. §22, which provides in part that "all process in such cases may be served in the district of which it [the corporate defendant] is an inhabitant, or wherever it may be found." If Philips sues Datarama in Massachusetts federal court, may she serve the complaint on Datarama in Texas by the mail/acknowledgment procedure in Rule 4(c)(2)(C)(ii)?

Harder than You Think

12. Philips sues Datarama, among others, under the Federal Interpleader Act, which also authorizes nationwide service of process. See 28 U.S.C. §2361, which provides (in part) that process in such actions "shall be . . . served by the United States marshals for the respective districts where the claimants reside or may be found." The suit is brought in the federal district court for the District of Massachusetts. Philips serves Datarama by mailing copies of the summons and complaint to it at its Texas headquarters, certified mail, return receipt requested. Is service proper?

13. Suppose that Philips sues Boswell in the federal district court for the District of Massachusetts under 28 U.S.C. §1983 for violation of her federal civil rights. Boswell is a natural person who lives in Connecticut and cannot be served in Massachusetts. Philips searches the United States Code but finds no special provision governing service of process in such cases. She therefore serves Boswell under Rule 4(c)(2)(C)(ii) by mailing copies of the summons and complaint and the notice/acknowledgment forms, with a return envelope, to Boswell in Connecticut. Is service proper?

Easier than You Think

14. Recall example 10, in which Herrick sues Poetic Truck Repair, Inc. in Massachusetts federal court. Suppose that Poetic is incorporated in New York, where it does most of its business, but also has a small truck repair shop in Revere, Massachusetts. May Herrick serve Poetic under the mail/acknowledgment procedure?

15. In the Schulansky case (see Part Six) Schulansky sued Richard Ronan and Ronan Construction Company, both from New Hampshire, in Massachusetts. If the suit were brought in federal court, what methods could Schulansky's attorney use to serve process on Ronan and Ronan Construction Company in that case?

EXPLANATIONS

A Comedy of Errors

1.   Service is improper because Marvell has only delivered a copy of the complaint itself. Rule 4(d) requires both the summons and the complaint to be served on the defendant. See also Rule 4(a) and 4(c)(2)(A), (B), and (C), which all refer to service of the summons and complaint.

This requirement makes sense. The complaint is simply the plaintiff's introductory pleading, stating the nature of the case and the relief sought. It is designed to inform the defendant of the events that gave rise to the plaintiff's claim and the nature of his claim. The summons, on the other hand, is an official court document, issued by the court and signed by the court clerk (see Fed. R. Civ. P. 4(b)), commanding the defendant to respond to the accompanying complaint and telling him the time within which it must be done. Look, for example, at the Schulansky summons, which warns the defendant that "[y]ou are hereby summoned and required to serve . . . an answer to the complaint which is herewith served upon you." It is the court itself, not the plaintiff, that has the authority to compel the defendant to respond to the complaint, and it is the summons by which the court exercises that power.

2.   This time Marvell has served the right documents but has done it in the wrong manner. Presumably, he is proceeding under Fed. R. Civ. P. 4(d)(1), which authorizes personal service on in-state defendants. However, Rule 4(c)(2)(A) provides that service of process may be made by any person who is not a party and is not less than 18 years of age. Marvell is a party; the rule bars him from serving the summons and complaint himself, presumably on the theory that such service might lead to immediate (but distinctly nonjudicial) settlement of the parties' differences.

Prior to the 1983 amendments to Rule 4, service could only be made by a United States marshal or a person specially designated by the court to serve process. The revised rule eliminates use of the marshals for routine service of process but preserves a limited role for them in special circumstances. See Rule 4(c)(2)(B).

3.   Technicalities, technicalities. Herbert has apparently relied again on Federal Rule 4(d)(1) but has not fulfilled the requirements of that subsection. *First,* it is doubtful that Donne's summer house constitutes his "dwelling house or usual place of abode"; it is apparently a vacation home. *Second,* the rule requires the process server to leave the summons and complaint with a person of suitable age and discretion residing therein. Herbert has clearly failed to meet this requirement.

Herbert might claim that service was proper under Mass. R. Civ. P. 4(d)(1). Remember that under Fed. R. Civ. P. 4(c)(2)(C)(i), he has the option to serve under the state service rules. Mass. R. Civ. P. 4(d)(1), unlike its federal counterpart, does not require that the summons and complaint be left with anyone. However, it does require them to be left at the "last and usual place of abode," which probably does not include a seasonal home. In addition, under the Massachusetts rule, service must be made by a sheriff or other official process server. Mass. R. Civ. P. 4(c). Service is therefore improper under either rule.

4.   It is difficult to fault Marple here, but Donne will probably win this round too. Here again, Herbert has apparently tried to comply with Rule 4(d)(1) of the Federal Rules. That rule allows him to leave the summons with a person other than the defendant but only if that person is of suitable age and discretion *and* resides at the defendant's dwelling house or usual place of abode. Presumably, Sister Donne has just flown in for the marathon and would not be held to "reside" at Donne's Boston home.

You well might ask, "How is Marple to know that Sister Donne doesn't live in the house?" Perhaps Sister will tell her if she asks; most people are fairly trusting and not expecting the process-server. If not, Marple takes a risk by serving in this manner; she might do better, time permitting, to serve the defendant personally or by mail under Fed. R. Civ. P. 4(c)(2)(C)(ii).

5.   He who laughs last laughs best. Although Herbert's latest attempt is insufficient under Fed. R. Civ. P. 4(d)(1) (because not left with a person of suitable age, etc.), that is not his only option. Fed. R. Civ. P. 4(c)(2)(C)(i) authorizes service under the Massachusetts provisions as well. Mass. R. Civ. P. 4(d)(1) allows service by leaving a copy of the summons and complaint at the defendant's last and usual place of abode. The state rule does not include a requirement that it be left with a family member or with any person at all. Thus, having the alternative of service under state law proves useful to effect service on an elusive defendant such as Donne.[7]

Service is proper here, unlike in example 4, because the papers were left at the defendant's last and usual place of abode, and they were served by the sheriff. The Massachusetts rule may be more liberal on the methods of delivery, but it is more restrictive on the issue of who delivers it. This is certainly appropriate if service is to be allowed without personal delivery. A sheriff or constable is a neutral party with a professional reputation to protect. His or her certification that service was actually made by leaving the papers at the last and usual place of abode is more trustworthy than that of a party or someone working for the party.

6.   Service is apparently improper here. Although Herbert got off to a good

---

7. While it is clear that leaving copies of the summons and complaint at the last and usual abode is sufficient under Mass. R. Civ. P. 4(d)(1), as incorporated by Fed. R. Civ. P. 4(c)(2)(C)(i), it is questionable whether such service is constitutionally sufficient. See *Greene v. Lindsey*, 456 U.S. 444, 452-456 (1982) (service in eviction proceeding by posting on door of apartment invalid under due process clause).

start by using the mail/acknowledgment procedure under Fed. R. Civ. P. 4(c)(2)(C)(ii), he failed to follow it through properly. Under the explicit terms of the mail/acknowledgment procedure, if the plaintiff sends the proper papers and the acknowledgment is not returned, the plaintiff is required to then serve the defendant "in the manner prescribed by subdivision (d)(1) or (d)(3) [of Federal Rule 4]." Since Donne is an individual defendant, Rule (d)(1) applies; that subsection does not authorize service by simply leaving the papers at Donne's home. Ironically, Herbert's second effort would have been sufficient under Rule 4(c)(2)(C)(i), if he had used it initially (see example 5), but is apparently improper as a follow-up to mail service. See *Billy v. Ashland Oil Inc.,* 102 F.R.D. 230, 233-234 (W.D. Pa. 1984); but see *Humana, Inc. v. Avram A. Jacobson, M.D., PA,* 804 F.2d 1390 (5th Cir. 1986) (approving service under state law despite the language of the statute).

At Your Service

7.   Since nothing in this example indicates that Marlowe's business is incorporated, we will assume that he is doing business as an individual and that Herrick is suing him individually. Apparently, Herrick's argument is that service is proper under Fed. R. Civ. P. 4(d)(1) because Daniel, as a manager at Marlowe's shop, is his agent for service of process. The argument fails, however, because 4(d)(1) (and its Massachusetts counterpart) only authorizes service on an agent "authorized by appointment or by law to receive service of process." Daniel may act generally for Marlowe in the shop, but this general authority to conduct his business is not the same as being specifically appointed to receive service of process.

This provision is meant to reach cases in which the defendant has specifically empowered another person to accept notice of suits. It does not apply to an employee who acts generally as the defendant's agent in the conduct of his business. See 2 Moore's at ¶4.12. Specific appointments to accept process are sometimes made in contracts, where one of the parties seeks to insure that he will be able to sue the other in a particular state. See, e.g., *National Equipment Rental v. Szukhent,* 375 U.S. 311 (1964) (approving service on agent for service appointed in contract between the parties). They may also occur by operation of law. For example, Massachusetts law provides that a nonresident who does business in any Massachusetts city or town appoints the clerk of that city or town his agent for service of process in actions arising out of business conducted there. Mass. Gen. L. ch. 227, §5A. In such a case, service on the city clerk would satisfy the provision in Rule 4(d)(1) for service on an agent "authorized . . . by law to receive service of process."

8.   This raises a fairly obvious issue but one that is not explicitly answered by the rule. Service is proper on Marlowe in this case, under Fed. R. Civ. P. 4(d)(1), but not on Daniel. Every defendant is entitled to direct notice of

suits against him, under the provisions of Rule 4. Just as the law refuses to presume that a general agent of Marlowe would inform him of a suit, it also refuses to rely on one defendant to inform others (who, in many cases, he may not even know) that they have been sued. Each defendant is entitled to proper service under the Rules. Herrick will have to serve Daniel separately under one of the provisions of Rule 4.

9.   By now you may be wondering how these rules can be so intricate yet leave so many questions unanswered. In this case, the defendant has brought in a new party, who clearly must be informed of the suit. It would appear that Rule 4 should apply since it governs service of summonses and complaints, and Rule 14(a) requires the impleading party to serve a summons and complaint on the third party. However, Rule 5(a) provides that "every pleading subsequent to the original complaint" shall be served on all parties, and Rule 5(b) authorizes such service by ordinary mail, which is insufficient under Rule 4.

While the Rules themselves are not explicit on the point, the policies that underlie service support the conclusion that the third-party complaint, like an original complaint, should be served under Rule 4. The purpose of Rule 4 is to insure adequate notice to parties who do not yet know that they have been sued. Rule 5, by contrast, is designed to provide a simple method for exchange of the many subsequent pleadings and papers that are filed in the case. It trades a little bit of certainty (under the stricter procedures of Rule 4) for a great deal of efficiency (under the ordinary mail provision of Rule 5). The rationale for doing so is that the defendant is already aware of the suit and, presumably, will stay in touch with subsequent developments. That rationale does not apply to the new third-party defendant; as to him, the third-party complaint is his first notice of the action, and he has the same right to notice of it under the due process clause as an original defendant. See *Adams Dairy Co. v. National Dairy Products Corp.*, 293 F. Supp. 1164, 1165 (W.D. Mo. 1968) (Rule 4 makes exclusive provision for service of all summonses and complaints, including third-party complaints); 3 Moore's at ¶14.18[2] (once motion to implead is granted, the third-party plaintiff should obtain summons from the clerk and have it served in accordance with Rule 4).

10a. Service on in-state corporations is governed by Rule 4(d)(3) rather than (d)(1). Subsection (d)(3) authorizes service on a "managing or general agent" of the corporation as well as various officers or appointed agents. Therefore, whether service on Daniel will suffice turns on whether his functions as service manager for the truck repair business make him a managing or general agent. This will depend on the specifics of Daniel's duties, but it is likely that he will satisfy this requirement. The rationale for allowing service on a general agent for a corporation is that an employee with general responsibilities is likely to realize the importance of the summons and complaint and inform the appropriate officers of the corporation of service. A service manager (once again, no pun intended) for a business that solely does repair work is likely to have that kind of general responsibility and awareness.

Note that under Rule 4(d)(3) service on a managing agent is sufficient, although example 7 indicates that it is not under Rule 4(d)(1). This distinction reflects the policy of the rule that when an individual is sued, service should be made on him personally (or on a family member) unless he has specifically consented to service on another on his behalf. A corporation, however, is not a flesh-and-blood defendant; it cannot be "personally" informed of the action. Instead, the Rule authorizes service on corporate employees sufficiently highly placed to make it probable that the corporate officers who must respond to the suit will learn of it.

Service on Daniel in this case might also be proper under Mass. R. Civ. P. 4(d)(2). Use of state procedure is proper for service on corporations as well as individuals. Fed. R. Civ. P. 4(c)(2)(C)(i). Mass. R. Civ. P. 4(d)(2) authorizes service on a domestic corporation by service on a managing or general agent, or on the person in charge of the corporate business at its principal place of business in the state. Depending on the particular facts, Daniel might well satisfy this provision.

b. In this case, it appears that Herrick has used the Rule 4(d)(1) procedure for service of process on an individual, by leaving the papers at Marlowe's house with a person of suitable age and discretion. Unfortunately, he is not serving Marlowe as an individual defendant: Herrick is serving Marlowe as an officer of the corporation in order to effect service on *the corporation itself.* It is certainly proper to serve the president of the corporation for this purpose, under Rule 4(d)(3), but that rule says nothing about leaving the papers with someone else. It speaks of "delivering [the papers] to an officer . . . ," suggesting that they must be served directly on the officer to comply with the rule.

Herrick could also serve under Mass. Rule 4(d)(2), but this does not help him, since it also requires personal delivery to the officer.

Crossing State Lines

11. As explained in the Introduction, service on out-of-state defendants is governed by Rule 4(e), rather than 4(c) and (d). Thus, the mail/acknowledgment procedure under Rule 4(c)(2)(C)(ii) is not directly applicable; it can only be used if Rule 4(e) incorporates it by reference. Under Rule 4(e) service may be made in the manner prescribed by a federal statute, or if such a statute authorizes out-of-state service but makes no provision as to how it is to be done, service may be made in a manner authorized by Rule 4. The statute at issue here authorizes nationwide service ("wherever [the corporate defendant] may be found") but prescribes no method for service. Service may therefore be made in "a manner stated in this rule" (Rule 4(e), first sentence). Thus, any of the three basic methods available for in-state service are proper, that is, service on an officer or agent under Rule (4(d)(3)), mail/acknowledgment under Rule 4(c)(2)(C)(ii), or state in-state service methods under Rule 4(c)(2)(C)(i). Philips's method is therefore proper.

Harder than You Think

12. In this case the federal statute does prescribe, at least in part, the method for service of process: The summons and complaint must be served by the United States marshal for the district where service is made. Philips has disregarded that requirement. Instead, she has served Datarama under one of the provisions for out-of-state service under Massachusetts law. See Mass. R. Civ. P. 4(e)(3). This is proper under the second sentence of Fed. R. Civ. P. 4(e), which authorizes service on nonresident defendants in the manner prescribed in a state statute or rule. The important point here is that the state methods authorized under the second sentence are an *alternative* to the federal methods under the first. See Advisory Committee Note to 1963 Amendment, 2 Moore's at ¶4.01[21]. Even if, as here, a federal statute applies and prescribes a particular method of service, the plaintiff has the option to use the state's out-of-state procedures instead.

13. Service is apparently improper here because the first sentence of Rule 4(e) does not apply at all. It is true that the last part of that sentence authorizes service by the methods in Federal Rule 4 (including the mail/acknowledgment procedure), but that only applies where a federal statute authorizes service on nonresident defendants ("[w]henever a statute of the United States or an order of court thereunder provides for service . . .") but fails to specify a method of service. When there is no federal statute authorizing such service, the only provision authorizing out-of-state service is the second sentence of the rule, which authorizes service in the manner provided for out-of-state service under the law of the state where the court sits. Mail/acknowledgment is not proper under Mass. R. Civ. P. 4(e), governing out-of-state service in actions in the Massachusetts courts, and is therefore not authorized here. Got that?![8]

Easier than You Think

14. The crux of the matter here is that while Poetic is a foreign corporation (i.e., incorporated outside the state), it is doing business in Massachusetts. Consequently, Rule 4(e), which applies to parties "not inhabitant of or found within the state," does not apply. Poetic is "found within the state" and may be served under the provisions governing in-state service, including the mail/acknowledgment procedure under Rule 4(c)(2)(C)(ii). This conclusion is

---

8. There is some debate about this as well. Despite the language of Rule 4(e), some courts have disagreed with the conclusion that the state service provisions are the exclusive means for out-of-state service. These courts would allow service under the provisions of Rule 4(c) and (d) as well. See, e.g., *McDougald v. Jenson*, 786 F.2d 1465, 1487 (11th Cir.), cert. denied, 479 U.S. 860 (1986); compare *Datskow v. Teledyne, Inc.*, 899 F.2d 1298, 1302-1303 (2d Cir. 1990) (mail service authorized only for service within the territorial limits of the state in which the court sits).

reinforced by the provisions of Fed. R. Civ. P. 4(d)(3). That provision, which details one method for serving in-state corporate defendants, specifies that service can be made under its provisions on a domestic *or foreign* corporation. The clear implication is that a "foreign" corporation (that is, one incorporated in another state) can be served under in-state procedures if it is found within the state.[9]

15. The defendants in *Schulansky* are both out-of-state defendants, one an individual and the other a corporation. The claims against them are common law negligence and breach of contract claims; no federal statute governs service of process in such cases. Consequently, the first sentence of Rule 4(e) does not apply at all, and the plaintiff's only option for service upon them is under the second sentence of that subsection, which authorizes service in the manner prescribed by Massachusetts law for service on out-of-state defendants. Those provisions are set forth in Mass. R. Civ. P. 4(e) and include any method for service on an in-state defendant (i.e., under Mass. R. Civ. P. 4(d)), any manner prescribed by the law of the state where service is made (i.e., New Hampshire's provisions for *in-state* service), any form of mail requiring a signed receipt, or any method ordered by the court. The simplest method will probably be service by certified mail, return receipt requested.

The provision for service under the law of the state where service is made is a little confusing. Fed. R. Civ. P. 4(e) incorporates the methods for out-of-state service under Massachusetts law, which allows plaintiff Schulansky to look to Mass. R. Civ. P. 4(e) (see supra p.266). However, subsection (2) of Massachusetts Rule 4(e) specifically allows the plaintiff to look to the methods provided for service in the state where service is to be made, so this opens up an additional set of options provided by the New Hampshire service rules.

And you thought you wanted to be a litigator.

---

9. Many states, including Massachusetts, have provisions for service on a state official in actions against foreign corporations arising from their in-state activities. See, e.g., Mass. Gen. L. ch.181, §4 (foreign corporation doing business in Massachusetts must designate Commissioner of Corporations as its agent for service of process in actions against it). Such statutes include a requirement that notice of the action be forwarded to the defendant corporation. See Mass. Gen. L. ch.181, §15 (providing for notice to be mailed to the corporation of all actions in which substituted service is made upon the commissioner). Statutes of this sort provide a means of effecting service on corporations even if they do not have a place of business within the forum state.

17

Getting Off Easy: The Motion to Dismiss

Introduction

The defendant usually responds to the plaintiff's complaint by filing an answer as provided in Fed. R. Civ. P. 12(a). (For an example, see the answer to the Schulansky complaint, Chapter 28.) However, the rules provide a second option in limited circumstances: If the defendant has certain preliminary objections to the suit, she may avoid answering immediately by filing a motion to dismiss the complaint instead under Fed. R. Civ. P. 12(b). See Jones's motion to dismiss in the Schulansky case, infra p.489.

Two important points about such "pre-answer motions" should be made at the outset. *First,* filing a pre-answer motion under Rule 12(b) is an *alternative* to answering the complaint. A defendant who moves to dismiss under Rule 12(b) need not answer the complaint until after the motion is decided. See Rule 12(a), last sentence. If she prevails on the motion, she may never have to answer. This can be a strong tactical advantage since filing an answer may require the defendant to admit damaging allegations in the complaint or, at a minimum, reveal much of her litigation strategy.

Second, filing a pre-answer motion is entirely optional. Defendants are not required to use it to raise the defenses listed in Rule 12(b); each may be raised in the answer instead. See Fed. R. Civ. P. 12(b), which provides that the listed defenses may, "at the option of the pleader," be raised by pre-answer motion. What, then, is the point of providing a separate device for raising these particular defenses?

Essentially, the Rules provide this device in order to short-circuit the usual litigation process in cases in which the defendant has a valid defense, evident from the outset, to the court proceeding with the case. These defenses are of two kinds. Some of the 12(b) defenses are immediately fatal to the plaintiff's case. For example, if the court lacks subject matter jurisdiction over the action (Rule 12(b)(1)), it has no power to render a valid judgment; it would be a useless charade for it to go any further with the action. The same is true if the court is not a proper venue (Rule 12(b)(3)) or lacks personal jurisdiction over the defendant (Rule 12(b)(2)). A defendant should not even be required to answer the allegations in the complaint if the case has been brought in the wrong court. To protect the defendant from such inappropriate suits, Rule 12(b) provides an avenue to secure immediate dismissal in cases where the court is powerless to do anything else.

Other defenses under Rule 12(b) raise defects in the procedure by which the plaintiff has initiated the action. The defense of insufficiency of service of process (Rule 12(b)(5)), for example, attacks the manner in which the complaint was served. Similarly, the Rule 12(b)(7) defense of failure to join an indispensable party asserts a defect in the scope of the suit as the plaintiff has framed it. Generally, these are curable defects that will not require dismissal of the suit but will have to be remedied before the case proceeds. If service of process was insufficient, for example, the court will order proper service of the complaint before proceeding. Similarly, if an indispensable party has not been joined, the court will not automatically dismiss the case but will order joinder of the indispensable party if feasible.[1] In these cases the Rule provides a mechanism to flush out preliminary problems and resolve them before getting into the substantive work of the lawsuit.

The 12(b)(6) dismissal, unlike the other pre-answer defenses, challenges the substantive merits of the complaint. The defendant who moves to dismiss "for failure to state a claim upon which relief can be granted" asserts that even if the plaintiff were to prove all the allegations in the complaint, she would still not be entitled to any relief. It hardly makes sense for the court to entertain the action and decide the facts if the law will not provide any relief to the plaintiff even if she proves everything alleged in the complaint. An example would be a suit for negligent infliction of emotional distress in a jurisdiction that does not recognize a right to recover for emotional distress unless the plaintiff also suffers physical injury. If physical injury is required, and the plaintiff cannot allege it, the court might just as well dismiss at the outset since the plaintiff will not be entitled to relief if she is allowed to proceed with the suit.

Although the 12(b)(6) motion is unique in attacking the substantive

---

1. In some cases these defects may not be curable. For example, joinder of an indispensable party might destroy diversity, thus undermining the federal court's subject matter jurisdiction. In such cases the court may have to dismiss.

merits of the plaintiff's claim, it is akin to the "fatal" defenses under 12(b)(1), (2), and (3), in that it can lead to dismissal if it is upheld by the court. However, a plaintiff whose *complaint* has been dismissed under Rule 12(b)(6) will virtually always be given at least one opportunity to amend the complaint to state a compensable claim, before her *case* is dismissed.[2] If the plaintiff had proper grounds to plead all the elements of a proper claim, but had simply failed to include them all in the original complaint, she can amend the complaint to state a compensable claim once the defect is brought to her attention. (For example, a plaintiff who had suffered a physical injury, but had simply failed to state that in the complaint for emotional distress, could amend to add an allegation of physical injury.) On the other hand, if the plaintiff is unable to amend to state a compensable claim because the facts do not support a necessary element of the claim, then the case will be dismissed. The Rule 12(b)(6) motion is explored in more detail in Chapter 18.

Waiver of Defenses Under Rule 12

So much for the consequences of raising 12(b) defenses. The more puzzling aspect of the rule is the consequences of *not* raising them. Rules 12(g) and (h), which govern those consequences, appear Byzantine at first but are more easily understood once their rationale is clear. Essentially, those subsections of the rule, read together (very carefully), provide that four of the 12(b) defenses will be waived if not raised in the defendant's first response to the complaint. If the defendant objects to personal jurisdiction, venue, the form of the process, or the method of service of process, she must raise those defenses in the pre-answer motion or (if she does not make a pre-answer motion) in the answer. If she fails to raise any of these four "disfavored" defenses in her initial response, she has waived that defense for all time.

This result, hard though it may be to extract from the language of these subsections, makes good sense. If the defendant has suffered any prejudice from these preliminary defects, she should become aware of it when the complaint is served upon her. For example, if the suit is filed in a state that has no personal jurisdiction over the defendant, she should be able to tell that from the caption of the complaint (indicating where the suit has been filed) and the facts alleged in it, which indicate what events gave rise to the claim. Thus, it is not unreasonable to put the burden on the defendant to raise these defects right away. If the rule did not require these objections to be raised immediately, the court and the parties might proceed to adjudicate the suit, only to learn down the road that the court has no right to do so. A defendant

---

2. Some circuits hold that the plaintiff has an absolute right to amend under Fed. R. Civ. P. 15(a). See, e.g., *Car Carriers, Inc. v. Ford Motor Co.,* 745 F.2d 1101, 1111 (7th Cir. 1984). Others allow such amendments as a matter of discretion. *Triplett v. Leflore County, Oklahoma,* 712 F.2d 444, 446 (10th Cir. 1983).

might even keep procedural objections in her back pocket and spring them on the court and the plaintiff later on if things go badly on the merits. To avoid such tactics and wasted judicial resources, the rule provides that the defendant must raise these defenses immediately or waive them by her failure to do so.

An Early Question

1.   Presumably, if the complaint fails to state a claim upon which relief can be granted, the defendant should be able to tell that from the complaint alone. Why, then, did the rulemakers not provide that the Rule 12(b)(6) defense is also waived if it is left out of a pre-answer motion?

These rules may seem fussy and technical to you, but it is well worth your while to learn them now. Many a lawyer has re-read Rule 12 in a cold sweat to find out if she has unwittingly waived her client's rights. It is one thing to lose a case by doing the wrong thing, but it is all the more embarrassing to lose it by doing nothing. Under Rule 12 the decision to do nothing is fraught with consequences for your client.

EXAMPLES

Traps for the Unwary

2.   David files a complaint for assault against Goliath. Goliath files a timely motion to dismiss for insufficient service of process. Several months later, the judge denies the motion to dismiss and so notifies the parties.

May Goliath, after being notified of the denial of his motion:
  a. move to dismiss for lack of personal jurisdiction?
  b. answer, including the defense of lack of personal jurisdiction in the answer?
  c. move to dismiss for failure to state a claim upon which relief can be granted?
  d. answer, including the defense of failure to state a claim upon which relief can be granted in the answer?
  e. move for a more definite statement under Rule 12(e)?
  f. move to dismiss for lack of subject matter jurisdiction?

3.   After the court denies his motion to dismiss for insufficient service of process, Goliath answers the complaint. May he include in his answer:
  a. a defense of improper venue?
  b. a claim that the court lacks subject matter jurisdiction over the action?
  c. a defense that David has given him a signed release from liability on all claims arising out of the alleged assault?

4. Suppose that Goliath decides to answer David's complaint instead of filing a Rule 12(b) motion to dismiss or any other pre-answer motion. May he include in his answer:
   a. a defense of insufficiency of service of process?
   b. a defense that the complaint fails to state a claim upon which relief can be granted?
   c. a motion for a more definite statement?
   d. a defense that the court lacks subject matter jurisdiction over the action?

5. Assume that Goliath's first response to the complaint is to move for a more definite statement. The judge grants the motion and orders David to file a clearer complaint within ten days. David complies. After Goliath receives the more definite statement, may he:
   a. move to dismiss for insufficiency of service of process?
   b. move to dismiss for failure to state a claim upon which relief can be granted?
   c. answer, raising the defense of insufficiency of service of process?
   d. answer, raising the defense of failure to state a claim upon which relief can be granted?

6. If Goliath responds to the complaint by moving to dismiss for insufficiency of service of process, may he move at the same time to dismiss for improper venue and lack of personal jurisdiction?

7. What is the difference between the defense of insufficiency of service of process (Rule 12(b)(5)) and insufficiency of process (Rule 12(b)(4))? See Rule 4(b).

8. Goliath does not raise *any* objections by pre-answer motion. He simply answers the complaint, denying the substance of the plaintiff's claims. Three months later, he files a motion to dismiss for lack of personal jurisdiction. What will the court do?

Permutations

9. Assume that Goliath answers the complaint and includes in his answer a counterclaim against David, seeking damages from David for calling him a bully. David contends that the counterclaim does not state a claim upon which relief can be granted. What should he do?

10. David files his claim for assault. Goliath moves to dismiss it under Rule 12(b)(3). While the motion is pending, David decides to amend his complaint to add a claim for battery. May he do so without leave of court? (Consider Rules 15(a), 7(a), and 7(b) in analyzing this example.)

11. One more variation, and then we will banish David and Goliath back to antiquity. David sues for assault, and Goliath files an answer, denying that he intentionally assaulted David. Several months later he realizes that the court

lacks personal jurisdiction over him and seeks to amend his answer, with leave of court, under Rule 15(a), to raise this defense. May he do so?

A Useful but Audacious Exercise

12. Students always express frustration with Rule 12(g) and (h) on the ground that they are unreadable and hypertechnical legalisms. If you agree, try to rewrite those two subsections in clearer terms without changing their meaning.

EXPLANATIONS

An Early Question

1. It is true that a defendant should be able to tell that a complaint is legally insufficient from the complaint itself, so that it would be arguably justifiable for Rule 12 to provide for waiver of the Rule 12(b)(6) defense unless it is asserted immediately. However, the defense of failure to state a claim is a fundamental challenge to the merits of the plaintiff's claim. If the defendant really has committed no legal wrong, she should not be held to waive this basic defense by the mere failure to raise it at the beginning of the suit. If this were the rule, we would be back to the rigidities of the common law, which forced the parties to stick to their original pleadings even if subsequent investigation uncovered basic defenses or theories that went to the merits of the dispute. The four disfavored defenses are distinguishable since these involve procedural objections, which should be apparent to the defendant as soon as she receives the summons and complaint.

In addition, it may not always be easy to determine whether a complaint fails to state a claim at the outset. It is clear enough in a case like my emotional distress hypo, but imagine a securities fraud case involving alleged violations of complex statutory filing and disclosure requirements. It might be very difficult to determine at the outset whether such a claim is legally sufficient. On balance, the system properly favors preservation of this basic objection over the efficiency gained from forcing defendants to raise it immediately.

Traps for the Unwary

2a. No. Rule 12(g) provides that a defendant who chooses to make a pre-answer motion must include in that motion all the 12(b) defenses she has at the time. Any of the listed defenses that are omitted from the motion are waived with the exception of the defenses preserved by Rule 12(h)(2) and (3). Here, Goliath must have known, if he received the complaint at all, that he was being ordered to appear before a court that might not have jurisdiction over him. Since that defense was "available" to him at the time he filed his first motion to dismiss, it could have been consolidated in the first motion. Rule 12(g), first sentence. Because Goliath omitted it, Rule 12(g) provides that he cannot make a second motion to dismiss on this ground.

This provision prevents the defendant from nickel and diming the plaintiff to death by repeated motions to dismiss on different grounds. Otherwise, Goliath might make three or four successive motions, each on a single ground, and unduly delay the proceedings.

b. No, again. Here, Goliath seeks to raise in his answer a defense that he could have included in his pre-answer motion. Rule 12(g) does not cover this; it only bars Goliath from making a second pre-answer motion on this ground. However, Rule 12(h)(1)(A) does prevent him from raising it because he made a pre-answer motion but omitted this defense from it. Goliath does not have to file a motion to dismiss at all, but if he decides to, the combination of Rule 12(g) and (h) forces him to put all four of these defenses in the motion or waive the ones he omits.

Don't be fooled by Rule 12(h)(1)(B), which appears to imply that these four defenses can be raised in either the motion to dismiss or the answer. True, they may be raised in either response, but a defendant can't raise some in a pre-answer motion and reserve others for the answer. Subsection (h)(1)(B) provides that these defenses are waived if: 1) the defendant makes a pre-answer motion and leaves them out; or 2) the defendant answers instead, and leaves them out. It does not authorize the defendant to leave some out of a motion and then insert them in her answer.

c. Probably not. Since Goliath has made a pre-answer motion to dismiss, Rule 12(g) requires him to include in that motion all 12(b) defenses "then available" to him. The second sentence of the rule states that he cannot make a new pre-answer motion based on such defenses.

This does not mean, however, that Goliath has waived his right to raise this defense entirely. As the first answer indicates, this objection is too fundamental to be subject to any rigid early waiver requirements. Rule 12(g) only prevents Goliath from making another pre-answer motion on this ground. Rule 12(h)(2) allows him to raise it in his answer or by another motion after pleading or at the trial on the merits.

I said above that Goliath would "probably not" be allowed to move to dismiss on this ground. It is possible that his objection to service of process was that no copy of the complaint was served on him. If that were the case he would not have known what the complaint alleged and could not have had grounds to move to dismiss under Rule 12(b)(6). On those facts he *would* be able to file a second pre-answer motion raising this defense since the 12(b)(6) defense was not "available" to Goliath when he filed the first one. The fact that the judge denied the first motion makes this unlikely, however.

d. Yes. The 12(b)(6) objection may be raised in the answer, even though it was omitted from an earlier pre-answer motion. Rule 12(h)(2) expressly provides that this defense may be raised "in any pleading permitted or ordered under Rule 7(a)." An answer is clearly permitted (indeed, required) by Rule 7(a).

e. Probably not. The motion for a more definite statement raises the defense that the complaint is so unclear that the responding party cannot frame a meaningful response to it. This defense is "available" to the pleader as soon as the complaint is served on her and therefore should be raised in the first pre-answer motion. Note that the carefully chosen language of Rule 12(g) requires consolidation of this 12(e) defense as well as the various 12(b) defenses.

There is a possibility, as in example 1c, that Goliath never received a copy of the complaint. If so, then he could hardly be expected to know that it would be incomprehensible when he did get it. If this were the case, the defense would not have been available to Goliath when he filed his first pre-answer motion, and he would be allowed to file a second motion on this ground.

f. The language of Rule 12(g) would support an argument that this motion is barred. Rule 12(g) provides that a party who makes a pre-answer motion must consolidate all 12(b) defenses in the first motion and may not make a further motion on any of these grounds "except as provided in subdivision 12(h)(2)." However, despite the puzzling lack of reference to it in Rule 12(g), Rule 12(h)(3) provides authority to raise the objection of lack of subject matter jurisdiction at any time. That subsection provides that "[w]henever" it appears, by "suggestion of the parties or otherwise," that subject matter jurisdiction is lacking, the court shall dismiss the action. Presumably, "whenever" includes before an answer but after a first pre-answer motion, and presumably "suggestion of the parties" may be by a second pre-answer motion. Because no court can act beyond its subject matter competence, a court will dismiss whenever the lack of jurisdiction is called to its attention.

3a. No. As soon as the complaint was served on Goliath, he was in a position to object to venue. Here Goliath made a pre-answer motion, and Rule 12(g) required him to include his venue defense in his pre-answer motion or waive it. Because he did not include the venue defense in his first response to the complaint, it is lost, waived, gone forever.

Actually, it may not always be that easy for defendants to determine from the complaint that they have an objection to venue or other preliminary defenses, such as personal or subject matter jurisdiction. It may not be possible to tell from the complaint, for example, whether a corporate defendant is subject to personal jurisdiction in a district for purposes of 28 U.S.C. §1391(c) or whether all defendants reside in the same state. See 28 U.S.C. §1391(a)(1), (b)(1). Yet the rule requires immediate assertion of the defense. Clearly, if there is doubt as to the propriety of venue the defense should be raised, subject to the ethical restraints on pleading in Rule 11. If more time is needed to investigate before responding, counsel may move for an extension of time to file a response under Fed. R. Civ. P. 6(b).

b. Yes. As previously stated in example 1f, Rule 12(h)(3) authorizes either party to raise this defense at any time.

c. Yes. This is not one of the preliminary defenses singled out in Rule 12(b) for special treatment. It is an affirmative defense on the merits to the plaintiff's claim, which properly should be raised in the answer. Indeed, it could not be raised in a pre-answer motion even if Goliath wished to: Rule 12(b) provides that all Goliath's defenses, except the seven listed in 12(b) itself, must be presented in the answer.[3] Since this defense may not be raised before answering, it is certainly appropriate to put it in the answer.

4a. Yes. Rule 12 does not require Goliath to raise his defense of improper service in a pre-answer motion. It only requires that *if he makes such a motion,* he include all his preliminary defenses. He may simply file an answer including this defense, and it will be considered by the court in the same manner as if it had been raised by pre-answer motion. (See the answer in the Schulansky case, infra p.460, which asserts an objection to personal jurisdiction that could have been presented by pre-answer motion under Rule 12(b)(2) instead.) The real difference is a tactical one: If Goliath answers, he must respond to the substantive allegations in the complaint. He must make his admissions and denials under Rule 8(b), raise his affirmative defenses under Rule 8(c), and assert his counterclaims under Rule 13. If he moves to dismiss, he may avoid, at least temporarily, the need to answer the plaintiff's allegations.[4]

b. Yes. As in the previous answer, Goliath has the choice to raise this in the answer instead of by pre-answer motion. Indeed, he may raise it in the answer even if he omitted it from a pre-answer motion. See example 1d.

c. No. The purpose of the motion for a more definite statement is to provide the defendant with a sufficiently clear statement of the plaintiff's allegations so that the defendant can meaningfully respond to it, either by filing a pre-answer motion or by answering the complaint. Consequently, Rule 12(e) requires the defendant to make this motion "before interposing his responsive pleading."

d. Yes. Rule 12(b) allows this to be raised by motion, but Rule 12(h)(3) makes clear that whether or not a pre-answer motion was made, this basic defense may be raised in the answer or at any other time as well.

5a. No. The defense of insufficiency of service challenges the manner in which the complaint and summons were served upon the defendant. Goliath

---

3. However, the defense of release could be raised by a motion for summary judgment even before answering. See Fed. R. Civ. P. 56(b), authorizing a defendant to move for summary judgment at any time.

4. Filing a Rule 12(b) pre-answer motion does not, however, suspend the litigation. For example, the parties are authorized to engage in discovery, even while a motion is pending challenging the court's authority to hear the case. See, e.g., Rules 31 and 33 (authorizing depositions and interrogatories any time after commencement of the action).

should have been aware of any defects in the method of service as soon as the papers were served upon him, even if the complaint itself was indecipherable. Since the defense was available to him when he filed the motion for a more definite statement, he should have joined it in that motion. Rule 12(g), read very carefully, says so; Rule 12(h)(1)(A) says that the defense is now waived.

b. Yes. This defense was presumably not "available" to Goliath when he filed his motion for a more definite statement because he couldn't figure out what the plaintiff's complaint was alleging. It is only after Goliath receives the clearer complaint that he is able to ascertain whether the plaintiff's allegations state a claim. Because this defense was not previously available, Rule 12(g) does not preclude Goliath from subsequently asserting it in another pre-answer motion, despite the usual command of Rule 12(g) that all pre-answer defenses be raised together.

c. No. Goliath should have been aware of defects in the method of service at the time he was served with the complaint. As in example 4a, this defense was available to him when he filed the earlier motion, and Goliath waived the defense by failing to raise it there.

d. Yes. *First,* the defense was not available at the time the first motion was made. See example 4b. *Second,* this defense can be raised in the answer, even if it was omitted from a pre-answer motion. Rule 12(h)(2).

6.   I threw this question in to see if you would stick to your guns and answer "absolutely." The defendant is not required to stake his case on one of these defenses if others may also be available to him. Not only may he assert multiple objections under Rule 12(b), he *must* do so to avoid waiving them. That is the purpose of Rule 12(g) and (h).

7.   The Rule 12(b)(4) motion challenges the adequacy of the summons itself, the court document served on the defendant that orders her to respond to the complaint. Rule 4(b) details the requirements of a proper summons. (For an example of a summons, see Chapter 26, p.438.) A motion to dismiss under Rule 12(b)(4) might allege that some requirement of that rule was omitted, such as the clerk's signature or the court seal.

By contrast, the Rule 12(b)(5) motion for insufficiency of service of process challenges the manner in which the complaint and summons were delivered to the defendant. See Chapter 16 concerning proper methods of serving process in the federal courts. A Rule 12(b)(5) motion by Goliath might be based, for example, on the ground that it was not left at his cave with a person of suitable age and discretion (see Rule 4(d)(1)) but at a neighbor's instead.

8.   The court will refuse to entertain the motion. Goliath has waived the personal jurisdiction defense by failing to raise it in his response to the complaint. The whole point of the complexities of Rule 12(g) and (h) is to provide for the automatic waiver of the four disfavored preliminary objections, unless they are brought forth in the first response to the complaint. Goliath did not include this defense in his answer (his first response to the complaint), and so it is waived by operation of the rule.

Permutations

9.   Rule 12(b) governs not only an original defendant's options in respond-ing to a complaint, but also those of other defending parties. Rule 12(b), first sentence (referring to defenses to "any pleading, whether a claim, counter-claim, cross-claim or third-party claim"). Here, David, as a defending party on Goliath's counterclaim, has the same options for responding to the coun-terclaim that Goliath had in responding to the original complaint. David may present his defense of failure to state a claim by a motion to dismiss or in his answer to the counterclaim, just as the original defendant may. The same would be true of a defendant responding to a cross-claim or a third-party complaint.

10. Rule 15(a) allows a party to amend her pleading once "as a matter of course" — that is, without leave of court — before her opponent files a re-sponsive pleading. Is Goliath's motion to dismiss a responsive pleading? No. Rule 7(a) enumerates permissible pleadings, including complaints, answers, and replies; motions are provided for in a separate subsection (7(b)). See *Car Carriers, Inc. v. Ford Motor Co.*, 745 F.2d 1101, 1111 (7th Cir. 1984). Since a motion is not a pleading, Goliath has not yet filed a responsive pleading, and David is free to amend without the court's permission. Indeed, if the court is slow to decide the motion, this period for an amendment as of right may go on for some time.

11.   Goliath's train of thought here is obvious. He has run afoul of the rule by failing to include the jurisdictional defense in his answer. Under Rule 12(h)(1), therefore, he has waived the personal jurisdiction defense. When Goliath realizes his oversight, he tries to get the defense into the answer by amendment under Rule 15, asking the court to accept the amendment and treat it as though it had been included in the original answer. (See Rule 15(c), which provides that an amendment "relates back" to the date of the original pleading if certain requirements are met.)

    If this worked, it would provide an easy end-run around the waiver provisions of Rule 12, at least if the judge granted the motion. It won't work though. Rule 12(h)(1)(B) provides that the defense is lost if it is left out of a pre-answer motion, a responsive pleading, "or an amendment thereof permit-ted by Rule 15(a) to be made as a matter of course."[5] As usual, the rule-makers thought about this possibility and impliedly rejected Goliath's tactic by limiting the use of amendments to cure such omissions to those filed as a matter of course. Goliath only had 20 days to amend as of right (Rule 15(a)); since several months have elapsed, he has waived his objection to personal jurisdiction. Even if the judge was willing to grant leave to amend, it would be inconsistent with the limitation in Rule 12(h)(1)(B) to allow the defen-dant to do so. *Morgan Guaranty Trust Co. of New York v. Blum*, 649 F.2d 342, 345 (5th Cir. 1981); 5A Wright and Miller §1391, p.752.

---

5. Amendments as a matter of course may only be made before a responsive pleading is served or within 20 days of filing the pleading. Fed. R. Civ. P. 15(a).

A Useful but Audacious Exercise

12. If you made a real effort to rewrite these subsections, you will have developed some grudging respect for the work of the rule-makers. Their version is elegant and precise, although difficult to understand without considerable study. Here is my rewrite; it may be clearer in some respects, but I still like their version better.

> **12(g).** A party who makes a motion under this rule may join with it any other motions authorized by this rule that the party then has available to him. If a party makes a pre-answer motion under this rule, he must include in it any defense then available to him under Rule 12(b)(2), (3), (4), or (5), or 12(e). Any of these defenses is waived if it was available and omitted from a pre-answer motion.
>
> **12(h)(1).** If a party does not make a pre-answer motion, he must include any defense he has under Rule 12(b)(2), (3), (4), or (5) in his responsive pleading or in an amendment to it permitted by Rule 15(a) as a matter of course. If he fails to do so, the omitted defenses are waived.
>
> **12(h)(2).** A defense of failure to state a claim upon which relief can be granted or failure to join a party indispensable under Rule 19 may be raised by pre-answer motion under Rule 12(b). If omitted from a pre-answer motion, these defenses may be raised in any pleading permitted or ordered under Rule 7(a) or by a motion for judgment on the pleadings or at the trial on the merits.
>
> **12(h)(3).** The defense of lack of subject matter jurisdiction may be raised in a pre-answer motion, in a responsive pleading, or at any time by suggestion of the parties or the court. Whenever it appears by suggestion of the parties or otherwise that the court lacks jurisdiction over the subject matter, the court shall dismiss the action.

My version sounds more like a civil procedure class than a provision of the Rules. In addition, if you read my version carefully, you will find a few cases that aren't so clearly dealt with.

18

Defective Allegation or Insufficient Proof?: Dismissal for Failure to State a Claim Compared to Summary Judgment

Introduction

One major theme of the civil procedure course is "The Perils of Plaintiff" or "all the ways you can bring a lawsuit and never get to trial." We have already explored a variety of purely *procedural* defects that may bring the suit to an untimely end, such as lack of jurisdiction, improper venue, and improper service of process. However, there are also several devices that defendants may use to challenge the merits of the plaintiff's case before trial, which may foreclose a trial if the court agrees with the defendant's objections. The principal devices for such pretrial resolution are the motion to dismiss for failure to state a claim upon which relief can be granted, or "12(b)(6) motion," and the motion for summary judgment under Rule 56. This chapter will examine these two motions in turn and offer some examples to help you distinguish them.

The Rule 12(b)(6) Motion

Under Rule 12(b)(6) of the Federal Rules (and the similar "demurrer" device in code pleading jurisdictions) a defendant may move to dismiss the plaintiff's complaint on the ground that it fails to state a claim that entitles the plaintiff to any form of relief. The gist of the defendant's objection in making the motion is that the "wrong" that the plaintiff describes in his complaint is not recognized as a violation of the plaintiff's legal rights. If that is true, the court would not be able to grant him damages or other relief even if he proved all the facts alleged.

Suppose, for example, that Ferraro sues Gramm for voting Republican, after he promised Ferraro that he wouldn't. The law does not currently recognize a right to have promises performed unless consideration, estoppel, or some other additional acts make the promise binding. Even if Ferraro proves that Gramm made the promise, a court could not grant her any relief for Gramm's failure to keep it. Since there is no right to relief on Ferraro's claim, it would simply place a pointless burden on the court and the parties to proceed with the action. On these facts Gramm could move to dismiss the complaint for failure to state a claim upon which relief could be granted.

Because the purpose of the Rule 12(b)(6) motion is to test whether the plaintiff's allegations (assuming they can be proved) state a claim for which a court might grant relief, the *only* question posed by the motion is whether the complaint itself states a legally sufficient claim. Consequently, the court does not consider any other pleadings or evidence in deciding the motion. It only addresses a purely legal question: whether, if the plaintiff can prove the allegations in the complaint, he will have established a cause of action entitling him to some form of relief from the court. In cases like Ferraro's, dismissal on the basis of the complaint alone is appropriate under this test. Since Ferraro's complaint does not state a legal wrong for which the court could grant her redress, allowing her to litigate the allegations through discovery and trial would be a waste of both the parties' and the court's time.

Dismissal of a suit for failure to state a claim is a drastic measure. If the court dismisses, the plaintiff will never have the opportunity to present his case to a jury, or even to gather evidence through the discovery process that might demonstrate that he has suffered a legally cognizable injury. Consequently, courts give every benefit of the doubt to the plaintiff in deciding the motion. The Supreme Court has held that a complaint should not be dismissed under Rule 12(b)(6) "unless it appears beyond doubt that the plaintiff can prove no set of facts in support of his claim which would entitle him to relief." *Conley v. Gibson,* 355 U.S. 41, 45-46 (1957). The court may not consider the likelihood that the plaintiff will be able to prove his factual allegations; it must assume for purposes of deciding the motion that the plaintiff *will* prove them.

In considering the motion, the pleadings must be liberally construed in favor of sustaining the complaint. Thus, if the allegations in the complaint are susceptible of two constructions, one of which would support relief while the other would not, the court must construe the complaint in favor of the pleader. For example, a complaint that alleges that the defendant "swerved and ran into me on Bleecker Street" might be construed to allege either negligent driving or an unavoidable accident. The court, under *Conley,* would likely infer that the plaintiff (who is suing the defendant, after all) is alleging that the collision resulted from the defendant's negligence.

In some cases a complaint will be vulnerable to dismissal under Rule 12(b)(6) because the plaintiff has sought relief for acts that are simply not proscribed under current law, as in the Ferraro case. In other cases, however, the complaint may be defective because the plaintiff (or his lawyer) has simply failed to allege the necessary elements of a claim that, if properly pleaded, would state a sufficient claim. Suppose, for example, that Berlin sues Porter for malicious prosecution, alleging that Porter filed a criminal complaint against him without cause, and that as a result he suffered damage to his reputation. To recover for malicious prosecution a plaintiff must allege that the original proceeding (in this example, the criminal case) was brought without probable cause, that it was terminated in his favor, that the defendant acted with an improper purpose, and that the plaintiff suffered resulting harm. See Restatement (Second) of Torts §653. If Berlin's complaint does not allege favorable termination, Porter may move to dismiss for failure to state a claim on the ground that Berlin has failed to allege all the necessary elements of a claim for malicious prosecution. Berlin's failure to plead favorable termination may simply be an oversight. If so, the court will allow Berlin to amend the complaint to add this allegation, and the suit will proceed.[1] However, if Berlin cannot allege favorable termination (if, for example, he was convicted or entered into a plea bargain), then his complaint is fatally defective. Since an essential element of the claim cannot be proved, it may be dismissed under Rule 12(b)(6).[2]

Before comparing the Rule 12(b)(6) motion with the motion for summary judgment, a few examples may help to clarify the function of the motion to dismiss for failure to state a claim. In considering the examples, assume that all actions are brought as diversity actions in federal court, that personal and subject matter jurisdiction are proper, and that state substantive law applies.

---

1. When a complaint is dismissed, the court will ordinarily give the plaintiff at least one opportunity to amend to cure defects in the original complaint. See 3 Moore's at §15.10.

2. The examples in this chapter all involve summary judgment motions by defendants. However, the motion may be also used by plaintiffs to establish elements of a claim or to defeat an affirmative defense. See Fed. R. Civ. P. 56(a).

EXAMPLES

Threshold Challenges

1.   While Gershwin and his wife, Comden, are jogging in Central Park in New York City, a car driven by Hart careens off the road and hits Gershwin. Comden is not hit herself but suffers severe emotional distress from seeing Gershwin seriously injured. She sues Hart, alleging the above facts in her complaint and claiming a right to damages for negligent infliction of emotional distress. Hart moves to dismiss under Rule 12(b)(6).

    a.   How would you phrase the issue posed by Hart's motion?

    b.   Assume that New York law does not recognize a right to relief for negligent infliction of emotional distress unless the plaintiff also suffered direct physical injury from the defendant's negligence. Will Hart's motion be granted?

2.   On the same facts as example 1, Comden sues for her emotional injuries and her husband joins as coplaintiff to recover for his physical injuries. If Hart moves to dismiss Comden's claim, will the motion be granted?

3.   Assume that Comden makes the same allegations but also includes in her complaint an allegation that there is a right to relief under New York law for negligent infliction of emotional distress. Hart moves to dismiss for failure to state a claim. Should the motion be granted?

4.   Assume, for purposes of this example only, that the right to recover for negligent infliction of emotional distress under New York law is not quite so clear. Early cases rejected such recovery, but recent appellate cases have granted a right to relief for intentional infliction of emotional distress. Comden can make a fair argument that the recent cases effectively overrule prior law and recognize a right to relief for negligently inflicted emotional injuries as well. Is a motion to dismiss for failure to state a claim a proper means for Hart to challenge the complaint?

Void for Vagueness?

5.   Assume that New York law bars recovery for emotional injuries without accompanying physical impact but that Comden words her complaint more generally. She alleges that Hart negligently drove his automobile in Central Park on the day in question and that Hart's negligence proximately caused personal injuries to her, for which she claims damages. Hart moves to dismiss for failure to state a claim. Will the motion be granted?

6.   Jones is arrested for vagrancy by Rogers, a police officer of the Town of Broadway. Rogers books Jones and places him in a cell. An hour later, Jones is found hanging from the bars of the cell, an apparent suicide. Kern, the administrator of Jones's estate, sues Broadway for wrongful death, claiming

that the town is liable for the failure of Rogers and other officers to take precautions to prevent Jones from taking his own life. Under applicable tort law, the town would be liable if its employees, acting in the scope of employment, failed to take precautions to protect Jones from suicide, provided they knew or had reason to know of the particular risk that Jones might attempt suicide.

The complaint alleges that Rogers arrested and booked Jones, that neither he nor the other officers took any precautions to assure Jones's safety, that Jones committed suicide in the cell, and that the Town is therefore liable to the estate for damages. Broadway moves to dismiss the complaint for failure to state a claim upon which relief can be granted. Should the motion be granted?

7.   Assume, on the facts of example 6, that Kern files an amended complaint, which properly alleges the necessary elements of the claim. Broadway answers the complaint, denying that its officers had any reason to know that Jones might attempt suicide. Shortly after answering, the Town files a motion to dismiss for failure to state a claim on this ground.

   a. Can Broadway make the motion at this point?
   b. Will the motion be granted?

Summary Judgment Distinguished

The first part of this chapter suggests that the plaintiff does not bear a heavy burden in avoiding dismissal under Rule 12(b)(6). He need not prove any facts nor even allege them in detail so long as the court can infer that he is alleging the elements of a proper claim. The motion offers no assistance in weeding out cases in which a proper cause of action has been alleged but the plaintiff cannot prove his claim.

The motion for summary judgment under Fed. R. Civ. P. 56 is designed to allow early resolution of cases in which the plaintiff meets the burden to plead the elements of a compensable claim, but cannot *prove* one or more of those elements. *Summary* judgment means entry of judgment by the court in favor of either the plaintiff or the defendant. Such resolution of the case (or a part of it) by the judge, without trial, is appropriate only if the evidence before the court demonstrates that there are no disputed issues of material fact to be tried and that the moving party is entitled to judgment on the undisputed facts. Fed. R. Civ. P. 56(c).

Suppose, for example, that Berlin, the malicious prosecution plaintiff introduced above, properly alleges that Porter brought a criminal action against him, that he had no probable cause, that it was brought without a proper purpose, and that it terminated in his favor. However, Porter knows that the case was "continued without a finding" by the court, rather than dismissed.[3] If this disposition does not constitute "favorable termination," Berlin cannot win his malicious prosecution case. Under Rule 56, Porter may challenge Berlin's ability to prove favorable termination by moving for summary judgment, supported by evidence to prove that the case was continued without a finding and a memorandum arguing that the continuance is insufficient to meet the "favorable termination" element of a malicious prosecution action.

Porter's motion challenges Berlin's ability to prove an essential element of his claim. When the motion is made and adequately supported, Berlin must respond by producing admissible evidence to prove that element. Fed. R Civ. P. 56(e). He might, for example, submit evidence that there were two charges against him and that one was continued but the one on which he relies was dismissed. He might submit evidence that the continuance the defendant relies on was simply to postpone the hearing and that the case was subsequently dismissed. Such evidence would demonstrate that there is a "genuine issue of material fact" as to whether the prior proceeding was terminated in Berlin's favor.

If Berlin produces such countervailing evidence, summary judgment must be denied. Summary judgment is not meant to try the facts but only to determine whether there are genuinely contested issues of material fact. Thus, the burden of the party opposing summary judgment is only to show that he has legally competent evidence upon which a jury could resolve the factual issues in his favor. If there is a genuine dispute as to the relevant facts, it is the jury's role to resolve it. The judge's role on summary judgment is only to determine whether the parties' evidence reveals such a factual dispute.

If Berlin does not produce countervailing evidence, he has not demonstrated that there is a factual dispute for the jury to try. If his action against Porter were allowed to go to a jury without any evidence to prove that the original action had terminated in his favor, the jury would have no legitimate basis upon which to find for Berlin. A verdict for him could only reflect irrational decision-making. Summary judgment avoids this risk, as well as the delay and expense of trying unprovable cases.

---

3. In some states, many minor criminal cases are "continued" for a period of time rather than dismissed or tried. Under this procedure the court can impose conditions on the defendant in exchange for suspending the prosecution, but the defendant does not plead guilty or acquire a criminal record. Since this practice is routinely used in cases in which the defendant's guilt is clear, it is doubtful that the court would hold that such a continuance constitutes "favorable termination" under the common law of malicious prosecution. At least one case has held that it does not. *Van Arsdale v. Caswell*, 311 S.W.2d 404 (Ky. 1958).

Some Interim Questions

8. Assume that Berlin has alleged that the prior suit was terminated in his favor but has no evidence to prove it. Could Porter obtain dismissal of Berlin's claim under Rule 12(b)(6) at the outset of the case?

9. Why might Berlin have filed the action if the case was continued indefinitely rather than dismissed? Isn't he wasting his time and money and flaunting the ethical constraints on pleading in Rule 11?

In many cases the parties agree on the underlying facts but disagree as to the legal implications of those facts. Summary judgment provides a needed avenue for resolution of such "legal" cases. In Porter's case, for example, the parties may agree that the case was decided by a continuance without a finding but disagree as to whether that disposition constitutes "favorable termination" for purposes of an action for malicious prosecution. If so, Berlin might move for summary judgment, supported by evidence that the case was continued without a finding. If Porter admits that the case was continued, he will not respond with countervailing evidence but instead with the legal argument that the continuance satisfies the "favorable termination" element of a malicious prosecution claim. On these facts, the motion has framed a single, dispositive legal issue for the court. If it finds that the continuance suffices for favorable termination, it will deny summary judgment and allow the case to proceed. If it finds that it does not satisfy the favorable termination requirement, it will enter judgment for Berlin because he is "entitled to judgment as a matter of law."[4]

The motion can also be used to resolve individual claims in a multiclaim lawsuit. Fed. R. Civ. P. 56(c), (d). See, for example, the motion in the Schulansky case, infra p.507, which sought summary judgment on one of the plaintiff's contract claims only. Or, claims by or against one party might be resolved on summary judgment, leaving others for trial. For example, Hart might get summary judgment on the emotional distress claim alleged by Comden on the facts of example 1, but still have to go to trial on Gershwin's physical injury claims.

Rule 56 provides that a motion for summary judgment may be supported by affidavits, depositions, answers to interrogatories, admissions, and admissible documents. Fed. R. Civ. P. 56(c), (e). These materials are not always admissible at trial themselves, but they demonstrate that the party has access to evidence that would be admissible. For example, an affidavit of Hart concerning the Central Park accident is a sworn statement, under the pains

---

4. Often the parties will stipulate to the relevant facts and submit the case for decision on "cross motions" for summary judgment, each arguing that he should get judgment as a matter of law on the undisputed facts.

and penalties of perjury. If the case went to trial, the affidavit would not be admissible, but Hart could come into court and give the same testimony. So the affidavit shows that Hart *has* admissible evidence to support his claim. The same is true for depositions, admissions, and answers to interrogatories, all of which represent sworn statements of parties or witnesses. Many documents, if shown to be authentic, are also admissible under the rules of evidence and therefore may also be used to support or oppose a summary judgment motion. In the Broadway case, for example, the police booking records would be admissible evidence. However, allegations in the pleadings, which represent the parties' *assertions* as to what they can prove, are not admissible evidence and therefore may not be used as supporting evidence on a summary judgment motion.

Another Interim Question

10. Why must the evidence presented in support of or in opposition to a motion for summary judgment be evidence that would be admissible at trial?

The function of the summary judgment motion is similar to that of the Rule 12(b)(6) motion, but there are important differences. The following examples should help you to understand summary judgment and its relationship to the motion to dismiss for failure to state a claim.

EXAMPLES

No Genuine Issue

11. Recall example 5, involving Comden's claim against Hart for negligent infliction of emotional distress. In that example Comden pleaded generally that she had suffered "personal injuries" and the complaint therefore survived a motion to dismiss.
   a. If New York law did not recognize a right to relief for negligent infliction of emotional distress, could Hart obtain judgment on a motion for summary judgment?
   b. If he seeks summary judgment, what supporting materials might he submit?

12. Suppose, on the same facts, that Hart moves for summary judgment on Comden's claim, supported by an excerpt from Comden's deposition in which she admits that she suffered no physical injury. Comden responds with an affidavit, which states in detail the emotional injuries she sustained and details lost earnings that resulted from her emotional reaction to the accident. She also submits authenticated bills for resulting psychiatric care. Should the motion be granted?

13. In Kern's action against Broadway arising from the jail suicide, assume that Kern's complaint properly alleges the elements of the claim. Broadway answers, denying that Rogers or the other officers knew or should have known of Jones's suicidal tendencies. It then moves for summary judgment, supported by an affidavit of Rogers, the booking officer, in which he testifies that Jones was sullen and uncommunicative when arrested, and that he never made any statement indicating an intent to take his life. In fact, Jones was strongly intoxicated and never said a word during the entire booking process. Kern opposes the motion, but does not submit any supporting materials. Should the motion be granted?

Point/Counterpoint

14. Broadway moves for summary judgment, supported by affidavits of all the police officers involved in the arrest and booking of Jones. Each testifies that Jones behaved normally during the process, cooperated with the officers, did not appear depressed, and made no statements suggesting that he might attempt suicide.

   a. Kern submits no opposing evidence but argues in opposition to the motion that he has alleged in his complaint that the officers knew or should have known that Jones was suicidal, thus placing that fact in dispute. Should the motion be granted?

   b. Kern submits his own affidavit in opposition to the motion, in which he states under oath that Officer Rogers "knew or should have known from Jones's behavior that Jones was depressed and suicidal." Should the motion be granted?

   c. Kern submits an opposing affidavit that states that Jones called him shortly after his arrest and was crying and threatening suicide on the phone. He also submits an affidavit from a witness to Jones's arrest, who states that Jones was irrational and made suicidal statements when Officer Rogers arrested him. Should the motion be granted?

   d. In response to the police officers' affidavits described in the beginning of the example, Kern submits an affidavit in opposition to the motion stating that the officers failed to take Jones's belt away from him, and that Jones hung himself with the belt. Broadway responds with a further affidavit of Rogers stating that Jones was not wearing a belt at the time of his arrest. Should the motion be granted?

Baring the Burden

15. Broadway moves for summary judgment. In support of the motion it submits Kern's answer to an interrogatory asking him to "state all facts upon which you base your allegations that the police officers knew or should have known that Jones was suicidal." Kern's response to this interrogatory states

that Jones had told him several days earlier that he wanted to die, and that Jones was in desperate financial circumstances and had just separated from his wife. Broadway also submits an excerpt from Kern's deposition, in which he is again asked what facts he relies on to establish the officers' knowledge that Jones might attempt suicide. Kern's response was, "It was obvious; he had been depressed for months, often talked of suicide, and was out of a job. Don't your officers have any common sense?" Broadway does not submit any evidence from its own witnesses but argues that this record demonstrates that Kern cannot support his claim that the officers knew of the risk of suicide. Kern offers no affidavits of his own. Should the motion be granted?

EXPLANATIONS
Threshold Challenges

1a. The issue posed by the motion is whether a party who suffers emotional distress from witnessing negligently caused injury to another but suffers no direct physical injury himself, has a right to recover damages for emotional distress from the negligent party. Note that the issue is not whether Comden actually suffered the emotional distress or whether Hart was negligent but only whether, assuming all the pleaded facts to be true, the law authorizes an award of damages for such injuries.

b. This motion should be granted. It is clear from the allegations in Comden's complaint that she is claiming relief based solely on emotional distress. If New York law does not recognize a right to relief for acts that only cause emotional distress to a defendant, Comden has asked for relief that the court cannot grant. If the court allowed Comden to proceed to trial, and Comden proved at trial that Hart was negligent and that she did suffer emotional distress as a result of Hart's negligence, the court would still be unable to grant Comden's demand for damages. The claim Comden has alleged is simply not recognized under the applicable law as a legal wrong entitling her to compensation. If that is true, there is no reason to proceed to trial. In such cases, the court can short-circuit the process by dismissing the case at the outset. That's what Rule 12(b)(6) is designed to do.

2. In this case, Comden's claim is joined with Gershwin's negligence claim for the physical injuries he suffered in the accident. Under any state's law, his allegations of physical injuries resulting from the defendant's negligence will entitle him to damages, if he proves the allegations. Comden's claim, however, is still solely for emotional distress. Her claim is not saved by the fact that another plaintiff alleges physical injuries; the rule stated in the example allows recovery for emotional suffering only if *that* plaintiff also suffered physical injury. The court will dismiss her claim, even though Gershwin has stated a compensable claim.

3.   Comden's train of thought here is creative, though unavailing. If the court must assume the truth of the allegations in the complaint, why not allege that the law allows relief for emotional distress? Unfortunately, Comden is singing the wrong tune. The court only accepts the *factual* allegations of the complaint as true for purposes of the motion. The legal issue of whether her allegations state a claim is exactly what the motion is intended to resolve. Rule 12(b)(6) would be useless if the plaintiff could simply allege that he has stated a compensable claim and thereby prevent the court from deciding whether he has.

4.   In this problem, it is difficult to determine whether Comden has stated a claim for relief because the state of the law on the crucial issue in the case is not definitively settled by the cases. If the recent cases have effectively overruled the old doctrine, Comden has stated a compensable claim and must be allowed a chance to prove her allegations. If, on the other hand, the old rule remains valid (perhaps because the recent cases limited the right to recover to emotional distress caused by intentional acts) Comden has not stated a claim.

Although the motion here requires close analysis of the relevant case law, Hart's motion to dismiss is still a proper means to challenge the sufficiency of Comden's complaint. The Rule 12(b)(6) motion is available to resolve difficult issues of law as well as clear ones, and whether Comden has stated a claim depends on a question of law. If the court determines that the recent New York cases have established a right to recover for negligent infliction of emotional distress without physical injury, it should deny the motion and allow Comden to go to trial. On the other hand, if the court concludes that the recent cases are limited to intentional acts, it should dismiss since Comden's allegations are based solely on negligence.

Admittedly, some courts may be reluctant to grant motions to dismiss if the state of the law is unsettled. The court may sense that the issue is a close one that could be better decided on a full record after discovery or trial. The judge might therefore allow the case to proceed to trial and allow the appellate court to clarify the law on appeal after a verdict. But if the court is convinced that the case law does not allow recovery, it has the power to dismiss under Rule 12(b)(6) since the issue, though difficult, is one of law for the court.

Void for Vagueness?

5.   Comden has phrased her allegations so generally here that the court cannot tell from the complaint that the "personal injuries" she has suffered are solely emotional. You and I may know it from the facts described in example 1. Hart may know it since he knows full-well his car only hit Gershwin. But for purposes of the motion to dismiss, the court only "knows" what is in the complaint. Under *Conley v. Gibson,* the court must ask whether the plaintiff, on the allegations of the complaint, could prove any set of facts

that would entitle her to relief. On these general allegations, Comden might prove that the "personal injuries" she suffered were physical injuries, clearly compensable under traditional negligence law. Thus, the complaint may state a claim upon which relief may be granted, and the motion must be denied.

If this tactic will avoid dismissal, and pleading this generally is sufficient under *Conley v. Gibson,* why would plaintiffs ever plead a questionable cause of action more specifically? One answer is that a more specific complaint is more helpful to the court and also will trigger more specific responses from the defendant in his answer. See Chapter 28, p.465. In addition, the plaintiff may prefer to put the difficult legal issue on the table from the beginning. After all, if the case will ultimately turn on the legal question, it may be desirable to resolve it at the outset rather than vigorously litigating the truth of the factual allegations only to discover down the line that proving them will still leave the plaintiff without any right to relief.

On the other hand, in many cases plaintiffs *do* plead their claims very generally, as *Conley v. Gibson* allows, in order not to reveal weaknesses in their cases or simply to avoid giving the opposing party any "free discovery." In some cases such generality may at least postpone the day of reckoning, but as we shall see, the defendant will likely use the summary judgment motion to flush out such weaknesses anyway.

6.   This complaint is insufficient for several reasons. To begin with, the Town is only liable if the police officers acted in the scope of employment, but Kern has not alleged that they did. However, most judges would not dismiss the complaint on this basis. Although the complaint does not explicitly include the scope-of-employment allegation, the complaint alleges that the police officers acted at the jail, performed acts that are part of ordinary police procedure, and that the Town is liable. It is a fair inference that the estate bases its claim on the fact that the officers acted in the scope of their employment for the Town. In ruling on the motion to dismiss, the court must resolve any ambiguities in the pleadings in favor of the nonmoving party. If the court, looking at the complaint, can reasonably infer that the plaintiff has stated a valid cause of action, it must deny the motion to dismiss. In this case, there is enough there for a court to conclude under the liberal pleading standard of *Conley v. Gibson* that the estate may have a compensable claim. Perhaps a judge who loves his rules will require the estate to amend to allege that the officers acted in the scope of employment, but the court should not dismiss the action on this ground.

The other defect, however, is substantive. Kern has not alleged that the officers had any reason to know that Jones was suicidal. Under the applicable tort law, the duty to take precautions arises once the officers in charge of Jones have reason to know that he might try to injure himself. If they don't know or don't have reason to suspect that, the Town is not liable, even if they could have prevented the suicide by greater vigilance. Unless Kern alleges that they had reason to believe there was a risk of suicide, he has not alleged a necessary element of the cause of action.

It may be that Kern's counsel simply neglected to allege this element clearly in the complaint. If so, he will certainly be allowed to amend to cure the defect. However, if he didn't allege it because he has no support for this theory, the complaint may be dismissed under Rule 12(b)(6) because, without such an allegation, there is no right to relief.

7a.   Broadway's motion is procedurally proper. Rule 12(h)(2) authorizes the defendant to raise the objection of failure to state a claim in any pleading, by motion for judgment on the pleadings[5] or even at trial. The rules allow this objection to be raised throughout the suit because it is pointless for a court to proceed if it cannot ultimately provide the plaintiff with any relief.

b.   Be careful to distinguish the issue of the legal sufficiency of the plaintiff's allegations from the factual issue of whether the allegations are true. Here, Broadway does not claim that Kern could not recover, even if he proved that its police officers should have taken precautions to prevent Jones's suicide. Rather, Broadway denies that the officers had any reason to know of the need for such precautions. Broadway has really asked the judge to determine the truth of this allegation in the complaint, not its legal sufficiency.

At this stage of the case the court has absolutely no basis to determine whether the officers knew of the need to take precautions to protect Jones. Kern has alleged that they did, and Broadway has denied it. But at this point *there is absolutely no evidence before the court on the issue.* All it has before it is Kern's allegations and Broadway's denial. The motion to dismiss for failure to state a claim, whether made before or after the defendant answers the complaint, still challenges only the legal sufficiency of those allegations. Broadway's assertion in its answer that the allegations cannot be proved does not change the fact that Broadway may be liable if they are proved. Whether in fact its officers should have realized the risk and taken precautions is a factual issue, which cannot be resolved on a 12(b)(6) motion.

Some Interim Questions

8.   Even if he knows that Berlin cannot prove his claim for malicious prosecution, Porter will not be able to obtain dismissal under Rule 12(b)(6). On a 12(b)(6) motion the court only considers whether the plaintiff has alleged the elements necessary to state a claim. Here, the facts state that Berlin alleged in his complaint that the original action terminated in his favor. The court cannot look beyond the plaintiff's allegations in deciding the Rule 12(b)(6) motion; therefore, such a motion would have been denied since Berlin has alleged all the elements of the claim. Porter needs to "pierce the pleadings,"

---

5. A judgment on the pleadings is authorized by Fed. R. Civ. P. 12(c). It may be used either as a delayed motion to dismiss, that is, a challenge to the sufficiency of the complaint standing alone, or as a challenge to the sufficiency of the complaint in light of particular defenses raised in the answer. See generally 2A Moore's at §12.15.

that is, go beyond the allegations in the complaint in order to convince the court that although Berlin has *alleged* a proper claim for malicious prosecution, he cannot *prove* the favorable termination element of his claim.

9.   People file lawsuits for many reasons. Berlin may have been unclear as to the necessary elements of the claim, or he may have had grounds to believe that under the applicable law a continuance is sufficient to satisfy the favorable termination requirement. He may have hoped to induce Porter to settle the claim, despite doubt as to its legal sufficiency. He may even have had little hope of winning, yet filed suit as a means of venting his anger or embarrassing the defendant. In some cases such suits may violate the ethical limitations on pleading in Fed. R. Civ. P. 11 or the Code of Professional Responsibility, as a misuse of court process. In others, however, they may simply reflect the uncertainties inherent in the application of general legal principles to particular cases.

For whatever reason, many suits are filed that, when tested on the merits, prove fatally defective. Summary judgment provides a means to probe for such defects without going to trial on all issues in the case.

Another Interim Question

10.   "Admissible" evidence is evidence that is deemed sufficiently reliable, under established rules of evidence, for a jury to consider in reaching a decision on the facts. If the party opposing summary judgment has no admissible evidence to prove his case (or any crucial element of the case), the jury would have no evidentiary basis upon which to render a verdict for him. If the case went to trial, the judge would have to order entry of judgment as a matter of law for the defendant for lack of proof. Fed. R. Civ. P. 50(a). The point of the summary judgment motion is to determine whether there is a basis to put the case before a jury. If there is no legally sufficient evidence to establish the plaintiff's case, there is no factual issue for the jury to consider.

No Genuine Issue

11a. This is exactly the type of situation in which summary judgment allows parties to obtain judgment without trial, despite the fact that the plaintiff's complaint alleges a proper claim for relief. Here, Hart knows that Comden cannot prove a compensable claim under New York law, but Hart has to show the court that this is true by demonstrating that Comden cannot prove physical injury, an essential element of her claim. By moving for summary judgment supported by admissible evidence that Comden suffered no physical injuries, Hart will flush out the fatal weakness in Comden's case. Presumably, Comden will be unable to counter Hart's evidence since it is true. The motion will therefore demonstrate that there is "no genuine issue" (Fed. R. Civ. P. 56(c)) as to whether Comden suffered physical injuries and that Hart is entitled to judgment as a matter of law, since psychic injuries do not give rise to a right to recover under applicable law.

Note that here, as on the motion to dismiss under Rule 12(b)(6), the case ultimately boils down to a legal issue. However, in the procedural posture of this case, a 12(b)(6) motion would have been denied because Comden has alleged a compensable claim, even though she cannot prove a crucial element of it. The summary judgment motion allows Hart to demonstrate this fatal weakness in Comden's case.

b. Hart may use any materials that demonstrate that he has admissible evidence to support his motion. A party's answers to interrogatories, for example, are sworn statements that the party could testify to at trial. Hart could send interrogatories to Comden asking whether she suffered physical injury in the accident. Comden will presumably answer "no," and that answer could be submitted in support of the motion. Hart could offer similar testimony from Comden's deposition or his own affidavit stating that his car did not hit Comden, that he observed Comden after the accident, and that she had no physical injuries. Sworn affidavits of other witnesses or a certified police report in which Comden stated that she suffered no physical injury would also constitute proper supporting evidence.

12. Assuming that New York law does not allow recovery for purely emotional injuries, Comden's claim will again end on a sour note. Hart has submitted admissible evidence in support of his motion that indicates that Comden did not suffer physical injury. Comden has filed an opposing affidavit, but the affidavit does not demonstrate that there is any issue as to whether she suffered physical injury. Her evidence goes to prove the severity of her psychic injury, but that is not enough to entitle her to take her case to a jury. She may be totally incapacitated and prove it by the testimony of 20 unimpeachable witnesses, but she will still not be entitled to relief if the law requires accompanying physical injury.

This example illustrates an important point. It is not enough to show that there is a dispute in the evidence on *some* fact; the dispute must be on an issue that is material to the right to recover. Here, Comden's opposing affidavits indicate that she can prove facts, but facts that are irrelevant under the governing law. Thus, there is no dispute of *material* fact (see Fed. R. Civ. P. 56(c)), and Hart is entitled to judgment as a matter of law.

13. You may have concluded that Broadway's motion should be granted on the purely procedural ground that Kern has filed no affidavits or other evidence in opposition to the motion. Rule 56(e) appears at first blush to require this result, since it provides that a party opposing summary judgment may not simply rest on the allegations in his pleading but is required to come forward with evidence in support of those allegations.

That conclusion, while understandable from an initial reading of Rule 56(e), is wrong. Summary judgment should only be granted under Rule 56(e) "if appropriate." It is never "appropriate" to grant the motion if the moving party's evidence itself raises doubts as to the facts. It is only where the moving party's materials would suffice to establish that party's version of the facts that the burden shifts to the opposing party to introduce contrary evidence.

In this example, Rogers's deposition indicates that Jones never stated that he intended to commit suicide, but surely that is not the only behavior that would put police officers on notice of such a risk. Maybe his sullenness, refusal to talk, and intoxication should be sufficient in themselves to suggest depression and reduced impulse control, factors commonly associated with suicide. This affidavit hardly suffices to eliminate the possibility that the officers were on notice of the risk. In deciding the summary judgment motion, the court will view the evidence submitted in the light most favorable to the party opposing the motion. If the evidence offered by the party opposing summary judgment could give rise to two inferences, one of which would support the opposing party's case, the court will assume that the jury would make that inference and deny summary judgment. *Anderson v. Liberty Lobby, Inc.,* 477 U.S. 242, 255 (1986). Thus, Broadway's supporting evidence does not demonstrate that there is no genuine issue of fact as to whether the officers knew of Jones's suicidal tendencies.[6] Since Broadway's own materials do not entitle it to summary judgment, the motion should be denied even if Kern does not file opposing materials.

Of course, it is hardly advisable for Kern to rest solely on the argument that there is ambiguity in Broadway's evidence. Kern should also respond with positive evidence to support his contention that the officers knew or should of known of the risk, rather than take the chance that Broadway has failed to meet its initial burden to adequately support the motion.

Point/Counterpoint

14a. Kern's response here is insufficient to keep the show on the road. Rule 56(e) specifically provides that a party may not avoid summary judgment by resting on contrary allegations in the complaint. All that Kern has done here is to say, "All right, you have evidence to prove that the officers didn't suspect that Jones was suicidal, but I say they did." This is mere persistence, not proof. The court knows that is Kern's position, but a summary judgment motion challenges him to show that he can prove it, not just allege it.

b.   Once again, Kern is whistling Dixie. He has simply taken the knew-or-should-have-known allegation in his complaint and restated it in his affidavit. If Kern cannot avoid summary judgment by resting on the allegation in his complaint, it hardly seems appropriate to let him achieve the same result by simply repeating the same allegation in an affidavit. This is not admissible

---

6. Similar ambiguities in their own evidence led Ronan's lawyers to decide not to file their motion for summary judgment in *Schulansky v. Ronan.* See Chapter 31.

evidence, but simply the opinion of an interested party as to how the factual issue should be resolved. If parties could avoid summary judgment by this tactic, it would hardly be an effective device.

If a party moves for summary judgment and properly supports the motion with admissible evidence, the opposing party must respond with countervailing evidence in order to avoid the entry of judgment against him. Fed. R. Civ. P. 56(e). It is not sufficient for the opposing party to respond by simply reiterating that he disagrees with the evidence proffered by the moving party. At the summary judgment stage the court wants to see what evidence the parties have to put before the jury if a trial is held, not a rehash of their positions in the pleadings. Otherwise, the motion would simply occasion a renewed swearing match between the parties, which would not probe their ability to prove their cases.

c. This is an entirely different situation. Here Kern has offered admissible evidence, his own testimony and that of another witness to relevant events, as to *facts* that tend to prove that the officers should have been aware that Jones might attempt suicide. These affidavits do not absolutely establish that awareness, but they do raise a question of fact on the issue. Summary judgment should be denied here because the evidence is contradictory, thus posing a triable issue of fact as to whether the officers were on notice of Jones's suicidal tendencies. In this case, the show must go on.

d. The parties' affidavits here certainly raise a factual issue as to whether Jones was wearing a belt. But the issue is not *material* to the cause of action alleged by Kern. His claim is that they should have taken precautions to protect Jones because they were aware that he might attempt suicide. The duty to take such precautions is premised on knowledge of the risk; absent that knowledge, the fact that they didn't take appropriate precautions, such as taking the belt away, is irrelevant. Unless Kern can prove notice of the risk, failure to avert it is legally irrelevant.

As Kern's lawyer, you would probably argue (as my students do when we study the case on which these examples are based)[7] that it is negligent not to take belts away from *all* prisoners, regardless of any reason to anticipate a risk of suicide. Maybe it is (though it was held not to be in the actual case), but that is a different theory of the case than the one alleged in Kern's complaint. If Kern wants to argue this, he should plead that the officers were negligent in their general booking procedures, as well as in failing to take special precautions because of their awareness of Jones's condition. If he pleaded that theory, the conflict in the evidence on the belt issue would be material to that theory, and would keep his case alive even if his claim based on their knowledge of Jones's suicidal tendencies failed on summary judgment.

---

7. *Slaven v. Salem,* 386 Mass. 885 (1982).

Baring the Burden

15. In this example, Broadway has not submitted any evidence to *disprove* Kern's allegation that its officers knew of Jones's suicidal tendencies. Instead, it has submitted materials to show that Kern cannot meet his burden to prove that they did. Broadway is saying, "Here, Court, look at this record. I've used the discovery tools the way they're supposed to be used, to probe the other side's case, and look what he's got: nothing. His statements in his deposition and answers to interrogatories do not contain any evidence to show that the police officers knew or should have known that Jones was suicidal. On this record, it is clear that the plaintiff has nothing whatsoever to prove that we knew of Jones's suicidal tendencies. Kern cannot prove an element of his case, so we win. Throw this case out."

Broadway is right, on this record. Kern's answers do not show that the officers had any reason to take special precautions to protect Jones. The facts that he was depressed, out of work, and separated tend to prove that he might be suicidal, but do not prove that the officers *knew or should have known* it. Whether the motion should be granted turns, then, on whether the moving party can get summary judgment by pointing out that the party with the burden of proof lacks adequate evidence to meet that burden, without producing any evidence of its own to disprove the alleged facts.

In *Celotex Corp. v. Catrett,* 477 U.S. 317 (1986), the Supreme Court held that a party can support a summary judgment motion with materials that show that the party who has the burden of proof on an essential fact cannot prove that fact. In *Celotex,* the issue was whether the plaintiff's decedent had been exposed to the defendant's asbestos products. The record suggested that the plaintiff could not prove such exposure. The Court held that, if the defendant demonstrated that there was no evidence in the record to support the plaintiff's claim of exposure to its product, and the plaintiff did not produce evidence tending to prove exposure, the defendant could get summary judgment without presenting any evidence to show lack of exposure. Celotex would be "entitled to judgment as a matter of law" because the plaintiff, who held the burden of proof on the issue, had no evidence to carry that burden.

This holding makes some sense: You can't very well carry the burden of proof at trial without any evidence. At the same time, however, it puts plaintiffs like Kern in a very difficult position. Broadway can move for summary judgment, supported by the interrogatory showing that Kern has no evidence to prove that the officers knew or should have known of the risk. The burden would then fall on Kern, in opposing the motion, to produce some evidence of that knowledge. If he can't, he will lose, even if they knew of the risk all along.[8]

---

8. It is sometimes said that summary judgment is not appropriate on issues involving state of mind, such as the officers' awareness of the risk of suicide in this case, because

Thus, after *Celotex,* Kern must aggressively develop the evidence before the motion, perhaps by taking the depositions of the officers to determine what they knew or suspected. If he doesn't, he may lose, not because his claim lacks merit, but because he has not yet gathered the evidence necessary to prove it. The moving party, on the other hand, can force his opponent (usually the plaintiff) to this effort without tipping his hand as to the contrary proof he will produce at trial if the plaintiff avoids summary judgment by producing admissible evidence on the issue.

---

they are subjective questions, which turn on credibility and difficult inferences about what people intend or know. However, summary judgment may be proper if there is no evidence from which those inferences can be made. In *Slaven,* for example, the court granted summary judgment because there was no evidence in the record to support the allegation that the officers were on notice of the decedent's suicidal tendencies.

19

The Judge and the Jury, Part One: Judgment as a Matter of Law (Directed Verdict)

Introduction

Every good citizen knows that the Constitution guarantees "the right to trial by jury." However, a good part of the civil procedure course is devoted to studying various hurdles that stand between the litigant who demands jury trial and actual jury decision of the merits of her case. As the last chapter demonstrates, the plaintiff's case may be cut short by a motion to dismiss under Rule 12(b)(6), which allows the judge to enter judgment for the defendant on the ground that the plaintiff's complaint does not state a legal claim for relief. If the plaintiff's case survives a Rule 12(b)(6) challenge, it may still meet an early demise on a motion for summary judgment if the judge concludes that there is "no genuine issue of material fact" for the jury to consider.

Although these two motions may preclude the parties from obtaining a jury trial, they are justifiable since both are based on the premise that there is really nothing for the jury to do. It comes as more of a surprise to students to learn that even after the beginning of trial and the presentation of evidence the judge may still snatch the case from the jury or even more invasively, allow the jury to render a verdict and then enter judgment for the party who *lost* the jury verdict. This chapter and the one that follows are intended to help you understand several devices that the judge may use to control the jury's decision-making process: judgment as a matter of law and new trial.

The Plaintiff's Burden of Production

In order to understand these devices, it helps to have a preliminary understanding of the plaintiff's burden to produce evidence at trial in support of her claim. Figure 19-1[1] represents varying degrees of evidence in support of the plaintiff's claim. At the extreme left is the case in which the plaintiff produces no evidence to prove her claim; as you move to the right along the line the strength of the plaintiff's evidence increases. The X line on the diagram indicates the point at which the plaintiff has produced evidence that is sufficiently persuasive that a jury, acting rationally, could find that she has proved each element of her case. If the plaintiff's evidence crosses this line, she is said to have satisfied her *burden of production*. Even though the judge may consider the plaintiff's evidence weak or less persuasive than the defendant's, if the evidence is sufficient to cross the X line the case falls in the realm of legitimate difference of opinion and must go to the jury for decision.

The Z line on the diagram represents the point at which the evidence is evenly balanced; that is, evidence of equal probative value supports the plaintiff's position and the defendant's. In a civil case the plaintiff's burden of proof is to establish that her version of events is more probably true than the defendant's — that is, that a simple preponderance of the evidence favors the plaintiff's version of events. In terms of the diagram, her evidence must fall to the right of the Z line to carry her burden of proof. The Y line represents the point at which the plaintiff's proof becomes so strong that any reasonable jury would have to conclude that the plaintiff has proved her case.[2]

Between the X and Y lines lies the arena for legitimate differences of opinion as to the proper outcome — and hence the arena for jury decision. Even though the judge concludes that the evidence falls at point Q, well to the left of the point where the balance of the evidence favors the plaintiff, she must allow the jury to decide the outcome. If the judge could take the case from the jury when the proof lies between X and Y, she could essentially usurp the role of the jury by substituting her own judgment for that of the jury at any time. General practice (and the constitutional right to jury trial) denies the judge such power: If reasonable minds can differ as to the result, the case is for the jury, not the judge.

---

1. A similar diagram in Landers and Martin, Civil Procedure (1981) was used, with permission, as the basis for this diagram.

2. In a criminal case, the state's burden of proof falls near if not on the Y line since the state must prove the defendant's guilt beyond a reasonable doubt.

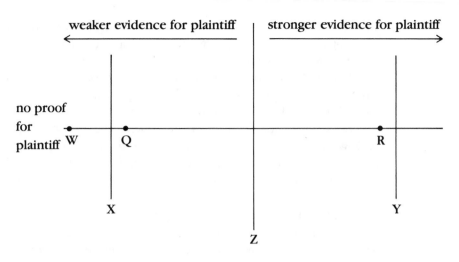

Figure 19-1

Similarly, if the judge concludes that the balance of the evidence falls at point R on the spectrum, where the plaintiff's evidence substantially outweighs the opposing evidence (but is not so persuasive that the only reasonable verdict is for the plaintiff), the case must also go to the jury. Even though the judge believes that the balance tips in the plaintiff's favor, at this point on the spectrum that conclusion is legitimately debatable, just as it is at point Q. If the jury could reasonably find for the defendant, it must be given the opportunity to consider the case, even though the judge believes that the preponderance of the evidence favors the plaintiff.

Old Wine in New Bottles: The Motion for Judgment as a Matter of Law

The courts have long provided a procedural means for judges to take cases away from the jury if the plaintiff's evidence does not reach the magical X line. If the judge concludes that the plaintiff's case[3] is so weak that no jury, acting rationally on the evidence before it, could find for her, allowing the case to go to the jury simply invites irrational decision-making based on irrelevant or prejudicial factors. The judge has traditionally had the authority to guard against such flawed verdicts by refusing to send cases to the jury if there is no legitimate doubt as to what the facts are. See *Rutherford v. Illinois Central R.R.,* 278 F.2d 310, 312 (5th Cir.), cert. denied, 364 U.S. 922

---

3. The motion may be granted for plaintiffs as well as defendants (if the plaintiff's evidence is so strong as to pass the hypothetical Y line), though for reasons discussed below this is much less common than directed verdicts for defendants.

(1960) (court's power to take case from jury provides "a method for protecting neutral principles of law from powerful forces outside the scope of law — compassion and prejudice.").

The traditional device for taking the case from the jury has been the "motion for a directed verdict." Under early procedure, the judge actually did "direct" the verdict: If she concluded that the evidence was too weak to support a verdict for the plaintiff, she ordered the jury to go out and come back with a verdict for the defendant.[4] Eventually, this pro forma (if not demeaning) reference to the jury was dropped; instead, the judge would "direct the verdict" for the defendant herself, and the case would not go to the jury at all.

In truth, this practice does not involve a "verdict" at all, which connotes a jury's finding of facts. However, the motion is still called a motion for a "directed verdict" in most state courts. The "directed verdict" terminology was also used in the federal courts until 1991, when the federal rulemakers changed the name without altering the substance of the motion. Now, in the federal courts, a party seeking to have the judge take the case from the jury on the ground that the evidence is too weak to support a verdict makes a "motion for judgment as a matter of law." Fed. R. Civ. P. 50(a). This is a good name for the motion for several reasons. First, it eliminates any implication that the jury has a role in the decision: As under directed verdict practice, if the judge grants the motion, the jury is discharged without deliberating or deciding anything. Second, the new name emphasizes that the judge, in theory, does not resolve factual issues when he withdraws the case from the jury but makes a legal judgment that the evidence is so lopsided that there really is no meaningful factual dispute for a jury to consider.

However, the change in terminology will create some confusion. The federal courts have developed a good half-century of "directed verdict" case law. Lawyers — like you — who will practice under the new rule must understand that the new rule really is old wine in a new bottle. The rulemakers have not changed the *substance* of Rule 50(a). They did not change the fact

---

4. See W. Blume, The Origin and Development of the Directed Verdict, 48 Mich. L. Rev. 555, 582 (1950). For a curious example of this practice, see *Cahill v. Chicago, Minneapolis & St. Paul Ry. Co.,* 74 F.2d 285 (7th Cir. 1896), in which the judge ordered the jury to return a verdict for the defendant and one juror refused to do it. The court of appeals was not pleased with such recalcitrance:

> The conduct of the juror in this instance was in the highest degree reprehensible, and might well have subjected him, and any who encouraged him to persist in this course, to punishment for contempt. His conduct was in violation of law, subversive of authority and obstructive of the orderly administration of justice.

74 F.2d at 290.

that the judge makes the decision, rather than the jury. They did not change the *standard* for deciding when the case should be decided by the judge. Thus, the case law under prior Rule 50(a) is still authoritative on most aspects of the motion. In addition, the change in terminology in Rule 50(a) only applies to the federal courts. State courts allow the judge similar latitude to control the jury, but most still use the "directed verdict" terminology. Thus, you will have to adjust to the schizophrenic need to make the same motion in federal court under one name and in state court under another. In this chapter I will generally use the term "judgment as a matter of law," since much of the discussion focuses on the federal rule, Fed. R. Civ. P. 50(a).

The Timing of the Motion

As Figure 19-2[5] indicates, the plaintiff in a civil case presents her evidence first at trial. She has the burden during her case-in-chief to produce enough evidence on each element of her claim to pass the X line and reach the jury. Typically, the defendant will move for judgment as a matter of law at the close of the plaintiff's evidence, on the ground that that evidence does not cross the X line, that is, does not satisfy the plaintiff's burden to produce credible evidence in support of each element of her claim. If the judge agrees that the plaintiff has not produced enough evidence to support a rational verdict in her favor, she may withdraw the case from the jury by entering judgment as a matter of law for the defendant at this point.

If the judge denies the motion, the defendant will present her evidence to rebut the plaintiff's case or to establish affirmative defenses. After the defendant rests she may move again for judgment as a matter of law. When the motion is made at this point it challenges the sufficiency of all the evidence, both plaintiff's and defendant's, to support a verdict for the plaintiff. As the diagram indicates, the plaintiff may also move for judgment as a matter of law at this point, though not at the close of her own case.

Two Fundamental Questions

1.   Why may the defendant, but not the plaintiff, move for judgment as a matter of law at the close of the plaintiff's case?
2.   What will happen next if the judge grants the defendant's motion at the close of the plaintiff's case?

---

5. The diagram and the accompanying discussion are a bit oversimplified. For example, after the close of the defendant's case, the court will often allow the plaintiff to reopen her case to offer rebuttal testimony.

Opening
statements

Plaintiff presents
her evidence

Defendant presents
his evidence

Closing
statements

Judge
instructs
jury

Jury
deliberates

Jury
renders
a
verdict

Judge
enters
judg-
ment
on
verdict

Defendant may
move for directed
verdict (judgment
as a matter of law)
here

Either party may
move for directed
verdict (judgment
as a matter of law)
here

Figure 19–2

The Standard for Entering Judgment as a Matter of Law

Because the judge risks encroachment on the role of the jury in taking the case away from it, it is important to have a clear picture of just where the X and Y lines fall. Unfortunately, while it is easy to draw diagrams conceptualizing the parties' burdens of production, it is a great deal harder to articulate a clear and workable *standard* for deciding when the evidence crosses those lines. The Federal Rules, as revised in 1991, now specify that judgment as a matter of law may be entered when "there is no legally sufficient evidentiary basis for a reasonable jury to find for" the nonmoving party. Fed. R. Civ. P. 50(a)(1). However, this really just poses the question of when the evidence is legally sufficient, rather than providing an answer.

A few courts hold that the case must go to the jury if there is even "a scintilla" of evidence to support the opposing party's case. See, e.g., Ala. R. Civ. P. 50(e). Under this test, if the plaintiff has any evidence to support the elements of her claim, she will get to the jury. This standard places point X almost on top of point W on the diagram. See, e.g., *Brown v. Turner,* 497 So. 2d 1119, 1120 (Ala. 1986) (case goes to jury if there is "'a mere gleam, glimmer, spark . . . or a scintilla'" in support of complaint). Obviously this stretches the area between X and Y, giving the greatest latitude to the jury but at the expense of effective judicial control of irrational jury decision-making.

Another suggested standard requires the judge to consider *only* the evidence proffered by the nonmoving party (usually the plaintiff). Under this standard, the judge must assume the truth of all evidence offered by the nonmoving party (usually the plaintiff), take all the inferences from the evidence in the light most favorable to that party, and direct a verdict (or, in federal court, enter judgment as a matter of law) only if that evidence would not support a verdict for the nonmoving party. *Wilkerson v. McCarthy,* 336 U.S. 53, 57 (1949). In passing on the motion, the judge may not determine the credibility of witnesses; the issue of which witnesses to believe is classically a jury decision. The test is not whether the judge believes the plaintiff's witnesses, but whether the jury, if it chooses to believe those witnesses, would have sufficient evidence to support a verdict for the plaintiff.

Suppose, for example, that Pavarotti sues Sills for negligence after he is hit by a red Chevrolet on Maple Street in Cleveland, Ohio. He presents evidence that Sills lives three blocks from the scene of the accident and owns a red Chevrolet bearing the license number 301-LJM. One of Pavarotti's witnesses testifies that she saw a red Chevrolet leave the intersection after the accident, driven by a blonde woman (assume that Sills is blonde) and read the first three numbers of the license number as 311. Although this evidence is hardly overwhelming, it may well be sufficient to allow a jury to make a rational inference that Sills was the driver. Under the "plaintiff's evidence" standard, the judge would probably allow this case to go to the jury, regardless of the evidence Sills presented in rebuttal.

A third standard for taking the case from the jury requires the judge to consider the nonmoving party's evidence in its most favorable light (just as in the second test) but also to consider any evidence put forward by the moving party, which is not impeached or contradicted by the opposing party's evidence. See *Carlson v. American Safety Equipment Corp.*, 528 F.2d 384, 385 (1st Cir. 1976) (when defendant moves for directed verdict, the court must examine the facts in the light most favorable to the plaintiff but without neglecting the uncontradicted evidence for the defendant). If, considering all of that evidence, "there can be but one reasonable conclusion as to the verdict," the judge must direct a verdict for the moving party. 5A Moore's at ¶50.02[1]. A frequent statement of the standard is as follows:

> [T]he Court should consider all of the evidence — not just that evidence which supports the non-mover's case — but in the light and with all reasonable inferences most favorable to the party opposed to the motion. If the facts and inferences point so strongly and overwhelmingly in favor of one party that the Court believes that reasonable men could not arrive at a contrary verdict, grant of the motions is proper. On the other hand, if there is substantial evidence opposed to the motions, evidence of such quality and weight that reasonable and fair-minded men in the exercise of impartial judgment might reach different conclusions, the motions should be denied, and the case submitted to the jury.

Boeing Co. v. Shipman, 411 F.2d 365, 374 (5th Cir. 1969). Most federal cases apply this standard under Fed. R. Civ. P. 50(a). For easy reference, I will call it the "federal standard," although this approach is very widely followed in state courts as well.

To illustrate the operation of this standard, assume that Sills (after the plaintiff, Pavarotti, presents the evidence described above) offers the undisputed testimony of two eyewitnesses to the accident that she was not the driver of the car and documentary evidence that indicates that she was performing in an opera in Minneapolis at the time of the accident. On this state of the evidence, her motion for judgment as a matter of law at the close of all the evidence should be granted under the federal standard. The plaintiff produced enough evidence to support a legitimate (but not compelling) inference that Sills had hit him. But that inference is negated by the defendant's uncontradicted, unimpeached evidence to the contrary and leaves the jury without a reasonable basis to conclude that Sills is liable.

The examples that follow should help you to get a sense of the court's role in controlling jury action by entering judgment as a matter of law. The examples are based on one of the classic cases on directed verdicts, *Pennsylvania R.R. Co. v. Chamberlain*, 288 U.S. 333 (1933). The relevant evidence in *Chamberlain* is set forth immediately below, but you may want to read *Chamberlain* before considering the examples.

The decedent in *Chamberlain* was killed when he fell from a train he was riding, while sorting groups of cars in a railroad yard.

> The lead track crossed a "hump," and the work of car distribution consisted of pushing a train of cars by means of a locomotive to the top of the "hump," and then allowing the cars, in separate strings, to descend by gravity, under the control of hand brakes, to their respective destinations in the various branch tracks. Deceased had charge of a string of two gondola cars, which he was piloting to track 14. Immediately ahead of him was a string of seven cars, and behind him a string of nine cars, both also destined for track 14. Soon after the cars ridden by the deceased had passed to track 14, his body was found on that track some distance beyond the switch. He had evidently fallen onto the track and been run over by a car or cars.

288 U.S. at 335-336. The plaintiff's theory was that the railroad's employees negligently caused the string of cars Chamberlain was riding to collide with the following string of nine cars, throwing him under the train.

EXAMPLES

The Plaintiff's Case

3. In *Chamberlain* the plaintiff offered the following evidence as to the cause of the accident:

> The plaintiff's only witness to the event, one Bainbridge, then employed by the road, stood close to the yardmaster's office, near the "hump." He professed to have paid little attention to what went on, but he did see the deceased riding at the rear of his cars, whose speed when they passed him he took to be about eight or ten miles. Shortly thereafter a second string passed which was shunted into another track and this was followed by the nine, which according to the plaintiff's theory, collided with the deceased's. After the nine cars had passed at a somewhat greater speed than the deceased's, Bainbridge paid no more attention to either string for a while, but looked again when the deceased, who was still standing in his place, had passed the switch and onto the assorting track where he was bound. At that time his speed had been checked to about three miles, but the speed of the following nine cars had increased. They were just passing the switch, about four or five cars behind the deceased. Bainbridge looked away again and soon heard what he described as a "loud crash," not however an unusual event in a switching yard. Apparently this did not cause him at once to turn, but he did so shortly thereafter, and saw the two strings together, still moving, and the deceased no longer in sight. . . . Until he left to go to the accident, he had stood fifty feet to the north of the track where the accident happened, and about nine hundred feet from where the body was found.

288 U.S. at 336-337.

Assume that the plaintiff in *Chamberlain* presents this evidence as to the cause of the accident and rests her case. The defendant moves for judgment as a matter of law.

   a. If the court applies the "plaintiff's evidence" standard, should the motion be granted?

   b. Assume that the case is tried instead in a court that applies the federal standard, which also allows consideration of the moving party's uncontradicted, unimpeached evidence. Should the railroad's motion at the close of the plaintiff's case be granted?

4.   Suppose that Bainbridge was again the only witness and gave the same testimony but that he had made his observations while riding on a third string of cars following the nine-car string. If the railroad moved for judgment as a matter of law at the close of the plaintiff's case, should the court grant the motion if the "plaintiff's evidence" standard applies?

5.   Assume that the employee in *Chamberlain* was seriously injured rather than killed, and the case therefore involved extensive evidence on damages (such as future pain and suffering, medical costs, lost earnings, and disability), as well as on liability. At trial, the plaintiff's evidence for liability is the same, again based on Bainbridge's testimony. After she presents her case on liability (but before she offers her evidence on damages), the railroad moves for judgment as a matter of law. Is the motion timely?

The Defendant's Case

6.   If the federal standard applies, should the railroad be allowed to move for judgment as a matter of law at the close of all the evidence if it failed to do so at the close of the plaintiff's case?

7.   Suppose that the plaintiff in *Chamberlain* rests her case, and the railroad rests its case without offering any evidence. The plaintiff moves for judgment as a matter of law. Should it be granted?

8.   Assume that the court refuses to enter judgment for the defendant in *Chamberlain* at the close of the plaintiff's evidence. Therefore, the railroad proceeds to present its case. (See Figure 19-2 supra.) As the case report indicates, the railroad's case was as follows. "Three employees, riding the nine-car string, testified positively that no such collision occurred. They were corroborated by every other employee in a position to see, all testifying that there was no contact between the nine-car string and that of the deceased." 288 U.S. at 336.

   a. After presenting its case, the railroad moves for judgment as a matter of law. Should the motion be granted under the plaintiff's evidence standard?

   b. Should the motion be granted under the federal standard?

A Few Variations

9.   Suppose that Bainbridge offered the same testimony as above, but there were only two trains, the two-car string and the nine-car string, in the yard at the time. How should the court rule if the railroad offers the same evidence as above and then moves for judgment as a matter of law at the close of all the evidence? Assume that the federal standard applies.

10. Suppose that Bainbridge's testimony was the same as that offered in the actual case, but that he testified that he actually saw the trains collide. Could the judge enter judgment for the railroad?

11. Suppose there had been only one witness for the defendant, the railroad yardmaster. Assume that he was standing near the spot where the decedent was found and testified unequivocally that no collision occurred. Could the judge enter judgment as a matter of law for the railroad?

Trial and Error

12. Assume that the Chamberlain case was tried to the judge instead of a jury. The defendant's counsel rises at the close of the plaintiff's case and moves "for judgment as a matter of law under Rule 50(a), on the ground that no reasonable jury could find for the plaintiff." What two grievous errors did defendant's counsel make? See Fed. R. Civ. P. 52(c).

A Retrospective

13. Let's back up a minute and assume that the railroad moved for summary judgment before trial and submitted affidavits in support of the motion from their employees. The affidavits all state that no collision took place between the two strings. The plaintiff submits an opposing affidavit of Bainbridge, stating his testimony as it is given in example 3. Should the railroad's motion be granted?

EXPLANATIONS

Two Fundamental Questions

1.   Due process of law entitles every litigant to an opportunity to be heard before a court adjudicates her rights. If the court could enter judgment as a matter of law for the plaintiff at the close of her case, the defendant would be deprived of her opportunity to present evidence, either to refute the plaintiff's proof or to establish an affirmative defense. Even if the judge concludes that the plaintiff's evidence has crossed the Y line, the defendant may well produce countervailing evidence that would leave legitimate doubt as to the facts, making the case an appropriate one for the jury. Thus, no matter how strong the plaintiff's evidence may be, the defendant will be given a chance to rebut it.

2.   The judge may only grant judgment as a matter of law for the defendant if she concludes that the plaintiff has not produced enough evidence to support a rational verdict in her favor. If the judge concludes that the plaintiff has not produced adequate evidence on each of the elements of her "prima facie case," there is no need to go on and hear the defendant's evidence. The judge will enter judgment for the defendant on the basis of the insufficiency of plaintiff's proof.

The Plaintiff's Case

3a.   Under the plaintiff's evidence standard, the motion should be denied if the jury, considering only the evidence supporting the plaintiff's case, could reasonably infer that the accident resulted from the railroad's negligence. Although the plaintiff's evidence that the two strings collided (thus indicating negligence by the railroad) is less than compelling, it is probably sufficient to support a rational inference that a collision caused the accident. If the jury credits Bainbridge's testimony, it would have evidence that a crash occurred, that the nine-car string was moving considerably faster than the two-car string before the crash, and that the two strings subsequently were seen moving in tandem. In addition, the fact that the decedent had fallen from the train supported the inference that a collision had knocked him off. If such an inference could rationally be made, the jury should be allowed to make it (or reject it). The defendant's motion should probably be denied.

b.   The result at this stage of the case should be the same under the federal test. At the close of the plaintiff's case the only evidence before the court is that offered by the plaintiff.[6] Thus, the defendant's motion at this point will usually be based on the position that the plaintiff's evidence is insufficient to cross the X line, that is, it does not satisfy her burden to produce evidence that would rationally support the conclusion that the accident resulted from the railroad's negligence. As indicated above, the plaintiff's evidence in *Chamberlain* was probably sufficient to defeat this motion.

It is conceivable that the railroad's attorney would elicit evidence from the *plaintiff's* witnesses that would foreclose a verdict in the plaintiff's favor. For example, the railroad might get Bainbridge to admit on cross-examination that he is unable to see farther than 25 feet without his glasses, which he was not wearing at the time. This evidence would be considered under the federal standard and, if not impeached or contradicted by other evidence for the plaintiff, it could force the plaintiff's case back over the X line and lead to a directed verdict (judgment as a matter of law) for the railroad even before it presents its own case. Absent such evidence, however, the result should be the same under either standard at this point.

---

6. Except, of course, for adverse testimony by the plaintiff's witnesses, elicited by defendant's counsel on cross-examination.

4.   Although the judge is required to view the case in the light most favorable to the plaintiff, there comes a point where the unlikely fades into the humanly impossible. As the case report indicates, Bainbridge apparently viewed the moving trains from a three-degree angle if he was standing *beside* the track. If he were actually on a train following the nine-car string (and there were no bend in the track) it would be impossible for him to observe a collision 900 feet in front of him on the same track. On this evidence the reasonable judge could reasonably conclude that only an unreasonable jury could find for the plaintiff.

It is true that the judge, by taking the case from the jury on these facts, exercises some judgment as to the strength of the plaintiff's case. In this sense, the term "judgment as a matter of law" is a bit of a misnomer because the judge has made a factual judgment here that the evidence is too far-fetched to justify a finding for the plaintiff. But a line must be drawn somewhere between the inherently incredible and the unlikely-but-possible. If the court abdicates the responsibility of doing so, the jury becomes the unrestrained arbiter of the parties' rights regardless of the inadequacy of their proof.

5.   The railroad's position here is that the evidence on damages is legally irrelevant if Chamberlain has not proved liability. Why should the parties and the court waste their time on lengthy damage evidence if Chamberlain has not met her burden of production on the liability issue?

While motions for a directed verdict are usually made after the plaintiff presents her entire case (see Figure 19-2), it may sometimes be appropriate to try a dispositive issue first and determine the legal sufficiency of the evidence on that issue. If Chamberlain has not passed the X line on the liability elements of her claim, there is no need to hear the damages evidence. The Advisory Committee notes to the 1991 revisions to Rule 50(a) emphasize that a motion for judgment as a matter of law may be appropriate "as soon as a party has completed a presentation on a fact essential to that party's case." Advisory Committee note to Rule 50(a), fifth paragraph. This suggestion is in line with the modern tendency to encourage judges to aggressively manage cases in order to speed their disposition. See, e.g., Fed. R. Civ. P. 16 (authorizing scheduling and pretrial conferences to streamline the trial process).

Under this approach, a judge might even order that an affirmative defense be tried first, if it appeared that the defense might be decisive. For example, if a defendant in a negligence case claims that the plaintiff gave him a release of the claim, and the evidence on the issue is strong, the judge might order this issue tried first, to determine whether there is a jury question as to whether the claim was released. If she concludes that the release defense is established as a matter of law, the case will be dismissed without trying the plaintiff's basic negligence case at all.

Some lawyers feel that this managerial approach unfairly encroaches on their traditional prerogative to present their cases in their own way. Chamberlain's counsel, for example, would doubtless prefer to put in his entire case, hoping that the judge's decision on the motion would be colored by the compelling evidence of Chamberlain's damages. Many courts will still defer the decision to the end of the plaintiff's evidence, but there is a marked tendency, especially in the federal courts, to curtail counsel's autonomy in litigation procedure in the interest of efficient resolution of cases. The federal rulemakers, in revising Rule 50, have given judges a green light to extend this tendency to directed verdict practice as well.

The Defendant's Case

6.   This motion is proper. There is no requirement that a defendant move for judgment as a matter of law at the close of the plaintiff's case in order to preserve her right to do so at the close of all the evidence. Nor should there be; as stated in the Introduction, the motion raises distinct issues depending upon when it is made. When the defendant makes this motion at the close of the plaintiff's case the issue is whether the plaintiff has produced so little evidence that no reasonable jury could conclude that she has carried her burden of proof. The defendant's motion at the close of all the evidence may, if the federal standard applies, be based on the argument that the plaintiff had initially presented a strong enough case to go to the jury, but the unimpeached and uncontradicted evidence that she has presented forces the case back to the left of the X line on the diagram, where the judge must enter judgment for the defendant. If that is true, then it would be improper to take the case from the jury at the close of the plaintiff's case, but appropriate at the end of all the evidence under the federal standard.

7.   A plaintiff's motion for judgment as a matter of law at the close of the case asserts that the uncontradicted, unimpeached evidence in support of her case is so strong that the proof falls to the right of the Y line, where no reasonable jury could reach a verdict for the defendant. In passing on the plaintiff's motion, the court must assume that the jury would believe all of the defendant's evidence and reject all evidence for the plaintiff that had been contradicted or impeached. If, upon these assumptions, the only rational conclusion is that the plaintiff has proved each element of her case, the verdict may be directed.

On the *Chamberlain* facts, the motion should be denied. Even though the railroad offered no evidence, it does not follow that the plaintiff has established her case beyond doubt. The jury would still have to infer from Bainbridge's circumstantial evidence that a crash occurred between the two-car string and the nine-car string. Reasonable jurors might make that inference, but they also might not. The evidence is strong enough to support a verdict for Chamberlain but not strong enough to compel it.

As a practical matter, the judge seldom orders judgment as a matter of law for plaintiffs because they bear the burden of proof as to each element of their claim. Most cases turn at least in part on the credibility of witnesses. If the credibility of the plaintiff's witnesses has been challenged, the court will have to assume for purposes of the motion that the jury will disbelieve them. If their testimony is necessary to establish any element of the plaintiff's claim, the motion will be denied.

8a. The analysis of example 3a suggests that the plaintiff's evidence, taken alone, was sufficient to place the *Chamberlain* case in the middle area of the diagram, between the X and Y lines, where the jury must decide the contested issues of fact. If the plaintiff's evidence standard is applied here, the court must disregard all of the railroad's opposing testimony, and the same result will follow in this case even though the defendant has introduced very strong contrary evidence.

b. If the federal standard is applied, the court must consider not only Bainbridge's testimony for the plaintiff but also the uncontradicted and un-impeached testimony for the defendant. The crucial question is whether the defendant's witnesses, who testify directly that no crash occurred (and therefore no negligence and no ground for recovery), are contradicted or impeached by the plaintiff's evidence.

The Court holds, and I think rightly, that Bainbridge's and the defendant's versions of the incident are not contradictory. Bainbridge's testimony indicates that there was a crash and that the trains were moving along at the same speed after the crash. A jury could infer from this that the nine-car string collided with the two-car string. Alternatively, they could infer that a collision took place someplace else in the yard, and that these two strings were moving at the same speed because each had been braked to the same speed. The defendant's witnesses do not contradict Bainbridge; their testimony that the nine-car and the two-car strings did not collide simply eliminates one of the two possible inferences from his testimony. Unless the jury has some rational basis for rejecting their testimony, it is no longer possible to infer from Bainbridge's circumstantial version of events that these two strings actually collided.

It might be argued that the jury could reject the testimony of the defendant's witnesses because they were all employed by the railroad and thus could be biased. The argument has some force, but the Court concluded in *Chamberlain* that the mere fact of employment by the defendant was insufficient to impeach their testimony. See also *Chesapeake & Ohio Railway Co. v. Martin*, 283 U.S. 209, 216-220 (1931). The case would likely be different if only one employee testified for the railroad and the evidence indicated that he was promoted the week after the accident.

Needless to say, application of these standards for taking the case from the jury is hardly scientifically precise. In *Chamberlain,* the trial judge directed a verdict for the railroad. The court of appeals reversed, in a two-to-one decision, on the ground that the case should have been left to the jury. The eminent Judge Learned Hand wrote for the majority, and Judge Swan, another respected jurist, registered a strong dissent. 59 F.2d 986 (1932). The Supreme Court then unanimously reversed the court of appeals. Clearly, reasonable judges may differ about when reasonable jurors may differ. Yet the fact that there are close cases does not change the fact that the motion provides needed control of irrational jury behavior.

A Few Variations

9.   This change in the facts introduces a direct contradiction between the plaintiff's and the defendant's evidence. Bainbridge testifies that he heard a crash of the type made by trains colliding, and there only were two in the yard. If you believe Bainbridge, the only possible inference is that those two strings of cars collided. Unlike the facts of the actual case, this testimony would directly contradict the testimony of the defendant's witnesses. Although there were six or seven witnesses for the defendant and only one, Bainbridge, for the plaintiff, the court may not pass on issues of credibility in ruling on a motion for judgment as a matter of law. If there is a legitimate conflict in the evidence, the jury must resolve it. If the jury believes Bainbridge over the railroad's employees, it could reasonably find for the plaintiff and should be given the opportunity to do so.

10. Here again Bainbridge's testimony directly contradicts that of the defendant's witnesses and should therefore raise a jury issue unless the Court concludes that his testimony is inherently incredible. The Supreme Court intimated that it may have been physically impossible for Bainbridge to actually see whether the two strings were in contact. *Chamberlain* at 342. Thus, it is not clear that direct testimony from Bainbridge of a collision would have changed the result. The court might disregard it as physically impossible and conclude that the plaintiff's case was built entirely on an inference, which was negated by the defendant's direct evidence to the contrary. Many judges, however, would conclude (as the court of appeals did in *Chamberlain*) that Bainbridge's acute angle of vision is a fact for the jury to weigh in deciding whether to believe his testimony, rather than making that testimony inherently incredible.

11. As suggested above, practice in this area is heavily fact-specific and unscientific. Consequently, distinctions that are conceptually clear do not always dictate results. In this case, the state of the evidence has not changed much when evaluated under the federal standard for taking the case from the jury. The plaintiff's case is still built upon inference, and it is still directly contradicted by evidence that the jury has little or no reason to discredit.

Yet many courts would not direct the verdict on these facts. There is not the same level of certainty about the defendant's case as there was in the real case, in which six witnesses unanimously denied a collision. A single witness might be unbiased but simply wrong. The argument for bias is stronger here as well since there is more incentive for a managerial employee of the railroad to testify falsely than for lower-level yard workers to do so.

Trial and Error

12. The railroad's attorney has made two mistakes here, one technical but the other substantial. *First,* he should not have sought judgment under Rule 50(a) at all. That rule addresses the judge's power to enter judgment in a case tried to a jury. See, e.g., Rule 50(a)(1) ("If, during a trial by jury. . ."). Here, the case was tried to the judge, so Rule 50(a) is not relevant; the proper motion would have been for judgment on partial findings by the court under Fed. R. Civ. P. 52(c).

Second, and more important, the railroad's attorney has inappropriately asked the judge to apply the standard for withdrawing a case from the jury to a case in which *the judge is the factfinder.* In a jury case the judge's role is to act as a gatekeeper, keeping obviously inadequate cases from the jury. However, when the defendant in a nonjury trial moves for judgment at the close of the plaintiff's case, the judge *is* the factfinder. The issue is not whether the evidence is strong enough that a reasonable jury could find for the plaintiff (i.e., whether it has passed the X line on the diagram), but rather whether the judge, as the factfinder, believes that the plaintiff has proved the elements of her cause of action by a preponderance of the evidence (i.e., whether the plaintiff's evidence has passed the Z line). If the plaintiff has not satisfied that standard, the judge may enter judgment without hearing the defendant's evidence, since the plaintiff has had a full opportunity to make her case and has not carried her burden of proof. See Fed. R. Civ. P. 52(c), as amended by the 1991 revisions to the Federal Rules, and the accompanying Advisory Committee note.

In determining whether the plaintiff has carried her burden of proof, the judge may also consider the credibility of the witnesses; she is not deciding whether the jury *could* believe plaintiff's witnesses but rather whether she, the judge acting as the factfinder, *does* believe them. In other words, in a judge-tried case, the motion for a finding allows the judge to determine whether the plaintiff has carried her burden of *proof,* while in a jury case the judge acts as a gatekeeper to prevent the jury from hearing insubstantial cases, and must confine herself to considering whether the plaintiff has carried her burden of *production.*[7]

---

7. The analogy in a jury case would be if the judge sent the jury out after the plaintiff rested her case to determine whether the plaintiff's evidence had moved the case over the Z line (that is, satisfied the plaintiff's burden of proof) and dismissed the action if the jury concluded that the plaintiff had not. I suppose jury trials could be run that way: The jury would deliberate twice, once after the plaintiff's case to determine whether she had carried her initial burden of proof by a preponderance of the evidence; and a second time after the defendant's evidence to determine if she had pushed the case back over the Z line. However, such a system would break the flow of the evidence and confuse the jury as well. But the judge *can* do this in a nonjury trial, since she is used to dealing with the concept of burdens of proof and can more easily break up the presentation of the evidence to consider the motion.

A Retrospective

13. Summary judgment is only appropriate if there is "no genuine issue of material fact" to be resolved by the jury. It is often said that if the evidence is so one-sided that a judge would be required to enter judgment as a matter of law at trial, then no genuine factual issue exists and summary judgment is appropriate. See, e.g., *Anderson v. Liberty Lobby, Inc.*, 477 U.S. 242, 250 (1986). Under this analysis, the difference between the Rule 50(a) motion and the summary judgment motion under Rule 56 is essentially procedural: The Rule 50(a) motion is raised during the trial and decided on the basis of the testimony and documentary evidence offered at trial, while the summary judgment motion is made before trial and determined solely on the basis of documentary evidence such as depositions, interrogatories, and affidavits. See *Anderson*, 477 U.S. at 251.

While this is conceptually consistent, many courts are more reluctant to grant summary judgment than judgment as a matter of law under Rule 50(a). Although in theory the judge asks the same question in passing on both motions — whether the party opposing the motion has offered enough evidence that a reasonable factfinder could find in her favor — the context of the motions is strikingly different. In most cases summary judgment motions are decided on the basis of affidavits and other documentary evidence. The opposing party may submit her own evidentiary materials but will not have the benefit of cross-examination. In addition, the motion often comes fairly early in the litigation, before the parties have exhaustively developed their cases. If the judge senses that the case will turn on questions of fact that are not fully elucidated by the record, she will likely conclude that the parties should have a full opportunity to present their evidence at trial before a decision is made to withdraw the case from the jury.

> In considering a motion for summary judgment, the district court must give the benefit of the doubt to the party who asserts he can prove a dubious proposition at trial. In considering a motion for a directed verdict, in contrast, the district court has had the benefit of seeing what the parties alleged they could prove prior to trial tested in the crucible of open court. Accordingly, the district court is entitled to grant a directed verdict even though some evidence supports the opposite position.

Kim v. Coppin State College, 662 F.2d 1055, 1059 (4th Cir. 1981). Consequently, it is not unusual for the court to deny summary judgment but subsequently grant judgment as a matter of law at trial for the same party. See 6 Moore's at ¶56.04[2] n.11.

In the *Chamberlain* case there is ample ground for a court to conclude that full trial of the issues might reveal a submissible case for the plaintiff. The evidence was largely testimonial; cross-examination might have revealed inconsistencies in the defendant's witnesses' testimony, or impeached their credibility. In such cases judges tend to give the party opposing summary judgment the benefit of the doubt by allowing the case to proceed to trial. See Field, Kaplan, and Clermont, Civil Procedure (6th ed. 1990) at 668 (motion for directed verdict "comes at a later stage in the litigation with lesser worry of prematurely interceding, and it is decided upon a more complete and effective airing of the evidence. The result is a practical difference in standards, with the test for directed verdict being slightly easier to meet."); see generally James and Hazard, Civil Procedure 273-277 (1985) (hereinafter cited as James and Hazard). Even if (as here) the judge ultimately takes the case from the jury, such forbearance gives the parties the fullest opportunity to satisfy their burden of production (and thus get to the jury) in close cases.

20

The Judge and the Jury, Part Two: Whose Case Is This, Anyway?

Introduction

A misguided minority of law students think that civil procedure is dull, but in truth it is full of surprises. You may well have been surprised to learn from the last chapter that a judge may snatch a case from the jury in the middle of trial by entering judgment as a matter of law. It is perhaps even more surprising that the judge may actually allow the jury to deliberate and reach its verdict on the evidence but refuse to enter judgment on the verdict rendered. At first blush this seems the ultimate affront to the jury system, to allow the jury to go through the entire trial process and reach its decision, and then disregard or reverse it. Yet, as we shall see, there are good reasons to allow the judge to do so.

Traditionally, the judge has had the authority to displace the jury's verdict by entering a "judgment notwithstanding the verdict," or j.n.o.v.[1] The j.n.o.v. motion is essentially a delayed (or, more accurately, renewed) motion for a directed verdict. The standard for granting the j.n.o.v. motion is the same as that for directing a verdict: Either motion will be granted if the

---

1. J.n.o.v., or judgment "*non obstante veredicto*," is Latin for judgment notwithstanding the verdict. The two terms are used interchangeably in practice.

opponent's evidence is so weak that no reasonable jury could have reached a verdict for him. Of course, when the losing party moves for j.n.o.v. after the jury's verdict, a jury *has* found for the opposing party. Thus, the j.n.o.v motion asserts that the jury acted irrationally, in disregard of the evidence in reaching a verdict for the party opposing the motion.

The j.n.o.v. motion has long been a fixture of trial practice in both the state and federal courts. However, the 1991 amendments to the Federal Rules changed the name of the j.n.o.v. motion: It is now called a motion for judgment as a matter of law, the same as the new name for the motion made during trial to take the case away from the jury. Fed. R. Civ. P. 50(b). Again, the change in the name makes sense because it emphasizes that the motion after verdict asks the judge to do exactly the same thing that the motion during trial does: take the case from the jury to prevent an irrational result. Again, as with the earlier motion, the new wine really is the same vintage as the old: The motion for judgment as a matter of law after verdict is the functional equivalent of a motion for j.n.o.v. And, again, the j.n.o.v. terminology persists in most state courts, so you will have to use both terms in practice. In this chapter, I will use the federal terminology. However, because the new name refers to both the pre-verdict and post-verdict motion, I will indicate in parentheses whether I am referring to a motion made before the case goes to the jury (d.v.) or after the verdict (j.n.o.v.).

You may well wonder what purpose is served by allowing the motion for judgment as a matter of law after the verdict (j.n.o.v.). If the standards for granting the motion before the jury deliberates (d.v.) and after (j.n.o.v.) are the same, why not simply grant the motion before the jury deliberates? This will save the jury the trouble of unnecessary deliberations and avoid the affront of having their findings disregarded.

If the decision to take the case from the jury was cut and dried, this argument would have considerable force. However, reasonable judges may differ — and often do — about whether a given case is strong enough to go to a jury. Because the decision that the evidence is too weak to go to the jury is often debatable, the judge's entry of judgment as a matter of law before the jury deliberates (d.v.) will frequently be appealed. If the appellate court concludes that the evidence was sufficient to send the case to the jury,[2] it will reverse the judge's entry of judgment and order a new trial. This will then require a wasteful repetition of the entire first trial. See scenario 1 in Figure 20-1.

If, on the other hand, the judge withholds decision on the sufficiency of the evidence by denying the motion for judgment as a matter of law (d.v.) at

---

2. Because the decision to grant a directed verdict motion is based on the conclusion that the evidence is too weak as a matter of law to support a verdict for the other party, it is reviewed de novo by the appellate court under the same standard used by the trial judge. See 9 Wright and Miller at §2536, p.595.

Figure 20–1

Scenario 1	Scenario 2
D seeks judgment as a matter of law (d.v.) at close of evidence	D seeks judgment as a matter of law (d.v.) at close of evidence
↓	↓
Judge grants, discharges jury, enters judgment for D	Judge denies or defers decision on motion
↓	↓
P appeals	Case goes to jury, which renders verdict for P
↓	↓
Appellate Court finds evidence legally sufficient, reverses, sends back to trial court	After verdict, D renews motion for judgment as a matter of law (j.n.o.v.)
↓	↓
Case must be retried from beginning	Judge grants renewed motion (j.n.o.v.)
	↓
	P appeals
	↓
	Appellate Court finds evidence legally sufficient, reverses
	↓
	Orders judgment entered on jury verdict (no retrial needed)

the close of the evidence, this scenario can frequently be avoided. If the evidence is weak enough to lead the judge to consider directing the verdict, it is likely that the jury will agree and return a verdict for the moving party anyway. This is the best possible result: It avoids any apparent intrusion on the right to jury trial, leads to a verdict that the judge finds supportable on the evidence, and avoids the appeal that would frequently have followed if the judge had taken the case from the jury.

If the jury returns a verdict for the party (usually the plaintiff) against whom the judge considered directing the verdict, the judge can still enter judgment as a matter of law (j.n.o.v.) for the other party. Here again, the party whose verdict has been taken away will frequently appeal on the ground that the evidence was strong enough to support a rational verdict in his favor. If the appeals court agrees and reverses the judge's order for entry of judgment as a matter of law (j.n.o.v.), it can simply order judgment entered on the jury's verdict. Thus, the need to retry the case is avoided by waiting until after the verdict to decide whether the case is jury-worthy. See scenario 2 in Figure 20-1.

Prerequisites to the Renewed Motion

There are several important limitations on the right to seek judgment as a matter of law (j.n.o.v.) after the verdict. Under Fed. R. Civ. P. 50(b) (and many state rules modeled on it) the motion must be made within ten days of the entry of judgment on the jury's verdict.[3] In addition, a party may only move for judgment as a matter of law (j.n.o.v.) after the verdict if he made the same motion (d.v.) before the verdict. See Fed. R. Civ. P. 50(b) (motion for judgment as a matter of law made at the close of all the evidence may be "renewed" after verdict).

There are two reasons for this second requirement, one historical and rather silly, the other policy-based and entirely sensible. The historical reason has to do with the seventh amendment to the United States Constitution, which provides that "no fact tried by a jury, shall be otherwise reexamined in any Court of the United States, than according to the rules of the common law." Early cases held that it was unconstitutional for the judge to allow the jury to decide the facts and then "reexamine" them through the j.n.o.v. motion. *Slocum v. New York Life Ins. Co.*, 228 U.S. 364 (1913). However, the Supreme Court retreated from this position in *Baltimore & Carolina Line, Inc. v. Redman*, 295 U.S. 654 (1935). In *Redman* the Court held that it was permissible for the trial court to grant judgment notwithstanding the verdict if the moving party had sought a directed verdict before the jury deliberated and the court had reserved decision on the motion.[4] The first sentence of Rule 50(b) embodies the *Redman* fiction that the judge who denies a directed verdict has simply delayed decision upon it, rather than "reexamined" the jury's findings.

The second reason for requiring a pre-verdict motion as a prerequisite for granting judgment as a matter of law (j.n.o.v.) after the verdict is more substantial. A party who moves for judgment as a matter of law at the close of the evidence must state his grounds for concluding that the case should not be submitted to the jury. Fed. R. Civ. P. 50(a); see also Fed. R. Civ. P. 7(a). Thus, the motion will alert the court and the opposing party to the defects in that party's case before the jury has gone out, while there is still time to offer

---

3. Entry of judgment occurs when the court clerk enters a notation of the judgment on the case docket. See Fed. R. Civ. P. 58, 79(a). It is also permissible to seek j.n.o.v. after the verdict but before entry of judgment; Rule 50(b) merely requires that the motion be made "not later than" ten days after entry of judgment.

However, the 1991 revisions to Rule 50 indicate that the practice of making oral motions for j.n.o.v. in open court immediately after the jury returns a verdict is no longer sufficient. See Rule 50(b) (requiring the motion to be served and filed).

4. This was regarded as permissible, despite the "reexamination" clause in the seventh amendment, because the court was deemed to have the power to direct the verdict for the defendant without ever sending the case to the jury. If the judge can do that, the *Redman* court reasoned, he should also be allowed to submit the case subject to a subsequent decision on the directed verdict motion. Instead of "reexamining" the jury's verdict, the judge is simply "examining" the sufficiency of the evidence for the first time, but a little late.

further evidence to cure the defect. By requiring the earlier motion in order to preserve the right to move for judgment after the verdict, the rule prevents a party from "sandbagging" his opponent by raising defects in the opponent's evidence after the jury has been discharged, when it is too late to cure those defects. See Advisory Committee Note to 1991 Revision of Rule 50(a)(2). It may be frustrating to a careful lawyer to be forced to help a less perceptive opponent make his case by pointing out those defects. However, remember that the entire thrust of the Rules is to ensure that suits are determined on the merits, not on the procedural skills of counsel.[5]

New Trial Distinguished

The judge may also deprive a party of a verdict by granting a new trial under Fed. R. Civ. P. 59. Unlike the motion for judgment as a matter of law, which leads to a judgment for the moving party, the grant of a new trial does not end the case but leads to a second trial on all or part of the case.

There are two general categories of cases in which the courts have traditionally granted new trials. The first is for errors in the trial process. Every litigant is entitled to "due process of law," including a fair trial procedure before his rights are determined. Any number of mistakes may be made in the course of trial, such as the improper admission or exclusion of evidence, improper instructions by the judge as to the legal principles the jury must apply, or juror contacts with witnesses outside the courtroom. Errors of this sort may taint the jury's decision-making process, leading it to consider inappropriate information in reaching a verdict or to use the wrong rules of law in assessing liability or damages. See generally James and Hazard at §§7.17-7.19.

If the losing party moves for a new trial on the basis of such errors immediately after trial,[6] Rule 59 allows the judge to vacate the verdict and order the case retried in order to assure the parties a fair trial procedure. If he doesn't grant a new trial, the party prejudiced by the error will doubtless appeal, the appellate court will reverse, and a new trial will be ordered anyway, after much additional effort and expense.[7] The judge can save this effort and expense by ordering the new trial himself if he is convinced that there was error in the first trial.

---

5. Despite this reasoning, many states do not follow the federal practice of requiring a directed verdict motion to preserve the right to seek j.n.o.v. See Cound, Friedenthal, and Miller at 543.

6. The motion for new trial, like the Rule 50(b) motion for j.n.o.v., must be made within ten days of entry of judgment. Fed. R. Civ. P. 59(b).

7. In many cases, however, erroneous decisions in the course of trial will not affect the substantial rights of the parties. Such "harmless error[s]" will not support a grant of a new trial, j.n.o.v., or reversal on appeal. See Fed. R. Civ. P. 61. An example might be the exclusion of evidence that would be merely cumulative or repetitive of other evidence on the issue.

In addition to new trials for procedural errors, the trial judge has traditionally had the power to grant a new trial if he believes the trial *process* was fair but the *result* is clearly wrong. The federal cases suggest various (but quite similar) standards for granting a new trial based on a dubious outcome. It is said that the judge may grant a new trial if the jury's verdict is "against the 'clear weight,' 'overwhelming weight,' or 'great weight' of the evidence" (*Goldsmith v. Diamond Shamrock Corp.*, 767 F.2d 411, 416 (8th Cir. 1985)); when it is "quite clear that the jury has reached a seriously erroneous result" (*Lind v. Schenley Industries, Inc.*, 278 F.2d 79, 89 (3d Cir. 1960)); or when a new trial "is necessary to prevent injustice" (*Whalen v. Roanoke County Board of Supervisors*, 769 F.2d 221, 226 (4th Cir. 1985)). Under such formulas the judge cannot displace the verdict simply because he disagrees with the jury. But he may order a new trial in cases in which the evidence is strong enough to rationally support the jury's verdict, but he believes that verdict is seriously erroneous (represented, perhaps, by point Q on the diagram in the last chapter, p.310; see also the comparative chart on p.348 infra).

In passing on the new trial motion, the judge *may* consider the credibility of the witnesses. Compare the motion for judgment as a matter of law, which, in both its incarnations, requires the judge to assume the truth of the evidence for the nonmoving party. Thus, the judge in passing on the motion for a new trial, acts to some extent as a "thirteenth juror," making an independent assessment of the evidence. The judgment to be made is not whether the verdict was totally irrational but whether the judge is convinced that it is so strongly suspect that it would serve the ends of justice to have another jury hear the case.

Arguably, the judge's power to grant a new trial on this ground is even more intrusive than the power to take the case away from the jury, since the standard for granting a new trial is less stringent than that for entering judgment as a matter of law. However, it may be defended on the ground that a new *jury*, not the judge, will reconsider the case if the motion is granted. In fact, if a new trial is granted, the next step in the case will be to hold the second trial. Under federal procedure, the party who won the verdict may not immediately appeal the judge's new trial grant. Parties are only entitled to appeal when the case is over in the trial court. When the judge enters an order to retry the case, there is no "final decision" from which to take an appeal. See 28 U.S.C. §1291; 6A Moore's at ¶59.15[1].

The judge may also grant partial new trials in appropriate cases. If, for example, the jury's verdict on liability is clearly supportable but the damages greatly exceed the losses reflected in the evidence, the judge may order a new trial as to damages only.[8] In other cases, the judge may find the verdict

---

8. In cases where the verdict is excessive, the judge may also offer the plaintiff a remittitur. Under remittitur practice, the court agrees to enter judgment for the plaintiff if he will accept a lesser sum than the jury's verdict. If the plaintiff refuses to accept the remittitur, the judge orders a new trial. See generally James and Hazard at §7.21, pp.395-400.

against one defendant clearly supported by the evidence but not against another and grant a new trial solely on the claims against the second defendant.

An important difference between new trials for trial error and for verdicts against the weight of the evidence is the standard of appellate review. Questions concerning the admission or exclusion of evidence or the proper instructions to the jury usually involve issues of law, which can be reviewed de novo by the courts of appeals. Appellate judges, after all, are specialists in such legal questions. However, whether the verdict goes against the great weight of the evidence is a delicate decision that requires a balancing of evidence, usually including live testimony, which only the trial judge has had a full opportunity to observe. Consequently, it is rare for appellate judges to second-guess the trial judge's on-the-spot judgment that a new trial is warranted on this ground. Early federal cases suggested that the grant of a new trial on this ground was "unreviewable," that is, committed completely to the discretion of the trial court. See *Fairmount Glass Works v. Cub Fork Coal Co.*, 287 U.S. 474, 481-482 (1933). The current trend, however, is for the courts of appeals to review new trial grants under an abuse of discretion standard. See Friedenthal, Kane, and Miller at §12.4, pp.559-560.

The first examples that follow illustrate the relationship between motions for judgment as a matter of law before the verdict (d.v.) and after the verdict (j.n.o.v.), and new trial. The second part of the chapter explores the procedural complexities of joint motions under Rule 50(c) and (d). Assume that all actions are brought in federal court.

EXAMPLES

Never Say Die

1.   Milne brings an action against Potter for interference with a copyright Milne holds on a book about a bear. The case is tried to a jury. Potter moves for judgment as a matter of law (d.v) at the close of Milne's evidence. The motion is denied. Potter renews the motion after presenting her own evidence. The motion is denied again. The jury is instructed, deliberates, and returns a verdict for Milne. May Potter now move again for judgment as a matter of law (j.n.o.v.)?

2.   Potter, the defendant, moves for judgment as a matter of law (d.v.) at the close of the evidence. The motion is denied. The jury returns a verdict for Potter. Milne believes that the jury's verdict is completely unsupported by the evidence.

   a. May Milne now move for judgment as a matter of law (j.n.o.v.)?
   b. May he move for a new trial?

3.   Assume, as in example 1, that Potter (the defendant) moved for judgment as a matter of law (d.v.) at the close of Milne's evidence but did not renew her motion at the close of all the evidence. The verdict went for Milne,

and Potter now moves again for judgment as a matter of law (j.n.o.v.). Is the motion proper under the Rule?

4.   Potter moves for judgment as a matter of law (d.v.) at the close of the evidence. The motion is denied, and the jury returns a verdict for Milne. Judgment is entered on the verdict. Potter believes that the verdict is completely unsupported by the evidence. Three days after judgment is entered, she renews her motion for judgment as a matter of law, under Rule 50(b). The judge denies the motion five weeks later. Potter now moves for a new trial, on the ground that the judge improperly excluded important evidence at trial and that the verdict is against the weight of the evidence. The judge, after research, agrees on the evidentiary point but not on the "weight of the evidence" point. What should the judge do?

Contingency Planning

5.   Assume the same basic facts as example 4, except that both parties have some complaints about the trial. The jury rendered a verdict for the plaintiff, Milne, but Potter believes that the judge should have granted her motion for judgment as a matter of law (d.v.). She also objects to the judge's instruction on the standard for liability. Milne is satisfied with the verdict but is also convinced that his case would have been stronger if the judge had not excluded important evidence that he offered at trial.
    a. How should Potter present her objections?
    b. What should Milne do about his objection to the exclusion of the evidence?

6.   After trial the jury returns a verdict for Potter. Milne moves for a new trial on the ground that the judge improperly instructed the jury on the application of the copyright statute. Potter argues strenuously that the instructions were proper. The judge concludes that Milne is right and orders a new trial. What happens next?

7.   Assume that Potter moves for judgment as a matter of law at the close of the evidence on the ground that Milne's evidence is too weak to support a verdict. The motion is denied, and the jury returns a verdict for Milne. In frustration, Potter reviews her trial notes and recalls that the judge allowed Milne to introduce hearsay evidence that probably should have been excluded. Although she did not object at the time, Potter researches the evidentiary issue and concludes that the evidence was indeed improperly admitted. Within the ten-day period, she makes two motions, one for a new trial on the ground that the evidence should have been excluded, and a second motion for judgment as a matter of law (j.n.o.v.) on the ground that without the inadmissible evidence, Milne's case was too weak to go to the jury.
    a. Should the judge grant the motion for a new trial?
    b. Should he grant the motion for judgment as a matter of law?

8.   Assume that *Milne v. Potter* was tried before the judge, instead of a jury.

After a full hearing, the judge finds for Milne and enters judgment accordingly. Potter believes that the judge improperly excluded important evidence she had offered on the liability issue.

    a. How should Potter present her objection before the trial court?

    b. What will the judge do if he agrees with Potter?

Combined Motions and Appellate Review

As the examples above suggest, counsel for both parties may have multiple objections to the course of the trial, which they will seek to raise after trial by combined post-trial motions. Subsections (c) and (d) of Rule 50 deal with the procedure for presenting such objections in motions for judgment as a matter of law (j.n.o.v.) and new trial, and for appellate review of such combined motions.

Under Rule 50(c)(1), the trial judge confronted with a combined motion for judgment as a matter of law (j.n.o.v.) and new trial must not only rule on the j.n.o.v. motion but must also make a conditional ruling on the alternative motion for new trial. The court of appeals can then address both arguments at once in one consolidated appeal, if the case is appealed. A similar purpose lies behind Rule 50(d), which allows a party who won the verdict below, but has it taken away on appeal, to assert objections to the original trial process.

The examples that follow should help you see how the use of combined motions under these two intimidating provisions facilitates the disposition of cases on appeal. For some very helpful background you may want to read *Montgomery Ward & Co. v. Duncan*, 311 U.S. 243 (1940), in which the Supreme Court established the broad outlines of the procedure later embodied in Rule 50(c) and (d). However, you should be able to answer the examples from a careful reading of these parts of the rule alone.

EXAMPLES

No Stone Unturned

9.   Carroll sues Alcott for breach of contract. The jury returns a verdict for Carroll and judgment is entered on the verdict. Alcott moves for judgment as a matter of law (j.n.o.v.) and, in the alternative, for a new trial on the ground that the verdict is against the weight of the evidence. The judge grants the j.n.o.v. motion and "conditionally" grants the new trial motion as well.

    a. May Carroll appeal at this point?

    b. Assume that the court of appeals holds that the evidence was sufficient to go to the jury, so that judgment as a matter of law (j.n.o.v.) should not have been granted. What will that court do next?

10. Alcott, the defendant, loses at trial and moves for judgment as a matter of law (j.n.o.v.) and for a new trial on the grounds that the verdict was against the weight of the evidence and that the judge's instructions to the jury

were improper. The judge denies both motions. Alcott appeals. What will the court of appeals do if

    a. it concludes that judgment as a matter of law (j.n.o.v.) should have been granted?

    b. it concludes that j.n.o.v. was properly denied and that the verdict was not against the weight of the evidence but that the instructions were improper?

Delayed Reaction

11. Assume that both Alcott and Carroll are unhappy with the trial. The jury returned a verdict for Carroll, but Alcott believes that the evidence was too weak to support the verdict. Carroll believes the verdict is proper but also believes that the judge improperly excluded evidence that would have strengthened his case. Alcott moves for judgment as a matter of law (j.n.o.v.); Carroll opposes the motion but makes none of his own. The motion is denied. Alcott appeals on the ground that j.n.o.v. should have been granted, and the court of appeals agrees. Where does the case go from here?

Practice Makes Perfect

12. Consider the following possible outcomes at the trial and appellate level. Assume in each case that the plaintiff won the verdict, and that the defendant seeks judgment as a matter of law (j.n.o.v.) on the basis that the evidence was too weak to support a plaintiff's verdict, and, in the alternative, a new trial on the ground of an error in the instructions to the jury.

    What should the appellate court do in each case?

	Trial court	Appellate court
a.	grants *D*'s motion for j.n.o.v., and his conditional motion for new trial	agrees that j.n.o.v. proper, but not new trial
b.	grants *D*'s motion for j.n.o.v. and grants his conditional motion for new trial	agrees with both decisions
c.	denies *D*'s motion for j.n.o.v. and grants his conditional motion for new trial	agrees on j.n.o.v., disagrees on new trial
d.	denies *D*'s motion for j.n.o.v., grants his new trial motion	disagrees on both
e.	grants j.n.o.v. for *D*, denies *D*'s conditional motion for new trial	disagrees on both

EXPLANATIONS

Never Say Die

1.   In this case Potter has already twice asked the judge to rule that Milne's evidence is too weak to go to the jury. Each time the judge has allowed the case to proceed. However, this does not bar Potter from renewing her challenge to the sufficiency of the evidence by seeking judgment as a matter of law (j.n.o.v.) after the verdict for Milne. As the Introduction indicates, the rule requires that the motion be made before verdict (d.v.) in order to preserve the right to make the motion after verdict (j.n.o.v.). Thus, every party who seeks judgment as a matter of law after the verdict will be renewing a similar motion made before the jury retires. The judge's denial of the first motion does not necessarily indicate that he believes the evidence poses a jury issue; he may simply wish to reserve judgment on the issue, so as to get the jury's verdict and save a complete retrial if the decision to grant judgment as a matter of law after verdict (j.n.o.v.) is reversed on appeal.

2a.   Rule 50(b) only authorizes a party who has moved for judgment as a matter of law before the verdict (d.v.) to renew the motion after the verdict (j.n.o.v.), for the reasons discussed in the Introduction. Although Potter sought judgment as a matter of law (d.v.) at the close of the case, Milne did not. Thus, Milne's failure to make a similar motion will bar him from seeking judgment notwithstanding the verdict after the jury finds for Potter.

Milne may not argue that his motion is proper because *Potter* sought judgment as a matter of law (d.v.) before the case went to the jury. As discussed in the Introduction, the motion must be made before the verdict in order to alert the opposing party to weaknesses in that party's case. Potter's motion was obviously directed to the weaknesses in Milne's case, not her own.

b.   Milne is barred from seeking entry of judgment in his favor under Rule 50(b), but Rule 59 contains no analogous requirement of a prior motion for judgment as a matter of law (d.v.) (or for a new trial) in order to move for a new trial on the ground that the verdict is against the weight of the evidence. 6A Moore's at ¶59.04[5]. Since Milne believes the evidence was too weak to support a rational verdict for Potter, he presumably also believes that the verdict is against the great weight of the evidence. Thus, Milne can at least ask the judge to vacate the verdict and grant a new trial on this ground. That will not get him the judgment but will at least give him the opportunity to convince another jury of the strength of his case.

3.   A party must move for judgment as a matter of law (d.v.) before the case goes to the jury in order to preserve the right to renew the motion after the verdict. Here Potter did make such a motion at the close of the plaintiff's case but did not renew it at the close of all the evidence. This is probably not sufficient to preserve the right to seek judgment as a matter of law after the verdict. See Rule 50(b), first sentence ("Whenever a motion for judgment as

a matter of law at the close of all the evidence is denied . . .") and second sentence ("Such a motion may be renewed . . .").[9]

Some cases before the 1991 amendment adopted a more flexible approach to this requirement and entertained motions for j.n.o.v. where the moving party had sought a directed verdict earlier in the trial but not at the close of all the evidence. See, e.g., *Bohrer v. Hanes Corp.,* 715 F.2d 213, 216-217 (5th Cir. 1983). Although these cases may have stretched the language of Rule 50, they were consistent with the purpose for requiring a pre-verdict motion because the motion, even when made earlier in the trial, puts the opponent on notice of the alleged weakness in his case. For example, if Potter moves for judgment as a matter of law (d.v.) at the close of Milne's evidence, Milne will have already offered all the evidence he believes is necessary to make a prima facie case. Thus, the motion should alert Milne to the unproved elements in his case and prevent him from being "sandbagged" by a renewed motion after the verdict.

However, the more precise language of the 1991 version of Rule 50(b)[10] suggests that the rulemakers have rejected this approach. See also the Advisory Committee note to the 1991 revisions to Rule 50(b), which repeatedly refers to the requirement of a motion "made at the close of all the evidence." The rule appears to require in all cases that the defects be raised after the whole case is in, to give the court a chance to consider the sufficiency of the entire evidence before sending the case to the jury.

4.   The judge must deny the motion despite his conclusion that Potter has a valid claim that the trial was unfair. Under Rule 59, as under Rule 50(b), the motion must be made within ten days of the entry of judgment. Potter's Rule 50(b) motion (j.n.o.v.) was timely, but her subsequent new trial motion was not, and the making of one post-trial motion does not suspend the time for making the other. Potter should have made both motions together within ten days of entry of judgment in order to assert all her objections in a timely fashion. See Rule 50(b), third sentence, which authorizes combined motions for new trial and judgment as a matter of law (j.n.o.v.).

Nor may the judge relieve Potter of her procedural mistake by granting the motion for a new trial "sua sponte" (on his own motion). Rule 59(d) authorizes the trial judge to grant a new trial sua sponte but requires him to do so within ten days of the entry of judgment. The implication is that he may not correct an error brought to his attention after this period has lapsed.

---

9. The revisers tightened up the language of the rule somewhat on this point. Before the 1991 revision the second sentence of the rule authorized "a party who has moved for directed verdict" to seek j.n.o.v. Now the second sentence refers back to the first, indicating that only a motion at the close of all the evidence ("[s]uch a motion") may be renewed. Even before the 1991 revision many courts held that the motion had to be made at the close of all the evidence. See 5A Moore's at ¶50.08.

10. See n.9.

This limitation seems unfortunate, at least where the judge becomes convinced of the error within the 30-day appeal period in Fed. R. App. P. 4(a)(1). If the judge is really convinced that he improperly excluded evidence that would have affected the result, it makes sense to allow him to grant the new trial. Otherwise, Potter will be forced to appeal, and the court of appeals will be forced to hear and decide an appeal that could have been avoided by the grant of a new trial as soon as the error became apparent.[11]

The strict limit on the time for granting a new trial reflects a strong policy in favor of finality of judgments. Parties must know at some point that the decision rendered in an action will not be revised, so they can order their affairs accordingly. If the judge could reconsider at any time, the outcome would still remain uncertain despite the entry of a "final" judgment.

Contingency Planning

5a. It is not unusual for both parties to have complaints about the conduct of a trial. Here, Potter believes that the outcome was unwarranted by the evidence and, in addition, that the process was tainted due to improper instructions. Milne is content with the outcome but believes that he could have made an even stronger case if all his evidence had been placed before the jury.

Potter, of course, should renew her motion for judgment as a matter of law (seek j.n.o.v.), since she believes that the evidence was too weak to support a rational verdict for Milne. In addition, if she believes the evidence was too weak to go to the jury, she must also believe it was against the great weight of the evidence. Consequently, she should join a motion under Rule 59 for a new trial on this ground with her Rule 50(b) motion. Finally, she should assert the improper jury instruction as an alternative ground for a new trial. She may assert all three grounds in a combined motion, but must do so within ten days of entry of judgment.

b. Milne is in a slightly different position. Because he won the verdict, he has no cause to press his objection to the exclusion of evidence (unless, of course, the evidence went to the size of the verdict and he is unhappy with that). He prevailed without the evidence and presumably has no interest in trying the suit again just to have a perfect process. However, Milne is still somewhat at risk since Potter has asked the judge to displace the jury's verdict. If the judge grants judgment for Potter (j.n.o.v.) on the ground that Milne did not produce sufficient evidence to pose a jury issue, Milne will surely wish to argue that he *could* have made a submissible case if the judge had not excluded important evidence.

---

11. The judge might be able to achieve the same result by granting relief from the judgment under Fed. R. Civ. P. 60(b), at least before the period for appeal of the judgment has run. See Chapter 21, example 17.

Of course, the rulemakers have thought of everything and provided for this contingency. If the judge deprives Milne of his victory by entering judgment as a matter of law (j.n.o.v.) for Potter, Rule 50(c)(2) allows Milne to move for a new trial within ten days after entry of that judgment, on the ground that the evidence was improperly excluded. Thus, he need not raise the objection until the verdict in his favor is taken away. At that point, it becomes apparent that the judge's evidentiary ruling has harmed Milne's case, and he may ask the court to grant a new trial on that ground.

6.   If Potter believes that the instruction was proper, she would like to appeal immediately, in hopes that the court of appeals will agree with her, reverse the new trial grant, and enter judgment on the jury's verdict. However, when a new trial motion is granted, the judge will enter an order for the case to be retried. As the Introduction states, parties in Potter's position may not appeal the grant of a new trial until after the new trial is held because a new trial grant is not considered a final judgment under federal practice. See 28 U.S.C. §1291 (authorizing appeal from "final decisions" of the district courts).

Thus, Potter will have to go through the second trial before appealing. If she wins at the second trial, she will presumably be satisfied with the result (though not the elongated process to reach it) and have no incentive to appeal the grant of the new trial. However, if she loses at the second trial, Potter will be entitled to appeal the judge's earlier decision to grant the new trial since the court will render a final judgment for Milne on the second verdict (assuming no further motions for new trial are granted after the *second* trial). The court of appeals will then review the disputed instruction from the first trial. If it agrees with Potter that the original instruction was proper, it will enter judgment on the original verdict for her. If it agrees that the trial judge's initial instruction was wrong, it will uphold the grant of the new trial and (assuming no reversible error in the second trial) affirm the judgment for Milne.

Although there is logic to delaying review of the new trial grant in these cases, there is also much to be said for immediate appeal. If the case is reviewed before the new trial and the new trial order is reversed, it will save the considerable effort of trying the case a second time, perhaps to no purpose.[12] For this reason some state systems allow interlocutory review of new trial grants. See Friedenthal, Kane, and Miller at pp.558-559.

---

12. In *Roy v. Volkswagen of America, Inc.,* 896 F.2d 1174 (1990), for example, the plaintiffs won a verdict of $3 million in a negligence action, and the judge ordered a new trial. The Roys attempted an appeal, which was dismissed because the new trial prevented a final judgment. At the new trial, the jury found for the defendant. On appeal by the Roys from this judgment, the court held that the evidence was "substantially balanced" (896 F.2d at 1179) so that the new trial should not have been granted in the first place. Consequently, the court ordered judgment entered on the original jury verdict for the Roys.

7a. The example here indicates that Potter did not object to the judge's error in admitting the evidence at the time that the error was made. In most cases the failure to object to the ruling during trial will foreclose relief on a motion for new trial afterwards. See 11 Wright and Miller at §2805, p.39 (in absence of a timely objection, new trial will not be granted "unless the error was so fundamental that gross injustice would result"). Although this rule seems draconian, especially given the pressures of trial, it makes good sense. If the error is brought to the judge's attention immediately, he may exclude the evidence and avoid a reversible error. If it is only raised after trial by the new trial motion, it is too late to save the trial.

If Potter could raise such objections without having objected during trial, it would open the door to manipulation of the trial process. She might deliberately withhold objection to one or more arguably prejudicial decisions of the trial judge. Then if she lost the verdict, she could undermine the unfavorable verdict by pulling these objections out of her hat as grounds for a new trial.

b. The judge will also deny Potter's motion for judgment as a matter of law (j.n.o.v.). Her argument here is that the evidence would have been too weak to go to the jury if the disputed evidence had not been admitted. Here again Potter should have avoided the error by a timely objection, rather than using it later to overturn the jury's verdict. Note that Potter made a motion for judgment as a matter of law (d.v.) before the case went to the jury, but *not on the ground of admission of the improper evidence*. Thus, neither the court nor Milne was given a chance to cure the problem.[13]

A Rule 50(a) motion at the close of all the evidence on one ground will not preserve the right to seek judgment as a matter of law (j.n.o.v.) on a different ground. The purpose for the prior motion is to point out the problem at a time when it can be cured. Here Potter raised the objection that the evidence before the jury was too weak to support a verdict but did not raise the hearsay problem. Thus, her motion did not alert the court or Milne to the other evidentiary problem at a time when it could have been cured. See *Lifshitz v. Walter Drake & Sons, Inc.,* 806 F.2d 1426, 1428-1429 (9th Cir. 1986) (prior directed verdict motion only preserves right to seek j.n.o.v. on the specific grounds raised in the prior motion).

8a. Parties have the same right to seek a new trial in cases tried to the judge as they do in jury cases. See Fed. R. Civ. P. 59(a)(2). Potter should make her motion for a new trial (often called a "rehearing" in nonjury cases) within ten days of entry of judgment, stating as her ground the exclusion of the disputed evidence.

b. Although the procedure for presenting the motion is similar, a re-

---

13. The court might have cured it by instructing the jury to disregard the evidence. Potter might have cured it by producing a proper foundation for the evidence, which would demonstrate that is was admissible.

hearing in a nonjury trial differs significantly from a new trial in a jury case. In a jury case, the jury is discharged after a verdict is reached. They cannot be called back after the new trial is granted to hear the additional evidence that had been wrongly excluded. Thus, the only way to provide both parties with a full opportunity to be heard is to start over and present all the evidence to a new jury in a complete new trial.

In a nonjury case the judge need not go back and start from square one. He has already heard all the evidence and decided the relevant legal rules to apply in reaching a decision. If Potter's only objection is that the judge failed to consider certain evidence (and if the judge concludes that she is right), the judge can reopen the hearing, hear that evidence, and reconsider the case, taking the additional evidence into account. Thus, the rehearing in such cases can be a relatively brief proceeding to simply augment the record with the additional evidence. See Fed. R. Civ. P. 59(a), second sentence.

If Potter's objection had been that the judge *admitted* evidence that should have been excluded, the "rehearing" might be even simpler. The judge could simply sustain the motion and reconsider the case without taking the inadmissible evidence into account. At least that's the theory. In practice it is obviously questionable whether the judge can really disregard persuasive evidence that he has already heard simply on the technical ground that it is inadmissible under the rules of evidence.[14]

No Stone Unturned

9a.   Carroll may appeal the judge's combined ruling, even though the new trial was "conditionally" (Fed. R. Civ. P. 50(c)(1)) granted. The judge has ordered judgment as a matter of law (j.n.o.v.) for Alcott. Rule 50(c)(1), second sentence, clearly states that the decision on the new trial motion does not prevent this from being a final judgment. Alcott is the winner and if no one appeals there will be no new trial. The purpose of requiring the judge to rule conditionally on Alcott's alternative motion for a new trial is to help the court of appeals decide how to dispose of the case if it reverses the decision to enter judgment as a matter of law for Alcott. If the j.n.o.v. stands, the conditional grant of the new trial has no effect.

b.   If Carroll appeals and the court reverses the entry of judgment as a matter of law for Alcott, the judge's conditional ruling on the new trial motion assists the appellate court in deciding what should happen next in the

---

14. If one party in a case has evidence that is extremely persuasive but probably inadmissible under the rules of evidence, this may be a strong tactical reason for the other party to seek a jury trial. The judge must often see the evidence that is offered in order to pass on its admissibility. If he is also the factfinder, it will be difficult for him to disregard what he has seen. If the case is tried to a jury, however, the judge will see such evidence, but the factfinder (the jury) will not.

case. The court of appeals can now review the judge's conditional decision that a new trial should be granted. If it concludes that the judge did not abuse his discretion in concluding that the verdict went against the clear weight of the evidence, the court can uphold the grant of the new trial and remand the case to the trial court for retrial. If, on the other hand, the court concludes that even the new trial motion should not have been granted (an unlikely decision, given the broad discretion accorded the trial court in making the new trial decision), it may reverse both decisions and order entry of judgment for Carroll. See Fed. R. Civ. P. 50(c)(1), third sentence.

The good sense of this procedure is highlighted by considering the alternative. If the trial judge decided only the Rule 50(b) motion, and that was reversed, the court of appeals would have to remand for the judge to consider whether a new trial should be granted. If he granted it on remand, the new trial would proceed since the grant of a new trial is an interlocutory decision. Only after a second trial would Carroll be able to challenge the new trial grant, on a second appeal.

On the other hand, if the judge denied the motion for a new trial on remand after reversal of the judgment as a matter of law (j.n.o.v.), Alcott would appeal that denial, and a second trip to the court of appeals would be needed to fully dispose of the case. The Rule 50(c) procedure for conditional rulings on both motions allows the appellate court to fully dispose of the case in a single appeal.

10a. If the court concludes that judgment should have been granted for Alcott because Carroll's evidence was too weak to go to the jury, it may enter judgment as a matter of law (j.n.o.v.) itself. Unlike the discretionary decision as to whether the verdict was contrary to the clear weight of the evidence, which involves consideration of the credibility of witnesses, the j.n.o.v. decision is a question of law that the appellate court reviews de novo. The court must review all the evidence, consider it in the light most favorable to the nonmoving party, and make its own judgment as to whether Carroll's case was legally sufficient to submit to the jury.

b. If the court of appeals concludes that judgment as a matter of law (j.n.o.v.) was properly denied and that the verdict is not against the weight of the evidence, it will then consider whether the new trial should have been granted due to legal error in the instructions. The issue of the proper rules for the jury to apply in deciding the case is a question of law, which the court of appeals decides de novo. If the court concludes that the jury was not properly instructed, it can remand for a new trial. If the instructions were correct, it can affirm the denial of the new trial and (since it had already ruled that j.n.o.v. was properly denied) affirm the entry of judgment for Carroll. Either way, the use of combined motions again allows the appellate court to consider all of the losing party's objections without remand for decision of further post-trial motions.

Delayed Reaction

11. The situation here is similar to that in example 5b, in which the plaintiff won the verdict but had the victory snatched away when the judge granted j.n.o.v. for the defendant. Here, the same thing happened, except that it was the court of appeals rather than the trial judge that displaced the verdict. Until judgment was granted for Alcott on appeal, Carroll was content with the result of the original trial. Although he believed his case would have been stronger if the excluded evidence had been admitted, it was already strong enough to win. Thus Carroll had no reason to seek a new trial due to the exclusion of the evidence.

It is only after the court of appeals deprives him of his judgment by holding that judgment as a matter of law (j.n.o.v.) should have been granted for Alcott that Carroll will wish to raise his objection to the evidentiary ruling. At that point, he will want to argue that the original trial was flawed and that he is entitled to a new trial at which the excluded evidence is placed before the jury. After all, it may be that his case was too weak to reach the jury precisely because that evidence was excluded.

Under Rule 50(d) Carroll may raise this argument at the appeal stage even if he did not seek a new trial in the district court. (Of course, he would have had to object at the time the evidence was excluded. See the answer to example 7.) If Carroll raises the issue on appeal, and the court of appeals reverses the denial of j.n.o.v., that court will consider the evidentiary point as well. It may order a new trial on this ground or remand to allow the trial judge to address the motion. Fed. R. Civ. P. 50(d). Or, of course, it may deny the new trial if the evidence was properly excluded.

Practice Makes Perfect

12a. The court enters judgment for the defendant, since it concludes that the plaintiff's case was too weak to support a verdict. Although the decision that the defendant is entitled to a new trial was erroneous, the error is harmless. The defendant has now prevailed; the last thing he wants is a new trial.

b. Judgment is entered for the defendant, since both trial and appellate courts agree that the plaintiff's case was too weak to support a verdict. Once again, the defendant has no further interest in a new trial, though both courts agree that he would be entitled to one if the plaintiff's case were strong enough to go to the jury.

c. Initially, of course, the appellate court will do nothing at all, since the plaintiff cannot appeal the new trial grant until after the second trial. When the plaintiff finally gets up on appeal the court will reverse the order for a new trial and order entry of judgment for the plaintiff on the original verdict.

d. Once again, the plaintiff will have to wait until after the second trial to appeal the decision to order a new trial. If he loses at the second trial and appeals, he is in for a rude shock on this scenario: The court will reverse the entry of the order for a new trial but order judgment for the defendant anyway. Because the evidence at the first trial was too weak to support a plaintiff's verdict, the appellate court will enter judgment for the defendant, since the defendant's motion for j.n.o.v. should have been granted at the end of the first trial.

If the plaintiff *wins* at the second trial, the defendant will likely appeal, on the ground that the j.n.o.v. motion should have been granted, making the new trial issue moot. Because (the answer assumes) the appellate court agrees that j.n.o.v. should have been granted at the end of the first trial, it will order entry of judgment for the defendant, based on the legal insufficiency of the evidence at the first trial.

e. Here, the case is immediately appealable, because the court has entered judgment as a matter of law for the defendant on the basis that the case was too weak to go to the jury. Because the appellate court disagrees with this conclusion, it should reverse the entry of judgment for the defendant. However, since it concludes that a new trial was warranted due to the erroneous instruction, it should remand the case to the trial court for retrial with proper instructions.

Figure 20–2: The Judge's Power to Displace the Jury's Verdict: A Schematic

(This chart is a trifle oversimplified, but it should help you see the general relation of the motions.)

Evidence Evenly Balanced

← weaker evidence for plaintiff   stronger evidence for plaintiff →

	Judge's assessment of the evidence	Judge's disposition of the case
X	Evidence too weak to support a rational verdict for plaintiff	Judge may enter directed verdict or j.n.o.v. for defendant
	A verdict for plaintiff is supportable, but against clear weight of the evidence	Judge may order new trial
	Judge does not agree with jury, but cannot say verdict for plaintiff is against clear weight of the evidence	Judge will order entry of judgment on the jury's verdict
Z	Judge and jury concur that preponderance of the evidence favors plaintiff	Judge will order entry of judgment on the verdict for plaintiff
	A verdict for defendant is supportable but against clear weight of evidence	Judge may order new trial
Y	Judge concludes that evidence is so compelling that no reasonable jury could find for defendant (rare — see infra pp.322-323)	Judge enters directed verdict or j.n.o.v. for plaintiff

PART FIVE

The Effect of the Judgment

21

Res Judicata: The Limits of Procedural Liberality

Introduction

Perhaps you are thoroughly tired of hearing how *reasonable* the Federal Rules of Civil Procedure are. Certainly, one of the recurrent themes of the Rules is to create a flexible procedural system in order to prevent procedure from dominating substance, to assure that the merits of the parties' claims, not procedural missteps, determine the outcome of lawsuits.

For example, parties are given broad power to join claims and parties in a single suit. Fed. R. Civ. P. 13, 14, 18, 20, 24. They are given the latitude to plead all their possible claims against opposing parties, within the limits of proper pleading. Fed. R. Civ. P. 8(a), 8(e)(2), 11. Pleadings are liberally construed, Fed. R. Civ. P. 8(f); *Conley v. Gibson,* 355 U.S. 41 (1957), and amendments freely allowed. Fed. R. Civ. P. 15(a). Even if amendments are not offered, the court can treat the pleadings *as though* they had been amended, when justice so requires, Fed. R. Civ. P. 15(b), and may grant parties the relief to which they are entitled even though they never asked for it. Fed. R. Civ. P. 54(c). If the process still goes awry, despite all these opportunities to correct procedural errors, the court may grant relief from judgment under Fed. R. Civ. P. 60(b) or a new trial under Fed. R. Civ. P. 59.

Given all this procedural liberality, you might expect that the rules governing relitigation of claims would be correspondingly indulgent. However, the exact opposite is true. Once the parties have had a full and fair opportunity to be heard under the flexible rules reviewed above, all this paternalistic indulgence comes to an abrupt halt. Regardless of a party's reason for wishing to relitigate a dispute, the doctrine of res judicata stands like a brutish, unreflecting myrmidon, guarding the doors of the courthouse.[1] While the Rules are liberal, res judicata is strict and uncharitable. No matter how unfair the result in the first suit may seem or indeed, no matter how unfair it may actually have been, the myrmidon will not step aside.

For example, suppose that the plaintiff in the Schulansky case recovers $7,000 from Ronan for breach of contract. If Schulansky believes that the verdict was too low, she cannot bring a second action against Ronan for more. Or, if she discovers a statute that allows a more generous measure of damages, she cannot bring a new action based on that statute. If Schulansky loses but believes that her lawyer did not litigate the case energetically, she will be barred by res judicata from trying again with a new lawyer.

In the traditional terminology, Schulansky's claim was said to be "merged" into the judgment she had won. That is, the claim was extinguished and replaced by the judgment. Restatement (Second) of Judgments §§17, 18 (1982). Once the judgment was entered, a suit could be brought to enforce that judgment if necessary (see Chapter 3, pp.44-45), but no further suit could be brought on the extinguished claim. Conversely, if Schulansky lost, her claim was said to be "barred" by the adverse judgment so that no further suit could be brought on the claim.

The rationale for the doctrine is ancient and fundamental. Litigation is burdensome enough the first time without redoing it again whenever one of the parties is unhappy with the result — as at least one will be in every case. Parties must also get on with their affairs; without the certainty provided by res judicata, parties would not be able to rely on court decisions in planning their future conduct. Finally, from the point of view of the system, there is no justification for multiplying the costs and delay of litigation by allowing parties to go at it again once they have had a full and fair opportunity to litigate a claim.

Of course, the efficiency of res judicata would not be justified if it were achieved at the expense of fairness to the parties in presenting meritorious claims. For example, it would be a hard system indeed that barred the plaintiff from amending her complaint in the first action to assert new theories for relief unearthed during discovery and also barred her from bringing a separate action based on those theories. But, if amendments are liberally allowed in the first suit, it is fair to bar a second action on theories left out of the first suit. Thus, it is precisely because the Rules of Civil Procedure are so liberal in facilitating presentation of claims in the first action that the res judicata

---

1. A myrmidon is a servant who mindlessly but doggedly obeys his master's every command. The first myrmidons were ants, who were changed into men by Zeus to repopulate the island kingdom of Aegina. They were known for their loyalty and courage in following their leader, Achilles, in the Trojan War. See E. Hamilton, Mythology 296 (1969).

myrmidon can so stubbornly bar a second try. Indeed, the specter of res judicata encourages parties to take full advantage of the Rules to present their claims initially since they know that they will not get a second chance to try the suit, that there will be no "second bite at the apple."

In most jurisdictions, there are four prerequisites for res judicata: (1) there must be a final judgment; (2) the judgment must be "on the merits"; (3) the claims must be the same in the first and second suits; and (4) the parties in the second action must be the same as those in the first (or in privity with a party to the prior action). Most of the interpretive issues in applying the doctrine concern the requirements that the claims be the same in both suits and that the original judgment be on the merits.

The "Same Claim" Requirement

The definition of a single "claim" for res judicata purposes varies from one jurisdiction to another. See generally Friedenthal, Kane, and Miller at §14.4. The federal courts and an increasing number of states have adopted the standard in the Restatement (Second) of Judgments §24 (1982), which essentially equates a party's claim for res judicata purposes with the "transaction or occurrence" test of the federal joinder rules. See 18 Wright and Miller at §4407, p.62. Under this approach, a party who has asserted a right to relief arising out of a particular transaction or occurrence must join all claims she has arising from it, or the omitted claims will be barred by res judicata.

There is good sense to a theory that makes the scope of preclusion mirror the test for allowing initial joinder under the Rules. If a party had the right to join two claims for relief arising from the same transaction in the first suit, it is reasonable to require her to do so, instead of bringing two suits that will rehash the same facts. Conversely, if the scope of preclusion is to mirror the scope of permissible joinder, res judicata should *not* bar claims that could not have been joined in the first action. For example, before the development of the unified civil action under the Rules, parties could not always seek legal and equitable relief in the same proceeding: They were often forced to split their claims between the law courts (for damage claims) and the equity courts (for claims to equitable relief, such as specific performance or injunctions). See generally James and Hazard at 14-17. In such cases, a party who had sought damages in an action at law was not precluded from seeking injunctive relief based on the same transaction or occurrence from a court of equity because she could not have obtained an injunction in the prior action at law. Under the Federal Rules, however, parties may almost always assert all their claims in a single suit, and res judicata is correspondingly broad.[2]

---

2. However, the right to join claims under the Rules does not automatically lead to the conclusion that res judicata will bar a separate suit on those claims. See Chapter 22.

Under the transaction or occurrence test, preclusion turns on the *right* to join the claim in the original action, not on whether the claim actually was asserted. Consequently, claims need not have actually been litigated to be barred in a later action; they need only have been *available* to the plaintiff in the first suit. For example, it is clear that Schulansky, after recovering $7,000 from Ronan in the contract action described in Part Six, could not sue Ronan again for this claim on a breach of contract theory. However, res judicata will also bar Schulansky from suing Ronan for fraud even though she had never pleaded fraud in her first suit, never tried the case on a fraud theory, and in fact never thought of it. Indeed, the message of res judicata is that Schulansky (or, more particularly, Schulansky's lawyer) had *better* think of it, sooner rather than later.

Judgment "On the Merits"

Another res judicata prerequisite that has raised interpretive problems is the requirement of a decision "on the merits" in the first action. Clearly, a full trial followed by a verdict and judgment is the paradigm of a decision on the merits. At the other extreme, some dismissals, such as dismissals for improper venue or lack of personal jurisdiction, do not bar a second action, on the rationale that the court never reached the merits in the first action, much less decided it after a full opportunity to be heard. The very basis of such dismissals is that the court does not have the power to reach the merits because the plaintiff has chosen an improper court under the "three ring" analysis.

The toughest cases fall between these extremes. For example, jurisdictions differ as to whether a dismissal for failure to state a claim (see Fed. R. Civ. P. 12(b)(6)) should bar a second action. The Restatement (Second) of Judgments concludes that such dismissals should bar relitigation on the theory that a plaintiff whose complaint is dismissed for failure to state a claim is allowed liberal opportunities to amend. Restatement (Second) of Judgments §19, comment d (1982). If she cannot amend to state a compensable claim on a second or third try, it is presumably because she has no right to relief under the law. If that is true, there is no reason to allow her to harass the defendant with a new action. This is the rule applied in the federal courts. *Federated Department Stores v. Moitie*, 452 U.S. 394, 399 n.3 (1981); 1B Moore's ¶0.409[1.-2]. However, some state courts allow a second action under these circumstances because comparatively little litigation effort goes into these preliminary dismissals, and hence a basic value underlying res judicata, preservation of scarce judicial resources, is not compromised by allowing a new action.

Actually, it is a bit of a misnomer to say that judgment must be "on the merits" to bar a second action. In fact, the court need not reach the merits at all for its judgment to have full res judicata effect. For example, if the plaintiff files suit, but does not pursue the case, it will eventually be dismissed for failure to prosecute. Clearly the parties have not litigated the merits in such cases; they haven't litigated anything at all. But such a dismissal is deemed "on the merits" in the sense that it will bar a subsequent action because the plaintiff had a full *opportunity* to litigate the merits in the first action. If she doesn't choose to take the opportunity, she must accept the res judicata consequences. Similarly, a defendant who defaults (that is, never answers to the merits and therefore loses by default), is also barred by res judicata on the same reasoning.

Final Judgment

A judgment must also be "final" before res judicata attaches. There is obviously little point in barring a second action on a claim that has not yet been fully resolved in the first. Suppose, for example, that Schulansky sues Ronan in federal court on breach of contract and fraud theories, and the court dismisses the fraud claim under Fed. R. Civ. P. 12(b)(6) but allows the contract claim to proceed. Generally, courts remain free to reexamine interlocutory rulings made in the course of suit, including a ruling dismissing one of the plaintiff's claims. See 18 Wright and Miller at §4478. Thus, the dismissal of the fraud claim might be reconsidered and vacated by the judge in the first action before the case is finally determined in the trial court. Thus, until final judgment is entered in the trial court, it remains too uncertain to support a res judicata plea in a separate action between the parties.

However, many courts give res judicata effect to a judgment once it has become final in the trial court, even if an appeal is pending. This is the Restatement view. Restatement (Second) of Judgments §13, comment f (1982). Under this approach, a judgment may bar relitigation even though the original case is still being litigated and is not yet enforceable by execution or otherwise. Other courts, however, only give res judicata effect to judgments if the time for appeal has passed or the case has been finally resolved by the appellate court. James and Hazard at §11.4, p.592.

In working through the examples that follow assume that all suits are brought in federal court and that the Restatement principles discussed above apply. If you want further background, Professor Wright has a good, short discussion of the doctrine. Wright at pp.678-682. For more detail, I recommend the Second Restatement itself, which is replete with helpful examples and comments. Restatement (Second) of Judgments §§13-26 (1982). But keep in mind (not for the examples below but for those long lawyering years ahead) that the doctrine varies from one jurisdiction to another. Even if the Restatement principles are generally followed, each jurisdiction is likely to have its own quirks and quiddities that can only be learned from studying local practice.

EXAMPLES

Fielder's Choices

1.   Rizzuto's eye is injured when his baseball glove breaks while he is field-ing a vicious grounder. He sues Allston Leather Company for negligent manufacture of the glove. The case is tried and judgment is entered for Allston. Later, Rizzuto sues again. He argues that the judge in the first suit erroneously excluded important evidence from Rizzuto's expert on baseball glove manufacturing standards and that he should have a chance to have a trial with all the admissible evidence properly before the jury. Allston pleads res judicata. Will the defense bar Rizzuto's second action?

2.   After the judgment for Allston in Rizzuto's case, Boyer tells Rizzuto that he was also injured using the same type of Allston glove and recovered judgment against Allston on a strict liability theory, which did not require proof that Allston was negligent. Rizzuto files a new action against Allston based on the original accident but asserting a right to recover only on the basis of strict liability. Will the claim be barred?

3.   Assume that Rizzuto won his first suit against Allston and recovered $3,000 in compensatory damages. Boyer subsequently tells him that he had claimed gross negligence by Allston in a prior suit based on the same defec-tive glove and recovered punitive damages. Rizzuto brings a second action against Allston for punitive damages based on gross negligence. Can Allston plead res judicata?

4.   Assume that Rizzuto recovered $15,000 dollars in an action against Allston, but Allston was in shaky financial condition and never paid. Rizzuto later brings a new action against Allston after learning that its financial condi-tion has improved. Does res judicata bar the second suit?

5.   Assume that Rizzuto presented evidence in the original action against Allston that he suffered impaired vision in his eye for several weeks as a result of the accident, missed two weeks of the baseball season, and had some pain from the injury. This is the only evidence he presented on damages. The jury finds for Rizzuto and awards him $10,000 damages. Three years later, after the judgment has been entered and paid, Rizzuto develops migraine head-aches. His doctor tells him that these often result from an eye injury and are likely to continue indefinitely. Can Rizzuto sue Allston for damages for these headaches?

An Absurd Hypothetical

6.   Imagine that Rizzuto's vicious grounder breaks through his glove, whacks him in the eye, and bounces off Kubek, injuring him as well. Kubek sues Allston and recovers. Rizzuto testifies in Kubek's suit. Rizzuto now takes the cue and brings an action to recover for his injuries in the same

accident. Allston pleads the inevitable res judicata. Is the suit barred?

7.   At the time Rizzuto was injured using Allston's glove, he had an endorsement contract with them to promote the glove in television commercials. He had made the ads but had not been paid by Allston.

Acting on the advice of his lawyers that asserting the contract claim in the negligence suit would confuse matters, Rizzuto did not assert his contract claim in the negligence suit against Allston. Instead, he sues separately on the contract claim after judgment in the negligence action. Allston pleads res judicata. Was the lawyers' advice sound?

8.   Assume that Rizzuto's contract calls for royalties (or "residuals" in the language of the trade) to be paid to Rizzuto for each year that the commercials are used. Allston pays the residuals in the first year at 5 percent, while Rizzuto claims it should be 10 percent. Rizzuto sues and wins. At the end of the next year, Allston pays Rizzuto again at the 5 percent rate. Rizzuto sues again and Allston pleads res judicata. Is the second action barred?

9.   Rizzuto sues Allston to collect under the endorsement contract. Allston defends the action and wins on the ground that Rizzuto had not performed his obligations under the contract because he abandoned filming after making several commercials. Allston subsequently brings a separate suit against Rizzuto for *his* breach of the contract. Is Allston's suit precluded by res judicata?

Judgment on the Merits

10. Rizzuto sues Allston on the negligence claim in federal court. Allston moves to dismiss under Fed. R. Civ. P. 12(b)(1) for lack of subject matter jurisdiction on the ground that complete diversity does not exist because its principal place of business is in New York (Rizzuto's home state). The court holds a full evidentiary hearing on the motion, including extensive testimony from officials of Allston as to the extent of Allston's business activities in New York and other states. After presentation of the evidence and briefs and argument by the parties, the court concludes that Allston's principal place of business is in New York and therefore dismisses the suit. Rizzuto now sues in a New York state court, and Allston pleads res judicata. Will the defense prevail?

11. Assume that the court in the case described in example 10 clearly has subject matter jurisdiction. Allston therefore answers Rizzuto's negligence complaint and subsequently moves for summary judgment on the ground that Rizzuto cannot prove any negligence of Allston. It submits supporting affidavits of its employees, stating under oath that they had examined the glove after the accident and it was not damaged or defective in any way. Rizzuto submits no opposing affidavit, and summary judgment is entered for Allston. Subsequently, Rizzuto sues again. Is the second suit barred?

Pendent or Independent?

12. Koufax sues Throneberry in state court under a state unfair competition statute. He claims that Throneberry wrote a book about great baseball heros of the 1950s, which plagiarized a similar book by Koufax. The court dismisses Koufax's claim on the basis that the statute of limitations on the unfair competition claim has run. Subsequently, he sues in federal court for violation of the federal copyright laws, based on the same acts. Is the second action barred by res judicata? Look at 28 U.S.C. §1338(a) before answering this example.

13. Suppose that Koufax sued first in federal court on the federal copyright claim, and the court held that Throneberry's book was sufficiently distinct that it did not violate Koufax's copyright. Koufax loses. Subsequently, Koufax sues Throneberry in state court under a state unfair competition statute, based on the same acts. Will the second action be barred?

14. Assume that Rizzuto brought his negligence case against Allston in a New York state court, and that New York law did not recognize strict liability claims under the circumstances of Rizzuto's injury. After losing on his negligence claim, Rizzuto brings a second action in Minnesota, where Allston manufactures its gloves. Minnesota recognizes strict liability, and Rizzuto sues solely on a strict liability theory. Is the suit barred by res judicata?

"The Game Ain't Over 'till It's Over"

15. Berra sues Durocher for intentional infliction of emotional distress, arising out of an altercation behind home plate at Yankee Stadium. The court dismisses the suit under Fed. R. Civ. P. 12(b)(6) on the ground that under the New York case law[3] there is no right to recover for infliction of emotional distress unless the plaintiff also suffered physical injury. Judgment is entered for Durocher. Six months later, the New York Court of Appeals overrules this approach in another case, holding that a plaintiff may recover for intentional infliction of emotional distress without proof of physical injury. Berra brings a new action to recover for the same incident. Is the suit barred?

16. Assume that Berra sued Durocher for intentional infliction of emotional distress in a New York state court. The court dismissed the suit on the ground that the applicable law did not allow recovery for infliction of emotional distress unless the plaintiff also suffered physical injury. Berra appealed. While the appeal was pending, the New York Court of Appeals held in a separate case that plaintiffs may recover for infliction of emotional distress without accompanying physical injury. Which rule should apply to Berra's case?

---

3. New York law would apply in this federal diversity action under *Erie Railroad v. Tompkins,* 304 U.S. 64 (1938).

17. Assume that Berra learns of the change in the law six months after the judgment in his original suit became final. Rather than bring a new action on the claim, Berra takes a different tack: He brings a motion for relief from the *original* judgment, under Fed. R. Civ. P. 60(b), asking the trial court to reopen the first case in light of the change in the applicable law. Should the court grant the motion?

EXPLANATIONS
Fielder's Choices

1.   Res judicata will bar Rizzuto's second action. A judgment need not be right to preclude further litigation; it need only be final and on the merits. "Res judicata reflects the policy that sometimes it is more important that a judgment be stable than that it be correct." Friedenthal, Kane, and Miller at 616. Here, Rizzuto tried his case and lost, and final judgment was entered for Allston "on the merits," that is, based on a verdict by the jury that Allston was not negligent. That judgment bars a second suit by Rizzuto on the same claim even if evidence was wrongly excluded. If that exclusion was improper, Rizzuto should have appealed it in the first suit, not attempted to relitigate it in a second. See *Federated Department Stores, Inc. v. Moitie,* 452 U.S. 394, 398 (1981).

     If Rizzuto could avoid the effect of the first judgment by claiming it was wrong, the res judicata doctrine would lose much of its value. A major purpose of the doctrine is to preserve judicial resources by barring rehearing of cases already litigated and decided. This purpose would be undermined if the evidence would have to be reheard in order to ascertain whether the first case was rightly decided. It would also place the judge in the second suit in the inappropriate position of reviewing the first trial to determine whether it was error-free in order to determine whether it should have res judicata effect.

2.   Res judicata bars not only those claims that were asserted in the first suit, but also any others arising out of that transaction or occurrence that could have been asserted but were not. Here, Rizzuto has simply switched theories of relief and sued again based on the same vicious grounder he complained of in the earlier suit. Since his suit arises out of the same occurrence as the first, it will be barred.

     The rigidity of this rule forces parties to litigate their claims fully in their first suit. Lawyers, knowing they will get only one bite at the apple, must consider all possible grounds for relief raised by the underlying facts and plead them in the first action. This is one reason why complaints often contain numerous counts based on different legal theories. It is better to be comprehensive in the original action (subject, of course, to the ethical constraints of Rule 11) than to try to battle the res judicata myrmidon in a subsequent action.

3.   Allston will also prevail on his res judicata defense here. In example 2, Rizzuto tried to "split his claim" by asserting one theory of relief in the first action and another in the second. Here he has tried a different type of claim-splitting, seeking different types of damages in different actions. Here too, the myrmidon says no. The claim for punitive damages could have been, and therefore should have been, asserted in the first action. No matter how clear Rizzuto's right to punitive damages, the court will not hear this claim.

In an earlier day many states allowed "claim-splitting" based on distinct types of damages. For example, plaintiffs in auto negligence cases were frequently allowed to seek recovery for their personal injuries and damage to their vehicles in separate actions, on the theory that these involved discrete rights protected by distinct causes of action. See, e.g., *Vasu v. Kohlers, Inc.*, 61 N.E.2d 707 (Ohio 1945). This rule has given way in many jurisdictions to the view that all damages from a single accident must be sought in a single suit. See *Rush v. City of Maple Heights,* 147 N.E.2d 599 (Ohio), cert. denied, 358 U.S. 814 (1958) (effectively overruling *Vasu*).

4.   Rizzuto's problem here is not dissatisfaction with the relief he obtained in the first action but difficulty in collecting it from the defendant. The fact that the defendant has not satisfied the judgment does not give the plaintiff the right to bring a second action on the original claim. Under res judicata theory, his claim is "merged into the judgment"; once he obtains the judgment, his right to sue on the original claim is replaced by a right to enforce the judgment. In most jurisdictions a judgment remains enforceable for many years, as long as an execution is issued promptly after judgment. See, e.g., Wis. Stat. Ann. §815.04 (West 1977) (20 years); S.D. Codified Laws Ann. §15-18-1 (1984) (20 years). There is no need for Rizzuto to bring a new suit and relitigate matters already settled in his favor. When Rizzuto learns that Allston is in a position to pay, he should seek execution on the original judgment or bring an action on the judgment in another state where Allston has assets that can be taken on execution. See Chapter 3, pp.44-45.

5.   This is a hard case indeed. Here Rizzuto sought all his known damages in his original suit but did not seek recovery for a potential future consequence of the injury. Naturally when that consequence arises he feels entitled to compensation for it as well. And since res judicata only bars claims that could have been joined in the original action, he has a good argument for a new action.

Rizzuto's position is certainly sympathetic, but it has generally been rejected by the courts. Imagine the havoc that would result if plaintiffs could relitigate claims whenever their disabilities or medical expenses turned out to be more than expected at the time of trial. Judgments would never be final because they would be subject to revision in the light of future events. Defendants would be unable to rely on the finality of judgments in planning their future conduct and estimating their liabilities. In most cases the benefit of providing full relief based on subsequent evidence would be far outweighed by the burden of renewed litigation and the uncertainty that would result.

Consequently, the usual rule is that a plaintiff must recover for all her damages in the original action, including those suffered prior to trial and all future damages that are reasonably likely to ensue. Restatement (Second) of Judgments §25, comment c (1982).[4] Here, for example, Rizzuto should have presented evidence in his original suit that victims of this type of eye injury are likely to develop headaches. The jury could then have assessed additional damages based on this probable consequence of the injury. Admittedly, this is a very rough measure of Rizzuto's actual damages, but it is the best that the system can do without retrying Rizzuto's case repeatedly in future years.

A related problem arises in many asbestos personal injury cases. Frequently, the plaintiff sues and recovers for asbestosis caused by exposure to asbestos, and later — often many years later — develops cancer. Under strict res judicata doctrine, a second suit for the cancer is barred. This is a hard result, in view of the long latency period for the cancer (often 30 to 35 years from date of exposure) and the uncertainty as to whether it will develop at all. Some courts have allowed the plaintiff to bring a second action in such circumstances,[5] but there is no doubt that in doing so they are bending the established rules of claim preclusion.

An Absurd Hypothetical

6.   The short answer to this example is that the four prerequisites for application of res judicata are not met since the parties are not the same in the second action. Rizzuto was not a party in the first suit; though Allston was, *both* parties must be the same (or in privity with the prior parties) for res judicata to apply. In addition, the "claim" is not the same in the second action. The rights of different plaintiffs to relief arising out of a single inci-

---

4. Rizzuto would have an alternative remedy if his headaches appeared within a year. See Fed. R. Civ. P. 60(b)(2), which allows a party to seek relief from the *original* judgment within one year on the ground that newly discovered evidence should be considered.

5. See, e.g., *Mauro v. Raymark Industries, Inc.*, 561 A.2d 257, 264-267 (N.J. 1989) (recognizing the right to bring a second action for cancer after prior recovery for asbestosis caused by the same exposure to asbestos); compare *Gideon v. Johns-Mansville Sales Corp.*, 761 F.2d 1129, 1136-1137 (5th Cir. 1985) (under Texas law asbestos victim must recover all resulting damages in a single action). See generally Note, Claim Preclusion in Modern Latent Disease Cases: A Proposal for Allowing Second Suits, 103 Harv. L. Rev. 1989 (1990).

A former student of mine who works in the area of asbestos litigation tells me that the problem is largely academic. The grim reality is that the court system has been so overwhelmed by the massive backlog of asbestos claims that the large majority of plaintiffs have died before their cases are resolved.

dent are not considered one "claim" simply because they arise out of one transaction or occurrence. Every potential plaintiff who suffers injury from a transaction or occurrence has a distinct claim for res judicata purposes. Here, for example, although Kubek's and Rizzuto's claims both arise out of the same incident, the two claims are distinct. The fact that Kubek has sued for his injuries does not bar Rizzuto from suing separately for his.

If res judicata barred a second suit in a situation like this, all plaintiffs with claims arising out of a single incident would be forced to sue together. The usual rule in American courts is to the contrary: The "plaintiff is master of her claim" and *may* sue jointly with other plaintiffs (see Fed. R. Civ. P. 20(a)) but need not. Even though he knew of Kubek's suit and appeared as a witness, Rizzuto still has the right to sue separately.

7.   The advice that Rizzuto may sue separately on the contract claim without fear of the myrmidon is sound. Even though the contract claim had accrued at the time of the negligence suit (that is, the breach had occurred and Rizzuto had a right to sue on it), Rizzuto is not required to assert it in the negligence action. Under the Restatement definition of a single "claim," these are separate claims because they arise out of separate transactions. Restatement (Second) of Judgments §24 (1982). Rizzuto's first action was based on an accident on the playing field. His second is based on a separate transaction, the contract to promote Allston gloves on television.

This example highlights several important points. *First,* it is important to understand that Rizzuto's right to sue separately on these claims is not based on the fact that one action is for tort and the other for contract. In many cases a plaintiff has a right to recover under both tort and contract theories, based on a single incident. In the Schulansky case, for example, Schulansky asserts contract and tort claims against the defendants, which both arise out of the construction of the addition on her house. See the Schulansky complaint infra p.432. If either of these were left out, res judicata would bar Schulansky from suing on it separately. By contrast, Rizzuto may sue separately here because his contract claim arises from a different set of historical facts.

Second, note that Rizzuto *could* have joined both of these unrelated claims in a single action under Fed. R. Civ. P. 18(a). It does not always follow that you must join claims in a single action simply because the Rules allow you to do so. See Chapter 22, which explores in more detail the relationship between res judicata and the joinder rules.

8.   On these facts Rizzuto's second action will not be barred. At the time of his first suit Rizzuto did not have a claim for the second year's royalties. He can hardly be expected to predict future defaults and sue for them before they occur. Even though the two suits arise out of a single contract, the separate breaches in successive years are different occurrences that may be sued on separately.

That would not be true, however, if Rizzuto had waited until the end of the second year to sue. At that point, the royalties for both years had accrued, and the usual rule is that Rizzuto must sue for them all as a single debt due on an account. Friedenthal, Kane, and Miller at 630-631; Restatement (Second) of Judgments §24, comment d. Similarly, a landlord who sues a tenant for back rent must seek recovery for all months' rent due but not future defaults. This reflects the basic premise that res judicata bars all claims arising out of a single transaction or occurrence that could have been raised in the original action. The claims for future nonpayment could not have been raised since the plaintiff has no right to sue for these claims until they accrue.

Although res judicata will not bar Rizzuto's second suit here, collateral estoppel will bar relitigation of issues that were litigated and decided in the first suit. For example, if the court held that the contract called for payment of all royalties at the 10 percent rate, Allston will be estopped from claiming that the rate should be 5 percent in the second action. See Chapter 23, p.382.

9.   If you focused carefully on the prerequisites for res judicata discussed in the Introduction, you should have concluded that the myrmidon will not bar Allston's suit against Rizzuto. As example 6 suggests, every separate party has a separate claim for res judicata purposes even though their claims arise out of the same incident. Thus, Allston's claim against Rizzuto is not the "same claim" as Rizzuto's claim against Allston.

However, while traditional res judicata doctrine does not bar Allston's claim, many jurisdictions provide by court rule that counterclaims arising out of the same transaction or occurrence must be brought in the original action. See, e.g., Fed. R. Civ. P. 13(a) (counterclaim is compulsory if it arises out of same transaction or occurrence as the opposing party's claim). If the defendant fails to join a compulsory counterclaim, she will then be barred from bringing it later, not because the common law res judicata doctrine applies, but in order to enforce the compulsory counterclaim rule. See James and Hazard at §11.14.

In a jurisdiction that does not have a compulsory counterclaim rule, Allston would remain free to assert its claim in a separate action. However, the crucial issues underlying its claim may have been decided in the original suit anyway. In this case, for example, the earlier action determined that Rizzuto had breached his contract. In Allston's separate action, collateral estoppel will bar Rizzuto from relitigating that issue.

Judgment on the Merits

10. Res judicata does not apply here because the claim has never been decided on the merits. Although an actual hearing was held and testimony and argument heard, the issue under consideration was the power of the court to hear the action, not the substance of Rizzuto's negligence claim. Since the court held that it lacked subject matter jurisdiction over the suit, it never reached the merits. Consequently, one of the prerequisites for res judicata is not met.

It would certainly be a hard rule if litigants in Rizzuto's position were barred from going to a second court after dismissal for lack of jurisdiction in the first. Under that approach, the second suit would be barred even though the first court never considered the merits of plaintiff's case and, in fact, never had the power to do so. To avoid this risk, the plaintiff would be forced to choose a court that definitely has jurisdiction, even though she would prefer to sue in another that *may* have it. The res judicata doctrine does not put the parties to such risks. The "on the merits" requirement assures that preliminary dismissals due to lack of jurisdiction or venue will not bar suit in another court that has the power to proceed.[6]

11.   In this case, although Rizzuto's claim has been resolved without trial, it has been decided on the merits. Summary judgment in Allston's favor was based on the court's conclusion that Rizzuto has no evidence to support his contention that his accident resulted from Allston's negligence, and therefore no jury could find for Rizzuto on the negligence issue. Because Rizzuto cannot prove an essential element of his claim, judgment for Allston is proper. This is "on the merits" because it represents an adjudication of Rizzuto's substantive claim for relief, not a preliminary issue. Similarly, a judgment as a matter of law under Rule 50 is given res judicata effect because it determines that the plaintiff's claim has so little "merit" that no reasonable jury could uphold it. Restatement (Second) of Judgments §19, comments g, h (1982).

Pendent or Independent?

12.   Under the four prerequisites Koufax's second action should be barred since he is suing the same defendant again on a claim arising out of the same events as the first suit. The procedural quirk here, however, is that Koufax could not have included the federal copyright claim in the state law action: The federal courts have exclusive jurisdiction over federal copyright claims under 28 U.S.C. §1338(a).

Most courts have held in these circumstances that the second suit is not barred. If it were barred, it would force Koufax to sue in federal court to avoid losing his federal copyright claim by operation of res judicata. Consequently he would lose the chance to have the state court decide his state unfair competition claim. Most courts have concluded that it is better to allow the second action in such cases so as to avoid interfering with the authority of state courts to hear claims created by their own law. See Restatement (Second) of Judgments §26(1)(c) and illustration 2 (1982); 18 Wright and Miller at §4412, pp.97-99 and 1991 Supp.

---

6. The only argument for preclusion here is that the plaintiff has already caused the defendant and the courts to expend substantial time and energy in considering her case by choosing an inappropriate court. But this consideration is outweighed by the premium the system places on deciding cases on their merits, rather than allowing procedural mistakes to dominate over substantive rights.

13. When the first suit is brought in federal court, the situation is somewhat different. The state unfair competition claim is a state law claim that would be within the court's supplemental jurisdiction in the federal copyright suit. See 28 U.S.C. §1367; Chapter 14, pp.234-235. However, under §1367(c) the court has discretion to hear or dismiss the supplemental claims. It might not have heard Koufax's state law claim even if he had tried.

The general rule is that plaintiffs in Koufax's position must assert their supplemental claims or lose them by operation of res judicata. If the federal court entertains the state unfair competition claim, it will contribute to judicial efficiency and consistency of decision making, two goals of the res judicata doctrine. If the court refuses to hear it, then Koufax will not be barred from suing separately on the claim in state court, since it could not be heard in the first action, and the plaintiff has therefore not had an opportunity to litigate that claim. All that Koufax can do is ask; if he does and the court refuses, he is protected.[7] If he doesn't ask, the potential benefits of joint litigation are lost through his own neglect, and the myrmidon will be characteristically unsympathetic.

14. It is easy to see the plaintiff's argument for allowing the second case here: Res judicata requires the plaintiff to assert in the first action all claims that were available to her in that action. In this case, the strict liability claim could not have been asserted in the New York suit because New York tort law does not recognize such claims. Thus, since he could not assert the strict liability claim in the first suit, he can bring a new one on it in another state that recognizes such claims. Right?

The argument has superficial appeal, but on closer examination it is inconsistent with the basic purposes of res judicata doctrine. If this second action were not barred, the plaintiff could give it a preliminary try in State A, with limited tort remedies, and then try again in a State B if he lost — and maybe even in State C with some further remedy not available in the first two. This would lead to wasteful relitigation, which would have been avoided had he sued in State B (or C) to begin with.

But (I can almost hear you protest) we didn't force Koufax to choose federal court first in example 12. To be consistent, shouldn't Rizzuto, as

---

7. For an interesting but dubious contrary holding, see *Mattson v. City of Costa Mesa*, 164 Cal. Rptr. 913 (1980). In *Mattson* the plaintiff sued in federal court on the federal claims and the supplemental state law claims, but the federal court declined in its discretion to hear the state law claims. When the plaintiff later sued on the state claims in state court, that court held that the plaintiff, once the federal court declined jurisdiction over the state law claims, had to choose either to waive those claims and litigate the federal claim in federal court, or dismiss the federal action and proceed on all claims in the state court, which had jurisdiction to hear them all in a single action. The *Mattson* approach has not met with general acceptance. It would not apply on these facts anyway: Koufax could not bring the copyright claim in state court since the federal court has exclusive jurisdiction over it.

"master of his claim," be entitled to sue in New York first if he chooses without losing the remedy that only Minnesota will give? Well, I don't think so. The rule that a plaintiff can bring state claims in state court and not lose related claims within exclusive federal jurisdiction preserves the right to use the state courts for state law claims and the federal court for related federal remedies. But plaintiffs do not have the right to have tort cases decided under the inconsistent tort law of two different states. Rizzuto could have chosen to sue in Minnesota first if its law was more favorable. He also could have argued in the New York court that it should apply Minnesota tort law to the case. See Chapter 11, pp.178-179. Having made his choice to bring the action in New York, the plaintiff must live with that choice. See Restatement (Second) of Judgments §18, comment d (states required to give full faith and credit to money judgments of sister states).

"The Game Ain't Over 'till It's Over"

15. As indicated in the Introduction, the federal courts give res judicata effect to dismissals under Fed. R. Civ. P. 12(b)(6) for failure to state a claim. See Fed. R. Civ. P. 41(b) (unless the court specifies otherwise, dismissals are with prejudice except for specified preliminary dismissals). Thus, Berra's second action will be barred unless the subsequent change in the substantive law provides a basis to avoid the usual effect of res judicata.

This subsequent change in the law will not allow Berra to start a new action. Parties are not entitled to have their cases decided under the law as it will be at some future time; each case must be decided under the law at the time it is considered. See 1B Moore's at ¶0.415. Imagine the confusion that would ensue if parties could bring new suits if the law changed after they lost a case. Finality of judgments would be meaningless since cases might be reopened (or nullified by the results in a later suit) at some indeterminate time in the future. How long would parties have to reopen the judgment? How much later could the law change and still be applied to a previously decided case?

Clearly, such a principle, even if circumscribed by some form of statute of limitations, would undermine two goals of the res judicata doctrine: judicial economy and certainty of judgments. Besides, rules may be fair at the time they are applied even though they change later, when conditions have changed. See Chapter 9, pp.137-138 (suggesting that Athenians of one generation may choose to live under different laws than those of their predecessors). Better to leave it at that than to undermine the finality of judgments by reconsidering them every time the underlying substantive law is reconsidered.

If Berra believed that the prior case law should be overruled, he should have appealed on that ground instead of waiting for a future plaintiff to carry the laboring oar. Perhaps the court would have changed the rule in his case instead of the next one six months down the line. See, for a case on point, *Federated Department Stores, Inc. v. Moitie,* 452 U.S. 394 (1981).

16. There is a crucial difference between this case and the last. Here, Berra's first action is still going on. Although he lost in the trial court under the old approach to intentional infliction, he has taken his appeal and asked the higher court to change the rule. If the court had not adopted the new rule in the other case raising the issue, it presumably would have done so in his. He should not be disadvantaged by the fact that the appeal in the other case was heard first. Consequently, the general rule is that the court will apply the law as it stands when the pending appeal is decided, not the law as it stood at the time of trial. The dismissal of Berra's case will be reversed, and it will be sent back for trial on the merits.

17. If Berra could get the trial judge to reopen the original action, it would undermine the finality of the judgment just as clearly as allowing a new action would in example 15. Instead of starting a new suit, he could simply revive the old one and ask the court to retry the case under the new state of the law. The general rule in the federal courts, therefore, is that the court may not grant relief from judgment due to a change in the substantive law once the period for appeal has passed. See, e.g., *Morris v. Adams-Millis Corp.,* 758 F.2d 1352, 1358-1359 (10th Cir. 1985); *Lubben v. Selective Service System Local Board No. 27,* 453 F.2d 645, 651 (1st Cir. 1972).

However, if the law changes while the period for appeal is still running (usually 30 days from entry of judgment in the trial court, see Fed. R. App. P. 4(a)(1)), many courts would allow Berra to seek relief from the judgment on this ground. This exception makes eminent good sense: If the trial judge could not acknowledge this change in the law and reopen the case during the appeal period, Rizzuto clearly would appeal. The appellate court would apply the new rule (see example 16), reverse the case for reconsideration under the new rule, and the case would be reopened anyway, after a wasteful appeal. Allowing the trial judge to grant relief from judgment during the appeal period (but only during this period) will save the parties the expense of an unnecessary appeal with a foregone conclusion. Cf. 7 Moore's at ¶60.22[3], pp.60-185 – 60-186 (discussing related right of trial judge to correct error within time for appeal).

22

Res Judicata and the Rules of Joinder: When Does May Mean Must?

Introduction

In any reasonable civil procedure world, there ought to be a close relationship between the parties' right to join claims in their first lawsuit and the scope of res judicata in subsequent suits between them. If, for example, the rules of joinder did not allow plaintiffs to join counts for property damage and personal injury in a single lawsuit, it would be a rigid system indeed that barred the plaintiff who had sued for his property damage in one suit from bringing a separate action to recover for his personal injuries. Similarly, if the joinder rules limited a plaintiff to proceeding on a single theory, such as negligence, in his first suit, it would be unfair to bar him from starting a second action on a strict liability theory. One way or another, the system ought to offer parties a chance to have all of their claims heard, either through limited claims in multiple suits or multiple claims in a single suit.

The early English common law followed the first course, allowing multiple actions on different theories or seeking different relief. Under the common law system, the rigid limitations on joinder of claims frequently prevented plaintiffs from seeking full relief in a single action. For example, a plaintiff who sued at law for damages for trespass could not get an injunction against further trespasses in the same suit; he had to go to an equity court for that. Because the plaintiff was forced by these limitations to split his cause of action, the preclusion rules did not bar him from bringing the second action even though it arose out of the same occurrence as the first.

The federal courts (and many state systems as well) have chosen the second course, allowing many claims to be heard in a single action. This approach is implemented by extremely broad rules governing pleading and joinder. See Rules 8(a)(3), 8(e)(2), 13, 14, 18, 20. Under these liberal joinder rules, plaintiffs have broad power to join all their theories of recovery in their initial suit. Consequently, they will seldom be able to argue that they should be allowed to start a new action based on the same occurrence because they were unable to assert an omitted claim in the first suit.

For example, Fed. R. Civ. P. 18(a) allows the plaintiff to join virtually all possible theories of recovery in a single action. It is hardly unreasonable therefore to hold that res judicata bars him from suing later on any theory that is omitted from the first suit. In this situation the *may* of the rules clearly means *must* when the effects of res judicata are considered. If Elbers sues Doe Chemical Company for negligently manufacturing a drug, Rule 18(a) allows but does not require him to assert a separate strict liability claim against Doe based on the same events. See also Fed. R. Civ. P. 8(e)(2) (authorizing alternative or inconsistent pleading). However, if Elbers leaves out the strict liability claim, res judicata will bar him from asserting it in a later action. This is simply another theory of recovery for the same injuries already sued upon, and any claims arising from that occurrence that are not joined in Elbers's first action will be barred by res judicata doctrine. See Chapter 21, example 2.

There are a few instances, despite Rule 18(a), when initial joinder of a particular claim is not available. In such cases the res judicata myrmidon[1] grudgingly steps aside to allow the plaintiff to reenter the courthouse door. Suppose, for example, that Allen sues Moser in state court under a state unfair competition statute. Suppose further that Allen might also recover against Moser for patent infringement, a federal claim over which the federal courts have exclusive jurisdiction. Here, Allen could not have included his federal theory in the first action because the federal courts have exclusive jurisdiction over patent claims. Consequently, he will not be barred from asserting the patent claim in a later suit. See generally Restatement (Second) of Judgments §26(1)(c) (1982).

It would make life a lot easier for civil procedure students, as well as for practicing lawyers, if it were invariably true that every claim that could have been joined in the initial action will be barred in a later action. Alas, though this would be neat and symmetrical, it just isn't so. Although *theories* that could have been joined are generally barred, the scope of permissible joinder of *parties* is much broader than the dimensions of a single "claim" for res judicata purposes. Thus, in many cases, claims against additional parties could be joined under the Rules but will not be barred by res judicata if they are not.

---

1. For a natural history of this creature, see Chapter 21, n.1.

For example, if Fellows is involved in a three-car collision with Rich and Rontowski, he could sue them as codefendants in a single lawsuit. Fed. R. Civ. P. 20(a). However, he doesn't *have* to: If he sues Rich alone, he is not precluded from suing Rontowski later in a separate action. A plaintiff's rights to recover from separate defendants are considered distinct "claims" under res judicata analysis, even though they arise out of the same occurrence. In addition, the "same parties" requirement of res judicata is not met in such cases since the defendants differ in the two actions.

This is puzzling at first, but if it were not true, the res judicata rules would convert permissive joinder under the Rules into compulsory joinder. Rule 20(a) says that Fellows *may* choose to sue Rich and Rontowski together. Clearly, the rulemakers have chosen to allow him to sue them jointly but also have given him the option not to. This reflects the traditional precept that the "plaintiff is master of his claim," free to choose when and where to sue each potential defendant. But, if res judicata barred Fellows from suing Rontowski because he had previously sued Rich without joining Rontowski, the *may* of Rule 20(a) would be converted to *must* by the preclusion rules: Fellows would be forced to sue them both in the first action. Although such a compulsory joinder of parties rule might make sense from an efficiency point of view, the rulemakers have favored freedom of choice over efficiency.[2] The res judicata rules should be crafted to protect that policy decision.

This principle that claims against different parties need not be joined even if the rules would allow it does not prevent the first action from having some preclusive effect, however. If Fellows loses his suit against Rich on the ground that he was contributorily negligent, Rontowski may be able to invoke collateral estoppel to establish Fellows's negligence if Fellows subsequently sues him. See *Blonder-Tongue Laboratories, Inc. v. University of Illinois Foundation*, 402 U.S. 313 (1971); Chapter 24, pp.398-400. Certainly, this inhibits Fellows's freedom of choice to some extent, since he cannot start his action against Rontowski with a completely clean slate.

The following examples will help you sort out the relationship between the joinder and res judicata rules. Assume that all actions are brought in federal court and that subject matter jurisdiction is proper in each case. Consider in each case whether the omitted claim could have been joined under the rules and, if so, whether res judicata will bar the second action.

EXAMPLES

A Few Warm-Ups

1.   Roosevelt is hit by a car while walking across Park Avenue in New York City. The only occupants of the car were Kefauver and Warren, but each denies that he was driving. Roosevelt sues Kefauver, a Tennessee citizen, in

---

2. Some of the reasons for that choice are discussed in Chapter 12, example 1.

the federal court for the Middle District of Tennessee. She loses. Now Roosevelt sues Warren, a New Yorker, in the Southern District of New York.

    a. Could Roosevelt have joined Kefauver and Warren in the first action?

    b. Is Roosevelt's second suit barred?

2. Roosevelt sues Kefauver in the Tennessee federal court for battery, based on the collision on Park Avenue. The jury finds that Kefauver did not hit Roosevelt intentionally, and judgment is entered for Kefauver. Subsequently, Roosevelt sues Kefauver in the Southern District of New York for negligently injuring her in the collision.

    a. Could Roosevelt have joined the negligence claim in the first suit?

    b. Is the second suit barred by res judicata?

3. Roosevelt sues Kefauver for battery and for negligence based on the accident. She later sues Kefauver again in the same court for a breach of contract that took place before the accident.

    a. Could Roosevelt have joined the contract claim in the first action?

    b. Is the second suit precluded by res judicata?

4. Stanton sues Anthony for her injuries in a two-car collision and recovers $17,000. Now Blatch, a passenger in Stanton's car, sues Anthony for her injuries in the collision.

    a. Could Stanton and Blatch have joined as coplaintiffs in the first action?

    b. Could Blatch have intervened in Stanton's suit against Anthony? See Fed. R. Civ. P. 24.

    c. Is Blatch barred by res judicata from bringing her suit?

A Hybrid Case

5. Grasso sues Adams for breach of contract, arising out of a contract for the delivery of livestock to Grasso. Grasso loses. Subsequently, Adams sues Grasso for breach of the contract, seeking to collect the balance due under the contract.

    a. Could Adams have joined his contract claim in the original action?

    b. Is Adams's action against Grasso barred by res judicata?

6. After Grasso sues Adams for breach of the livestock contract, could Adams start a separate action against Grasso on an unrelated fraud claim that accrued before the contract dispute?

7. Grasso sues Adams and Johnson Drug Co. for personal injuries suffered as a result of using a drug made by Johnson and sold to her by Adams. She recovers judgment for $35,000 against each defendant. Adams pays the judgment and then sues Johnson for indemnification, claiming that since the

negligent manufacture of the drug caused Grasso's injuries, Adams should be indemnified by the manufacturer for the damages he paid to Grasso.

    a. Could the claim have been asserted in the first action?

    b. Is Adams barred from bringing the second suit?

A Myrmidon in the Labyrinth

8.   Assume that Grasso sued Adams alone on the drug claim and recovered. Now Adams sues Johnson for indemnification.

    a. Could Adams have asserted this claim in the original action?

    b. Is his action against Johnson precluded?

9.   Smith, from South Dakota, sues Bryan, from Minnesota, for breach of a contract to construct a home for him. Smith claims that the foundation of the house was improperly poured. Bryan impleads Coolidge, a South Dakota subcontractor who poured the foundation, for indemnification. The court holds that the foundation meets the specifications, and therefore judgment is entered for Bryan on the main claim and for Coolidge on the third-party claim. Subsequently, Bryan sues Coolidge to collect the wages of five laborers Bryan had lent to Coolidge to help him perform the foundation work.

    a. Could Bryan have asserted the new claim in the first action?

    b. Is the second suit barred by res judicata?

10. Assume the same facts as example 9, but that the claim Bryan asserted in the second action was for a previous breach of another contract between him and Coolidge.

    a. Could Bryan have asserted the second contract claim in the first action?

    b. Is he barred from bringing it in the second suit?

When Does *May Not* Mean *Must*?

11. Suppose that Smith sued Bryan for breach of the contract, as a result of defects in the foundation. Three years into the suit, when the parties have completed discovery and trial is imminent, Smith moves to amend the complaint to assert a second claim against Bryan for negligence, on the ground that the foundation was inadequately poured. The court denies the motion to amend on the ground that it is untimely, since it could have been asserted earlier in the suit, and that allowance of the motion would delay the trial and prejudice Bryan's ability to prepare his defense. See *Foman v. Davis,* 371 U.S. 178, 181-182 (1962)(delay in seeking amendment and prejudice to opponent may justify denial of leave to amend).

    The breach of contract claim is tried and Smith loses. He then brings a second action against Bryan, asserting only the negligence claim. (Assume that the applicable statute of limitations is six years, so that the action is not yet barred on this ground.) Bryan pleads res judicata.

    a. If you represented Smith, how would you argue that the second action is not barred by res judicata?

    b. How will the judge rule on the res judicata defense?

EXPLANATIONS

A Few Warm-Ups

1.   Joinder: Yes   Res judicata: No

    a. This is a simple case of one plaintiff who has claims against two defendants. Rule 20(a) allows Roosevelt to sue them together because the claims arise from the same accident and will involve the common issue of who was driving the car. However, Rule 20(a) does not require Roosevelt to sue the defendants together; the rule says *may* and means it. In this case Roosevelt might have been well advised to sue them jointly. As it is, the first jury may conclude that Warren was driving, and the second that Kefauver was, leaving Roosevelt a double loser. For one reason or another, Roosevelt has chosen to take that risk, as the joinder rules allow her to do.

    b. Roosevelt's second action is not barred because her claim against Warren is distinct from her claim against Kefauver, and they are not the same parties. If res judicata did bar the second action, it would force Roosevelt to sue the two defendants together, thus undermining the choice given to Roosevelt by the rules. Consider the consequences that such a result would have for Roosevelt's case. It is unlikely that she could get personal jurisdiction in Tennessee over Warren for this New York accident. Consequently, if the res judicata rules forced her to sue the two together, Roosevelt would lose her choice of forum against Kefauver. She would be forced to sue in New York where she could obtain personal jurisdiction over both defendants because the claim arose there.

    This is another example of the intricate interrelations of various civil procedure doctrines. A change in this aspect of the res judicata rules would directly affect the joinder rules and the choice of forum rules. The rulemakers have chosen to preserve one value — the plaintiff's right to choose his forum against each defendant — and have had to mold the related joinder and preclusion rules accordingly.

    As indicated in the Introduction, however, it is still possible that the first suit will affect the second if the court in the second action allows Warren to invoke nonmutual collateral estoppel to bar relitigation of any issues decided in the first.

2.   Joinder: Yes   Res judicata: Yes

a. The issue here is joinder of "claims" (in the sense of theories of recovery) rather than joinder of parties. Rule 18(a), the epitome of liberality, allows a plaintiff to join any claims he has against a defending party. But again, the rule is permissive; under Rule 18(a) Roosevelt has the option but is not required to join the negligence claim in the first action.

b. The myrmidon[3] will stubbornly resist Roosevelt's efforts to bring this second action. Joinder of these "claims" may be permissive under the rules but is made mandatory by the res judicata principles applied in the federal courts. Under those principles, all theories for recovery arising out of a single transaction or occurrence constitute a single "claim" for preclusion purposes. See Chapter 21, p.353. A party who seeks relief based on a particular set of historical facts must join all his grounds for recovery on those facts in the first action or face the res judicata defense if he tries to sue later on one of these grounds. Thus, Roosevelt's second suit for negligence will be barred even though Rule 18(a) appears to give her the option to join or withhold it in the first action. Here, unlike the joinder of parties situation in example 1, the preclusion doctrine demands what the rule merely permits.

It makes no difference that Roosevelt's second action is brought in a different court. Under full faith and credit principles, each court within the system will honor the judgments of its sister courts by giving them full res judicata effect.

3.   Joinder: Yes   Res judicata: No

a. Rule 18(a) authorizes joinder of "claims," both in the sense of different theories arising out of the same events and also completely unrelated claims arising out of completely separate events. Thus, Roosevelt could have joined her contract claim with her other claims in the first action even though it arises from a separate transaction.

b. Roosevelt's second action is not barred. Unlike example 2, in which the omitted "claim" simply asserted a different theory of recovery for the same loss litigated in the first suit, the contract claim here arose out of a separate incident from the negligence and battery claims. Roosevelt's prior suit based on the accident will bar all future suits against Kefauver based on that accident but not other suits based on separate events.

Thus Roosevelt is free to bring a separate action on the contract claim even though she could have joined it in the first suit. Here, the *may* of the rule does not mean *must* under res judicata because the claim does not satisfy the res judicata definition of a single "claim." See Restatement (Second) of Judgments §24 (1982) (single claim under res judicata analysis includes all grounds for relief arising out of a single transaction).

---

3. I will drop this metaphor eventually. There's no point in beating a dead myrmidon.

4.   Joinder: Yes   Intervention: Maybe   Res judicata: No

a. Rule 20(a) authorizes, but does not require, Stanton and Blatch to sue jointly since they seek relief arising from the same occurrence, and their claims will involve a number of common questions of law or fact, including the central question of the cause of the accident.

b. Blatch could at least have tried to intervene under Rule 24(b) since her claim and Stanton's will involve a common question of fact — whether Anthony's negligence caused the accident. But intervention under Rule 24(b) is permissive; the court might have declined to allow Blatch into the suit for a variety of reasons.

It is unlikely that Blatch could have intervened in Stanton's suit as a matter of right under Rule 24(a). She will not be prejudiced by the Stanton/ Anthony litigation unless she will be barred from bringing her own action against Anthony. As explained immediately below, she will not be barred from doing so. In addition, even if Blatch meets the criteria for intervention as of right, she is still under no duty to intervene since Rule 24(a) authorizes intervention as of right but does not force parties to intervene even when they would have a right to do so. Last, there may be jurisdictional problems if there is not complete diversity among the parties. See 28 U.S.C. §1367(b) (barring supplemental jurisdiction over intervening parties in diversity cases if inconsistent with requirements of §1332).

c. Blatch's suit against Anthony is not precluded by Stanton's because she is a different party from the original parties and because her claim against Anthony is not the same as Stanton's claim against Anthony. Thus, two of the prerequisites to res judicata are not met. While Blatch had several avenues for getting into the first action, they are both permissive, and *may* is not converted to *must* here because the separate requirements for preclusion are not met.

Blatch may obtain some benefit from Stanton's action, however: Because Stanton has proved Anthony's negligence, Blatch may be able to invoke offensive nonmutual collateral estoppel to bar Anthony from relitigating the issue. See Chapter 24, pp.401-403.

A Hybrid Case

5.   Joinder: Yes   Res Judicata: In a way

a. Adams's claim for the payments due under the contract was a compulsory counterclaim in the first action since it arose out of the same events as Grasso's original claim. Under Rule 13(a), Adams was *required* to assert this claim in the original action. The drafters of Rule 13(a) decided that the gain in litigation efficiency from hearing a defendant's related claims in the original action outweighed the defendant's usual right to choose his own forum. Consequently, they required such related claims to be asserted in the original action.

b. The rulemakers' goal will only be achieved if Adams is barred from suing separately on the omitted counterclaim. Under res judicata doctrine, however, Adams would not be precluded from suing separately on this claim because Adams's claim against Grasso is not the "same claim" as Grasso's claim against him. In this situation the courts have estopped parties in Adams's position from suing separately on the omitted counterclaim, simply to enforce the policy underlying the compulsory counterclaim rule. This form of "rule-based res judicata" applies even though the same claim requirement of res judicata is not met. See Friedenthal, Kane, and Miller at §14.6, p.638.

In some state systems counterclaims are not compulsory, whether or not they arise out of the same transaction as the main claim. In those systems Adams would not be barred from starting a second action on the counterclaim. However, such jurisdictions sometimes hold that a party waives his right to sue separately on an omitted counterclaim if the same issues were raised defensively in the prior action. Id. at 639-640.

6.   In this example, Adams's claim was available at the time of the original action and could have been joined as a permissive counterclaim under Rule 13(b). However, Adams need not join it in the first suit, and it will not be barred by res judicata if he omits it. By definition, a permissive counterclaim arises out of a separate transaction from the main claim. See Fed. R. Civ. P. 13(b). Thus, it is not part of the "same claim" as the plaintiff's claim, nor is it barred by rule-based preclusion, as a compulsory counterclaim would be. Here, *may* really means *may*; Adams's fraud claim will not be barred.

If the claim were barred by res judicata if omitted from the first action, the preclusion rules would make permissive counterclaims compulsory, undermining the rulemakers' choice and raising serious jurisdictional problems in many federal cases.

7.   Joinder: Yes   Res judicata: No

a. Adams could have joined his indemnification claim as a cross-claim in the original action, under Rule 13(g), which authorizes but does not require him to assert any related claim he has against the codefendant in the original action.

b. Res judicata will not bar Adams from seeking indemnification from Johnson in a second suit. Under the res judicata analysis, Adams's claim against Johnson is not the same as Grasso's claim against Adams, so that the assertion of the latter does not bar the subsequent assertion of the former. Again, this result is consistent with the policy of the Rules. The rulemakers have chosen to make cross-claims permissive; if res judicata barred subsequent assertion of omitted cross-claims they would effectively be compulsory.

Compulsory cross-claims actually might not be a bad idea. As long as all the parties are already in the case, why not force them to litigate all claims among them arising out of the same transaction? The Rules make defendants do it under Rule 13(a) but draw the line at forcing the assertion of other related claims such as cross-claims and third-party claims.

A Myrmidon in the Labyrinth

8.   Joinder: Yes   Res judicata: No

a. Adams could have impleaded Johnson for indemnification under Rule 14(a) since he seeks recovery from Johnson for the damages Grasso seeks from him.

b. If Adams is free to refrain from asserting his claim against Johnson in the last example, in which they are both already in the suit, he should similarly be free *not* to implead Johnson when sued by Grasso. Impleader is permissive, and Adams is free to sue Johnson separately for indemnification if he prefers. Res judicata will not bar the suit.

Tactically, it may be preferable to implead Johnson to prevent the risk of inconsistent judgments, but Adams may have his reasons for failing to do so, such as lack of personal jurisdiction over Johnson in the court where Grasso sued him. It would certainly be inappropriate to force Adams to join Johnson if he couldn't obtain personal jurisdiction over him. Such problems were undoubtedly in the minds of the rulemakers when they decided not to make Rule 14 impleader claims compulsory.

However, if Adams did implead Johnson, res judicata obviously would bar him from bringing a separate action against Johnson on the same claim. Further, Johnson may still be able to invoke collateral estoppel in the second action on some issues decided against Adams in the first.

9.   Joinder: Yes   Res judicata: Yes

a. Bryan could have asserted this claim against Coolidge under Rule 18(a), which provides that a party seeking relief from an opposing party may assert as many claims as he has against that opposing party. Granted, Bryan could not have impleaded Coolidge on the basis of this claim alone because it does not satisfy the Rule 14(a) requirement that Coolidge may be liable to Bryan for all or part of the plaintiff's claim. See Chapter 13, pp.215-216. Once Bryan has properly impleaded Coolidge on the indemnification claim, however, he may assert whatever claims he has against Coolidge, related or unrelated.

However, there would also have to be a basis for subject matter jurisdiction over Bryan's additional claim for it to be asserted in the original action. The supplemental jurisdiction statute, 28 U.S.C. §1367, provides a basis for jurisdiction, since Bryan's wage claim arises from the same foundation work as the main claim brought by Smith. There may not even be a need to invoke §1367, since the parties to the wage claim are diverse and Bryan may aggregate his claims against Coolidge. If Bryan sought more than $50,000 in damages on the combined claims the amount-in-controversy requirement would be met, and the court would have jurisdiction based on diversity.

b. Assuming that there was subject matter jurisdiction over the wage claim in the original suit, res judicata will bar Bryan from suing on the claim later. Res judicata applies not only to a plaintiff who has asserted claims against a defendant, but to other parties in the suit who have asserted claims. Here, Bryan has asserted a claim against Coolidge by impleading him on the foundation claim. Having done so, the res judicata rules require him to assert all claims he has against Coolidge arising out of that occurrence. Bryan omitted the wage claim, which also arose from the construction of the foundation, and he is therefore barred from asserting it in a new action.

Bryan had the option not to implead Coolidge at all, in which case he could have asserted the indemnification and wage claims in a separate suit (but *not* in two separate suits). However, once he has joined issue with Coolidge on the foundation question, he must get it all out in that suit. Although Rule 18(a) says he *may* assert his related wage claim, the res judicata rules convert that to *must* in this situation.[4]

10. Joinder: Yes, with a caution   Res judicata: No

a. As in example 9, Rule 18(a) authorizes Bryan to assert this claim along with his third-party indemnification claim. Here, of course, the claim is completely unrelated to the impleader claim, but Rule 18 doesn't seem to care. However, there would not be supplemental jurisdiction over this claim since it arises from an unrelated contract breach. Bryan would have to establish independent diversity jurisdiction over the added claims based on diversity.

b. Bryan is not barred from suing separately on this claim, since the claim asserted in the second action does not arise out of the same transaction or occurrence as the impleader claim against Coolidge in the first suit. Therefore, it does not satisfy the "same claim" requirement of res judicata, and Bryan was not required to assert it in the prior action.

If Bryan were forced to join this unrelated claim, the symmetry of the res judicata and jurisdiction rules would be lost. The court would not have supplemental jurisdiction over the unrelated claim, since it is not part of the same "case or controversy" under §1367(a). If there were no independent basis for subject matter jurisdiction, Bryan would be forced by the preclusion rules to join this claim but prevented by the jurisdiction rules from doing so.

---

4. Of course, if jurisdiction were based on 28 U.S.C. §1367, the court might have declined to exercise jurisdiction, in its discretion, under §1367(c). However, the court in the second action is likely to hold that Bryan should have asserted the wage claim in the first suit. That would have given the first court the opportunity to hear the wage claim with the related impleader claim, since it arose from the same transaction as the impleader claim, and the court had the power to hear it under §1367. If the court refused, then the claim would not be barred. See Chapter 21, example 13.

When Does *May Not* Mean *Must?*

11a. Ordinarily, Smith's negligence claim would be barred because it arose out of the same transaction as the breach of contract claim. However, Smith may argue that he should be allowed to bring a second action on the negligence claim because he tried to join it in the first action, but the court refused to hear it. The situation is roughly analogous to the case of supplemental claims, which must be asserted in the original action but will not be barred if the court refuses in its discretion to entertain them. See Chapter 21, example 13. Similarly, in this case Smith will argue that he sought but was denied the right to assert the claim in the original suit and should therefore be allowed to resurrect it here.

b. Smith's argument is clever, but the analogy is a bit too rough to carry the day. Here, the negligence claim was disallowed because it was asserted in an untimely manner. Once Smith brought suit against Bryan, Smith had to assert all his claims properly in that action. Although the amendment rules are liberal, Smith has no right to hold back some claims arising from the construction and spring them on Bryan just before trial. At some point the defendant has a right to focus his trial preparation on those issues that have been properly placed in dispute and let the others go. See 18 Wright and Miller §4412, p.105. This claim will be barred because it arose from the same transaction as the original claim and was available to Smith if timely asserted in the first suit.

The irony here, of course, is that if Smith had waited for three years to bring the entire suit, he could have asserted all of his claims, since the limitations period had not expired. But, once the suit has been commenced and the case approaches trial, fairness to the defendant and the need to expedite litigation may prevent the assertion of additional claims even though they would not be barred by the statute of limitations. In this case, the court's conclusion that Smith may not amend means that the omitted claim is lost.

23

Collateral Estoppel: Fine-Tuning the Preclusion Doctrine

Introduction

If law is a mysterious profession, it is partly because lawyers have such a knack for attaching intimidating names to relatively commonsense principles. Names such as "res judicata" and "collateral estoppel," for example; handles like these are enough to intimidate any client and most lawyers. But once you rub elbows with these related doctrines for a while, they will lose their power to intimidate, and you will recognize them for what they are, essential and sensible tools of the trade.

Although they serve related functions, these two tools are different in character. Res judicata acts like a bludgeon, indiscriminately smashing all efforts of a party to relitigate events that have already been litigated and decided in a prior suit. Collateral estoppel, by contrast, operates like a scalpel, dissecting a lawsuit into its various issues and surgically removing from reconsideration any that have been properly decided in a prior action.

Speaking less metaphorically, res judicata bars Smith from suing Jones for any kind of relief arising from a particular transaction or occurrence if Smith had previously brought an action against Jones based on that transaction or occurrence, and the prior action was decided on the merits. Restatement (Second) of Judgments §24 (1982).[1] Res judicata bars any relitigation

---

1. The discussion in this chapter is based on the principles of the Second Restatement of Judgments. These principles have been widely applied in the federal courts (see, e.g., *Montana v. United States*, 440 U.S. 147, 153, 162 (1979); *United States v. Stauffer Chemical Co.*, 464 U.S. 165, 171 (1984)) and have been increasingly adopted by state courts as well.

of Smith's rights against Jones based on those events, including not only the claims that Smith did raise the first time around but also any other claims arising out of the same set of facts that Smith could have raised (but did not) in the first action.

Collateral estoppel is more narrowly focused. It only precludes Smith from relitigating issues that were actually litigated and decided in a prior action with Jones. If an issue could have been raised in the first case but was not explicitly raised and decided, collateral estoppel will not bar Smith from litigating that issue in a subsequent action against Jones.

An example will help to distinguish the two. Smith sues Jones for trespass on her property. Jones defends on the ground that she holds an easement to enter on the land to cut firewood. The court concludes that the easement is valid and enters judgment for Jones. Res judicata would bar Smith from suing Jones again based on the same wood-cutting incident. For example, Smith could not bring a new action on the theory that an implied condition of the easement was that Jones pay fair value for the timber cut. Nor could she seek damages for property damage done to her land during the cutting. When Smith sues Jones for that occurrence, res judicata forces her to bring forth all claims she has arising from it in the original action, rather than plaguing Jones with successive suits based on the same incident but asserting new theories for recovery or different types of relief.

Collateral estoppel, by contrast, would bar Smith from relitigating specific issues decided in the first action, such as the validity of Jones's easement. If Jones returns to cut wood again on Smith's land and Smith sues, this second suit will not be barred by res judicata because she is not suing for the same incident as the original action. However, Smith will be collaterally estopped from trying again to prove that Jones's easement is invalid because that issue was litigated and decided in the original action. But Smith would be free to litigate other issues not resolved in the earlier action. For example, Smith could still claim in the later suit based on the second incident that an implied condition of the easement required payment for the timber. This issue would not be barred by collateral estoppel because it was not raised and decided in the first action.

At this point you may be asking, "Well, who needs collateral estoppel?" If res judicata so broadly precludes relitigation, whether or not an issue was previously raised, what is the need for a separate doctrine with another mysterious name?[2] The answer is that collateral estoppel is needed because issues already litigated may come up again in later litigation based on separate events. Smith's second action against Jones for the second wood-cutting incident would not be barred by res judicata since this is a new "claim" that has not been litigated before. See Restatement (Second) of Judgments §24

---

2. With *two* mysterious names, actually. Collateral estoppel is also frequently referred to as "issue preclusion," and res judicata as "claim preclusion."

(1982) (defining "claim" to include all rights arising out of a single transaction or occurrence). But the issue of whether Smith has an easement to cut timber will arise again in the new action. Collateral estoppel will preclude litigation of that issue even though res judicata is inapplicable.

This example shows that collateral estoppel is both broader and narrower than res judicata. It is narrower in that it does not preclude all possible issues that might have been raised in a prior action but only those actually decided in that action. But it is also broader in that it can foreclose litigation of a particular issue in an entirely new context. Once the validity of Jones's easement has been determined between the parties, estoppel may preclude either party from relitigating that issue in suits arising out of completely different underlying facts. Suppose, for example, that Jones went to cut wood again on Smith's property and was injured when she fell in an abandoned well. Under common law negligence principles, the duty of care Smith owed to her might depend on whether she was a trespasser. In her negligence action Jones could estop Smith from defending on the ground that Jones was a trespasser, since the prior suit determined that the easement allowed her to enter the property. Although the context is different in the second action (in fact, the original plaintiff is now the defendant), Jones's right to be on the land is at issue in both suits and there is no reason to allow Smith to relitigate it.

Prerequisites for Estoppel

Collateral estoppel is a flexible doctrine, which varies in its application from one jurisdiction to another. However, the basic prerequisites are fairly uniform. *First,* the issue in the second case must be the same as the issue in the first. In the example above, the issue in both suits is whether Jones has a legal right to enter upon Smith's property to cut wood. But if Smith sues Jones for breach of a contract made in June of 1988, and Jones is held to have been incompetent to make the contract because she was a minor, it does not follow that Jones was incompetent to make another contract in October of 1990. Here, the issues are not the same, and the resolution of one should not preclude litigation on the other.

Second, the issue must have been actually litigated. Restatement (Second) of Judgments §27 (1982). This requirement will obviously not be satisfied when a party failed to raise an issue in a previous action, such as Smith failing to assert a right to be paid for the wood Jones cut in the first suit. But an issue may not have been "actually litigated" even though it *was* raised in a prior action. Suppose, for example, that Smith sues Jones for breach of contract and Jones admits in her answer that she made the contract but defends the action on another ground. Under the Restatement view, Jones may defend a second suit for a later breach of the same contract on the ground that she never made the contract, since she never actually litigated that issue in the original suit.

> There are many reasons why a party may choose not to raise an issue, or to contest an assertion, in a particular action. The action may involve so small an amount that litigation of the issue may cost more than the value of the lawsuit. Or the forum may be an inconvenient one in which to produce the necessary evidence or in which to litigate at all. The interests of conserving judicial resources, of maintaining consistency, and of avoiding oppression or harassment of the adverse party are less compelling when the issue on which preclusion is sought has not actually been litigated before. And if preclusive effect were given to issues not litigated, the result might serve to discourage compromise, to decrease the likelihood that the issues in an action would be narrowed by stipulation, and thus to intensify litigation.

Restatement (Second) of Judgments §27, comment e (1982).

Third, even if an issue was litigated in a prior action, collateral estoppel will not bar relitigation unless the issue was actually decided in that action. Restatement (Second) of Judgments §27 (1982). Suppose, for example, that Smith sues Jones on copyright infringement and breach of contract theories, and the case goes to trial on both issues. If the court finds for Smith on the ground that Jones breached the contract, collateral estoppel will not bar relitigation of the copyright infringement issue in another context even though both sides fully presented their evidence on the copyright issue in the first case. The parties have fully litigated the issue, and it seems wasteful to have them relitigate it in another suit. However, it is a little hard to apply collateral estoppel without knowing which party to estop. Without a winner or loser on the copyright issue, the court in the later action has no choice but to rehear it.

Fourth, it is usually said that collateral estoppel will not apply unless the decision on the issue in the prior action was necessary to the court's judgment. Restatement (Second) of Judgments §27 (1982). This requirement of the doctrine has raised some problems of interpretation. Suppose, for example, that the court in Smith's copyright and contract action finds that Jones breached her contract with Smith *and* that she infringed Smith's copyright. Each issue has been actually litigated and actually decided, but the Restatement would deny collateral estoppel effect to either decision since it is impossible to tell which decision was necessary to the judgment:

> First, a determination in the alternative may not have been as carefully or rigorously considered as it would have been if it had been necessary to the result, and in that sense it has some of the characteristics of dicta. Second, and of critical importance, the losing party, although entitled to appeal from both determinations, might be dissuaded from doing so because of the likelihood that at least one of them would be upheld and the other not even reached. If she were to appeal solely for the purpose of avoiding the application of the

rule of issue preclusion, then the rule might be responsible for increasing the burdens of litigation on the parties and the courts rather than lightening those burdens.

Restatement (Second) of Judgments §27, comment i (1982). See *Halpern v. Schwartz,* 426 F.2d 102, 105-106 (2d Cir. 1970). However, this rationale has not been universally accepted; some courts have given collateral estoppel effect to *both* alternative determinations in these circumstances. See, e.g., *Winters v. Lavine,* 574 F.2d 46, 67 (2d Cir. 1978), in which the Second Circuit appeared to limit *Halpern* to bankruptcy cases. Other cases and commentators have suggested a flexible middle ground between these extremes, which would apply estoppel if the second court can determine from the record of the first that both holdings were given full consideration. See *Malloy v. Trombley,* 427 N.Y.S.2d 969 (1980); 18 Wright and Miller at §4421, p.208.

There are further wrinkles to the collateral estoppel doctrine. In particular, the issues of "offensive" use of estoppel and nonmutual estoppel, considered in *Parklane Hosiery Co., Inc. v. Shore,* 439 U.S. 322 (1979), add an additional level of complexity to the analysis, which is explored in the following chapter. For the moment, however, we will focus on the basics. In analyzing the following examples, assume that all actions are brought in federal court and that the "modern" Second Restatement principles of collateral estoppel apply.

EXAMPLES

First Principles

1.   Vanderbilt enters into a contract with Fisk for the delivery of five tons of coal per week to Vanderbilt's power plant, for the period from January 1985 to December 1990. In 1987 Vanderbilt sues Fisk for breach of contract. He claims that the coal delivered from March to August 1985 was "grade AB" rather than "first quality" coal, as required by the contract. Fisk denies the allegation that he delivered grade AB coal instead of first quality coal and prevails in a jury trial.

Subsequently, Vanderbilt again sues Fisk for breach of contract on the ground that the coal delivered between February and June 1988 was grade AB. Fisk denies the breach.
    a. Why is Vanderbilt's second suit not barred by res judicata?
    b. Does collateral estoppel bar relitigation of any issue decided in the first suit?

2.   Assume that Vanderbilt claims in the first suit that Fisk delivered grade AB coal from March to August of 1985, which did not comply with the contract specification for "first quality" coal. Fisk admits that he delivered grade AB coal during that period but defends on the ground that AB coal

satisfies the contract specification. The case is tried to a jury, which finds for Vanderbilt and awards him damages.

    a. Vanderbilt sues Fisk again for delivering grade AB coal from February to June 1988. Will collateral estoppel apply to any issue?

    b. If Vanderbilt sues for the second (1988) breach, could Fisk defend on the ground that the contract is void because the parties entered into it on the basis of a mutual mistake as to the type of coal to be delivered?

    c. Assume that in Vanderbilt's second action Fisk defends on the ground that AB coal satisfies the contract specifications. He offers expert testimony, not offered in the original action, that AB coal is universally accepted in the industry as "first quality" coal. Will the court bar him from relitigating the issue?

    d. Assume that Vanderbilt's second suit against Fisk is for delivering grade AB coal from September to December 1989. Fisk defends on the ground that Vanderbilt had agreed to an oral modification of the contract allowing delivery of grade AB coal due to a national shortage of "first quality" coal during those months. Will collateral estoppel bar Fisk from relying on this defense?

3.   Vanderbilt sues Fisk for breach of the coal delivery contract, claiming that Fisk delivered AB coal from March to August 1985. Fisk defends on the ground that the contract was invalid due to mutual mistake and, in the alternative, that AB coal complies with the contract specifications. The jury renders a general verdict[3] for Fisk.

    a. In 1989, Vanderbilt sues Fisk for a subsequent breach of the contract by delivering AB coal from February to June 1988. Fisk again defends on the ground that AB coal satisfies the contract specifications. Does collateral estoppel bar relitigation of this issue?

    b. Assume that in the original suit described in this example Vanderbilt moved for judgment as a matter of law on Fisk's mutual mistake defense, and the court granted the motion. The case went to the jury on the defense that AB coal was adequate under the contract, and the jury rendered a verdict for Fisk. Subsequently, Vanderbilt sues Fisk for the 1988 breach. Fisk raises the same defenses. May Fisk estop Vanderbilt from claiming that AB coal does not meet the contract specifications?

    c. On the preceding facts, may Vanderbilt bar Fisk from relitigating the mutual mistake defense?

    d. Assume that the case went to the jury on both defenses, and the jury rendered a verdict for Vanderbilt in the first suit. Now Vanderbilt sues for the second breach during 1988, and Fisk defends on the ground that the parties entered into the contract under a mutual mistake. May Vanderbilt estop Fisk from relitigating the issue of mutual mistake?

---

3. A general verdict is a simple verdict for the plaintiff or defendant without specifying the ground upon which the decision is based.

Isn't This Example in the Wrong Chapter?

4.   Morgan sues Gould for violation of the federal antitrust laws, in the federal district court for the Southern District of New York. Gould moves to dismiss for lack of personal jurisdiction. The court allows discovery on the jurisdictional issue, takes evidence on the issue at a hearing, hears oral argument, and subsequently denies the motion. Gould defaults on the merits, and Morgan gets judgment. Morgan then brings an action to enforce the judgment in Florida. Gould opposes enforcement of the judgment.

   a. Will collateral estoppel bar relitigation of the personal jurisdiction issue?

   b. Will collateral estoppel bar relitigation of the merits of the antitrust claim?

5.   Carnegie sues Astor in California for manufacturing a type of railroad engine in that state. Carnegie bases his suit on two claims. First, he alleges that he has a patent on the engine under the federal patent laws and that Astor is infringing his patent by building the engine without his permission. Second, he claims that Astor is violating California's unfair competition laws by using Carnegie's engine design. The case is tried to a jury, which renders a general verdict for Carnegie and awards him damages.

   Subsequently, Astor resumes making the same engines in Nevada, which (we will assume) has no unfair competition statute. Carnegie sues him for patent infringement. Does collateral estoppel bar relitigation of the infringement issue?

A Brainteaser with a Commonsense Answer

6.   Assume the same facts as example 5, except that Astor resumed making the engines in California. Carnegie sues him there again. He seeks to enjoin Astor from making the engines and argues that the decision in the prior suit establishes his right to the injunction. Will collateral estoppel bar Astor from relitigating the legality of his conduct?

7.   Assume that Carnegie's first suit against Astor was tried to the court rather than the jury and that the judge's written decision expressly finds that Astor is liable on both theories. Astor then begins production of the engines in Nevada, and Carnegie brings a second action against him there. Will collateral estoppel bar Astor from claiming that he has not infringed Carnegie's patent?

Mega-Hypo: Exercise for the Enthusiast

8.   The examples above illustrate particular issues in the application of collateral estoppel. Often, though, cases are not so conceptually clean; it is necessary to cull through a long procedural history and voluminous record to prove that the requirements of collateral estoppel are met. Indeed, it may take as much litigation to prove that the issue is precluded as it would to relitigate

it, thus undermining one of the policy reasons for allowing issue preclusion. For a taste of these complexities, try the following example.

Hill buys two identical blast furnaces from Villard. One of them explodes, and Hill sues Villard for his injuries. He asserts claims for negligent design, breach of warranty, and strict liability. He seeks compensatory damages on all three counts and punitive damages, which are only available on the negligence claim. Villard admits that he made the furnace but denies that the design was negligent. He admits that a warranty of fitness for its intended use arose upon the sale but denies that he breached the warranty. He also denies that he is strictly liable for injuries resulting from the furnace. In addition, he raises contributory negligence as a defense on the negligence claim (a complete defense under applicable law) and claims that Hill's negligence claim is barred by the statute of limitations. The judge dismisses the strict liability claim under Rule 12(b)(6), on the ground that the applicable law does not allow recovery on a strict liability theory. Villard moves for summary judgment on the statute of limitations defense, but the judge denies the motion. At trial Hill moves for judgment as a matter of law on the negligent design issue. The judge denies it. The jury returns a verdict for the plaintiff and awards compensatory and punitive damages.

Two weeks after the judgment in the original suit, the second furnace explodes, and Hill sues Villard on the same theories. What issues will be precluded in the second action?

EXPLANATIONS
First Principles

1a.   It is important at the outset to distinguish the relitigation of claims from the relitigation of issues. Res judicata only bars relitigation of the same claim, that is, the same transaction or occurrence that was the subject of the first suit. See Chapter 21, p.353. Vanderbilt is not seeking to relitigate his original claim for the breach of contract that took place in 1985. Rather, he is litigating a new claim for a later breach of the same contract. This second breach is not the same transaction or occurrence as the first, even though it involves the same contract. Indeed, since it had not occurred when Vanderbilt first sued Fisk, it obviously could not have been joined in the first action.

b. Collateral estoppel, in contrast to res judicata, precludes relitigation of issues in a second suit that have previously been litigated in a prior action. Even though the second suit is for a separate claim, so that res judicata does not apply, a subsequent suit may involve issues already settled in an earlier suit between them. If so, it makes no sense to allow the same parties to relitigate those issues.

However, the first prerequisite for collateral estoppel is that the issues in the two suits must be the same. Therefore, analysis of collateral estoppel issues should always begin with a determination of what was decided in the first action. In this case the issue in the first suit was whether Fisk had delivered first quality coal from March to August 1985. The issue in the second suit was whether Fisk delivered first quality coal during a subsequent period. This is a different factual issue, which was not raised in the prior suit and must be litigated in the new one.

2a. The issue in the first suit was not whether Fisk actually delivered AB coal (he admits that he did), but whether AB coal was insufficient under the contract specifications. Since this was the basis for Vanderbilt's claim that Fisk breached the contract, and the jury found for Vanderbilt, they must have concluded that AB coal did not satisfy the specifications. Since that issue was litigated and decided in the first suit, the court in Vanderbilt's second action for a later breach will estop Fisk from defending the second suit on the ground that AB coal satisfies the specifications. Here, although the issue arises in the second suit on a claim resulting from a new transaction or occurrence (and thus would not be barred by res judicata), it will be barred by collateral estoppel since the issue was previously litigated and decided between the parties.

b. As indicated above, the issue that was raised and decided in the first suit was whether AB coal satisfied the contract specifications. Although the separate defense of mutual mistake at the time of entering into the contract was available to Fisk in the prior action, he failed to raise it. However, collateral estoppel does not bar him from doing so later in a second suit for a new breach of the contract. Collateral estoppel only bars issues that were litigated and decided in the prior action; it does not affect claims or defenses that *could have been* raised but were not.

Compare res judicata doctrine, which bars litigation of any issues that could have been raised in a prior suit on the same claim. Res judicata does not apply in this hypothetical because Vanderbilt's second suit is for a separate claim, the 1988 breach.

c. Essentially, Fisk's position here is that he should be able to relitigate the AB coal issue because, while he failed to prove his defense the first time, he can prove it now. This argument will fall on deaf ears. This testimony could presumably have been offered in the original suit and should have been. There is no reason why preclusion should operate against parties who litigated carefully the first time around but not against those who did not. Nor is there a requirement that the original finding has to be "right" to preclude relitigation. If that were true, the second court would have to rehear the issue to decide whether it was correctly decided the first time, thus completely undermining the purpose of the doctrine itself.

In limited situations, a party who discovers new evidence on an issue may move for relief from judgment under Fed. R. Civ. P. 60(b)(2). Under this rule, Fisk could seek to reopen the *original* action and overturn the finding that AB coal was insufficient. If he succeeded, of course, that original finding would no longer be entitled to collateral estoppel effect in subsequent suits.[4]

d. In this case the original finding that AB coal did not comply with the specifications could not be relitigated. However, Fisk's defense is not that AB coal is sufficient under the original contract but that a subsequent modification of the contract allows him to deliver AB coal. This is a new issue, which was not raised in the original action, has never been litigated or decided, and is available to Fisk as a defense to the new action.

3a. Collateral estoppel does not apply unless the issue was decided in the prior suit. In this case Fisk raised two defenses to Vanderbilt's first claim. If the jury accepted either defense, they would have had to find for Fisk. Obviously, they did accept one of those defenses, but it is impossible to tell from the jury's general verdict for Fisk which one it was. When a case is submitted to a jury with a general verdict form, the jury is simply asked to find for the plaintiff or for the defendant (and if it finds for the plaintiff, to find the amount of the plaintiff's damages). In this case, the jury's general finding "for the defendant" does not indicate whether it found the contract void or, alternatively, that AB coal complied with the specifications. Because it is impossible to tell which issue was decided, Fisk will not be able to demonstrate that the issue of whether the coal was sufficient was actually decided or necessary to the judgment. Consequently, collateral estoppel will not bar relitigation of that issue.

b. The result here is different because the procedural history of the suit clearly indicates what issues were decided. The judge's entry of judgment as a matter of law for Vanderbilt on the mutual mistake defense is a decision on that issue; it constitutes a finding that on the evidence produced by the parties no reasonable jury could find for Fisk on that issue. Thus, that issue was actually litigated and decided in Vanderbilt's favor. That left only one defense, that the AB coal complied with the contract specifications. The jury's verdict for Fisk must have been based on this defense.

In this case, therefore, unlike example 3a, it is clear that the AB coal issue was decided in Fisk's favor in the previous action and that it was the basis for the jury's verdict for Fisk. Consequently, Vanderbilt will be estopped from relitigating that issue; the court will grant judgment for Fisk if Vanderbilt

---

4. Fisk will have an uphill fight in obtaining relief from judgment under Rule 60(b)(2), which only allows the court to reopen the suit due to newly discovered evidence within one year after judgment. In addition, the moving party on such a motion must show that the new evidence could not have been discovered in the exercise of due diligence in time for presentation at the original trial.

In a few cases, courts have refused to apply collateral estoppel because new scientific evidence on a complex issue has been developed since the prior action. See Madden, Issue Preclusion in Products Liability, 11 Pace L. Rev. 87, 117 (1990) (describing several complex medical causation cases which refused estoppel on this ground).

sues him for damages on the ground that the coal was inadequate under the contract.

As this example indicates, collateral estoppel can work for either party. In example 2a, Vanderbilt used it to establish an issue crucial to obtaining relief. In this case Fisk uses it to establish a defense that had been previously litigated and decided in his favor.

c. If Fisk raises the defense of mutual mistake again, Vanderbilt will argue that he is estopped from relitigating the issue since it was litigated and decided adversely to Fisk in the first suit. Unfortunately for Vanderbilt, this will not work, since the finding for Vanderbilt that there was no mutual mistake was not necessary to support the original judgment. That judgment was for Fisk and was based on the jury's finding that Fisk had proved his defense that AB coal was adequate under the contract. Vanderbilt lost even though the contract was valid because the AB coal complied with it. Presumably, the court could have reached the result it did without even reaching the mutual mistake issue. Thus, although the mistake issue was litigated and decided, the court will deny collateral estoppel effect to the prior decision since it was not essential to the decision of the case.

Although this seems artificial, consider Fisk's point of view. Even if he believes that the court wrongly decided the mistake issue, he has no incentive to appeal since he won the verdict. If he did appeal for fear of the potential collateral estoppel effect of the decision on the mutual mistake issue, the appellate court would probably refuse to hear the appeal since Fisk won below and review of the mutual mistake issue would therefore serve no purpose. In a sense, then, there has been no final decision on the issue; Fisk should not be estopped by a potentially erroneous decision that he has no opportunity or incentive to correct.

d. Here, Vanderbilt may invoke collateral estoppel to bar Fisk from relitigating the mutual mistake issue. In this example Fisk raised two defenses in the first suit. If the jury accepted either one they would have found for Fisk. Because they found for Vanderbilt, they must have considered each of the defenses and concluded that Fisk had not proved either one. In addition, the decision on each defense was necessary to the judgment since they had to consider and reject each defense raised by Fisk in order to find for Vanderbilt: If the jury had found either a mutual mistake in making the contract or that AB coal was sufficient, Fisk would have won.

Isn't This Example in the Wrong Chapter?

4a. This situation should sound familiar: It echoes example 5 from Chapter 3. If you look at that example, you will see that the defendant was barred from relitigating whether the rendering court had personal jurisdiction over him or not because he had already raised and litigated that issue in the rendering court. Now it should be clear to you that this result is a straightforward application of collateral estoppel principles: The personal jurisdiction issue was raised, litigated, and decided in the original action and was necessary to the judgment as well, since the court would not have entered judgment for Morgan if it had concluded that it lacked jurisdiction over Gould. Thus, all the requirements for collateral estoppel are met, and Gould will be barred from relitigating the issue.

Note that in this case Morgan invokes collateral estoppel on an issue that has nothing to do with the merits of the lawsuit, indeed, in a situation where the merits were never litigated at all. But a decision "on the merits" of the plaintiff's substantive claim is not necessary before collateral estoppel applies: So long as the particular issue, be it procedural or substantive, was litigated and decided and necessary to the judgment, issue preclusion will bar it from being raised again. This result makes good sense. Gould should not be allowed to relitigate the personal jurisdiction question if it has been fully and fairly decided in another court.

Distinguish res judicata, however. That doctrine only bars relitigation of *claims* once they have been decided on the merits. When a case is dismissed on procedural grounds, the merits have never been litigated, and the plaintiff may sue again in a court that can properly reach the merits.

b. Collateral estoppel will not bar relitigation of the merits since the case was not litigated on the merits in the original suit. However, res judicata will bar Gould from litigating the merits. A default judgment is entitled to res judicata effect, and (unlike collateral estoppel) there is no requirement that claims have been "actually litigated" for res judicata to attach.

5.   Carnegie will have to relitigate the patent infringement issue. Although he won the first suit, it is impossible to tell from the general verdict which claim prevailed before the jury. Thus, both the "actually decided" and "necessary to the judgment" requirements are not clearly met.

Because a general verdict obscures the basis of the jury's decision, one or both of the parties may want to request use of a special verdict form, under Fed. R. Civ. P. 49, if they foresee the possibility of future litigation involving the same issues. A special verdict asks the jury to make findings on particular issues, rather than finding generally for the plaintiff or defendant. See Friedenthal, Kane, and Miller at §12.1. In this case, for example, the jury could be asked specifically whether they find that Astor infringed Carnegie's patent and whether they find that he violated California's unfair competition laws. If they answer "yes" on the patent infringement issue but "no" on the unfair competition issue, then it would be possible to prove in subsequent actions that the patent question was actually decided and necessary to the decision of the original suit.

The situation would be different if Carnegie had lost the first case. Then it would be clear — even with a general verdict — that the jury had rejected both Carnegie's theories, and collateral estoppel could prevent relitigation of either.

A Brainteaser with a Commonsense Answer

6. At first glance, it seems that the answer here ought to be "no" in light of the answer to example 5. It is unclear whether the jury in the first suit found for Carnegie on the patent claim or the unfair competition claim. However, it is clear that they found that Astor's conduct infringed on Carnegie's rights on one ground or the other. This should be sufficient to preclude relitigation in some contexts, at least. Carnegie may invoke collateral estoppel to bar relitigation of Astor's right to make the engines, on the ground that the original judgment necessarily decided that he had no right to do so. The court may not need to decide which of Carnegie's theories the jury accepted in the first action; it may be enough to support the injunction that they accepted one.

However, if Carnegie seeks damages from Astor in the second suit, it may not be possible for him to rely on the previous judgment. If the measure of damages under the two claims differs, it will be necessary to determine which theory of liability applies in order to assess the damages. Because Carnegie can only show that the first suit determined that Astor was barred from making the engines, but not which theory that determination was based on, the jury in a second damage action would have to decide anew whether Astor is liable and, if so, on which ground.

7. This example raises the "alternative holdings" problem discussed in the Introduction. The judge's opinion leaves no doubt that both the patent and unfair competition issues were actually litigated and decided. However, there is a problem as to whether either is "necessary to the judgment" when each is sufficient to support the judgment: Presumably, if either of the alternative holdings had been left out, the outcome would have been the same anyway, based on the other ground.

The Second Restatement of Judgments takes the position that neither holding is entitled to preclusive effect because it is impossible to tell whether each received full consideration and because the losing party has no incentive to appeal on one arguably incorrect ground if the other would support the judgment. As indicated in the Introduction, however, some courts take the exact opposite view, that *both* holdings are entitled to collateral estoppel effect.

Mega-Hypo: Exercise for the Enthusiast

8. This is not a particularly unusual scenario for a products liability action, yet it takes some doing to unravel the procedural history and ascertain whether any issues will be barred in the second suit.

A good place to start is to determine what issues were decided in the original action. Villard admitted that he made the furnace and that a warranty of fitness for use arose upon the sale. However, as the Introduction points out, these admissions do not satisfy the "actually litigated" requirement for collateral estoppel purposes.

The denial of the motion for summary judgment on the limitations issue does not "actually decide" that issue; it simply indicates that both parties have some evidence on that issue and therefore ought to have the opportunity to go to trial on it. See Chapter 18, p.294. Similarly, the denial of the motion for judgment as a matter of law on negligent design does not satisfy the requirement that the issue be "actually decided." That denial simply indicates that there is enough evidence to support a rational verdict for Villard, the nonmoving party, on that issue.

By contrast, the judge's dismissal of the strict liability claim clearly indicates that he decided as a matter of law that there is no strict liability claim arising out of the sale. A dismissal under Rule 12(b)(6) is a decision "on the merits" that may bar future litigation on the same issue.

How about the verdict; can we discern what the jury actually decided in reaching their verdict for Hill? The case went to trial on breach of warranty and negligence (but not on strict liability since the judge dismissed that claim), and the jury's general verdict does not expressly indicate whether the jury found for Hill on one or both theories. However, the jury awarded punitive damages, which were only available on the negligent design claim. Thus, the jury must have found for Hill on that claim. And in order to do so it must have rejected the defense that the negligence claim is barred by the statute of limitations and that Hill's contributory negligence bars relief.

The jury *may* have also found for Hill on the breach of warranty claim, but we can't tell, since compensatory damages are available on both theories. Even if the jury found for Hill on both theories, it would only award him his actual losses as compensatory damages. Thus, the amount of the compensatory damages does not reveal whether the jury accepted both theories or only one.

We have identified four issues as actually litigated and decided: whether the statute of limitations barred the negligence claim, whether Hill's contributory negligence barred the negligence claim, whether the furnace was negligently designed, and whether Villard is strictly liable for the injuries resulting from the explosion. The first three were necessary to the judgment since the injury could not have found for Hill on the negligence claim without rejecting the statute of limitations and contributory negligence defenses and finding that the design was negligent. The dismissal of the strict liability claim is not necessary to the judgment, however, and Hill should be able to relitigate it in the second suit. After all, he *won* the first action on other grounds, so he had no incentive to appeal the dismissal of his strict liability claim.

Only three issues, then, satisfy the prerequisites. But two of those, the statute of limitations and contributory negligence issues, are not likely to be the same in the two suits since the two explosions took place at different times and perhaps under different circumstances.[5] Only the negligent design issue remains. That issue will presumably be the same since the two furnaces are identical.

Even though Hill will have to go through all of that to invoke collateral estoppel, he will still have a strong incentive to do so. If he can get the judge to travel this long road, at the end of it he will have established an issue crucial to his right to relief, without relitigating the merits of that issue and without the risk of losing on it before the second jury. For Hill, the value of invoking collateral estoppel is not merely to save litigation time, but to assure the same favorable result he obtained in the first suit. Ironically, he may be willing to spend as much litigation time to obtain that result as it would take to try the issue again.

---

5. In some circumstances, the contributory negligence issue might be the same, so that the rejection of the defense in the first action would bar Villard from asserting it in the second. Suppose, for example, that Hill installed the two furnaces in the same way at the same time, and Villard claimed in the first suit that inadequate installation contributed to the explosion. On those facts the issue would be the same in the second suit, and Villard would be barred by collateral estoppel from raising the defense again. But Hill would still have to prove that the furnaces *were* installed in the same way in order to support estoppel.

24

The Obscure Kingdom: Nonmutual Collateral Estoppel

Introduction

We began this journey at the beginning (see p.3), and we should end at the end . . . but nothing is quite that simple in civil procedure. A lawsuit "ends" when a final judgment is entered or an appeal of the trial court judgment is decided. But the suit may send out waves that break on very distant shores. Under collateral estoppel doctrine, issues decided in one lawsuit may have effects in another suit between the parties at a later time or in a different court. And, beyond this fairly well-mapped terrain lies the more obscure kingdom of nonmutual collateral estoppel.

Under traditional issue preclusion principles, a party may be estopped from relitigating an issue that he had litigated in a prior suit and lost. Restatement (Second) of Judgments §27 (1982); Chapter 23, p.382. Assume, for example, that Cartier sues La Salle, a tenant in his shopping center, for breach of a provision in the standard lease signed by all Cartier's tenants. If the court finds that the lease provision is invalid, La Salle may estop Cartier in a future suit involving the same lease from claiming that the disputed provision is enforceable. Conversely, if the provision had been held valid, Cartier could estop La Salle from defending a future action based on the same lease on the ground that the provision was invalid.

Nonmutual collateral estoppel goes a step beyond this basic doctrine by allowing a new party to invoke collateral estoppel against a party who litigated and lost on an issue in a prior action. Suppose, for example, that Cartier, after losing his suit against La Salle on the ground that the lease provision was unenforceable, sues Cortez, another tenant who had signed the same standard lease. Under nonmutual preclusion principles, Cortez, the new defendant, could estop Cartier from claiming that the disputed provision was enforceable, since Cartier had previously litigated that issue against La Salle and lost.

For many years, this frontier concept remained, if not undiscovered, at least unexplored by most courts. The general rule was that estoppels must be mutual, that is, the only parties who could invoke collateral estoppel were those who were involved in the suit in which the issue was initially decided. This "doctrine of mutuality" allowed La Salle to estop Cartier on the issue of the validity of the lease provision but would not allow Cortez, a stranger to the first suit, to do so. The courts reasoned that La Salle had litigated in the first action; he took the risk that, if he lost on the issue, he would be bound by that finding in subsequent suits, under basic collateral estoppel doctrine, and therefore he — and only he — had earned the right to assert estoppel if he won. But Cortez was not a party to the first action; he took no risk of being bound by an adverse judgment if Cartier proved that the lease provision *was* valid. Consequently, since he would not be bound by an unfavorable finding, the mutuality doctrine barred Cortez from taking advantage of a favorable finding in the La Salle/Cartier suit.

A Fundamental Question

1.   Why is it true, whether or not the mutuality rule applies, that Cortez could not be bound by a finding in the original suit that the lease provision was valid?

Courts that applied the mutuality rule were also influenced by an additional reason in confining estoppel to the original parties. If the litigants know that findings will only affect other suits with the same adversaries, they can usually anticipate the future implications of an adverse decision in the original suit. However, if estoppel is available to new parties, the litigants may be forced to over-litigate issues in the original action for fear of unknown risks of estoppel in future actions involving new parties.

While the mutuality rule has had a respectable history and widespread acceptance, it has been abandoned in many jurisdictions since the landmark case of *Bernhard v. Bank of America National Trust & Savings Assn.,* 122 P.2d 892 (Cal. 1942). In *Bernhard,* Mrs. Bernhard claimed that certain funds held by Cook, the executor of an estate, belonged to the estate. Cook claimed they were a gift to him from the decedent, which he need not include in the assets of the estate. Bernhard challenged Cook's claim in a probate proceeding during the course of the settlement of the estate, and the court held that the funds were a gift to Cook. Bernhard then sued the bank that had been holding the funds and paid them to Cook, alleging again that the funds were assets of the estate that should have been paid to the estate rather than to Cook.

The bank pleaded collateral estoppel, arguing that Bernhard had already adjudicated the right to the funds in the probate proceeding, had lost, and should be precluded from relitigating the issue against the bank.

Who's Who?

2.   Why was the bank's invocation of collateral estoppel in *Bernhard* "non-mutual"?

In *Bernhard,* Justice Traynor concluded that it was not categorically improper to allow a new party to take advantage of findings in an earlier suit to estop a party who had litigated the issue in the prior action. Instead of focusing on the "free ride" that the bank received by borrowing the favorable result achieved by Cook in the earlier case, Justice Traynor emphasized the fact that Bernhard, the party *against* whom the estoppel was asserted, had been a party to the first action and had had a full and fair opportunity to litigate the issue there. *Bernhard* at 895. In such circumstances, the court saw no reason to allow her to relitigate the decided issue by simply switching adversaries.

The United States Supreme Court first endorsed the use of nonmutual estoppel in the federal courts in *Blonder-Tongue Laboratories, Inc. v. University of Illinois Foundation,* 402 U.S. 313 (1971). The situation in *Blonder-Tongue* was analogous to *Bernhard.* The University of Illinois Foundation sued one defendant for infringing a patent but lost on the ground that its patent was invalid. It then "switched adversaries," bringing suit against another defendant for infringement of the same patent. The Supreme Court reversed its long-standing rule allowing such relitigation and approved use of nonmutual collateral estoppel against the university on the issue of the validity of the patent. The Court noted the unfairness and waste of judicial resources that flows from allowing "repeated litigation of the same issue as long as the supply of unrelated defendants holds out." *Blonder-Tongue* at 329.

Like the *Bernhard* court, the Court in *Blonder-Tongue* emphasized that preclusion was only appropriate if the precluded party had had a full and fair opportunity to litigate the issue in the first action. *Blonder-Tongue* at 332-334. In addition, the Court emphasized the unique burdens that patent infringement actions impose on the courts. However, the lower federal courts have not construed the Court's holding as limited to patent cases.

Subsequent cases have applied nonmutual collateral estoppel in a wide variety of cases, at least when the posture of the parties in the successive actions is similar to that of the parties in *Blonder-Tongue* and *Bernhard*. See generally 18 Wright and Miller at §4464.

Defensive Nonmutual Estoppel

This matter of the posture of the parties introduces a further wrinkle to the nonmutual preclusion problem. In both *Blonder-Tongue* and *Bernhard*, the new party in the second action was a defendant who invoked estoppel to prevent the plaintiff from establishing a fact that the plaintiff had been unable to establish in the first suit. Bernhard, for example, had essentially been a plaintiff in the first probate proceeding, trying to establish the estate's right to the funds held by Cook. In the second action, she was again the plaintiff, attempting to prove the same issue in order to recover from the bank. The bank asserted estoppel "defensively," to prevent her from proving an essential element of her claim. Similarly, in *Blonder-Tongue,* the university foundation had brought the first suit and lost and was also the plaintiff in the second suit. The new defendant asserted defensive nonmutual estoppel to prevent the foundation from establishing the validity of a patent previously held invalid. See *Parklane Hosiery v. Shore,* 439 U.S. 322, 326 n.4 (1979) ("[d]efensive use occurs when a defendant seeks to prevent a plaintiff from asserting a claim the plaintiff has previously litigated and lost against another defendant"). This use of estoppel is "nonmutual" because the party asserting the estoppel on the issue was not a party to the action in which the issue was first litigated. Visually the sequence looks like this:

Suit 1:   P————————→ D$_1$ (plaintiff loses on Issue A)

Suit 2:   P————————→ D$_2$ (new defendant pleads collateral estoppel to bar plaintiff from relitigating Issue A)

This defensive assertion of nonmutual estoppel is more easily justified than the offensive use of estoppel discussed in *Parklane.* In defensive estoppel cases, the party being estopped was usually the plaintiff in the original suit and chose the forum and the defendant against whom to initially litigate the issue. When that is true, it hardly seems unfair to bind the plaintiff to the first resolution of the recurring issue.

Offensive Nonmutual Estoppel

By contrast, offensive use of collateral estoppel usually involves a new plaintiff who seeks to borrow a finding from a prior action to impose liability on a party who was a defendant in the prior action. See *Parklane* at 326 n.4 ("offensive use of collateral estoppel occurs when the plaintiff seeks to foreclose the defendant from litigating an issue the defendant has previously litigated unsuccessfully in an action with another party"). For example, suppose that La Salle had brought suit against Cartier to enjoin him from enforcing the disputed provision of the standard lease, and the provision was held invalid. If Cortez now sued Cartier for damages resulting from the invalid provision and invoked collateral estoppel to prevent Cartier from relitigating the validity of the provision, that would be offensive, nonmutual estoppel. The new plaintiff, Cortez, would be taking advantage of the finding against Cartier, a defendant in the prior action, to establish a claim against Cartier in a new suit.

This is exactly what the plaintiff did in *Parklane*. In the first case to go to judgment, the Securities and Exchange Commission had claimed — and the court had held — that Parklane Hosiery had issued a false and misleading proxy statement. Subsequently, the plaintiffs in a class action suit against Parklane, based on the same proxy statement, invoked collateral estoppel against Parklane on the question of whether the statement was false and misleading. Since Parklane had litigated and lost that issue in the S.E.C. suit, the class plaintiffs argued that it had had its day in court on the issue and should be barred from relitigating it. The plaintiffs' use of estoppel was "offensive," since they sought to use it to establish the defendant's liability in a new action. It was nonmutual, because they were not parties to the action in which the issue was first litigated. The sequence of suits looks like this:

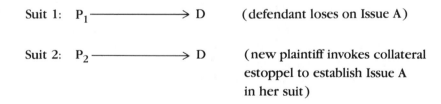

In these offensive nonmutual estoppel situations, there are a number of reasons for the courts to exercise particular caution in deciding whether to apply nonmutual collateral estoppel. For one thing, the party against whom estoppel is asserted in the second action (i.e., Parklane in the *Parklane* case and Cartier in the preceding example) was a defendant in the first suit and did not choose the forum in which the issue was initially decided. While it is possible to say that the losing party in a defensive-use situation gave it his best shot in the original action, this is not so clear in the offensive-use situation, in which the estopped party did not choose the time and place of the first suit or the adversary against whom to try the issue.

The Supreme Court in *Parklane* noted several other risks posed by offensive use of estoppel. *First,* the prospect of taking advantage of another plaintiff's victory to establish crucial issues without trial may lead plaintiffs to "wait and see," that is, to hold back from joining in the first plaintiff's suit. After all, if La Salle lost the first action against Cartier because the lease provision was held valid, Cortez would not be barred from relitigating the issue because he has never litigated it, and no party can be estopped until he (or someone in privity with him) has had his day in court on the issue. But if La Salle wins and the court recognizes nonmutual collateral estoppel, Cortez may be able to establish this crucial issue without trial and the resulting risk of losing on the issue altogether.

Second, the *Parklane* Court recognized that a party might not have litigated the issue aggressively in the first action if the stakes were small or the forum inconvenient. It may be inappropriate to apply estoppel in a second suit if the estopped party did not have the incentive to litigate the issue fully in the first. *Third,* the Court noted that it may not have been possible for the losing party to litigate effectively in the first action if the procedural rules of the court that decided the first case were more restrictive than those of the court hearing the second.[1] *Last,* one or more prior inconsistent judgments on the issue may suggest that it would be unfair to give conclusive effect to any one of them.

In *Parklane* the Supreme Court did not categorically endorse or reject offensive nonmutual collateral estoppel. As modern courts are wont to do, the Court held that lower courts should exercise discretion in deciding whether to allow such offensive assertions of estoppel. The court should consider, on the unique facts of each case, all the factors described above and any other factors that may indicate that the issue was not fully and fairly decided in the first suit. If, considering all the circumstances, the court is convinced that the issue was fully adjudicated in the first action, then it may allow preclusion, including offensive nonmutual estoppel. If, on the other hand, the court is doubtful, for whatever reason, that the party being es-

---

1. This could be true in a number of ways. For example, the second court's civil procedure rules might allow broader discovery. The rules of evidence might allow crucial evidence that was excluded in the first case. The long-arm statute might authorize personal jurisdiction over defendants who could not be brought into the first case. Or the rules governing the subpoena power might authorize the court to order the appearance of witnesses from a broader area.

topped had a full "bite at the apple" in the first action, it should deny estoppel.[2]

Although the *Parklane* case goes into more detail than *Blonder-Tongue* concerning the risks of nonmutual collateral estoppel, the two cases are entirely consistent. The Court in *Blonder-Tongue* emphasized that the court in the second action must be convinced that the estopped party had a full opportunity to litigate the issue in the first case. *Parklane* emphasizes the same fundamental prerequisite but spells out in more detail the factors to be considered in making that determination. In fact, most of the cautionary factors discussed in *Parklane* are equally applicable to defensive use situations, such as whether the estopped party had a strong incentive to litigate in the first suit, whether the procedural opportunities to do so were as broad in that action, and whether there are any prior inconsistent judgments. Other factors, however, such as whether the plaintiff should have joined in an earlier action, are unique to offensive estoppel.

Let me end this introduction with a truism. Nonmutual collateral estoppel, whether of the offensive or defensive persuasion, *is* a form of collateral estoppel. As such, it must meet all of the basic prerequisites for application of estoppel discussed in the last chapter. In every case, mutual or nonmutual, the court must find that the issue is the same, that it was actually litigated and decided in the prior action, and that it was necessary to the judgment in the first action before it can apply estoppel in a second action. However, in nonmutual preclusion situations, the court must consider not only these basic requirements for estoppel but also the additional factors discussed above in order to determine whether it would be fair to preclude relitigation of findings from the prior action in a new suit involving a new party.

In analyzing the following examples, assume that contributory negligence constitutes a complete defense if it is proved. Also, assume that all actions are brought in state court unless otherwise specified.

---

2. When the Supreme Court takes cases in which to adopt a new principle, they often take ones that present good facts for application of the new principle. *Parklane* is an example. On the facts of the case, all of the factors the court discussed argued for estoppel: there were no prior inconsistent judgments; the procedural opportunities available in the two cases were the same, since both were filed in federal court; and the plaintiffs in the second action could not have joined in the first, since private litigants are not able to join in securities actions brought by the government. See *Parklane* at 332 n.17. Finally, Parklane had every incentive to litigate aggressively in the first suit: Corporations can expect shareholder suits in the wake of a government action for securities violations, and in this case the class action against Parklane was filed *before* the government's suit, though the latter went to judgment first.

EXAMPLES

Charting the Terrain

3.   Lewis sues Clark for trespassing on his property. Clark denies that Lewis owns the land. The court determines that Lewis owns the land and awards him damages for the trespass.

Subsequently, Lewis sues Fremont for trespass on the same piece of land.

a. Who would be likely to invoke collateral estoppel in the second action?
b. Would estoppel be allowed in a mutuality jurisdiction?
c. Would estoppel be allowed in a jurisdiction that allows nonmutual estoppel?

4.   Suppose that Lewis sued Clark for the trespass, and the court found for Clark on the ground that Lewis does not own the land. Subsequently, Lewis sues Fremont for trespassing on the same property.

a. Who would be likely to invoke collateral estoppel?
b. Would this be mutual or nonmutual use of collateral estoppel?
c. Would it be defensive or offensive use of estoppel?
d. Could the court apply collateral estoppel in the second suit if the suits were brought in a jurisdiction that has abandoned the mutuality doctrine?

5.   Earhart brings a negligence action against Lindbergh for serious injuries suffered when a plane Lindbergh was piloting crashed. The jury finds for Earhart and awards her damages. Subsequently, Wright, another passenger in Lindbergh's plane, brings a separate action against Lindbergh for his injuries in the same accident. Wright invokes collateral estoppel to prevent Lindbergh from relitigating the issue of his negligence.

a. Is this offensive or defensive collateral estoppel?
b. Is it mutual or nonmutual?
c. Could the court apply collateral estoppel in the second action if both suits were brought in federal court?

New Frontiers

6.   Mr. and Mrs. Byrd sue Da Gama for serious injuries suffered in a collision involving three cars: the Byrds', Da Gama's, and Vespucci's. Da Gama pleads contributory negligence as a defense against Mr. Byrd, who was driving the Byrd car, but not against Mrs. Byrd. The jury returns a verdict for Da Gama on Mr. Byrd's claim but for Mrs. Byrd on her claim for her own injuries.

Mr. Byrd now sues Vespucci, the third driver involved in the collision, to recover for injuries. Vespucci pleads contributory negligence.

    a. Who would seek to invoke collateral estoppel in the second action? On what issue?

    b. Would this be offensive or defensive use?

    c. Would it be permissible in a jurisdiction that requires mutuality?

    d. Would it be permissible in a jurisdiction that has abandoned the mutuality doctrine?

7.   In 1981 Carol Burnett brought a libel suit in California against the *National Enquirer*, arising out of a story in the *Enquirer* about her behavior in a Washington restaurant. One of the *Enquirer*'s defenses was that it had printed a retraction of the story; under a California statute a newspaper can avoid substantial liability by printing a timely retraction. See Cal. Civ. Proc. Code §48(a) (West 1982). A major issue in the case was whether the *Enquirer* was a newspaper, which enjoys the protection of the statute, or a magazine, which would not. The court held that the *Enquirer* was a magazine and thus not entitled to the protection of the retraction statute. Burnett recovered a very substantial verdict.

The *Boston Globe* reported the verdict in a story on March 27, 1981, and went on to state:

> Burnett's case has been watched closely by other celebrities who have sued, or want to sue, the tabloid and other gossip publications over items they consider fiction and harmful to their careers.
> Singer Helen Reddy and her manager-husband Jeff Wald were the most recent to sue the *National Enquirer*, asking $30 million this week for a March 3 article about them.

Boston Globe, March 27, 1981, p.4.

Assume that the *Enquirer* printed a similar retraction of the Reddy/Wald article. After the decision in the Burnett case, Reddy and Wald bring suit against the *Enquirer*, and assert collateral estoppel on the issue of whether the *Enquirer* is a magazine or a newspaper.

    a. Would this be offensive or defensive use of estoppel?

    b. Would this be allowed if both actions were brought in courts that applied the mutuality doctrine?

    c. Would it be allowed if both suits were brought in courts that have abandoned the mutuality approach?

Outer Space

8.   Armstrong sues Ride and Gagarin in federal court for injuries arising out of a three-car auto accident. Each defendant denies negligence and claims that Armstrong was negligent. After trial, the jury finds for Armstrong against Ride but finds Gagarin not liable.

Subsequently, Gagarin sues Ride for his injuries in the accident. Ride pleads contributory negligence. Visually, the two cases look like this:

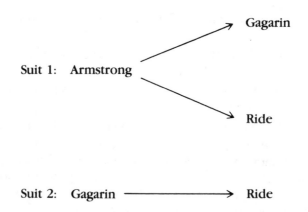

a. Could Gagarin have joined his claim against Ride in the first suit?
b. Who would seek to invoke collateral estoppel in the second action? On what issues?
c. Is this mutual or nonmutual estoppel?
d. Which party would invoke defensive estoppel and which would invoke offensive estoppel?
e. Will the court allow use of estoppel on any issues?

EXPLANATIONS

A Fundamental Question

1.   We began this voyage by emphasizing that every litigant is entitled to due process of law before a court adjudicates his rights. See Chapter 1, p.3. The very essence of due process is an opportunity for the parties to be heard, to litigate the issues before those issues are resolved for or against them. If Cartier won his suit against La Salle and then sued Cortez for violating the same lease provision, Cortez would be a new party who has never had an opportunity to litigate the validity of the provision. It would come as quite a surprise to Cortez to learn that he had effectively lost his action (because the crucial issue was already decided in Cartier's favor) before he had even reached the courthouse, simply because La Salle had previously lost his suit. Cortez may well believe that he can litigate the lease question more effectively than La Salle, who may not have had the resources to litigate the issue aggressively or may have made a tactical decision to focus his defense on other grounds. Maybe Cortez won't do better but under the due process clause every party gets one chance to try, and Cortez has not yet had his "bite at the apple."

Although it would promote efficiency to estop Cortez from relitigating decided issues (just as it promotes efficiency to bar La Salle from doing so under traditional estoppel doctrine), efficiency is only one goal of the procedural system. In this case it is outweighed by the countervailing value of fairness to new parties.

Who's Who?

2. The *Bernhard* case is an example of nonmutual collateral estoppel because the party seeking to invoke estoppel was not a party to the suit in which the issue was initially decided. That action was between the heirs (including Bernhard) and Cook. Under mutuality doctrine, only they could assert estoppel in subsequent cases; the bank, a new party, is unable to assert estoppel because it was not a party to the original suit and hence took no risk of being estopped on the issue if it were decided in Bernhard's favor. Since the bank could not be burdened by the result in the original case (see the explanation above for example 1), courts that adhered to the mutuality rule concluded that it should not be able to benefit from the prior decision if Bernhard lost.

Charting the Terrain

3a. The issue that is common to both actions is whether Lewis owns the land. Lewis won on this issue in the first suit and is therefore the party likely to assert estoppel in the second to establish his ownership of the property.

   b. Lewis will not be allowed to estop Fremont on the ownership issue because Fremont, like Cortez in the earlier example, has never had his day in court on the question of Lewis's title, and no court will estop him from litigating that issue until he has had a full and fair opportunity to do so. Besides, Fremont was not a party to the original action, and the mutuality doctrine confines estoppel to the parties to the original suit or those in privity with the original parties.

   c. It is crucial to understand that estoppel would also be denied on these facts in a nonmutuality jurisdiction. As indicated above, Fremont has never had an opportunity to litigate the issue of Lewis's title to the land; due process entitles Fremont to an opportunity to do so. The abandonment of mutuality has *not* changed this basic tenet of the system. In every nonmutual estoppel situation, the estopped party must have been a party in the first suit and therefore had his chance to litigate the issue. Thus, the crucial question in such cases is the one emphasized in *Bernhard*: whether the party being estopped litigated the issue in the prior action. Because Fremont was not a party in the first suit and did not litigate and lose on the issue, estoppel would not bar him from litigating the issue in the second action.

4a. In this case, Fremont would seek to take advantage of the finding in the prior action that Lewis did not own the land. If Fremont can estop Lewis from trying to prove that he owns the land, Fremont will defeat Lewis's claim, since a plaintiff must prove that he has an interest in the property to recover for trespass.

   b. Fremont would be invoking nonmutual collateral estoppel since he was not a party to the prior action. The only parties who could use mutual collateral estoppel are Lewis and Clark, the parties to the first suit. Here estoppel is invoked against a prior party by a stranger to the original action.

c. This would be defensive collateral estoppel since Fremont, the defendant, would invoke estoppel to prevent Lewis, the plaintiff in the first suit, from relitigating the ownership issue that he had previously litigated and lost. Lewis is analogous to the university foundation in *Blonder-Tongue,* which was barred from relitigating the validity of its patent against a second defendant after failing to prove it in a prior action. See the diagram on p.400.

d. In a jurisdiction that has abandoned mutuality, the court would have the authority to apply defensive nonmutual collateral estoppel to bar Lewis from relitigating the ownership issue. Under *Bernhard* and *Blonder-Tongue,* a court may allow the use of defensive estoppel by a new party, so long as the party being estopped was a party to the prior action and litigated the issue there. Those criteria are met here because Lewis was a party to the prior suit against Clark and litigated and lost on the ownership issue in that action.

However, the court would not automatically apply defensive estoppel to bar Lewis from relitigating. As the *Bernhard* court pointed out, and the Supreme Court reiterated in *Blonder-Tongue,* a party who has already litigated an issue should not be estopped from relitigating it unless he had a full and fair opportunity to contest the issue in the first action. Thus, the court will only apply estoppel if it is convinced, after review of the proceedings in the first suit, that Lewis had the incentive and opportunity to litigate the ownership issue tenaciously against Clark.

The burden to establish that the issue was fully litigated falls on Fremont, the party invoking estoppel. Friedenthal, Kane, and Miller at §14.11. Thus, the abandonment of mutuality opens the door to preclusion in situations like this, but the court must exercise caution in deciding who to let in.

5a. This is an example of offensive estoppel. Here, Wright invokes the negligence finding from the first action to *establish* an issue necessary for recovery against Lindbergh, the defendant in both the first and second suits. Wright seeks to use estoppel "as a sword," to establish a fact necessary to recovery, rather than as a "shield" against liability, as in example 4. See the diagram on p.401 supra.

b. Because estoppel is invoked by Wright, a new party who did not litigate the negligence issue in the first action, this is nonmutual estoppel. Of course, Lindbergh *was* a party to the first suit; in every nonmutual estoppel case *one* of the parties in the second suit will have been a party (or in privity with a party) to the first, since estoppel may only be invoked against a party who litigated and lost on the issue before.

c. The Supreme Court held in *Parklane* that the federal courts may apply offensive nonmutual collateral estoppel in situations such as this in which a new plaintiff invokes estoppel to establish an issue that was decided against the defendant in a prior suit. Although Wright, the new party invoking estoppel, was not a party to the original action, the party against whom it was invoked (in this case Lindbergh) was there and litigated the issue in the first suit. Lindbergh has had an opportunity to be heard on the issue, the fundamental prerequisite to barring relitigation.

However, as in the defensive estoppel cases, the court will not automatically bar Lindbergh from relitigating. The court must examine the circumstances of the first case to determine whether Lindbergh had an adequate opportunity to litigate and whether other cautionary factors (such as whether Wright sat out the first suit to see how Earhart would fare) counsel against application of estoppel.

In this case, several of these factors favor application of estoppel. *First,* since Earhart's injuries were serious, Lindbergh presumably had a strong incentive to defend her action vigorously to avoid paying substantial damages. In addition, Wright was a passenger in the same plane; surely Lindbergh would foresee that he would sue as well. *Second,* the example indicates that both suits were brought in federal court. Thus, there are not likely to be procedural advantages available to Lindbergh in the second suit that were not available in the first; both will be governed by the Federal Rules of Civil Procedure. Absent other factors suggesting unfairness to Lindbergh, this case looks like a good candidate for application of nonmutual offensive collateral estoppel.[3]

New Frontiers

6a. The first step in analyzing this case, as in every collateral estoppel case, mutual or otherwise, is to determine what issues were decided in the first action that may recur in the second. In this case the verdict for Mrs. Byrd indicates that the jury found Da Gama negligent. However, their verdict for Da Gama against Mr. Byrd indicates that they also found Mr. Byrd contributorily negligent.[4] It is this finding that is relevant to the second action: If Vespucci pleads contributory negligence as a defense to Mr. Byrd's suit and is able to invoke collateral estoppel to establish it, he will escape liability regardless of his own negligence.

b. This example looks partly like offensive estoppel and partly like defensive estoppel. It is like defensive use because the defendant in the second action invokes estoppel to preclude Byrd, a plaintiff in both the first and second suits, from relitigating an issue that he litigated and lost in the prior suit.

However, the case is like offensive use in that Vespucci uses estoppel to establish a fact — in this case, the *affirmative defense* of Byrd's negligence —

---

3. The four factors discussed in *Parklane* are not exclusive. Other factors may also counsel against giving the prior determination preclusive effect. See Restatement (Second) of Judgments §29; 1B Moore's ¶0.441[4].

4. This assumes that the evidence of Mr. Byrd's injuries eliminates the possibility that the jury found that he had suffered no damages. Compare *Illinois Central Gulf R.R. Co. v. Parks,* 390 N.E.2d 1078 (Ind. App. 1979).

that Byrd lost on in the first case. In cases such as *Blonder-Tongue,* the plaintiff lost on an issue that was an element of his prima facie case and was precluded in a later action from proving that element. In this case, Vespucci is not trying to use estoppel to prevent Byrd from proving an element of his case; he is using it to establish a defense against the claim based on Byrd's contributory negligence. In one sense he uses it as a "sword" to establish a fact, Byrd's negligence. In another, he uses it as a "shield," to prevent Byrd from proving that he is liable by borrowing the finding from an earlier suit in which Byrd lost on the same issue. Thus, it is a hybrid case, not quite like the classic defensive or offensive situation. Most courts would probably call this defensive estoppel, based on the fact that the party invoking estoppel is a defendant, as in *Bernhard* and *Blonder-Tongue,* and that the defendant invokes estoppel to avoid liability.[5]

c. Vespucci would not be able to assert collateral estoppel in a mutuality jurisdiction since he was not a party to the first suit and therefore was not allowed to take advantage of favorable findings in that action.

d. A court in a nonmutuality jurisdiction could allow Vespucci to invoke collateral estoppel even though he was not a party to the Byrd/Da Gama suit in which Byrd's negligence was initially established. As in all nonmutual estoppel cases, however, estoppel would be discretionary. The court will only apply estoppel if it is convinced that Byrd had a full opportunity and incentive to litigate the issue of his negligence in the first action.

7a. The *Enquirer* was the defendant in the first action, and lost on the issue of whether it is a newspaper within the meaning of the California statute. In the second action, two new plaintiffs try to use the finding from the first case to help establish their case against the *Enquirer,* a defendant in each suit. Based on the configuration of the parties, this would likely be classified as offensive collateral estoppel.

Just as example 6 represents a twist on the typical defensive estoppel case, this is not quite the classic example of offensive nonmutual estoppel. Here the new plaintiff asserts estoppel to preclude the defendant from proving a defense that failed in the first action. In the more typical offensive use situation, the plaintiff asserts collateral estoppel to establish an element of his prima facie case (such as the defendant's negligence) after another plaintiff proved that element against the same defendant in a prior action. In *Parklane,* for example, the plaintiffs in the second suit had to prove that the proxy statement was false and misleading in order to recover. They sought to do so by borrowing the court's finding to that effect in the earlier action.

b. Estoppel would be denied in a mutuality jurisdiction since Reddy

---

5. This is not entirely a matter of semantics. The characterization can make a difference, since some courts are more receptive to defensive nonmutual estoppel than to offensive nonmutual estoppel.

and Wald were not parties to the prior action or in privity with the plaintiff in that action.

c. The answer to this example is a cautious "maybe." The analysis must start with the truism at the end of the Introduction. Nonmutual estoppel is a species of collateral estoppel; as such, it is only applicable if the basic prerequisites for estoppel are satisfied. Before collateral estoppel can ever be applied, the court must determine that the issue in the first and second actions is the same. Here, it is clear that the issue of the *Enquirer*'s status as a magazine or newspaper under the California statute was litigated and decided in the first action. But obviously, estoppel will only apply if the issue in the Reddy/Wald suit is the same, that is, if the California statute applies. If Reddy and Wald reside in Virginia and suffered most of their damages there, a court might not apply the California statute to their suit at all; it might apply Virginia law, which might authorize magazines as well as newspapers to escape liability by printing a retraction or not allow the retraction defense at all. Thus, the issue may be different in the second suit or irrelevant to it.

Assuming that the California statute would apply in the Reddy/Wald suit, the court would still have to consider the various factors that may make offensive nonmutual estoppel inappropriate. Although it certainly appears that the *Enquirer* had a strong incentive to litigate the issue in the Burnett case, it might not be fair to apply estoppel if the procedural system in which the second suit was brought was more flexible, or if important witnesses were unavailable to the *Enquirer* in the first case but can be produced in the second. Or the court could deny preclusion if it determined that Reddy and Wald had deliberately decided *not* to join in the Burnett case in order to get the advantage of nonmutual estoppel without taking the risk of losing on the issue in the first action. (This would not be a problem on the facts here because the incident involving Reddy and Wald took place long after the Burnett case was filed.) Once again, the point is that the abandonment of mutuality opens the door to case-by-case consideration of whether estoppel should be available to the new party; it does not automatically lead to preclusion.

Outer Space

8a. Gagarin could have cross-claimed against Ride for his injuries in the first action, under Fed. R. Civ. P. 13(g), but was not required to do so. Because he did not have to do so, he may bring the claim separately. Res judicata does not bar the separate suit because Gagarin's claim against Ride was never adjudicated in the first suit; he never asserted a right to relief against her. See Chapter 22, example 7.

b. The verdicts in the first action indicate that the jury found Ride negligent, but not Gagarin or Armstrong. If Armstrong was negligent, he would have lost against Ride. If Gagarin was negligent, he would have been held liable along with Ride. In the second action, Gagarin would assert collateral estoppel to estop Ride from relitigating both her own negligence and Gagarin's.

c. This could be either mutual or nonmutual estoppel, depending on what Ride and Gagarin actually attempted to prove in the first action. Although they were both parties to the prior suit, they were not adversaries, and neither had to try to prove the other's negligence. Ride, for example, may have defended by trying to show that she acted with due care and that Armstrong's negligence caused the accident. If that is true, then she has not litigated the issue of Gagarin's negligence. Similarly, Gagarin may have simply tried to show that he was careful and Armstrong was not. If that is true, then he has not litigated the question of Ride's negligence. On these assumptions, use of estoppel in the second action would be nonmutual, since (while Ride and Gagarin were both parties to the first suit) neither has litigated the other's negligence. Consequently, they would not be able to assert preclusion against each other in a mutuality jurisdiction. The key to "mutuality" is not just having been a party to a prior suit but actually having litigated issues against one another.

Suppose, however, that Ride and Gagarin had each defended against Armstrong by trying to show that the other was negligent. Then they *would* have litigated each other's negligence in the prior suit, even though they did not assert claims for relief against each other. On this assumption, they would each be bound by the decision on those issues, even in a mutuality jurisdiction.

d. Gagarin's assertion of estoppel on the issue of Ride's negligence is an offensive use of estoppel: He invokes estoppel as a "sword" to establish Ride's negligence, a fact necessary to impose liability on Ride, which was established in the prior action. Assuming that Gagarin had not tried to prove Ride's negligence in the prior action, this would be nonmutual offensive collateral estoppel since he would be seeking to establish Ride's negligence on the basis of the fact that Armstrong had proved it in the first case.

Gagarin might also invoke defensive estoppel to defeat Ride's contributory negligence defense. That is, he would claim that since he was found free of negligence in the first action, estoppel should bar relitigation of the issue. Assuming again that Gagarin and Ride did not try to prove each other negligent in the first suit, this would be nonmutual estoppel. Gagarin would be trying to estop Ride from proving his negligence because Armstrong (the plaintiff in the prior action) had failed to prove it.

e. First, let's consider Gagarin's use of defensive estoppel against Ride. If Ride and Gagarin did not attempt to prove each other's negligence in the prior action, the court will not allow Gagarin to estop Ride from relitigating Gagarin's negligence. Ride was under no duty to litigate Gagarin's negligence to defend the first suit, and she chose not to do so. Although they were both parties to the suit, they were not adversaries and were not required under the procedural rules to assert claims against each other. Although

Armstrong was unable to prove Gagarin's negligence, Ride will be entitled to her opportunity to do so unless it is clear from the record of the first action that she tried to in that suit.

The situation is different as to Gagarin's use of offensive estoppel on the issue of Ride's negligence. Ride did fully litigate that question in the prior action and lost. Gagarin now seeks to use offensive estoppel to establish Ride's negligence in his own action for damages. The court will have to review the proceedings in the first action to determine whether it would be appropriate, under the *Parklane* analysis, to apply collateral estoppel based on it.

Ride will no doubt argue that Gagarin decided to "wait and see" whether Ride was found negligent in the first action, in hopes of using offensive collateral estoppel in the second. See *Parklane* at 330. Gagarin could have asserted his claim for damages as a cross-claim in the prior action and the court would have had supplemental jurisdiction over it. See Chapter 14, example 3. Although he had the right to withhold the claim in the first action, since cross-claims under Fed. R. Civ. P. 13(g) are permissive, the court (Ride will argue) should deny him the further benefit of offensive collateral estoppel since he chose this less efficient course.

Few cases address whether a party will be barred from using offensive collateral estoppel because he failed to assert a claim in a prior action. This seems like a particularly strong case for denying estoppel, since Gagarin was already in the suit and the negligence issues were already being litigated against another party. However, refusing to apply estoppel in this case, in order to deprive Gagarin of the benefit of holding back his claim, also burdens the court system with additional litigation on an issue already resolved. If all the other prudential factors favor preclusion, it seems doubtful that the court will refuse to apply it simply because Gagarin exercised his right under the rules to bring his own action against Ride.

PART SIX

Thinking Procedurally: The Rules in Action

25

An Introduction to the Pretrial Litigation Process: Setting the Stage for the Schulansky Case

The first five parts of this book have dealt with the "substance" of civil procedure, that is, the various judicial rules and doctrines that govern the litigation process. The chapters that follow are intended to give you a sense of how the process actually works by chronicling the early stages of a typical (though hypothetical) civil case, *Schulansky v. Ronan*. Each chapter includes the court papers filed at a certain stage of the Schulansky suit, including typical pleadings, motions, and supporting documents. In addition, the materials provide a look at the legal and tactical questions that the attorneys considered in drafting those documents.

Preparation for Filing Suit

In most cases the litigation process begins well before the parties get to court. Obviously, the first step is for the client to bring a dispute to a lawyer. The plaintiff's lawyer will obtain as much information as possible from the client. On the basis of this information and her assessment of the client, the lawyer must make a judgment as to whether to take the case. If she does agree to take it, she will propose a fee arrangement, and if the client accepts, a contract for services will be signed. In damage actions the agreement will frequently provide for a contingent fee, that is, an attorney's fee based on a percentage of any eventual recovery, frequently set at one-third of the amount recovered. The expenses of the action, such as deposition costs, expert witness fees, and other out-of-pocket expenditures, will also be paid out of the recovery.

Once the plaintiff's lawyer has agreed to handle the case, she will conduct a preliminary investigation of the events giving rise to the claim. She will obtain as much information as possible from her client and from other witnesses who are willing to discuss the case. She will gather and review documentary evidence, such as accident reports, business records, government reports, or other available materials. She will also do preliminary legal research if the case involves novel theories of recovery or other critical issues of law, in order to ascertain whether her client's injuries give rise to a right to relief.

On the basis of this preliminary development of the case, the plaintiff's attorney will usually send a claim letter to the defendant or discuss the claim with the defendant's counsel in order to explore the possibility of settling the claim without bringing suit. Many claims can be settled without the expense of litigation, particularly if there is little question as to liability and the only issue is the extent of the plaintiff's damages. However, in other cases the settlement value of a claim will depend on facts that have not yet been fully explored at this early stage. In the Schulansky case, for example, the defendant's judgment of the settlement value of the claim will turn in part on the parties' testimony as to their negotiations before the construction work began. The plaintiff's testimony as to those negotiations will only be available to the defendant through court-supervised "discovery" in the course of litigation. In such cases the parties will be less likely to reach an agreement until suit is brought and the facts are more fully developed.

The plaintiff's attorney must also consider a number of tactical issues in deciding whether to file suit. She must consider whether the case is strong enough and the value of a potential judgment high enough to justify the considerable expense of litigation. She must assess whether the client is patient enough and financially solvent enough to await a judgment several years down the road. She must consider possible alternative means of obtaining a remedy, such as invoking the assistance of a state agency, seeking an administrative remedy, or agreeing to mediation or arbitration.

Drafting the Complaint

Assuming that informal settlement efforts fail, and the plaintiff's attorney concludes that it makes sense to file suit on the claim, she will begin the lawsuit by filing a complaint, the first "pleading" required under the Federal Rules (and many similar state rules). Pleadings are the papers filed by the parties at the beginning of the action, in which they set forth their positions as to the facts in issue. Pleadings are not evidence; they are not even sworn testimony by the parties or their attorneys. They are simply statements of the parties' positions on the factual and legal issues in dispute.

In the simplest two-party suit the only pleadings required will be a complaint, in which the plaintiff sets forth her claim, and an answer, in which the defendant responds by stating her position as to each of the allegations in the complaint and asserting any other defenses she may have to the plaintiff's claim. See the plaintiff's complaint in the Schulansky case, infra p.432, and Ronan's answer, infra p.460. But further pleadings may be necessary if additional parties are brought into the suit or if counterclaims are asserted. See, e.g., Chapter 29, which includes a third-party complaint; see also Fed. R. Civ. P. 7(a), which describes the various pleadings that may be filed in appropriate circumstances.

Both the form and the content of the complaint are governed by the rules of procedure applicable in the court where the suit is filed. Because the Schulansky case was filed in the Massachusetts Superior Court, it must comply with the Massachusetts Rules of Civil Procedure, which are quite similar to the Federal Rules. Chapter 26 illustrates in detail how the complaint was drafted to comply with those rules. In addition, most courts have local rules of procedure that supplement the general civil rules. For example, the Massachusetts Superior Court has its own supplementary rules that cover numerous details of practice before that court. Thus, all applicable local rules must be checked in order to comply with any additional requirements.

In drafting the complaint, counsel must also consider whether the procedural rules allow joinder of all the desired parties as plaintiffs or defendants. (The joinder rules are analyzed in Chapters 12-15.) The substantive law governing the plaintiff's claims must also be analyzed to ascertain whether there is good ground to file suit on the claims asserted in the complaint. A large part of the attorneys' memos in the following chapters is devoted to considering whether the law of contracts and negligence will support the claims for relief in the Schulansky case, and, if so, how those claims should be asserted in the pleadings.

Tactical Considerations in Choosing the Forum

The plaintiff's counsel faces a number of "real world" tactical issues in deciding where to bring a lawsuit. To begin with, she must choose a court that has subject matter jurisdiction, personal jurisdiction over the defendant, and satisfies the applicable rules of venue. See Part One for a detailed analysis of those requirements. It may not always be clear from the facts whether jurisdiction and venue are proper in a particular court. (In the Schulansky case, for example, there is some doubt as to whether the Massachusetts court has personal jurisdiction over the defendants.) If so, the attorney will have to make a judgment as to whether the advantages of litigating in her chosen forum are outweighed by the risk that the suit will be dismissed on one of these grounds, causing additional expense to the client and possible statute of limitations problems.

The plaintiff's counsel must also decide whether to file suit in federal or state court, assuming, as will frequently be the case, that jurisdiction and venue are satisfied in both. Numerous factors may be important in making that choice. For example, the scope of pretrial discovery may be broader in federal court. Federal courts also have broader power to transfer cases than do state courts. On the other hand, the scope of interlocutory review may be broader in state court than federal court. (See Chapter 3, example 9, concerning interlocutory appeal of decisions on motions to dismiss for lack of personal jurisdiction.) The right to join additional parties may differ, as may the court's power to exercise personal jurisdiction over them.

Other differences involving the trial process itself may be important in a case. For example, the rules of evidence in the state and federal courts may differ in crucial respects. The power of the court to subpoena witnesses will differ. The ethnic and economic characteristics of the jury will differ because a federal court jury will be drawn from a broader geographical area. The judges in one system may be more familiar with the type of case in suit. It may be possible to get to trial a good deal more quickly in one system than another (or in one state than another).

Convenience may also play an important role in the decision. The plaintiff's lawyer may be more familiar with practice in one system. One court may be more conveniently located for the plaintiff (or her attorney) or more inconvenient for the defendant (or her attorney). Attorney Slater's initial memo in the Schulansky case does not reveal all of the factors she considered in deciding to go to state court, but proximity to her client's home and her own office was undoubtedly an important one in such a relatively small case. Innumerable other such factors may also be significant in a particular case.[1]

Filing the Complaint

In view of all these considerations, the attorney will draft the complaint, file it with the clerk of the appropriate court, and serve it on the defendant. (As to the proper methods of service, see Chapter 16.) If the defendant is already represented by counsel, the plaintiff's lawyer may as a matter of courtesy call the defendant's lawyer to let her know that suit is being filed. In turn, the defendant's counsel may agree to accept service of the complaint and summons without compliance with the formal service rules. (As Chapter 17

---

1. For a more detailed discussion of the tactical reasons for choosing state or federal court, see Steinglass, The Emerging State Court §1983 Action: A Procedural Review, 38 U. Miami L. Rev. 381, 412-424 (1984); see also 1A Moore's at ¶0.157[13].

indicates, the defendant may waive any objection to the manner of service by failing to object to it.)

It is only upon the filing of the complaint that the court gets involved in the case. At least initially, its involvement will be minimal. The clerk will assign a docket number to the case and establish a case file. All subsequent pleadings and other papers filed in the case will be "docketed," that is, entered on a docket sheet kept with the case file, and added to the file. In federal courts, the case will usually be assigned to a judge when the complaint is filed; that judge will then preside over the case for the duration.

In some state courts, however, the case is not permanently assigned; different proceedings will be heard by different judges depending on which judge is "sitting" at the time a motion comes up for hearing or when the case is reached on the trial list. For example, if the Schulansky case had remained in Massachusetts state court, the motion to dismiss might have been heard by Judge A, but the motion for summary judgment (had it been filed and marked up for hearing) by Judge B. Judge B would have no previous knowledge of the case but would have to review the pleadings and other papers before or during the hearing to familiarize herself with the suit. When the case reached trial, it might be tried before Judge C, who was assigned to the civil jury session at the time the case was reached on the trial list. By contrast, in federal court the same judge would preside over the suit from the outset and would develop a "feel" for the case through hearings on motions, discovery conferences, and other pretrial proceedings. As Chapter 31 indicates (see infra p.521), knowing which judge will preside over the case can have an important effect on the attorneys' tactical decisions.

Responding to the Complaint

Once the defendant or her counsel receives the complaint, she must respond. In most cases, the defendant will answer the complaint. If the defendant has certain preliminary objections to the suit, however, she may move to dismiss instead. See the motion to dismiss for lack of personal jurisdiction filed by Jones, the third-party defendant in the Schulansky case, infra p.489. Chapter 17 reviews in detail the circumstances in which a motion to dismiss may be filed instead of an answer.

It is important to understand the difference between a pleading and a motion. A motion is not a pleading. See Fed. R. Civ. P. 7(a) and (b), which provide separately for pleadings and motions. The pleadings set forth the positions of the parties on the claim. A motion, by contrast, is a direct application to the court for an order. Whenever a party seeks action from the court, a motion is the appropriate way to do so. For example, a defendant's motion to dismiss for lack of personal jurisdiction is a direct request to the court to dismiss the case.

Although many types of motions are specifically provided for in the rules (see, e.g., Fed. R. Civ. P. 12(b), (e); 56), the motion is a flexible device for seeking any type of action from the court. Other common examples are motions for further discovery, motions to place a case on the trial list, to convene a discovery conference, to implead a third party, to amend the complaint or answer, to extend the time to answer, or for any other assistance in the litigation process. (One well-known pro se litigant in Massachusetts is rumored to have filed a "Motion for a Landmark Decision"!)

If the defendant answers the complaint instead of moving to dismiss, her answer must set forth her position on the allegations in the complaint. As Chapter 26 demonstrates, the Federal Rules of Civil Procedure require the plaintiff in federal suits to set forth her allegations in numbered paragraphs. The defendant's answer must respond to each allegation, paragraph by paragraph. The defendant may also assert affirmative defenses or counterclaims in the answer, as Ronan has done. The answer must be filed with the court and served on the plaintiff. The rules require the answer or motion to dismiss to be filed within 20 days, but extensions of time to answer are frequently granted, often with the consent of the opposing party.

Discovery

Once the pleadings are complete, the case will move into the *discovery phase*. Discovery is the process by which the parties obtain information from each other and outside witnesses through several commonsense devices authorized by the rules of procedure. In the federal courts, three primary discovery devices are used to develop factual evidence in preparation for trial. *Interrogatories,* authorized by Fed. R. Civ. P. 33, are written questions sent by one party to another, which must be answered under oath. *Requests for production of documents,* under Fed. R. Civ. P. 34, are requests from a party for an opposing party to produce documents that may be relevant to the issues in suit, for inspection or copying by the requesting party. The third basic discovery tool[2] is the *oral deposition,* authorized by Fed. R. Civ. P. 30. A deposition is a procedure for taking oral testimony from a witness.

Usually counsel will take the depositions of crucial witnesses for the other party, in order to prepare for trial and to get the witness's testimony "on the record." The deposition is taken before a licensed court reporter, usually at the office of one of the parties' attorneys. The witness testifies under oath and may be represented by counsel. Counsel for opposing parties are entitled to cross-examine but usually do not do so extensively. Chapter 31 contains an excerpt from the plaintiff's deposition in the Schulansky case.

---

2. Two other basic discovery devices are the *request for admission,* under Fed. R. Civ. P. 36, used to narrow the scope of trial by obtaining admission of undisputed facts, and the *physical or mental examination,* authorized by Fed. R. Civ. P. 35, in cases in which a party's mental or physical condition is at issue in the lawsuit.

Many cases involve complex technical issues, sophisticated reconstruction of accidents, complex statistical or economic projections, or specialized knowledge of medical procedures. In such cases, a crucial aspect of trial preparation is the hiring and preparation of expert witnesses. Both sides will retain, often at considerable expense, recognized experts in the relevant discipline to testify as to such issues as causation, proper technique for industrial or medical procedures, and probable future damages. Both sides will seek discovery of the other side's experts. Much time will also be spent educating their own experts about the case, conducting experiments or calculations, and preparing them for direct and cross examination.

Despite the emphasis in this book on procedural rules and doctrines, the most crucial phase of a lawsuit is the development of the evidence through the discovery process and investigation by the attorneys. Most cases are won, lost, or settled on the basis of the strength of the facts, and it is through discovery that the facts and the credibility of the crucial witnesses can be evaluated. Typically, the discovery phase will take at least a year in a reasonably substantial case, but it may take considerably longer.

Attorney Cooperation in the Discovery Process

Throughout this period, it is the attorneys who conduct the litigation by using the discovery tools provided in the rules, responding to discovery requests from the other side, and developing the evidence to support their cases at trial. In many cases judicial involvement may be minimal right down to the time of trial. The attorneys carry the laboring oar by filing their pleadings, sending and responding to requests for discovery, scheduling and conducting depositions, and, where possible, agreeing to stipulations of the undisputed facts to shorten the trial.

Because discovery is conducted primarily by the attorneys, it is important for opposing counsel to cooperate in the discovery process. The formality of the civil procedure rules and the adversary nature of litigation practice frequently lead beginning attorneys to conclude that they are not serving their clients unless they resist every request of opposing counsel. In the long run, however, unrestrained belligerence is counterproductive. It is entirely feasible for counsel to work together to facilitate moving a case to trial without in any way compromising their clients' substantive rights.

For example, many questions will arise during the pleading and discovery phases of the suit that can be resolved by agreements of counsel. Extensions of time to file pleadings can be agreed to, saving the need to argue a contested motion for an extension. Stipulations of agreed facts can be drawn up to obviate the need to prove those facts at trial. Disagreements as to the scope or timing of discovery, claims of attorney-client privilege, or limits imposed by a preliminary injunction may often be worked out by counsel instead of taking court time. In addition, scheduling of depositions and hearings on pretrial motions can be arranged with opposing counsel. In these and other ways, the process will run much more smoothly (and inexpensively) for all concerned if the attorneys cooperate.

The Changing Judicial Role in Litigation

Under the traditional model (still followed to a degree in many state courts) the court itself plays a largely passive role in litigation. The parties file the pleadings, conduct discovery, initiate settlement discussions, and seek a trial when ready. Under this system, there is no active, periodic judicial review of pending cases. For example, a judge will not review complaints as they are filed to determine whether the court has personal jurisdiction over the defendant or the complaint states a claim upon which relief can be granted. It is up to the attorneys to seek court decision of such questions by filing an appropriate motion. The court is simply there as a referee to respond to motions by the parties if the pleading or discovery process goes awry and to supply a judge to preside over the trial when and if a trial is necessary. If the attorneys choose to litigate at a leisurely pace, the court under this model does little to force them to trial.

However, the litigation process is moving away from this "hands off" model as the volume of litigation increasingly strains court resources. Particularly in the federal courts, judges are taking an activist role in managing cases by monitoring the discovery process, limiting the issues in pretrial conferences, and setting deadlines for discovery and trial. For example, the court in federal cases is now required to enter a scheduling order in many cases, setting deadlines for the joinder of additional parties, amendment of pleadings, and completion of discovery. See Fed. R. Civ. P. 16(b). The court may also schedule discovery conferences with the attorneys to monitor the progress of discovery, to narrow the issues, and to encourage settlement discussions. See Fed. R. Civ. P. 26(f).

Moving Towards Trial

As discussed in Chapter 18, lawsuits may be cut short by pretrial dismissal or summary judgment. However, most cases survive these hurdles and, if not settled during the discovery phase, continue on track toward the culmination of the litigation process: a trial on the merits. As the discovery process nears completion, the court will usually hold a pretrial conference to resolve pending motions, address evidentiary issues, encourage stipulations as to undisputed facts, determine the issues and witnesses for trial, explore the possibility of settlement, and set a final schedule for trial. See Fed. R. Civ. P. 16. In some systems, trials may be fairly prompt, but in others the court's caseload forces long delays before the case is reached on the trial list. If the parties persevere, they will eventually get a trial, but it is almost impossible in many systems to predict or control exactly when that will be.

Most cases, even if they are actively litigated through the discovery phase and are set down for trial, are never tried. Upwards of 90 percent of all civil actions are ultimately settled, many on the eve of trial. However, the considerable effort that goes into discovery and pretrial preparation in such cases is not wasted. It is the intensive development of the facts and the parties' increasingly sophisticated understanding of the strengths and weaknesses of their positions that make an equitable settlement possible. As trial approaches, settlement discussions become more focused, and the parties usually begin to move toward an acceptable middle ground. In addition, the incentive to settle increases markedly as trial becomes an impending reality rather than a distant possibility.

The Attorney's Experience of Litigation

All of this is very well, but it still gives little impression of what the experience of litigation is like for the lawyers who conduct it. In practice, litigation is episodic. A lawyer may have anywhere from 20 to 50 or more active cases at a time, at various stages from pre-filing investigation to post-trial motions. At any given time, there will not be much happening in many of those cases: The lawyer might be awaiting responses to discovery requests in one, awaiting judicial action on a motion to dismiss in another, discussing responses to interrogatories with her client in another, drafting an answer in another, awaiting a trial date in another, and so on.

Much of the average litigator's time is spent in detailed factual investigation: reviewing depositions and documents produced under discovery requests, interviewing witnesses, meeting with clients, tracking down other sources of proof, and preparing and organizing testimony for trial. The work requires a painstaking attention to detail; a good memory and a methodical approach to trial preparation helps. In addition, a good deal of time is spent drafting pleadings and motions, supporting affidavits, and other materials. There is frequently legal research to be done (especially by junior attorneys in the office) and memoranda to be written in support of or in opposition to pending motions.

A litigator's cases have a way of "acting up" unexpectedly. The morning mail may bring a motion for summary judgment in a case that has been sitting on the back burner, a motion for sanctions in a case based on allegedly inadequate response to a request for production of documents, notice of a deposition of an important witness, or an order from the court to appear for a pretrial conference. Often these litigation events require a prompt response — a memorandum in opposition to a motion, an appearance in court to argue a motion, a conference with a client to draw up answers to interrogatories, or preparation for and attendance at a deposition.

Thus, a litigator is constantly juggling a number of cases, trying to keep all the balls in the air at once. The unexpected happens frequently, and a constant procession of deadlines beckons. Periodically, the process is punctuated by trials, which usually involve intensive periods of long hours and single-minded attention to one case (with consequent reshuffling of commitments in other cases). However, for most litigators, trials are infrequent; litigation practice resembles continuously preparing for exams, most of which are then called off at the last minute. Some lawyers find it exhilarating; others, simply nerve-wracking. Few find it dull.

26

First Moves: Schulansky Goes to Court

The Drafting Request

MEMORANDUM

TO: David E. Howard
          Associate

FROM: Phyllis Slater

RE: Schulansky construction dispute
          Our file No. 90-1248

DATE: November 20, 1990

   Deborah Schulansky, a client of ours, has consulted me concerning a dispute that has arisen between her and a contractor who recently built an addition to her vacation home. It appears that this problem cannot be resolved without filing suit. I would like you to help me with the case.

   Although Schulansky lives here in Plymouth, Massachusetts, she also owns an antique colonial home in Alton, New Hampshire, which she uses as a vacation home. The house dates from 1782 and is listed in the National Register of Historic Places. Last spring, Ms. Schulansky met Richard Ronan, a New Hampshire contractor, while he was restoring a house in Plymouth. After some negotiations at her home in Plymouth, the parties agreed that Ronan would build an addition on the back of the Alton house. Ronan mailed a "Proposal and Estimate" to Schulansky in Plymouth, and she signed and returned it. I have attached a copy of the Proposal and Estimate for the job, signed by both parties. [See p.436. — ED.]

The work involved taking out part of the back wall of the house and building an 18′ × 25′ addition behind the living room, with a full cellar under the addition. The contractor was to excavate the earth from the original foundation, excavate the adjacent area to be occupied by the addition, lay a cellar floor and foundation walls in the excavated area to support the addition, and build the addition above the new cellar area. In order to provide access to the new cellar, the contractor was to break a doorway through the original foundation of the main house adjacent to the addition.

There were problems from the beginning of the construction work. Ronan hired a bulldozer operator, named Jones, to do the excavation work, as he had told Schulansky he would. When Jones excavated the earth from the original foundation with his bulldozer, he discovered that the lower part of the foundation was simply loose rubble. Evidently, in colonial days it was fairly common to simply pile large rocks around the perimeter of the house site and build brick and mortar foundations on top of the rocks. These rubble foundations apparently last remarkably well as long as they are undisturbed, but are less stable if exposed, as was necessary here to construct the cellar for the new addition.

Apparently, there was some discussion during the negotiations about possible problems with the old foundation. Schulansky asked Ronan if he anticipated any problems due to disturbance of the foundation. He responded that he doubted that it would be a problem, but if anything was loose he would do whatever was needed to provide adequate support for the addition. When Schulansky visited the site during construction and observed the excavation, she became concerned about the stability of the original foundation. For one thing, she could see that the foundation was just loose rubble, with no mortar or other support except the surrounding earth. For another, the bulldozer had repeatedly ploughed into the old foundation in the course of excavating the new cellar, and loose rocks from the foundation were lying in the ditch next to the foundation. Schulansky asked Ronan several times if the old foundation was adequate and asked him to reinforce or rebuild it. Ronan refused to do any major reconstruction, on the ground that he had not agreed to do so and that it was unnecessary. Instead, he simply poured some cement in between the rocks and left it at that.

In May, when the job was virtually complete, Schulansky began to notice cracks in the plaster walls of the living room, in the bedroom above it, and in the addition itself. She also observed some sagging in the floor at the joint between the main house and the addition. She had a friend who is a structural engineer come and look at the house. He concluded that the cracks resulted from settling of the old foundation, evidently due to shifting of the rubble after exposure during the excavation. He is unsure whether the settling resulted from negligent excavation (that is, the rubble being disturbed by the bulldozer), or from the removal of the supporting earth on the outside of the old foundation.

In either case, his opinion is that the settling will continue, causing major structural damage, unless the foundation is rebuilt. Because the addition is now completed, that reconstruction will be substantially more expensive than it would have been if it had been done during construction of the addition. He estimates that it could cost as much as $25,000 to jack up the house and reconstruct the foundation, and another $35,000 to repair the damage to the house due to settlement of the foundation.

Schulansky has tried to work this out with Ronan, but he denies any responsibility. Consequently, she refused to make the final payment under the contract. I have talked to Ronan myself, and written him a demand letter, but it is clear that he will refuse to provide any satisfaction to our client. Instead, he has threatened to file suit himself if Schulansky does not pay him the last progress payment under the contract.

I intend to initiate suit against Ronan personally and against Ronan Construction Company for breach of contract and negligence. Although we could probably bring suit in federal court on the basis of diversity (Ronan lives in Nashua, Ronan Construction is incorporated in New Hampshire, and its principal place of business is probably in New Hampshire), I would prefer to litigate here in Plymouth Superior Court.

I realize that we may have a claim against Jones as well. At the moment, however, I am not even sure of Jones's full name, much less where he lives, whether he is solvent, and whether he is subject to personal jurisdiction here. We will have to learn more about Jones through discovery and amend to add him if necessary. But I have some hope that this can be settled quickly without the expense of lengthy, multi-party litigation.

Please draft a complaint and summons to initiate this suit in the Superior Court for Plymouth County. If you need further information, talk to me or call Ms. Schulansky directly. As you know, Rules 8-11 of the Massachusetts Rules of Civil Procedure are similar to Rules 8-11 of the Federal Rules of Civil Procedure. One important distinction for our purposes is that it is unnecessary under the Massachusetts version of Rule 8 to allege the basis for subject matter jurisdiction. Compare Fed. R. Civ. P. 8(a)(1).

We will also want to assert our right to a jury trial. See Mass. R. Civ. P. 38(b) (identical in relevant part to Fed. R. Civ. P. 38(b)).

The Associate's Response

MEMORANDUM

TO: Phyllis Slater

FROM: David E. Howard

RE: Complaint in *Schulansky v. Ronan*
            Our file No. 90-1248

DATE: December 1, 1990

I have attached a draft complaint and summons in the Schulansky matter. Please note that I have made both Richard Ronan and Ronan Construction Company defendants in the suit. (I refer to them collectively as "Ronan" in this memo.) The contract is signed by Richard Ronan, but on the stationery of Ronan Construction Company. At this stage, it is not clear whether Ronan signed on behalf of the corporation or individually, or both. Since either or both may be liable, I have named both as defendants.

As my draft complaint indicates, Schulansky may be entitled to relief on two separate theories, breach of contract and negligence. Ronan may have breached the contract in several ways. First, Ronan may have agreed to reconstruct the foundation if necessary, but failed to do so. The Proposal and Estimate is hardly clear on this; the only relevant provision is paragraph two, which requires construction of ". . . foundation walls to support 18′ × 25′ addition." However, an argument can be made that the old foundation wall at the juncture of the house and the addition is part of the foundation of the addition, and therefore the contractor had a duty to make sure that that part of the foundation was solid as well. Paragraphs 23 and 24 of the draft complaint assert this basis for recovery for breach of contract.

Our argument that paragraph two required Ronan to reconstruct the foundation is bolstered by the negotiations between Ronan and Schulansky concerning possible reconstruction of the foundation if it turned out to be inadequate. The potential problem here is that these discussions took place before the Proposal and Estimate was signed. The defendants will no doubt argue that the written contract embodies the entire agreement between the parties, that on its face it does not include any obligation to reconstruct the old foundation, and that the parol evidence rule bars evidence of prior negotiations to vary the terms of the contract. See generally, Farnsworth, Contracts §7.12 (1982). We will have to argue that paragraph two is ambiguous, so that evidence of the prior negotiations is proper to demonstrate the intent of the parties.

Alternatively, it may turn out that the settling resulted from damage done to the foundation by Jones in the course of excavating the cellar. If this is true, Ronan would still be liable on a breach of contract theory. Certainly, an implied term of the contract between Ronan and Schulansky is that the work will be carried out in a careful manner, including the work that Ronan chooses to delegate to his employees or agents. See Restatement (Second) of Contracts §318(3) (1981) (delegation of duties under contract does not discharge delegating party from its duty to perform those duties). Even if it was Jones who damaged the foundation with the bulldozer, this would constitute a breach of Ronan's duty to perform the contract work carefully. Thus, even if we cannot prove that Ronan had agreed to rebuild the foundation, this would constitute a separate breach of the contract, which gives rise to a claim for whatever subsidence resulted from the damage. I have included this allegation in paragraph 25 of the draft.

The second claim for relief in my draft complaint asserts a tort claim for negligence, based on the allegation that the negligent excavation by Jones led to the subsidence. If Jones acted as Ronan's employee in performing the excavation work, Ronan will be liable for Jones's negligent acts, since employers are liable for the torts of their employees in the scope of employment. Restatement (Second) of Agency §219 (1958). It is not clear at this stage whether Jones operated as an employee or independent subcontractor in performing the excavation work. The legal distinction between an employee and independent contractor turns on the employer's right to control the details of the work. *Cowan v. Eastern Racing Assn.*, 330 Mass. 135, 141-142 (1953); Restatement (Second) of Agency §220 (1958). If Ronan exercised detailed control over Jones in the manner of digging the new cellar, Jones acted as Ronan's employee, and Ronan would be liable for Jones's negligence. However, if Ronan simply hired Jones to complete the excavation work in his own manner for an agreed price, Jones may have acted as an independent subcontractor.

There is some reason to believe that Jones acted as Ronan's employee, since (according to Schulansky) Ronan appeared to direct him in the course of the excavation work. Thus, I have drafted the second claim for relief on this theory. An important goal of discovery on our second claim for relief will be to ascertain the exact course of dealing between Ronan and Jones, to determine whether Jones acted as Ronan's employee or as an independent contractor.

Once you have reviewed the draft and made any changes, I will arrange for filing of the complaint and service on the defendants in New Hampshire.

The Resulting Documents

1.

COMMONWEALTH OF MASSACHUSETTS

PLYMOUTH COUNTY   SUPERIOR COURT DEPARTMENT
                                         CIVIL ACTION NO.

DEBORAH SCHULANSKY

            Plaintiff
                                         COMPLAINT AND
        v.   DEMAND FOR
                                         JURY TRIAL
RICHARD L. RONAN
RONAN CONSTRUCTION CO.

            Defendants

2. ——————————————————→ <u>PARTIES</u>

3.

1. The plaintiff, Deborah Schulansky, is an individual residing at 219 Parker Street, Plymouth, Plymouth County, Massachusetts.

2. The defendant Ronan Construction Company is a corporation incorporated in New Hampshire with offices at 1124 Newark Road, Nashua, New Hampshire.

3. The defendant Richard L. Ronan is an individual residing at 3 Carleton Drive, Nashua, New Hampshire, and the president of Ronan Construction Company.

4. At all relevant times, the defendant Richard L. Ronan acted as the authorized agent of Ronan Construction Company.

4. ——————————————————→ <u>FACTS</u>

5.

5. The plaintiff owns an antique colonial house located at 53 School Street, Alton, New Hampshire. The house was built in 1782, and is listed in the National Register of Historic Places.

6. In February, 1990, the plaintiff met the defendant, Richard L. Ronan, while Ronan was working on a restoration project in Plymouth, Massachusetts.

7. At this first meeting, Ronan represented to the plaintiff that he was experienced at restoration of historic houses in New Hampshire and Massachusetts.

8. In early March, 1990, the plaintiff met with Ronan at her home in Plymouth, Massachusetts, to discuss the possibility of hiring him to build an addition on her house in Alton, New Hampshire.

9. During that meeting, the parties discussed the need for extensive rebuilding of the foundation of the main house adjacent to the planned addition.

10. During that meeting, the defendant Richard L. Ronan agreed that any necessary reconstruction of the old foundation would be included as part of the construction of an adequate foundation for the addition.

11. After the March meeting, Richard L. Ronan sent a Proposal and Estimate to the plaintiff in Plymouth, Massachusetts, describing the work to be done and offering to perform the work for $40,000. A copy of the Proposal and Estimate is attached to this complaint as Exhibit A.

6. ————→

12. The plaintiff accepted the defendants' offer by signing and mailing the Proposal and Estimate and mailing it to the defendants, at their office in Nashua, New Hampshire, on April 3, 1990.

13. The defendants commenced work on the addition on April 15, 1990, and continued until June 3, 1990.

14. In the course of the work, the defendants or their agents excavated the earth from the outside of the foundation of the main house to a depth of approximately seven feet.

15. This excavation revealed that the base of the foundation consisted of loose rocks piled on top of each other and held in place by the surrounding earth.

16. In the process of excavation, the defendants or their agents damaged the foundation of the main house by digging up and displacing large boulders, which formed part of that foundation.

17. As a result of the removal of the supporting earth outside the foundation, or the damage done to it during the excavation, or both, it became necessary to reconstruct this part of the foundation to adequately support the main house and the addition.

18. Despite their agreement to do so, the defendants failed to reconstruct the original foundation to provide adequate support for the house and the addition.

19. Even after the plaintiff brought the problem to the defendants' attention during construction, and demanded that they reconstruct the foundation in accordance with their agreement, the defendants refused to do so.

20. As a result of the inadequate foundation work, the main house and the addition have sustained major structural damage, including cracks in the walls and sagging of the first floor immediately above the affected area.

7. ————————————————→ FIRST CLAIM FOR RELIEF:

BREACH OF CONTRACT

8. ————→ 21. The plaintiff repeats and realleges the allegations in paragraphs 1-20 of the complaint.

22. The Proposal and Estimate signed by the defendant Richard L. Ronan and the plaintiff constitutes a written contract for a valuable consideration between the defendants and the plaintiff.

23. Under paragraph two of the contract, the defendants agreed to construct an adequate foundation to support the addition and adjacent portion of the main house.

24. The defendants breached the contract by failing to perform their obligation to construct an adequate foundation for the addition.

25. The defendants also breached the contract by failing to perform the excavation work required by the contract in a careful manner, which resulted in damage to the existing foundation of the house.

26. The plaintiff made all progress payments under the contract in a timely manner, until she became aware of the defendants' breach.

27. As a result of the defendants' breach, both the main house and the addition have sustained severe structural damage, which will require extensive repair and reconstruction.

SECOND CLAIM FOR RELIEF:

NEGLIGENCE

28. The plaintiff repeats and realleges the allegations in paragraphs 1-20 of the complaint.

29. In the course of the construction of the addition, the defendants or their employees negligently excavated the area adjacent to the foundation of the main house.

30. As a result of this negligent excavation, the foundation of the main house was displaced and damaged, causing subsidence of the foundation and structural damage to the main house and the addition.

9. ———————————————————→ <u>DEMAND</u> <u>FOR</u> <u>RELIEF</u>

WHEREFORE, the plaintiff demands judgment in the amount of her actual damages plus interest and costs, and such other relief as the court finds just and equitable.

10. ——————————————————→ <u>DEMAND</u> <u>FOR</u> <u>JURY</u> <u>TRIAL</u>

Pursuant to Mass. R. Civ. P. 38(b), the plaintiff demands jury trial of all issues triable of right by a jury.

11. ——————————————————→ *Phyllis Slater*

Phyllis Slater
Gomez, Robbins and Slater
Attorney for Plaintiff
322 Puritan Road
Plymouth, MA 02360
(508) 293-7024

RONAN CONSTRUCTION CO.
1124 Newark Road
Nashua, New Hampshire 03061

TO: Deborah Schulansky
         219 Parker Street
         Plymouth, MA 02360

RE: Addition to premises at 53 School Street,
         Alton, New Hampshire

DATE: March 15, 1990

PROPOSAL AND ESTIMATE

1. Excavate 18' x 25' x 7' deep area at right rear of house;
   remove fill.

2. Construct footings, cellar floor, and foundation walls to
   support 18' x 25' addition.

3. Cut doorway through present foundation into new cellar
   area.

4. Construct one-story addition with peaked roof and
   unfinished attic crawl space — standard frame
   construction, including cedar clapboard siding and
   asphalt shingle roof.

5. Two standard double-hung windows each side (west and
   east), and two 6' bay windows (double glazed) on main south
   wall.

6. Interior walls standard drywall construction; clear maple
   finish floor and baseboards.

7. Remove wall where addition abuts house; support upper
   floors with steel beam spanning opening.

8. Clean-up of site; broom clean, no seeding or planting.

9. Electrical work to be done by separate contractor hired
   by owner.

10. Contractor reserves the right to sub-contract excavating
    and concrete work.

11. Work to be completed by June 20, 1990.

Estimated Cost: $40,000

Payment schedule: $5,000 on completion of excavation
                         $5,000 on completion of foundation
                         $5,000 on completion of framing
                         $10,000 on completion of exterior finish
                         work
                         balance upon completion of job.

                         _____
                         Richard L. Ronan

Bid accepted: _____
                         Deborah Schulansky

COMMONWEALTH OF MASSACHUSETTS

PLYMOUTH, ss.

SUPERIOR COURT DEPARTMENT OF THE
TRIAL COURT OF THE COMMONWEALTH

CIVIL ACTION

NO.

Deborah Schulansky , Plaintiff(s)

vs.

Richard L. Ronan
Ronan Construction Company , Defendant(s)

SUMMONS

To the above-named defendant   :

You are hereby summoned and required to serve upon Phyllis Slater, Gomez, Robbins &
plaintiff   attorney, whose address is 322 Puritan Rd, Plymouth, MA 02360, Slater an answer to the
complaint which is herewith served upon you, within 20 days after service of this summons upon you,
exclusive of the day of service. If you fail to do so, judgment by default will be taken against you for
the relief demanded in the complaint. You are also required to file your answer to the complaint in the
office of the Clerk of this court at Brockton either before service upon plaintiff   attorney or within a
reasonable time thereafter.

Unless otherwise provided by Rule 13(a), your answer must state as a counterclaim any claim which
you may have against the plaintiff   which arises out of the transaction or occurrence that is the subject
matter of the plaintiff   claim or you will thereafter be barred from making such claim in any other action.

Witness, Esquire, at Brockton, the   Eighth   day of
December , in the year of our Lord one thousand nine hundred and Ninety .

Franos R. Powers

CLERK.

NOTES

1. This summons is issued pursuant to Rule 4 of the Massachusetts Rules of Civil Procedure.
2. When more than one defendant is involved, the names of all defendants should appear in the caption. If a separate summons is used for each defendant, each should be addressed to the particular defendant.
3. To plaintiff's attorney: please circle type of action involved — Tort — Motor Vehicle Tort — Contract — Equitable Relief — Other.

PROOF OF SERVICE OF PROCESS

I hereby certify and return that on , 19 , I served a copy
of the within summons, together with a copy of the complaint in this action, upon the within-named
defendant   , in the following manner (See Mass. R. Civ. P. 4 (d) (1-5)):

Dated: , 19

N. B.   TO PROCESS SERVER:—
PLEASE PLACE <u>DATE</u> YOU MAKE SERVICE ON DEFENDANT IN THIS BOX <u>ON</u>
THE ORIGINAL AND ON COPY SERVED ON DEFENDANT.

, 19   .

FORM 1 RP 5M

Comments on the Schulansky Complaint

Although Schulansky's complaint has been drafted to comply with the pleading requirements of the Massachusetts Rules of Civil Procedure (Mass. R. Civ. P. 8-11), those rules are very similar to Rules 8-11 of the Federal Rules of Civil Procedure. The following comments therefore refer to the rules generically unless the federal and state versions differ on the particular point under discussion.

1.   While some of the contents of pleadings are a matter of custom in a particular court or personal preference of the drafting attorney, the Rules specifically govern many aspects of pleading. For example, Rule 10(a) requires every pleading to have a caption such as that in Schulansky's complaint. Under Rule 10(a), the caption must include the name of the court (*Commonwealth of Massachusetts, Plymouth County, Superior Court Department*), the docket number of the action (*Civil Action No.*), the names of the parties, and a designation of the pleading (*Complaint and Demand for Jury Trial*).

The docket number is a number assigned to each case by the court clerk, for administrative purposes. On Schulansky's complaint, the docket number is left blank because the case will not be assigned a docket number until the complaint is filed with the clerk.

2.   Note that Howard has included a number of subheadings in the complaint. While these are not required by the Rules, such subheadings are frequently included for the sake of clarity. Particularly in a lengthy complaint that asserts a number of claims, or where the factual allegations are complex, separate sections for *Parties, Facts,* and *Claims for Relief* make it easy for the court and the parties to quickly find and review parts of the complaint during motion arguments and other proceedings.

In federal actions, a *Jurisdiction* subheading is frequently added because Fed. R. Civ. P. 8(a)(1) specifically requires the plaintiff to allege the basis for subject matter jurisdiction over the action. Such an allegation is not required under Massachusetts Rule 8 because, unlike the federal district courts, the Superior Court is a court of general jurisdiction.

For many simple cases, such as an action on a note or a straightforward motor vehicle tort case, the complaint may be so brief that subheadings are unnecessary. See the Appendix of Forms accompanying the Federal Rules of Civil Procedure, Forms 3-18 for examples of such complaints.

3.   The Federal Rules do not explicitly require separate paragraphs identifying the parties to the action.[1] However, it is customary to begin the com-

---

1. The Massachusetts rules do, however, require that the residence or place of business of the parties be specified. Mass. R. Civ. P. 10(d).

plaint with descriptions of the plaintiff(s) and the defendant(s). This information is important to various issues, including personal jurisdiction, venue, capacity to sue and be sued, and (particularly in federal diversity actions) subject matter jurisdiction. In Schulansky's complaint, for example, the allegation that Schulansky resides in Plymouth County indicates the plaintiff's basis under state law for laying venue there. See Mass. Gen. L. ch. 223, §1 (venue proper in county where plaintiff lives).

4.   Many complaints will include a subheading entitled *Facts,* or *Factual Allegations,* setting forth a brief description of the events that gave rise to the plaintiff's claim for relief. This type of breakdown is useful, particularly in complex cases, to distinguish the underlying facts giving rise to the claim from the plaintiff's asserted claims for relief arising out of those facts.

In Schulansky's case, for example, there is enough factual background that a separate facts section facilitates a clear understanding of her claims. It is true that Rule 8(a)(2) only requires a "short and plain statement of the claim," and that very brief, general allegations will suffice to avoid dismissal. *Conley v. Gibson,* 355 U.S. 41, 47-48 (1957). But a little more detail than the absolute minimum needed under the pleading rules will give the court a clearer picture of the case, from the plaintiff's point of view. And since Rule 8(b) requires the defendant to respond paragraph by paragraph to the allegations in the complaint, a more detailed complaint will elicit more specific denials or admissions in the defendant's answer.

5.   The Rules require all allegations in the body of the complaint to be set forth in numbered paragraphs. Rule 10(b). This facilitates quick reference to the allegations in the complaint. It also allows defendants to respond to each of the plaintiff's allegations by number and allows the plaintiff to incorporate allegations by number in later parts of the complaint, as Howard has done in paragraphs 21 and 28 of the Schulansky complaint.

Rule 10(b) also provides that the allegations in each paragraph of the complaint "shall be limited as far as practicable to a statement of a single set of circumstances. . . ." However, reducing specificity to the atomic level (for example, by breaking Schulansky's paragraph five into three paragraphs), would make the complaint unduly tedious. The allegations in paragraph five all relate closely to the issue of the age and value of the house and form a logical grouping for a single paragraph. The Rule does not limit each paragraph to a single fact, but to a single "set of circumstances," and calls for a commonsense breakdown of allegations "to the extent practicable."

6.   The Rules authorize parties to attach exhibits to their pleadings, as Schulansky has done here. Rule 10(c). Parties should exercise care in incorporating documents in the complaint, however, since doing so may constitute an admission at least of the authenticity of the documents, if not their

accuracy. Here, for example, Schulansky's inclusion of the Proposal and Estimate, together with her allegation that it constitutes the contract between her and Ronan, may weaken her argument that Ronan had an additional duty, arising from their prior discussions, to repair the old foundation. See the Third Defense in Ronan's answer, infra.

7.   In paragraphs 21-27 and 28-30, Howard has recast the factual allegations in terms of claims for relief for breach of contract and negligence. These sections of the complaint are intended to show the court that the facts alleged satisfy the elements of legally recognized claims that, if proved, entitle Schulansky to relief.[2] The subheading *Claim for Relief* tracks the language of Rule 8(a)(2), which requires the complaint to include a "short and plain statement of the claim showing that the pleader is entitled to relief." Here, Schulansky has asserted a right to relief under two distinct theories. If the court concludes that she has proved a right to recovery on either her contract theory or her tort theory, it will grant her whatever relief is proper under that claim. This "pleading in the alternative" is expressly authorized by Rule 8(e)(2).

The rules do not require the pleader to state the legal theory on which he claims a right to relief. A brief description of the "claim," that is, the events giving rise to the action, is sufficient. See 2A Moore's at ¶8.14 (1991). However, it is certainly appropriate and helpful to allege the elements of each claim clearly, especially in cases involving multiple theories of relief based on the same underlying facts. See *O'Donnell v. Elgin, J. & E. Ry. Co.*, 338 U.S. 384, 392 (1949) ("We no longer insist upon technical rules of pleading, but it will ever be difficult in a jury trial to segregate issues which counsel do not separate in their pleading, preparation or thinking.").

Separate pleading theories are often labeled as different "counts" instead of Claims for Relief. In simple complaints, such subdivisions are unnecessary. See, e.g., Appendix of Forms accompanying Federal Rules of Civil Procedure, Form 17, which asserts two theories of relief quite clearly without separate counts or subheadings.

8.   Rule 10(c) authorizes a pleader to incorporate prior allegations by reference in later parts of his pleading. Here Howard has done so in order to make clear that the breach of contract claim is based on the facts alleged in the cited paragraphs.

---

2. Schulansky might have other claims for relief in addition to the two asserted in the complaint. For example, other claims might be based on the failure of Ronan to properly supervise Jones or negligent selection of Jones as the subcontractor. For illustration purposes, however, I have tried to keep the complaint to a manageable length.

9.   At the end of the complaint, Howard includes a demand for the relief Schulansky seeks on both claims, as required by Rule 8(a)(3). In this case, the relief sought is damages, but in other actions different types of relief are also commonly sought, such as specific performance, an injunction, or a declaration of the rights of the parties.

Attorneys differ as to whether to put a demand for relief after each claim for relief, or to place a single demand at the end of the complaint. Clearly, if the relief requested differs on the different claims, separate demands for relief are appropriate. For example, if Schulansky were seeking specific performance of the contract with Ronan, inserting separate demands for relief after each claim for relief would help to make it clear that specific performance is sought under the contract claim rather than the negligence claim (which would not support a demand for specific performance). Because she seeks only damages on each claim, however, and the measure of damages on each theory is apparently the same, either a single demand at the end of the complaint or demands after each claim would be appropriate. Compare the separate demands for relief in Ronan's third-party complaint, infra p.477-479.

Note that the demand for relief in the *Schulansky* complaint does not state a specific dollar amount requested. This is because a recent Massachusetts statute bars plaintiffs from stating a specific dollar demand. Mass. Gen. L. ch. 231, §13B. Several states have enacted such statutes, apparently aimed at avoiding adverse publicity and possible jury prejudice from inflated damage figures in pleadings.

10.   Rule 38(b) provides that a demand for jury trial "may be indorsed upon a pleading," which means, in plain English, that it may be put at the end of the complaint. Because the right to trial by jury is waived if not demanded within ten days of the close of the pleadings (see Rule 38(b)), it is wise to insert the demand for jury trial in the complaint. Otherwise, plaintiff's counsel may forget about it, and the period for seeking jury trial may slip by unnoticed.

11.   Rule 11 governs signature of the complaint and other pleadings.[3] It requires the attorney to sign the complaint and state his address. The rule also imposes important ethical duties on attorneys who sign complaints and other court papers. Under Federal Rule 11, an attorney's signature on a complaint certifies to the court that the attorney has read it and believes, after reasonable inquiry, that it is well-grounded in fact and warranted by existing law or an argument for change in the existing law, and that the complaint is not filed for any improper purpose.

The "reasonable inquiry" requirement was added to Federal Rule 11 in

---

3. The complaint is shown here with the attorney's signature affixed. Subsequent pleadings and motions have not been signed because they are suggested pleadings for the partner's review and have not yet been filed in court.

1983 to strengthen the attorney's obligation to the court to avoid frivolous or unethical pleadings. See Advisory Committee Note to 1983 Amendment to Rule 11, U.S.C.S. Rules of Civil Procedure R. 11, p.343 (1984). This language does not require Slater and Howard to complete their research or investigation before filing suit against Ronan, but it does require them to have a factual basis beyond mere opinion or speculation to support the pleaded facts, as well as a colorable argument for the legal positions asserted in the complaint.

The factual standard in Rule 11 would be met by the information Schulansky gave her attorneys about the construction problem before they drafted the complaint. They knew that the damage appeared shortly after the construction work began, in the area where the work was being done. They also knew that an engineer had viewed the damage and concluded that it resulted from the inadequate construction work. That is a reasonable basis to support the factual allegations in the Schulansky complaint. The rule does not require certainty or admissible evidence at this early stage of the suit, only a reasonable pre-filing inquiry.

The legal standard in Rule 11 would also be satisfied in the Schulansky case. Howard and Slater had a copy of the contract, which required Ronan to construct walls to support the addition. If the damage to the house resulted from inadequate support, that would arguably constitute a breach of the contract. In addition, the discussions between Ronan and Schulansky during the negotiations may well support a claim that Ronan had agreed to reinforce or rebuild the foundation. Similarly, if the engineer's alternative conclusion that the bulldozer damaged the foundation is accurate, that would certainly constitute actionable negligence.

Interestingly, Massachusetts has not chosen to impose the stringent pleading requirements of Federal Rule 11. Under Massachusetts Rule 11, the attorney's signature certifies that "to the best of his knowledge, information and belief there is good ground to support" the pleading, and that it is not interposed for delay. It does not impose a requirement of pre-filing inquiry and does not make reference to improper purposes other than delay (as, for example, escalating the expense of litigation to the point where the opponent cannot sustain it). In addition, the Massachusetts version makes sanctions optional and authorizes them only for "wilful violations." The Massachusetts rulemakers have been unwilling to impose the stricter requirements of Federal Rule 11. Consequently, sanctions for improper pleading are invoked much less frequently in the Massachusetts state courts than in the federal courts.

Comments on the Summons

Rule 4 requires both a summons and complaint to be served on the defendant. The complaint is written by the plaintiff or his attorney, setting out the allegations against the defendant. The summons, by contrast, is an official order from the court requiring the defendant to respond to the complaint. Hence, Rule 4(b) requires that the summons bear the seal of the court and be signed by the clerk.

In many courts printed summonses like the one used here, already signed and sealed, may be obtained in blank from the clerk's office. The plaintiff's attorney fills in the blanks and arranges for service of the summons with the complaint. Compare the printed summons with the detailed requirements of Rule 4(b). (Mass. R. Civ. P. 4(b) closely parallels Federal Rule 4(b).) The summons includes the seal of the court,[4] the name of the court, space for the names of the parties, and the name and address of the plaintiff's attorney. It also warns the defendant, as required by Rule 4(b), that he must answer within 20 days or default judgment will be entered against him. See Rule 55, which authorizes entry of a default judgment if the defendant fails to respond to the complaint.

The first paragraph of the summons quite properly distinguishes between service and filing of the defendant's answer. Rule 12(a) requires the defendant to *serve* his answer on the plaintiff within 20 days of service of the complaint. See Chapter 16 for a discussion of methods of service of process, particularly example 15, which discusses proper methods for service of the Schulansky complaint. Rule 5(d) also requires the defendant to file the answer (and all other papers in the case) with the clerk of court, so that a complete official record of the documents in the case is available to the court and the parties. As the summons states, the answer must be filed before it is served or within a reasonable time thereafter.

Nothing in Rule 4(b) requires inclusion of the second paragraph of the summons, warning defendants that they must assert compulsory counterclaims under Rule 13(a). Other courts, operating under the same version of the rule, do not include it. The purpose of the warning is obviously to remind defendants, who must respond within a short time, that they must assert any compulsory counterclaims in their answer or risk loss of those claims.

The printed summons usually includes space (here, at the bottom of the page) for the sheriff, constable, or other process server to provide proof of service. See Rule 4(g). The server fills out the form, indicating the date and manner in which service was made, and files it with the court.

If service is made directly by the plaintiff's attorney (for example, in a case such as this one, where service on the out-of-state defendants will likely be made by mail), a separate, sworn affidavit must be filed setting forth the time and manner in which service was made.

---

4. In some courts, the seal is actually printed on the summons; in others, the court clerk embosses the seal on the summons by hand. The Plymouth County clerk's office uses an embossed seal, so it does not show up on the form illustrated here.

27

A Change of Forum: Ronan Removes to Federal Court

The Drafting Request

MEMORANDUM

TO: Marcia Losordo
Associate

FROM: Arthur Ackerman

RE: *Schulansky v. Ronan*
Plymouth Superior Court No. 90-2982

DATE: December 19, 1990

As you know, this office frequently handles litigation for Federal Security Insurance Company, a large insurer specializing in construction accounts. Federal Security has just asked us to represent one of their insureds, a New Hampshire contractor named Richard Ronan. On December 10 Ronan was served with process in a suit commenced against him and Ronan Construction Company in the Plymouth Superior Court. Copies of the complaint and summons are attached.

Ronan was in this morning for an initial interview on the case. (I would have asked you to sit in, but you were in court.) Although I didn't have much time, I did get the relevant background information on the case. The suit arises out of some work Ronan did for the plaintiff, Deborah Schulansky, on her second home in Alton, New Hampshire. Schulansky claims that Ronan agreed to build an addition to the house but failed to reinforce the foundation adequately, causing the main part of the house to settle. Ronan denies that the house has settled or, if it has, that it resulted from his work.

My initial reaction was that it seems doubtful that Ronan is subject to personal jurisdiction in Massachusetts for this claim, since the work was done out of state and Ronan is from New Hampshire. However, he did negotiate the contract with the plaintiff in Massachusetts, so he does at least have some relevant contacts here.

If Ronan is subject to jurisdiction in Massachusetts, I would prefer to litigate in federal district court here in Boston rather than down in Plymouth. Ronan lives in Nashua, New Hampshire, and Ronan Construction Company is incorporated in New Hampshire with its principal place of business in Nashua, so the case is removable on diversity grounds.

I need some quick information on removal of this case. Could you please write me a short memo answering the following questions:

1.   Should the petition be filed in the state or federal court?
2.   What documents must be filed with the removal petition?
3.   Can we file our motion to dismiss for lack of personal jurisdiction in the state court and wait for a decision on that motion before removing the suit?
4.   Do we have to answer or move to dismiss before removing? If not, when is our response due in federal court?
5.   The plaintiff has demanded trial by jury in her state court complaint. If we also want a jury, do we have to request it again in the federal court after removal?

If we have to remove right away, rather than waiting for the state court to resolve the personal jurisdiction issue, please draft a petition for removal as well. Even though the holidays are imminent, please get to this during the next week; I believe there is a 30-day limit on removal, and we've already lost nine of them.

The Associate's Response

MEMORANDUM

TO: Arthur Ackerman

FROM: Marcia Losordo

RE: Removal of *Schulansky v. Ronan*
            Plymouth County Superior Court No. 90-2982

DATE: December 23, 1990

I have researched your questions on removal of the *Schulansky* case. In addition, since I conclude that we must remove the case within 30 days even if the state court lacks personal jurisdiction, I have also drafted a notice of removal and other required documents, which I attach for your review.

Please note that there have been some changes in the removal statute recently. The removing party no longer files a "petition to remove"; instead, 28 U.S.C. §1446(a) (as amended in 1988) provides that the removing party must file a "notice of removal." I have used this terminology in the accompanying draft. In addition, the 1988 amendment eliminated the need to file a bond with the removal and to verify the petition.

The answers to your questions are as follows:

1. Should the petition be filed in the state or federal court?

The notice of removal must be filed in the federal district court "for the district and division within which such action is pending." 28 U.S.C. §1446(a). A copy of the notice must then be filed in the state court. 28 U.S.C. §1446(d). The case is only properly removed when the state court has been notified. Id.

2. What must be filed with the removal petition?

Under 28 U.S.C. §1446(a), copies of "all process, pleadings, and orders" served upon the defendants must be filed with the notice of removal. In this case that includes only the summons and complaint served on each defendant.

A party who removes to federal court must give written notice of the filing to all other parties to the action "promptly after the filing such of petition and bond." 28 U.S.C. §1446(d). (This reference to a "petition and bond," instead of the "notice" of removal, is apparently a legislative oversight. When Congress eliminated the bond requirement and "petition" terminology, it failed to amend this section to eliminate these references.) I have prepared a notification form, as well as copies of the notice for service on the plaintiff and filing in the state court.

3. Can I file my motion to dismiss for lack of personal jurisdiction in the state court and wait for a decision on that motion before removing the suit?

It is certainly permissible to file the motion to dismiss before removing. Until removal is sought, the case is governed by the state court rules, which require a response to the complaint within 20 days. Mass. R. Civ. P. 12(a).

However, §1446(b) provides that the notice of removal must be filed within 30 days after the defendant is served with the complaint. Nothing in the statute suggests that the 30-day period is suspended by any pending motions, and it is very unlikely that the motion to dismiss would be acted on before the 30 days elapse. Therefore, we cannot await decision on the motion before removing the case. We should remove the case now; the federal court will then decide whether to grant the motion to dismiss.

4. Do I have to answer or move to dismiss before removing? If not, when is my response due in federal court?

As indicated in the previous answer, the Massachusetts rules require a response within 20 days after service of the complaint and summons. If we do not remove within the first 20 days, a response to the complaint will be due, and we will have to file one or be in default. We should either remove before the response is due or file an answer or motion to dismiss in the state court. If we do answer before removing, the answer will stand as the answer in federal court, unless that court orders otherwise. Fed. R. Civ. P. 81(c).

One reason why we might wish to remove before answering is that some authorities suggest that a defendant may waive the right to remove by taking some actions in state court, such as filing a counterclaim. See Friedenthal, Kane, and Miller, Civil Procedure, p.65. The rationale for this approach is that the defendant has demonstrated her willingness to have the state court adjudicate the case by taking affirmative steps in the state court. Removing and then answering in federal court will avoid any risk of raising this issue.

If we remove before responding to the complaint, Fed. R. Civ. P. 81(c) provides that we must answer within 20 days of service of the complaint or 5 days after the notice of removal is filed, whichever is longer. Thus, we had better begin preparing an answer immediately or move for an extension of time in which to answer, under Fed. R. Civ. P. 6(b).

5. The plaintiff has demanded trial by jury in her state court complaint. If we also want a jury, do we have to request it again in the federal court after removal?

Rule 81 (c) provides that a party who has properly requested jury trial prior to removal need not renew the request in the federal court. Once the case is removed, the federal rules will govern the action (Fed. R. Civ. P. 81(c)), including Fed. R. Civ. P. 38(d), which provides that a jury trial demand cannot be withdrawn without the consent of the parties. Therefore, this action will be tried to a jury unless both sides later consent to trial before the court.

However, I am not sure whether the plaintiff's general demand for jury trial would apply to any counterclaim we may assert in our answer. If the case reaches the point of filing an answer, and we decide to assert any counterclaims, a separate demand for jury trial should be made as to them.

The Resulting Documents

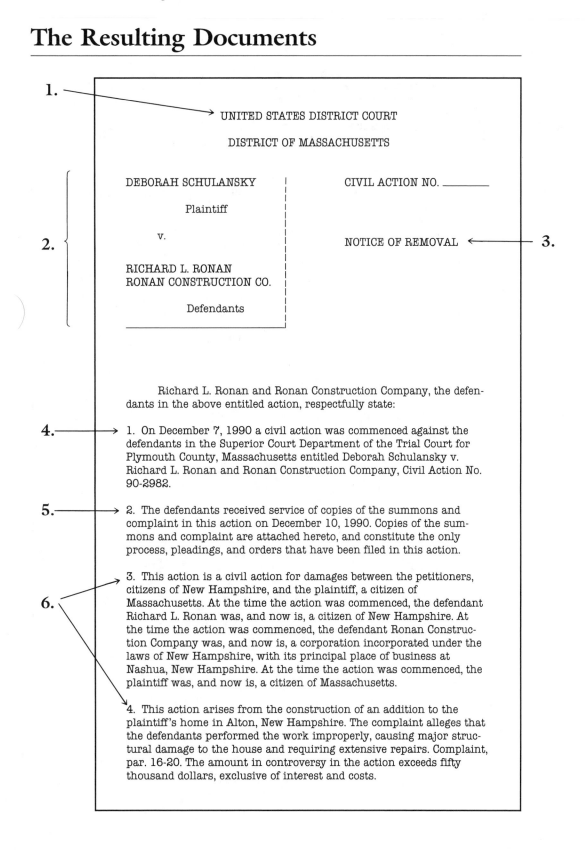

1.

UNITED STATES DISTRICT COURT

DISTRICT OF MASSACHUSETTS

2.

DEBORAH SCHULANSKY	CIVIL ACTION NO. _____
Plaintiff	
v.	NOTICE OF REMOVAL
RICHARD L. RONAN RONAN CONSTRUCTION CO.	
Defendants	

3.

Richard L. Ronan and Ronan Construction Company, the defendants in the above entitled action, respectfully state:

4.   1. On December 7, 1990 a civil action was commenced against the defendants in the Superior Court Department of the Trial Court for Plymouth County, Massachusetts entitled Deborah Schulansky v. Richard L. Ronan and Ronan Construction Company, Civil Action No. 90-2982.

5.   2. The defendants received service of copies of the summons and complaint in this action on December 10, 1990. Copies of the summons and complaint are attached hereto, and constitute the only process, pleadings, and orders that have been filed in this action.

6.   3. This action is a civil action for damages between the petitioners, citizens of New Hampshire, and the plaintiff, a citizen of Massachusetts. At the time the action was commenced, the defendant Richard L. Ronan was, and now is, a citizen of New Hampshire. At the time the action was commenced, the defendant Ronan Construction Company was, and now is, a corporation incorporated under the laws of New Hampshire, with its principal place of business at Nashua, New Hampshire. At the time the action was commenced, the plaintiff was, and now is, a citizen of Massachusetts.

4. This action arises from the construction of an addition to the plaintiff's home in Alton, New Hampshire. The complaint alleges that the defendants performed the work improperly, causing major structural damage to the house and requiring extensive repairs. Complaint, par. 16-20. The amount in controversy in the action exceeds fifty thousand dollars, exclusive of interest and costs.

7. ———→ 5. This court has original jurisdiction of this action on the basis of diversity of citizenship, under 28 U.S.C. §1332, and removal jurisdiction under 28 U.S.C. §1441(a).

8. { 6. The petitioner will give written notice of the filing of this notice and the accompanying bond to the plaintiff, as required by 28 U.S.C. §1446(d).

7. A copy of this notice will be filed with the clerk of the Superior Court Department for Plymouth County, Massachusetts, as required by 28 U.S.C. §1446(d).

WHEREFORE, the defendants request that this action proceed in this Court as an action properly removed hereto.

9. ————————————→ Arthur Ackerman
Ackerman, Sloan and Cariotis
Attorney for the Defendants
59 State Street
Boston, MA 02114
(617) 228-6301

UNITED STATES DISTRICT COURT

DISTRICT OF MASSACHUSETTS

DEBORAH SCHULANSKY | CIVIL ACTION NO. _____
                                      |
         Plaintiff |
                                      |
         v. | NOTIFICATION OF FILING OF   —10.
                                      | NOTICE OF REMOVAL   ←
RICHARD L. RONAN |
RONAN CONSTRUCTION CO. |
                                      |
         Defendants |
_____|

TO: Phyllis Slater
      Gomez, Robbins and Slater
      Attorney for Plaintiff
      322 Puritan Road
      Plymouth, MA 02360

      Please take notice that the defendants in the above-entitled
action have this date filed their notice of removal of this action in the
Office of the Clerk of the United States District Court for the District of
Massachusetts. A copy of the notice is attached hereto.

      You are further advised that the defendants, upon filing of the
notice of removal, also filed a copy of the notice with the Clerk of
the Superior Court Department for Plymouth County, thus effecting
removal under 28 U.S.C. §1446(d).

Date: _____

                              _____
                              Arthur Ackerman
                              Ackerman, Sloan and Cariotis
                              Attorney for the Defendants
                              59 State Street
                              Boston, MA 02114
                              (617) 228-6301

Comments on the Notice of Removal

1.   The heading of the notice of removal reflects the fact that the notice is filed in the federal district court, not in the state court in which Schulansky filed suit.

2.   Although Fed. R. Civ. P. 10(a) only governs the caption for pleadings, and a notice of removal is not a pleading (see Fed. R. Civ. P. 7(a)), it is customary to use the same type of caption in all papers filed in the suit. (Indeed, this may be required by local rules of the federal district, as it is in Massachusetts. See United States District Court, District of Massachusetts, Local Rule 5.1(a).) Of course, the title of the paper will change, but the court, names of the parties, and docket number will appear on all filed papers. Note again that the docket number has not been filled in since the case will receive a new federal court docket number when the notice of removal is filed.

3.   As Losordo's memo states, Congress recently amended §1446, which addresses the procedure for removal. One change was to require a "notice" of removal rather than a "petition" for removal. The change reflects the basic fact that removal is not at the discretion of the federal court: If the federal court has jurisdiction over the action, it must hear it upon removal. The "petition" terminology suggested that the defendant was requesting the federal court to hear the case, and that it might choose to grant or refuse that request. The substituted term, "notice," reflects the fact that the defendant has a *right* to remove if the case falls within the federal court's removal jurisdiction and is "notifying" the court that she is exercising that option.

4.   Although the removal statutes are not entirely clear on the point, the courts have held that all defendants must agree to the removal. See Chapter 6, example 7. Paragraph one indicates to the court that this requirement is met.

5.   The allegation as to the date of service of the complaint indicates to the court that removal is timely, since the 30-day removal period begins to run on the date of service of the summons and complaint on the defendants. 28 U.S.C. §1446(b). This paragraph of the notice also indicates that the defendants have complied with the requirement of 28 U.S.C. §1446(a), that "a copy of all process, pleadings, and orders served upon such defendant or defendants" be filed with the notice.

6.   It will not always be clear from the plaintiff's complaint that a case meets the requirements for original or removal jurisdiction of the federal court. For example, Schulansky's state court complaint did not allege where Ronan

Construction Company's principal place of business was, since it was not necessary to do so to invoke the state court's jurisdiction over the action.

Section 1446(a) authorizes the removing defendant to state facts in the notice of removal that are necessary to demonstrate that the federal court has jurisdiction. The information in paragraphs three and four of the notice of removal is intended to show the court that this is a proper diversity case, which could have been brought originally in federal court. These paragraphs also demonstrate that none of the defendants is a citizen of the forum state, a separate requirement in 28 U.S.C. §1441(b) for removal of diversity cases.

As was noted in Chapter 26, the Demand for Relief in Schulansky's complaint does not state a specific dollar demand — in fact, a statute barred her from including a dollar figure in the demand. This poses an awkward situation for the defendants. *First,* how is Ronan to know if the amount in controversy exceeds $50,000, as required by 28 U.S.C. §1332(a), when he contends that Schulansky hasn't suffered any damages at all from his work? Ronan is an experienced construction contractor, and he is familiar with the house and the work he did on it. In addition, he has the factual allegations as to the nature of damages and the type of repair needed, so he should have a factual basis for roughly estimating the possible damages. Naturally, he can't be very accurate about it, but the *St. Paul Mercury* rule doesn't require him to be. So long as there is a possible basis for damages in excess of $50,000, the requirement is met. Section 1446(a) requires Ronan to put in the notice of removal the basic facts that lead him to believe the amount-in-controversy requirement has been met, as he has done in paragraph four.

Including this statement is also awkward for Ronan for another reason. By alleging that the amount requirement is satisfied, he in some sense lends credibility to the argument that the plaintiff has suffered extensive damages, an allegation he will presumably deny in his answer. But again, remember that the amount-in-controversy requirement refers to the amount that is *in dispute between the parties,* not to the actual damages the plaintiff has suffered. See Chapter 4, p.62. Ronan does not concede, by asserting in the notice of removal that the dispute concerns more than $50,000, that the plaintiff has actually suffered that great a loss, or any loss at all. Nor will the jury likely be aware of the amount-in-controversy requirement or that Ronan has invoked federal jurisdiction on the basis that a particular amount is disputed.

7. The fundamental requirement for removal is that the case could have been brought initially in federal court. 28 U.S.C. §1441(a). In paragraph five, the defendants state that original jurisdiction existed and that removal is therefore proper under §1441(a).

8. Paragraphs six and seven indicate that the removing defendants will comply with the requirements of 28 U.S.C. §1446(d), that the plaintiff be notified of the removal, and that a copy of the notice be filed in the state court.

9.   Section 1446(a) now explicitly states that the representations made in the notice of removal are subject to the ethical requirements of Rule 11. Thus, as with Slater's signature on the complaint, Ackerman's signature certifies to the court that he has made a preliminary inquiry both as to the supporting facts and legal right to remove and concluded that he has adequate grounds to support the statements made in the notice of removal.

10.   The Notification of Filing of Notice of Removal is a fairly commonsensical document drawn up to comply with the requirement of 28 U.S.C. §1446(d), that the defendant give notice to the adverse parties of the filing of the notice. As with the notice itself, it is intended to demonstrate to the court and the plaintiff that the defendants have complied with the removal requirements.

The third question Ackerman asks in his memo is interesting. It seems like an unnecessary hassle to go through the formalities of removal if the action is likely to be dismissed for lack of personal jurisdiction anyway. However, as the answer indicates, the removal statute does not allow the defendants to litigate preliminary objections in the state court before exercising their right to remove; removal must take place within 30 days, regardless of objections the plaintiff may have to jurisdiction, venue, or other matters relating to the court's competence to entertain the action.

Thus, even if Ackerman believes that he might fare better on some issues in the case in state court, he does not have the choice to litigate some issues there and then remove to federal court. Removal must be done immediately and brings the entire action into the federal court. Thus, he must make a quick decision as to whether the overall advantages of litigating in federal court outweigh those of staying in state court. (Some of the many considerations that may influence that decision are discussed in Chapter 25, pp.419-420.) This is a difficult position to be in, particularly if the suit was not expected. When the case came into Ackerman's office nine days of the removal period had already elapsed, leaving little time to research all of the strategic ramifications of removal.

28

The Defendants' Perspective: Ronan's Answer and Counterclaim

The Drafting Request

MEMORANDUM

TO: Marcia Losordo
          Associate

FROM: Arthur Ackerman

RE: Answer and Counterclaim in *Schulansky v. Ronan*
          U.S. District Court No. 90-6719

DATE: December 26, 1990

- -

Thank you for your informative memo and removal documents in this case. I have filed the notice of removal today and notified the plaintiff and the state court, so we are officially in federal court.

I have decided to file an answer to the complaint (instead of a Rule 12(b) motion) and would appreciate your assistance in drafting it. I realize that you have not yet had any Christmas vacation, but as your memo indicates, we are under the gun because Fed. R. Civ. P. 81(c) requires us to respond to the complaint within five days of removing the case.

Not surprisingly, Dick Ronan's version of the facts in this case differs significantly from the allegations in Schulansky's complaint. First of all, although there was some discussion about the old foundation during their negotiations, Ronan's position is that he never assumed responsibility for any extensive reconstruction work. He never said anything about rebuilding the foundation, except that he doubted it would be necessary. He did say he would pour cement into any gaps in the exposed boulders but definitely did not agree to anything more than that. He points out that reconstructing the foundation on a house that old is a very substantial job; he could never have quoted her the price he did if such reconstruction were included in the work.

Second, according to Ronan, he and Schulansky discussed the problem again after the old foundation had been exposed. She asked him whether it ought to be rebuilt, and Ronan said that he did not think it was necessary and that it was beyond the scope of the contract. He specifically recalls telling her at that time that he thought the foundation would be sufficient if he filled in the gaps with concrete, but "you can never be 100 percent sure — old houses are unpredictable." She agreed to his suggestion, and that is what he did.

Ronan also denies any negligence in excavating the foundation. There were some loose boulders in the excavated area near the foundation, which Schulansky assumed had been knocked out by the bulldozer. Ronan admits that the bulldozer hit the foundation a number of times, but he thinks those rocks were probably excavated from the new cellar area instead. He also states that digging the earth away from the foundation did not weaken it. According to him, it is the direct downward pressure of the structure on top of the rocks in the foundation, not the surrounding earth, that keeps the foundation — and the house itself — in place.

Last, Ronan denies that Schulansky's house has settled as a result of his construction work or any defect in the old foundation. He claims that most of the cracks she refers to were already there when he inspected the house before he bid on the job; after all, the house is over 200 years old, and there is evidence of settling in every room of the house. While he does not doubt the good faith of the plaintiff, he thinks she simply had not noticed these problems until the construction work caused her to take a close look at the structure of the house.

Please draft an answer to the Schulansky complaint, based on Ronan's understanding of the facts outlined above. Feel free to contact Ronan directly for any further information you need.

Our answer should not only respond to the individual allegations in Schulansky's complaint, but also raise several additional defenses. First, I think we should take the position that the Proposal and Estimate constitutes the entire agreement between the parties and that Ronan is under no duty to rebuild the foundation if the Proposal and Estimate does not require it. Even if there was some prior discussion in which Ronan arguably agreed to rebuild the foundation, it is the contract itself, not the discussions leading up to it, that defines the parties' obligations. As you know, where a contract is clear and complete on its face, the parol evidence rule bars either party from varying or contradicting the terms of the contract by evidence of prior inconsistent negotiations. Here, the contract is clear: Paragraph two requires Ronan to build a foundation for the addition, not to rebuild the preexisting foundation.

Second, Ronan states (and the plaintiff's complaint admits) that Schulansky was present when the foundation was exposed. Ronan told her what he planned to do, and she evidently accepted his proposal to reinforce it rather than rebuild it. Thus, I think we can make a strong argument that Schulansky has waived any right to reconstruction of the old foundation.

Our answer should also raise the objection that the court lacks personal jurisdiction over both defendants. I realize that we could postpone answering by filing a motion to dismiss on this ground, but I have decided to answer instead. I am somewhat doubtful that the court will dismiss on this ground. If the court postpones decision on the motion (as it may under Fed. R. Civ. P. 12(d)), I would rather have our answer to the complaint, setting forth our position on the merits, before the court from the beginning of the litigation.

Please also include a counterclaim for the final payment under the contract, which Schulansky has never made. In addition, it is our position that Richard Ronan signed the contract as an agent of Ronan Construction Company, not on his own behalf. Consequently, he was not a party to the contract and is not personally liable for any breach of that contract. Please be careful in drafting the answer to observe this distinction in responding to the allegations in the complaint and in drafting the counterclaim.

We may also wish to file a third-party complaint against the excavation subcontractor, Arlen Jones. Please let me know whether this must be filed with the answer. I certainly would prefer to have more time to decide whether to file a third-party claim and, if so, whether there will be any jurisdictional problems involved. (Jones is apparently from New Hampshire, but I am not sure whether he may be subject to personal jurisdiction here on some ground.)

The Associate's Response

MEMORANDUM

TO: Arthur Ackerman

FROM: Marcia Losordo

RE: Answer and Counterclaim in *Schulansky v. Ronan*
U.S. District Court No. 90-6719

DATE: December 28, 1990

I have attached a proposed answer and counterclaim in the Schulansky case.

I have based my responses to the plaintiff's allegations on the facts as you set them out in your memo and on direct conversations with Dick Ronan. In responding to the plaintiff's first claim for relief, for breach of contract, I have consistently taken the position that Ronan's only obligation was to construct foundation walls for the addition, not for any part of the main house.

The plaintiff's second claim for relief on a negligence theory is evidently premised on the assumption that Jones was an employee of either Ronan personally or Ronan Construction Company, so that one or the other would be liable for his negligence. However, it is not at all clear that Jones was an employee, as opposed to an independent contractor with Ronan. The decision turns on whether Ronan had the right of control over Jones in the detailed performance of the work. Restatement (Second) of Agency §220 (1958). If he did, Jones was an employee; if not, he acted as an independent contractor.

From what Ronan tells me, it is unclear whether the court would characterize Jones as an employee of Ronan or as an independent contractor. On the one hand, Jones was paid a flat fee for the job and used his own bulldozer, factors that suggest that he was independent. Restatement (Second) of Agency §227 (1958). On the other, Jones worked for Ronan on a regular basis, did not have any written agreement for the work, and generally did whatever Ronan told him to do. These facts would support a finding that Jones was an employee. Where the facts could reasonably support the conclusion that Jones was independent, I conclude that it is proper under Fed. R. Civ. P. 11 to deny that he was Ronan's employee, and I have done so. See paragraph 29 of the First Defense and the Sixth Defense.

If you decide to file a third-party complaint against Jones, it need not be filed with the answer. You may serve a third-party complaint without leave of court within ten days of serving the answer in the original action. Fed. R. Civ. P. 14(a). After that you will need leave of court, after notice to the plaintiff, to file any third-party claims. Id. However, even if we file within the ten-day period for filing as of right, the court does not have to entertain the third-party claim. The decision to allow or dismiss a third-party claim is a discretionary one in each case. Wright at 509. If the court concludes that entertaining the additional claim would not advance the efficient and fair resolution of the entire dispute, it may dismiss it at any time.

As I read the technicalities of Fed. R. Civ. P. 6(a), our answer is due on January 3: We have to answer within five days. Wednesday the 26th, the day on which the case was removed, does not count under the rule, but the 27th and 28th do. Saturday the 29th and Sunday the 30th don't count because weekend days don't count when the period is less than eleven days. See Rule 6(a), fourth sentence. New Year's Eve, the 31st, makes three days, but New

Year's Day, a holiday, does not count. So Tuesday the 2nd is the fourth day, and our answer is due on Wednesday the 3rd. Even though the holiday is coming up, please remember to save time to review the documents before that date.

One last point you may wish to consider. Is it possible that, by seeking affirmative relief from Schulansky in our counterclaim, we will waive our objection to personal jurisdiction? I have not researched this point but will do so if you think this is a possible problem.

The Resulting Documents

1.

UNITED STATES DISTRICT COURT

DISTRICT OF MASSACHUSETTS

CIVIL ACTION NO. 90-6719

DEBORAH SCHULANSKY

Plaintiff

v.

RICHARD L. RONAN, et al.

Defendants

ANSWER AND

COUNTERCLAIM

2. FIRST DEFENSE

1. The defendants admit the allegations in paragraph one of the complaint.

2. The defendants admit the allegations in paragraph two of the complaint.

3. The defendants admit the allegations in paragraph three of the complaint.

4. The defendants admit the allegations in paragraph four of the complaint.

3. 5. The defendants admit that the plaintiff owns a colonial home in Alton, New Hampshire, but are without sufficient knowledge or information to form a belief as to the truth of the remaining allegations in paragraph five of the complaint.

6. The defendants admit the allegations in paragraph six of the complaint.

4. 7. The defendants admit that Richard Ronan told the plaintiff that he had worked on older houses in both states, but deny that he represented himself as an expert in restoration of historic houses.

8. The defendants admit the allegations in paragraph eight of the complaint.

9. The defendants admit that the parties discussed the condition of the old foundation at the March meeting, but deny that there

was any discussion of a possible need for extensive reconstruction of the foundation.

10. The defendants deny that they, or either one of them, agreed to reconstruct the foundation, or that such reconstruction was part of the construction of the foundation for the addition agreed to in the contract between the plaintiff and Ronan Construction Company.

11. The defendants admit that the defendant Richard Ronan sent a Proposal and Estimate to the plaintiff. The defendants further state that the Proposal and Estimate constituted an offer by the Ronan Construction Company, not by the defendant Richard Ronan individually.

12. The defendants admit that the plaintiff signed and returned the Proposal and Estimate on or around April 3, 1990, but further state that the Proposal and Estimate constituted an offer solely by Ronan Construction Company.

13. The defendants admit the allegations in paragraph thirteen of the complaint.

14. The defendants admit the allegations in paragraph fourteen of the complaint.

15. The defendants admit that the foundation consisted of loose boulders without mortar, but deny that they were held together by the surrounding earth.

16. The defendants deny the allegations in paragraph sixteen of the complaint.

17. The defendants deny the allegations in paragraph seventeen of the complaint.

18. The defendants admit that they did not completely reconstruct the preexisting foundation, but deny that they had agreed to do so, or that such reconstruction was necessary to provide adequate support for the house or the addition. The defendants did heavily reinforce the preexisting foundation with concrete in the course of constructing the addition.

19. The defendants deny that the plaintiff demanded that they reconstruct the foundation or that the contract required them to do so.

20. The defendants deny the allegations of paragraph twenty of the complaint.

5. → 21. The defendants repeat and reallege their responses to the allegations in paragraphs one to twenty of the complaint.

22. The defendants admit that the Proposal and Estimate constitutes contract between Ronan Construction Company and the plaintiff. The defendants deny that Richard L. Ronan is a party to the contract.

23. The defendants admit that, under the contract, the defendant Ronan Construction Company agreed to construct an adequate foundation for the addition. They deny that the contract imposed any obligation upon Ronan Construction Company to reconstruct the foundation of the main house. They deny that Richard L. Ronan personally undertook any obligations under the contract.

24. The defendants deny the allegations in paragraph twenty-four of the complaint.

25. The defendants deny the allegations in paragraph twenty-five of the complaint.

26. The defendants admit that the plaintiff made the first four progress payments under the contract, but deny that they breached the contract. The defendants further state that the plaintiff has refused to make the final payment due under the contract, in the amount of $15,000, although the defendant Ronan Construction Company has performed all of its obligations under the contract in a timely and satisfactory manner and has demanded payment of the balance due under the contract.

27. The defendants deny the allegations in paragraph twenty-seven of the complaint.

28. The defendants repeat and reallege their responses to paragraphs one to twenty of the complaint.

29. The defendants deny that the area adjacent to the foundation of the main house was negligently excavated. They further deny that the excavation was performed by employees of either defendant.

30. The defendants deny the allegations of paragraph thirty of the complaint.

6. ⟶ SECOND DEFENSE

This action must be dismissed because the court lacks personal jurisdiction over the defendants under the Fourteenth Amendment and the Massachusetts Long-Arm Statute, Mass. G.L. c. 223A, §3.

THIRD DEFENSE

The plaintiff's first claim for relief fails to state a claim upon which relief can be granted, because the Proposal and Estimate constitutes the entire agreement between the parties, and does not require any reconstruction of the original foundation.

7. ⟶ FOURTH DEFENSE

If the defendants had any obligation under the contract to reconstruct the preexisting foundation, the plaintiff waived performance of that obligation on or about April 15, 1990, when she agreed that the defendants could fulfill their obligations under the contract by reinforcing the preexisting foundation with cement.

FIFTH DEFENSE

The plaintiff's first claim for relief fails to state a claim upon which relief can be granted against the defendant Richard L. Ronan, because he was not a party to the contract.

SIXTH DEFENSE

If there was any negligence in the excavation of the foundation, that negligence was solely the act of Arlen Jones, an independent contractor for whose negligence the defendants cannot be held liable.

8. ⟶ WHEREFORE, the defendants request that the court dismiss the plaintiff's complaint and award the defendants their costs, together with such other relief as the court finds just and equitable.

9. ⟶ ## COUNTERCLAIM OF RONAN CONSTRUCTION COMPANY —

BREACH OF CONTRACT

The defendant Ronan Construction Company counterclaims against the plaintiff as follows:

10. ⟶ 1. This court has subject matter jurisdiction of this action under Article III, §2 of the United States Constitution and 28 U.S.C. §1332. This counterclaim is a compulsory counterclaim under Fed. R. Civ. P. 13(a). This court has supplemental jurisdiction over the counterclaim under 28 U.S.C. §1367(a).

11.

2. The signed Proposal and Estimate attached to the plaintiff's complaint constitutes a valid contract between the plaintiff and the defendant Ronan Construction Company.

3. Under that contract, the plaintiff agreed to pay Ronan Construction Company $40,000 for the construction of an addition to her home at 53 School Street, Alton, New Hampshire.

4. The defendant Ronan Construction Company has fully performed all of its obligations under the contract.

5. Although the defendant Ronan Construction Company has demanded payment of the final balance due under the contract, the plaintiff has failed to pay Ronan Construction Company the final progress payment of $15,000.

11.

WHEREFORE, the defendant Ronan Construction Company demands judgment from the plaintiff in the amount of $15,000 and interest and costs and such other relief as the court finds just and equitable.

DEMAND FOR JURY TRIAL

12.

Under Fed. R. Civ. P. 38(b), the defendants demand jury trial of all issues raised by the plaintiff's complaint and the defendant Ronan Construction Company's counterclaim.

_____

13.

Arthur Ackerman
Ackerman, Sloan and Cariotis
Attorney for the Defendants
59 State Street
Boston, MA 02114
(617) 228-6301

14.

CERTIFICATE OF SERVICE

I hereby certify that on this date I served a true copy of the above answer and counterclaim upon Phyllis Slater, Gomez, Robbins and Slater, 322 Puritan Road, Plymouth, MA 02360, by First Class mail, postage prepaid.

Date: _____

_____

Arther Ackerman
Ackerman, Sloan and Cariotis
59 State Street
Boston, MA 02114
(617) 228-6301

Comments on the Answer and Counterclaim

1.   Rule 10(a) governs the caption of the answer as well as the complaint and all other pleadings. Note that the federal docket number is now known and will be used in all subsequent pleadings and other papers.

2.   Rule 8(b) specifically requires the defendant to respond to each allegation in the complaint by admitting or denying the allegations, stating the parts that are true and denying the remainder, or stating that the defendant does not have enough information to assess the truth of the allegation. In his *First Defense,* Ronan complies with this requirement by responding, paragraph by paragraph, to the allegations in the plaintiff's complaint. Rule 10(b) requires these responses to be set forth in numbered paragraphs, and the drafting attorney here has numbered her admissions and denials to correspond to the appropriate paragraphs in the complaint. This will make it easy for the parties and the court to compare the pleadings during the course of the suit, in order to quickly ascertain the positions of the parties on the various issues.

In some cases, the defendant may group his responses to parts of the complaint in a single sentence. For example, the answer might state that "the defendant admits the allegations in paragraphs one to eleven and sixteen to twenty-one of the complaint." See, e.g., Official Form 20, accompanying the Federal Rules of Civil Procedure. This saves space and time, but in cases with a large number of paragraphs and varied responses it is less helpful for quick reference in comparing the complaint and the answer.

3.   It is permissible for a party to respond by stating that he lacks sufficient information to admit or deny an allegation. Fed. R. Civ. P. 8(b). The defendants here probably have no particular knowledge of the National Register of Historic Places and are under no duty to scurry around and verify this allegation in order to answer the complaint.

4.   Rule 8(b) requires the defendant to respond clearly and forthrightly to the allegations of the complaint. ("Denials shall fairly meet the substance of the averments denied. When a pleader intends in good faith to deny only a part or a qualification of an averment, the pleader shall specify so much of it as is true and material and shall deny only the remainder.") It would not be proper for the defendants here to simply deny the entire allegation in paragraph seven because Ronan had told the plaintiff that he had worked on old houses. However, the defendants do not accept the plaintiff's characterization of Ronan's statements and have therefore crafted their response to paragraph seven to negate any inference that Ronan represented himself as an expert in this area. A number of the defendants' other responses also admit

some parts of the allegations but deny other parts or recharacterize allegations in the complaint. See, e.g., paragraphs 11, 15, 18, and 26.

5.   Rule 10(c) authorizes adoption by reference of parts of a pleading in another part of the pleading. The language of the rule is general, so it is clear that a defendant — or any other pleader — may do so as well as a plaintiff. Because Schulansky incorporated all of her factual allegations by reference into her First Claim for Relief, Ronan has similarly incorporated his answers to the earlier paragraphs in his answer to her First Claim for Relief.

6.   As you are probably aware, defending parties will frequently have further defenses to the plaintiff's claims, in addition to denials of the allegations in the complaint. After responding in the First Defense to each of the allegations of the complaint, the answer goes on to set forth several further defenses. This breakdown is proper under Rule 10(b), which provides in part that "each defense other than denials shall be stated in a separate count or defense whenever a separation facilitates the clear presentation of the matters set forth."

The defendants' Second Defense here is an objection to the court's power to adjudicate, on the ground that it lacks personal jurisdiction over the defendants. This objection could be raised by pre-answer motion under Rule 12(b), but it does not have to be. It is always proper to include this objection in the answer instead of raising it by pre-answer motion, so long as no pre-answer motion is made. See Chapter 17, p.277. As Ackerman's comments indicate, the decision to answer rather than move to dismiss is a tactical one.

7.   The defendants' Fourth Defense raises an affirmative defense. The defendants take the position that, even if the contract required reconstruction of the foundation and the defendants failed to do so, the plaintiff waived performance of this obligation by her assent to Ronan's alternative suggestion. An affirmative defense asserts new facts that avoid liability even if the plaintiff proves her basic allegations. It is akin to the old common law "confession and avoidance" device, except that the defendant need not admit the plaintiff's allegations ("confess") in order to allege additional facts that avoid liability.

Under Rule 8(e)(2), a defendant may plead inconsistently, and the *Schulansky* defendants have done so in their answer. In their First Defense, they deny that they agreed to reconstruct the foundation. In their Fourth Defense, they assert that, even if they did agree to do so, the plaintiff waived performance of that obligation.

The order of the various defenses is not prescribed by the rules. On occasion, you will see an answer that begins with objections and affirmative defenses and leaves the admissions and denials until later. Of paramount importance, of course, is that all defenses be raised in the answer, to avoid waiving any by omission.

8.   Defendants frequently include a paragraph like this at the end of the answer, asking the court, on the basis of the defenses and denials in the answer, to dismiss the complaint. In the federal courts (and state systems as well) a prevailing party is entitled to recover certain costs of suit, such as witness fees and the cost of transcripts. See 28 U.S.C. §1920. It is customary to ask for these in the answer and, in a lawyerly excess of caution, to append a request for any other relief the court finds "just and equitable" as well.

9.   It is entirely proper to include a counterclaim within the answer. It should be set apart from the rest of the answer, however, and clearly labeled as a counterclaim. If a counterclaim is not clearly labeled as such, it may look a good deal like an affirmative defense. (Compare, for example, paragraph 26 of the answer, which could be construed to seek relief from Schulansky for the unpaid balance under the contract.) Unless it is clearly labeled as a counterclaim and set apart from the various defenses, it may be unclear whether Ronan is defending on the basis of Schulansky's failure to fulfill her obligations under the contract or seeking independent, affirmative relief by way of counterclaim.

Note that Losordo has consistently taken the position in drafting the answer that the contract is between Ronan Construction Company and Schulansky. See paragraphs 10, 11, 12, 22, 23, and 26 of the First Defense. Thus, the company is the proper party to assert the counterclaim for breach of the contract. Indeed, Losordo might have chosen to emphasize the difference in the positions of Ronan and Ronan Construction Company by filing completely separate answers for them. The rules do not require the defendants to file a joint answer, and in cases where their interests are clearly divergent, they will not do so.

10.   Federal Rule 8(a) requires "a pleading which sets forth a claim for relief" to include a statement of the grounds for the court's jurisdiction. A counterclaim is such a pleading, and Losordo has accordingly asserted here that the court has supplemental jurisdiction over it. Supplemental jurisdiction is proper for this claim because it is a compulsory counterclaim. See Chapter 14, example 4.

Strictly speaking, this is probably overpleading. Rule 8(a)(1) does not require a jurisdictional allegation if the court already has jurisdiction (i.e., if an earlier pleading has already provided a basis for jurisdiction over the action), and the new pleading does not require "new grounds" for jurisdiction. In this case, the court has jurisdiction over the main claim based on diversity, and supplemental jurisdiction over the related counterclaim is arguably not a "new ground." However, since Schulansky's complaint was originally filed in state court, it contained no explicit allegation as to the basis of jurisdiction, and it is certainly appropriate, even if not required, to assert the ground of jurisdiction in the counterclaim.

The Rule 8(a)(1) requirement to state the ground of the court's jurisdiction refers to subject matter jurisdiction, not personal jurisdiction. *Sterling Homex Corp. v. Homasote Co.*, 437 F.2d 87, 88 (2d Cir. 1971). It is not necessary to assert in a pleading that the court has personal jurisdiction over the defendant, but, of course, the court must have it in order to proceed.

11. The general rules of pleading govern the allegations in a counterclaim, including the use of numbered paragraphs and inclusion of a demand for relief.[1] Like an original complaint, a counterclaim may include a number of claims for relief based on different theories. It is even permissible to assert completely unrelated counterclaims (see Fed. R. Civ. P. 13(b)), although there will not be supplemental jurisdiction over such claims.

Unlike the common law, where the parties might plead back and forth a number of times before a single issue is reached, the answer usually ends the pleadings under the Federal Rules. However, Fed. R. Civ. P. 7(a) does require the plaintiff to reply to a counterclaim if it is "denominated as such." This means that if the defendant does not clearly label the counterclaim in the answer, the plaintiff need not file a reply. Thus, he need not guess whether vague allegations in an answer are affirmative defenses, denials, or counterclaims. Schulansky would be required to file a reply to this counterclaim, since Ronan's counsel has clearly labeled it as such, putting Schulansky on notice that Ronan is claiming affirmative relief from her.

The plaintiff's reply is governed by the same pleading requirements as Ronan's answer and should include responses to each of the paragraphs in the counterclaim as well as affirmative defenses. Of course, the reply will only address the allegations in the counterclaim itself, since the parties' positions on the main claim are already established by the complaint and the answer. The reply must be served within 20 days after service of the answer. Fed. R. Civ. P. 12(a).

12. Losordo has followed her own suggestion in her memo on removal (see infra p.448) and included a demand for jury trial on the counterclaim. It may be that the jury demand is unnecessary, but at most it is redundant. Rather than invest substantial research time (and the client's money) in finding a definitive answer to this question, Losordo has simply erred on the side of

---

1. In putting a dollar demand in his counterclaim, Ronan has not ignored Mass. Gen. L. ch. 231, §13B, the statute that bars putting a dollar demand in a complaint. That statute only bars a dollar demand in cases of unliquidated damages, that is, damages that cannot easily be calculated. In cases where the damages can be easily ascertained by calculation, a specific demand is proper. Here, all Ronan has to do to ascertain the damages is to subtract the earlier progress payments from the contract price. However, if a specific dollar demand is included, the statute requires the pleader to append a sworn statement to the pleading showing how the calculation was made.

caution by including it in the answer. Just to cover all the bases, she has also demanded jury trial on the main claim as well.

13. The answer, like the complaint and all other pleadings and motions, must be signed by the attorney and is subject to the ethical constraints and sanctions set forth in Fed. R. Civ. P. 11.

14. The elaborate service provisions of Fed. R. Civ. P. 4 only govern service of the complaint. Subsequent papers may be served under the simpler provisions of Fed. R. Civ. P. 5(b), which authorizes service by personal delivery or regular mail to the attorney for the opposing party. Once properly notified that the suit has been commenced, the parties should be in contact and should watch the docket for subsequent filings. But a party who never receives initial notice of a suit cannot take such precautions.

The certificate of service constitutes a representation by the serving attorney that he has complied with the service requirements of Rule 5(b). It is often drafted as a separate document, but the local rules for the District of Massachusetts provide that the certificate of service must appear in the margin of the pleading or motion itself, rather than on a separate sheet. Local Rule 5.2(b)(2).

———————————————

Losordo raises an interesting question at the end of her memo, concerning the possibility that asserting the counterclaim might waive the defendant's objection to personal jurisdiction. In fact, if Ronan's attorneys look into this issue, they will find that the courts are split on this question. Some cases have held that a defendant waives his objection to personal jurisdiction by asking the court to adjudicate a counterclaim. Others, however, have recognized that this puts the defendant in an awkward position, because Fed. R. Civ. P. 13(a) *requires* him to assert any counterclaim that arises out of the same events as the plaintiff's claim. (Of course, the defendant could present the personal jurisdiction issue by pre-answer motion, thus obtaining resolution of that issue before answering.) See generally 5A Wright and Miller at §1397, which reviews this issue and suggests that assertion of a compulsory counterclaim should not waive the personal jurisdiction defense.

One of the things that makes a litigation practice unnerving is the number of uncertainties that arise in the course of a case, in circumstances that make it impossible to give those issues the full attention they deserve. Here, the attorneys are under the gun to get their responsive pleading in and are doubtless handling many other matters as well. Many lawyers would never even have thought of this rather subtle ramification of the counterclaim. Even if their client could afford to have exhaustive research done on this point, it would have been hard for Ronan's lawyers to find the time to do it before answering. They probably would not have found a definitive answer even if they had researched the point.

It is also interesting to compare the facts as stated in the Slater memo (p.427) and Ackerman's memo in this chapter. The dispute looks quite different from the two parties' points of view. It is unlikely that either is lying or deliberately distorting the facts, they just see things from different perspectives, like Republicans and Democrats, or Mainers and Californians. The truth, if there is such a thing in a case like this, is likely to be ambiguous and elusive. If there is a trial, the system will resolve the dispute one way or the other, but it is unlikely that it will definitively determine who is "right" or leave either party feeling fully satisfied for the effort and emotional stress it engenders.

Naturally, the attorneys' job in drafting the pleadings, and in representing the parties generally, is to state the case most strongly from their clients' viewpoints. Hopefully, providing vigorous advocacy will not prevent them from seeing the facts as they are likely to play out at trial and advising their clients accordingly. But even if they keep some perspective on the case, there is little doubt that the lawyer's duty in an adversary system tends to accentuate the differences in the parties' views rather than the search for common ground. This has spawned an increasing emphasis on alternatives to litigation, such as mediation, which try to educate the parties about each others' views and bring the parties together rather than focus, as the litigation system tends to, on the differences in their points of view.

29

Chain Reaction: Ronan Brings In Jones

The Drafting Request

MEMORANDUM

TO: Marcia Losordo
Associate

FROM: Arthur Ackerman

RE: Third-party complaint in *Schulansky v. Ronan*
U.S. District Court No. 90-6719

DATE: January 4, 1991

I have reviewed and filed your answer and counterclaim in the Schulansky case. I have also discussed with Dick Ronan the possibility of filing a third-party complaint against Arlen Jones, the bulldozer operator who did the excavation work on the job. On the basis of that discussion, I have decided to proceed with the third-party complaint.

As you are no doubt aware, Fed. R. Civ. P. 14(a) allows us to implead Jones if he "is or may be liable to [our clients] for all or part of the plaintiff's claim" against them. In other words, we can implead Jones if we have a right to reimbursement from him for any damages Schulansky recovers from us. In my judgment, we may be able to obtain indemnification from Jones if Schulansky recovers on either her breach of contract claim or her negligence claim.

Please let me know if you agree with the following line of reasoning, which leads me to that conclusion.

As you suggested in your earlier memo, it is not clear whether Jones acted as a subcontractor to Ronan or as Ronan's employee in doing the excavation work. The accepted test is the extent of control Ronan could exercise over Jones in the course of the work, and the facts on this are ambiguous. On the one hand, Ronan did not have a written contract with Jones for the excavation work; he simply called Jones up and asked him to do the work for $3,000. The facts that Jones worked for a flat price and used his own equipment support the argument that he acted as an independent contractor. On the other hand, according to Ronan, he consistently directed Jones in the course of the work and considered Jones (who worked quite regularly for Ronan) an employee, even though he usually paid him by the job. In addition, the informality of their arrangement suggests an employment relationship more than a contract. Given the ambiguity in the evidence, it will likely be a jury question whether Jones should be characterized as an employee or independent contractor. Restatement (Second) of Agency §220, comment c (1958).

If the jury were to find that Jones was Ronan's employee, Ronan would be liable for his negligence, under respondeat superior principles (Restatement (Second) of Agency §219 (1958)), but would have a right to indemnification from Jones. Thus, if Schulansky proves that Jones negligently disturbed the existing foundation during the excavation, and the jury concludes that Jones acted as an employee in doing the work, Schulansky will recover judgment from us, but Jones will be liable to indemnify us for the entire judgment.

Alternatively, if the jury finds that Jones was not directly under Ronan's control and therefore acted as a subcontractor to Ronan, Ronan should still have a right of indemnification from him under contract principles. If Jones's negligent excavation caused a breach of the main contract between Ronan and Schulansky, Ronan would be liable directly to Schulansky for the breach by his subcontractor. However, Jones would have breached his (unwritten) subcontract with Ronan by failing to perform the work properly, so Ronan would have a cause of action against him for breach of the subcontract. The damages for this breach would include the judgment Ronan incurred to Schulansky, as well as his attorneys' fees (to us) incurred in defending her claim. Thus, if Schulansky recovers on her breach of contract claim, we should be entitled to recover both the damages to Schulansky and our fees for defending the action from Jones.

If you agree with my reasoning, please draft a third-party complaint against Jones for indemnification on both of the plaintiff's claims. I realize that our theories for indemnification are based on inconsistent allegations, since we will allege on the negligence claim that Jones was an employee, but on the contract claim that he was a subcontractor. However, Rule 8(e)(2) expressly allows us to plead inconsistent versions of our claim. Nor do I view this as inappropriate under the ethical pleading requirements in Rule 11, since there is factual support for characterizing Jones either as an employee or an independent contractor. Where the jury could properly reach either conclusion, it is appropriate to assert whatever rights we may have against Jones based on either theory.

As you pointed out in our discussions, it is a little awkward to deny that the foundation was damaged at all during the excavation (as we did in our answer) but to turn around and implead Jones for causing that damage. Ronan tells me that he is not convinced that Jones's excavation work destabilized the foundation, or that anything did. But there is some evidence to support a finding that Jones was negligent. Apparently Jones did hit the foundation a number of times with his bulldozer, and the excavation turned up some loose rocks along the edge of the foundation. Schulansky was present at the time, and this is probably what is behind her negligence claim.

I do not think the Rules require us to disregard our possible rights against Jones just because we denied in our answer that any negligence took place. As indicated above, the Rules specifically authorize inconsistent pleading. Of course, we must have reasonable grounds to support the allegations under Rule 11, but I believe Ronan's observations about Jones's encounters with the foundation during the excavation meet this test, since it suggests that Jones may have damaged the foundation in the course of the excavation. We shouldn't have to abandon a possible right to indemnification against Jones just because we think the stronger argument is that there was no negligence in the first place.

We may have a serious problem obtaining personal jurisdiction over Jones in Massachusetts. Jones lives in New Hampshire, agreed to do the work in a telephone conversation with Ronan, and performed all the work in New Hampshire. According to Ronan, Jones does work occasionally in Massachusetts, but I doubt that this occasional work in the state is sufficient to support personal jurisdiction over Jones for a claim unrelated to his work here in the state. On the other hand, since Jones occasionally works for contractors here in Massachusetts perhaps we can serve process on him while he is working here and obtain jurisdiction based on in-state service. Please do a little research to determine whether this would establish personal jurisdiction over Jones here.

I realize you have not yet had a chance to open your Christmas presents, but please get on this right away. I would like to file this within the ten-day limit for filing the third-party complaint without leave of court.

The Associate's Response

MEMORANDUM

TO: Arthur Ackerman

FROM: Marcia Losordo

RE: Third-party complaint in *Schulansky v. Ronan*
            U.S. District Court No. 90-6719

DATE: January 7, 1991

I have attached a draft third-party complaint against Jones in the Schulansky case. I agree with your analysis of Jones's potential liability to us, but I have several additional observations. First, it is conceivable that Schulansky would recover from us for breach of contract on both grounds alleged in her complaint. It may turn out that the structural damage resulted in part from Ronan's failure to rebuild the foundation, and in part from damage caused by Jones's bulldozer. If the jury finds that both causes contributed to the settling, we would have a right to partial indemnification from Jones: Presumably the court would apportion the damages between the two causes, and Jones only contributed to one of them.

It is proper to implead a third party for partial as well as full indemnification; Rule 14(a) authorizes impleader of a party who "is or may be liable to the third-party plaintiff for all *or part* of the plaintiff's claim . . ." (emphasis supplied). Thus, I have asserted two claims for relief based on the theory that Jones breached his subcontract with Ronan, one for full indemnification and a separate claim for partial indemnification.

Second, note that our claim against Jones for the attorneys' fees Ronan must pay us to defend Schulansky's claim against him does not satisfy the Rule 14 requirement, since this is not reimbursement for damages Ronan must pay Schulansky. These fees represent separate consequential damages Ronan has suffered as a result of Jones's breach of the subcontract, and the resulting need to defend Schulansky's lawsuit. However, it is proper to assert this additional claim in the third-party complaint. Once a defendant has asserted a proper impleader claim under Rule 14(a), she may also assert independent claims against the third-party defendant under Fed. R. Civ. P. 18(a).

As you suggest, the fact that Jones does occasional business in Massachusetts is not sufficient under the *International Shoe* minimum contacts test to support personal jurisdiction over him for a claim unrelated to the in-state business. See *Helicopteros Nacionales de Columbia, S.A. v. Hall*, 466 U.S. 408, 414-415 (1984) (where claim does not arise out of contacts with forum state, the defendant must have continuous and systematic contacts there to support jurisdiction). Since Jones only works in Massachusetts occasionally, it is doubtful that he would be subject to general in personam jurisdiction here. However, personal jurisdiction can be obtained over Jones by serving process on him here in Massachusetts, under the hoary doctrine of *Pennoyer v. Neff*. The Supreme Court recently reaffirmed the sufficiency of such "transient personal service" in *Burnham v. Superior Court of California*, 495 U.S. 604 (1990). Of course, this requires us to keep track of Jones's movements, locate him on the job site in Massachusetts, and actually serve him in person in the state.

Alternatively, it may be possible to serve Jones in New Hampshire under Fed. R. Civ. P. 4(f), the "100-mile bulge" provision for service on certain additional parties to actions in federal court. Under Rule 4(f), a defendant may be served with process outside the forum state but within 100 miles of the courthouse. This provision authorizes service on Jones in New Hampshire, as long as he is served within 100 miles of the courthouse in Boston. However, while the 100-mile bulge provision authorizes service of process within the bulge, it is unclear whether the defendant must still meet fourteenth amendment standards of personal jurisdiction. In other words, even if we serve Jones in New Hampshire, within the bulge area, he may not be subject to personal jurisdiction here unless he has minimum contacts with Massachusetts or the bulge area. See 4A Wright & Miller §1127 at n.6.

This is a very sophisticated personal jurisdiction issue, which could require extensive research and briefing if it is contested. But the issue won't arise if we serve Jones in Massachusetts, or if we serve him in New Hampshire under Rule 4(f), and he does not raise an objection to personal jurisdiction. I suggest that we serve him on the job in Massachusetts if possible, and if not, within the 100-mile bulge. (Please note that the complaint and summons must be served under the provisions of Fed. R. Civ. P. 4, not under Rule 5.) If he submits to jurisdiction, we may save our clients a good deal of expense in a relatively small-stakes case.

The Resulting Documents

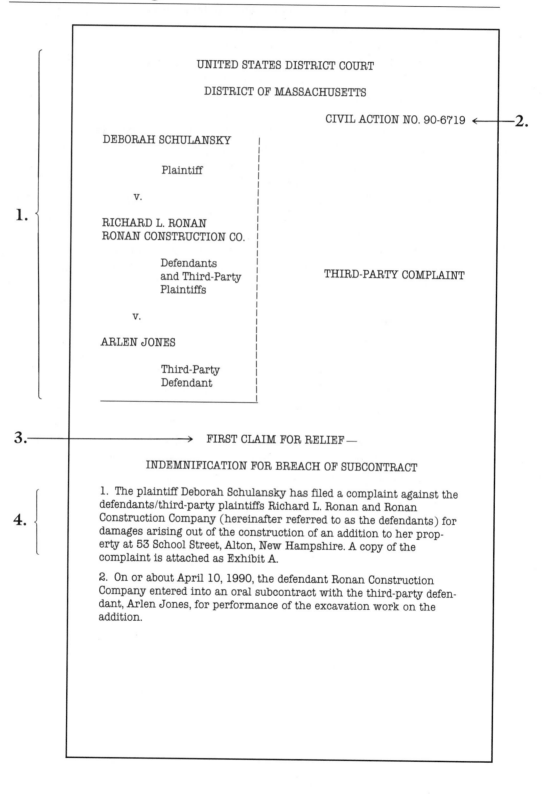

1.

UNITED STATES DISTRICT COURT

DISTRICT OF MASSACHUSETTS

CIVIL ACTION NO. 90-6719   ← **2.**

DEBORAH SCHULANSKY

Plaintiff

v.

RICHARD L. RONAN
RONAN CONSTRUCTION CO.

Defendants
and Third-Party
Plaintiffs

THIRD-PARTY COMPLAINT

v.

ARLEN JONES

Third-Party
Defendant

3. ⟶   FIRST CLAIM FOR RELIEF—

INDEMNIFICATION FOR BREACH OF SUBCONTRACT

4.

1. The plaintiff Deborah Schulansky has filed a complaint against the defendants/third-party plaintiffs Richard L. Ronan and Ronan Construction Company (hereinafter referred to as the defendants) for damages arising out of the construction of an addition to her property at 53 School Street, Alton, New Hampshire. A copy of the complaint is attached as Exhibit A.

2. On or about April 10, 1990, the defendant Ronan Construction Company entered into an oral subcontract with the third-party defendant, Arlen Jones, for performance of the excavation work on the addition.

3. Under the contract, the third-party defendant agreed to perform all the excavation work required by the main contract, using his own labor and equipment, and the defendants agreed to pay the third-party defendant the sum of $3,000 upon completion of the work.

4. The excavation work was performed entirely by the third-party defendant, on or about April 15-18, 1990.

5. The First Claim for Relief in the plaintiff's complaint alleges a right to relief for breach of contract, on the ground that the defendants breached their contract with her by failing to perform the excavation work in a careful manner, resulting in damage to the existing foundation of the house.

6. If defendants breached their contract with the plaintiff by failing to perform the excavation work in a careful manner, that breach and any resulting damage was caused solely by the acts of the third-party defendant.

7. If the third-party defendant failed to perform the excavation work in a careful manner, that failure constituted a breach of the contract between the defendants and the third-party defendant.

5. 8. If the plaintiff recovers against the defendants on the ground that the damage to the foundation in the course of excavation constituted a breach of their contract, the third-party defendant is liable to the defendants for any damages adjudged against them in the main action described in paragraph one.

6. WHEREFORE, the defendants demand judgment against the third-party defendant as follows:

  a. For any and all sums that may be adjudged against them in the plaintiff's main action against them.

7. b. For all costs, including attorneys' fees, incurred in defense of this action.

  c. For such other relief as the court deems just and proper.

SECOND CLAIM FOR RELIEF —

PARTIAL INDEMNIFICATION FOR BREACH OF SUBCONTRACT

9. The defendants repeat and reallege the allegations in paragraphs one to seven of the third-party complaint.

10. If the plaintiff recovers from the defendants both on the ground that they breached their contract with the plaintiff by negligently excavating the foundation and on the ground that they failed to rebuild

it, the third-party defendant is liable to the defendants under the subcontract for that part of the damages resulting from the negligent excavation.

WHEREFORE, the defendants demand judgment from the third-party defendant as follows:

a. For any and all sums that may be adjudged against them for breach of contract resulting from the third-party defendant's negligent excavation.

b. For that part of the defendants' attorneys' fees and costs in defending this action attributable to the plaintiff's claim for negligent excavation.

c. For such other relief as the court deems just and proper.

THIRD CLAIM FOR RELIEF—

INDEMNIFICATION FOR NEGLIGENCE

11. The defendants repeat and reallege the allegations in paragraph one of the third-party complaint.

12. The Second Claim for Relief in the plaintiff's complaint alleges a right to recover from the defendants on the ground that the defendants were negligent in excavating the area in which the addition was to be constructed.

8.

13. On or about April 10, 1990, the defendants employed the third-party defendant Jones to perform the excavation work for the addition.

14. The excavation work was done entirely by the third-party defendant in the course of his employment for the defendants.

15. If the excavation work was negligently performed, any negligence in the work was due solely to acts of the third-party defendant.

16. If the plaintiff recovers from the defendant on her Second Claim for Relief, the defendants are entitled to indemnification from the third-party defendant for any and all damages that they are ordered to pay to the plaintiff on that claim.

WHEREFORE, the defendants demand judgment from the third-party defendant as follows:

a. For all damages that the defendants are ordered to pay to the plaintiff on her second claim for relief.

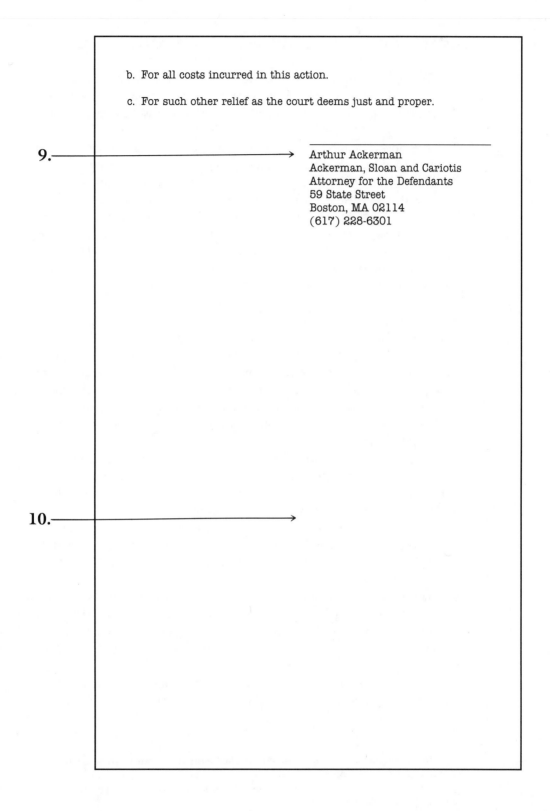

b. For all costs incurred in this action.

c. For such other relief as the court deems just and proper.

9.
Arthur Ackerman
Ackerman, Sloan and Cariotis
Attorney for the Defendants
59 State Street
Boston, MA 02114
(617) 228-6301

10.

Comments on the Third-Party Complaint

1.   The contents of the caption of the third-party complaint are again governed by Rule 10(a), which applies to "every pleading." Note that the title of the action has grown to include the third party as well as the original parties.

2.   The docket number on the third-party complaint is the same as that assigned to the original action. This reflects the very important fact: The third-party action is *not* a separate action, but an additional claim asserted by the defendant against a new party in the original action. This new claim will be litigated along with the main claim unless the court orders separate trials. Thus, all three parties will be entitled to seek discovery from each other (see, e.g., Fed. R. Civ. P. 33, 34, 36), all motions and other papers will be served on all other parties, all parties will participate in any hearings or pretrial proceedings, and all claims will be tried at the same time.

3.   A third-party complaint is a pleading that asserts a right to relief against a new defendant. Thus, its contents are governed by Rule 8(a), which applies to any "pleading which sets forth a claim for relief, whether an original claim, counterclaim, cross-claim, or third-party claim. . . ." Like an original complaint, the third-party complaint must contain an allegation as to the court's basis for subject matter jurisdiction (unless the ground for jurisdiction appears in a previous pleading),[1] a short and plain statement of the plaintiff's claim, and a demand for relief.

   Because it is subject to the regular pleading rules, the defendants' third-party complaint is organized much like an original complaint, with separate claims for relief asserting the defendants' various theories for holding Jones liable to them, and demands for relief following each claim. The defendants have not included a separate *Facts* section as in Schulansky's complaint because most of the relevant facts are already in the original complaint, and the additional facts can be set forth clearly within the *Claim for Relief* sections.

4.   The underlying premise of the defendants' impleader claims is a right to recover from Jones for damages they are ordered to pay Schulansky in this lawsuit. They therefore begin their third-party complaint by alleging the existence of the primary suit, which gives rise to their claims for indemnification.

   A third-party claim requires an answer conforming to the same rules as the original answer. See Fed. R. Civ. P. 7(a), which specifies that proper

---

1. The defendants have not included an allegation of jurisdiction, since there is supplemental jurisdiction over third-party claims. Thus the claims do not need "new grounds" (Fed. R. Civ. P. 8(c)) to support them. See my comment 10 on the answer and counterclaim, supra p.467.

pleadings include an answer to a third-party complaint. In order to properly respond to Ronan's claim against him, Jones will need to have Schulansky's original complaint before him as well as the third-party complaint. For example, Rule 14 allows Jones to raise defenses that *Ronan* may have to Schulansky's primary complaint, on the theory that, if Ronan is not held liable to her, then Jones cannot be held liable to Ronan. Jones can only do this if he has the original complaint to work with in formulating an answer. The defendants should therefore append a copy of the original complaint to the third-party complaint.

5.   The defendants may bring in Jones if he is or may be liable to them for all or part of Schulansky's claim against them. The third-party complaint properly seeks recovery from Jones for those damages that the defendants are ordered to pay Schulansky.

6.   Since the third-party complaint is governed by the pleading requirements of Rule 8(a), it must include a demand for relief. Again, since Ronan seeks recovery over against Jones, his main demand for relief (subsection a) is for the damages he must pay Schulansky. Here the defendants have included separate demands for damages after each claim for relief. Since the potential damages differ under at least the first two claims, including separate demands after each claim makes it easier to understand each claim. Compare the original complaint, supra p.432, which includes a single demand at the end of the entire complaint, and comment 9 following it.

7.   The associate's point about the right to attorneys' fees is a perceptive one. While Ronan's claim to recover from Jones any damages he pays to Schulansky is derivative under Rule 14, his claim for fees is for a separate loss he suffered as a result of Jones's acts. Essentially, Ronan's fees claim is based on the theory that he would not have had to defend Schulansky's suit if Jones had done his job properly. Thus, the fees expended in the defense are a consequential loss resulting from Jones's breach, although they are paid to Ronan's lawyer, not to Schulansky. They constitute a distinct claim that does not satisfy Rule 14 but may be asserted along with it under Fed. R. Civ. P. 18(a). Compare Chapter 13, example 6. It is quite likely that the court would have jurisdiction over this related claim under the supplemental jurisdiction statute, 28 U.S.C. §1367(a).

8.   In paragraphs 13 and 14 of the third claim for relief, Ronan alleges that Jones acted in the scope of his employment for Ronan. Compare paragraphs two and three of his first claim for relief against Jones, which allege a contractual relationship. As Ackerman's memo indicates, the two theories of relief are premised on differing underlying factual conclusions that the jury might reach. Consequently, the factual allegations in the two claims for relief reflect these inconsistent positions.

9.   The attorney's signature on the third-party complaint, as on any other pleading or motion, is subject to the ethical requirements of Rule 11. As Ackerman's memo indicates, he gave considerable thought to those requirements before including inconsistent allegations concerning Jones's status in the third-party complaint.

10.   Note that there is no attorney's certificate of service at the end of the third-party complaint. The reason is that the third-party complaint must be served on Jones, a new party who has no prior notice of the action, under the more exacting provisions of Rule 4, not Rule 5. Proof of service will thus be made in the manner provided by Rule 4(g), not by a simple attorney's certificate.

Losordo's suggestion in her memo that they postpone research on the issue of personal jurisdiction over Jones is a good one. Any practicing lawyer will attest that innumerable complex issues arise in the practice of law. Sometimes it is evident from the outset that a case will turn on such an issue. Most of the time, however, issues arise that may turn out to be important or may not, depending on the course of the suit, the evidence turned up in discovery, whether the opposing party raises the issue, and whether the case goes to trial. Attorneys constantly make pragmatic judgments about which issues to spend their time and their clients' money researching. Frequently, those complex issues just go away for one reason or another.

In this case, for example, the issue of Jones's amenability to jurisdiction under Fed. R. Civ. P. 4(f) could be a complicated one. But it may never need to be decided, if Jones is served in Massachusetts, or if he does not object to jurisdiction, or if he does but the case settles before the issue is litigated. Here, Losordo has noted the potential problem but quite sensibly delayed extensive research on the issue until it becomes clear that it will have to be resolved.

30

Preliminary Objections: Jones Seeks a Way Out

The Drafting Request

MEMORANDUM

TO: Phillip Torres
Associate

FROM: Don Philbrook

RE: Arlen Jones Construction Case

DATE: January 21, 1991

    I represent Arlen Jones, a neighbor of mine who is in the excavation business. He has just been served with process in a federal court suit down in Boston, arising out of some work he did on a house over in Alton. I have attached the original complaint in the action and the third-party complaint against Jones. He is surprised and puzzled by the suit, since he thought the job went fine and the owner was happy. He is also concerned about defending an action down in Boston. Arlen is a local guy with a small business; he is hardly in a position to pay big city legal fees. (I'm not even sure he'll be able to manage mine . . . I'll probably have to put in a pool so he can pay me off by doing the excavation!)

    Naturally, Jones would rather litigate up here than down in Boston, or, better still, get out of this suit entirely. It seems to me that we may have several grounds for dismissal of this action by motion. First, it seems dubious to me that Jones should be subject to personal jurisdiction in Massachusetts on this claim. He negotiated with the general contractor, Ronan Construction Company, here in New Hampshire. He did the work in New Hampshire. The job was a small one at that, only a few days' work for something like $3,000. Whatever damages the owner suffered were suffered here. Thus, this claim does not arise out of any "minimum contacts" Jones has with Massachusetts. Nor is he subject to general in personam jurisdiction there — he lives next door to me here in Littleton, and though he works in Massachusetts once in a while, he does not do business there regularly.

Jones wasn't even served with process in the suit in Massachusetts; Ronan had the summons and complaint served on Jones while he was working on a job down in Dover. Now, I'm just an old country lawyer, and you young fellas may know more about these things than I do, but it seems dubious to me that Jones could be served with process here in New Hampshire, and dragged down to defend a federal court case in Massachusetts, if he lacks minimum contacts with that state. Please do a little research on this issue. Don't go overboard on it — we're not talking million dollar damages here, and Jones can't afford to pay for overkill — but give it a few hours to see if we may have grounds for filing a Rule 12(b) motion to dismiss based on lack of personal jurisdiction and draft an appropriate motion for my signature if there is reasonable support for it.

We may also be able to move to dismiss for lack of subject matter jurisdiction, since we are from the same state as Ronan, the third-party plaintiff, and this is a state law claim. There is a new statute on bringing such ancillary claims in federal court. I just looked at it briefly when it was enacted, but I thought it barred claims brought under Rule 14. Please research and advise me on this as well.

If we can't get the claim against Jones dismissed under Fed. R. Civ. P. 12(b)(1) or (2), perhaps we can convince the court to transfer this action to the District of New Hampshire under 28 U.S.C. §1404(a). It seems to me that it makes much more sense to litigate this case here than in Boston. The work was done here, both of the defendants and the third-party defendant live and do business here, and any damages resulting from the job were suffered here. I assume that most of the witnesses other than Schulansky will be from New Hampshire, since Jones tells me that all of Ronan's employees are also local.

Please take a quick look at the case law on the grounds for transfer of venue. If the cases support our argument for transfer, please draft a separate motion to transfer this action to the District of New Hampshire and advise me as to whether you think we should file it along with our motion to dismiss or hold off until decision of that motion. Be sure to check the local rules of the District of Massachusetts for any special requirements pertaining to motions filed in that court. Feel free to call Jones directly if you need further information from him.

Our response is due within 10 days (the 20-day period under the rule minus the 10 days it took Jones to come to me), so please take care of this right away.

The Associate's Response

MEMORANDUM

TO: Donald Philbrook

FROM: Phillip Torres

RE: Preliminary Motions in *Ronan v. Jones*
         Ma. Federal Dist. Ct. Civil Action No. 90-6719

DATE: January 24, 1991

I have done preliminary research on the three issues you raised in your memo. I conclude that we do not have grounds to move to dismiss for lack of subject matter jurisdiction. On the personal jurisdiction issue, I conclude that we have a colorable argument for dismissal but that we are very unlikely to prevail. The strongest argument is for transfer under 28 U.S.C. §1404(a). I recommend making a motion to transfer only.

1. Subject Matter Jurisdiction

It appears that we do not have a valid objection to subject matter jurisdiction over Ronan's claim against Jones. Before the passage of the new federal statute governing "supplemental jurisdiction," it was clear that the citizenship of an impleaded third party was not relevant to establishing diversity jurisdiction. Several prominent authorities supported the proposition that, if the original action was a proper diversity action, the addition of a third party did not affect the court's jurisdiction. See 3 Moore's Federal Practice ¶14.26 (1985); Glannon, Civil Procedure: Examples and Explanations 152 (1st ed. 1987). Jurisdiction over such claims was based on "ancillary jurisdiction." *Owen Equipment & Erection Co. v. Kroger,* 437 U.S. 365, 375-376 (1978).

Under the new "supplemental jurisdiction" statute, enacted in 1990, state law claims that are related to a case properly before the federal court may also be heard by the court. See 28 U.S.C. §1367(a), which provides that claims that are part of the same "case or controversy" as the main claim may be brought in federal court along with it. There is little question that the statute authorizes supplemental jurisdiction over third-party claims where there is no independent basis for subject matter jurisdiction. See now Glannon, Civil Procedure: Examples and Explanations 242-243 (2d ed. 1992). Consequently I have not included this defense in the motion to dismiss.

Your memory is correct that the statute contains a special provision governing certain Rule 14 claims. See §1367(b). This provision bars supplemental jurisdiction over claims by *plaintiffs* against persons made parties under Rule 14 (and other rules), but it does not apply to claims by a defendant against an impleaded party.

2. Personal Jurisdiction

I spent several hours researching whether Jones is subject to personal jurisdiction in the Massachusetts federal court on the basis of personal service in New Hampshire. My preliminary analysis is as follows:

In *Burnham v. Superior Court of California,* 495 U.S. 604 (1990), the Supreme Court reaffirmed that personal jurisdiction may be based on service of process within the forum state, but *Burnham* does not authorize personal jurisdiction in Massachusetts based on service in New Hampshire. However, service in this case may be proper under Fed. R. Civ. P. 4(f), the "100-mile bulge" provision of Rule 4. Frankly, I had never heard of Rule 4(f) until I started to research this issue. It provides that certain parties (including parties like Jones who are brought in under Rule 14) may be served anywhere within 100 miles of the courthouse. Dover, where Jones was served, is well within that limit. So it is clear that Ronan was authorized to serve Jones in this manner.

It is less clear, however, that a person can be forced into court in Massachusetts just because they are served in New Hampshire within the 100-mile bulge: We can argue that Rule 4(f) addresses only the method of service, not amenability to jurisdiction, and that Jones still cannot be ordered into court in Massachusetts if he lacks minimum contacts with Massachusetts which give rise to the claim.

This argument makes some sense: Why should the court have broader power to exercise jurisdiction over Jones just because the statute authorizes service of the summons and complaint in a broader area? Unfortunately, a quick look at the cases reveals that most courts have held that a defendant served within the "bulge" area is subject to personal jurisdiction, so long as they have minimum contacts *with the bulge area itself.* One early case (*Karlsen v. Hanff,* 278 F. Supp. 864 (S.D.N.Y. 1967)) required that the defendant have minimum contacts with the forum state, but it was later overruled. *Coleman v. American Export Isbrandtsen Lines, Inc.,* 405 F.2d 250, 251-253 (2nd Cir. 1968). Most of the cases I located on a quick look agreed with *Coleman.*

This issue has apparently not been resolved in the First Circuit, but my sense is that this view of Rule 4(f) is now very firmly established and would be followed by the First Circuit. Certainly, there is a respectable legal argument in favor of the position taken in *Karlsen;* I don't see any Rule 11 problem with filing the motion and making the argument. But I think we are very unlikely to get out on this basis, and it is not worth the expense to the client of pursuing it.[1]

I have drafted a motion to dismiss for lack of personal jurisdiction for your consideration. If you want to pursue this objection, I will research it more fully.

3. Transfer under 28 U.S.C. §1404(a)

Our strongest argument is for transfer of the case under 28 U.S.C. §1404(a). Under §1404(a), the court may transfer cases "for the convenience of parties and witnesses, in the interest of justice." The primary factors to be considered are those established in *Gulf Oil Corp. v. Gilbert,* 330 U.S. 501 (1947) (decided under the related doctrine of forum non conveniens), including the plaintiff's choice of a forum, relative ease of access to sources of proof, availability of compulsory process, convenience of witnesses, possibility of a view, and advantages of enforceability of a judgment. See generally 1 Moore's at ¶0.145[5].

Many of these factors support an argument for transfer of this action. As you indicate, the events that gave rise to the suit took place in New Hampshire, and all witnesses and parties except for Schulansky live here. In fact, it will not be possible to compel all of Ronan's employees to testify in Massachusetts because several of them are not subject to the subpoena power of the Massachusetts court and Jones tells me that they no longer work for Ronan. It may also be necessary for the court and the jury to view the house, which would obviously make trial here more appropriate.

In addition, while I have not yet had the time to research the issue, it seems likely that the Massachusetts federal court, applying Massachusetts conflicts of law doctrine (see *Klaxon Co. v. Stentor Electric Mfg. Co.,* 313 U.S. 487 (1941)) would apply the contract and tort law of New Hampshire to this case, since most of the events giving rise to the action took place here, the property is located here, and the damage was suffered here. A number of cases have concluded that the need to apply the law of another state is a factor in favor of transfer. See, e.g., *Hotel Constructors, Inc. v. The Seagrave Corp.,* 543 F. Supp. 1048, 1052 (N.D. Ill. 1982); but cf. *Houk v. Kimberley-Clark*

---

1. There is another argument we could make here. Even if jurisdiction is proper if the defendant has minimum contacts with the "bulge" area, Jones's contacts, which gave rise to this claim, are with Alton, New Hampshire. A quick look at the atlas indicates that Alton is about 75-80 *air miles* from Boston, but probably over a hundred by road. We could argue that the miles should be measured by road, since this is how people usually get from place to place.

Believe it or not, this esoteric issue has also been litigated. See, e.g., *Sprow v. Hartford Ins. Co.,* 594 F.2d 412, 417-418 (5th Cir. 1979), which concluded that the better approach is to measure the hundred miles "as the crow flies." Wright and Miller also advocate this approach. 4A Wright & Miller §1127 n.1. So I think this argument is also likely to be a loser.

Corp., 613 F. Supp. 923, 932 (W.D. Mo. 1985) (applicable law not given great weight unless it is complex or unsettled).

Because a major reason for transfer under §1404(a) is for the convenience of the parties, it would certainly bolster our position if the defendants were willing to join in the motion to transfer. You may wish to call Ronan's counsel to see if he is willing to do so. Ironically, while it would be more convenient for Ronan personally to litigate up here, it would be less so for his lawyers because Ackerman, Sloan and Cariotis only have offices in Boston. You might get a more enthusiastic reception if you could suggest this directly to Ronan. However, I realize this would be improper under the Code of Professional Responsibility.

I have attached draft motions to dismiss and to transfer, along with supporting affidavits from Jones. Tactically, we could file the motion to dismiss under Fed. R. Civ. P. 12(b)(2) and hold our motion to transfer, as there is no requirement that the transfer motion be filed before answering the complaint. However, since the argument based on lack of personal jurisdiction looks doubtful, we may want to file both motions together. Perhaps the judge will latch on to the transfer motion as a means of avoiding the more complicated personal jurisdiction question. Last, since we will have to participate in discovery while the motions are pending, we should present both motions in hopes of getting out of the Massachusetts court as soon as possible.

Thank you for reminding me to check the local district court rules. Rule 7.1(a) of the Local Rules of the District of Massachusetts provides that affidavits and other supporting materials, including supporting memoranda, must be filed with the motion. Otherwise, they may only be filed with leave of court. In view of this rule, I suggest that we file a motion for an extension of time to file a responsive pleading under Fed. R. Civ. P. 6(b) or ask Ronan's counsel to assent to an extension, to give us adequate time to prepare a supporting memorandum of law to file with these motions. Alternatively, I have included a request in each motion for leave to file supporting memos at a time specified by the court.

The Resulting Documents

UNITED STATES DISTRICT COURT

DISTRICT OF MASSACHUSETTS

CIVIL ACTION NO. 90-6719

DEBORAH SCHULANSKY

Plaintiff

v.

RICHARD L. RONAN
RONAN CONSTRUCTION CO.

Defendants

v.

ARLEN JONES

Third-Party
Defendant

THIRD-PARTY DEFENDANT'S

MOTION TO DISMISS THE

THIRD-PARTY COMPLAINT FOR

LACK OF PERSONAL

JURISDICTION

The third-party defendant, Arlen Jones, moves to dismiss the third-party complaint against him under Fed. R. Civ. P. 12(b)(2) on the ground that the court lacks personal jurisdiction over him on this claim. In support of the motion the third-party defendant states as follows:

1. The third-party defendant is not domiciled in Massachusetts or doing business in Massachusetts on a regular basis, as more fully appears from the Affidavit of Arlen Jones, paragraphs one and three, attached as Exhibit A to this motion.

2. This claim arises out of construction work performed by the third-party defendant in Alton, New Hampshire, as more fully appears from paragraphs one to four of the Third-Party Complaint, and paragraphs four and five of the attached Affidavit of Arlen Jones.

3. The third-party defendant has no contacts with Massachusetts that are related to this claim, as further appears from the Affidavit of Arlen Jones.

4. The exercise of personal jurisdiction over the third-party defendant in these circumstances is barred by the Due Process Clause of the Fourteenth Amendment to the United States Constitution.

<u>REQUEST</u> <u>FOR</u> <u>ORAL</u> <u>ARGUMENT</u>

The third-party defendant requests twenty minutes for oral argument on this motion, pursuant to Local Rule 7.1(c), and leave to file a supporting memorandum at a time specified by the court.

_____

Donald R. Philbrook
Attorney for Third-Party
  Defendant
11A Grove Street
Littleton, New Hampshire 03561
(603) 471-8200

UNITED STATES DISTRICT COURT

DISTRICT OF MASSACHUSETTS

CIVIL ACTION NO. 90-6719

DEBORAH SCHULANSKY

    Plaintiff

v.

RICHARD L. RONAN
RONAN CONSTRUCTION CO.

    Defendants

v.

ARLEN JONES

    Third-Party
    Defendant

AFFIDAVIT OF ARLEN JONES

IN SUPPORT OF MOTION TO

DISMISS THIRD-PARTY

COMPLAINT

State of New Hampshire
County of Littleton
     ss.:

Arlen Jones, being first duly sworn, states as follows:

1. On January 11, 1991, I was personally served with a summons and Third-Party Complaint in the above-captioned action. Service was made at Dover, New Hampshire, while I was engaged in a small excavating project for a condominium complex there.

2. At the time of service and at all other times relevant to this action I resided at 88 Warner Avenue, Littleton, New Hampshire, and conducted a small excavating business from that address as a sole proprietor.

3. Although I occasionally (approximately once per year) do small excavation jobs in Massachusetts, I am not licensed to do business in

Massachusetts, do not conduct business there on a regular basis, and receive less than 5% of my income from Massachusetts business.

4. This action arises out of renovation work performed by Richard Ronan on the plaintiff's house in Alton, New Hampshire. The third-party complaint alleges a right to relief for faulty excavation work performed as part of the renovation work at the Alton site.

5. All negotiations, agreements, preparation, and performance of the work giving rise to this claim took place in New Hampshire. I did not solicit this job in Massachusetts nor perform any act related to the events in suit in Massachusetts, nor was I aware until I received process in this action that the plaintiff resided there.

6. I have never consented to suit in Massachusetts on this claim.

———————————————————
                              Arlen Jones

    Subscribed and sworn to before me this ___ day of ————————, 1991.

———————————————————
                              Notary Public

My commission expires:

———————————————

UNITED STATES DISTRICT COURT

DISTRICT OF MASSACHUSETTS

CIVIL ACTION NO. 90-6719

DEBORAH SCHULANSKY

    Plaintiff

v.

RICHARD L. RONAN
RONAN CONSTRUCTION CO.

    Defendants

v.

ARLEN JONES

    Third-Party
    Defendant

THIRD-PARTY DEFENDANT'S

MOTION TO TRANSFER UNDER

28 U.S.C. §1404(a)

The third-party defendant, Arlen Jones, moves to transfer this action to the federal district court for the District of New Hampshire, under 28 U.S.C. §1404(a), for the convenience of the parties and in the interest of justice. In support of the motion, the third-party defendant states as follows:

1. This action arises out of construction work performed on the plaintiff's home in Alton, New Hampshire, as more fully appears from paragraphs 5 and 14-20 of the plaintiff's complaint and paragraphs 7-9 of the Affidavit of Arlen Jones, attached hereto as Exhibit A.

2. The defendants on the main claim are a New Hampshire resident and a New Hampshire corporation, as more fully appears from paragraphs 2-3 of the plaintiff's complaint.

3. All negotiations between the defendant and the third-party defendant concerning the excavation work took place in New Hampshire, as more fully appears from the Affidavit of Arlen Jones, paragraph 8.

4. All of the construction work giving rise to both the plaintiff's claims against the defendants and the defendants' claims against the third-party defendant took place in Alton, New Hampshire, as more fully appears from the Affidavit of Arlen Jones, paragraph 9.

5. Any damages suffered by the plaintiff or the defendants were suffered in New Hampshire, where the premises involved in this action are located and the defendants are located.

6. All potential witnesses who worked on the construction of the addition reside in New Hampshire, as more fully appears from the Affidavit of Arlen Jones, paragraph 10.

7. At least some of the potential witnesses in this action are beyond the subpoena power of this court, as more fully appears from the Affidavit of Arlen Jones, paragraph 10.

8. This claim could have been brought in the District of New Hampshire because the events giving rise to the claim took place there and all defendants are subject to service of process in that district.

REQUEST FOR ORAL ARGUMENT

The third-party defendant requests one half hour for oral argument of this motion, and leave to file a supporting memorandum at a time specified by the court.

Donald R. Philbrook
Attorney for Third-Party
  Defendant
11A Grove Street
Littleton, New Hampshire 03561
(603) 471-8200

UNITED STATES DISTRICT COURT

DISTRICT OF MASSACHUSETTS

CIVIL ACTION NO. 90-6719

DEBORAH SCHULANSKY

Plaintiff

v.

RICHARD L. RONAN
RONAN CONSTRUCTION CO.

Defendants

v.

ARLEN JONES

Third-Party
Defendant

AFFIDAVIT OF ARLEN JONES

IN SUPPORT OF MOTION TO

TRANSFER UNDER

28 U.S.C. §1404(a)

State of New Hampshire ⎱
                       ⎰ ss.:
County of Littleton

Arlen Jones, being first duly sworn, states as follows:

1. I reside at 88 Warner Avenue, Littleton, New Hampshire, approximately 125 miles from Boston, and have resided there at all times relevant to the events involved in this action.

2. I operate a small excavation business, as a sole proprietor. The business is operated out of my home and grosses about $60,000 per year.

3. Over 90% of my business is done in New Hampshire, most of it in the Littleton area of northern New Hampshire. While I occasionally

do small jobs in Massachusetts, I do not work there more than approximately once a year. I do not currently have any orders for future jobs in Massachusetts.

4. I am currently booked solid for the new construction season with jobs all over New Hampshire. Since I am a small proprietor, and must attend to my business every day, it would seriously inconvenience me to litigate this action, which arises out of one of the smallest jobs I did last year, in Massachusetts.

5. At no time did I have any direct negotiations with the plaintiff in this action, nor was I apprised of the fact that she lives in Massachusetts or of any other facts which would have led me to expect to have to defend this claim in a Massachusetts court.

6. On information and belief, the defendants Richard Ronan and Ronan Construction Company are primarily engaged in residential construction in New Hampshire.

7. Sometime during the first week of April 1990, Richard Ronan called me in Littleton concerning an excavation job on the Schulansky house in Alton, New Hampshire.

8. After several phone calls between Ronan and me, all of which took place in New Hampshire, I agreed to do the excavation work on the Alton job, for $3,000.

9. I commenced work on the Schulansky job on April 15, 1990, and completed the work on April 17. All preparation and performance of the work took place in either Littleton, New Hampshire or Alton, New Hampshire.

10. I have done at least twenty excavation jobs for Ronan and/or Ronan Construction Company during the past three years. I am acquainted with all of Ronan's employees who worked on the Schulansky job. All of those employees live in New Hampshire, and at least four of them in the Littleton area, more than 100 miles from Boston.

11. Since the Schulansky job in April 1990, several of the carpenters who worked on the job have left Ronan's employ.

_____

Arlen Jones

Subscribed and sworn to before me this ___ day of _____, 1991.

_____

Notary Public

My commission expires:

_____

Comments on the Third-Party Motions

1.   The same formal rules that govern captions for pleadings also apply to motions and to affidavits as well. See Fed. R. Civ. P. 7(b)(2). In addition, the ethical constraints on pleadings in Rule 11 also apply to motions. Fed. R. Civ. P. 7(b)(3). Under Rule 11, as amended in 1983, attorneys must investigate both the factual and legal bases for filing motions before doing so. Under earlier practice, defense counsel would frequently respond to a complaint with a motion to dismiss, including a long laundry list of dubious objections. Such habits, while they die slowly, are now clearly inconsistent with the Rule 11 requirements for reasonable inquiry and supporting grounds.

2.   Rule 7(b) provides that a motion shall "state with particularity the grounds therefor." In both the motion to dismiss and the motion to transfer, Jones's counsel has set forth briefly the reasons that support the particular order sought in the motion. This satisfies the requirement of "particularity" and assists the court in understanding the basis of the motions. A motion must also "set forth the relief or order sought." Rule 7(b)(1). Torres's draft motions do this as well: The first seeks dismissal and the second, transfer. See the first paragraph of each motion.

However, the motion itself is not the right place to *argue* the merits of the motion, or to set forth in detail the facts that support the motion. The supporting arguments and discussion of authority should be set forth in an accompanying memorandum of law. Any facts necessary to support the motion should be provided in accompanying affidavits, deposition transcripts, interrogatories, business records, or other evidentiary documents.

3.   An affidavit is a sworn statement by a witness. It is usually notarized and is signed subject to the pains and penalties of perjury. The "ss." in the heading is a legal formalism frequently found in affidavits. It stands for "silicet," which roughly means "to wit" or "let it be known," and simply indicates that the affiant publicly asserts the facts in the affidavit.

It is entirely proper to submit affidavits in support of a motion, to establish the facts necessary for the court to rule on the motion. See Fed. R. Civ. P. 43(e). In the case of Jones's motion to dismiss for lack of personal jurisdiction, for example, the earlier pleadings do not indicate whether Jones has sufficient contacts with Massachusetts to support jurisdiction over him for this claim. Jones's affidavit provides the court with admissible evidence (since it is sworn personal testimony of the affiant), which supports the position taken in his motion.

If the other parties have countervailing evidence, they may submit their own affidavits or other materials in opposition to the motion. The court may decide the motion on the basis of the facts presented or, if issues of credibility are involved or further evidence needed, may take testimony from the witnesses in a full evidentiary hearing on the motion.

4.   You may have been puzzled as to why Jones's lawyers have included a paragraph in the affidavit stating that several potential witnesses no longer work for Ronan and do not live within 100 miles of Boston. These facts are relevant to the motion to transfer: If these witnesses still worked for Ronan they would presumably be subject to his control and therefore would appear to testify at a trial in Massachusetts. If they no longer work for Ronan, however, and are outside the subpoena power of the Massachusetts federal court, they will probably not be available to testify at a trial in Boston. See Fed. R. Civ. P. 45(b)(2) (authorizing service of subpoenas within the judicial district where suit is pending or within 100 miles of the place of trial). A New Hampshire court, however, could subpoena witnesses from any place within New Hampshire, thus supporting the argument for transfer.

5.   It is entirely proper to file combined motions for more than one form of action by the court. Jones's lawyers could, for example, decide to file a combined "Motion to Dismiss for Lack of Personal Jurisdiction, or in the Alternative to Transfer Venue under 28 U.S.C. §1404(a)." Torres drafted the two separately because the tactical decision whether to file them together or separately had not yet been made.

6.   Torres's suggestion that Philbrook contact Ronan's counsel is interesting. It would certainly lend credence to the motion if the original defendants also sought transfer. Although Jones and Ronan are adversaries on the merits, their interests may coincide on this issue or others in the suit. As Chapter 25 indicates (supra p.423), it is appropriate to contact Ronan's counsel to discuss a possible joint motion or any other such issues that arise in the course of the litigation.

Further, the point that Torres makes about the potential difference in interests between Ronan and his attorneys is a delicate and interesting one. If the case is transferred, the insurance company may retain local counsel in New Hampshire to handle it, and the Boston firm may lose the case. However, Ronan's counsel is there to represent his clients' interests, not his own, and should join in the motion to transfer if Ronan prefers to litigate in New Hampshire, or if other tactical considerations point to New Hampshire as the preferable forum.

7.   This book writing business is frustrating. I started out to create a fairly straightforward case for illustration purposes, but like all lawsuits, *Schulansky v. Ronan* refuses to be simple. The motion to transfer presents a good example. There is some authority for the proposition that the third-party defendant has no standing to object to venue or, apparently, to move to transfer.

Instead, the court should consider any inconvenience to the third-party defendant in deciding whether to allow him to be impleaded in the first place. See *Pelinski v. Goodyear Tire & Rubber Co.*, 499 F. Supp. 1092, 1095 (N.D. Ill. 1980) ("some question" whether a third-party defendant can seek transfer under §1404(a)); 6 Wright and Miller §1445.

To be truthful, your humble author never knew that arcane bit of procedural lore until his research assistant stumbled on the point in researching the standards for transfer. It is hardly surprising that Jones's attorneys have not yet discovered it. They well may when they reach the stage of briefing the transfer issue. Or they may not. If they don't, the issue may be raised by one of the other parties or the judge. Or it may not. If the court decides that Jones lacks standing to seek a transfer (or that transfer is not warranted, since the plaintiff and defendants are happy with the forum), he may still take the course suggested by Wright and Miller, and dismiss the third-party claim in his discretion under Rule 14(a). Or, Jones can try to convince Ronan to sponsor the motion, since Ronan clearly has standing to seek a transfer.

8.   An important limitation on transfer is the requirement that the suit "might have been brought" in the transferee district. 28 U.S.C. §1404(a). In *Hoffman v. Blaski,* 363 U.S. 335, 342-343 (1960), the Supreme Court held that this phrase limits transfer to districts in which venue was proper and service could have been made on the defendant. This requirement is obviously met here, since venue in the initial action would be proper under several subsections of 28 U.S.C. §1391(a) and all defendants would be subject to personal jurisdiction in New Hampshire. In paragraph eight of his motion, Torres represents that this requirement for transfer is satisfied.

9.   It is fortunate that Philbrook, a New Hampshire practitioner,[2] remembered to have Torres check the local rules for the District of Massachusetts. Most federal districts have their own rules, in addition to the Federal Rules of Civil Procedure, and they frequently cover important aspects of local practice. In this case, Rule 7.1(a) of the Local Rules for the District of Massachusetts specifically requires that supporting affidavits and memoranda be filed with the motion, or else only with leave of court.[3] Rule 7.1(c) further requires that

---

2. Philbrook will not automatically have the right to appear on behalf of Jones in the Massachusetts Federal District Court, unless he is a member of the Massachusetts bar. However, Rule 83.5.3 of the Massachusetts District Court Local Rules authorizes the district court to allow an attorney admitted to practice in another state to appear in particular cases.

3. One effect of this requirement is to discourage "shotgun" motions raising a long laundry list of possible objections. Since counsel must brief all the issues at the outset, they are much more likely to separate the wheat from the chaff in raising preliminary objections. If there is no viable argument for an objection, that will become clear to counsel when he tries to support the argument in a brief. Thus, the need to brief the question right off will often lead counsel to drop the objection instead.

a request for a hearing be included in the motion if the moving party wants one and that the party seeking a hearing indicate in the motion the amount of time needed for oral argument, as Torres has done at the end of each motion.

Rule 7.1(a) imposes another requirement that may trap the unwary litigant. Under that Rule, a party who *opposes* a motion must file an opposition to the motion within ten days. There is nothing in the Federal Rules of Civil Procedure that requires that an opposition be filed. It is thus essential for counsel to be familiar with the local rules as well as the Federal Rules themselves, which apply generally to *all* federal district courts.

10. Note that the draft motion to dismiss for lack of personal jurisdiction says nothing about Rule 4(f) or the line of cases Torres unearthed in his research. It simply asserts the position that there is no jurisdiction because Jones lacks minimum contacts with Massachusetts. However, because the local rule requires a supporting memorandum of law, Jones would have to set out his argument as to why such contacts are necessary. Thus, he would have to cite the few cases in support of his argument, and this would doubtless trigger a response from Ronan with a wealth of contrary cases. Torres is probably right to suggest that, given the strength of the opposing case law and the expense of the motion, it is better to let this one go. While the lawyer's job is to raise arguments that benefit his clients, that does not require him to abandon good judgment in tilting at litigation windmills. Such unrestrained aggressiveness will simply raise the stakes of litigation and induce similar unproductive conduct from the opposition.

31

A Tactical Dilemma: Ronan's Motion for Summary Judgment

The Drafting Request

MEMORANDUM

TO: Marcia Losordo

FROM: Arthur Ackerman

RE: Summary judgment in *Schulansky v. Ronan*
U.S. District Court No. 90-6719

DATE: September 8, 1991

Now that the judge has denied Jones's motion to transfer this action (somewhat to my surprise, actually), I think we should review the file to determine whether we might be able to get at least some of the claims in this case dismissed on a motion for summary judgment.

In particular, it seems to me that we may be able to get summary judgment on Schulansky's claim (see Complaint, paragraphs 23 and 24) that Ronan agreed to rebuild the old foundation wall. Schulansky virtually admits in her complaint (paragraphs 11-12, 22-23) that the Proposal and Estimate is the entire contract between the parties. If that is true, Schulansky will have to prove that the terms of the Proposal and Estimate itself required Ronan to rebuild the old foundation. The only provision of the contract that arguably addresses this issue is paragraph two. We may be able to convince the court that the interpretation of that paragraph is a question of law for the court and that the only reasonable reading of the paragraph is that it required Ronan to build supporting foundation walls for the three walls of the addition itself, but not to rebuild the original foundation as well.

Schulansky will probably argue that the Proposal and Estimate did not embody the entire agreement between the parties and that she and Ronan had a separate understanding about the scope of the work to be done on the old foundation wall. However, as I recall, Schulansky's deposition testimony strongly supports our position that there were no other agreements or implied terms of the agreement apart from the written terms of the contract.

If the court agrees that the contract is complete on its face, won't the parol evidence rule bar Schulansky from introducing evidence of any prior representations by Ronan concerning rebuilding the foundation? And if such evidence is inadmissible, shouldn't we be entitled to summary judgment based on the language of paragraph two, which only requires Ronan to build walls to support the new addition itself?

In order to determine whether this motion has a reasonable chance of success, I think we should go over the evidence relevant to this issue in detail. Please review the Schulansky deposition and pull out her testimony concerning the negotiations on the foundation problem. Also, talk to Ronan and draw up an affidavit that we could submit in support of our motion, setting out his testimony as to the course of their discussions. Last, please draw up a draft motion for summary judgment and briefly give me your assessment of the likelihood of prevailing on the motion, based on the evidence set forth in the affidavit and deposition. Please do not draft a memorandum in support of the motion at this time, in case we decide not to file the motion.

The Associate's Response

MEMORANDUM

TO: Arthur Ackerman

FROM: Marcia Losordo

RE: Partial Summary Judgment in *Schulansky v. Ronan*
U.S. District Court No. 90-6719

DATE: September 16, 1991

As you requested, I have reviewed Deborah Schulansky's deposition and pulled out her testimony concerning the negotiations on the reconstruction of the old foundation and the signing of the Ronan contract. I have attached the relevant pages of the deposition to this memo. I have also discussed this aspect of the case in detail with Richard Ronan and drawn up an affidavit for his signature that sets forth his version of the facts. I also attach a draft motion for partial summary judgment on the issue of Ronan's contractual duty to rebuild the foundation.

After reviewing the documents and spending about four hours researching Massachusetts law on the parol evidence rule and contract interpretation, my preliminary conclusion is that the court will probably deny our motion for summary judgment in this case. Summary judgment will only be granted if our evidence demonstrates that there is no disputed issue of fact for the jury to resolve and that, on the undisputed facts, we are entitled to judgment as a matter of law. Fed. R. Civ. P. 56(c). I doubt that we will be able to make that showing in this case. Given the expense to the client, it may not be worth litigating the motion in a case of this size.

You are correct in stating that Schulansky would be barred from proving any separate agreement with Ronan if the Proposal and Estimate is "fully integrated," that is, constitutes the complete and final agreement of the parties. *Shain Investment Co. v. Cohen,* 15 Mass. App. Ct. 4, 13 (1982); Restatement (Second) of Contracts §215 (1981). A fully integrated contract is one that includes "all the matters agreed upon." Restatement (Second) of Contracts §210, comment a (1981). If a contract is fully integrated, prior negotiations (like the March discussion in this case) are irrelevant, since they have been superseded by the contract, which includes all the rights and obligations of the parties. *Thomas v. Christenson,* 12 Mass. App. Ct. 169, 176 (1981); Restatement (Second) of Contracts §215 (1981). If the contract is not fully integrated, evidence of other agreements would be admissible.

The fact that the contract in issue here is so short, and obviously drafted by Ronan himself rather than counsel, will weaken the argument that it was intended as a fully integrated contract. In addition, the court may hear evidence of prior negotiations to determine whether a contract was meant to comprehensively set forth the obligations of the parties. Restatement (Second) of Contracts §214 (1981); see *Wang Laboratories Inc. v. Docktor Pet Centers, Inc.,* 12 Mass. App. Ct. 213, 219-220 (1981). Thus, (somewhat ironically) the court will hear the evidence as to the negotiations between Ronan and Schulansky about the old foundation, if only to determine whether a separate agreement existed that covered additional matters not addressed in the written contract.

In deciding whether the Proposal and Estimate constitutes the complete agreement of the parties, the court will probably not give too much weight to Schulansky's answers to your questions in the deposition (pp.9-10) about the existence of additional agreements. Although she does appear to concede that there was no separate agreement about the foundation, her answers indicate some confusion as to exactly what you were asking. She probably was not aware of the legal significance of your questions; she may have thought you were asking whether there were any other formal contracts, rather than an oral understanding between the parties. Slater's objections suggest that she is aware that the issue of a possible separate agreement regarding the foundation is crucial. If we file our motion, supported by the deposition testimony, Slater will doubtless file a counter-affidavit of Schulansky stating that she did not fully understand your questions, that she did not mean that there was no separate understanding about rebuilding the old foundation, and that such a separate oral agreement did in fact exist.

Our strongest argument for summary judgment is that the plaintiff's complaint itself relies exclusively on the Proposal and Estimate as the source of the contractual duty to rebuild the old foundation. See paragraphs 22 and 23. Frankly, I don't understand why her counsel wrote the complaint so narrowly. If the court does not allow an amendment, Schulansky may effectively be barred from proving that she and Ronan had a separate agreement about the old foundation, since she has based her right to relief exclusively on the terms of the Proposal and Estimate. We can argue that any proof of collateral agreements is outside the scope of the complaint. Therefore, if no obligation is created by the terms of the written contract, Ronan is entitled to judgment on the contract claim.

However, this argument may still not carry the day. First, Slater is likely to move to amend the complaint, to add an allegation that the parties had an additional oral agreement concerning the old foundation. At this stage of the case, the court is likely to allow the motion. (Indeed, Schulansky's deposition itself indicates that we are already litigating the issue of possible additional agreements; thus it will be hard to argue that the amendment should be denied due to surprise or prejudice to us.)

Second, even if the court accepts our argument that it is solely the Proposal and Estimate that governs the work, there is still a question as to the interpretation of the second paragraph, requiring Ronan to build foundation walls "to support the addition." This might mean only the three new walls, or it could be construed to include the fourth wall, the old foundation wall adjoining the addition. If the term is ambiguous, and there is conflicting evidence as to the intended meaning, the issue is for the jury, and summary judgment will be denied. Restatement (Second) of Contracts §212(2) (1981).

After review of the deposition, I think that Judge Meliotis would likely find that there is a genuine issue of material fact as to the meaning of paragraph two. Although Schulansky did not testify that Ronan explicitly agreed to rebuild the old foundation, if the jury believed her testimony they could find that Ronan agreed to do whatever was necessary to make the foundation solid. Schulansky understood him to say that he would do whatever had to be done to stabilize the old foundation. See Schulansky deposition at 12 (Ronan "would take care of it"); pp.12-13 (she got the impression that "he would rebuild it if it had to be done"). Ronan himself admits that they discussed the subject, although he has a very different view of their understanding on it.

See Ronan affidavit, par. 4-8. Thus, I conclude that the judge will find issues of fact as to what Ronan agreed to here — even under the Proposal and Estimate itself — which have to be resolved at trial.

I agree with you that Ronan's testimony is more precise and is supported by the fact that he did exactly what he says he agreed to do, stabilize the foundation with concrete. See Affidavit of Ronan, paragraphs 7, 12. In addition, Schulansky's own testimony tends to support Ronan's version of their discussions. Deposition, p.12 (Ronan said he would "use concrete to fix" the foundation). This suggests that we may prevail on this factual issue at trial, but it does not make the issue a question of law appropriate for summary judgment. As long as a reasonable jury *could* infer from Schulansky's testimony that Ronan had agreed to do more, a factual issue is posed and summary judgment must be denied. See Fed. R. Civ. P. 56(c) (summary judgment appropriate where there is "no genuine issue of material fact").

Please let me know whether you intend to file the motion; I assume you will want me to write a memorandum in support of the motion if you do.

MEMORANDUM

TO: Marcia Losordo

FROM: Arthur Ackerman

RE: Summary judgment in *Schulansky v. Ronan*
            U.S. District Court No. 90-6719

DATE: September 19, 1991

Thank you for your memo on the complexities of contract interpretation in this case. Given the expense of briefing and arguing the motion and the obstacles to prevailing on it, I have decided not to seek summary judgment at this time. Although I think we have a very strong case for our interpretation of the contract, I reluctantly agree that getting a judge to say as a matter of law that there was no separate agreement on the foundation, or that paragraph two of the Proposal and Estimate *must* carry our meaning, is unlikely.

Several other points in your memo also suggest that we might be better advised not to file the motion, at least at this stage of the case. Your memo reminded me that Judge Meliotis has this case. Judge Meliotis is affectionately referred to as "Try It" Meliotis among experienced members of the local bar, for her well-known propensity to give plaintiffs their "day in court" by denying pretrial motions to dismiss.

In addition, I agree that the plaintiff's allegations in the complaint may ultimately limit her right to prove a collateral agreement at trial. She has not alleged a separate oral agreement to rebuild the foundation in the complaint as it stands. If we move for summary judgment this early in the case, you quite rightly point out that the court is likely to allow an amendment. However, if the plaintiff does not amend before trial, the court might refuse to allow her to do so at trial. At that point, we will be able to argue that the motion is unduly delayed and that our trial preparation has been shaped by the original pleadings. Under the circumstances, we should probably not educate the plaintiff now about possible defects in those pleadings.

Since the Parnell case has just settled unexpectedly, and we will not be filing the summary judgment motion in the Schulansky case, maybe you should try to catch a few days off. Don't we owe you some time from last Christmas?

The Resulting Documents

UNITED STATES DISTRICT COURT

DISTRICT OF MASSACHUSETTS

CIVIL ACTION NO. 90-6719

DEBORAH SCHULANSKY

Plaintiff

v.

RICHARD L. RONAN et al.

Defendants

v.

ARLEN JONES

Third-Party
Defendant

DEFENDANTS' MOTION FOR

PARTIAL SUMMARY JUDGMENT

The defendants move for summary judgment under Fed. R. Civ. P. 56 on the plaintiff's Claim for Relief for breach of contract set forth in paragraphs twenty-one through twenty-four of the complaint. In support of this motion, the defendants state that, based on the complaint (including the Proposal and Estimate, attached as Exhibit A to the complaint), the answer, the attached excerpt from the deposition of Deborah Schulansky, and the attached affidavit of Richard L. Ronan, there is no genuine issue of material fact as to this claim and the defendants are entitled to judgment as a matter of law.

In support of this motion, the defendants state:

1. The plaintiff's complaint alleges a right to relief for breach of a contract between her and the defendants, dated March 15, 1990, and entitled "Proposal and Estimate."

2. The plaintiff admits that she signed the Proposal and Estimate (see complaint, paragraphs eleven, twelve) and that it constitutes the final and complete contract between the parties for the work to be done on

the Alton house. Complaint, paragraph twenty-two; Deposition of Deborah Schulansky, pp. 9-10.

3. Paragraph two is the only provision of the Proposal and Estimate that covers foundation work to be done under the contract.

4. Paragraph two does not create any obligation on the part of the defendants to rebuild the foundation of the main house.

REQUEST FOR ORAL ARGUMENT

Pursuant to Rule 7.1(c) of the Local Rules of the District Court of Massachusetts, the defendant requests one half hour for oral argument on this motion.

Arthur Ackerman
Ackerman, Sloan and Cariotis
Attorney for the Defendants
59 State Street
Boston, MA 02114
(617) 228-6301

UNITED STATES DISTRICT COURT

DISTRICT OF MASSACHUSETTS

CIVIL ACTION NO. 90-6719

DEBORAH SCHULANSKY

    Plaintiff

    v.

RICHARD L. RONAN et al.

    Defendants

    v.

ARLEN JONES

    Third-Party
    Defendant

DEPOSITION OF DEBORAH SCHULANSKY, taken on behalf of the defendants Richard Ronan and Ronan Construction Company, pursuant to notice under the Federal Rules of Civil Procedure, before Alexander Barlow, a Registered Professional Reporter and Notary Public in and for the Commonwealth of Massachusetts, at the office of Ackerman, Sloan and Cariotis, 59 State Street, Boston, Massachusetts, on Wednesday, May 14, 1991, commencing at 10:00 a.m.

Q. Now, Mrs. Schulansky, I show you this document, headed "Proposal and Estimate," which is attached to your complaint and marked Exhibit A. Are you familiar with that document?

A. Yes, that's the paper Richard Ronan sent me to sign about the job.

Q. Is this the contract between you and Ronan Construction Company for the construction of the addition?

A. Yes, that's it.

Q. Did you make any additions or changes to this agreement before you signed it and returned it to Ronan?

A. No, I didn't change anything on it.

Q. Did you make any written changes or modifications in the agreement after it was signed, either before the work commenced or while it was being done?

A. No.

Q. Is this the only contract you had with Ronan or Ronan Construction Company relating to the construction of the addition?

A. Yes.

Q. You didn't enter into any other agreements with Ronan concerning the work?

A. I'm not sure just what you mean. . .

Q. Did you sign any other documents describing the work to be done or other terms of the agreement?

A. No, that was the only thing I signed.

Q. Did you have any other oral agreements about the job, apart from the Proposal and Estimate?

Ms. Slater: Objection. You are asking for a legal characterization of the negotiations between the parties.

Q. Well, I think the plaintiff is qualified to testify to her own understanding of what happened. Let me rephrase the question.

Was it your understanding that there were other agreements between you and Ronan Construction Company, or between you and Richard Ronan, governing the work to be done on the addition?

A. No, I didn't have any other agreements with him. Just that contract you have there that I signed in March. But I'm still not sure I know what you mean.

Q. So this Exhibit A, the Proposal and Estimate, was the only agreement you had for the construction?

A. Yes, it was the only thing I signed.

Q. And it represents the complete agreement between you as to how much you would pay, the work to be done, the timing, all the terms of the contract?

Objection: The question calls for a legal conclusion.

A. That's the only agreement I signed, if that's what you're getting at.

Q. Now, Mrs. Schulansky, could you tell us what was the first time that you discussed the foundation of the house with Richard

-10-

Ronan?

A. It was the second time we talked. He came to my house —
the one in Plymouth, that is — to go over the details of the project.

After we met the first time, he went over and took a look at
the house in Alton so we could talk more specifically about what had
to be done. Then we sat down in Plymouth to go over the details.

Q. Who brought up the subject of the foundation at that time?

A. Well, I don't really remember. I remember that it was a
concern of mine, and I planned to ask him about it, but I can't say
whether I brought it up or he did. I think probably I did, but I'm not
sure.

Q. Could you tell me as accurately as you can recall just what
the sequence of the conversation was about the foundation?

A. Well, I think I asked him whether he thought there would
be any problem with the foundation, and he said he didn't think so.

Q. Did you specify problems with the old foundation, as
opposed to the foundation to support the addition?

A. Well, I don't think I was as specific as that, but I'm sure he
knew what I was talking about. In fact, I remember saying that one
reason I had some concerns about it was that we were going to cut a
door through it into the new cellar.

Q. Exactly what did you ask him about the foundation?

A. As I said, I asked him whether it would be O.K., whether it
would be disturbed by the construction and whether it would have to

-11-

be rebuilt when he dug a new cellar.

Q. Did you use the word "rebuilt"?

A. I really couldn't say what words I used, but that was the gist of what I was asking.

Q. And what did Ronan answer?

A. Well, he said that he didn't think it would be a problem, that it had been there for 200 years and would probably be there for 200 more, something like that. But if there was a problem he would take care of it.

Q. Were those his exact words?

A. I really don't remember exactly what he said, but it was something about if anything was loose he would take care of it, or fix it, or something like that.

Q. Did he say he would rebuild the foundation?

A. I don't remember whether he used those exact words, but I do remember him saying he would use concrete to fix it. He definitely said he would use concrete, he would fix it with concrete, which I assume means the same thing as rebuilding it.

Q. But he didn't use the word "rebuild"?

Ms. Slater: Objection as to the form of the question.

A. I can't swear that he used that exact word, but that was the impression I got, that he would rebuild it if it had to be done.

Q. Did he say he would "reinforce" the foundation?

A. Again, I just can't say, it was over a year ago and I didn't

-12-

expect to get in a lawsuit over this thing. I can't say he said "re-build" or "reinforce" but it was clear to me that he was going to take care of any problems with the foundation, because that was part of the job.

Q. Was there any discussion about the type of foundation that was there, what it was made up of or how it was put together?

A. I think he said he couldn't tell for sure until it was exposed during the excavation, but that it was probably stones and cement, or I guess they called it mortar back then.

Q. Did Ronan say that he would fix it no matter what he found when he got in there?

A. I already told you, he said he didn't think it would be a problem, but he would take care of it.

Q. Did he discuss any different methods he would use to fix it, depending on what he found when it was exposed?

A. Well, he said he would reinforce it, fix it with concrete.

Q. But he didn't make any distinction between what he would do if it was a mortar foundation or a rock foundation, anything like that?

Ms. Slater: Objection as to the form.

A. No, he just assured me it would be all right.

Q. Was that all of the discussion you had concerning the old foundation?

A. At that time, yes.

-13-

Q. Did you discuss it again later?

A. Yes, when they were doing the excavating and that guy with the bulldozer started tearing it to pieces. . .

Q. But you didn't discuss it again at any time before the job started, before you signed the Proposal and Estimate?

A. No, just the one time. I thought we had a clear understanding on it; I didn't bring it up again.

Q. Was there anything in the Proposal and Estimate about rebuilding the foundation?

Ms. Slater: Objection, the question calls for a legal interpretation.

Q. I will withdraw the question. When you got the Proposal and Estimate from Ronan did you have any question about whether the proposal covered rebuilding the foundation?

A. No, it seemed to me to cover the ground . . . he was going to build the addition as we discussed and I was going to pay him $40,000, or whatever it was.

Q. Did you contact Ronan with any questions about the Proposal and Estimate?

A. No, I just looked it over and signed it. It looked all right to me, but I'm a stockbroker, not a lawyer. I wasn't planning on getting into a lawsuit over this thing. He seemed like he knew what he was talking about, and he did a good job for my neighbor, so I assumed he would do the job right.

-14-

Q. Now, Mrs. Schulansky, moving on, when was the next time, after your March meeting, that you discussed possible problems with the old foundation with Ronan, or any other employee of Ronan Construction Company?

A. Well, I guess it was when I drove up to Alton, when they started the work, in mid-April.

Q. You didn't discuss it with Ronan between signing the Proposal and Estimate and the time the work started?

A. No, I didn't see him again until then.

Q. No phone discussions prior to the beginning of the work?

A. No.

Q. Could you tell me how the subject arose when you went to the job site?

A. Well, I went there when they started the job, to check out any last minute problems and see how the excavation went. When I arrived the bulldozer man was already in there digging out the new cellar, and I started to get nervous about the foundation problem. So I stayed to see what the foundation was like. It wasn't until after lunch that he really started to excavate around the foundation, but as soon as he did I could see there were going to be problems.

Q. Did you talk to Ronan at that point about the foundation?

A. Yes. I was upset because the bulldozer kept smashing into the rock foundation, and I could see he was loosening up the rocks that hold up the house. So I spoke to Ronan about it.

-15-

UNITED STATES DISTRICT COURT

DISTRICT OF MASSACHUSETTS

CIVIL ACTION NO. 90-6719

DEBORAH SCHULANSKY

    Plaintiff

    v.

RICHARD L. RONAN et al.

    Defendants

    v.

ARLEN JONES

      Third-Party
      Defendant

AFFIDAVIT OF

RICHARD L. RONAN

IN SUPPORT

OF MOTION FOR

SUMMARY JUDGMENT

Commonwealth of Massachusetts

Suffolk County

} ss:

I, Richard L. Ronan, being first duly sworn, depose and say:

1. I am the president of Ronan Construction Company, a New Hampshire corporation with offices at 1124 Newark Road, Nashua, New Hampshire.

2. Ronan Construction Company is engaged in residential construction work in New Hampshire and Massachusetts.

3. In March of 1990, I entered into negotiations, on behalf of Ronan Construction Company, with Deborah Schulansky, the plaintiff in this case, concerning an addition that she wished to build onto the back of her home in Alton, New Hampshire.

4. During one of the meetings I had with the plaintiff concerning the work to be done as part of the construction of the addition, the plaintiff asked me about possible reconstruction of the old house foundation, where the addition adjoined the living room of the main house.

5. At that time, I stated that such reconstruction would probably not be necessary, because the foundation appeared to be stable, had been there for many years and was unlikely to shift.

6. However, I further stated that you can never be sure about a foundation that old, and that it was impossible to tell for sure what the foundation was like until we uncovered it in the process of excavating the new cellar.

7. I further stated that it was likely that it was a rock and mortar foundation, or a plain rock foundation, and that if there were holes in it I would fill them in with cement.

8. At no time during this conversation did I indicate that I would completely rebuild the foundation, or that I could guarantee that the foundation would last for any period of time or never be subject to subsidence.

9. This was the only discussion that I or anyone else on behalf of Ronan Construction Company had with the plaintiff concerning the old foundation until the actual excavation began.

10. Complete reconstruction of even a small part of the original foundation, without disturbing the structure above it, is a delicate and expensive job, that could easily cost as much as the entire bid I made on the Schulansky job.

11. Such reconstruction would normally be done separately, by a masonry contractor, not as part of a construction job such as the one in issue in this case.

12. After exposure of the foundation, it became clear that the foundation was stable, although no mortar had been used in the original construction. In accordance with my earlier statements to the plaintiff, I had the mason pour cement into the holes among the rocks.

13. At no time did I state that I would rebuild the old foundation, or do anything more than add small amounts of concrete to the existing foundation.

_____
Richard L. Ronan

Subscribed and sworn to before me this 12th day of
September, 1991.

_____
Notary Public

My commission expires:

_____

Comments on the Motion for Summary Judgment

1.   A motion for summary judgment, like any other motion, is governed by Rule 7(b) of the Federal Rules of Civil Procedure. It must be in writing and must state "with particularity" the grounds of the motion. The four numbered paragraphs of Ronan's motion briefly state the supporting reasons for the motion.

2.   As the motion indicates, the defendants only seek summary judgment on part of Schulansky's first claim for relief. Even if they prevail on their argument that Ronan had no duty to rebuild the old foundation, Schulansky also seeks relief for breach of contract on the ground that Jones, acting on behalf of the defendants in performing the contract work, damaged the foundation with the bulldozer. See Complaint, paragraph 25, supra p.434. That issue (and, of course, the negligence claim in the second claim for relief) would still have to be litigated, even if summary judgment were granted on the duty-to-rebuild issue.

3.   As Chapter 18 indicates, a motion for summary judgment is based on the assertion that there is no "genuine issue" as to the material facts. To support that position, the moving party must submit admissible evidence that supports its version of the facts.[1] In this case, Losordo has reviewed the deposition, pulled out those pages that contain relevant testimony, and attached them to the motion. The defendants' position, if they file the motion, is that Schulansky's testimony (at pp.9-10), when read together with the Ronan affidavit, demonstrates that the Proposal and Estimate constitutes the complete agreement of the parties and that, as a matter of law, it cannot be construed to require Ronan to rebuild the foundation.

4.   As the Introduction to these materials indicates, depositions are arranged by the parties. The evidence is taken under oath by a licensed court reporter. After the deposition, the reporter prepares a transcript and sends it to the party who scheduled the deposition, with a copy to opposing counsel if requested. The parties usually agree that the deposition will not be filed with the court.
   Depositions are an extremely effective means of discovery, since they

---

1. In cases in which summary judgment is sought against the party who bears the burden of proof, the moving party may rely on the absence from the record of any admissible evidence to support the opposing party's case. See *Celotex Corp. v. Catrett*, 477 U.S. 317 (1986). But in most cases the moving party will submit evidence to establish its own version of the facts.

provide the opportunity to examine the witness in person and to follow up immediately on issues that arise from the deponent's answers. However, they are also expensive. A typical deposition might run anywhere from 50 to 200 pages or more. As of September 1991, court reporters in Boston were charging $2.50 to $3.00 per page for taking a deposition and providing the transcript to the attorney who took the deposition. Preparation for taking the deposition takes time, and of course the lawyer charges for her time during the deposition. In view of the expense involved, counsel must exercise judgment in deciding whether the size of the case and the likelihood that the deposition will be productive justify such expense.

5.   Tactically, the defendants should probably submit only that part of the Schulansky deposition (pp.9-10) that deals with the existence of other agreements. They would probably not submit the following pages (pp.11-14) of the deposition, since the testimony about the March negotiations may raise a question of fact as to whether the parties had a separate agreement about the old foundation or, if not, about the meaning of paragraph two of the Proposal and Estimate.

Of course, if the defendants did not submit this part of the testimony, Schulansky's lawyers probably would. When a motion for summary judgment is made and supported by evidence that tends to establish the movant's version of the facts, the party opposing summary judgment must come forward with evidence that shows that there is a factual dispute for the jury. As Losordo's memo suggests, Schulansky's testimony about the March discussions probably is sufficient to raise a factual question as to whether a separate agreement existed and, if so, what it required Ronan to do.

6.   Losordo's memo points out a real problem with the plaintiff's complaint. Paragraphs 22-24 of the complaint allege that Ronan had a duty under the Proposal and Estimate to rebuild the foundation. No mention is made of a possible separate understanding regarding this part of the work. Ackerman's questions in the Schulansky deposition have undoubtedly alerted Schulansky's counsel to the fact that the defendants will argue that any obligation to rebuild must be based on the Proposal and Estimate. Slater might well seek to amend the complaint to assert, in the alternative, that the parties had a separate oral agreement regarding reconstruction of the foundation.

Such an amendment would likely be granted at this stage of the case. The spirit of the federal "notice pleading" system is to have the parties set forth their positions at the outset but to allow them to clarify those positions as the discovery process provides more detailed information about their claims and defenses. That is precisely what has happened here. As the parties proceed with discovery and focus in on the pivotal issue of the exact terms of the agreement between the parties, Schulansky's counsel will refine their understanding of both the facts and the (somewhat amorphous) law of contract formation.

Absent undue delay or other demonstrable prejudice to the defendants, they should be allowed to amend their pleadings to reflect that clearer understanding of the case. However, as Ackerman's second memo suggests, the likelihood that such an amendment will be allowed decreases as trial approaches. If Schulansky's attorneys do not seek an amendment promptly, they risk the possibility that the court will deny a motion to amend later on. If that happens, they could be precluded from proving that a separate understanding required Ronan to rebuild the foundation, because they failed to give the defendants timely notice that the issue would be raised.

7.   Ackerman's comment about Judge Meliotis raises an interesting tactical point. As the Introduction indicates, cases in federal court in Massachusetts are assigned to one judge, who presides over the case from start to finish. Thus, Ronan's attorneys know who will hear their motion for summary judgment and will naturally take into account whatever they know about that judge's predilections.

While ours is supposedly "a government of laws, not of men [and women]," any practicing lawyer will tell you that it makes a difference which judge hears your case. If Judge Meliotis is conservative in interpreting the rules of procedure, she may be less likely to grant summary judgment. Or, if she is particularly sensitive to reversal on appeal, she may see denial of the motion as the safest course, since denial of the motion is much less likely to be reversed than a grant of summary judgment. These and many other considerations may influence a judge's decision, and hence must be taken into account (to the extent they are known) by the parties litigating before that judge.

8.   Obviously, an essential component of the defendants' motion for summary judgment will be an accompanying memorandum of law, explaining why there are no material facts in dispute and why, as a matter of law, the court should enter judgment in their favor. See Local Rule 7.1(a)(1) of the District of Massachusetts, which requires that a supporting memorandum be filed along with the motion.

Although *Schulansky* is a relatively low-stakes case, the legal issues involved are not correspondingly simple. For example, Losordo's memo demonstrates that the summary judgment motion raises complex issues of contract interpretation. In addition, an even more complex issue may be lurking: Which state's contract law should apply to this case?

Under *Erie Railroad Co. v. Tompkins,* 304 U.S. 64 (1938), the federal court must apply state law to this diversity case — but which state's law, Massachusetts's or New Hampshire's? In *Klaxon Co. v. Stentor Electric Mfg. Co.,* 313 U.S. 487 (1941), the Supreme Court held that the court must apply the law that the state court would apply if the case were in state court. Under

Klaxon, the federal judge must determine whether the Massachusetts court would apply Massachusetts or New Hampshire law, under "choice of law" principles. See Chapter 12, p.181. The defendants' lawyers might spend a good deal of their clients' money to research that issue and still only come up with an educated guess. The plaintiff's counsel will also have to research these issues and write a memorandum in opposition to the motion for summary judgment.

One of the difficult calls lawyers make all the time is how much time to put into particular issues, given the client's ability to pay, the likelihood that the issue will arise, the likelihood that research will yield helpful results, and the amount at stake in the case. Losordo could easily spend 20 hours researching the contract issues raised above and drafting an effective memorandum in support of the motion. At $75 per hour, that amounts to $1,500 just to file the motion. Additional time will have to be spent preparing to argue the motion, arguing it in court, and writing a reply to the plaintiff's memorandum in opposition to the motion.

Obviously, this is only one stage in the case; trial will doubtless involve substantially more hours (often billed at a higher rate), and other time has already gone into the pleadings and discovery. As every lawyer knows, litigation provides a means for resolving disputes, but it is neither simple nor fast in most cases.

Index